# UNDERSTANDING OTHER

# UNDERSTANDING OTHER MINDS

*Perspectives from Developmental
Cognitive Neuroscience*

## Second Edition

Edited by

SIMON BARON-COHEN

*Lecturer in Psychopathology,
University of Cambridge*

HELEN TAGER-FLUSBERG

*Professor of Psychology,
University of Massachusetts*

and

DONALD J. COHEN

*Professor of Child Psychiatry, Pediatrics, and Psychology,
Director, Child Study Center,
Yale University*

OXFORD
UNIVERSITY PRESS

# OXFORD

UNIVERSITY PRESS

Great Clarendon Street, Oxford OX2 6DP
Oxford University Press is a department of the University of Oxford.
It furthers the University's objective of excellence in research, scholarship,
and education by publishing worldwide in

Oxford New York

Auckland Cape Town Dar es Salaam Hong Kong Karachi
Kuala Lumpur Madrid Melbourne Mexico City Nairobi
New Delhi Shanghai Taipei Toronto

With offices in

Argentina Austria Brazil Chile Czech Republic France Greece
Guatemala Hungary Italy Japan Poland Portugal Singapore
South Korea Switzerland Thailand Turkey Ukraine Vietnam

Oxford is a registered trade mark of Oxford University Press
in the UK and in certain other countries

Published in the United States
by Oxford University Press Inc., New York

British Library Cataloguing in Publication Data

Data available

Library of Congress Cataloging in Publication Data

Understanding other minds: perspectives from developmental cognitive
neuroscience/edited by Simon Baron-Cohen, Helen Tager-Flusberg.
and Donald J. Cohen.—2nd ed.
Includes bibliographical references and index.
1. Autism in children.   2. Philosophy of mind in children.
I. Baron-Cohen, Simon   II. Tager-Flusberg, Helen.
III. Cohen, Donald J.
[DNLM: 1. Autistic Disorder.   2. Developmental Biology.
3. Psychophysiology.   WM 203.5 U55 1999]
RJ506.A9U5   1999   618.92'8982—dc21   99-37353

ISBN 0 19 852446 3 (Hbk)
ISBN 0 19 852445 5 (Pbk)

7 9 10 8

Printed in Great Britain
on acid-free paper by
Antony Rowe Ltd.,
Chippenham, Wiltshire

# Preface

During the first few years of life, children acquire an understanding of the relations between their own mental states, the world (particularly, the social world), and action. They use this to understand themselves and others. Without obvious effort or formal instruction they learn that other people, just like themselves, have minds and that the behaviour of others, just like their own, reflects their knowledge, thoughts, beliefs, and desires. In the scientific literature, this has been called the child's acquisition of a 'theory of mind'. This term underlines the intellectual achievement of a theory upon which a child can rely. Other investigators have preferred the term 'folk psychology' or a 'concept of mind'. We have used the more neutral term 'understanding other minds' in the title of this book. Learning about the minds and actions of others is of course related to learning about how one's own thoughts and actions are inter-related; our title could thus have been 'Understanding Minds'.

The child's acquisition of a theory of mind has been a central and exciting domain of scientific inquiry for more than a decade. The process that allows a normally-developing child to achieve this profoundly important understanding is fascinating in its own right. In addition, a major impetus for research has been the way the findings from normal development cast a light on the psychological and neurological development of children with serious disturbances in the emergence of social competence. In this way, studies of theory of mind represent one of the best examples of the broader field of developmental psychopathology in which the principles of normal development are used to unravel the basis of problems and disorders.

Disturbances in the formation of social relations are at the core of autism, and studies on autism have represented the major application of research methods and theories on theory of mind. Investigators from many different scientific disciplines and orientations, in different parts of the world, have examined whether individuals with autism are impaired in the development of a theory of mind. In pursuing this research, they have advanced the basic understanding of the ontogenesis and evolution of this capacity.

The first book, *Understanding Other Minds: Perspectives from autism* (henceforth, *UOM-1*) was published in 1993 and reflected the state of knowledge that is now almost a decade old. This second book, *Understanding Other Minds: Perspectives from developmental cognitive neuroscience* (henceforth, *UOM-2*) reflects rapid advances in theory, method, and data.

During this past decade, the field of research into the origins and functions of a theory of mind has developed exponentially. Over the same period, there has been great advance in research on autism and closely associated conditions within the autistic spectrum. Finally, the field of psychology has, in quite interesting ways, become reconceptualized in large part as cognitive science and, more recently, cognitive neuroscience. This shift in nomenclature suggests that theory of mind is no longer studied almost exclusively by developmental psychologists. This area is increasingly a focus for basic and clinical investigators concerned about the relationship between brain systems, information processing, and complex behavioural systems.

The topic of theory of mind brings together scholars from a range of disciplines, including developmental psychopathology, child psychiatry, cognitive science, neuroscience, primatology, special education, developmental psycholinguistics, and philosophy. Clinicians and educators find the field of great relevance to them, too, as it provides a way of understanding the problems of their students and patients. The topic has become an interest, as well, in child psychoanalysis, a field that pioneered the study of the child's understanding of others.

Thus, just as in *UOM-1*, the current book brings together a broad range of disciplines and perspectives. Probably the major change between the first and this edition is the whole section on the cognitive neuroscience of understanding other minds. These chapters convey the excitement within the broad field of developmental sciences that has come with new research methods and the integration of behavioural and biological approaches. These methods include new approaches to functional neuroimaging, electrophysiological monitoring of brain functioning, single cell recording, and neuropsychology. Ten years ago, there was a paucity of suggestions about the neurobiological substrate of socialization and theory of mind. Today, there are important, testable hypotheses about brain regions and systems involved in these processes. Equally, the study of theory of mind in non-human primates was just beginning at the time of *UOM-1*, while today there is a wealth of new data about this domain in primates. This research has, in turn, fueled speculation about the biological evolution of a theory of mind.

New data are also now available relating to theory of mind in autism, as well as in other clinical populations. *UOM-2* describes some of the work from the field of schizophrenia, as well as in relation to individuals with autism with higher intellectual ability and variants of autism (including Asperger's Syndrome). While autism remains a critical testing ground for the application and extension of theory of mind hypotheses, the study of other disorders suggests that the methods and theories have broader application.

The theory of mind hypothesis has not been static within the field of autism. Indeed, the vitality of the hypothesis is supported by the number of studies it has generated and the continuing debates it has generated. Among the most interesting debates during the last decade are the following: whether the theory of mind deficit (also known as mindblindness) is specific to autism; whether it is core (in the sense of being universally seen in individuals across the autistic spectrum); and the relationship between theory of mind deficits and other cognitive deficits in individuals with autism (such as difficulties in maintaining central coherence, in executive function, in language development, and in imitation). All of these debates find their place in *UOM-2*.

Finally, the study of normal development of theory of mind has been a fast moving field of investigation. No longer are there just one or two theories of how theory of mind may develop. *UOM-1* included discussions of the modular theory, but the chapters in *UOM-2* make it clear that this is not the only proposal on the table. As in *UOM-1*, the field shows evidence of strong cross-fertilization between the studies of normal and abnormal functioning, enriching the theories that emerge from both.

'Mindreading' may seem like a mysterious phenomenon. Yet, understanding the actions of others and of one's self in terms of agency and intentional states is central to a child's socialization and to the capacity of adults to empathically and correctly understand each other. The capacity to read the minds of others rests upon a long evolutionary history, is grounded in neurobiology, and becomes expressed in the first intimate social relations. The study of this essentially human competence aims to integrate the perspectives of psychological and neurobiological research. We are seeing the first steps in the scientific understanding of the biological and psychological origins and functioning of a theory of mind in normal and atypical development, in humans and non-humans. We look forward to seeing this field mature over the next decade as scientific knowledge continues to expand the understanding of social understanding.

| | |
|---|---|
| *Cambridge* | S.B-C. |
| *Boston* | H.T-F. |
| *New Haven* | D.J.C. |

January 2000

# A Note on Nosology

Whilst this book does not focus specifically on autism, many chapters discuss this as a clear example of a clinical syndrome involving degrees of difficulty in understanding other minds.

The concept of 'autism' as a specific, clinical diagnosis is rooted in the clinical observations of Leo Kanner and others of young children who were seriously and persistently impaired in the emergence of normal social and communicative abilities. The validity of the core features of this clinical disorder and of the possibility of highly reliable diagnostic agreement have been sustained by clinical research over the course of fifty years and in nations throughout the world (Rutter 1989).

Two classification systems and diagnostic guidelines have achieved virtually international acceptance in science and clinical work: the World Health Organization International Classification of Diseases (ICD, tenth edition) (WHO 1993) and the American Psychiatric Association Diagnostic and Statistical Manual (DSM, 4th edition) (APA 1994). Fortunately, on the basis of close collaboration between the working groups, the last editions of these two systems converged in the diagnostic guidelines for autism. Thus, at present, there is an international convention for the diagnosis of Autistic Disorder (DSM IV) or Childhood Autism (ICD 10). Virtually all studies and research publications since the publication of these documents – including this volume – claim to adhere to these diagnostic guidelines. The publication of ICD 10 and DSM IV, however, has not eliminated all nosological difficulties and these remain reflected in this volume.

Even within the scope of the published and accepted diagnostic systems, autism as a clinical disorder is exceedingly heterogeneous. Individuals with autism vary greatly in the following domains:

- age (from the first year or two of life through old age)

- evenness of impairment (with some individuals impaired to the same general degree in all three core domains — social, communicative and imaginative, and others showing markedly uneven profiles)

- severity of social, communicative and imaginative impairment (in the mildest degree, the individual can live comfortably within the mainstream of society; in the most severe forms, normal social and vocational functioning is impossible)

- additional symptoms or co-morbid conditions (including hyperactivity, aggression to self and others, anxiety, sleep disturbances, etc.)

- intellectual competence (from intellectual abilities within the normal range to profound mental retardation)

- adaptive functioning (with some individuals having better adaptive skills in one or more domains but all having substantial impairments in socialization)

- the presence of medical conditions (including seizure disorders, chromosomal/genetic findings, metabolic disorders, neurological findings on clinical and laboratory testing, etc.)

- family history (with most individuals having no family history of autism and others with higher rates than expected).

Individuals with autism fall along the full spectrum of these dimensions. For some scientific and clinical purposes, these distinctions within the population are of crucial importance and the population quite naturally should be split into subgroups. For example, treatment planning depends a great deal on age, severity, associated problems, etc. For other purposes, differences in one or other domain may be less critically important; 'lumping' of individuals with some degree of diversity may be appropriate, for example, in epidemiological studies. The broadly accepted endorsement of multiaxial classification, embodied by DSM IV and ICD 10, suggests that, ideally, investigators would provide the specific characteristics for the individuals studied, the basis for their choice of sample or population, and the reasons for splitting and lumping that they have used. This would help sort out differences in findings, between groups and across measures and methods, and might lead to more rational classification systems. Unfortunately, most research studies do not provide detailed diagnostic information; this difficulty is evidenced, also, in studies on theory of mind and in this volume.

Individuals with autism frequently are sub-grouped into 'high functioning' and 'low functioning'. In general, the concept of 'high functioning autism' is applied to individuals with Autistic Disorder who have intellectual abilities in the normal range (above IQ 70, more or less) and equivalent adaptive skills (with social skills generally lower than communication, daily living, or self care). Broadly speaking, the 'high functioning' individuals with autism are verbal and do not have Mental Retardation or the major, impairing associated behavioural symptoms (aggression, self-mutilation, etc). In most studies of theory of mind, the individuals are either 'high functioning', as just described, or have a mild degree of mental retardation and somewhat lower adaptive skills. Most importantly, virtually all studies are restricted to individuals at the relatively higher range (and, as necessary for this type of research, with verbal abilities).

There is no term of science or clinical art that captures 'intermediate functioning autism'. Thus, there is less clarity about where to draw the lines for 'low functioning' and if 'low functioning' encompasses all individuals with autism who are not 'high functioning'. The term itself has an unpleasant connotation. In general, 'low functioning' seems to be used primarily for individuals with Severe Mental Retardation and little or no communicative speech. These individuals are more likely to have severely impairing behavioural symptoms and are excluded from studies of theory of mind.

DSM IV and ICD 10 use the broad rubric of Pervasive Development Disorders (PDD) as the over-arching diagnostic concept. While no specific diagnostic criteria are provided for PDD, this concept is sometimes used diagnostically. Interestingly, it is not commonly applied in research studies. Instead, other terms have come into common usage, without systematic clarification. These include 'autistic spectrum' and 'broader phenotype'.

'Autistic spectrum' appears roughly to correspond with the major features of PDD as described in DSM IV: 'severe and pervasive impairments in several area of development: reciprocal social interaction skills, communication skills, or the presence of stereotyped behavior, interests, and activities'. The DSM category of 'PDD-not otherwise specified' or the ICD category 'Atypical Autism' may cover some of the individuals in this 'autistic spectrum' class.

At times, the phrase 'autism and associated disorders' is used to convey the group consisting of individuals with Autistic Disorder and individuals with PDD who are quite similar to them. This usage generally excludes the other pervasive developmental disorders – Rett's Disorder and Childhood Disintegrative Disorder. One simply cannot be diagnostically secure when 'autistic spectrum' or 'associated disorders' is used since specific criteria are rarely provided.

More recently, the concept of 'broader phenotype' or 'extended phenotype' has been used to convey the observation that within families in which there is an individual with autism, other relatives may also have symptoms of social, communicative, or other psychiatric or developmental problems (including disturbances in arousal regulation, anxiety, or mood). It is not clear at this point which, if any, of these individuals are suitably classified from the perspective of their relationship to autism (that is, as reflecting an alternate or related expression of the same, underlying, autistic genotype or pathogenesis). It is even less clear when, if ever, this concept should be applied in relation to individuals who do not have a first degree relative with autism. The concept of 'broader phenotype' conveys a sense of the current state of thinking about genetics and the spectrum of expression of the underlying diathesis. The ambiguities of this term, however, are a source of confusion in the scientific literature. These difficulties, we hope, will be reduced with additional research.

DSM IV and ICD 10 introduced Asperger's Syndrome as a new nosological entity within the Pervasive Developmental Disorders. Asperger's Syndrome shares the major PDD characteristics with Autistic Disorder but is differentiated on the basis of early history and current findings. The published criteria state that Asperger's Disorder is not associated with significant delays in language, cognitive development, adaptive skills, and curiosity during childhood (with no specific age range provided for 'childhood'). It is remarkable that DSM excludes, by definition, the use of this developmental diagnosis for individuals with mental retardation or intellectual disability; it is the only place in DSM where this occurs. However, clinicians and researchers are now aware that this is an error: Asperger's Syndrome occurs in individuals with (mild) mental retardation.

The DSM IV and ICD 10 specifications for Asperger's Syndrome have not been universally accepted or used. Some clinicians and investigators feel that the distinction between Autism and Asperger's Syndrome is arbitrary – that is, that a subgroup of individuals with Autistic Disorder has been carved out on the basis of some of the dimensions noted above. Other investigators have provided evidence of the usefulness and validity of the concept that led to its acceptance by the DSM and ICD working groups. Thus, at present there are differences in the use of the concept of Asperger's Syndrome. Some investigators remain scrupulous in following the published guidelines (although they, also, are willing to diagnose the disorder in the presence of at least mild degrees of retardation). In practice, other clinicians and investigators seem to use the term Asperger's Syndrome interchangeably or synonymously with 'high functioning autism' (as described above). At times, Autistic Disorder and Asperger's Syndrome are lumped together within 'autistic spectrum' or 'autism and associated disorders'. This lack of clarity poses serious methodological problems (Volkmar and Klin 1999). Unfortunately, these issues are also reflected in publications in major journals and in contributions to this volume where we have not been able to constrain usage according to the published criteria.

The diagnostic terminology for individuals with Mental Retardation – as defined by DSM and ICD – has also raised scientific and social policy issues. Indeed, clinicians, families, advocates and individuals with retardation have criticized the diagnostic term itself.

DSM and ICD retain the term 'Mental Retardation'. DSM emphasizes two diagnostic features: significantly sub-average general intellectual functioning and significant limitations in adaptive functioning (p. 39). The concept 'significantly sub-average' is operationalized by reference to IQ score. ICD emphasizes 'intelligence' – 'arrested or incomplete development of the mind' – and notes that impairment may be minimal or altogether absent in individuals with mild retardation. There remains considerable debate about the meaning and measurement of intelligence or types of intelligences. Both DSM and ICD, however, retain the established subgroups of Mild, Moderate, Severe and Profound, based primarily on IQ and associated behavioural/linguistic features. A minority of investigators have questioned both cognitive and adaptive domains in the diagnosis and have argued for using a strict IQ measure.

On the other side, during the last years, the entire diagnostic approach and terminology have been seriously questioned. Investigators have pointed to the many different mental and behavioural activities that are encompassed by 'intelligence'. Advocates have argued that the classification is stigmatizing, discriminatory, and likely to lead to adverse life opportunities.

In response to these criticisms, other terms and approaches have been used to refer to individuals in this population. These terms include 'intellectual disability', 'intellectually challenged', 'mentally handicapped', and 'individuals with learning difficulties'. However, the scientific literature continues, predominantly, to use Mental Retardation and the two-factor approach (IQ and adaptive skills). In public discourse, 'intellectual disability' is often used. Authors in this volume generally have used the conventions of DSM and ICD in relation to the use of the term, 'Mental Retardation'; however, some have also used the term 'intellectual disability' in recognition of the social policy concerns. A few authors have adopted the term 'learning difficulties' for essentially the same referents as Mental Retardation; this term should, of course, be differentiated from the standard terms for denoting more circumscribed academic difficulties – 'learning disabilities' or 'learning disorders' (DSM IV).

These issues are important to studies of autism since the majority of individuals with Autistic Disorder also suffers from Mental Retardation, as defined by DSM and ICD. Until quite recently, an accepted notion was that about 80% of individuals with Autistic Disorder were retarded as well. However, as the 'autistic spectrum' becomes broadened through epidemiological studies, studies of relatives of individuals with autism, and changes in clinical sensitivity, awareness or practice, there are more individuals with Autistic Disorder who are not retarded. But, here too, there are issues around the diagnosis of Mental Retardation and the weight given to both IQ and adaptive functioning. Research on theory of mind has been restricted to individuals with normal intelligence or Mild Mental Retardation.

Advances in developmental behaviour science and neuroscience – including the developmental cognitive and social sciences that are the focus of this volume – are likely to transform diagnostic and classification systems and guidelines. In the future, the current diagnostic terms are likely to fade into history as we learn more about the basic science of developmental psychopathology. With new knowledge, researchers and clinicians will discuss and study children with serious, early onset and persistent disorders in social and communicative functioning in terms of classes of genes; patterns of gene-environment interactions; underlying neurocognitive dimensions, modules and systems of development; the multiple pathways leading to types of impairments and the multiple pathways of development and natural history; and so on.

Future clinicians and researchers also will be able to provide far greater specificity about pathogenesis, natural history, and individual differences that will be true to the obvious heterogeneity of the clinical disorders. Increasing knowledge about the development and functioning of the brain and associated behavioural/cognitive systems will provide the same type of knowledge that has allowed medicine to move from surface manifestations of disease towards the understanding of disorders on the basis of pathophysiological mechanisms. In this new clinical epistemology, the types of concepts, methods and social-cognitive and neurocognitive findings described in this volume are likely to play a contributing role.

In the field of developmental psychopathology, just as in general pediatrics and medicine, these types of scientific advances stand in a dialectical relationship with categorical diagnostic systems. Categorical diagnoses, such as Autistic Disorder and Asperger's Syndrome, are usually and necessary in defining samples and populations for research; without clarity in their boundaries, it is less likely that any cognitive, biological, or behavioural markers or dysfunctions will be explicated. Thus, this note highlights a major concern in the field: the need for increasingly rigorous and specific information on the individuals who are being studied in various types of research.

While there have been advances in nosology and diagnostic guidelines in the field of autism, this note on nosology and chapters in this volume reflect the remaining challenges in achieving clarity and broad acceptance of diagnostic conventions and criteria (Volkmar et al. 1997). We are confident that systematic, rigorous research – of the type exemplified by current studies noted in this volume and ongoing in the field of research on autism and associated disorders – will help meet these challenges.


REFERENCES

American Psychiatric Association (1994). DSM IV. *Diagnostic and statistical manual of mental disorders* (4th ed.). Washington, DC: Author.

World Health Organization (1993). *International classification of diseases*: Tenth revision. Chapter V. Mental and behavioral disorders (including disorders of psychological development). Geneva.

Rutter, M. (1989). Annotation: Child psychiatric disorders in ICD-10. *Journal of Child Psychology and Psychiatry*, **30**, 499–513.

Volkmar, F. R., Klin, A., and Cohen, D. J. (1997). Diagnosis and classification of autism and related conditions: Consensus and issues. In *Handbook of Autism and Pervasive Developmental Disorders* (ed. D. J. Cohen and F. R. Volkmar). John Wiley and Sons, New York.

Volkmar, F. R. and Klin, A. (1999). Diagnostic issues in Asperger's Syndrome. In *Asperger's Syndrome*. (ed. A. Klin, F. R. Volkmar and S. S. Sparrow). Guildford Press, New York.

# Acknowledgments

We would like to thank Alison Clare for her secretarial support in the preparation of this edition, Martin Baum, Vanessa Whiting and Hannah Kenner, of Oxford University Press for their patient advice and editorial support, and Bridget Lindley for her encouragement and help at all levels. We are grateful to the Medical Research Council and the Wellcome Trust who supported the first editor during preparation of this book. The cover illustration shows the Corleck Head, and is reprinted with kind permission of the National Museum of Ireland. Finally, we thank Sam David, Kate Hannah and Robin Louis for their help with the front cover design.

# Contents

# Contributors

*Professor Janet Wilde Astington*
Institute of Child Study, University of Toronto, 45 Walmer Road, Toronto, Ontario, Canada M5R 2X2.

*Dr Simon Baron-Cohen*
Departments of Experimental Psychology and Psychiatry, University of Cambridge, Downing Street, Cambridge CB2 3EB, UK.

*Professor Hiram Brownell*
Department of Psychology, Boston College, Chestnut Hill, MA 02467, USA.

*Dr Lisa Capps*
Department of Psychology, University of California at Berkeley, Berkeley, California 94720, USA.

*Dr Tony Charman*
Institute of Child Health, Behavioural Sciences Unit, University College London, 30 Guilford Street, London WC1N 1EH, UK.

*Professor Donald J. Cohen*
Child Study Center, Yale University, 230 South Frontage Road, New Haven, Connecticut 06520, USA.

*Dr Rhiannon Corcoran*
Psychology Department, University of Liverpool, Eleanor Rathbone Building, Bedord Street South, Liverpool L69 3BX, UK.

*Dr Nathan J. Emery*
Center of Neuroscience and Department of Psychiatry, University of California, Davis, CA 95616, USA.

*Ori Friedman*
Department of Psychology, Boston College, Chestnut Hill, MA 02467, USA.

*Professor Chris Frith*
Wellcome Department of Cognitive Neurology, Institute of Neurology, Queen Square, London WC1, UK.

*Professor Uta Frith*
Institute of Cognitive Neuroscience and Department of Psychology, University College London, Alexandra House, 17–19 Queen Square, London WC1N 3AR, UK.

*Professor Alison Gopnik*
Department of Psychology, University of California at Berkeley, Berkeley, California 94720, USA.

*Richard Griffin*
Department of Psychology, Boston College, Chestnut Hill, MA 02467, USA.

*Dr Francesca Happé*
MRC Social, Genetic, and Developmental Research Centre, Institute of Psychiatry, Denmark Hill, London SE5 8AF, UK.

*Professor Paul Harris*
Department of Experimental Psychology, University of Oxford, South Parks Road, Oxford OX1 3UD, UK.

*Dr Ami Klin*
Child Study Center, Yale University, 230 South Frontage Road, New Haven, Connecticut 06520, USA.

*Dr Kristin H. Lagattuta*
The University of Michigan, Centre for Human Growth & Development, 300N Ingalls Building, 10th Level, Ann Arbor, Michigan 48109–0406, USA.

*Mag. Birgit Lang*
Institut für Psychologie, Universitaät Salzburg, Helbrunnerstrasse 34, A–5020 Salzburg, Austria.

*Dr Hilary Leevers*
Center for Molecular & Behavioral Neurosciences, Aidekman Research Center, Rutgers University, 197 University Avenue, Newark, NJ 07102, USA.

*Professor Andy Meltzoff*
Department of Psychology, University of Washington, WJ–10 Seattle, Washington 98195, USA.

*Dr Steven Mithen*
Department of Archaeology, University of Reading, Whiteknights, P O Box 218, Reading RG6 6AA, UK.

*Professor Daniela K. O'Neill*
Department of Psychology, University of Waterloo, Waterloo, Ontario N2L 3G1, Canada.

*Professor Josef Perner*
Institut für Psychologie, Universitaät Salzburg, Helbrunnerstrasse 34, A–5020 Salzburg, Austria.

*Professor David I. Perrett*
School of Psychology, University of St. Andrew's, Fife, KY16 9JU, Scotland.

*Dr Kate Plaisted*
Department of Experimental Psychology, University of Cambridge, Downing Street, Cambridge CB2 3EB, UK.

*Professor Daniel J. Povinelli*
Institute of Cognitive Science, University of Southwestern Louisiana, 100 Avenue D, New Iberia, LA 70560, USA.

*Dr Robert Schultz*
Child Study Center, Yale University, 230 South Frontage Road, New Haven, Connecticut, 06520, USA.

*Professor Valerie Stone*
Department of Psychology, University of Denver, 2155 South Race St, Denver, CO 80208–2478, USA.

*Dr John Swettenham*
Department of Human Communication Science, University College London, Chandler House, 2 Wakefield Street, London WC1, UK.

*Professor Helen Tager-Flusberg*
Research on Neurodevelopmental Disorders, The Eunice Kennedy Shriver Center, Behavioral Sciences Division, 200 Trapelo Road, Waltham, MA 02254, USA.

*Professor Jill de Villiers*
Department of Psychology, Clark Science Center – Bass Hall 401, Smith College, Northampton, MA 01063, USA.

*Dr Penelope G. Vinden*
Frances L. Hiatt School of Psychology, Clark University, 950 Main Street, Worcester, MA 01610–1477, USA.

*Professor Henry M. Wellman*
The University of Michigan, Center for Human Growth & Development, 300N Ingalls Building, 10th Level, Ann Arbor, Michigan 48109–0406, USA.

*Professor Ellen Winner*
Department of Psychology, Boston College, Chestnut Hill, MA 02467, USA.

# Part 1 Theory of mind in normal development and autism

# 1

# Theory of mind and autism: a fifteen year review

SIMON BARON-COHEN

There is a danger when something gets discussed too much, its importance gets overlooked. 'Theory of mind' as a topic in developmental psychology may be facing that danger. Fifteen years ago, the topic was relatively under-researched, and its arrival into science opened a floodgate of research, much of which has been summarized in a number of influential books (Astington 1994; Astington *et al.* 1988; Baron-Cohen 1995; Baron-Cohen *et al.* 1993*b*; Mitchell and Lewis 1995; Moore and Dunham 1996; Perner 1991; Wellman 1990; Whiten 1991). Fifteen years later, the field is that much more mature, and many of the relevant findings from normal development are summarized in the chapter by Wellman, this volume (Chapter 2). But readers should be on their guard not to consider the topic any less important today: a theory of mind remains one of the quintessential abilities that makes us human (Whiten 1993). By theory of mind we mean being able to infer the full range of mental states (beliefs, desires, intentions, imagination, emotions, etc.) that cause action. In brief, to be able to reflect on the contents of one's own and other's minds.

Abnormalities in understanding other minds is not the only cognitive feature of autism spectrum disorders—two other prominent ones being weak central coherence (see Happé, this volume, Chapter 9), and executive dysfunction (Russell 1997)—but it seems to be a core and possibly universal abnormality among such individuals. This chapter describes some of the manifestations of this abnormality, and emphasizes how developmentally appropriate tests of this are needed in order to reveal it. In this chapter we use the terms 'theory of mind', 'mindreading', and 'understanding other minds' synonymously.

Our earlier volume (Baron-Cohen *et al.* 1993*b*) summarized the work investigating theory of mind in autism that had been published prior to 1991 (because of the familiar publication lag). In this chapter, I survey the work over the period from 1985 to the present. Whilst this is not exhaustive, it gives a good flavour of the studies from this time, summarizing many different experiments. These are also listed in Table 1.1.

## THE MENTAL–PHYSICAL DISTINCTION

Perhaps the best place to start this review is with the mental–physical distinction since many consider that this distinction is a fundamental cornerstone of our folk psychology,

**Table 1.1** Some tests of theory of mind in people with autism

---

1. The mental-physical distinction (Baron-Cohen 1989a).
2. Understanding of the *functions of the mind* (*ibid*).
3. The *appearance–reality distinction* (*ibid*).
4. *First-order false-belief tasks*, (Baron-Cohen *et al*. 1985, 1986; Leekam and Perner 1991; Perner *et al*. 1989; Reed and Peterson 1990; Swettenham 1996; Swettenham *et al*. 1996).
5. *'Seeing leads to knowing'* tests (Baron-Cohen and Goodhart 1994; Leslie and Frith 1988).
6. Tests of *recognizing mental-state words* (like 'think', 'know', and 'imagine') in a wordlist (Baron-Cohen *et al*. 1994).
7. Tests of production of the same range of *mental-state* words in their spontaneous speech (Baron-Cohen *et al*. 1986; Tager-Flusberg 1992).
8. Tests of the production of spontaneous *pretend play* (Baron-Cohen 1987; Lewis and Boucher 1988; Ungerer and Sigman 1981; Wing and Gould 1979).
9. Tests of understanding more *complex causes of emotion* (such as beliefs) (Baron-Cohen 1991; Baron-Cohen *et al*. 1993).
10. Tests of recognizing the *eye region of the face* as indicating when a person is thinking and what a person might want (Baron-Cohen and Cross 1992; Baron-Cohen *et al*. 1995).
11. Tests of being able to *monitor their own intentions* (Phillips *et al*. 1998).
12. Tests of *deception* (Baron-Cohen 1992; Sodian and Frith 1992; Yirmiya *et al*. 1996).
13. Tests of *understanding metaphor, sarcasm, and irony* (Happé, 1993).
14. Tests of *pragmatics* in their speech (Baron-Cohen 1988; Tager-Flusberg 1993).
15. Tests of recognition of violations of pragmatic rules (Surian *et al*. 1996).
16. Tests of *imagination* (Scott and Baron-Cohen 1996).
17. Correlation with real-life social skills, as measured by a modified version of the Vineland Adaptive Behaviour Scale (Frith *et al*. 1994).
18. *Second-order false-belief* tests (Baron-Cohen 1989b; Bowler 1992; Happe 1993; Ozonoff *et al*. 1991).
19. *Understanding stories* in which characters are motivated by complex mental states such as bluff and double bluff (Happe 1994).
20. Decoding complex mental states from the expression in *the eye region of the face* (Baron-Cohen and Hammer 1997; Baron-Cohen *et al*. 1997a,b).

---

and one that is not explicitly taught by parents or teachers. The test for this involves the child listening to stories in which one character is having a mental experience (e.g. thinking about a dog) whilst a second character is having a physical experience (e.g. holding a dog). The experimenter then asks the subject to judge which operations the two characters can perform (e.g. which character can stroke the dog?). Whilst Wellman and Estes (1986) found that three- to four-year-old normal children could easily make these judgments, thereby demonstrating their good grasp of the ontological distinction between mental and physical entities and events, it was found that children with autism were significantly impaired at making such judgments (Baron-Cohen 1989a).

## UNDERSTANDING OF THE FUNCTIONS OF THE BRAIN

This test was also originally devised by Wellman and Estes, and involves asking the child what the brain is for. They found that normal three- to four-year-olds already knew that the brain has a set of mental functions, such as dreaming, wanting, thinking, keeping secrets, etc. Some also knew it had physical functions (such as making you move, or helping you stay alive, etc.). In contrast, children with autism (but who have a mental age above a four-year-old level) appeared to know about the physical functions, but most failed to mention any mental function of the brain (Baron-Cohen 1989*a*).

## THE APPEARANCE–REALITY DISTINCTION

Flavell and colleagues (Flavell *et al.* 1986) found that children from about the age of four years old normally are able to distinguish between appearance and reality, that is, talk about objects which might have misleading identities. For example, they may say, when presented with a candle fashioned in the shape of an apple, that it looks like an apple but is really a candle. Children with autism presented with the same sorts of tests tended to commit errors, saying the object really is an apple, or really is a candle, but not capture the object's dual identity in their spontaneous descriptions (Baron-Cohen 1989*a*). Given that this requires being able to simultaneously keep track of what an object looks like, versus what it actually is—how it appears subjectively versus how it is objectively—it is an additional clue that in autism there is a deficit in the development of their theory of mind. Note that alternative interpretations of this deficit are certainly possible, since this task relies on quite complex language skills.

## FIRST-ORDER FALSE-BELIEF TASKS

These are the by now well-known tests of understanding that different people can have different thoughts about the same situation. They are called first-order tests because they only involve inferring one person's mental state. (See below for discussion of second-order tests.) Wimmer and Perner (1983), among others, had demonstrated that normal four-year-olds could keep track of how different people might think different things about the world. We have similarly found that when interpreting well-known stories such as Little Red Riding Hood or Snow White, that even four-year-olds will say in response to the picture shown in Fig. 1.1 that 'Little Red Riding Hood *thinks* that it's her grandmother in the bed, but really it's the wicked wolf!'; or in response to the picture shown in Fig. 1.2, that 'Snow White *thinks* the old woman is giving her a nice juicy apple. She doesn't *know* that it's really her wicked step-mother all dressed up, and that the apple is poisoned!' A large number of studies have repeatedly demonstrated that children with autism have difficulties in shifting their perspective to judge what someone else might think, instead simply reporting what they

**Fig. 1.1.** A false-belief scene in 'Little Red Riding Hood'. Reproduced with permission from Ladybird.

**Fig. 1.2.** A false-belief scene from 'Snow White'. Reproduced with permission from Ladybird.

themselves know (Baron-Cohen *et al.* 1985, 1986; Leekam and Perner 1991; Perner *et al.* 1989; Reed and Peterson 1990; Swettenham 1996;. Swettenham *et al.* 1996).


## 'SEEING LEADS TO KNOWING' TESTS

Yet another corner-stone of the normal child's theory of mind is understanding where knowledge comes from, so that they can work out who knows what, and more importantly, who doesn't know what. This is a key development simply because it underpins appropriate communication (telling people what they don't know—inform-ing others—rather than telling them what they already know. The latter would violate one of the Gricean maxims of conversation: Be informative) (Grice 1975). It also underpins understanding of deception, since before considering changing someone's beliefs about what is true, one first has to work out what they know or don't know about. Deception obviously fails if you cannot keep track of what the other person might know or not know. (We will return to discuss deception later.)

Pratt and Bryant (1990) established that normal three-year-olds can understand the seeing-leads-to-knowing principle, in that when given a story about two characters, one of whom looks into a box and the other of whom touches a box, they can infer that the one who looked, knows what's in the box, whilst the other one does not. In contrast, children with autism are virtually at chance on this test, as likely to indicate one character or the other when asked 'Which one knows what's in the box?' (Baron-Cohen and Goodhart 1994; Leslie and Frith 1988). See Fig. 1.3 for a schematic illustration of the experiment.


## TESTS OF RECOGNIZING MENTAL-STATE WORDS

It turns out that by four years old, normally-developing children can also pick out words from a word list that refer to what goes on in the mind, or what the mind can do. These words include 'think', 'know', 'dream', 'pretend', 'hope', 'wish', and 'imagine'. These are easily distinguished from other kinds of (non-mental) verbs like 'jump', 'eat', or 'move'. Children with autism have much more difficulty in making this judgment (Baron-Cohen *et al.* 1994). Note that this is really a test of their mental lexicon, rather than their ability to infer the contents of a mental state; but their deficient mental-state lexicon may well be an indicator that conceptual development in this domain is also less well developed than would be expected for the child's general mental age.


## TESTS OF PRODUCTION OF THE SAME RANGE OF MENTAL-STATE WORDS IN THEIR SPONTANEOUS SPEECH

The previous finding dovetails with reports that children with autism produce fewer mental-state words in their spontaneous descriptions of picture stories involving

The question:
Which one knows what is in the box?

Sally touches the box   —   Anne looks inside the box

**Fig. 1.3.** A schematic illustration of the seeing-leads-to-knowing test. After Pratt and Bryant (1990).

action and deception, and in their conversational discourse, compared with their normal counterparts (Baron-Cohen *et al.* 1986; Tager-Flusberg 1992). All the usual caveats regarding what we can infer from speech alone apply to these studies (i.e. does production reflect competence? etc.), but when taken together with other experimental evidence summarized in this chapter, the likelihood is that this reflects delays or deficits in comprehension of mental-state concepts, or at the very least, reduced attention to such phenomena.

## TESTS OF THE PRODUCTION OF SPONTANEOUS PRETEND PLAY

Many studies over twenty years have reported a lower frequency of pretend play in the spontaneous play of children with autism (Baron-Cohen 1987; Lewis and Boucher 1988; Ungerer and Sigman 1981; Wing and Gould 1979). This is interpreted in various ways (see Harris and Leevers, this volume). For example, it might reflect a failure to reflect on one's own imagination—a mindreading deficit (Leslie 1987). Or it might reflect a failure to switch attention flexibly from 'reality mode' to 'pretend mode', as a result of some aspect of executive dysfunction (Russell 1997). Or both. Note that the executive account strains a bit to explain why the normal twenty four-month-old child should find such switching so easy (and fun) during pretence, whilst the normal child at this stage is largely incapable of many other executive switching tasks, such as solving the Detour Reaching Task (Diamond 1991).

## TESTS OF UNDERSTANDING MORE COMPLEX CAUSES OF EMOTION (SUCH AS BELIEFS)

Emotions can be caused by physical events or situations (e.g. falling over causes you to cry, or being given a present causes you to feel happy). But emotions can also be caused by mental states such as desires and beliefs (Harris *et al.* 1989). Thus, you can be happy because you got what you wanted, or because you think you are getting what you wanted. Harris and colleagues found that normal four- to six-year-olds understand all three types of emotional causation. In contrast, children with autism with this mental age have difficulty with the more complex (mental states as) causes of emotion (Baron-Cohen 1991; Baron-Cohen *et al.* 1993*a*). As with all of the previous studies, the deficits in autism are typically demonstrated relative to a comparison group of children without autism but with general developmental delay, suggesting that the deficit is autism-specific.

## TESTS OF INFERRING FROM GAZE-DIRECTION WHEN A PERSON IS THINKING, OR WHAT A PERSON MIGHT WANT

Why do we spend so much time looking at people's eyes? Why not at their ears, chins, or elbows? The question may strike you as odd, because it makes no intuitive sense that these other parts of the body should contain any information that we might find important. But until recently, it was not clear what the information around someone's eyes conveyed to another person. We now know that from gaze-direction even young normal children (age four years) can work out when someone is thinking about something (e.g. gaze directed upwards and away, at nothing in particular, strongly signifies the person is thinking—see Fig. 1.4). Gaze-direction also allows young normal children of the same age to work out which of several objects a person wants (see Fig. 1.5). Children with autism in contrast are relatively blind to such information from gaze-direction, even though they can answer the explicit question 'What is Charlie looking at?' (Baron-Cohen 1989*c*; Baron-Cohen and Cross 1992; Baron-Cohen *et al.* 1995; Hobson 1984; Leekam *et al.* 1997). Mentalistic interpretation of the eyes of another person does not seem to come naturally to them.

## TESTS OF BEING ABLE TO MONITOR ONE'S OWN INTENTIONS

We have covered a number of tests of understanding other people's thoughts, but another important class of mental states is intentions. Working out why people behave as they do involves keeping track of people's intentions, since tracking actions alone gives you a description of what people do, but not why they do it. In a novel test of

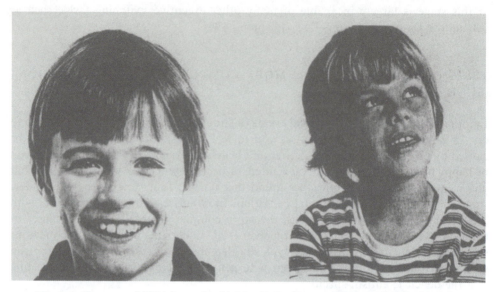

**Fig. 1.4.** The test of 'Which one is thinking?'. See Baron-Cohen and Cross (1992).

**Fig. 1.5.** The test of 'Which one does Charlie want?'. See Baron-Cohen *et al*. (1995).

this, four-year-old normal children were asked to shoot a toy gun at one of six targets, stating their intended target. Then, unbeknownst to the child, the outcome was manipulated by the experimenter, such that sometimes the child hit their chosen target, and sometimes they did not. Normally-developing four-year-olds could correctly answer the question 'Which one did you mean to hit?', even when they did not get what they intended, but children with autism often made the error of answering by reference to the actual outcome (Phillips *et al.* 1998). The equipment to assess this understanding is shown in Fig. 1.6.

## TESTS OF DECEPTION

Deception is relevant to understanding other minds because it involves trying to make someone else believe that something is true when in fact it is false. In other words, it is about trying to change someone else's mind. Clearly it must involve knowing that there are such things as beliefs, and that beliefs can be true or false; but it also involves knowing that beliefs are manipulable, that people will form their beliefs on the basis of what they know about, either through what they have directly witnessed or what they have heard about. Finally, deception requires motivation: recognizing that there might

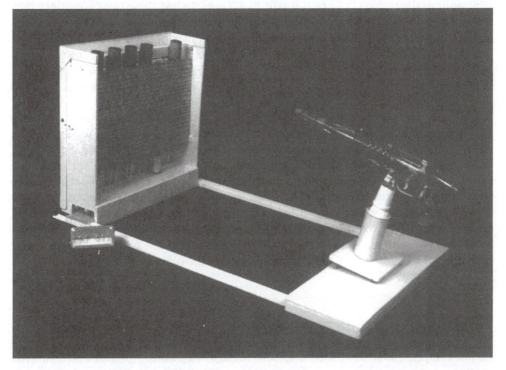

**Fig. 1.6.** The target shooting equipment (for testing recall of one's intentions). From Phillips *et al.* (1998).

be some pay-off to making someone else believe something to be the case, even when this does not match reality. We tend to think of deception as morally reprehensible, which in many cases it is. Society and communication are rightly predicated on the basis that we are all being truthful to each other, since otherwise we would never be able to trust each other's actions or communications. Some kinds of deception are morally less clear cut (such as saying how much you like someone's haircut, when you don't, or how much you like a gift you've received, when you don't), since in these cases it may be worse to hurt someone else's feelings by telling the truth, than to lie. Being able to distinguish such white lies from others is part of developing social skill and social cognition in the normal case.

A number of studies demonstrate that by the age of four years old the normally-developing child is both showing an interest in deception, and beginning to be more adept at it (Sodian *et al.* 1992). Leaving the moral aspects aside, such signs of deception can be taken as a yardstick that the child understands other minds. Of course, early attempts at deception may be clumsy and ineffective, such as the young child claiming that he did not take the chocolate cookies, whilst the tell-tale evidence is all over all over his face; or the young child in a game of hide-and-seek calling out from her hiding place behind the curtains to 'come and find me!' In these instances, the child is arguably trying to deceive, but is not keeping track of the clues that would lead the other person to know the truth. Most workers in this area would code a behaviour as deception (1) when it is effective (i.e. excluding these two cases, since they do not clearly demonstrate an understanding of the need to conceal the essential information); and (2) when there are multiple examples of it (i.e. excluding a single instance which could always be explained through the learning of some rule, as in 'go behind the curtain and stay quiet'). When there are multiple examples for which there is no single underlying rule, then the more parsimonious explanation is that the child understands what deception is.

Children with autism, when studied under experimental conditions, have been shown to have difficulties both in production of deception, but also in understanding when someone else is deceiving them (Baron-Cohen 1992; Sodian and Frith 1992; Yirmiya *et al.* 1996). An example of one test is the 'penny-hiding game', where the aim of the game is not to reveal in which hand you have hidden a penny. Young children with autism, despite having a mental age above a four-year-old level, often make errors in this game, which suggest they do not understand how to deceive very well. Examples of their errors include hiding the penny in one hand, but leaving the other hand open; or between trials, transferring the penny from one closed fist to the other; or putting the penny out of sight, and then telling the other person 'it's in here!', etc. (Baron-Cohen 1992).

## TESTS OF UNDERSTANDING METAPHOR, SARCASM, AND IRONY

Happé (Happé 1994) has tested whether children with autism understand figurative speech using a story comprehension technique. Figurative speech requires an understanding of the speaker's intentions, in order to move beyond the literal level of simply mapping words onto their referents. Examples of figurative language include sarcasm ('How clean your room looks today!', uttered by an exasperated parent to her child), and metaphor ('she's got a sharp tongue!'). Results suggest that this more advanced mindreading test (pitched at the level of a normal eight-year-old) reveals more subtle deficits in higher-functioning individuals with autism spectrum disorders. A similar finding using a simpler test comes from a study of normal preschoolers based on testing whether they can understand someone's intention to joke. Children heard utterances like 'This is a shoe', spoken by the experimenter whilst pointing at a cup, and were asked why the experimenter said that. Whereas normal children as young as three years old referred in their explanation to 'joking' and 'pretending', children with autism tended to refer to the speaker having got it wrong ('it's not a shoe, it's a cup' etc.) (Baron-Cohen 1997).

## TESTS OF PRAGMATICS

Understanding figurative speech and humour is a subset of pragmatics, or the use of language appropriately to the social context (Tager-Flusberg, this volume, Chapter 6). Pragmatics includes the following:

- tailoring one's speech to a particular listener;

- adapting the content of one's speech to what your listener already knows or needs to know;

- respecting conversational maxims (Grice, 1975/1957) such as being truthful, relevant, concise, and polite;

- turn-taking so that there is space for both participants in the dialogue;

- being sensitive to the other person's contribution to the conversation;

- recognizing what is the wrong or right thing to say in a particular context;

- staying on topic; and

- helping your listener to follow when a topic change is occurring.

Almost every aspect of pragmatics involves sensitivity to speaker and listener mental states, and hence mindreading, though it is important to note that pragmatics also involves using context. This means that a deficit in pragmatics could occur for at least two different reasons: some degree of mindblindness, or some degree of weak central coherence (use of context). Two experimental studies of pragmatics in children with autism have included (1) a test of whether the Gricean maxims of conversational relevance can be recognized (Surian *et al.* 1996); and (2) a test of recognizing when someone said the wrong thing (*faux pas*) (Baron-Cohen *et al.*, in press, *a*). Both studies suggest that children with autism have difficulties in this area.

## TESTS OF IMAGINATION

We discussed the relevance of pretend play earlier, but this is only one way that imagination can be expressed. Imagination is relevant to theory of mind since it involves building an unreal world that exists purely in your own mind, and being able to reflect on this virtual world. The virtual world is the content of one's mental state of imagining. One study of children with autism investigated the ability to draw pictures of unreal or impossible objects (such as two-headed people), and found that children with autism were either reluctant or less able to produce such drawings (Scott and Baron-Cohen 1996). Paul Harris and Hilary Leevers (this volume, Chapter 8) suggest that this may be due to executive function (the need to suppress routine approaches to drawing, and override these with novel approaches), and report that when the task is simplified sufficiently to eliminate such executive factors, no deficit in autism is seen (Leevers and Harris 1998).

However, Craig and colleagues have gathered fresh evidence for persisting imagination impairments in children with autism and children with Asperger's Syndrome, on a range of tasks not restricted to drawing (such as story telling, and standard creativity measures), for which an executive dysfunction explanation is not the most parsimonious account (Craig 1997; Craig and Baron-Cohen, 1999), and which may be better accounted for by positing a basic deficit in the use of the imagination *per se*. This experimental evidence is in line with clinical descriptions of impaired imagination in people with an autism spectrum condition, as specified in the standard diagnostic classification system (APA 1994).

## CORRELATION WITH REAL-LIFE SOCIAL SKILLS

One might raise the concern that theory of mind tasks measure aspects of social cognition under laboratory conditions, and have little relevance to social impairment in the real world. For this reason, Frith and colleagues have examined the correlation of theory of mind skills in children with autism in relation to real-world behaviour, as measured by a modified version of the Vineland Adaptive Behaviour Scale (Frith *et al.* 1994). They report that these are indeed significantly correlated, providing some measure of validity of the tests.

## SECOND-ORDER FALSE-BELIEF TESTS

The universality of theory of mind deficits in autism has been questioned because a proportion of children with autism or Asperger's Syndrome pass first-order tests. First-order tests, including most of those reviewed above, involve inferring one person's mental state. Happé points out that this need not challenge the universality claim, since there are no reported cases of autism spectrum disorder who pass first-order theory of mind tests at the right mental age. Thus, an individual with an autism spectrum condition (e.g. with Asperger's Syndrome) who has normal intelligence, should be able to pass such tests at three to four years of age. Typically however, they are older than this when they pass such tests. Equally, with children with autism, Happé finds that on average a verbal mental age of nine years old is needed before passing of such tests is seen, and that the youngest mental age of an individual with autism passing such tests is five and a half years (Happé 1995).

As one might expect, as a result of a delay in acquiring first-order theory of mind competence, these individuals often fail *second-order false-belief tests* (Baron-Cohen 1989*b*). Second-order tests involve considering embedded mental states (i.e. one person's mental states about other mental states). Whereas first-order tests correspond to a four-year-old mental age level, second-order tests correspond to a six-year-old mental age level. This may be another way of revealing if there is a *specific developmental delay* in theory of mind at a point later in development. But note that some individuals with autism or Asperger's Syndrome who are high functioning (in terms of IQ and language level), and who are usually adults, may pass even second-order false-belief tests (Bowler 1992; Happé 1993; Ozonoff *et al.* 1991). Those who can pass such second-order tests however may have difficulties in more advanced theory of mind tests, such as inferring complex mental states such as bluff and double bluff in story characters—an eight year mental age level test—(Happé 1994), or in decoding complex mental states from the expression in the eye region of the face (Baron-Cohen *et al.* 1997*a*,*b*).

## SPECIFICITY ISSUES

Deficits on theory of mind tests are not diagnostic. This is because a child might fail such tests for a variety of reasons. As Yirmiya *et al.* (1999) point out, in their meta-analysis, children with mental retardation but without autism may also fail such tests. Although many studies also show that performance in theory of mind is in line with mental age levels in such groups (Baron-Cohen *et al.* 1985, 1986; Perner *et al.* 1989), it is likely that a variety of types of comprehension problems might interfere with success on these tasks. Such children may also have equivalent difficulty on 'control' tasks such as the False Photograph Task (Charman and Baron-Cohen 1995; Leekam and Perner 1991; Leslie and Thaiss 1992), whilst children with autism may show a specific deficit only on the theory of mind task. The same point can be made in relation to deaf or blind children, whose development in theory of mind may be slowed down presumably due to not receiving enough of the right perceptual input (Brown *et al.* 1997; Peterson and Siegal 1995). Interestingly, in the case of the deaf, this deficit is not seen when children have been taught signing by signing parents (Peterson and Siegal 1997), the implication being that communication problems are in their case interfering with task performance.

People with autism-spectrum conditions appear to have mentalizing difficulties for different reasons from those seen in people with mental retardation or those who are blind or deaf, since a deficit can be revealed even in the highest-functioning individuals with an autism spectrum condition, in whom general comprehension problems can be ruled out. For example, adults with Asperger's Syndrome (AS) or High Functioning

Autism (HFA) show reduced performance on the Reading the Mind in the Eyes Task (Baron-Cohen *et al.* 1997). An even more dramatic demonstration of this is the deficit on this task reported in a University Mathematics Professor with AS, who had won the equivalent of the Nobel Prize (Baron-Cohen *et al.*, in press *b*). Mentalizing deficits in such 'pure' cases of AS may seem diagnostic, especially given their specific nature (such individuals having no identifiable deficits in any other domain). However, caution is still needed in not treating such tests as diagnostic since, as Corcoran (this volume, Chapter 16) shows, adults with schizophrenia can also fail such tests (Age-of-onset may be an important difference in these two disorders).

## CONCLUSIONS

Mindreading deficits in autism spectrum conditions appear to be early occurring (from at least the end of the first year of life, if one includes joint attention deficits) and universal (if one tests for these either at the right point in development, or in the case of high-functioning, older subjects by using sensitive, age-appropriate tests). Parents of children with AS may also show difficulties in attributing mental states when just the eye-region of the face is available (Baron-Cohen and Hammer 1997), suggesting that, for genetic reasons, mild degrees of mindblindness may be one aspect of the broader cognitive phenotype.

Some clues relating to the brain basis of the theory of mind deficit in autism are being gathered from both functional neuroimaging and studies of acquired brain damage (see Stone, this volume, Chapter 11; and Frith and Frith, this volume, Chapter 14). It is hoped that future research in this area will both refine the techniques for studying this skill across the lifespan, and make further headway in understanding the underlying mechanisms essential for mindreading. Finally, most importantly, much of the basic research in this field may have clinical applications in the areas of either intervention or diagnosis (see Swettenham, Chapter 18, and Charman, Chapter 17, this volume). This is an area which needs systematic exploration.

### Acknowledgments

SBC was supported by the MRC during the period of this work. This chapter elaborates on an article by the author which appeared in *Communication* 1998.

## REFERENCES

APA (1994). *Diagnostic and statistical manual of mental disorders*, 4th Edn. DSM-IV American Psychiatric Association, Washington, DC.
Astington, J. (1994). *The child's discovery of the mind.* Harvard University Press, Cambridge, MA.
Astington, J., Harris, P. and Olson, D. (1988). *Developing theories of mind.* Cambridge University Press, New York.

Baron-Cohen, S. (1987). Autism and symbolic play. *British Journal of Developmental Psychology*, **5**, 139–48.

Baron-Cohen, S. (1988). Social and pragmatic deficits in autism: cognitive or affective? *Journal of Autism and Developmental Disorders*, **18**, 379–402.

Baron-Cohen, S. (1989*a*). Are autistic children behaviourists? An examination of their mental–physical and appearance–reality distinctions. *Journal of Autism and Developmental Disorders*, **19**, 579–600.

Baron-Cohen, S. (1989*b*). The autistic child's theory of mind: a case of specific developmental delay. *Journal of Child Psychology and Psychiatry*, **30**, 285–98.

Baron-Cohen, S. (1989*c*). Perceptual role-taking and protodeclarative pointing in autism. *British Journal of Developmental Psychology*, **7**, 113–27.

Baron-Cohen, S. (1991). Do people with autism understand what causes emotion? *Child Development*, **62**, 385–95.

Baron-Cohen, S. (1992). Out of sight or out of mind: another look at deception in autism. *Journal of Child Psychology and Psychiatry*, **33**, 1141–55.

Baron-Cohen, S. (1995). *Mindblindness: an essay on autism and theory of mind*, Bradford Books, MIT Press, Cambridge, MA.

Baron-Cohen, S. (1997). Hey! It was just a joke! Understanding propositions and propositional attitudes by normally developing children and children with autism. *Israel Journal of Psychiatry*, **34**, 174–8.

Baron-Cohen, S. and Cross, P. (1992). Reading the eyes: evidence for the role of perception in the development of a theory of mind. *Mind and Language*, **6**, 173–86.

Baron-Cohen, S. and Goodhart, F. (1994). The 'seeing leads to knowing' deficit in autism: the Pratt and Bryant probe. *British Journal of Developmental Psychology*, **12**, 397–402.

Baron-Cohen, S. and Hammer, J. (1997) Parents of children with Asperger Syndrome: what is the cognitive phenotype? *Journal of Cognitive Neuroscience*, **9**, 548–54.

Baron-Cohen, S., Leslie, A. M. and Frith, U. (1985). Does the autistic child have a 'theory of mind'? *Cognition*, **21**, 37–46.

Baron-Cohen, S., Leslie, A. M. and Frith, U. (1986). Mechanical, behavioural and intentional understanding of picture stories in autistic children. *British Journal of Developmental Psychology*, **4**, 113–25.

Baron-Cohen, S., Spitz, A. and Cross, P. (1993*a*). Can children with autism recognize surprise? *Cognition and Emotion*, **7**, 507–16.

Baron-Cohen, S., Tager-Flusberg, H. and Cohen, D. (ed.) (1993*b*). *Understanding other minds: perspectives from autism*. Oxford University Press.

Baron-Cohen, S., Ring, H., Moriarty, J., Shmitz, P., Costa, D. and Ell, P. (1994). Recognition of mental state terms: a clinical study of autism, and a functional neuroimaging study of normal adults. *British Journal of Psychiatry*, **165**, 640–9.

Baron-Cohen, S., Campbell, R., Karmiloff-Smith, A., Grant, J. and Walker, J. (1995). Are children with autism blind to the mentalistic significance of the eyes? *British Journal of Developmental Psychology*, **13**, 379–98.

Baron-Cohen, S., Jolliffe, T., Mortimore, C. and Robertson, M. (1997*a*). Another advanced test of theory of mind: evidence from very high functioning adults with autism or Asperger Syndrome. *Journal of Child Psychology and Psychiatry*, **38**, 813–22.

Baron-Cohen, S., Wheelwright, S. and Jolliffe, T. (1997*b*). Is there a 'language of the eyes'? Evidence from normal adults and adults with autism or Asperger Syndrome. *Visual Cognition*, **4**, 311–31.

Baron-Cohen, S., O'Riordan, M., Jones, R., Stone, V. and Plaistead, K. (in press *a*). Can children with Asperger Syndrome detact *faux pas*? *Journal of Autism and Developmental Disorders*.

Baron-Cohen, S., Wheelwright, S., Stone, V. and Rutherford, M. (in press *b*). A mathematician, a physicist, and a computer scientist with Asperger Syndrome: performance on folk psychology and folk physics tests. *Neurocase.*

Bowler, D. M. (1992). Theory of mind in Asperger Syndrome. *Journal of Child Psychology and Psychiatry*, **33**, 877–95.

Brown, R., Hobson, P., Lee, A. and Stevenson, J. (1997). Are there 'autistic-like' features in congenitally blind children? *Journal of Child Psychology and Psychiatry*, **38**, 693–704.

Charman, T. and Baron-Cohen, S. (1995). Understanding models, photos, and beliefs: a test of the modularity thesis of metarepresentation. *Cognitive Development*, **10**, 287–98.

Craig, J. (1997). *An investigation of imagination and creativity in autism.* Unpublished PhD thesis, University of Cambridge.

Craig, J. and Baron-Cohen, S. (1999). Creativity and imagination in autism and Asperger Syndrome. *Journal of Autism and Developmental Disorders*, **29**, 319–26.

Diamond, A. (1991). Neuropsychological insights into the meaning of object concept development. In *The epigenesis of mind*, (ed. S. Carey and R. Gelman), pp. 67–110. Lawrence Erlbaum Associates., Hillsdale, N.J.

Flavell, J. H., Green, E. R. and Flavell, E. R. (1986). Development of knowledge about the appearance–reality distinction. *Monographs of the Society for Research in Child Development*, **51**.

Frith, U., Happé, F. and Siddons, F. (1994). Autism and theory of mind in everyday life. *Social Development*, **3**, 108–24.

Grice, H. P. (1975/1957). Logic and conversation. In *Syntax and semantics: speech acts*, (ed. R. Cole and J. Morgan). Academic Press, New York.

Happé, F. (1993). Communicative competence and theory of mind in autism: a test of Relevance Theory. *Cognition*, **48**, 101–19.

Happé, F. (1994). An advanced test of theory of mind: understanding of story characters' thoughts and feelings by able autistic, mentally handicapped, and normal children and adults. *Journal of Autism and Development Disorders*, **24**, 129–54.

Happé, F. (1995). The role of age and verbal ability in the theory of mind task performance of subjects with autism. *Child Development*, **66**, 843–55.

Harris, P., Johnson, C. N., Hutton, D., Andrews, G. and Cooke, T. (1989). Young children's theory of mind and emotion. *Cognition and Emotion*, **3**, 379–400.

Hobson, R. P. (1984). Early childhood autism and the question of egocentrism. *Journal of Autism and Developmental Disorders*, **14**, 85–104.

Leekam, S. and Perner, J. (1991). Does the autistic child have a metarepresentational deficit? *Cognition*, **40**, 203–18.

Leekam, S., Baron-Cohen, S., Brown, S., Perrett, D. and Milders, M. (1997). Eye-direction detection: a dissociation between geometric and joint-attention skills in autism. *British Journal of Developmental Psychology*, **15**, 77–95.

Leevers, H. and Harris, P. (1998). Drawing impossible entitities: a measure of the imagination in children with autism, children with learning disabilities, and normal 4-year-olds. *Journal of Child Psychology and Psychiatry*, **39**, 399–410.

Leslie, A. M. (1987). Pretence and representation: the origins of 'theory of mind'. *Psychological Review*, **94**, 412–26.

Leslie, A. M. and Frith, U. (1988). Autistic children's understanding of seeing, knowing, and believing. *British Journal of Developmental Psychology*, **6**, 315–24.

Leslie, A. M. and Thaiss, L. (1992). Domain specificity in conceptual development: evidence from autism. *Cognition*, **43**, 225–51.

Lewis, V. and Boucher, J. (1988). Spontaneous, instructed and elicited play in relatively able autistic children. *British Journal of Developmental Psychology*, **6**, 325–39.

Mitchell, P. and Lewis, C. (1995). *Origins of an understanding of mind*. Cambridge University Press, Cambridge.

Moore, C. and Dunham, P. (1996). *The role of joint attention in development*. Lawrence Erlbaum Associates, Hillsdale, N.J.

Ozonoff, S., Pennington, B. and Rogers, S. (1991). Executive function deficits in high-functioning autistic children: relationship to theory of mind. *Journal of Child Psychology and Psychiatry*, **32**, 1081–106.

Perner, J. (1991). *Understanding the representational mind*. Bradford Books, MIT Press, Cambridge, MA.

Perner, J., Frith, U., Leslie, A. M. and Leekam, S. (1989). Exploration of the autistic child's theory of mind: knowledge, belief, and communication. *Child Development*, **60**, 689–700.

Peterson, C. and Siegal, M. (1995). Deafness, conversation and theory of mind. *Journal of Child Psychology and Psychiatry*, **36**, 459–74.

Peterson, C. and Siegal, M. (ed.) (1997). Domain specificity and everyday biological, physical, and psychological thinking in normal, autistic, and deaf children. *New Directions for Child Development* (Vol. 75). Jossey Bass, San Francisco.

Phillips, W., Baron-Cohen, S. and Rutter, M. (1998). Understanding intention in normal development and in autism. *British Journal of Developmental Psychology*, **16**, 337–48.

Pratt, C. and Bryant, P. (1990). Young children understand that looking leads to knowing (so long as they are looking into a single barrel). *Child Development*, **61**, 973–83.

Reed, T. and Peterson, C. (1990). A comparative study of autistic subjects' performance at two levels of visual and cognitive perspective taking. *Journal of Autism and Development Disorders*, **20**, 555–68.

Russell, J. (ed.) (1997). *Autism as an executive disorder*. Oxford University Press, Oxford.

Scott, F. and Baron-Cohen, S. (1996). Imagining real and unreal objects: an investigation of imagination in autism. *Journal of Cognitive Neuroscience*, **8**, 400–11.

Sodian, B. and Frith, U. (1992). Deception and sabotage in autistic, retarded, and normal children. *Journal of Child Psychology and Psychiatry*, **33**, 591–606.

Sodian, B., Taylor, C., Harris, P. and Perner, J. (1992). Early deception and the child's theory of mind: false trails and genuine markers. *Child Development*, **62**, 468–83.

Surian, L., Baron-Cohen, S. and Van der Lely, H. (1996). Are children with autism deaf to Gricean Maxims? *Cognitive Neuropsychiatry*, **1**, 55–72.

Swettenham, J. (1996). Can children with autism be taught to understand false belief using computers? *Journal of Child Psychology and Psychiatry*, **37**, 157–65.

Swettenham, J., Baron-Cohen, S., Gomez, J.-C. and Walsh, S. (1996). What's inside a person's head? Conceiving of the mind as a camera helps children with autism develop an alternative theory of mind. *Cognitive Neuropsychiatry*, **1**, 73–88.

Tager-Flusberg, H. (1992). Autistic children's talk about psychological states: deficits in the early acquisition of a theory of mind. *Child Development*, **63**, 161–72.

Tager-Flusberg, H. (1993). What language reveals about the understanding of minds in children with autism. In *Understanding other minds: perspectives from autism*, (ed. S. Baron-Cohen, H. Tager-Flusberg, and D. J. Cohen). Oxford University Press.

Ungerer, J. and Sigman, M. (1981). Symbolic play and language comprehension in autistic children. *Journal of the American Academy of Child Psychiatry*, **20**, 318–37.

Wellman, H. (1990). *Children's theories of mind*. Bradford Books, MIT Press, Cambridge, MA.

Wellman, H. and Estes, D. (1986). Early understanding of mental entitites: a reexamination of childhood realism. *Child Development*, **57**, 910–23.

Whiten, A. (1991). *Natural theories of mind.* Basil Blackwell, Oxford.

Whiten, A. (1993). Evolving a theory of mind: the nature of non-verbal mentalism in other primates. In *Understanding other minds: perspectives from autism* (ed. S. Baron-Cohen, H. Tager-Flusberg, and D. J. Cohen). Oxford University Press.

Wimmer, H. and Perner, J. (1983). Beliefs about beliefs: representation and constraining function of wrong beliefs in young children's understanding of deception. *Cognition,* **13,** 103–28.

Wing, L and Gould, J. (1979). Severe impairments of social interaction and associated abnormalities in children: epidemiology and classification. *Journal of Autism and Developmental Disorders,* **9,** 11–29.

Yirmiya, N., Solomonica-Levi, D. and Shulman, C. (1996). The ability to manipulate behaviour and to understand manipulation of beliefs: a comparison of individuals with autism, mental retardation, and normal development. *Developmental Psychology,* **32,** 62–9.

Yirmiya, N., Erel, O., Shaked, M. and Solomonica-Levi, D. (1998). Meta-analyses comparing theory of mind abilities of individuals with autism, individuals with mental retardation, and normally developing individuals. *Psychological Bulletin,* **124,** 283–307.

# 2

# Developing understandings of mind

## HENRY M. WELLMAN AND KRISTIN H. LAGATTUTA

Humans are social creatures: we raise and are raised by others, live in family groups, co-operate, compete, and communicate. We not only live socially, we think socially. In particular, we develop numerous conceptions *about* people, about relationships, about groups, social institutions, conventions, manners and morals. The claim behind research on 'theory of mind' is that certain core understandings organize and enable this array of developing social perceptions, conceptions and beliefs. In particular, the claim is that our everyday understanding of persons is fundamentally mentalistic; we think of people in terms of their mental states—their beliefs, desires, hopes, goals, and inner feelings. Consequently, an everyday mentalism is ubiquitous and crucial to our understanding of the social world. Consider the following: you want to make someone happy, so you give her something she wants; you want an object that someone else also wants, so you deceive him into believing it is unavailable; you know something that others do not, so you tell them. These themes—wanting, pleasing, deceiving, informing—provide the fabric of everyday life, as well as that of great fiction and drama, and manifest our everyday understanding of persons as desiring, believing, emoting fellow beings.

Not only is a mentalistic construal of persons fundamental for adults, but in the last fifteen years considerable evidence has emerged to show that this construal, or some essential parts of it, is early-developing in children. In this chapter we review this evidence, thus outlining the psychological understandings of normally-developing children. Since the evidence is most abundant and clearest for three-, four-, and five-year-olds, we begin there and then go forward and backward to consider later and earlier developments.

Beginning with studies of preschool children's understanding of cognitive mental states such as beliefs, thoughts and knowledge, research on theory of mind has expanded to include an increasingly wide range of topics, ages, and accounts. In the past five years, especially, there has been increased focus on (a) children's developing psychological explanations; (b) their reasoning about people in natural contexts and everyday conversations; (c) their understanding of consciousness and mental ideation; (d) family and social-interactional influences on the development of understandings about mind and emotion; and (e) the early social understandings of infants. These emerging focuses figure prominently in our review.

To preview: this research shows that a mentalistic understanding of persons emerges rapidly in most normal children and characterizes a large part of children's reasoning about people. It is thus evident not only in a variety of laboratory tasks but also in children's spontaneous comments on and explanations about human life during their conversations with parents and friends. At the same time, thinking and reasoning about people mentalistically undergoes extensive development; early insights set the stage for a cascade of notions, conceptions, and ideas, as initial mentalistic construals give way to later revised ones. This developmental description raises the intriguing question of what social cognition and interaction would be like for persons who do not share in, or are seriously deficient in, our everyday mentalism. The theory of mind hypothesis for autism, explored in this volume, suggests that individuals with autism represent just such persons. The research on normative development, that we consider, is not only important in its own right, it also provides a framework for evaluating findings and debates about autism.

## PRESCHOOLERS AND TODDLERS

Consider two separable aspects of an everyday understanding of mind. One concerns the nature of mental entities or states—for example, the ordinary belief that thoughts and ideas are nonmaterial, subjective, mental 'things' in contrast with substantial, objective, physical objects. The second concerns the causal-explanatory aspect of mind—for example, our notions of how a person's goals, beliefs, and desires work together to produce their intentional actions or how various states and experiences shape their emotional reactions.

### Mental–physical distinctions

Unlike the tangible, manifest, public world of physical objects and overt behaviours, thoughts and ideas are insubstantial, transparent, and private. Thus, traditionally, mental phenomena were considered quite confusing for young children (e.g. Laurendeau and Pinard 1962; Piaget 1929; Shantz 1983). Piaget, for example, argued that pre-schoolers are realists, that is, they do not honour a distinction between mental and physical phenomena and hence think of mental entities as tangible, physical ones. 'The child cannot distinguish a real house, for example, from the concept or mental image or name of the house' (Piaget 1929, p. 55). In contrast, contemporary research demonstrates that children as young as three years firmly distinguish between the mental and physical worlds. For example, if told about one person who has a dog and another one who is thinking about a dog, three-, four-, and five-year-old children correctly judge which 'dog' can be seen, touched, and petted (Harris *et al.* 1991; Wellman and Estes 1986). Moreover, if told about someone who has a dog that ran away and about someone else who is thinking of a dog, such young children know that although neither 'dog' can be seen or petted, one is mental ('only imagination') whereas the other is physically real but unavailable (Estes *et al.* 1989). If asked to consider a thought about a raisin 'in the head' versus a swallowed raisin 'in the stomach', three-, four-, and five-year-olds know which one is literally inside the person and which is only metaphorically 'in his mind' (Watson *et al.* 1998).

Relatedly, from three to five years of age, young children grasp something of the subjectivity of thoughts. For example, three-year-olds are able to state that while they think a particular cookie tastes yummy, someone else could think it's yucky (e.g. Flavell *et al.* 1990), or that while Mary thinks a particular box has a doll in it, Bill thinks it contains a teddy bear (Wellman *et al.* 1996). Three- and four-year-olds also distinguish thinking from doing. They see the former as internal, private, and 'just' mental, while the latter is overt, public, and physically consequential (e.g. Flavell *et al.* 1995; Wellman *et al.* 1996). Moreover, by four and five years preschoolers understand various reality appearance distinctions—that a physical object can look one way to the eyes, yet be something altogether different 'in reality' (e.g. Flavell *et al.* 1986).

## Psychological causes and explanations

Mental states and entities are not only non-physical, they provide the causes and explanations for persons' actions and experiences. Philosophers and psychologists have often characterized this causal–explanatory system as a belief–desire reasoning framework (D'Andrade 1987; Fodor 1987; Wellman 1990). According to this analysis, at the centre of our everyday psychology is a basic triad: beliefs, desires, and actions. Why did Jane go to the swimming pool? She *wanted* to swim and *thought* the pool was open. The fundamental, albeit common, idea is that people engage in actions because they believe those actions will satisfy certain desires. Psychological explanation and attribution go beyond this basic triad in a variety of ways. For example, it encompasses reasoning such as: 'Why did John go to the candy machine? He wanted a candy bar, and thought he'd seen the kind he liked in that machine; boy, will he be disappointed'. That is, naive psychology incorporates a variety of related constructs such as preferences (e.g. 'the kind he likes') that ground one's desires, perceptual experiences (e.g. 'he'd seen that kind') that ground one's beliefs, and emotional reactions (e.g. 'he will be disappointed') that result from these desires, beliefs, and perceptions. Moreover, psychological reasoning involves a coherent system of mental-state constructs in which beliefs, desires, actions, emotions, and the like are causally intertwined: because an actor has certain beliefs and desires, he or she engages in certain intentional acts, the success and failure of which have certain consequences such as various emotional experiences.

Many demonstrations that young children can reason according to some of the connections inherent in this mentalistic system are based on children's predictions and attributions. In classic false-belief tasks, for example, participants are given information about a character's beliefs and desires and then must predict action. Thus, if four- and five-year-olds see a person notice where an object is placed, and then see that the person is absent (and thus cannot observe) when the object is moved to a new location, they can accurately predict that the person will mistakenly look for the object in the original location, and falsely think that it is there (Avis and Harris 1991; Moses and Flavell 1990; Wimmer and Perner 1983). Or, if four- and five-year-olds are shown a distinctive candy box that actually contains pencils, they can correctly attribute to a naive viewer of the box the belief that it contains candy, not pencils (Gopnik and Astington 1988; Perner *et al.* 1987). In other tasks three-, four-, and five-year-olds can use information about what a person perceives to predict what he or she knows or believes (Pillow 1989; Pratt and Bryant 1990; Wimmer *et al.* 1988), and can judge how various sources of information shape distinctive mental states (O'Neil and Gopnik 1991; Woolley and Bruell 1996). Similarly, children of this age can use information about what a character desires to predict his or her happiness, sadness, and anger at various outcomes (Stein and Levine 1989; Yuill 1984), or information about what a character believes to predict his or her surprise or puzzlement (Hadwin and Perner 1991; Wellman and Banerjee 1991).

If children's ordinary construal of persons is mentalistic, however, they should do more than make elicited predictions and attributions in tasks that force their attention to these states. They should also spontaneously explain human actions in terms of the actors' mental states. Indeed, children's explanations have recently become the focus of revealing experimental and natural language research. If preschool children are asked to explain simple human actions (e.g. Jane is looking for her kitty), they, like adults, predominantly advance belief–desire explanations (she wants her kitty, she thinks the kitty is missing) (Bartsch and Wellman 1989; Schult and Wellman 1997). Children offer such psychological explanations for emotional reactions as well, to explain characters' happiness, sadness, or surprise (Wellman and Banerjee 1991). Moreover, when presented with action scenarios, for example a picture of a boy holding a paintbrush, young children offer and prefer mental-state descriptions of the action rather than behavioural descriptions (e.g. preferring 'he's thinking about painting' to 'he's holding a paintbrush') (Lillard and Flavell 1990). Such mental–psychological explanations are apparent not only in laboratory studies but also in children's everyday conversations (Bartsch and Wellman 1995; Dunn and Brown 1993; Wellman *et al.* 1997). Moreover, young children's understandings of psychological causes and explanations are differentiated from contrasting understandings of physical causes and explanations. For example, whereas by three years children report that physical causes and forces are necessary to manipulate physical objects (e.g. to open and close a real pair of scissors), they assert that 'just thinking' is sufficient to affect mental changes (e.g. to open and close the image of a pair of scissors in your mind) (Estes *et al.* 1989). And while they give belief–desire explanations for intentional human actions (e.g. a person deciding to stand up) they give physical explanations for physical object-like human movements (e.g. a person being blown around by the wind) (Schult and Wellman 1997).

## Development

Although young children can reason about persons using an interlocking network of related mental-state constructs, children's psychological understanding develops significantly during the preschool years. Consider their reasoning about persons' beliefs, false beliefs, and mental representations. While four-year-olds often pass false-belief tasks, thereby evidencing an understanding that a person's actions are shaped by his or her beliefs about reality rather than simply by reality itself, younger children, typically three-year-olds, fail such tasks. In this, three-year-olds do not just answer randomly, they say that the person's actions or beliefs will correspond to what is really true (e.g. the person will look for the object in the new correct location; the other person will think that the candy box contains pencils). That is, they do not distinguish between the person's subjective belief and objective reality. This developmental difference from younger to older preschool children has been found when the questions are about mental states directly or when they are about behaviour (e.g. where the person will search or look), when the target person is a story character, a video-taped character, a puppet, a child, or an adult, and even in tasks that focus on the child's own beliefs (Wellman *et al.*, in preparation). Based on such findings children have been claimed to develop from an understanding of connections to an understanding of representations (Flavell 1988), from a situationist to a representational understanding of persons (Perner 1991), or from a desire to a belief–desire naive psychology (Wellman 1990).

At times these developmental claims have been framed in terms of a representational understanding 'absent' in three-year-olds and emerging 'only' in four- and five-year-olds. However, several studies now show that, at least in some situations, three-year-olds, too, can perform correctly on false-belief tasks. For example, downplaying the salience of the real state of affairs (e.g. that the candy box contains real pencils, not candy) or making salient the prior mental state (e.g. that the child first thinks it is a candy box) helps young children correctly identify the character's false belief (Mitchell and LaCohee 1991; Woolley 1995; Zaitchik 1991). In addition, three-year-olds at times perform well if they are more actively engaged in deceiving the target person (Chandler *et al.* 1989; Sullivan and Winner 1993; but see Sodian 1994), if the key features of the false-belief narrative are overlearned (Lewis *et al.* 1994), or if certain ways of phrasing the false-belief question are used rather than others (e.g. Lewis and Osborne 1990; Siegal and Beattie 1991). Yet, despite these variations, a recent meta-analysis of more than five hundred false-belief conditions with a variety of ages and procedural details shows that, overwhelmingly, two and a half- and early three-year-old children significantly make the false-belief error, whereas with increasing age they become significantly correct (Wellman *et al.*, in preparation).

Analysis of children's everyday conversations provides other evidence of a genuine shift in children's understanding of mental states. Children increasingly use such words as 'happy', 'sad', 'want', 'think', and 'know' in the preschool years (Bretherton and Beeghly 1982; Furrow *et al.* 1992; Ridgeway *et al.* 1985). Yet, while children use such words as 'want' and 'mad' to apparently refer to desires and emotions by eighteen months or so, they do not use words such as 'think' and 'know' to refer to thoughts and beliefs until about three years of age (Bartsch and Wellman 1995; Brown and Dunn 1991). This absence of references to thinking and knowing in children under three is striking considering that parents often talk to them about beliefs and thoughts as well as desires and emotions (Bartsch and Wellman 1995). Thus, natural language data are consistent with claims that children developmentally advance to a representational understanding of mind, or a belief–desire naive psychology, in the course of the preschool years.

By this description: (1) young children acquire an understanding of representational mental states over several years; but (2) at the start of the preschool years children already evidence a subjective, psychological understanding of persons. This is apparent for example, in their understanding of persons' desires and emotions. Thus, in laboratory judgement tasks two-year-olds show that they know that people may have different emotions (e.g. Denham 1986) and moreover judge that people may have different emotions about and different desires for the exact same object or event (e.g. Wellman and Woolley 1990). Not only do children produce such words as 'happy', 'sad', 'want', and 'like' by late in the second year of life, but systematic analyses show that, by two years, children use these terms to refer to persons' internal experiential states distinct from their external behaviours, physical features, and facial expressions. These conceptual distinctions are clear when young children explicitly contrast desires and reality, or two individuals' different desires or preferences (e.g. 'I don't like shaving cream; Daddy like shaving cream'). A variety of such contrastives—evident shortly after the second birthday—convincingly demonstrate an early subjective, psychological rather than objective, situational understanding of desires and emotions (Bartsch and Wellman 1995; Wellman *et al.* 1995).

Indeed, an understanding of desires—a person's wants and intentions—as subjective and as distinguished from overt behaviours may well be in place even earlier than two years. Repacholi and Gopnik (1997) had eighteen-month-old toddlers taste two snacks: broccoli, and goldfish crackers. Then an adult, facing the child, tasted each snack, saying, 'Mm' and smiling to one snack, and saying, 'Eww' and frowning to the other. In a 'Match' condition the adult liked the crackers and disliked the broccoli, matching the child's preference. In a 'Mismatch' condition she liked the broccoli instead. When the adult then held her hand halfway between the two snacks and said 'I want some more, can you give me some more?', eighteen-month-olds overwhelmingly gave the adult more of what she, the adult, had liked. In doing so in the Mismatch condition, the children demonstrated an understanding of desires as subjective—realizing that the adult wanted broccoli, contrary to their own preference for crackers. Moreover, Meltzoff (1995) demonstrated that eighteen-month-olds understand the intentions that lie behind overt actions. These toddlers imitated a model's actions by producing the intended, successful action, an action they had never actually observed, rather than the failed unsuccessful action that had been displayed (see also Carpenter *et al.* 1998).

Potentially, young children's engagement in and understanding of pretence may also reveal an early understanding of mental states (e.g. Leslie 1987), because, for adults at least, a person's pretend actions demand explanation in terms of that person's fictional representations. Before their second birthday most children begin to pretend, and by two years they engage in various pretence actions—e.g. pretending to sleep, treating a block as a car (e.g. McCune-Nicolich 1981). By two or two and a half years children often begin to use the term 'pretend', and show that they understand others' pretence actions as not-real (Harris and Kavanaugh 1993). However, children at this age may understand pretence simply as distinctive overt actions (e.g. Eric is *acting as* a rabbit acts, because he's hopping up and down), devoid of a more mentalistic interpretation of these peculiar behaviours (e.g. Eric is *thinking* he is a rabbit and so is hopping up and down). In fact, it is controversial how much, if any, even older three- and four-year-olds understand of the mental states involved in pretend actions (Lillard 1993). Some investigators claim that three-year-olds show an early mentalistic understanding of pretence (e.g. Custer 1996; Hickling *et al.* 1997) but others claim that this is not achieved until four or five years, well after a comparable mentalistic understanding of beliefs, imaginings, and knowledge (Lillard 1993). Regardless of these controversies, however, as we will discuss shortly, children's *participation* in pretend play likely provides an important occasion for learning about mental states.

## Summary

During the preschool years most normal children evidence a burgeoning mentalistic construal of persons. Even as toddlers children go beyond person's external appearances and overt behavioural movements to consider the intentions, desires, and emotions that underlie and cause overt action and expression. By the time they are four and five, many children further consider persons in terms of representational mental states, such as their thoughts, imaginations, and knowledge. These understandings are not mere fragmented attributions of this desire, or that belief, or yet some other emotion. Instead, and as increasingly evident in both laboratory tasks and everyday conversations, in the years from two to five children use a network of mental-state constructs in concert to come to sensible, coherent psychological understandings of persons' lives, experiences, and actions.

## INDIVIDUAL DIFFERENCES

Although variability in the expression, timing, and utilization of mentalistic understanding is only slowly being addressed and understood, it is clear that the overall developmental trajectory described above manifests itself only in the midst of considerable individual differences. For example, the age when children can first solve false-belief tasks (Astington and Jenkins 1995; Dunn *et al.* 1991*c*; Wellman *et al.*, in preparation) or start to talk about persons in terms of beliefs as well as desires (Bartsch and Wellman 1995) can vary from two and a half to five years. Whereas some children can reason about both external–situational and internal–mental causes of emotions at three years of age, others have difficulty interpreting why people feel they way they do at four and five years (Denham 1986; Lagattuta *et al.* 1997; Russell 1990). An increasing appreciation of such individual differences has encouraged several recent investigations into the connection between differing social experiences and early psychological understanding.

In several of these investigations children's understanding of false beliefs has again served as a marker for a developing understanding of mind. Perner *et al.* (1994) report that three- to five-year-old children with one or more siblings pass false-belief tests at higher rates than children with no siblings (see also Jenkins and Astington 1996). Further studies have pointed to co-operative play between siblings (Dunn *et al.* 1991*b*), play experiences with older versus younger siblings (Ruffman *et al.* 1998; Youngblade and Dunn 1995), or to interactions with older people in general (Lewis *et al.* 1996), as promoting children's early understandings of belief and mental representation.

Family experiences of these sorts may be significant because of their connection to pretend play. Namely, more siblings equals more opportunities to pretend (Perner *et al.* 1994), and pretending arguably provides a context for learning about mental states that are contrary to reality (see Leslie 1987; Harris 1991). Indeed, children who engage in frequent pretence more often discuss roles, negotiate scenes, transform objects, *and* use mental-state language in their play (Howe *et al.* 1998). Consistent with this, Taylor and Carlson (1997) found that three- and four-year-olds with extensive fantasy experiences (e.g. imaginary playmates, frequent pretend play, several fantasy toys) are more likely to pass false-belief tasks than children with less involvement in fantasy play. Further, the use of joint proposals and role assignments during pretence (Astington and Jenkins 1995) as well as role enactments with older siblings (Youngblade and Dunn 1995) can predict children's false-belief understanding as well.

Individual differences in children's knowledge about other mental states, especially emotions, have also been linked to early social experiences, particularly to family conversations. Although emotion talk typically occurs in all households, these conversations vary from family to family in terms of which feeling states are discussed, the tendency to provide causal explanations, the number of emotional themes, and in parental encouragement for child participation and evaluation (Dunn *et al.* 1991*b*; Fivush 1991; Reese *et al.* 1993). Gender of the child may also contribute to the frequency and content of these conversations (Haden *et al.* 1997; Reese and Fivush 1993), with several studies reporting that parents talk more about the causes and consequences of feelings, particularly sadness, with daughters than with sons (Fivush 1991; Kuebli and Fivush 1992), that by age two girls converse more extensively about emotions than boys do (Dunn *et al.* 1987), and that these gender differences continue until at least six years of age (Brown and Dunn 1996; but see Dunn and Brown 1993 and Dunn *et al.* 1991*a* for no gender differences).

This variability in how families talk about feelings is predictive of children's ability to identify emotional expressions and to connect emotions to common eliciting situations. For example, Dunn *et al.* (1991*a*) found that two-year-olds in families who frequently talked about emotions, particularly their causes, then evidenced more sophisticated knowledge about emotions at three years than did children whose families seldom discussed feelings. Related research by Dunn *et al.* (1991*b*) reported similar results, with talk about emotions at three years being predictive of children's affective-perspective taking at seven years (see also Brown and Dunn 1996).* Most importantly, early family conversations about emotion predict children's later understanding of mental states more generally. In particular, early frequent conversations about emotion predict later understandings of belief and false belief as well (Dunn *et al.* 1991*b*; see also Bartsch and Wellman 1995).

Understanding differences across individuals in the timing and strength of everyday psychological reasoning is undeniably important. Yet amidst this tapestry of individual differences, certain milestone achievements in a psychological understanding of

---

* Of course certain family experiences can negatively affect the development of emotion knowledge as well. For example, families with high negative affect or with parents who have high need to control children's aversive behaviours are associated with children who evidence less developed emotion knowledge (Camras *et al.* 1988; Cummings *et al.* 1985; Denham 1996; Denham *et al.* 1992; Dunn and Brown 1994).

persons typically emerge in the preschool years. Four- and five-year-olds in the US, Canada, UK, Australia, Turkey, and Japan solve appropriately simplified false-belief tasks. Non-literate, hunter-gathering sub-Saharan Africa four- and five-year-olds do so as well (Avis and Harris 1991). Moreover, so do mentally-handicapped Down's Syndrome children of four years' mental age (e.g. Baron-Cohen *et al.* 1985). Not only do English-speaking children talk about persons' desires well before later conversations about their beliefs, so too do Beijing and Hong Kong children learning Mandarin and Cantonese (Tardif and Wellman in press). Similarly, British, American, Japanese, and Chinese preschoolers share similar ideas about the time course of emotions (Harris *et al.* 1985) and the distinction between real, inner emotions versus apparent, displayed emotions (Gardner *et al.* 1988; Gross and Harris 1988). The achievement of these basic aspects of a mentalistic construal of persons in so many of the world's three-, four-, and five-year-olds thus raises at least two other intriguing questions: What later developments stem from these preschool achievements? and, What earlier developments precede them and enable them?

## LATER DEVELOPMENTS—THINKING

Children's understanding of mind and of persons continues to mature in important fashions beyond the age of four or five. Starting around age six, for example, children in literate Western societies not only understand that a person can have desires, beliefs, and preferences, but also that these mental attributes can be person-specific, enduring, and consistent across situations in the form of personality traits (e.g. Gnepp and Chilamkurti 1988; Heyman and Dweck 1998; Heyman and Gelman, 1998; Miller and Aloise 1989). Further achievements involve a deepening appreciation of the mind as an active interpreter and constructor of knowledge (e.g. Flavell 1988; Pillow 1988; Wellman 1990), and as a 'homunculus', or processing centre, that can be partly independent with a 'mind of its own' (Flavell *et al.* 1998; Wellman and Hickling 1994). For example, children of seven years and older appreciate that people's expectations or biases can distort their interpretations of ambiguous perceptual events (Carpendale and Chandler 1996; Pillow 1995; Pillow and Henrickson 1996; Taylor 1988).

   Children's improving understanding of thinking—in particular the ongoing mental ideation involved in actively thinking—is particularly noteworthy because it exemplifies how preschoolers' understanding of the mind can be both constrained and sophisticated at the same time. To reiterate, three- and four-year-olds know that thinking is an internal mental event that is different from seeing, talking, or touching an object; that a person can think of something she cannot see or touch; and that the contents of one's thoughts (e.g. a thought about a dog) are not physical or tangible (Flavell *et al.* 1993, 1995; Watson *et al.*1998; Wellman and Estes 1986). Moreover, three- and four-year-olds believe that a person is likely to be thinking during effortful cognitive tasks as long as obvious facial and gestural cues are displayed, such as a pensive look and stereotypical 'thinking pose' (Flavell *et al.* 1993, 1995).

   However, unlike older children, four- and five-year-olds do not see the mind as experiencing a 'stream of consciousness' (James 1890) or more or less constant flow of ideas and thoughts. Seven-year-olds and adults know that a person sitting quietly with a blank expression is still experiencing 'some thoughts and ideas' and that it is nearly impossible to have a mind completely 'empty of thoughts and ideas' for very long; but children younger than five do not share these intuitions (Flavell *et al.* 1993, 1995, 1998). Moreover, it is not until six to eight years of age that children consistently assert that people are thinking when engaged in apparently cognitive tasks such as pretending (Lillard 1993), reading, listening, and talking (Flavell *et al.* 1995). Even when preschoolers do acknowledge that a person is having thoughts, they find it difficult to report the content of those thoughts. This is true even when they are reporting their own thoughts (Flavell *et al.* 1995). Thus, coherent introspective reports of thinking activities are at first quite limited, and young children are surprisingly unaware that thoughts sometimes take the form of 'inner speech' or covert verbal talk (Flavell *et al.* 1997) or that thoughts can be unpredictable, automatic, involuntary, and difficult to suppress (Flavell *et al.* 1998).

Still, emotionally-laden thinking may be a distinct and important exception to any claim that preschoolers are 'generally poor at determining both when a person is thinking and what a person is thinking about' (Flavell *et al.* 1995, p. 79). For example, in one of the fourteen studies in the Flavell *et al.* (1995) monograph, children's understanding of thinking in emotional situations (e.g. waiting to get a shot) was compared with their knowledge about thinking during perceptual and cognitive situations including reading, looking, talking, and deciding. Whereas, in general, five- and seven-year-olds judged people as engaged in thinking less often than adults, children's and adults' responses for the emotional situations were comparable. Indeed, when presented with characters sitting quietly before or after emotionally arousing events, even five-year-olds asserted that they must be thinking nearly one hundred per cent of the time.

Perhaps the importance of affectively-laden thinking should not be surprising. Thoughts or memories about emotional experiences can be especially salient and have obvious consequences. For example, thinking about a past sad experience, such as a lost pet, can often re-engender the same negative feelings, despite the passing of days, months, or years since the actual event transpired. This interconnection between thoughts and emotions is stressed in scientific theories as well as everyday ones. Notably, cognitive theories of depression focus on the causative role of thinking with therapy aimed at changing negative ideation to improve emotional well-being (e.g. Abramson *et al.* 1978; Beck 1976; Nolen-Hoeksema 1991). Considering how inseparable thoughts and emotions can be, perhaps children's first inklings of the presence and influence of mental activity are intimately connected to emotional situations. Certainly, both talk about emotions and reminiscing about personal experiences are ubiquitous intertwined features of children's everyday conversations (Bretherton *et al.* 1986; Dunn *et al.* 1987; Dunn and Brown 1993; Fivush 1991; Hudson 1991; Kuebli and Fivush 1992; Reese *et al.* 1993).

Lagattuta *et al.* (1997) explored this possibility by investigating three- to six-year-olds' understanding of how being suddenly reminded, or cognitively cued, about a past emotional event, can change a person's current feelings. Cognitive cueing provides an informative measure of mind and emotion because it incorporates: (1) an understanding that people's emotional reactions to current situations can be shaped by past experiences; (2) knowledge that thoughts can influence emotional well-being; and (3) awareness that memories can be triggered by visual reminders, or cues. In several studies children listened to a series of stories that feature characters who feel sad after experiencing a negative event (e.g. a circus clown steps on, and destroys, Anne's favourite doll), and who many days later feel sad again after seeing a reminder, or cue to the past, during a positive situation (e.g. Anne later sees a clown at a birthday party). Children were asked to explain the current emotion: '*Why does [Anne] start to feel sad right now?*' Preschoolers' explanations evidenced sophisticated knowledge about thinking and cognitive cueing. For example, when cues were exact objects from past events (Anne now sees the exact same clown as before), 83% of three-year-olds and 100% of four- and five-year-olds were able to explain that a person's sadness was caused by thinking about the past (e.g. 'She's sad because she's remembering her broken doll'). Many three- (39%) and most four- (83%) and five-year-olds (100%) further linked these thoughts to the cue by offering one or more cognitive cueing explanations (e.g. 'She's sad because the clown makes her remember her doll'). By age five, children provided such cognitive cueing explanations for characters' emotions the large majority of the time. Further studies (Lagattuta and Wellman, submitted) have revealed that early insights about thinking and cognitive cueing may be particularly connected to explanations for *negative* emotions.

**Summary**

Advances in psychological understanding during the grade-school years include an understanding that people's mental states (e.g. desires and beliefs) are often consistent across situations in the form of personality traits, a greater appreciation of the mind as an active constructor and interpreter of knowledge, and a growing awareness of the presence, influence, and sources of ongoing thoughts—that is, active mental ideation. These later developments are preceded by significant insights during the preschool years. In particular, although older children and adults typically evidence a much richer appreciation of thinking and cognitive cueing than preschoolers do, four- and five-year-olds can demonstrate consistent knowledge about these concepts in certain *emotional* situations. Indeed, provocative emotional experiences may provide an important entryway into more sophisticated understandings of mind.

EARLIER DEVELOPMENTS—INFANTS

Preschoolers' achievements thus engender further, elaborated understandings about self and others, mind and mentalism. At the same time these preschool achievements are developmental outcomes. If two-year-olds and even eighteen-month-olds demonstrate some genuine appreciation of a person's desires, emotions, and intentions, then this suggests a developmental story beginning in infancy.

Even young infants are social creatures. They begin to become emotionally attached to others, they preferentially attend to faces—or, at first, the sorts of complex, detailed, high-contrast stimuli that faces represent (Banks and Salapatek 1983; Johnson and Morton 1991; Nelson 1987)—and in various other ways attend to people as a special sort of object. Consequently, infants develop certain expectations about persons that contrast with their expectations about physical objects. For example, within the first year of life infants will imitate the actions of persons (Meltzoff and Moore 1983) but not the similar activities of mechanical objects (e.g. Legerstee 1991), and they become visibly upset when people do not behave actively and contingently, or when they maintain a 'still face' (see review by Muir and Haines 1993). From about three months on infants discriminate animate–biological motions versus random or mechanical ones (e.g. Bertenthal 1993; Rochat *et al.* 1997), and toward the middle of the first year may distinguish persons as self-propelled movers in contrast to physical objects that must be launched by external forces. For example, at seven months (and perhaps earlier) infants appear surprised if objects begin moving without some external force causing them to do so as, but not if people do so (Spelke *et al.* 1995).

Understanding that certain objects move on their own, whereas others do not, helps infants to separate animate from inanimate things and encourages the recognition that infants 'are like other human beings as opposed to inanimate stimuli' (Legerstee 1992, p. 65). Yet conceiving of persons as animate in the sense of self-moving does not necessarily require a distinctive psychological conception. For example, an amoeba is an animate entity, and steam engines can be self moving, but neither requires a theory of mind in order to be understood. Indeed, many writers insist that a psychological conception of persons further requires an understanding of intentionality (Baldwin and Moses 1994; Brentano 1874; Dennett 1987; Perner 1991; Wellman 1993). An ordinary intentional act—deliberately reaching for an apple—is intentional because it is purposeful *and* because it manifests internal experiences about or towards some object or event, such as desire (*for* an apple) or a belief (*about* apples). Intentional acts, therefore, are very different from merely self-propelled motions; intentional acts are goal-directed—in the service of and directed toward some target or goal—and experiential—based on experiences of the goal, perception of the surrounding situation, and so on.

Traditionally, researchers studying infants describe a transition in social interaction evident in the period from eight to fourteen months, in which the infant comes to see self and others in notably different terms. Infants at this age are said to show a sense of subjectivity (Stern 1985), secondary intersubjectivity (Trevarthen and Hubley 1978), intentional communication (Bates *et al.* 1979), triadic awareness (Adamson and Bakeman 1985), or even an implicit theory of mind (Bretherton *et al.* 1981). If infants were coming to view persons in intentional terms at this age, it would be consistent with these claims and it could help account for a variety of findings whereby older infants (ten to fourteen months or so) show emerging understanding of others' visual gaze (Butterworth 1991; Scaife and Bruner 1975), use pointing to refer to nearby objects (Murphy and Messer 1977), engage in social referencing (Feinman 1982; Sorce *et al.* 1985), and begin to comprehend words and engage in simple communicative interchanges with words and gestures (Bates *et al.* 1979).

Currently, however, there is no consensus as to when infants come to understand

infants' understanding in terms of rationality—the ball's indirect path is attention-worthy because it is seen as irrational. However, these results could be consistent with a simpler interpretation of a budding infantile understanding of object-directedness. A more recent study with human actors and live behaviours provides some relevant evidence.

Phillips and Wellman (submitted) habituated six-, nine-, and twelve-month-old infants to a person who reached over a barrier and grasped an object, as shown in Fig. 2.1. Then they were shown two test events in which the barrier was *removed*: one showed a direct reach for the object, the other showed an indirect reach for the object. These test events were designed to contrast two possible understandings of the initial habituation movement. If infants attend to and code the initial habituation action in terms of physical movements of the arm, then they should look longer at the *direct reach* test event (which shows a new arm movement). However, if they code and attend to the habituation action in terms of an object-directed act—reaching directly for the object—then they should look longer at the *indirect reach* test event. In fact, on test trials, infants looked longer at the indirect reach. Even six-month-olds dishabituated to the indirect reach—even though it was showing the exact same arm movement as in habituation. And they remained habituated to the direct reach even though it actually showed a different physical arm movement. Thus at as early as six months these infants understood reaches as object-directed, as motions toward a target.

### Summary

By the last half of the second year, we believe, toddlers demonstrate an intentional understanding of persons. They understand that persons have subjective experiences such as desires and emotions (e.g. Repacholi and Gopnik 1997; Bartsch and Wellman 1995; Wellman *et al.* 1995). Moreover, they understand persons' actions in terms of the actors' underlying intentions or goals (Carpenter *et al.* 1998; Meltzoff 1995). These intentional understandings are preceded by several developments in infancy. Even as young as six months, infants may well understand some simple actions (e.g. reaches) as being directed toward certain target objects. By twelve months or so they understand a person's line of sight as being directed toward various objects and their

Habituation                     Direct reach test event              Indirect reach test event

**Fig. 2.1.** Displays used in Phillips and Wellman (submitted).

emotional displays as providing specific information about some objects and not others. Perhaps these early understandings, along with the infant pointing, social referencing, and early use of words that emerge at around twelve months, are manifestations of an important infant construal of persons in intentional terms—that is, by this age infants understand persons to be actors and experiencers who possess certain psychological states and goals about and for objects, states such as emoting, perceiving, and desiring. Alternatively, these early competencies may index a more modest, accumulating infantile knowledge about behavioural regularities—persons are beings whose reaches are overtly directed to objects, whose gazes are overtly directed to objects, and whose facial displays take on certain informative configurations.

Increasingly we favour a richer rather than leaner interpretation of year-old infant social competence; but this remains an open empirical issue. It is important to note, however, that, even under the leanest interpretation, six-month-old infants are coming to appreciate something very important: persons' actions and expressions are not only self-initiated, they are object-directed. At a minimum these early understandings support a deeper intentional understanding that will develop in the second year.

## CONCLUSIONS

The data base for understanding the development of a theory of mind encompasses evidence and theorizing from normal and impaired individuals, adults and children, humans and nonhuman primates, normative trends and individual differences, and persons raised in a variety of different cultural contexts. It is admittedly artificial and constrained to limit ourselves, as we have done in this chapter, essentially to describing normative developmental achievements of children growing up in middle class homes in literate societies. Nonetheless these data have proven provocative and informative to developmentalists, philosophers, linguists, primatologists, and more. Of special relevance to this volume, the studies and findings that we have reviewed have directly inspired the now voluminous literature on the impairments and achievements of individuals with autism. Moreover, they have shaped and amended theoretical hypotheses as to the mechanisms accounting for development of theories of mind.

Consider the two-pronged hypothesis of Leslie, Baron-Cohen, and colleagues (Baron-Cohen *et al.* 1985; Leslie 1987). More than ten years ago, these authors proposed that the rapid development of person-understandings apparent in normal children depends on a specialized mental module for representing mental states— ToMM, or the theory of mind mechanism. This module enables the child to represent not just objects or states of the world, but also representational states themselves (e.g. another person's belief about the world). If such a module existed, they argued, it could be impaired, resulting in failures to understand persons in terms of mental states and leading to distinctive deficits in social cognition and interaction, such as the impairments found in individuals with autism.

This initial hypothesis yielded considerable fruitful research on autism. As reviewed elsewhere in this volume, many studies now show impairment in reasoning about mental states in high-functioning individuals with autism who at the same time show very good reasoning about physical phenomena. These sorts of deficits in psychological reasoning are not apparent in control groups of subjects with Down Syndrome, mental retardation, or specific language delays.

At the same time, however, research of the sort we have reviewed, showing a rich and extended *series* of developmental achievements in infants', young children's, and older children's mental-state understandings, has strongly challenged the hypothesized activation of a single mental module (see e.g. the arguments in Gopnik and Wellman 1994). In response, both Leslie (1994) and Baron-Cohen (1995) recently proposed that there is a developmental *sequence* of mental modules. This series of modules, triggered or maturing at separate points in development, might then underlie the developmental data.

One implication of positing theory of mind modules, however, is that individuals who are *not* impaired in the relevant modules—that is, who do not have autism—should achieve landmark mental-state understandings on a roughly standard maturational timetable. In this regard, consider deaf individuals raised by hearing parents. Three recent studies of such deaf preschool children's performance on theory of mind tasks show delays and deficiencies comparable to those of children with autism (Gale *et al.* 1996; Peterson and Siegal 1995; Peterson and Siegal 1997). Since these deaf children presumably have not suffered the same sort of neurological damage that individuals with autism have, these data challenge accounts of theory of mind development relying solely on neurological–maturational mechanisms. Rather, they inspire alternative experiential–conversational accounts because deaf children of hearing parents have relatively little exposure to mental-state conversation early in life (Marschak 1993; Peterson and Siegal 1995). Consistent with more conversational accounts, whereas deaf children of hearing parents show impairments, deaf children raised by fluent signers do *not* show comparable theory of mind delays or deficits (Peterson and Siegal 1997).

More generally, modular accounts of development of theory of mind are complemented and opposed by a variety of other accounts that emphasize various crucial developmental experiences and/or conceptual constructions: conversational accounts (e.g. Dunn *et al.* 1991 *a,b*; Siegal 1991) that emphasize children's conversational experiences, Vygotskian accounts (e.g. Astington 1996) that emphasize other social–interactional influences, simulation accounts (Harris 1992) that emphasize children's experiences and abilities at using their own mental states to simulate those of others, and theory–theory accounts (e.g. Gopnik and Wellman 1994) that emphasize how later mental-state constructs (e.g. an understanding of beliefs) build on and transform earlier ones (e.g. an understanding of desire or perception). We will not review and evaluate these proposals here (but see Wellman and Gelman 1997). We emphasize only that all of these accounts stem from and are tested against the increasingly rich and detailed descriptive findings as to children's developing understandings. These descriptive findings also continue to provide inspiration for further research on the theory of mind hypothesis for autism. Indeed, we see at least four different emphases that might prove especially intriguing and informative for further research.

**Early developments: object-directedness**

Suppose that autism represents, in part, a serious delay or impairment in the normal progression of a sequence of conceptual understandings, as proposed by the theory of mind hypothesis. Then, understanding early developments in this sequence is of special importance. For example, early impairments could aid in early diagnoses. At present, research and hypotheses directed to this question concentrate on younger autistics' understanding of eyes, faces, and visual attention. Thus research has shown that young individuals with autism have difficulties with joint attention (Mundy and Sigman 1989), deficits in using pointing to direct attention (Baron-Cohen 1989), difficulties in attending to and understanding the significance of eyes (Baron-Cohen *et al.* 1995), and in recognizing facial displays of emotion (Hobson 1986).

The findings we have reviewed with infants suggest another line of inquiry: a focus on object-directed *actions*. As noted above, recent research on normal infants' understanding of intentionality suggests that knowledge about hands, reaches, and related actions may be an early breeding ground for intentional understandings. That is, as with eyes and faces, people's intentional states are also revealed in their actions. As we argued previously, infants' early focus on the actions of hands and arms may be significant because these movements overtly display object-directedness, and understanding of object-directedness foreshadows later knowledge about goal-directedness. Therefore, research on whether children with autism can recognize deliberate object-directed and goal-directed actions may provide an important alternative avenue for assessing their early intentional understandings.


**Thinking**

Normal development as we have outlined it proceeds from earlier understanding of intentional action and reference to later understandings of active, conscious, thinking minds. Thus, if research on intentional understandings might be fruitful with younger, less able autistics, then research on thinking may yield important insights about older and more high-functioning autistics.

A subset of children with autism (20–25%) come to pass false-belief tasks, thereby attributing to persons thoughts such as 'she thinks her ball is in the cupboard'. Yet Flavell's recent research demonstrates that in the normal case an understanding of thinking goes far beyond attributing such punctate thoughts. Older preschool and school age children come to view thinking as an incessant, ongoing cognitive activity. Thus they conceive of persons as having continuous inner thoughts, veritable streams of conscious experience, and they become able to report fluently and introspectively on their own streams of thought. A broadened consideration of conceptions and experiences of thinking might be useful for understanding autism as well. For example, Hulburt *et al.* (1994) solicited reports of inner experience from three individuals with Asperger's syndrome. These individuals were paged periodically throughout the day and asked to report their experiences in the course of their everyday activities. Normal adult controls engaged in this procedure reported a complex mixture of inner speech, emotional reactions, mental images, and 'pure thought'. The Asperger's individuals,

however, although verbally fluent and competent in other ways, reported only perceptions and actions, almost completely devoid of thoughts, emotions, or inner speech.

In rare instances Hulburt *et al.*'s individuals with Asperger's syndrome would
describe some inner experiences, and then they described these solely in terms of
pictures in their head. Temple Grandin, a high-functioning adult with autism, also
describes her thinking as largely pictures in the head (Grandin 1995). These reports
inspire an intriguing hypothesis. Perhaps encouraging high-functioning individuals
with autism to conceive of thoughts as pictures in the head may provide them an
avenue for understanding such elusive mental states and experiences. Research with
normal preschoolers adds some strength to this conjecture. Three-, four-, and five-
year-olds often talk about thoughts and dreams as pictures in the head (Estes *et al.*
1989). In addition, pictorial conventions such as thought-bubbles that depict thoughts
as pictures are easily understood by three-year-olds, and such thought-bubble depictions can help young children to reason more effectively about mental states
(Wellman *et al.* 1996). Consequently, three recent studies (Swettenten *et al.* 1996;
Baron-Cohen *et al.* 1997; McGregor *et al.*, 1998) have begun to explore this 'picture-
in-the-head' hypothesis with autistic children with promising initial results. Several
high-functioning autistics who at first failed false-belief tests later passed after being
trained to consider thoughts as 'pictures in the head'.

## Emotion and thinking

Part of the logic of using thought-bubbles or pictures-in-the-head to aid children with
autism to understand the mind is based on evidence that people with autism often
have a good understanding of pictures and drawings as representations (Leekam and
Perner 1991; Leslie and Thaiss 1992). Thus a relatively developed set of conceptions—
e.g. understanding of pictures—might be used to provide a compensatory strategy for
addressing or circumventing an impaired or undeveloped set of conceptions—e.g.
deficits in understanding mental states. Relatedly, research with normal children
suggests that early understandings of simple desires or emotions may be helping
children develop subsequent understandings of thoughts, beliefs, and knowledge. To
reiterate, in normal children early talk about and understanding of emotion not only
precedes, it *predicts*, later competence with beliefs, false beliefs, and knowledge.

Our knowledge of how individuals with autism understand emotion is controversial,
but several sources have shown that high-functioning autistics often have some awareness of simple desires and emotions (e.g. Baron-Cohen 1991) while failing to understand beliefs, false beliefs, and knowledge. Indeed, natural language data show that
whereas children with Down Syndrome and high-functioning children with autism
both talk about simple emotions and emotional expressions, only the language of
children with autism is strikingly lacking in cognitive mental terms such as 'think',
'know', 'remember', and 'dream' (Tager-Flusberg 1992). Perhaps, therefore, high-
functioning autistics' earlier, more adequate understanding of simple emotions could
be used to help bootstrap or encourage better understanding of epistemic mental states.
Alternatively, it may be that it is this key developmental connection—the interplay

between mind and emotion, and hence utilizing understanding of emotion to build a larger awareness of mind—that is particularly problematic for individuals with autism.

## The importance of explanation

Tager-Flusberg's (1992) data suggest that although *references* to emotions and desires are similar in the conversations of children with autism and with Down Syndrome, children with autism rarely offer *explanations* for emotions. Yet for normal children, in the research we reviewed earlier, it seems that discourse about and understanding of the causes and explanations of emotion may especially contribute to increased insights about the mind. This observation again underscores the importance of explanations for children's normal developing understanding of persons and minds. Mental-state understandings provide explanations for human actions, words, and expressions. They critically allow normal individuals to make sense of human action, reaction, and interaction. Research with normal children is thus increasingly focusing on children's explanations.

In contrast, research on children with autism has essentially confined itself to judgement or prediction tasks, such as standard false-belief tasks. In one early exception to this trend, Baron-Cohen *et al.* (1986) found that individuals with autism could not correctly order picture sequences depicting mental-state causality and experiences. In contrast, they were well able to correctly sequence pictures involving mechanical causality and outcome. Moreover, in narrating the mental-state picture sequences, children with autism not only failed to use mental-state terms, they also failed to relate the pictures together causally in any fashion, simply describing the pictures one by one in sequence. Such deficits are also found in the story retellings of children with autism (Loveland and Tunali 1993), leading to claims that they 'lack a grasp of how to *narrate*, as opposed to merely *describe*, a series of events' (p. 248).

Psychological understandings, of the normal belief–desire kind, require and manifest a coherent appreciation of a variety of mental states and especially of their connections to one another and to action. These connected understandings are importantly manifested in explanations, and importantly contrasted with physical explanations and reasoning. At the least, it would be intriguing to know more about how conceptions of causality and explanation develop in autistic individuals both inside and outside the realm of psychological understanding.

In conclusion, acquiring a theory of mind is a foundational human development, the impairment of which leads to serious consequences, as the evidence from typical and atypical children begins to make clear. Normally, the acquisition of a mentalistic understanding of persons begins early in life with certain social–cognitive appreciations of infants, is evident in a rapidly unfolding yet extended sequence of developments in childhood, and is manifest in children's judgements and explanations both in laboratory tasks and in their everyday conversations and social interactions. Understanding the developmental course of these achievements, then, provides critical information about an integral feature of normal development. Moreover, knowledge about normal development sheds light on the developmental impairments of individuals with autism, yielding insights that can aid both in diagnosis and in potential programmes to help autistics learn more about the mental world.

## Acknowledgements

Support for the preparation of this chapter was provided by NICHD grant HD-22149 to WellmanREFERENCES

Abramson, L. Y., Seligman, M. E. P. and Teasdale, J. D. (1978). Learned helplessness in humans: critique and reformulation. *Journal of Abnormal Psychology*, **87**, 49–74.

Adamson, L. B. and Bakeman, R. (1985). Affect and attention: infants observed with mothers and peers. *Child Development*, **5**, 582–93.

Astington, J. W. (1996). What is theoretical about the child's theory of mind? A Vygotskian view of its development. In *Theories of theory of mind*, (ed. P. Carruthers and P. K. Smith), pp. 184–99. Cambridge University Press.

Astington, J. W. and Jenkins, J. M. (1995). Theory of mind development and social understanding. *Cognition and Emotion*, **9**, 151–65.

Avis, J. and Harris, P. L. (1991). Belief–desire reasoning among Baka children. *Child Development*, **62**, 460–7.

Baldwin, D. A. and Moses, L. J. (1994). Early understanding of referential intent and attentional focus: evidence from language and emotion. In *Children's early understanding of mind*, (*ed.* C. Lewis and P. Mitchell). Erlbaum, Hove.

Baldwin, D. A. and Moses, L. J. (1996). The ontogeny of social information gathering. *Child Development*, **67**, 1915–39.

Banks, M. S. and Salapatek, P. (1983). Infant visual perception. In *Handbook of child psychology*, Vol. 2: Infancy and developmental psychology, (ed. M. Haith and J. Campos). Wiley, New York.

Baron-Cohen, S. (1989). Perceptual role-taking and protodeclarative pointing in autism. *British Journal of Developmental Psychology*, **1**, 113–27.

Baron-Cohen, S. (1991). Do people with autism understand what causes emotion? *Child Development*, **62**, 385–95.

Baron-Cohen, S. (1995). *Mindblindness: an essay on autism and theory of mind*. MIT Press, Cambridge, MA.

Baron-Cohen, S., Leslie, A. M. and Frith, U. (1985). Does the autistic child have a 'theory of mind?' *Cognition*, **21**, 37–46.

Baron-Cohen, S., Leslie, A. M. and Frith, U. (1986). Mechanical behavioral, intentional understanding of picture stories in autistic children. *British Journal of Developmental Psychology*, **4**, 113–25.

Baron-Cohen, S., Campbell, R., Karmiloff-Smith, A. and Grant, J. (1995). Are children with autism blind to the mentalistic significance of the eyes? *British Journal of Developmental Psychology*, **13**, 379–98.

Baron-Cohen, S., Wellman, H. M., Gomez, J. C., Swettenhan, J. and Toye, E. (1997). Using thought-bubbles helps children with autism acquire an alternative to a theory of mind. Unpublished manuscript.

Bartsch, K. and Wellman, H. M. (1989). Young children's attribution of action to beliefs and desires. *Child Development*, **60**, 946–64.

Bartsch, K. and Wellman, H. M. (1995). *Children talk about the mind*. Oxford University Press, New York.

Bates, E., Bonigni, L., Bretherton, I., Camaioni, L. and Volterra, V. (1979). *The emergence of symbols: cognition and communication in infancy.* Academic Press, New York.

Beck, A. T. (1976). *Cognitive therapy and emotional disorders.* International Universities Press, New York.

Bertenthal, B. I. (1993). Perception of biomechanical motions by infants. In *Visual perception and cognition in infancy*, (ed. C. Granrud), pp. 175–214. Erlbaum, Hillsdale, NJ.

Brentano, F. (1874/1973). *Psychology from an empirical standpoint*, (trans. A. C. Rancurello, D. B. Terrell and L. L. McAlister). Routledge and Kegan Paul, London.

Bretherton, I. and Beeghly, M. (1982). Talking about internal states: the acquisition of an explicit theory of mind. *Developmental Psychology*, **18**, 906–21.

Bretherton, I., McNew, S. and Beeghly-Smith, M. (1981). Early person knowledge as expressed in gestural and verbal communication: when do infants acquire a 'theory of mind?' In *Social cognition in infancy*, (ed. M. Lamb and L. Sherrod), pp. 333–73. Erlbaum, Hillsdale, NJ.

Bretherton, I., Fritz, J., Zahn-Waxler, C. and Ridgeway, D. (1986). Learning to talk about emotions: a functionalist perspective. *Child Development*, **57**, 529–48.

Brown, J. R. and Dunn, J. (1991). 'You can cry, mum': The social and developmental implications of talk about internal states. *British Journal of Developmental Psychology*, **9**, 237–56.

Brown, J. R. and Dunn, J. (1996). Continuities in emotion understanding from three to six years. *Child Development*, **67**, 789–802.

Butterworth, G. E. (1991). The ontogeny and phylogeny of joint visual attention. In *Natural theories of mind*, (ed. A. Whiten), pp. 223–32. Basil Blackwell, Oxford.

Camras, L. A., Ribordy, S., Hill, J., Martino, S., Spaccarelli, S., and Stefani, R. (1988). Recognition and posing of emotional expressions by abused children and their mothers. *Developmental Psychology*, **24**, 776–81.

Carpendale, J. I. and Chandler, M. J. (1996). On the distinction between false belief understanding and subscribing to an interpretive theory of mind. *Child Development*, **67**, 1686–706.

Carpenter, M., Aktar, N., and Tomasello, M. (1998). Fourteen- to 18–month-old infants differentially imitate intentional and accidental actions. *Infant Behavior and Development*, **21**, 315–30.

Chandler, M., Fritz, A. S., and Hala, S. (1989). Small scale deceit: deception as a marker of 2-, 3-, and 4-year-olds' early theories of mind. *Child Development*, **60**, 1263–77.

Csibra, G. and Gergely, G. (1996). Origins of naive psychology: understanding rational actions in infancy. Paper presented at the ISSBD Biennial Meetings, Quebec City, Canada.

Cummings, E. M., Iannotti, R. J., and Zahn-Waxler, C. (1985). Influence of conflict between adults on the emotions and aggression of young children. *Developmental Psychology*, **21**, 495–507.

Custer, W. L. (1996). A comparison of young children's understanding of contradictory representations in pretense, memory, and belief. *Child Development*, **67**, 678–88.

D'Andrade, R. (1987). A folk model of the mind. In *Cultural models in language and thought*, (ed. D. Holland and N. Quinn), pp. 1121–48). Cambridge University Press.

Denham, S. A. (1986). Social cognition, prosocial behavior and emotion in preschoolers. *Child Development*, **57**, 194–201.

Denham, S. A., Zoller, D., and Couchoud, E. A. (1992). Socialization of preschoolers' emotion understanding. *Developmental Psychology*, **30**, 928–36.

Dennett, D. C. (1987). *The intentional stance.* Bradford Books, MIT Press, Cambridge, MA.

Dunn, J. and Brown, J. (1993). Early conversations about causality: content, pragmatics and developmental change. *British Journal of Developmental Psychology*, **11**, 107–23.

Dunn, J., and Brown, J. R. (1994). Affect expression in the family, children's understanding of emotions, and their interactions with others. *Merrill-Palmer Quarterly*, **40**, 120–37.

Dunn, J., Bretherton, I. and Munn, P. (1987). Conversations about feeling states between mothers and their young children. *Developmental Psychology*, **23**, 132–9.

Dunn, J., Brown, J., and Beardsall, L. (1991a). Family talk about feeling states and children's later understanding of others' emotions. *Child Development*, **27**, 448–55.

Dunn, J., Brown, J., Slomkowski, C., Tesla, C. and Youngblade, L. (1991b). Young children's understanding of other people's feelings and beliefs: individual differences and their antecedents. *Child Development*, **62**, 1352–66.

Estes, D. (1998). Young children's awareness of their mental activity: The case of mental rotation. *Child Development*, **69**, 1345–60.

Estes, D., Wellman, H. M., and Woolley, J. D. (1989). Children's understanding of mental phenomena. In *Advances in child development and behavior*, (ed. H. Reese), pp. 41–87. Academic Press, New York.

Feinman, S. (1982). Social referencing in infancy. *Merrill-Palmer Quarterly*, **28**, 445–70.

Fernald, A. (1993). Approval and disapproval: infant responsiveness to vocal affect in familiar and unfamiliar languages. *Child Development*, **64**, 657–74.

Fivush, R. (1991). Gender and emotion in mother-child conversations about the past. *Journal of Narrative and Life History*, **1**, 325–41.

Flavell, J. H. (1988). The development of children's knowledge about the mind: from cognitive connections to mental representations. In *Developing theories of mind*, (ed. J. Astington, P. Harris, and D. Olson), pp. 244–67. Cambridge University Press, New York.

Flavell, J. H., Green, F. L. and Flavell, E. R. (1986). Development of knowledge about the appearance-reality distinction. *Monographs of the Society for Research in Child Development*, **51**, (Serial No. 212).

Flavell, J. H., Green, F. L., Flavell, E. R. and Grossman, J. B. (1997). The development of children's knowledge about inner speech. *Child Development*, **68**, 39–47.

Flavell, J. H., Flavell, E. R., Green, F. L. and Moses, L. J. (1990). Young children's understanding of fact beliefs versus value beliefs. *Child Development*, **61**, 915–28.

Flavell, J. H., Green, F. L. and Flavell, E. R. (1993). Children's understanding of the stream of consciousness. *Child Development*, **64**, 387–98.

Flavell, J. H., Green, F. L. and Flavell, E. R. (1995). Young children's knowledge of thinking. *Monographs of the Society for Research in Child Development*, entire serial No. 243.

Flavell, J. H., Green, F. L. and Flavell, E. R. (1997). The development of children's knowledge about inner speech. *Child Development*, **68**, 39–47.

Flavell, J. H., Green, F. L. and Flavell, E. R. (1998). The mind has a mind of its own: developing knowledge about mental uncontrollability. *Cognitive Development*, **13**, 127–38.

Fodor, J. A. (1987). *Psychosemantics: the problem of meaning in the philosophy of mind*. Bradford Books, MIT Press, Cambridge, MA.

Furrow, D., Moore, C., Davidge, J. and Chiasson. (1992). Mental terms in mothers' and children's speech: similarities and relationships. *Journal of Child Language*, **19**, 617–31.

Gale, E., de Villiers, P., de Villiers, J. and Pyers, J. (1996). Language and theory of mind in oral deaf children. Paper presented at the Boston University Conference on Language Development, Boston, MA.

Gardner, D., Harris, P. L., Ohomoto, M. and Hamazaki, T. (1988). Japanese children's understanding of the distinction between real and apparent emotion. *International Journal of Behavioral Development*, **11**, 203–18.

Gergely, G., Nadasdy, Z., Csibra, G. and Biro, S. (1995). Taking the intentional stance at 12 months of age. *Cognition*, **56**, 165–93.

Gnepp, J. and Chilamkuri, C. (1988). Children's use of personality attributions to predict other people's emotional and behavioral reactions. *Child Development*, **59**, 743–54.

Gopnik, A. and Astington, J. W. (1988). Children's understanding of representational change and its relation to the understanding of false belief and the appearance-reality distinction. *Child Development*, **59**, 26–37.

Gopnik, A. and Slaughter, V. (1991). Young children's understanding of changes in their mental states. *Child Development*, **62**, 98–110.

Gopnik, A. and Wellman, H. M. (1994). The theory theory. In *Domain specificity in cognition and culture*, (ed. L. Hirschfeld and S. Gelman). Cambridge University Press, New York.

Grandin, T. (1995). *Thinking in pictures*. Doubleday, New York.

Gross, D. and Harris, P. L. (1988). Understanding false beliefs about emotion. *International Journal of Behavioral Development*, **11**, 475–88.

Haden, C. A., Haine, R. A. and Fivush, R. (1997). Developing narrative structure in parent-child reminiscing across the preschool years. *Developmental Psychology*, **33**, 295–307.

Hadwin, J. and Perner, J. (1991). Pleased and surprised: children's cognitive theory of emotion. *British Journal of Developmental Psychology*, **9**, 215–34.

Harris, P. L. (1991). The work of the imagination. In *Natural theories of mind*, (ed. A. Whiten), pp. 283–304. Basil Blackwell, Oxford.

Harris, P. L. (1992). From simulation to folk psychology: The case for development. *Mind and Language*, **7**, 120–44.

Harris, P. L. and Kavanaugh, R. D. (1993). Young children's understanding of pretense. *Monographs of the Society for Research in Child Development*, **58**, entire serial No. 231.

Harris, P. L., Guz, G. R., Lipian, M. S. and Man-shu, Z. (1985). Insight into the time course of emotion among Western and Chinese children. *Child Development*, **56**, 972–88.

Harris, P. L., Brown, E., Marriot, C., Whithall, S. and Harmer, S. (1991). Monsters, ghosts and witches: testing the limits of the fantasyreality distinction in young children. *British Journal of Developmental Psychology*, **9**, 105–23.

Heyman, G. D. and Dweck, C. S. (1998). Children's thinking about traits: implications for judgments of self and others. *Child Development*, **69**, 391–403.

Heyman, G. D. and Gelman, S. A. (1998). Young children use motive information to make trait inferences. *Developmental Psychology*, **34**, 310–21.

Hickling, A. K., Wellman, H. M., and Gottfried, G. (1997). Preschoolers' understanding of others' mental attitudes toward pretend happenings. *British Journal of Developmental Psychology*, **15**, 339–54.

Hobson, R. P. (1986). The autistic child's appraisal of expressions of emotion. *Journal of Child Psychology and Psychiatry*, **27**, 321–42.

Hornick, R., Risenhoover, N., and Gunnar, M. (1987). The effects of maternal positive, neutral, and negative affective communications and infant responses to new toys. *Child Development*, **58**, 937–44.

Howe, N., Petrakos, H. and Rinaldi, C. M. (1998). 'All the sheeps are dead. He murdered them': sibling pretense, negotiation, internal state language, and relationship quality. *Child Development*, **69**, 182–91.

Hudson, J. (1991). Learning to reminisce: a case study. *Journal of Narrative and Life History*, **1**, 295–324.

Hulburt, R., Happe, F. and Frith, U. (1994). Sampling the inner experience of autism: a preliminary report. *Psychological Medicine*, **24**, 385–95.

James, W. (1890). *The principles of psychology*. Henry Holt, New York.

Jenkins, J. M. and Astington, J. W. (1996). Cognitive, linguistic, and social factors associated with theory of mind development in young children. *Developmental Psychology*, **32**, 708.

Johnson, M. H. and Morton, J. (1991). *Biology and cognitive development: the case of face recognition*. Basil Blackwell, Oxford.

Kuebli, J. and Fivush, R. (1992). Gender differences in parentchild conversations about past emotions. *Sex Roles*, **27**, 683–98.

Lagattuta, K. H., Wellman, H. M. and Flavell, J. H. (1997). Preschoolers' understanding of the link between thinking and feeling: cognitive cueing and emotional change. *Child Development*, **68**, 1081–104.

Lagattuta, K. H. and Wellman, H. M. (submitted). Reminiscing about the past: Early knowledge about links between prior experience, thinking, and emotion.

Laurendeau, M. and Pinard, A. (1962). *Causal thinking in the child: a genetic and experimental approach*. International Universities Press, New York.

Leekam, S. and Perner, J. (1991). Does the autistic child have a 'metarepresentational' deficit? *Cognition*, **40**, 203–18.

Legerstee, M. (1991). The role of person and object in eliciting early imitation. *Journal of Experimental Child Psychology*, **51**, 423–33.

Legerstee, M. (1992). A review of the animateinanimate distinction in infancy. *Early Development and Parenting*, **1**, 59–67.

Leslie, A. M. (1987). Pretense and representation: the origins of 'theory of mind'. *Psychological Review*, **94**, 4124–26.

Leslie, A. M. (1994). ToMM, ToBy, and agency: core architecture and domain specificity in cognition and culture. In *Mapping the mind: domain specificity in cognition and culture*, (ed. L. Hirschfeld and S. Gelman), pp. 119–48). Cambridge University Press, New York.

Leslie, A. M. and Thaiss, L. (1992). Domain specificity in conceptual development: neuropsychological evidence from autism. *Cognition*, **43**, 225–51.

Lewis, C. and Osbourne, A. (1990). Three-year-olds' problems with false belief: conceptual deficit or linguistic artifact? *Child Development*, **61**, 1514–19.

Lewis, C., Freeman, N. H., Hagestadt, E. and Douglas, H. (1994). Narrative access and production in preschoolers' false belief reasoning. *Cognitive Development*, **9**, 397–424.

Lewis, C., Freeman, H., Kyriakidou, C., Maridaki-Kassotaki, K. M. and Berridge, D. M. (1996). Social influences on false belief access: specific sibling influences or general apprenticeship? *Child Development*, **67**, 2930–47.

Lillard, A. S. (1993). Young children's conceptualization of pretense: action or mental representational state? *Child Development*, **64**, 372–86.

Lillard, A. S. and Flavell, J. H. (1990). Young children's preference for mental state versus behavioral descriptions of human action. *Child Development*, **61**, 731–41.

Loveland, K. and Tunali, B. (1993). Narrative language in autism and the theory of mind. In *Understanding other minds*, (ed. S. Baron-Cohen, H. Tager-Flusberg, and D. Cohen), pp. 247–66). Oxford University Press.

Marschak, M. (1993). *Psychological development in deaf children*. Oxford University Press, New York.

McCune-Nicolich, L. M. (1981). Toward symbolic functioning: structure of early use of pretend games and potential parallels with language. *Child Development*, **52**, 785–97.

McGregor, E., Whiten, A. and Blackburn, P. (1998). Teaching theory of mind by highlighting intention and illustrating thoughts. *British Journal of Developmental Psychology*, **16**, 281–300.

Meltzoff, A. N. (1995). Understanding the intentions of others: re-enactment of intended acts by 18-month-old children. *Developmental Psychology*, **31**, 838–50.

Meltzoff, A. N. and Moore, M. K. (1983). Newborn infants imitate adult facial gestures. *Child Development*, **54**, 702–19.

Miller, P. H. and Aloise, P. A. (1989). Young children's understanding of the psychological causes of behavior. *Child Development*, **60**, 257–85.

Mitchell, P. and Lacohee, H. (1991). Children's early understanding of false belief. *Cognition*, **39**, 107–27.

Moore, C. (1996).Theories of mind in infancy. *British Journal of Developmental Psychology*, **14**, 19–40.

Moore, C. and Corkum, V. (1994). Social understanding at the end of the first year of life. *Developmental Review*, **14**, 349–72.

Moses, L. J. and Flavell, J. H. (1990). Inferring false beliefs from actions and reactions. *Child Development*, **61**, 929–45.

Muir, D. W. and Haines, S. M. J. (1993). Infant sensitivity to perturbations in adult facial, vocal, tactile, and contingent stimulation during face to face interactions. In *Developmental neuro-cognition: speech and face processing in the first year*, (ed. B. de Boysson-Bardies, S. de Schonen, P. Jusczyk, P. McNeilage, and J. Morton). Kluver, Dordrecht.

Mumme, D. L., Fernald, A. and Herrerra, C. (1996). Infants' responses to facial and vocal emotional signals in a social referencing paradigm. *Child Development*, **67**, 3219–37.

Mundy, P. and Sigman, M. (1989). The theoretical implications of joint-attention deficits in autism. *Development and Psychopathology*, **1**, 173–84.

Murphy, C. M. and Messer, D. J. (1977). Mothers, infants and pointing: a study of a gesture. In *Studies in motherinfant interaction*, (ed. H. R. Schaffer). Academic Press, London.

Nelson, L. A. (1987). The recognition of facial expressions in the first two years of life: mechanisms of development. *Child Development*, **58**, 889–909.

Nolan-Hoeksema, S. (1991). Responses to depression and their effects on the duration of depressive episodes. *Journal of Abnormal Psychology*, **100**, 569–82.

O'Neill, D. K. and Gopnik, A. (1991). Young children's ability to identify the sources of their beliefs. *Developmental Psychology*, **27**, 390–7.

Perner, J. (1991). *Understanding the representational mind*. MIT Press, Cambridge, MA.

Perner, J., Leekam, S. R. and Wimmer, H. (1987). Three-year-olds' difficulty with false belief. *British Journal of Developmental Psychology*, **5**, 125–37.

Perner, J., Ruffman, T., and Leekam, S. R. (1994). Theory of mind is contagious: you catch it from your sibs. *Child Development*, **65**, 1228–38.

Peterson, C. C. and Siegal, M. (1995). Deafness, conversation and theory of mind. *Journal of Child Psychology and Psychiatry*, **36**, 459–74.

Peterson, C. C. and Siegal, M. (1997). Domain specificity and everyday biological, physical, and psychological thinking in normal, autistic, and deaf children. *New Directions for Child Development*, **75**, 55–70.

Phillips, A. T. and Wellman, H. M. Infants recognize goal directed actions. (submitted).

Piaget, J. (1929). *The child's conception of the world*. Routledge and Kegan Paul, London.

Pillow, B. H. (1988). The development of children's beliefs about the mental world. *Merrill-Palmer Quarterly*, **34**, 132.

Pillow, B. H. (1989). Early understanding of perception as a source of knowledge. *Journal of Experimental Child Psychology*, **47**, 116–29.

Pillow, B. H. (1995). Two trends in the development of conceptual perspective-taking: a elaboration of the passiveactive hypothesis. *International Journal of Behavioral Development*, **18**, 649–76.

Pillow, B. H. and Henrickson, A. J. (1996). There's more to the picture than meets the eye: young children's difficulty understanding biased interpretation. *Child Development*, **67**, 803–19.

Pratt, C. and Bryant, P. E. (1990). Young children understand that looking leads to knowing (so long as they are looking into a single barrel). *Child Development*, **61**, 973–82.

Premack, D. (1990). The infant's theory of self-propelled objects. *Cognition*, **36**, 116.

Reese, E. and Fivush, R. (1993). Parental styles of talking about the past. *Developmental Psychology*, **29**, 596–606.

Reese, E., Haden, C. A. and Fivush, R. (1993). Mother-child conversations about the past. *Cognitive Development*, **8**, 403–30.

Repacholi, B. M. and Gopnik, A. (1997). Early reasoning about desires: evidence from 14- and 18-month olds. *Developmental Psychology*, **33**, 12–21.

Ridgeway, D., Waters, E. and Kuczaj, S. (1985). Acquisition of emotion-descriptive language: receptive and productive vocabulary norms for ages 18 months to 6 years. *Developmental Psychology*, **21**, 901–8.

Rochat, P., Morgan, R. and Carpenter, M. (1997). Young infants' sensitivity to movement information specifying social causality. *Cognitive Development*, **2**, 537–61.

Ruffman, T., Perner, J., Naito, M., Parkin, L. and Clements, W. A. (1998). Older (but not younger) siblings facilitate belief understanding. *Developmental Psychology*, **34**, 161–74.

Russell, J. A. (1990). The preschooler's understanding of the causes and consequences of emotion. *Child Development*, **61**, 187–281.

Russell, J., Mauthwer, N., Sharpe, S. and Tidswell, T. (1991). The 'windows task' as a measure of strategic deception in preschoolers and autistic subjects. *British Journal of Developmental Psychology*, **9**, 331–49.

Scaife, M. and Bruner, J. S. (1975). The capacity for joint visual attention in the infant. *Nature*, **253**, 265.

Schult, C. A. and Wellman, H. M. (1997). Explaining human movements and actions: children's understanding of the limits of psychological explanation. *Cognition*, **62**, 291–324.

Shantz, C. U. (1983). Social cognition. In *Handbook of child psychology*, Vol. 3: Cognitive development. Wiley, New York.

Siegal, M. (1991). *Knowing children: experiments in conversation and cognition.* Erlbaum, Hove.

Siegal, M. and Beattie, K. (1991). Where to look first for children's understanding of false beliefs. *Cognition*, **38**, 112.

Sodian, B. (1994). Early deception and the conceptual continuity claim. In *Children's early understanding of mind*, (ed. C. Lewis and P. Mitchell). Erlbaum, Hove.

Sorce, J. F., Emde, R. N., Campos, J. J. and Klinert, N. D. (1985). Maternal emotional signaling: its effect on the visual cliff behavior of 1–year-olds. *Developmental Psychology*, **20**, 195–200.

Spelke, S. S., Phillips, A. T. and Woodward, A. L. (1995). Infants' knowledge of object motion and human action. In *Causal understanding in cognition and culture*, (ed. A. Premack). Clarendon Press, Oxford.

Stein, N. L. and Levine, L. J. (1989). The causal organization of emotional knowledge: a developmental study. *Cognition and Emotion*, **3**, 343–78.

Stern, D. N. (1985). *The interpersonal world of the infant.* Basic Books, New York.

Sullivan, K. and Winner, E. (1993). Three-year-olds' understanding of mental states: the influence of trickery. *Journal of Experimental Child Psychology*, **56**, 135–48.

Swettenham, J., Baron-Cohen, S., Gomez, J. C. and Walsh, S. (1996). What's inside a person's head? Conceiving of the mind as a camera helps children with autism develop a theory of mind. *Cognitive Neuropsychiatry*, **1**, 73–88.

Tager-Flusberg, H. (1992). Autistic children's talk about psychological states. *Child Development*, **63**, 161–72.

Tardif, T. and Wellman, H. W. (1997). Acquisition of mental state language in Chinese children. Paper presented at the Biennial Meeting of the Society for Research in Child Development, Washington, DC.

Taylor, M. (1988). Conceptual perspective taking: children's ability to distinguish what they know from what they see. *Child Development*, **59**, 703–18.

Taylor, M. and Carlson, S. M. (1997). The relation between individual differences in fantasy and theory of mind. *Child Development*, **68**, 436–55.

Tomasello, M. (1995). Joint attention as social cognition. In *Joint attention*, (ed. C. Moore and P. Dunham), pp. 103–30. Erlbaum, Hillsdale, NJ.

Trevarthen, C. and Hubley, P. (1978). Secondary intersubjectivity: confidence, confiding and acts of meaning in the first year. In *Action, gesture and symbol: the emergence of language*, (ed. A. Lock), pp. 183–229. Academic Press, New York.

Walden, T. A. and Ogan, T. A. (1988). The development of social referencing. *Child Development*, **59**, 1230–40.

Watson, J. K., Gelman, S. A. and Wellman, H. M. (1998). Young children's understanding of the non-physical nature of thoughts and the physical nature of the brain. *British Journal of Developmental Psychology*, **16**, 321–35.

Wellman, H. M. (1990). *The child's theory of mind.* Bradford Books, MIT Press, Cambridge, MA.

Wellman, H. M. (1993). Early understanding of mind: the normal case. In *Understanding other minds: perspectives from autism*, (ed. S. Baron-Cohen, H. Tager-Flusberg, and D. J. Cohen), pp. 10–39. Oxford University Press.

Wellman, H. M. and Banerjee, M. (1991). Mind and emotion: children's understanding of the emotional consequences of beliefs and desires. *British Journal of Developmental Psychology*, **9**, 1912–4.

Wellman, H. M. and Estes, D. (1986). Early understanding of mental entities: a reexamination of childhood realism. *Child Development*, **57**, 910–23.

Wellman, H. M. and Gelman, S. A. (1997). Knowledge acquisition in foundational domains. In *Handbook of child psychology*, Vol. 2: Cognition, perception and language, (5th edn), (ed. D. Kuhn and R. Siegler), pp. 523–73. Wiley, New York.

Wellman, H. M. and Hickling, A. K. (1994). The mind's 'I': children's conception of the mind as an active agent. *Child Development*, **65**, 1564–80.

Wellman, H. M. and Woolley, J. D. (1990). From simple desires to ordinary beliefs: the early development of everyday psychology. *Cognition*, **35**, 245–75.

Wellman, H. M., Harris, P. L., Banerjee, M. and Sinclair, A. (1995). Early understanding of emotion: evidence from natural language. *Cognition and Emotion*, **9**, 117–49.

Wellman, H. M., Hickling, A. K. and Schult, C. A. (1997). Young children's explanations: psychological, physical, and biological reasoning. In *The emergence of core domains of thought: physical, psychological, and biological thinking*, (ed. H. M. Wellman and K. Inagaki). Jossey Bass, San Francisco.

Wellman, H. M., Hollander, M. and Schult, C. A. (1998). Young children's understanding of thought-bubbles and of thoughts. *Child Development* **67**, 768–88.

Wellman, H. M., Cross, D. and Watson, J. A meta-analysis of theory of mind development: The truth about false belief. (In preparation.)

Wimmer, H. and Perner, J. (1983). Beliefs about beliefs: representation and constraining function of wrong beliefs in young children's understanding of deception. *Cognition*, **13**, 103–28.

Wimmer, H., Hogrefe, J. and Perner, J. (1988). Children's understanding of informational access as source of knowledge. *Child Development*, **59**, 386–96.

Woodward, A. (1996). Infants' reasoning about the goals of a human actor. Paper presented at the International Society for Infant Studies (ISIS), Providence, RI.

Woodward, A. (1998). Infants selectively encode the goals of a human actor. *Cognition*, **69**, 1–34.

Woolley, J. D. (1995). The fictional mind: young children's understanding of pretense, imagination, and dreams. *Developmental Review*, **15**, 172–211.

Woolley, J. D. and Bruel, M. J. (1996). Young children's awareness of the origins of their mental representations. *Developmental Psychology*, **32**, 335–46.

Youngblade, L. M. and Dunn, J. (1995). Individual differences in young children's pretend play with mother and sibling: links to relationships and understanding of other people's feelings and beliefs. *Child Development*, **66**, 147–292.

Yuill, N. (1984). Young children's coordination of motive and outcome in judgments of satisfaction and morality. *British Journal of Developmental Psychology*, **2**, 73–81.

Zaitchik, D. (1991). Is only seeing really believing? Sources of true belief in the false belief task. *Cognitive Development*, **6**, 91–103.

# 3

# Early theories of mind: what the theory theory can tell us about autism

ALISON GOPNIK, LISA CAPPS, AND ANDREW N. MELTZOFF

In the first edition of this book we presented a hypothesis about the early development of children's understanding of the mind (Meltzoff and Gopnik 1993).We suggested that normally-developing children are born linking their own minds and the minds of others. This ability is most clearly evidenced in the innate capacity to imitate facial expressions. This primitive link means that, later on in development, further discoveries about other people's minds are easily and naturally extended to knowledge of our own minds, and vice versa. We suggested that this initial link between the self and others may be missing in at least some cases of autism.

In this chapter we want to extend that earlier chapter in several ways. First, we will place our hypotheses about autism in the context of the broader theoretical debate about the nature of our developing understanding of the mind, and particularly in the context of the theory theory. We and others have recently articulated the theory in much more detail than had been done in the previous chapter (Gopnik and Meltzoff 1997; Gopnik and Wellman 1994; Wellman and Gelman 1997). Mind-reading deficits in autism are often taken as evidence for a 'modularity' view of cognitive development. Part of what we will do is argue that a biologically-based mind-reading deficit is equally compatible with a theory theory account. We will also consider another approach to the child's developing understanding of the mind, simulation theory, and show that the early existence of imitative abilities does not by itself provide any special support for such a theory. In particular, early imitation does not suggest any special privilege for one's own experience in making mental-state judgements. Second, we want to present new evidence, particularly evidence from recent studies of children with autism, in support of the hypothesis we put forward in our earlier chapter. This includes evidence about imitation and the perception of ambiguous figures in children with autism. Finally, we want to raise a hypothesis about part of the deficit in autism that has not been raised before. It is at least possible that some children with autism have a more general difficulty in theory-formation rather than a more specific problem with theory of mind. At a minimum, this possibility needs to be excluded before we can draw firm conclusions about a more specific deficit. We will present some preliminary evidence of a study of 'folk biology' in children with autism that supports this view.

## AUTISM AND THE THEORY THEORY

The fact that there is a mind-reading deficit in autism has often been taken to be support for a nativist 'modular' theory of our developing understanding of the mind (Baron-Cohen 1995; Leslie and Roth 1993). The logic of the argument is as follows: we know that autism is the result of an innately determined biological disorder, rather than the result of some particular pattern of experience, for example, some type of defective mothering. In fact, this is one of the most important empirical discoveries in the modern research on the disorder. Therefore, if theory of mind is specifically affected, there must be an innate basis for theory of mind. Therefore, there must be a theory of mind module, a genetically-determined and indefeasible way of understanding the mind. While we would agree that the first two claims are correct—that autism is biologically based and there is an innate basis for theory of mind—we don't agree with the modular conclusion.

Instead, we propose that our ordinary understanding of the mind proceeds by the formation, revision and replacement of successive theories of the mind. Rather than being determined by some innate maturational schedule, this succession of theories is the result of the operation of more general inferential mechanisms. Like scientists, children understand the world by constructing coherent views of it and changing those views in the light of new evidence that they obtain. Children play an active role in this process by making predictions, seeking explanations and considering evidence that is relevant to the mind. Moreover, theories in one domain can influence theories in other domains, though they need not necessarily do so. The information encoded in theories, unlike that encoded in modules, can be influenced by other types of knowledge.

This view, however, does not mean that there is no innate or domain-specific basis for our understanding of the mind. On the contrary, there are two important ways in which the theory theory proposes innate structure. First, the theory-formation mechanisms themselves are innate. These mechanisms are rich, powerful and substantive. They constitute an evolutionarily-determined machinery that allows us to infer the underlying structure of the world, particularly its causal structure, on the basis of the events we observe. We might, in fact, think in terms of an innate theory-formation system, like the visual system, which develops particular types of causal representations given particular types of evidence. This system is specifically designed to construct abstract, coherent and revisable 'causal maps' of the world (see Gopnik 1998; Gopnik, in press).

In fact, in many respects we attribute richer cognitive structure to infants than is attributed on other views. For example, our view is that theory-formation mechanisms are richer and more substantive than the very general learning mechanisms proposed by classical Piagetian theory. They are also much richer than those proposed by recent empiricist theories such as those inspired by connectionist models.

A second and equally important part of the view, particularly relevant to autism, is that, according to the theory theory, there are innate, initial, 'starting-state' theories about the mind, as well as about other particular aspects of the world (Astington and Gopnik 1991; Gopnik and Meltzoff 1997; Gopnik and Wellman 1994). These theories are present literally at birth. And they are genuinely theoretical. They are specific substantive, coherent, abstract, representations of the world that allow babies to make predictions, and to interpret, and even perhaps explain, what they see around them. These initial theories are also domain-specific; they include, for example, an initial theory of the movement of objects in space as well as an initial theory of people (Gopnik and Meltzoff 1997; Meltzoff and Moore 1998). These theories exist innately in addition to the general theory-formation mechanisms.

In fact, theory-formation is possible largely just because there are innate theories. Theory-formation is, on our view, always a process of revision. We think babies and children revise their abstract, coherent, structured representations of the world, their theories, in the light of evidence. We do not think they derive abstract, coherent, structured representations of the world from incoherent, unstructured raw data itself. Rather, new data are always interpreted and selected in the light of an existing theory. The innate theory-formation mechanisms have to have some equally innate initial structure to operate on. To perform theory-revision we need to have theories to revise.

How is this kind of nativism different from modularity views? Of course, 'modularity' views differ in the strength of their claims. A weak version might simply consist of the claim that there is innate domain-specific knowledge that is specifically relevant to the mind. This claim seems perfectly right and important, and we think that currently most 'theory of mind' investigators would agree on it. But philosophical modularity theories, for example, the views originally articulated by Fodor (1983) and Chomsky (1980), and echoed by Leslie (Leslie and Roth 1993), make a much stronger claim. These modularity theories propose that modules are cognitively impenetrable and indefeasible. They constitute a strong set of constraints on the final state of the cognitive system.

The classical examples of 'modules' are syntax and visual perception and it is claimed that these types of knowledge are not revisable. Modules determine the final character of our understanding of the mind. They are not revisable in the light of new evidence or information. Once a syntactic parameter has been set or a perceptual algorithm is implemented, it is fixed. In fact, phenomena like creoles and perceptual illusions, where we hold on to a particular construal of the world, in spite of massive evidence, and even specific beliefs to the contrary, are typically taken to be support for modularity views. Developmental changes, on this view, just consist of the replacement of one module by another through a maturational process, or relatively narrow 'parameter-setting' or 'triggering', or the lifting of 'performance constraints' (see e.g. Fodor 1992). Information from other cognitive systems is not used in the construction of modular representations.

Our view is that while there are innate domain-specific theories, those theories do not themselves constitute the final architecture of the representational system. Rather those theories can be and are radically revised in the light of new evidence. They are the starting state of the system but they are not the final state of the system. Moreover, we think successive theories are inferentially related to one another. New theories are derived from old theories and new data. And while theories are substantively specific to a particular domain, they can be influenced by information from any domain.

On the theory theory view, then, there are several ways that an innately determined biological disorder could lead to cognitive deficits and differences. Such a disorder could lead children to have a radically different initial theory, or no initial theory at all. It could alter the kind of evidence that is available to them (as in the case of blind children or deaf children of hearing parents). Or it could lead to deficits in the theory-formation process itself.

The first possibility is what we proposed earlier (Meltzoff and Gopnik, 1993). We suggested that some children with autism may lack an initial theory of persons, or at least have a very different theory. In normally-developing children, that theory is the foundation for later theory of mind development. Even if the learning mechanisms are at least largely intact in these children, the route they take towards understanding the mind might be radically different.

A scientific analogy might be helpful. In doing science we begin from a strong set of everyday beliefs, an everyday theory, about how objects work. That initial theory allows us to interpret and select evidence and to make predictions. In fact, it provides the vocabulary with which we describe the evidence. Physicists began by talking about heat as a single concept before they differentiated heat and temperature; they began by talking about burning and rusting differently before they saw that they were both the result of oxidation; and so on. The everyday theory of objects enabled scientific physicists to begin the process of hypothesis-testing that eventually led to new and quite different theories. Eventually, many aspects of the everyday theory were over-thrown. For instance, we were forced to revise our common intuitions that heavy objects fall faster than light objects, that heat and temperature are the same, and that rusting and burning are different. But without that everyday theory to start with, the progress and history of science would have been very different. New theories of physical objects would have been much more difficult to come by.

In fact, theories of some aspects of the physical world developed particularly late, and they were just those aspects where no everyday intuitions were available. For example, evolution and everyday experience did not provide us with an appropriate initial theory of the behaviour of very small objects moving at very fast speeds. Developing theories of that behaviour followed after, and depended on, theories of the movement of larger objects at slower speeds, objects and movements that we evolved to deal with.

Suppose those rarefied aspects of the physical world, like the behaviour of small objects moving at high speeds, translated into selection pressures. In that case, we might well have had an initial everyday theory of, say relativistic effects, and our understanding of these aspects of physics would have proceeded much more quickly and easily. The physicist George Gamow wrote a series of books in which he explained relativistic physics and quantum theory by describing worlds in which the effects of those theories influenced everyday life (for instance, where the speed of light was sixty miles per hour). People in this Gamow world had everyday intuitions about such things as the fact that your bicycle would shrink as you pedalled faster, and that mass and energy were similar. They were 'folk Einsteinians'.

One possibility is that people with autism are in the same position physicists would be if there were no initial everyday theory of objects, or indeed the position we are in in comparison with the people in Gamow's imaginary world. We did eventually get to understand Einsteinian physics but it took us much longer than it would take Gamowians. Without the right evolutionarily-determined innate theory of persons, children with autism take a much more laborious route toward understanding of the mind than do typically-developing children.

## THE INITIAL THEORY OF PERSONS AND ACTIONS: THE CASE OF BODY IMITATION

Postulating innate initial theories makes it easier to explain later development; if children did have such theories it would make it much simpler for them to develop new theories later. The real reason for thinking that there are innate theories, however, is empirical. The past twenty five years of infancy research have demonstrated that even young infants already have abstract, complex, coherent representations of various aspects of the world. They have theories, or something very like them. These theories are evident in a number of surprisingly complex behaviours that can be found empirically in young infants.

One such behaviour is facial imitation. Very young infants, even newborns, imitate a range of facial gestures including tongue protrusion, mouth opening and lip-pursing (Meltzoff and Moore 1977; Meltzoff and Moore 1983). While this finding was initially surprising, it has since been replicated widely. Moreover, there are a number of features of these behaviours which suggest that infants actively try to match the gesture they produce to the gesture they see. In particular, infants gradually converge on the correct gesture, rather than producing a fully-fledged imitation at their first attempt. Furthermore, they will make attempts to imitate even a gesture they cannot themselves produce, like a large tongue protrusion to one side (Meltzoff and Moore 1994). Finally, there is even some evidence for distinctive affective reactions to these imitation problems. When babies converge on the right response they show signs of positive affect like eye brightening. When they are presented with a gesture they cannot successfully imitate they show distress. (See Meltzoff and Moore 1995, 1997 for reviews.)

What kind of cognitive structure underpins these behaviours? It seems that newborn babies already have some beliefs about the relation between themselves and other people. In particular, these infants seem to map their own internal kinesthetic sensations, the way that their own faces feel, on to the perceived actions of others. They seem to represent the way it feels to stick out your own tongue in the same way that they represent the visual spectacle of someone else's protruding tongue. This abstract representation allows infants to make systematic inferences. If I see a protruding tongue, I can infer that a particular set of motor movements will eventually lead me to produce a gesture with the same structure. If I feel my own tongue kinesthetically, I can judge whether or not it matches the tongue I see visually.

We think, then, that babies are born assuming an important link between themselves and others. Babies automatically seem to assume that their own internal feelings and the actions of others can be represented in the same way. Imitation is nature's way of solving the other minds problem and the mind/body problem in one fell swoop.

Moreover, we think these representations also underpin other very early social behaviours. Very young infants respond in distinctive ways to human faces and voices, stimuli that they can match to their own internal representation of their own bodies (Meltzoff and Kuhl 1994). From very early on, they seem to prefer these stimuli and pay more attention to them than to other stimuli. Early in infancy babies engage in what have been called 'conversational dances' or 'primary intersubjectivity' (Brazelton and Tronick 1980; Trevarthen 1979). In these interactions babies and adults act in a co-ordinated way, with a burst of gesture and vocalization from the adult matched by a parallel burst from the baby. The interactions look like the co-ordination of gesture and speech in adult conversations between intimates. Basically, babies flirt. These early behaviours may reflect the same sort of underlying link between the self and others that we see most dramatically in early imitation. These behaviours occur well before the later abilities to engage in joint attention or social referencing.

## FURTHER THEORIES OF MIND: ATTITUDES, DESIRES, PERCEPTION, BELIEF, AND AMBIGUITY

We also think that this initial link between the baby and others, this innate theory, forms the basis for further theoretical progress in the child's understanding of the mind. This initial theory is both enriched and revised in the succeeding months and years.

### Nine months—attitudes towards objects

In particular, there is an important change when, towards the end of the first year, babies begin to integrate objects into their understanding of people. Newborns seem to think there is a link between their own internal feelings and the actions of other people. Initially, though, their understanding of objects does not seem to enter into this understanding of feelings and actions. At around nine months, babies enrich their earlier conception of the mind to include the idea that feelings and actions are directed at objects, we might say that children discover that mental states are attitudes towards objects. While newborns simply imitate actions, nine-month-olds will also imitate actions on objects, sometimes over as much as a week's delay (Meltzoff 1988). Children also seem to be able to produce more complex object-directed actions themselves at about this point.

Other behaviours like social referencing and joint attention also indicate this conceptual change. The early social referencing studies were ambiguous and many could have been interpreted as showing a kind of 'emotional contagion' rather than genuine understanding (Baldwin and Moses 1994). More recent, methodologically rigorous studies, however, continue to show a change towards the end of the first year. In one particularly convincing recent demonstration, for example, Repacholi (1998) showed children two closed boxes. The experimenter looked into each box and made a disgusted or happy face, and then gave the closed boxes to the babies. Babies handled both boxes equally, but were reluctant to open the disgust box. The babies had never seen the emotion in conjunction with the object in the box, just with the outside of the box itself. Nevertheless, they seemed to infer that the object should be avoided though the outside of the box itself should not be.

### Eighteen months—desires

We have demonstrated further important changes in children's understanding of intentions and desires at about eighteen months (Meltzoff *et al.*, in press). In particular, at this age, babies begin to appreciate how their own intentions and those of others may fail to produce a result, and that other people may have different desires than they do. Children at this age begin to imitate complex goal-directed behaviours, and at about the same time they produce these behaviours themselves. They also will 'read through' failed attempts to achieve a goal. If they see another person unsuccessfully try to do something, they will themselves produce the correct behaviour to reach that goal (Meltzoff 1995). In a recent experiment we also showed that eighteen-month-olds, though not fourteen-month-olds, understand that their own desires may be different from those of others. If they see another person express disgust towards an object they themselves like (like goldfish crackers) and pleasure towards an object they themselves do not like (like raw broccoli), they will give that person the broccoli and not the crackers (Repacholi and Gopnik 1997).

   This discovery has mixed results in real life. On the one hand it leads to 'the terrible twos' in which children intentionally differentiate their own desires from those of others. On the other hand it also may lead to empathic behaviours. In real empathy, as opposed to mere emotional contagion, the empathizer has to recognize that the other person is in distress and needs comfort, even if they are not in the same distress themselves. Empathic behaviours also emerge at around this age (Zahn-Waxler *et al.* 1992). Both the best and the worst of life with toddlers seems to stem from these first discoveries of the differences between the self and others.

### Thirty months—perceptions

Further, we think there are important changes in how children understand perception somewhat later in development. During this period children gradually develop the 'non-egocentric' understanding of perception that is finally manifested in their visual perspective-taking abilities at three (Gopnik *et al.* 1994). There is some evidence that this is a development; twenty four- and thirty-month-olds are more likely to produce 'egocentric' visual perspective-taking than thirty six-month-olds (Esterly *et al.* 1996; Gopnik *et al.* 1994; Lempers *et al.* 1977). The changes in children's understanding of belief between three and four are, of course, well-documented. (For a detailed account of all these successive changes from birth until four see Gopnik and Meltzoff (1997) Chapter 5.)

## SIX YEARS ON—INTERPRETATION, INFERENCE, AND AMBIGUITY

We also think there may be further changes in the theory later in development. Between five and seven years old, children begin to understand that people might draw different interpretations from the same ambiguous stimuli. For example, in the 'droodles' task children are presented with an ambiguous picture, such as a picture that is hidden except for a small triangle, and are given an interpretation of it (they turn the page and see that the triangle is part of a witch's hat). Then they are asked how another person will interpret the triangle. Children under about six or seven think that the other person will give the same interpretation they do (Chandler and Helm 1984; Taylor 1988). There are other findings which suggest that an understanding of interpretation, inference and ambiguity only develops at this age (Carpendale and Chandler 1996; Gopnik and Graf 1988; Sodian and Wimmer 1987). Similarly, Perner and Winner have documented a later understanding of 'second-order' false-belief tasks, tasks that involve beliefs about beliefs (Perner and Winner 1985). Happé (1994) has found that even adults vary in their responses to a more subtle mentalistic task involving 'strange stories'.

Recently, we have found some interesting parallels between children's developing understanding of ambiguity in others and their own experience of ambiguity. When adults see an ambiguous figure, like the famous duck/rabbit, they both understand its ambiguity and experience a distinctive phenomenological shift from one interpretation to another. The figure 'reverses' from a duck to a rabbit and back again. In earlier work we found that young children do not spontaneously reverse ambiguous figures, and, in fact, do not even experience reversals when they are informed in detail about their ambiguity (Rock *et al.* 1994). In fact, in recent studies we found that this capacity to reverse developed surprisingly late. Most children only reversed at all at age six. Only even older children spontaneously reversed without being informed that the object was ambiguous.

Moreover, this ability to perceive ambiguous figures in two ways was correlated with the ability to understand ambiguity in others, and more generally seemed related to an understanding of other minds. Only children who passed a false-belief task reversed at all. Further, there was a .86 phi correlation between five- and six-year-olds' performance on a 'droodle' task and their prompted reversals; only two of twenty eight children performed differently on the two tasks (Gopnik and Rosati 1996). Similarly, there was a correlation between the older children's spontaneous reversals and their performance on a second-order false-belief task (Mitroff 1998).

## HOW THE INITIAL THEORY INFLUENCES LATER THEORY-FORMATION

There are several interesting things about the effect of the innate initial theory on this succession of changing beliefs about the mind. First, when the theory is enriched, babies seem to assume automatically that the enrichment will apply both to themselves and to others. For example, at nine months babies seem to understand both that other people can have attitudes towards objects, and that they themselves have such attitudes (as evidenced in their object-oriented behaviour). At eighteen months they begin to appreciate that both their own intentions and those of others can fail to be fulfilled. At three years they understand that their own beliefs may be false at the same time that they discover that the beliefs of others may be false. In particular, three-year-olds fail to report changes in their own beliefs (Gopnik 1993; Gopnik and Astington 1988). Our recent work even suggests that later in childhood children begin to understand how other people interpret ambiguity at about the same time that they first experience reversals of ambiguity themselves.

These last two findings are particularly striking because as adults the phenomenology of belief change or perceptual reversal of ambiguous figures seems so striking and immediate. We do not feel that we infer that our own beliefs have changed or that the figure is ambiguous, we just introspect and 'see' the change in belief or in our representation of the duck/rabbit. In contrast, we do seem to infer the beliefs or perceptions of others. In fact, the developmental data suggest that this phenomenology may be misleading. It seems that our capacity to 'see' changes in our beliefs or to 'see' the ambiguity of our representations is linked to our capacity to understand the minds of others (see Gopnik 1993).

Second, many of the accomplishments of infancy and early childhood seem to involve discovering that the states of other people are different from yours, rather than discovering they are similar. In each case, desires, perceptions, beliefs, and interpretations, babies seem to begin by assuming that they and other people have the same internal states and gradually develop an understanding of differences. As we have seen, children only discover that their desires are different from those of others at two, that their perceptions are different at three, that their beliefs are different at four, and that their interpretations of ambiguous situations are different at six or seven. In each case, children do discover these differences eventually, but that discovery requires empirical and theoretical work, and that work has consequences for their view of themselves as well as their view of others.

In other words, the evidence suggests to us that children continue to make the fundamental assumption they are given at birth. They assume that they are like others and that their internal states map on to the behaviour of others. This link does not have to be discovered empirically. Children do postulate increasingly complex mental concepts, from feelings to desires to perceptions to beliefs to ambiguity, to deal with the empirical evidence they see around them, but at first they seem to assume that these states also are shared by themselves and others. Their initial view, however, has to be revised when, in fact, their mental states and those of others are not similar. Children are confronted by empirical evidence that challenges their innate theory. They come to understand quite gradually that their mental states can differ from those of others.

The initial theory, then, seems to have important cascading effects on later development. The initial theory specifies the kinds of evidence that will be available for later theory-formation. In particular, it leads babies to describe and understand the world in terms of cross-modal and cross-person representations. These representations are the input for later theory-formation. What we can perceive in the world is strongly influenced by what we already know and believe.

At the same time, new evidence can itself lead the initial theory to be revised. It allows children to postulate more and more complex types of mental states. And even if the first theories assume a link between self and other, children modify this assumption in the light of new evidence.

## IMITATION AND SIMULATION

The view we have been arguing for may sound in some respects like a 'simulation' account. In fact, the existence of early imitation has been taken as support for such an account. There are many varieties of simulation theories but they have in common the idea that people use their own minds as models for understanding the minds of others, and in particular for making predictions about the minds of others. We 'simulate' what we would do or feel in various circumstances and project that on to others. In some versions of simulation this projection involves a special introspective access to our own mental states (Goldman 1993; Harris 1991). In others it is a more automatic and non-conscious process; we may generate a prediction through something like an 'ascent routine' without actually introspectively experiencing our own mental states (Gordon 1986). But all the versions of simulation rely on the idea that I can predict your behaviour by extrapolating from my own mind. The fact that we have difficulty understanding cases where our beliefs are different from those of others is consistent with this account.

It is also, however, equally consistent with a very different account. On our view it is not that we understand the behaviour of others by projecting our own feelings on to them. Rather we have an initial representational system which is equally applicable to ourselves and others. It is not that we introspect the feeling of our own tongue, observe our tongue protrusion behaviour visually, and then project that feeling on to others when we observe similar behaviour. Very young babies do not observe their own tongues visually. Rather we have a representational system that indifferently represents both our kinesthetic sensations and the visual perception of another person's face. A tongue protrusion is a tongue protrusion in either case. From the very beginning we give the same representation to our own experiences and the behaviour of others, without having to project our experiences on to them. These more abstract cross-modal and cross-person representations license particular kinds of inferences.

One consequence of having these cross-modal representations is that we can make inferences about others based on our own experience. I might conclude, for example, that the emotion of happiness I feel when I make a smiling face is similar to the emotion that another person will feel when they smile. These inferences are predicted by simulation theories and by the theory theory (see Gopnik and Meltzoff 1997; Meltzoff and Gopnik 1994). But equally, on our view, I can make the inferences the other way around. When I postulate some mental state to explain the actions of others, I also attribute that state to myself. These inferences can not be explained by the simulation theory.

The phenomenon of social referencing is an excellent example of such an inference. In social referencing babies observe the facial expression of another person that is directed at a particular object. If that facial expression is negative, scared or disgusted, for example, babies will themselves avoid that object. They seem to assume that the behaviour of another person towards an object is itself a reason for they themselves to have the same mental state towards that object. They take on the emotion they observe in the behaviour of the other person. Similarly, I may decide that mental states are directed at objects, as a way of trying to make sense of what I see people do, and then infer that my own actions have that character. That discovery may even allow me to understand my own capacities in a new way, and so to use tools differently. Similarly, later on in development, my understanding of the perceptions, desires, and beliefs of others may deeply influence my understanding of my own perceptions, desires, and beliefs (Gopnik 1993).

The innate bridge between ourselves and others bears two-way traffic. We may either make inferences about others based on our experience of ourselves, or make inferences about ourselves based on our experience of others.

## IMITATIVE DEFICITS AND IMPAIRMENTS IN UNDERSTANDING PERSONS IN AUTISM: NEW DATA

On the basis of the arguments presented so far, we would predict that children with autism should show deficits on imitation tasks, and we would predict that deficits in imitation might be correlated with other measures of social cognition. There has been a great deal of interest in imitation in children with autism (Ritvo and Provence 1953; Charman and Baron-Cohen 1994; Charman *et al.* 1997; Hobson and Lee 1997; Rogers *et al.* 1996; Smith and Bryson 1994). The bulk of this work, however, has been with children whose mental age was well beyond the infant and preschool period. Some of these studies have found that these older children can imitate the actions of others (e.g. Charman and Baron-Cohen 1994; Charman *et al.* 1997) though others have not.

In order to look at the foundations of theory of mind, a recent study tested children with a mean mental age of about twenty eight months (Dawson *et al.* 1998). A total of 59 children were examined, 20 with autism, 19 with Down Syndrome, and 20 typically-developing. The children from the three groups were matched both on their receptive language mental age (Preschool Language Scale-3) and the communication scale of the Vineland Adaptive Behavior Scales. Moreover, the children with Down Syndrome and autism were matched for chronological age and verbal IQ (M = 57 and 59 respectively). Nonverbal mental ability was assessed by visual-spatial tasks derived from the Bayley Scales and the Stanford Binet IV.

Several measures of social cognition were taken, including assessments of imitation, empathy, orienting, and shared attention. The imitation battery was adapted from Meltzoff's (1988; 1995) tests of normally-developing infants. There were fifteen items; ten immediate imitation and five deferred. The tasks included facial and manual movements (e.g. mouth opening, tongue protrusion, hand opening), novel actions on objects (e.g. touching a head to a panel), and familiar acts (e.g. banging blocks). The test of empathy was adapted from Sigman *et al.* (1992)and consisted of an adult who appeared to hurt herself while using a hammer as a tool. She showed intense distress and pain in both facial and vocal reactions. The question was whether the children would show concern, ranging from no interest to active comforting (1–4 point scale). The test of orienting consisted of two social (voice, clap) versus two nonsocial (rattle, music) auditory signals of six seconds duration, matched in loudness (Dawson *et al.*, 1988). Shared attention was assessed using an adaptation of Butterworth and Jarrett's procedure (Butterworth and Jarrett 1991). The adult pointed to or looked at four objects in distal space, both in and out of the child's immediate visual field, and the child's visual gaze was videotaped to assess whether they followed the adult's attentional cues and also looked at these objects. The question was whether children with autism would show a deficit in orienting to the social signals relative to the controls.

The results showed that children with autism performed more poorly on all four measures of social cognition than did either the normally-developing or Down's Syndrome children (Dawson *et al.* 1998). The children were also given a test of object permanence designed for use with children with Down Syndrome (Rast and Meltzoff 1995). There was no significant difference among the groups in object permanence performance. This is especially interesting because it showed that the young children with autism were on task and paid attention to the movements of the experimenter when he hid toys under cloths—the same children who succeeded on one nonverbal test involving objects (object permanence) failed when it came to another nonverbal test (imitation). This type of specificity, rather than cross-the-board impairments of equal magnitude, is consistent with the idea that problems of social cognition and the understanding of people and their actions are central to autism even at the very young mental ages tested here.

It is of special interest that for the autistic children there was a correlation between an individual child's imitation score and how that child responded on the test of empathy. Individual children who were good imitators were the ones who showed a higher the degree of concern/helping for the distressed adult ($p < .05$) and also spent more time looking at the experimenter during the distressing episode ($p < .05$). This relation held even when the child's nonverbal mental age was treated as a covariate, for example, partialling out the children's performance on object permanence and the other nonverbal mental tests (Dawson *et al.* 1998).

We also hope to test these children when they are older on more traditional theory of mind tests and ambiguous figure tests (discussed below). Our prediction is that the children who were high imitators and showed empathy early in development will be those who pass various theory of mind tests later.

Another finding from this study concerns the orienting tests. These results showed that children with autism are poorer at orienting to auditory signals than the other groups, but that they have a special deficit in orienting to auditory social signals. The children with Down's Syndrome and typical development showed few errors in orienting to either the social or nonsocial stimuli ($< .40$ errors out of a maximum of 4); similarly, the children with autism showed few errors (.55) when orienting to the nonsocial stimuli. However, these same autistic children show significantly more errors when orienting to social stimuli, making 1.8 (out of a maximum of 4) errors. These data again suggest a fairly basic deficit in responses to people. Whereas children with autism have the motor and auditory skills to orient (as manifest in their reaction to the inanimate stimuli), they show deep inattention to social signals.

Both these cases, the deficit in imitation and the deficit in orienting to social signals, involve abilities that are present in very young normally-developing infants. They are indicative of an innate theory of persons and action. The absence of these very early abilities in young children with autism might have profound developmental consequences. It is not just that these young children lack a generalized ability (e.g. good eyesight), which would equally affect their relation to people and things, but that they lack a specific initial theory of persons, a theory that is taken for granted in the development of normal social cognition. If a child does not orient toward adults when they enter the room and greet them, they will cut themselves off from a nexus of information. For example, deficits in joint attention among older children with autism, widely reported in the literature, might stem from this more basic impairment in paying attention to people to begin with. You cannot learn to follow the point of another if you don't have experiences in orienting toward the show-and-tell when a caregiver says, 'Oooh, look at that!' Normally-developing infants instantly alert to the mother's voice and direct their attention to the show-and-tell; autistic children do not. Similarly, the deficits in basic imitative abilities will cut off young children with autism from other people. Imitation provides a rich source of information about what people do and how what they do is related to what you do yourself. Linking your own internal feelings to the behaviour of others allows for more sophisticated empathic behaviour later in development.

## UNDERSTANDING AMBIGUITY IN AUTISM: NEW DATA

So, there is empirical evidence that very young retarded children with autism have difficulty understanding and carrying out imitation and orienting to social signals. We also have evidence that, at the other end of the spectrum, much older high-functioning children with autism also have difficulty experiencing ambiguity. We are currently carrying out a number of studies involving non-retarded children with autism, ages eight to thirteen, and typically-developing comparison children matched on Verbal IQ ($M = 96$, $M = 104$, respectively).

In the first study, children were presented with ambiguous or reversible figures (i.e. a picture that could be construed as a rabbit or duck, a man in a hat or a mouse, a vase or a pair of faces). They were then asked to report what they saw. Some children spontaneously reversed the figures (i.e. identified both images without being informed of the ambiguity). Those who reported seeing only one of the figures (e.g. rabbit) were asked, 'Is there anything else this could be a picture of?' Children who still did not see the alternative (e.g. duck) were given an unambiguous picture of the image. They were then given the ambiguous figure again, and were asked if they could now see the alternate image (e.g. duck), and if so, to point to various features.

As we described above, typically-developing children under five, using just this procedure, rarely reversed ambiguous figures, even when they were informed of the second image, and they never spontaneously reversed the images (Gopnik and Rosati 1997; Rock *et al.* 1994). By six most children became able to reverse the figures when they were informed of the ambiguity. Children older than six also began to reverse spontaneously. Informed reversals were correlated with passing the 'droodles' task and spontaneous reversals were correlated with the more difficult 'second-order belief' task.

In the present study, eight to thirteen-year-old non-retarded children with autism were as capable as comparison children of reversing the ambiguous figures when both images were pointed out to them (Sobel *et al.* 1999). They also passed the standard false-belief task. The children with autism were significantly less likely, however, to spontaneously reverse the figures than control children. Further, among children with autism, those who spontaneously reversed the figures were also more likely to succeed in interpreting vignettes requiring advanced understanding of other minds (Strange Stories, Happé 1994). Moreover, while both performance on the Strange Stories task and the proclivity to spontaneously reverse the figures were positively correlated with Verbal IQ (as has been the case in several studies, see Happé (1995) for review, the association between them remained significant after controlling for verbal ability.

## AUTISM AND DEVELOPING THEORIES OF MIND

Our results and others in the recent literature suggest a different picture of the mind-reading deficit in autism than the strong modularity view would suggest. Instead these studies seem to suggest that there is, in fact, a developing conception of the mind in autism. That conception, however, starts from a different place. Our studies suggest that very young children with autism do not have the same initial state, the same first link between self and other, that other children have. That initial difference has cascading consequences for later development.

Our studies show that very young children with autism, children with a mental age between one and three, have specific difficulties with imitation and social orienting, abilities that do appear in even younger, normally-developing infants. We know from earlier studies that children with autism with a higher mental age have specific difficulties with joint attention and social referencing, and also have difficulty with false belief (Baron-Cohen 1995). It is important to point out, however, that older, high-functioning children with autism can eventually pass false-belief tasks, and even pass second-order false-belief tasks. However, they seem to arrive at these concepts in a more laborious manner, and require more well-developed verbal abilities to do so, than is the case among typically-developing children (Bowler 1992; Eisenmajer and Prior 1991; Happé 1995). And, in our studies, even high-functioning children with autism who pass false-belief tasks continue to have difficulty with developments that also occur later in typically-developing children, such as 'Strange Story' understanding and the spontaneous reversal of ambiguous figures.

The children in our studies do not seem to be inalterably 'missing' a particular piece of cognitive architecture, in the way that one might biologically fail to develop a leg or a visual system. The picture that emerges does not seem to be that one or perhaps even two modules are damaged. Rather, the whole unfolding series of developing theories of mind, from imitation to ambiguity, seems to be different. Very young children with autism do not seem to be capable of the same sorts of imitation as normally-developing newborns. Older high-functioning children do not seem capable of the sorts of higher-level understanding we see in normally-developing school-age children.

## DO CHILDREN WITH AUTISM HAVE A THEORY-FORMATION DEFICIT?

We mentioned above that the theory theory posits two kinds of innate structure, initial theories and an innate theory-formation system. In our earlier chapter (Meltzoff and Gopnik, 1993) we suggested that the difficulties in autism might be due to the absence of the initial theory, and we still think that is the most likely possibility. On the other hand there is another possibility that we think has not been sufficiently explored. Some children with autism may have a difficulty with theories in general, rather than with theories of mind in particular. In addition to lacking an initial theory of the mind, these children may not be able to construct and revise theories in the ways that normally-developing children do. Instead, they may use radically different methods to understand and learn about the world.

For example, some children with autism might make much more specific 'empirical generalizations' or perceptual transfers, or might rely much more heavily on specific 'scripts' or rote responses to gain an understanding of the world. These capacities might underpin 'correct' responses on tasks like false-belief or others even while the processes that lead to those responses are quite different. The important point about theory-formation is not just that children learn about the world; there are many atheoretical ways of learning about the world. Rather the point is that the process of learning about the world is distinctive. In particular, normally-developing children seem to have a drive to understand the world in a deep, causal, explanatory way. They ignore surface patterns of events and generate genuinely novel predictions and explanations.

We can see this contrast between superficially 'correct' knowledge and a deeper explanatory understanding in some high-functioning autistic children's identification and understanding of emotion. Early results suggested that children with autism might not be impaired in identifying emotions. For example, a study involving children with autism, children with mental retardation, and typically-developing children, whose mental ages ranged between four and eight years, tested children's understanding of the causes of two basic emotions: happiness and sadness (Baron-Cohen 1991a). Results suggested that individuals with autism were quite able to report that a protagonist would feel happy while having a birthday party and sad after scraping her knee (situation as cause), and happy when given the cereal they like, and sad when given the cereal they don't like (desire as cause), and to justify their responses. Similarly, in a study of empathic responsiveness involving the presentation of video-taped stimuli, Yirmiya and colleagues (Yirmiya *et al.* 1992) found that high-functioning children with autism were surprisingly good at labelling the emotion experienced by the protagonists and often reported sharing this emotion.

In some sense these children 'passed' an emotion recognition task. But closer examination of the responses in the study by Yirmiya *et al.* yielded a different picture. Children with autism tended to explain their responses by describing parts of the vignette. In contrast, typically-developing children generally made explicit inferences about the protagonists' emotions and about how they would feel or had felt in a comparable situation. Similarly, in studies underway in our laboratory, high-functioning children with autism frequently refer to generic definitions and behavioural manifestations of emotion not only in labelling, but in accounting for their own and others' emotional experiences (Capps *et al.* 1999; Rasco and Capps, 1999; see also Capps *et al.* 1992). And they struggle in the process. When asked to describe a time in which he felt embarrassed, for example, a high-functioning older child with autism said, 'Um, well, um when I was ashamed.' And when asked to recount a time in which he felt sad, another child with autism replied, 'Hm . . . Oh. Well. Uh. I felt sad when I was crying' (Capps *et al.* 1999). In like manner, when asked to explain why a video-taped protagonist felt angry, a child with autism responded, 'Because he was yelling' (Rasco and Capps 1999). Thus, in many cases, autistic children's theories about the nature, causes, and consequences of emotions appear undifferentiated from definitions and observable manifestations of these emotions. These impoverished understandings are of limited utility in interpreting, predicting, and explaining human behaviour, and differ dramatically from the well-developed theories available to typically-developing children with comparable intellectual abilities.

It is conceivable that children with autism have acquired somewhat scripted knowledge of generic happy and sad situations and responses (i.e. birthday parties and skinned knees, or tears and smiles). In prior and current investigations we have found that children with autism more frequently produced generic scripts when asked to recount specific times when they experienced various emotions (Capps *et al.* 1992; Capps *et al.* 1999). Moreover, in selecting the video-taped stimuli used in our current investigations, we deliberately avoided vignettes that could be interpreted according to scripts in an attempt to better understand the *processes* through which individuals with autism interpret and experience emotions. The elicitation of rich explanations is essential to illuminating developing theories of emotions. Explanation and theory-formation are closely connected (Gopnik 1998).

These children with autism may never come to understand the mind in a genuinely theoretical way, although they acquire a great deal of knowledge about human behaviour. This might indicate a more general difficulty with theoretical thinking. The hypothesis that children with autism have a difficulty with theories in general rather than with theories of mind in particular may seem unlikely given the general impression that these children understand physical objects relatively well. Baron-Cohen (1997) suggests that at least some high-functioning children with autism may have unimpaired and even superior understanding of 'folk physics'. In support of this idea he cites reports from clinicians and parents that are rife with descriptions of children with autism who are obsessed by machines. Family studies complement such portrayals in that parents of children with autism appear to be over-represented in professions such as engineering that rely on folk physics and require minimal intuitive understanding of psychology. Other types of evidence include the fact that children with autism are accurate in predicting where an object photographed with a Polaroid camera in a particular location will appear in the photo, despite its having been moved while the picture was developing. Autistic individuals' superior performance on embedded figures tasks and their failure to succumb to visual illusions have been interpreted in the same way (Baron-Cohen 1997). In addition, in an empirical study using a picture sequencing paradigm Baron-Cohen, Leslie, and Frith (1985) found that children with autism were as apt as mental-age matched controls in sequencing familiar physical–causal stories. They were also more likely to produce physical–causal justifications than intentional ones in accounting for their sequencing of the picture sets.

A recent study directly assessed 'folk physics' in a group of fifteen non-retarded children with Asperger's Syndrome (Baron-Cohen *et al.* 1998). Participants with autism performed significantly better on a multiple-choice folk physics test than did age-matched, typically-developing comparison children, and significantly less well on an advanced test of theory of mind.

However, there have been very few systematic attempts to determine whether children with autism understand the physical or biological world in a genuinely theoretical way. It would be perfectly possible to score well on an IQ task or a multiple-choice test of physical knowledge without that type of understanding. Similarly, the fact that children with autism often are interested in, even obsessed by, machines does not indicate that they understand those objects in a theoretical way, for example, in terms of their underlying causal structure or their novel inductive potential. In fact, some of the typical 'obsessive' encyclopedic kinds of knowledge, like having entire railway time-tables committed to memory or knowing the names of every possible variety of dinosaur, seem strikingly atheoretical, even anti-theoretical. Just as children with autism may be able to identify emotions without being able to explain them, they may have pieces of specific physical or causal knowledge without having deeper explanations of that knowledge. They may know that cameras take pictures without knowing (or caring) how they take pictures, or know typical sequences of events without understanding the underlying laws that govern those events. Moreover, their motivation for understanding the physical world, and the techniques they use to do so, may be quite different from the 'theory-driven' character of learning in other children (see Gopnik 1988).

In fact, it is possible that some people with autism prefer things to people just because things can be dealt with in an atheoretical way, without reference to their underlying structure, while understanding minds positively requires the postulation of unseen underlying causal entities. The 'scripted' character of much social cognition in autism seems obvious in social interaction, while an equally superficial understanding of physical objects would have less obvious consequences.

Many of the more general features of autism that are often discussed in terms of a 'central coherence' deficit (Frith 1989) are also consistent with the idea that some children with autism have difficulties with theories in general, as well as theories of mind in particular. These include the typical preoccupation with surfaces and details rather than coherent interpreted wholes, for example. They also include these children's general aversion to novelty and change, and their repetitive behaviour. The predictive and explanatory power of theories allows us to deal with new situations as well as familiar ones, and to see beyond the surfaces of things to their underlying causal structure.

## AUTISM AND 'FOLK BIOLOGY': A PRELIMINARY SET OF RESULTS

No one to our knowledge has systematically tested children with autism on their deeper understanding of 'folk biology' or 'folk physics', knowledge that has been claimed to be theoretical in normally-developing children (Carry 1985; Gelman and Wellman 1991; Wellman and Gelman 1997). Given the hypothesis that children with autism have difficulty with theories in general, one might predict impoverished folk biology as well as folk psychology. In a prior study of the animate/inanimate distinction, Baron-Cohen (1991*b*) used a card-sorting task and found that individuals with autism were quite able to distinguish mechanical objects such as cars and vacuum cleaners from animate objects such as mice and men (Baron-Cohen 1991*b*). We extended this work, with the same high-functioning children as in the previous study of ambiguity, by presenting a battery designed to tap biological concepts that required explanation (Carey 1985). As part of this battery, children were presented with twenty photographs of objects drawn from the categories of animals, plants, inanimate natural kinds, and artefacts. They were asked to judge whether the object was alive or not, and to explain why. Responses were analyzed both in terms of the accuracy of the judgements and the nature of the explanations given. In contrast to previous research, preliminary results suggest that individuals with autism were more often incorrect in their classification of objects with respect to animacy. Furthermore, their reasoning revealed less sophisticated understanding of biological concepts. In accounting for their judgements of animacy, individuals with autism were significantly less likely to refer to biological processes such as breathing, eating, and growing than were comparison children. In addition, they were significantly more likely than comparison children to designate objects as alive or not alive on the basis of autonomous movement, as in the following examples: 'the tractor is alive because it moves'; 'the crystal is not alive because it's not moving'. The explanations of children with autism were also significantly different in that they frequently attributed human characteristics to objects deemed alive, whereas this was never the case among comparison children. For example, a child with autism who correctly identified a tree as being alive explained, 'It's alive because it has leaves, it's not fake, it's conscious.' Similarly, another child stated that a bird is alive 'because it has a conscience'. And yet another child with autism deemed a flower to be alive 'because it feels happy'. As with theory of mind and other representational tasks, performance on the life concepts battery—both with respect to classification of objects and reference to biological concepts in explanatory accounts—was positively correlated with verbal IQ among children with autism but not among comparison children.

How do we reconcile these discrepant findings? The stimuli included in the present study included plants and natural artefacts that may have been more ambiguous than those used by Baron-Cohen, such as dried flowers and crystals. Further, the nature of children's theoretical understanding of biology may be best assessed through *analysis of explanations* in addition to the accuracy of categorical knowledge. As we have learned in studies of high-functioning individuals with autism who labour their way to success on measures of theory of mind and emotional understanding, correct responses to a given task are not necessarily undergirded by a strong theoretical foundation. Explanatory accounts also yield insight into the processes through which theoretical understandings are tested and revised. The nature of the explanations given in our study suggest that some children with autism may possess a less well-developed theory of biology than do typically-developing children.


CONCLUSIONS

We have every reason to believe that the answer to the riddle of autism will not be a simple one. The syndrome is complex and heterogeneous and it may well turn out that there is no such thing as 'autism' in general, in the way that there is no single disorder like 'inflammation' or 'fever'. Instead, various genetic and biological processes may lead to a variety of developmental patterns with overlapping similarities. Different children with autism may, and probably do, have different underlying deficits, and the biological disruptions that cause autism may, and probably do, lead to differences in many types of otherwise unrelated abilities. Nevertheless, problems in understanding people are one distinctive part of the syndrome. Knowing how typically-developing children develop an understanding of people, then, may help us to understand children with autism, and vice-versa. Our view is that the picture that emerges from both types of studies is a fundamentally developmental picture. This is true whether we see autism as a deficit in an initial state, a first theory, with cascading developmental consequences, or as a deficit in the developmental process of theory-formation itself. We develop theories of mind, not just a theory of mind, and that process may go on throughout childhood and, indeed throughout adult life.


**Acknowledgements**

We thank Andrea Rosati, David Sobel, Stephen Mitroff, Molly Losh, Erin Heerey and Lisa Rasco for their assistance with the studies reported here, as well as the children we studied and their parents. This research was supported by a grant to L. C. from the Spencer Foundation and to A. N. M. from NIH (NS26678, HD34565, HD22514).


REFERENCES

Astington J. W. and Gopnik, A. (1991). Theoretical explanations of children's understanding of the mind. *British Journal of Developmental Psychology*, **9**, 7–31.

Baldwin, D. A. and Moses, L. J. (1994). Early understanding of referential intent and attentional focus: evidence from language and emotion. In *Children's early understanding of mind: origins and development*, (ed. C. Lewis and P. Mitchell), pp. 133–56. Erlbaum, Hillsdale, NJ.

Baron-Cohen, S. (1991a). Do people with autism understand what causes emotion? *Child Development*, **62**, 385–95.

Baron-Cohen, S. (1991b). The theory of mind deficit in autism: How specific is it? *British Journal of Developmental Psychology*, **9**, 301–14.

Baron-Cohen, S. (1995). *Mindblindness: an essay on autism and theory of mind*. MIT Press, Cambridge, MA.

Baron-Cohen, S. (1997). Are children with autism superior at folk physics? In *Children's theories*, (ed. H. M. Wellman and K. Inagaki). Joosey-Bass, San Francisco.

Baron-Cohen, S., Leslie, A. M. and Frith, U. (1985). Does the autistic child have a 'theory of mind'? *Cognition*, **21**(1), 37–46.

Baron-Cohen, S., Wheelwright, S., Spong, A., and Scahill, V. (1998). Are children with Asperger's Syndrome superior in intuitive physics? Unpublished manuscript.

Bowler, D. M. (1992). 'Theory of mind' in Asperger's syndrome. *Journal of Child Psychology and Psychiatry*, **33**, 877–93.

Brazelton, T. B. and Tronick, E. (1980). Preverbal communication between mothers and infants. In *The social foundations of language and thought*, (ed. D. R. Olson), pp. 299–315. Norton, New York.

Butterworth, G. and Jarrett, N. (1991). What minds have in common is space: spatial mechanisms serving joint visual attention in infancy. *British Journal of Developmental Psychology*, **9**, 55–72.

Capps, L., Rasco, L., Losh, M. and Heerey, E. (1999). Understanding of self-conscious emotions in high-functioning children with autism. Paper presented at the Biennial Meeting of the Society for Research in Child Development. Albuquerque, NM., April.

Capps, L., Yirmiya, N. and Sigman, M. (1992). Understanding of simple and complex emotion in high-functioning children with autism. *Journal of Child Psychology and Psychiatry*, **33**, 1169–82.

Carey, S. (1985). *Conceptual change in childhood*. MIT Press, Cambridge, Mass.

Carpendale, J. and Chandler, M. (1996). On the distinction between false belief understanding and subscribing to an interpretative theory of mind. *Child Development*, **67**(4), 1686–706.

Chandler, M. and Helm, D. (1984). Developmental changes in the contribution of shared experience to social role-taking competence. *International Journal of Behavioral Development*, **7**, 145–56.

Charman, T. and Baron-Cohen, S. Another look at imitation in autism. *Development and Psychopathology*, **6**, 403–13.

Charman, T., Swettenham, J., Baron-Cohen, S., Cox, A., Baird, G. and Drew, A. (1997). Infants with autism: an investigation of empathy, pretend play, joint attention and imitation. *Developmental Psychology*, **33**, 781–9.

Chomsky, N. (1980). *Rules and representations*. Columbia University Press, New York.

Dawson, G., Meltzoff, A. N., Osterling, J. and Rinaldi, J. (1998). Children with autism fail to orient to naturally occurring social stimuli. *Journal of Autism and Developmental Disorders*, **28**, 479–85.

Eisenmajer, R. and Prior, M. (1991). Cognitive linguistic correlates of 'theory of mind' ability in autistic children. Special Issue: Perspectives on the child's theory of mind: II. *British Journal of Developmental Psychology*, **9**, 351–64.

Esterly, J., Gopnik, A., and Meltzoff, A. (1996). Changes in children's understanding of visual perspective between 24 and 36 months. Poster presented at the meeting of the Western Psychological Association, San Jose.

Fodor, J. A. (1983). *The modularity of mind: an essay on faculty psychology*. MIT Press, Cambridge, Mass.

Fodor, J. A. (1992). A theory of the child's theory of mind. *Cognition*, **44**(3), 283–96.

Frith, U. (1989). Autism: explaining the enigma. Blackwell, Oxford.

Gelman, S. A. and Wellman, H. M. (1991). Insides and essence: early understandings of the non-obvious. *Cognition*, **38**(3), 213–44.

Goldman, A. (1993). The psychology of folk psychology. *Behavioral and Brain Sciences*, **16**(1), 15–28.

Gopnik, A. (1988). Conceptual and semantic development as theory change: The case of object permanence. *Mind and Language*, **3**, 197–216.

Gopnik, A. (1993). How we know our minds: the illusion of first-person knowledge of intentionality. *Behavioral and Brain Sciences*, **16**(1), 29–113.

Gopnik, A. (1998). Explanation as orgasm. *Minds and Machines*, **8**(1), 101–18.

Gopnik, A. Explanation as orgasm and the drive for causal understanding: the evolution, function and phenomenology of the theory-formation system. *Cognition and explanation*, (ed. F. Keil and R. Wilson). MIT Press, Cambridge, MA. (In press.)

Gopnik, A. and Astington, J. W. (1988). Children's understanding of representational change and its relation to the understanding of false belief and the appearance–reality distinction. *Child Development*, **59**(1), 26–37.

Gopnik, A. and Graf, P. (1988). Knowing how you know: young children's ability to identify and remember the sources of their beliefs. *Child Development*, **59**(5), 1366–71.

Gopnik, A. and Meltzoff, A. N. (1997). *Words, thoughts and theories*. Bradford Books, MIT Press, Cambridge, Mass.

Gopnik, A. and Rosati, A. (1997). Perception, cognition, and young children's reversal of ambiguous figures. Paper presented at the Biennial Meeting of the Society for Research in Child Development, Washington, DC, April.

Gopnik, A. and Wellman, H. M. (1994). The theory theory. In *Mapping the mind: domain specificity in cognition and culture*, (ed. L. Hirschfield and S. Gelman), pp. 257–93. Cambridge University Press, New York.

Gopnik, A., Slaughter, V., and Meltzoff, A. (1994). Changing your views: how understanding visual perception can lead to a new theory of the mind. In *Children's early understanding of mind: origins and development*, (ed. C. Lewis and P. Mitchell), pp. 157–81. Erlbaum, Hillsdale, NJ.

Gordon, R. M. (1986). Folk psychology as simulation. *Mind and Language*, **1**, 158–71.

Happé, F. (1994). An advanced test of theory of mind: understanding of story characters' thoughts and feelings by able autistic, mentally handicapped, and normal children and adults. *Journal of Autism and Developmental Disorders*, **24**, 129–54.

Happé, F. (1995). The role of age and verbal ability in the theory of mind task performance of subjects with autism. *Child Development*, **66**, 843–55.

Harris, P. L. (1991). The work of the imagination. In *Natural theories of mind: evolution, development and simulation of everyday mindreading*, (ed. A. Whiten), pp. 283–304. Basil Blackwell, Oxford.

Hobson, R. P. and Lee, A. (1995). Imitation and identification in autism. Poster presented at the Biennial Meeting of the Society for Research in Child Development.

Lempers, J. D., Flavell, E. R. and Flavell, J. H. (1977). The development in very young children of tacit knowledge concerning visual perception. *Genetic Psychology Monographs*, **95**(1), 3–53.

Leslie, A. and Roth, D. (1993). What autism teaches us about metarepresentation. In *Understanding other minds: Perspectives from autism*, (ed. S. Baron-Cohen, H. Tager-Flusberg, and D. Cohen), pp. 83–111. Oxford University Press.

Meltzoff, A. N. (1988). Infant imitation after a 1–week delay: long-term memory for novel acts and multiple stimuli. *Developmental Psychology*, **24**(4), 470–6.

Meltzoff, A. N. (1995). Understanding the intentions of others: re-enactment of intended acts by 18–month-old children. *Developmental Psychology*, **31**(5), 838–50.

Meltzoff, A. N. and Gopnik, A. (1993). The role of imitation in understanding persons and developing a theory of mind. In *Understanding other minds: perspectives from autism*, (ed.

S. Baron-Cohen, H. Tager-Flusberg, and D. J. Cohen), pp. 335–66. Oxford University Press.

Meltzoff, A. N. and Kuhl, P. K. (1994). Faces and speech: intermodal processing of biologically relevant signals in infants and adults. In *The development of intersensory perception: comparative perspectives*, (ed. D. J. Lwekowica and R. Lickliter), pp. 335–69. Lawrence Erlbaum, Hillsdale, NJ.

Meltzoff, A. N. and Moore, M. K. (1977). Imitation of facial and manual gestures by human neonates. *Science*, **198**(4312), 75–8.

Meltzoff, A. N. and Moore, M. K. (1983). Newborn infants imitate adult facial gestures. *Child Development*, **54**(3), 702–09.

Meltzoff, A. N. and Moore, M. K. (1994). Imitation, memory, and the representation of persons. *Infant Behavior and Development*, **17**(1), 83–99.

Meltzoff, A. N. and Moore, M. K. (1995). Infants' understanding of people and things: from body imitation to folk psychology. In *The body and the self*, (ed. J. Bermudez, A. J. Marcel, and N. Eilan), pp. 43–69. MIT Press, Cambridge, MA.

Meltzoff, A. N. and Moore, M. K. (1997). Explaining facial imitation: a theoretical model. *Early Development and Parenting*, **6**, 179–92.

Meltzoff, A. N. and Moore, M. K. (1998). Object representation, identity, and the paradox of early permanence: steps toward a new framework. *Infant Behavior and Development*, **21**, 201–35.

Meltzoff, A. N., Gopnik, A. and Repacholi, B. Toddlers' understanding of intentions, desires and emotions: explorations of the dark ages. In *Developing theories of intention*, (ed. P. Zelazo). Lawrence Erlbaum, New Jersey. (In press.)

Mitroff, S. (1998). The relationship between spontaneous reversals of ambiguous figures and theory of mind development. Senior honors thesis. University of California at Berkeley.

Perner, J. and Wimmer H. (1985). 'John thinks that Mary thinks that . . .': attribution of second-order beliefs by 5- to 10-year-old children. *Journal of Experimental Child Psychology*, **39**, 437–71.

Rasco, L. and Capps, L. (1999). Affective knowledge in high functioning children with autism. Poster presented at the Biennial Meeting of the Society for Research in Child Development. Albuquerque, NM., April.

Rast, M. and Meltzoff, A. N. (1995). Memory and representation in young children with Down syndrome: exploring deferred imitation and object permanence. *Development and Psychopathology*, **7**, 393–407.

Repacholi, B. M. (1998). Infants' use of attentional cues to identify the referent of another person's emotional expression. *Developmental Psychology*, **34**(5), 1017–25.

Repacholi, B. M. and Gopnik, A. (1997). Early understanding of desires: evidence from 14 and 18–month-olds. *Developmental Psychology*, **33**(1), 12–21.

Ritro, S., and Provence, S. (1953). Form perception and imitation in some autistic children. *Psychoanalytic Study of the Child*, **8**, 155–63.

Rock, I., Gopnik, A., and Hall, S. (1994). Do young children reverse ambiguous figures? *Perception*, **23**(6), 635–44.

Rogers, S. J., McEvoy, R., Bennetto, L. and Pennington, B. F. (1996). Imitation and pantomine in high-functioning adolescents with autism spectrum disorders. *Child Development*, **67**, 2060–73.

Sigman, M., Kasari, C., Kwon, J. and Yirmiya, N. (1992). Responses to the negative emotions of others by autistic, mentally retarded and normal children. *Child Development*, **63**, 796–807.

Smith, I. M. and Bryson, S. E. (1994). Imitation and action in autism. A critical review. *Psychological Bulletin*, **116**, 259–73.

Sobel, D., Capps, L., and Gopnik, A. (1999). Exploring the relationship between autistic children's perceptions of ambiguous figures and theory of mind. Poster presented at the Annual Conference of the American Psychological Society. Denver, CO., June.

Sodian, B. and Wimmer, H. (1987). Children's understanding of inference as a source of knowledge. *Child Development*, **58**(2), 424–33.

Taylor, M. (1988). Conceptual perspective-taking: children's ability to distinguish what they know from what they see. *Child Development*, **59**, 703–18.

Trevarthen, C. (1979). Communication and cooperation in early infancy: a description of primary intersubjectivity. In *Before speech: the beginning of interpersonal communication*, (ed. M. Bullowa), pp. 231–347. Cambridge University Press, New York.

Wellman, H. and Gelman, S. (1997). Knowledge acquisition in foundational domains. In *Handbook of child psychology*, (5th edn), (ed. D. Kuhn and R. Siegler). Wiley, New York.

Yirmiya, N., Sigman, M., Kasari, C., and Mundy, P. (1992). Empathy and cognition in high-functioning children with autism. *Child Development*, **63**, 150–60.

Zahn-Waxler, C., Radke-Yarrow, M., Wagner, E. and Chapman, M. (1992). Development of concern for others. *Developmental Psychology*, **28**, 126–36.

# 4

# Autism: deficits in folk psychology exist alongside superiority in folk physics

SIMON BARON-COHEN

This volume concerns our everyday understanding of other minds, and how neuro-developmental factors can interfere with this ability. Our understanding of other minds is sometimes referred to as our folk psychology. According to Pinker, among others, the evolution of the human mind should be considered in terms of its evolved adaptedness to the environment (Pinker 1997). On this view, the brain needed to be able to maximize the survival of its host body in response to at least two broad challenges: predicting the physical and the social environment. The specialized cognitive domains of folk physics and folk psychology can be seen as adaptations to each of these. In this chapter I explore the possibility that a cognitive profile of superior folk physics alongside impaired folk psychology could arise for genetic reasons. This assumes that some brains are equally well adapted to understanding both the social and physical environment, whilst others are better adapted to under-standing the physical environment and yet others are better adapted to understanding the social environment. Both clinical and experimental tests of this profile in children with autism and Asperger's Syndrome (AS) will be reviewed.

Brentano's thesis is that in this universe there are only two kinds of entities: those that have intentionality, and those that do not (Brentano 1874/1970). This roughly corresponds to the distinction between animate and inanimate, in that inanimate things appear to have no intentionality, whilst most animate things are treated as if they do. Intentionality is defined as the capacity of something to refer or point to things other than itself. A rock cannot point to anything. It just is. In contrast, a mouse can 'look' at a piece of cheese, and can 'want' the piece of cheese. The animate–inanimate distinction doesn't quite cover the intentional/non-intentional distinction in that plants are animate, so the distinction is probably better covered by the concept of agency (Premack 1990). Agents have intentionality, and non-agents do not. This also means that when agents and non-agents move, their motion has different causes. Agents can move by self-propulsion, driven by their goals, whilst non-agents can be reliably expected not to move unless acted upon by another object (e.g. following a collision).

The task for us as information processors is to compute the causes of these two classes of motion. Dennett's (1978) claim is that humans from birth use their *folk* (or *intuitive*) *psychology* to deduce the cause of agents' actions, and use their *folk* (or *intuitive*) *physics* to deduce the cause of the movement of any other entity. Why did the rock roll down the hill? If an agent was involved, then the event is interpreted as being caused by an intention (to throw it, roll it, kick it, etc.). If no agent was involved, then the event is interpreted in terms of a physical causal force (it was hit by another object, gravity, etc.). Sperber *et al.* (1995) suggest that humans alone have the reflective capacity to be concerned about causality, and that 'causal cognition' broadly falls into these two types.

## DEVELOPMENTAL EVIDENCE

Folk psychology (searching for the mental or intentional causes behind agent-type events) appears to be present at least from twelve months of age (Baron-Cohen 1994; Gergely *et al.* 1996; Premack 1990; Rochat *et al.* 1997). Thus, infants show dis-habituation to actions of 'agents' that appear to violate goal-directedness. They also expect agents to 'emote' (express emotion), and expect this to be consistent across modalities (between face and voice). They are also highly sensitive to where another person is looking, and will strive to establish joint attention.

Folk physics (searching for the physical causes of any other kind of event) is present even earlier in human ontogeny (Baillargeon *et al.* 1995; Leslie and Keeble 1987; Spelke *et al.* 1995) as manifested in the infant's sensitivity to apparent violations of the laws of physics. Thus, infants show dishabituation to the unexpected events of larger objects going into smaller ones, objects being unsupported, two objects occupying the same space, one object passing through another, or one inanimate object moving without being touched by another. Leslie (1995) interprets these data by proposing that two innate, independent modules are part of the infant cognitive architecture: a theory of mind mechanism (ToMM) and a theory of bodies mechanism (ToBy)[1].

## AUTISM: PREDICTIONS

Since the first test of folk psychology in children with autism (Baron-Cohen *et al.* 1985), there have been more than thirty further experimental tests, the vast majority revealing profound impairments in the development of folk psychological under-standing in autism. These are reviewed in Chapter 1, this volume, and elsewhere (Baron-Cohen 1995; Baron-Cohen *et al.* 1993). These include deficits in understanding that 'seeing-leads-to-knowing' (Baron-Cohen and Goodhart 1994; Leslie and Frith 1988), distinguishing mental from physical entities (Baron-Cohen 1989*a*; Ozonoff *et al.* 1990), and making the appearance–reality distinction (Baron-Cohen 1989*a*). This deficit in their folk psychology is thought to underlie the difficulties such children have in social and communicative development (Baron-Cohen 1988; Tager-Flusberg 1993), and the development of imagination (Baron-Cohen 1987; Leslie 1987).

Clearly a crucial contrast case in terms of understanding cognition in autism would be to look at their folk physics. We know that in autism there is an impairment in folk psychology. How circumscribed is this? Does it leave their folk physics intact? Or might their folk physics be super-developed, either in compensation or for other (possibly genetic) reasons?

## AUTISM AND FOLK PHYSICS: CLINICAL EVIDENCE

If children with autism had an impairment in their folk physics, this might suggest that the cause of their problems in the intentional domain was a problem in 'theory-building' per se (Carey 1985). However, there are reasons to suspect not only that their folk physics is intact, but that it may even be *superior*, relative to normally-developing children.

There is no shortage of clinical descriptions of children with autism being fascinated by machines (the paragon of non-intentional systems). One of the earliest clinical accounts was by Bettelheim (1968) who describes the case of 'Joey, the mechanical boy'. This child with autism was obsessed with drawing pictures of machines (both real and fictitious), and with explaining his own behaviour and that of others in purely mechanical terms. On the face of it, this would suggest he had a well-developed folk-physics. The clinical literature reveals hundreds of cases of children obsessed by machines. Parents' accounts (Hart 1989; Lovell 1978; Park 1967) are a rich source of such descriptions. Indeed, it is hard to find a clinical account of autism that does *not* involve the child being obsessed by some machine or another. Typical examples include extreme fascinations with electricity pylons, burglar alarms, vacuum cleaners, washing machines, video players, trains, planes, and clocks. Sometimes the machine that is the object of the child's obsession is quite simple (e.g. the workings of drain-pipes, or the designs of windows).

Of course a fascination with machines need not necessarily imply that the child *understands* the machine, but in fact most of these anecdotes also reveal that children with autism have a precocious understanding too. The child (with enough language, such as is seen in children with Asperger's Syndrome (AS)) may be described as holding forth, like a 'little professor', on their favourite subject or area of expertise, often failing to detect that their listener may have long since become bored of hearing more on the subject. Showing an apparently precocious mechanical understanding, whilst being relatively oblivious to their listener's level of interest, suggests that their folk physics might be outstripping their folk psychology in development.

The anecdotal evidence includes not just an obsession with machines, but with other kinds of physical systems. Examples include obsessions with the weather (meteorology), the formation of mountains (geography), motion of the planets (astronomy), and the classification of lizards (taxonomy). That is, their folk physics embraces both artefactual and natural kinds. In this article we use the term 'folk physics' both in the narrow way, to refer to our understanding of physical causality, and in the broader way, to encompass all of these non-intentional aspects of the physical world, whether causal or not.

## AUTISM AND FOLK PHYSICS: EXPERIMENTAL EVIDENCE

Leaving clinical/anecdotal evidence to one side, experimental studies converge on the same conclusion, that children with autism not only have an intact folk physics, but also have accelerated or superior development in this domain (relative to their folk psychology). First, using a picture-sequencing paradigm, we found that children with autism performed significantly better than mental-age matched controls in sequencing physical–causal stories (Baron-Cohen *et al.* 1986). The children with autism also produced more physical–causal justifications in their verbal accounts of the picture sequences they made, compared with intentional accounts.

Second, two studies (Leekam and Perner 1991; Leslie and Thaiss 1992) found that children with autism showed good understanding of a camera. In these studies, the child is shown a scene where an object is located in one position (A). The child is encouraged to take a photo of this scene, using a Polaroid camera. Whilst the experimenter and the child are waiting for the photo to develop, the scene is changed: the object is now moved to a new position (B). The experimenter then turns to the child and asks where in the photo the object will be. These studies found that children with autism could accurately infer what would be depicted in a photograph, even though the photograph was at odds with the current visual scene. Again, this contrasted with their poor performance on false-belief tests.

What was particularly important about these experiments was that the structure of the 'False Photo Task' exactly paralleled the structure of the false-belief task. The key difference is that in the false-belief test, a *person* sees the scene, and then the object is moved from A to B whilst that person is absent. Hence the person holds a belief that is at odds with the correct visual scene. In the False Photo task a *camera* records the scene, and then the object is moved from A to B whilst the camera is not in use. Hence the camera contains a picture that is at odds with the current visual scene. The pattern of results by the children with autism on these two tests was interpreted as showing that whilst their understanding of mental representations was impaired, their understanding of physical representations was not. This pattern has been found in other domains (Charman and Baron-Cohen 1992, 1995). But the False Photo Test is also evidence of their mechanical understanding (their folk physics) outstripping their folk psychology.

A third piece of evidence is a study examining children's understanding of the functions of the brain: significantly more children with autism mentioned the brain's causal role in action, compared with matched MA controls (Baron-Cohen 1989*a*). In contrast, in the same study, children with autism were significantly less likely to mention *mentalistic* functions of the brain. Once again the same pattern of superior folk physics and inferior folk psychology is seen. Our concept of the brain involves physical–causal events, whilst our concept of the mind involves intentional–causal events.

Fourth, in a study of the animate–inanimate distinction in autism (Baron-Cohen 1989*a*) it was found that school age children with autism were perfectly able to distinguish two different kinds of moving object: mechanical versus animate. (Mechanical objects were things like vacuum cleaners and cars. Animate objects were things like mice and men). This is additional evidence that their folk physics was intact.

Two final clues that there may be superior folk physics in autism spectrum conditions come from an experimental investigation, and a postal survey. In the former, fifteen children with AS were given a physics test and results found that they outperformed age- and IQ-matched controls on this, whilst not differing in terms of a control test of general (Baron-Cohen *et al.*, submitted). Regarding the latter, we have collected information from parents on the content of their children's obsessions, and found that children with either autism or AS tended to have obsessions that would fall into the area of folk physics far more often than any other folk domain (Baron-Cohen and Wheelwright, in press).

## FAMILY STUDIES

Family studies add to this picture. Parents of children with AS also show mild but significant deficits on an adult folk psychology task, mirroring the deficit in folk psychology seen in patients with autism or AS (Baron-Cohen and Hammer 1997*b*). Of critical relevance to the current argument, since autism and AS appear to have a strong heritable component (Bailey *et al.* 1995; Bolton *et al.* 1994; Folstein and Rutter 1977; Le Couteur *et al.* 1996), one should expect that parents of children with autism or AS should be over-represented in occupations in which possession of superior folk physics would be an advantage, whilst a deficit in folk psychology would not necessarily lead to any disadvantage. The paradigm occupation for such a cognitive profile is engineering.

A recent study of 1000 families found that fathers and grandfathers (patri- and matrilineal) of children with autism or AS were more than twice as likely to work in the field of engineering, compared with control groups (Baron-Cohen *et al.* 1997). Indeed, 28.4% of children with autism or AS had at least one relative (father and/or grandfather) who was an engineer. Related evidence comes from a survey of students at Cambridge University, studying either sciences (physics, engineering, or maths) or humanities (English or French literature). When asked about family history of a range of psychiatric conditions (schizophrenia, anorexia, autism, Down's Syndrome, or manic depression), the students in the science group showed a six-fold increase in the rate of autism in their families, and this elevation of risk was specific to autism (Baron-Cohen *et al.* 1998).

## CONCLUSIONS

In this chapter, we have summarized predictions from the model that the human brain has evolved two modes of causal cognition: folk psychology and folk physics[3]. In the extreme case, severe autism may be characterized by almost no folk psychology (and thus 'mindblindness'), but as autism spectrum conditions (including AS) come by degrees, so different points on the autistic spectrum may involve degrees of deficit in folk psychology. In those individuals who have no accompanying mental retardation (i.e. whose intelligence is in the normal range), the child's folk physics could develop not only normally, but at a superior level. We tested this most directly in a group of children with Asperger's Syndrome (AS). Children with AS were functioning significantly above their mental age (MA) in terms of folk physics, but significantly below their MA in terms of folk psychology (Baron-Cohen *et al.*, submitted). This could be the result of both genetic liability and the development of expertise in non-social learning environments.

If it was partly the result of a genetic liability, there is every reason to expect that individuals with this sort of cognitive profile would have been selected for in hominid evolution, since good folk physics confers important advantages (e.g. tool use, hunting skills, construction skills). Indeed, it is a tautology that without highly developed folk physics (e.g. engineering), Homo Sapiens would still be pre-industrial. It may be that the 'male brain' is an instance of this cognitive profile, given the evidence from the experimental studies of sex differences (female superiority in folk psychology, and male superiority in folk physics) (Baron-Cohen and Hammer 1997a; Halpern 1992). On this view, the autistic brain may be an extreme form of the male brain (Asperger's 1944; Baron-Cohen and Hammer 1997a).

If a brain has a genetically-based impairment in folk psychology, or a genetically-based talent for folk physics, this could lead the individual to spend less time interacting with the social environment, and more time interacting with the physical environment, since at least it can understand the latter. A simple mass-practice or expertise model (i.e. a gene-environment interaction) could then explain why such a brain, developing along an abnormally one-sided trajectory, could then lead to a superiority in folk physics. Alternatively, if we take seriously the notion of a module for folk physics (Leslie 1995), then it is possible that in autism spectrum conditions we see the twin genetically-based anomalies of impaired folk psychology co-occurring with superior folk physics. Future research will need to attempt to test the extent of learning and innate factors in this profile.

What is the extra explanatory scope of documenting superior folk physics in autism spectrum conditions, over and above the (now standard) demonstration of a theory of mind (or folk psychology) deficit in autism? The theory of mind account has been virtually silent on why such children should show 'repetitive behaviour', a strong desire for routines, and a 'need for sameness'. To date, the only cognitive account to attempt to explain this aspects of the syndrome is the executive dysfunction theory (Ozonoff *et al.* 1994; Pennington *et al.* 1997; Russell 1997). This paints an essentially negative view of this behaviour, assuming that it is a form of 'frontal lobe' perseveration or inability to shift attention.

Whilst some forms of repetitive behaviour in autism, such as 'stereotypies' (e.g. twiddling the fingers rapidly in peripheral vision) may be due to executive deficits, the executive account has traditionally ignored the *content* of 'repetitive behaviour'. The current account draws attention to the fact that much repetitive behaviour involves the child's 'obsessional'[4] or strong interests with mechanical systems (such as light switches or water faucets) or other systems that can be understood in physical–causal terms. Rather than these 'behaviours' being a sign of executive dysfunction, these may reflect the child's intact or even superior development of their folk physics. The child's 'obsession' with machines and systems, and what is often described as their 'need for sameness' in attempting to hold the environment constant, might be signs of the child as a superior folk-physicist: conducting mini-experiments in his or her surroundings, in an attempt to identify physical–causal principles underlying events. Certainly, our recent study of obsessions suggests that these are not random with respect to content (which would be predicted by the content-free executive dysfunction theory), but that these test to cluster in the domain of folk physics (Baron-Cohen and Wheelwright, in press).

This article has focused on folk physics and folk psychology, because they are the two forms of causal cognition. But as has been widely discussed (Hatano and Inagaki 1994; Sperber *et al.* 1995; Wellman 1990) other universal cognitive domains may also exist. The principal others are folk mathematics (counting) and folk biology (classification of the animate world into species, predators, prey, etc.). We remain to be convinced that these are independent domains, since it is plausible that folk mathematics is simply part of folk physics, for example. However, in the same way that a deficit in folk psychology should leave folk physics either unaffected or superior in autism, by the same arguments it should lead to unaffected or superior development of folk mathematics and folk biology in such individuals. This model of the independence of folk physics and folk psychology (corresponding to social and non-social intelligences) also predicts the existence of very high-functioning individuals with AS, who may be extreme high achievers in domains such as mathematics and physics but with deficits in folk psychology. Some recent single case studies confirm the existence of such pure cases (Baron-Cohen *et al.*, in press).

Finally, Happé (this volume, Chapter 9) notes that the superior folk physics theory may explain some islets of ability in the visual domain, but is limited in not being able to explain other patterns of skills in non-visual domains such as language. She makes the case for the weak central coherence theory having greater explanatory power. Note that folk physics relies on analysis of contingencies in the physical world, noticing spatial and temporal relations which may be causal. This is not confined to the visual world. More important, these two accounts are not necessarily mutually exclusive, as it may well be the case that weak central coherence is a prerequisite for having good folk physics. Future experiments could test the relationship between these two aspects of cognition.

## Acknowledgements

SBC was supported by the MRC during the period of this work.

## Notes

1. Baron-Cohen (1994) suggests that although a full-blown theory of mind may take several years to develop, a more restricted Intentionality Detector (or ID) along the lines proposed by Premack (1990) does appear to be part of our causal cognition in infancy.

2. Asperger's Syndrome is thought to be a subgroup of high-functioning individuals on the autistic spectrum.

3. In this paper we have used the terms 'folk psychology', 'intuitive psychology', 'theory of mind', and 'mentalizing' interchangeably. We also intend 'folk physics' and 'intuitive physics' to be interchangeable terms.

4. Elsewhere (Baron-Cohen, 1989*b*) we review the argument for why the term 'obsession' can only with difficulty be used in the context of autism. This centres on the traditional definition of an obsession being 'egodystonic' (or unwanted). In autism, there is no evidence that the child's strong interests are unwanted. Rather, those individuals with autism or AS who can report on why they engage in these activities report that they often derive some pleasure from them. They are therefore probably egosyntonic.

## REFERENCES

Asperger, H. (1944). Die 'Autistischen Psychopathen' im Kindesalter. *Archiv fur Psychiatrie und Nervenkrankheiten*, **117**, 76–136.

Bailey, T., Le Couteur, A., Gottesman, I., Bolton, P., Simonoff, E., Yuzda, E. and Rutter, M. (1995). Autism as a strongly genetic disorder: evidence from a British twin study. *Psychological Medicine*, **25**, 63–77.

Baillargeon, R., Kotovsky, L. and Needham, A. (1995). The acquisition of physical knowledge in infancy. In *Causal cognition: a multidisciplinary debate* (ed. D. Sperber, D. Premack, and A. Premack). Oxford University Press.

Baron-Cohen, S. (1987). Autism and symbolic play. *British Journal of Developmental Psychology*, **5**, 139–48.

Baron-Cohen, S. (1988). Social and pragmatic deficits in autism: cognitive or affective? *Journal of Autism and Developmental Disorders*, **18**, 379–402.

Baron-Cohen, S. (1989*a*). Are autistic children behaviourists? An examination of their mental–physical and appearance–reality distinctions. *Journal of Autism and Development Disorders*, **19**, 579–600.

Baron-Cohen, S. (1989*b*). Do autistic children have obsessions and compulsions? *British Journal of Clinical Psychology*, **28**, 193–200.

Baron-Cohen, S. (1994). How to build a baby that can read minds: cognitive mechanisms in mindreading. *Cahiers de Psychologie Cognitive/Current Psychology of Cognition*, **13**, 513–52.

Baron-Cohen, S. (1995). *Mindblindness: an essay on autism and theory of mind*. Bradford Books, MIT Press, Cambridge, Mass.

Baron-Cohen, S. and Goodhart, F. (1994). The 'seeing leads to knowing' deficit in autism: the Pratt and Bryant probe. *British Journal of Developmental Psychology*, **12**, 397–402.

Baron-Cohen, S. and Hammer, J. (1997*a*). Is autism an extreme form of the male brain? *Advances in Infancy Research*, **11**, 193–217.

Baron-Cohen, S. and Hammer, J. (1997*b*). Parents of children with Asperger Syndrome: what is the cognitive phenotype? *Journal of Cognitive Neuroscience*, **9**, 548–54.

Baron-Cohen, S. and Wheelright, W. (in press). Obsessions in children with autism or Asperger Syndrome: a content analysis in terms of core domains of cognition. *British Journal of Psychiatry.*

Baron-Cohen, S., Leslie, A. M. and Frith, U. (1985). Does the autistic child have a 'theory of mind'? *Cognition*, **21**, 37–46.

Baron-Cohen, S., Leslie, A. M. and Frith, U. (1986). Mechanical, behavioural and intentional understanding of picture stories in autistic children. *British Journal of Developmental Psychology*, **4**, 113–25.

Baron-Cohen, S., Tager-Flusberg, H. and Cohen, D. (ed.) (1993). *Understanding other minds: perspectives from autism.* Oxford University Press.

Baron-Cohen, S., Wheelwright, S., Scott, C., Bolton, P. and Goodyer, I. (1997). Is there a link between engineering and autism? *Autism*, **1**, 153–63.

Baron-Cohen, S., Bolton, P., Wheelwright, S., Short, L., Mead, G., Smith, A. and Scahill, V. (1998). Autism occurs more often in families of physicists, engineers, and mathematicians. *Autism*, **2**, 296–301.

Baron-Cohen, S., Wheelwright, S., Stone, V. and Rutherford, M. (in press). A mathematician, a physicist, and a computer scientist with Asperger Syndrome: performance on folk psychology and folk physics tests. *Neurocase*.

Baron-Cohen, S., Wheelwright, S., Scahill, V. and Spong, A. Are children with Asperger syndrome superior in intuitive physics? University of Cambridge. (Submitted).

Bettelheim, B. (1968). *The empty fortress.* The Free Press, Chicago.

Bolton, P., MacDonald, H., Pickles, A., Rios, P., Goode, S., Crowson, M., Bailey, A and Rutter, M. (1994). A Case-control family history study of autism. *Journal of Child Psychology and Psychiatry*, **35**, 877–900.

Brentano, F., von (1874/1970). *Psychology from an empirical standpoint.* Routledge and Kegan Paul, London.

Carey, S. (1985). *Conceptual change in childhood.* Bradford Books/MIT Press, Cambridge, Mass.

Charman, T. and Baron-Cohen, S. (1992). Understanding beliefs and drawings: a further test of the metarepresentation theory of autism. *Journal of Child Psychology and Psychiatry*, **33**, 1105–12.

Charman, T. and Baron-Cohen, S. (1995). Understanding models, photos, and beliefs: a test of the modularity thesis of metarepresentation. *Cognitive Development*, **10**, 287–98.

Dennett, D. (1978). *Brainstorms.* Sussex: Harvester.

Folstein, S. and Rutter, M. (1977). Infantile autism: a genetic study of 21 twin pairs. *Journal of Child Psychology and Psychiatry*, **18**, 297–321.

Gergely, G., Nadasdy, Z., Gergely, C. and Biro, S. (1995). Taking the intentional stance at 12 months of age. *Cognition*, **56**, 165–93.

Halpern, D. (1992). *Sex differences in cognitive ability.* Lawrence Erlbaum, Hillsdale, N.J.

Hart, C. (1989). *Without reason.* Harper and Row, Inc., New York.

Hatano, G. and Inagaki, K. (1994). Young children's naive theory of biology. *Cognition*, **50**, 171–88.

Le Couteur, A., Bailey, A., Goode, S., Pickles, A., Robertson, S., Gottesman, I. and Rutter, M. (1996). A broader phenotype of autism: the clinical spectrum in twins. *Journal of Child Psychology and Psychiatry*, **37**, 785–801.

Leekam, S. and Perner, J. (1991). Does the autistic child have a metarepresentational deficit? *Cognition*, **40**, 203–18.

Leslie, A. (1995). ToMM, ToBy, and Agency: core architecture and domain specificity. In *Domain specificity in cognition and culture* (ed. L. Hirschfeld and S. Gelman). Cambridge University Press, New York.

Leslie, A. and Keeble, S. (1987). Do six month old infants perceive causality? *Cognition*, **25**, 265–88.

Leslie, A. M. (1987). Pretence and representation: the origins of 'theory of mind'. *Psychological Review*, **94**, 412–26.

Leslie, A. M. and Frith, U. (1988). Autistic children's understanding of seeing, knowing, and believing. *British Journal of Developmental Psychology*, **6**, 315–24.

Leslie, A. M. and Thaiss, L. (1992). Domain specificity in conceptual development: evidence from autism. *Cognition*, **43**, 225–51.

Lovell, A. (1978). *In a summer garment.* Secker and Warburg, London.

Ozonoff, S., Pennington, B. and Rogers, S. (1990). Are there emotion perception deficits in young autistic children? *Journal of Child Psychology and Psychiatry*, **31**, 343–63.

Ozonoff, S., Rogers, S., Farnham, J. and Pennington, B. (1994). Can standard measures identify subclinical markers of autism? *Journal of Autism and Developmental Disorders.*

Park, C. (1967). *The Siege.* Hutchinson, London.

Pennington, B., Rogers, S., Bennetto, L., Griffith, E., Reed, D. and Shyu, V. (1997). Validity Test of the Executive Dysfunction Hypothesis of Autism. In *Executive functioning in autism* (ed. J. Russell). Oxford University Press.

Pinker, S. (1997). *How the mind works.* Penguin, London.

Premack, D. (1990). Do infants have a theory of self-propelled objects? *Cognition*, **36**, 1–16.

Rochat, P., Morgan, R. and Carpenter, M. (1997). Young infants' sensitivity to movement information specifying social causality. *Cognitive Development*, **12**, 537–61.

Russell, J. (1997). How executive disorders can bring about an inadequate theory of mind. In *Autism as an executive disorder* (ed. J. Russell). Oxford University Press.

Sigman, M., Ungerer, J., Mundy, P. and Sherman, T. (1987). Cognition in autistic children. In *Handbook of autism and pervasive developmental disorders* (ed. D. Cohen and A. Donnellan). Wiley and Sons, New York.

Spelke, E., Phillips, A. and Woodward, A. (1995). Infants' knowledge of object motion and human action. In *Causal cognition: a multidisciplinary debate* (ed. D. Sperber, D. Premack, and A. Premack). Oxford University Press, Oxford.

Sperber, D., Premack, D. and Premack, A. (ed.) (1995). *Causal cognition: a multidisciplinary debate.* Oxford University Press, Oxford.

Tager-Flusberg, H. (1993). What language reveals about the understanding of minds in children with autism. In *Understanding other minds: perspectives from autism* (ed. S. Baron-Cohen, H. Tager-Flusberg, and D. J. Cohen). Oxford University Press, Oxford.

Wellman, H. (1990). *Children's theories of mind.* Bradford Books, MIT Press, Cambridge, MA.

# 5

# Language and theory of mind: what are the developmental relationships?

JILL DE VILLIERS

## INTRODUCTION

In this chapter I will try to ground the claim, both theoretically and empirically, that false-belief reasoning requires a sophisticated command of syntax. One of the oldest philosophical questions asks whether one can have thinking without language, and if so, what are its limits? In the domain of theory of mind this question achieves new significance. Is this what distinguishes us from the rest of the animal kingdom? Is this what language is good for? And not just words, but syntax?

The first section of this chapter grapples with the fundamental issue of the contribution language makes, if any, to the formation of concepts. A tentative distinction will be drawn between concepts that require no language and concepts that are formed with the help of language. In that latter case, the question arises about whether language is strictly necessary, or just helpful in the normal course of development.

The second section of the paper considers phenomena under theory of mind, and asks how the categories and distinctions formed there connect to language. A brief review of the theoretical discussions of the connections of language and certain theory of mind developments is undertaken, and then a specific alternative proposal is examined.

The third section is a summary of the empirical data related to the role of language, specifically syntax, in false-belief reasoning. Data are reviewed from the course of development in preschool children, and also from the delayed acquisition seen in deaf children who are learning oral language.

The fourth section of the paper points to some interesting new results in language acquisition, inspired and motivated by the work on theory of mind in child development. In this section, the focus of interest is the changes that become possible in language itself as a function of the child's ability to take on different speaker perspectives.

Finally, the implications of this framework for children with autism are discussed.

## CAN LANGUAGE ASSIST CONCEPTS AT ALL?

The standard account of the relationships of concepts to language contends that concepts necessarily provide the foundation for linguistic meanings. We can form infinitely many concepts, and each language chooses a few tens of thousands of those to attach labels to. That is, language maps onto some non-linguistic concepts. How could it be otherwise? Fodor, beginning with his *Language of thought* (1975), has argued cogently that we must possess a rich, symbolic and propositional representational medium for our thought, nothing less elaborate than a language of thought, and this we share with non-human animals, infants, and other language-less beings, who need it in order to think at all. Furthermore, all the concepts within our language of thought must be innate, or made up by recombination of primitive and innate components. Concepts, according to Fodor, cannot be acquired by experience. In the face of this absolute framework, it is tempting to rattle the bars.

The theoretical point of this chapter is to argue that the acquisition of a natural language is foundational for the concept of false beliefs. To show why this is the case, it becomes necessary first to contrast other areas in which language and concepts might interrelate. Table 5.1 is a rough outline of a continuum of relationships between conceptual and linguistic development. As we shall see, the case of false beliefs is at one end of the continuum, and for good reason. Nelson (1991) makes a related case for proposing different levels of influence of language on cognition in considering the acquisition of time concepts.

Fodor (1975) argued that the idea of language preceding concepts is conceptually incoherent. How could you possibly learn the word for something if you didn't have a way of forming the concept first? But one can have the capacity to discriminate among an infinite number of pairs, one taken from set A and one taken from set B, such that it is always the case that any A can be distinguished from any B. Thus, the ability to distinguish on the basis of the fundamental difference between As and Bs can be present. But the ability to discriminate is not necessarily the same as the ability to conceptualize A-ness versus B-ness. Even if A and B always differ, that does not necessarily mean that all As *cohere* compared with all Bs. That latter is what is meant by concepts: classing stimuli together by some dimension, not telling stimuli apart along that dimension. This difference can be illustrated by considering the following pairs:

**Table 5.1.** Concepts at different levels and their linguistic (in)dependence

| | |
|---|---|
| **level zero:** | The difference between A and B can be detected (any A versus any B). Language is not necessary. |
| **level one:** | All As (versus all Bs) can be classed together because of their functional equivalence for some behaviour. Language could accelerate this process, but is not necessary. |
| **level two:** | For all As, language is under normal circumstances the only functional behaviour that ties them together, but it isn't necessarily the only possible act that could do so. |
| **level three:** | Language is an example of a representational system that could capture the equivalence of all As, because it is symbolic and can therefore capture second-order relations. |
| **level four:** | Language is the only representational system that could capture the equivalance, because it is not just symbolic but propositional, and can therefore capure falsity and embeddedness of propositions. |

Can you tell the difference between:
a jigsaw puzzle piece in its puzzle (A) and a frog in a tank (B),
a topped fountain pen (A) and a chocolate in a box (B),
a cassette in its case (A) and a mop in a bucket (B),
a telephone in its handset (A) and a man in a phone booth (B).

The task is a trivial one—there is no doubt you can respond differently to each. But now suppose I tell you that list A have something in common and list B have something in common. It isn't so obvious that you would naturally see the coherence, the commonality, among the instances of A and B that you have so willingly discriminated. In fact, the difference is that list A all involve the 'tight fit' of pieces to wholes, whereas list B involves 'loose fit'. Once I give you the words, you can generate a thousand more examples. Do the words in fact matter, or could I simply reward you for always picking from list A until you get it right? In this case, no-one has tried the experiment, but the reinforcement procedure might work: you might be able to make the A-ness versus B-ness functional by this artificial means. The point here is to illustrate simply that making a reliable discrimination does not necessarily entail classification on the basis of that detectable difference. Let us agree with Fodor that differentiation of any A from any B on some basis is prerequisite for forming a concept, and must, logically, be language-independent. The real question is, is perceiving the *coherence* of A versus B always necessarily prior to language, or can language ever direct this classification?

Consider the evidence first on the acquisition of basic-level concepts in infancy. Surely in this case, one could argue for acquisition of the concepts prior to language for them, because basic object level kinds have behavioural as well as perceptual equivalence (Rosch and Mervis 1975). Furthermore, research suggests laboratory pigeons have some ability to form perceptual equivalence classes of basic-object level natural kinds (Herrnstein 1984). Some perceptual classification of such categories as dog, cat, horse has been observed with three-to six-month-old human infants in habituation paradigms that consider looking time (Eimas and Quinn 1994). However, Mandler and McDonough (1993) argue that detecting perceptual similarity alone does not prove conceptual classification. Mandler and McDonough (1993) found very poor ability to categorize at the basic object level among older infants of seven to eleven months. The difference is that Mandler and McDonough studied how the babies picked up and handled toy objects, and compared their examination times in a habituation/dishabituation paradigm. For example, the babies might be handed a series of little animals and then an airplane, or a series of toy dogs and then a toy cat. Mandler and McDonough concluded that although babies probably 'saw' the perceptual differences among say, cats and dogs, the differences were not important enough to cause them to handle them differently. Instead, Mandler and McDonough found evidence of 'superordinate' classification—a differential treatment of animate versus inanimate things. Although one must question whether toy exemplars constitute an adequate basis for judging categorization in infants, the suggestion is that basic object level categories even of natural kinds may only be established at the perceptual level at the end of the first year of life. But much work remains to be done.

Next consider action categories, that slippery set of concepts encoding event structure, captured in our verb system. Simplifying enormously from the real state of affairs, consider behaviourally distinct actions such as jumping and running. To give evidence of coherence of either conceptual class, we require the infant to make some common response to all acts of jumping, regardless of actor, situation, motive, and so forth. Again, it seems unlikely that any natural contingency exists that would encourage the formation of such a similarity class, even though we may have no doubt that the infant could discriminate any particular act of jumping from any particular act of running. Why do adults detect any similarity? Language again has provided the common behavioural response, verbs have solidified the discriminable dimension into a symbol for a class of events. The philosopher Davidson (1993) has argued that because of our linguistic habits, we are prone to overlook the fundamental difference between events, which are particular (e.g. a specific occasion of a man sitting down), and types, which are only present given language (e.g. the concept of sitting as an action). Is that empirically true? We should ask if there is any event class, like basic object-level categories for objects, towards which the infant might make a common response prior to labelling. Some possible candidates are feeding, reaching, pointing, sleeping, smiling, and crying. These classes have behavioural coherence as gestures, or as signals, and may indeed get organized prior to labels on that basis. Interestingly, they are also part of the infant's own repertoire, and imitation might provide the foundation for the classification.

It is an empirical question of considerable importance to discover whether certain basic object-level classes (natural kinds, primarily) are given to human infants, as well as certain behavioural classes, perhaps intentional acts that babies can mimic—the equivalent of 'natural kinds' in action. On the basis of current literature and speculation, it is a reasonable guess that certain special categories exist prior to language.

But for which other categories can we find evidence for common responses prior to language, in the natural world of the child? For example, take a superordinate, such as fruit: is there any common response the baby makes to that class that they do not make to competing classes, like vegetable? Rosch found it unlikely that adults had common responses beyond the basic object level, so babies probably do not behave in distinctive ways to the class either, until labels arrive. It is labels that provide the behavioural signal that there is something to class: language invites the baby to form a category in the case of a superordinate. Indeed, the literature provides little evidence for superordinate classification in the first year of life, prior to labels. Mandler and McDonough (1996) find behavioural separation of vehicles and animals in a toy-based imitation task by fourteen months of age, but nevertheless argue that the term 'global' is more appropriate than superordinate, since their subjects do not show behavioural evidence of hierarchical sub-class relationships under the global category (Mandler *et al.* 1991).

What of properties, such as colour? There is ample evidence that infants perceive colours and can respond to them differentially in laboratory experiments, just as many species can be trained to do (Bornstein 1985). In real life, colours are attached to objects, and it is possible that there are no natural contingencies that reward the infant for responding one way to all red things, and another way to all green things. That is, no natural contingencies except one—the use of labels. Labels provide an invitation to divide the world in a different way: not by thing-hood, but by property. It is not clear outside of the laboratory that any other invitation arises to so do.

Consider also spatial relations. Investigation of the myriad ways in which languages of the world divide up and classify the space around us has provided a major challenge to writers who consider all concepts exist in full-fledged coherence prior to labelling. So, for instance, even apparently widely shared notions like containment (in) and support (on) are quite distinctly marked in closely related languages such as Dutch, English, and German (Bowerman 1996). The evidence belies the claim that infants first form the concept then map a label onto it, because the labels map different classes, each of which feels 'natural' to a member of that language community. Casting a wider net from European languages, Korean provides evidence that containment and support are not necessarily the most obvious basis for organizing spatial relations: Korean organizes space by the type of connection; by loose and tight fit (Bowerman 1996). We are obviously capable of responding to that difference (remember the example above) but we don't use it to form a coherence class until pushed, by examples organized to test us, like the one above, or by learning a label. Nothing in our ordinary, non-Korean-speaking environment causes us to form that class.

In sum so far: certain basic object-level categories of object, and certain significant human actions, are likely to form coherence classes based on behavioural equivalence witnessed and enacted by human infants. These form the stock of concepts prior to any labelling at all, and are quite likely shared with other species, at least relative to their own species' needs. There is a further level of classification: superordinate object classes, properties, actions, event sequences, spatial relationships, that infants can undoubtedly discriminate, and that under appropriate experimental presentation could form coherence classes, but for which the natural environment provides nothing by way of invitation. Nothing, that is, except labelling. Labelling is usually the mechanism by which the coherence classes get formed, though it is not necessary that language be the mechanism.

Let us take the argument a step further. Is there any concept for which language is *necessarily* the mechanism? Premack (1983) argued yes: second-order categories such as *same* or *different* rely on symbolic mediation for their formation, and are hence out of reach of symbol-less species. In fact, he argued that his chimps who acquired a symbol system (admittedly well short of a true language) were capable of forming these categories but chimpanzees who had not acquired symbols could not be trained to do so. A brief discursion on the categories is necessary to explain why they might extend the demands of behavioural response.

The most trivial case of responding to 'same' is the classic match to sample procedure: the subject is given a sample, say a blue patch, and then a pair of patches, one blue and one red, and must find the 'match' to the original sample. Once the procedure is established, the dimensions of similarity can be switched continually, and the subject just has to match to the sample e.g. a square versus a triangle with colour constant, or plastic versus wood with colour and shape constant . . . Isn't this all there is to demonstrating that the subject knows the concept 'same'? Premack says no: it is at the level of discriminating, or detecting the dimension, but not forming a coherence class equivalent to seeing what the match to sample trials have in common. To do that, Premack argues, we need to probe with a further challenge. Having been trained on match to sample procedures, can the subject perceive the second-order relationship of same versus different? For example, can the subject answer the following type of question, namely which of the pair following it is more like the first stimulus?

$$\frac{\text{AA}}{\text{AB} \quad \text{BB}}$$

That is, can the subject see that the relationship of the two As is one of *sameness*, which is also the relationship between the two Bs? A response based just on resemblance, or overlapping attributes, would probably select AB as the nearest, though imperfect, match. To select BB requires seeing the second order relationship of sameness that AA and BB have in common. Premack argues that this requires a symbolic code, such as language; 'a second-order judgement—a judgement about the relation between relations—can only be made on items that are represented in the abstract code' (p. 128).

What other second-order relations might there be? Negation is one such case, i.e. *not*–A is hard to conceptualize without a symbol for *not*. As Fodor (1983*a*) put it, try to form a picture of a man *not* scratching his nose, or a person not smoking a pipe. These pictures can only be recognized as such in connection with the symbol, they cannot stand alone. Other candidate second order relations might be '*more than*', '*bigger than*', '*to the left of*', '*cause*' and the like (Spelke 1998), but the question is an empirical one. Premack argued that second-order relations require symbolic mediation: if proven true, this would be a powerful case for language not just being the usual form of invitation to form a category, but the only way to do it.

The final case to consider brings us (finally) closer to the heart of the matter of concern for this chapter. The last case suggests that language is powerful because it can symbolize a class. This symbolic function provides the anchor around which similarities coalesce, and then this coalition of diverse stimuli can function economically within the reasoning system, united by the symbol. Even Fodor conceded in *Language of thought* that language could serve this economical, mnemonic-type function for concepts, though he denied that concepts depended on language in any essential way, arguing as we have noted, that the only coherent position was that all concepts pre-date language.

But language does more than provide symbols. Natural languages also have rich syntax, grammatical devices that permit the construction of propositions, and those propositions can encode relationships that stretch beyond word meanings. Sentences extend the meaning-making to allow the differentiation and coalescence of concepts to an infinite degree: we have the component parts, and sentences allow us to play with these infinitely. We are not restricted to things we might have seen, so we can invent concepts as playful as five-legged pink frogs, or as profoundly unlikely as a universe the size of an orange. Language opens up possible worlds and holds them up for our imagination. But this function too, does not necessitate language: art can do the same thing. Whether art can do the same thing in the absence of language, is an important but unanswered question. Are mute artistic savants inevitably realists in their art?

The combinatorial potential of natural language is not, however, restricted to simple propositions. A certain class of linguistic constructions known as complements are embedded under main verbs of communication and mental state, allowing one proposition to be embedded within another, recursively:

The girl said she saw a pink frog.
The girl thought she saw a pink frog.

For such a sentence to be true, it is immaterial whether or not the girl saw a pink frog. In other words, the embedded proposition (*she saw a pink frog*) might be true or false without affecting the truth value of the whole. This class of sentence is somewhat unique, because in the usual case the falseness of part of a sentence renders the whole false (de Villiers 1999). Consider the contrast among the following sentences, each of which has a false proposition in italics:

The girl laughed and *saw a pink frog.*
The girl laughed before *she saw a pink frog.*
When the girl laughed *she saw a pink frog.*
The girl *who saw a pink frog* laughed.

The falsity of the embedded proposition renders each of these whole sentences false, unlike the case of the complement. It is true that logical operators such as *or, if, then, can,* and metalinguistic forms such as *it is not the case that* also have the requisite property, but they do not open worlds that are true in someone else's mind. It is the critical conjunction of a word referring to mental state, together with the syntactic/semantic structure of a complement, that makes reference to false beliefs possible. The special embedded property of the complement under the verb also makes possible certain syntactic operations such as long-distance wh-movement, in which a wh-question refers to the lower verb. In a sentence such as:

Where did the girl think the train was going?

it is clear that the wh-question can connect to the verb *going,* but in a question such as:

Where did the girl sit when the train came?

the question has to refer to the place of sitting, not the train's movements. The complement is embedded under the verb and therefore in the right syntactic relationship for many syntactic and semantic operations that are blocked in other forms that are merely adjoined to a verb. Notice that this very property makes possible a distinction between things in the world and things that are thought, or talked about:

What did the girl say she caught?

Here the question explicitly asks for a distinction between what happened in reality and what someone said happened. To answer the question correctly means integrating the information across two verbs: not answering what was *caught,* but answering what the girl *said* was caught.

The complement structure invites us to enter a different world, the world of the girl's mind, and suspend our usual procedures of checking truth as we know it. In this way, language captures the contents of minds, and the relativity of beliefs and knowledge states. These sentence forms also invite us to entertain the possible worlds of other minds, by a means that is unavailable without embedded propositions. Pictures cannot capture negation, nor falsity, nor the embeddedness of beliefs-that-are-false, unless we have a propositional translation alongside. So this special property of natural languages allows the representation of a class of events—the contents of others' minds —that cannot be captured except via a system as complex as natural language.

Does that mean we can only think about false beliefs in natural language? Fodor argues that we must have a language of thought as representationally rich, and propositional and symbolic, as natural language, but distinct from it. How else, he argues, could infants and animals think? However, something must activate the diverse and very indirectly visible class of events that requires us to posit contents of other minds. Surely only natural language provides the invitation to form such a class, first via the verb labels for the events 'think', 'know', believe', forgot', then, most importantly, for the structures that uniquely allow the representation of false propositions under those verbs.

Thus only the syntax of natural languages normally provides the anchor around which the concept of the propositional contents of other minds can coalesce, and that is not just the normal case, but the necessary case, given the properties that the representational medium must have. This reasoning does not require that natural language *eventually* be the medium in which such ideas are represented, but it must be the medium that invites the formation of a coherence class (de Villiers and de Villiers, 1999). Lacking access to that, infants and animals might in fact *not* think about others' false beliefs.

## THEORIES OF LANGUAGE AND THEORY OF MIND

Other researchers and writers have argued about the connection between language of the mind and theory of mind, without making this exact connection between complement structures and the potential for an increase in representational power. In part that is because the various theories carry with them other ontological commitments concerning the nature of language, the nature of mind, and the role of the environment in shaping each. It can be argued that accounts of the relationship between language and thinking in the development of a mature theory of mind lie on a continuum between quite diverse philosophical viewpoints. In what follows I discuss the extreme versions each in turn, and try to spell out their implications and associated traditions. Then I suggest that compromise is possible between the extremes, and that more work needs to bring these very different traditions together to provide a convincing and coherent picture.

### Learning the discourse about mind

At one end of the continuum lies a tradition in which language is regarded as a part of the nexus of social communication skills that the child encounters as part of a

| Subject | Attitude | Proposition |
|---------|----------|-------------|
| I | think(s) | that the cake is in the fridge |
| He | remember(s) | that the girl has the sticker |
| | believe(s) | |
| | hope(s) | |
| | pretend(s) | |

Intentionality theorists contend that propositional attitudes are real, and causally connected to behaviour, not fictional or purely theoretical. The child must infer them in other people, and on different accounts uses either behavioural evidence, or self-reflection, or some of both, to succeed at these inferences.

The important work of Bartsch and Wellman (1995) can be seen from this point of view. In their exhaustive tally of the uses of mental language by young English-speaking children, they primarily see their work as uncovering the first natural reflections of the child's developing theory of mind, at an earlier point than standardized tests reveal. Bartsch and Wellman spend considerable time defending the children's early uses as genuine mental-state references, rather than just empty uses reflective of cultural discourse. In fact, they argue that the consistent finding of earlier uses of desire terms than of belief terms reflects the ontogeny of those concepts, and is not easily explained by invoking the style of discourse that the children heard.

Having pointed out the lines of tension and the different paradigms of approaching the language/thought issue, consider two theorists who have attempted a synthesis of these extremes.

## Attempted syntheses

Olson (1988) argues, like many others, that the direction of change from infancy to age four years or so moves the child from a behaviourist to an 'intentional' stance (Dennett 1971). In infancy, Olson characterizes the child as engaging in sets of behavioural procedures such as 'if A do B', or expectancies, such as 'if A then B'. In neither case it is necessary to invoke any kind of representational states such as beliefs or desires. However, the child who develops words and sentences must be credited with intentional states, according to Olson. So, 'if they ask for *x*, they desire *x*, if they say that *p*, then they think that *p*'. At the final stage of a theory of mind, they 'begin to see their utterances as expressions of belief', 'to distinguish beliefs from reality'. How do they achieve this change? According to Olson, it is by learning the metalanguage of the culture, by learning to talk about the states of mind that have motivated the toddler in actual talk at a much earlier stage. In this way, the intentional states of the child are no longer merely part of the folk psychology of the culture used to explain behaviour, they become real: 'the child now possesses the structures that can serve as the objects of higher order representations' (p. 424). According to Olson, although one can infer intentional states in the child as soon as he learns to speak, the child develops a theory based on intentionality as he acquires the metalanguage, and he does that via participating in social discourse.

So Olson represents a compromise point of view as a representationalist who credits the social acquisition of language with providing the child a new metalanguage that allows him to represent the states of mind of other persons, and hence use these metarepresentations in a more developed theory of other minds. Olson thus sees language as causally related to the child's metarepresentations, but falls short of claiming that it must be so, and the precise mechanism remains mysterious.

Karmiloff-Smith (1992), like Olson, attempts a synthesis of a representationalist stance and a Vygostkyan view of language as social speech moved inwards to serve a cognitive function. Karmiloff-Smith borrows heavily from Perner's view that there is a representational change occurring at about age four, though in her own terminology. Perner (1991*a*) was concerned to explain the two-year gap between the competencies that Leslie (1987) argues exist in pretence, and those that show up in false belief. The child seems to have the representational competence—a separation of reality from another possible world—in pretence, long before they demonstrate understanding of belief states. Perner argued that the child at age three can recognize two different propositional contents; one about reality, one about the pretend world, and can map these contents on to two protagonists—one real, one imagined. The three-year-old tries to do the same thing with belief, namely to recognize the mismatch of two propositional contents. But the three-year-old cannot handle this information within a causal theory about knowledge, that is, cannot predict what it will mean for a person's behaviour. But the four-year-old recognizes not just that the proposition is false, but that the holder of that attitude regards it as true. So the older child acknowledges not just propositional contents, but propositional attitudes. From this arises a representational theory of mind, in other words that people act according to their representations of the situations, not just the situations themselves. Perner considers this change at age four years critical in being a new representational stage that incorporates a causal theory of knowledge, and does not just invoke the same structures of propositional attitudes and propositional contents that pretend play does.

In Karmiloff-Smith's theory, cognitive development proceeds from purely procedural knowledge, to a form of representation she calls implicit knowledge, then to explicit (conscious) knowledge, the most developed form of which is usually verbal. She proposes that the movement to an explicit theory of mind equivalent to Perner's metarepresentational stage is due to a process of 'redescription' into different representational formats. She argues that, in this one domain at least, the acquisition of the terms themselves for mental states, desires, and so forth, may be essential to this redescription process. In particular, she argues that linguistic representations may provide something of a privileged format for encoding propositional attitudes, and when children are not given a linguistic narrative about a complex behavioural event, they may fail to spontaneously generate one (Norris and Millan 1991, cited in Karmiloff-Smith 1992).

This compromise position places language in a central role not just in exposing the child to the ways in which culture encodes mental events but more essentially, in providing the representational structures that enable the child to reason efficiently about human behaviour. However, Olson and Karmiloff-Smith differ in their view of the mechanism by which language changes representations. Karmiloff-Smith argues that growth in false-belief understanding reflects the child's increasing capacity for using and generating symbolic representations elaborate enough to overcome 'otherwise compelling interpretations generated by direct experience'. Because language 'scaffolds' this symbolic representation, it is crucial. In her account, three-year-olds fail at standard tasks because their rudimentary symbolic representations are not sufficient to override 'experience-based' interpretations.

Karmiloff-Smith's account suggests the relationship between false beliefs and language is at level 3 in Table 5.1. Language ordinarily, and necessarily, organizes experiences under a symbol that marks an abstract relationship. But above I have argued that 'thinks that' is not the same kind of abstract relationship as 'same as'. The representation of the relation '*X* thinks *p*' is an order of magnitude more complex than representing second order relations like 'same as' or 'not', because it involves the embedding of propositions, and those propositions can be false. The power of language as a code lies not just in its symbolic function but in its syntax. In the next section the existing evidence is reviewed about how the necessary lexicon (symbols) and syntax develop, and how these developments connect to the child's abilities in reading minds.

## EXISTING NATURALISTIC EVIDENCE ON LANGUAGE AND THEORY OF MIND

The term 'theory of mind' encompasses a wide range of phenomena, the culmination of which is generally considered to be the understanding of others' false beliefs (Premack and Woodruff 1978). Which of these phenomena might be connected to language developments, and in which ways? Reading others' intentions has been discussed as one of the earliest manifestations of theory of mind, that is, following another's eye gaze, and following points, reaches and so forth (Baron-Cohen 1991; Leslie 1994). Within the first year of life, infants seem to follow another's intentions by following eye gaze, responding appropriately to points, and handing people objects towards which they are reaching. These achievements may be language-independent, though it is hard to tell in the normal case as rudimentary language acquisition—labelling and social rituals—is proceeding during the same interval. It is now clear that infants by the middle of the second year of life—around eighteen months or so—begin using these intentional signals to figure out reference (Baldwin 1991, 1993). Several researchers have now documented that toddlers narrow the possible meaning of new words by using signals such as eye gaze. They have also been shown to reject possible meanings when the person gives evidence that their intention was not met, e.g. when the object was not the expected one, or when the intended action backfired (Tomasello and Kruger 1992). In this early realm of theory of mind development it seems evident that intentionality, perceived nonverbally, assists in the acquisition of early language, particularly reference. It is not completely clear whether language (here: speech) assists in the acquisition of intentionality, but if it does, it is probably facilitative but not necessary. The best guess would be that the relationship of the concept of intentionality to language is level 1 from Table 5.1.

It is claimed that, sometime in the third year of life, children begin to appreciate the different desires of another individual, and predict what a person will do on the basis of a desire (Wellman and Woolley 1990) All the two-year-old really needs is the ability to read intention 'on the fly' as another child reaches for a toy or grabs at food. Around the same time, the child's vocabulary begins to include meanings referring to these behavioural tendencies, such as 'want', 'like', 'doesn't like', and so forth (Bartsch and Wellman 1995). These relatively abstract terms are among the earliest lists of verbs (Dale 1991). Notice that verbs of desire do not take full tensed propositions as arguments, but rather they take noun phrases (NPs):

I want an apple.

or events or states, that have yet to occur, coded in English by infinitive forms:

I want to go home.
I want her to like me.

or states true at present or habitually, coded with a gerundive form:

I like Mom tickling me.

In no case are the embedded forms 'false', that is, referring to current states of affairs that conflict with reality.

It seems probable, though not empirically tested, that the linguistic terms facilitate the child's conceptual access to understanding behaviour in these terms. That would place desire concepts and terms into a level 2 relationship: language is normally the way that the situations get tied together, but it doesn't have to be. Once language does encode these concepts, however, the child can acquire the information about another individual without having to undertake observation: the child can be told 'I want that cup' or 'He likes teddy bears' and respond appropriately (or not, this being a two-year-old). So, language could 'shortcut' sometimes elaborate inferencing.

Gopnik and Meltzoff (1997) propose that conceptual and semantic development may go hand in hand: at particular periods of development, when children are actively engaged in solving specific conceptual problems (such as those to do with a theory of mind), their attention may be drawn to learning words that are relevant to those problems. The advances that we are most interested in occur in the fourth year of life, towards the end of which the child becomes capable of reasoning about the contents of other people's minds on standard and well-controlled tests. Yet it is still in the third year that the child has the first uses of mental terms such as 'think', and 'know', and 'forget'. How do we account for the early uses of the mental verbs, before false-belief understanding on standard tasks?

First, it is evident that the mental verb uses do not always reflect genuine mental reference (Bartsch and Wellman 1995). In the beginning, these terms are most often used in what could be stereotyped routines, e.g. 'I don't know' in answer to a question. However, they begin to appear attached to propositions at least by the end of the third year, such as 'I think $p$'. Bartsch and Wellman code their data very conservatively, yet find convincing evidence that the early use of these verbs has genuine mental reference. The majority of uses are self-referent rather than other-referent, and the vast majority of the mental verbs occur in front of propositions that are true, which raises the question as to whether they are 'opinion-markers' rather than genuine references to mental contents. However, the verbs clearly do occur in every child transcript studied by Bartsch and Wellman in occasional sentences that refer to mistakes, and then one can be sure they do mark mental contents separate from reality e.g. 'I thought *p*' where *p* is false. Some examples of contrastive uses of this sort are as follows:

Abe (2;11): I painted on them. (His hands.)
Adult: why did you?
Abe: I thought *my hands are paper.*

It is only on average one month later that the same children start talking about the false contents of others' minds. Thus the spontaneous speech data, admittedly from a skewed sample of mostly privileged children, suggests that talk about false beliefs, that seems genuinely motivated by understanding, comes in around the age of three. This is at least several months in advance of successful performance on standard false-belief reasoning tasks found in experimental studies.

Our own work suggests that it is quite difficult for the average young three-year-old to formulate or understand a sentence that involves reference to another's false beliefs, when the situation is a controlled experimental one (de Villiers and Pyers 1997). By the end of the fourth year, children can do so much more reliably. There are two possible explanations for the discrepancy between spontaneous speech prowess and controlled situational testing. Note that, in the spontaneous speech samples, the children were in familiar surroundings, with familiar interlocutors, and were free to speak or not as the mood or the competence struck them. In experiments, the interlocutors are relatively unknown, the situations are new, and usually some response is expected. Performance demands alone might create the discrepancy, but it is also probable that there is some meaning, even in the mental arena, to the notion of skill or productive mastery (see Karmiloff-Smith 1992). That is, doing something once in a while, when everything is right and you are in control, is a lot different to summoning the performance successfully every time. So the time discrepancy between consistent performance in controlled production and comprehension of the verbs, and performance on false-belief tasks, may not be as drastic as spontaneous speech measures might lead us to believe.

Consider then how the acquisition of mental verbs and their complements might proceed. Very probably, the first mental verb uses are markers of uncertainty:

I think it's in here.

can be rephrased as:

It's in here, I think.

(Shatz, 1994) and then it is revealed as an adjunct, not a genuine complement, equivalent to:

It's in here, maybe.

The routinized forms:

I don't know.
I think so.

also enter the child's lexicon as markers of the speaker's uncertainty or stance towards some state of affairs, then develop into more genuine mental verbs as Bartsch and Wellman detail (1995).

It is likely that the earliest forms in production do not represent full productive mastery; that is, they might not be elicited in controlled circumstances in which the experimenter sets the scene. In addition, it is difficult to assess from the forms in production whether they are genuine complements with all the attendant syntactic/semantic properties that are evidenced in complements rather than adjuncts. These are best assessed via comprehension, and evidence from wh-question comprehension would suggest that children are in the process of mastering the complement/adjunct distinction between age three and four years (de Villiers *et al.* 1990; Roeper and de Villiers 1994). In particular, children in this age range still evidence difficulty with forms such as:

What did the girl say she bought?

to which they are prone to answer what she actually bought. Notice that this is not a question involving mental states at all, but overt acts of speech, and that neither does it require any inferences about hidden mental processes, as the information is given overtly in the story. All the child needs to do is to interpret the structure correctly as a complement in which the question concerns the joint effect of two verbs: both saying and buying. As such, we regard it as a good index of whether the child really has the structure of complements in the grammar (de Villiers 1999). The evidence of both command of the comprehension and controlled elicitation of complements jointly provide the best assurance of the mastery of the fundamental syntax of complements.

Notice that mastery of the verbs of communication has been a relatively neglected part of the story of 'language of the mind' development, because the verbs are not ostensibly about the mind. Nevertheless, I have argued (de Villiers 1995*a,b*) that the problem of acquiring the complement structures with mental verbs might be partially solvable by considering the parallels between the behaviour of verbs of communication ('say', 'ask', 'tell') and verbs of mental state ('think', 'believe', 'guess'). Verbs of communication can also be used entirely redundantly:

I say put your clothes on!

but also in discrepant situations where what is said does not match reality:

You said you ate your peas!

where the peas are still much in evidence. Fortunately in the case of 'say', there is no inference required about covert states: saying is an overt act, and can be witnessed. So, in principle, all of this machinery—that is of a matrix verb, that can take either a true or a false proposition—can be mastered with verbs of communication (or perception). Bartsch and Wellman give evidence that the order of development proceeded in this direction in three of the four children they studied intensively. Then verbs like 'think', that refer to covert states of mind, can inherit the identical complement structures. By this process the child can achieve a mastery of the syntax/semantics interface of mental verbs, even before the contexts that require them are really recognized. A rough depiction of the parallels between communication and mental verbs is provided in Table 5.2, and of the steps to mastery in Table 5.3.

So with the mental verbs learned as referents to 'invisible' states, perhaps even self-referential, and the critical complement structures learned by analogy with overt states of communication, the child has now acquired the representational structure for encoding states of false belief.

In de Villiers (1999) I argue that at the final step in which the child acquires the representational structure for false complements, there is some formal property of the grammar that gets set (or re-set from a default). Many linguists have argued that factive verbs ('know', 'forget') require some formal feature that reflects that their complements are obligatorily true: I argue that it is necessary for the child to set a equivalent feature in the grammar to indicate that the complement of a non-factive communication or mental-state verb can be false. The most obvious place to locate such a formal feature in the grammar is in the position called CP, which is where complementizers ('that', 'for', 'to', 'if', 'what') are located between clauses. Every sentence and subordinate sentence is headed by a CP, and the CP site carries information relevant to such properties as quantification, questions, focus, topic, and, most critically for our analysis, 'point of view'—perspectives on time, place, and reference (Kratzer 1997). Acquisition of the formal properties of the CP may begin with the step

**Table 5.2.** Parallels between communication and mental verbs

| **Words for speech:** | **Words for mental state:** |
|---|---|
| say | think |
| ask | pretend |
| tell | guess |
| **Structures for speech verbs:** | **Structures for mental verbs:** |
| imperatives: | imperatives: |
| say p | *think p |
| ask X | pretend p |
| tell X | guess p (?restricted) |
| direct speech: | direct quotes |
| he says 'X' | he thinks 'X' |
| he says 'p' | he thinks 'p' |
| he asked/told her 'p' | ?he pretends 'p' |
|  | ?he guesses 'p' |
| indirect speech-true p complements | indirect speech-true p complements |
| he says (that) p | he thinks (that) p |
| he asked (p) | he pretends (that) p |
| he told Y (that) p | he guesses (that) p |
| indirect speech-false p complements | indirect speech-false p complements |
| he says (that) p | he thinks (that) p |
| he asked (p) | he pretends (that) p |
| he told Y (that) p | he guesses (that) p |

**Table 5.3.** Proposed stages of mastery of complements of communication and mental verbs

---

*Step 1*: The child masters the basic sentence forms: a simple sentence is mapped on to a simple event. The child encounters true sentences  that match reality.

| situation | (matrix verb) | complement |
|---|---|---|
| x | — | x |
| dog on chair | — | dog on chair |

*Step 2*: The child first encounters discrepancy between sentence and reality: the child learns to recognize pretence as well as mistakes.

| situation | (matrix verb) | complement |
|---|---|---|
| x | — | y |
| dog on chair | — | cat on chair |

*Step 3*: The child masters the first embedded structures under verbs of communication/mental state/desire: child acquires the fundamental syntax of embedding but makes no accommodation of meaning within that structure: the complement retains its truth value as a simple sentence independent of the matrix verb. This structure may or may not be available simultaneously for communication verbs and mental-state verbs.

| situation | matrix verb | complement |
|---|---|---|
| a, x | a | x |
| mother says something | | |
| dog on chair | mother says | dog on chair |

AND

| | | |
|---|---|---|
| mother believes something | | |
| dog on chair | mother believes | dog on chair |

*Step 4*: The child first notices occasions with verbs of communication that suggest the complement can be false when embedded e.g. reports of lying, mistakes. The relation of statement to fact makes the semantic accommodation evident.

| situation | matrix verb | complement |
|---|---|---|
| a, x | a | y |
| mother says something | mother says | cat on chair |
| dog on chair | | |

This development may have two parts:
 i) Understanding the direct speech of the mother: 'a cat is on the chair' despite what is actually true: i.e. that what the mother said is false.
ii) Understanding that it is true that *the mother said that a cat is on a chair*. So, a false clause can become part of a true statement, if and only if it is syntactically embedded.

*Step 5*: The special semantic accommodation of complements is extended to verbs of mental states: beliefs.

| situation | matrix verb | complement |
|---|---|---|
| b, x | b | y |
| mother believes something | mother believes | cat on chair |
| dog on chair | | |

---

of appropriately marking the complement of the verb as potentially false, with the other features then gradually accreting.

Linguistic details aside, it is argued that acquisition of the syntax for representing false complements is the step that allows the child to use and generate symbolic representations elaborate enough to overcome 'otherwise compelling interpretations generated by direct experience', to borrow from Karmiloff-Smith (1992).

The claim made here can be reconciled with several other accounts of the changes occurring in the preschool years. For example, consider Perner's (1991*b*) account of the stages of false-belief development, which is an account in terms of the changing quality of representations. To Perner, the two-year-old is a 'situation theorist', who has no true representation of mental states, but is developing representations of e.g. pictures and drawings. The three-year-old understands that others have minds but does not have a concept of mental representation. Such a child can form a representation of desired objects or states of affairs, but simply imagines the other person related to them but not representing them. By four years old, the child can represent the contents of other minds, a kind of metarepresentation: a concept of representation. Perner's argument that children's early representations are akin to regarding 'belief' as equivalent to 'thinking of *x*' rather than 'thinking that *p*' is compatible with the idea that the full complement structure, rather than the incomplete representation of a mental verb as taking an NP argument, is what enables the more sophisticated metarepresentation.

Consider also Fodor's (1992) claim, that the two-year-old has a full 'desire–belief psychology' innately, but lacks the computational ability to resist certain inferences. Basically the child has two hypotheses, with H1 as the default:

H1 = predict agent will act in such a way as to satisfy desires.
H2 = predict agent would satisfy desires if his beliefs were true.

The difference is that the four-year-old can cancel the desire-based reasoning of H1, and take account of the agent's false belief via H2. The current proposal is not at odds with Fodor's argument that the child is unable to resist the desire/true-belief reasoning, but, instead of proposing a general change in 'computational power', the present theory suggests that the ability to represent false complements linguistically is what boosts the child's computational skill up a notch.

There are also several theories with which the present account is less easily accommodated. Harris (1996), proposing a simulation theory approach to false-belief reasoning, argues that the two-year-old can simulate desire and belief in others on the basis of projection of what he might feel or think in such a situation. Harris predicts that understanding the self is easier than understanding others because the self is just directly experienced then reported, but the feelings or thought of another must be simulated, experienced, and then reported. In achieving this latter understanding, Harris claims that there are two default settings to be overcome: the child's own intentional states and the state of reality. Both can interfere with the output of this simulation process. Within a simulation theory account, it is not at all clear how a change in representational power could affect a greater resistance to default settings, since simulation theory disavows representations.

Bartsch and Wellman (1995) argued that the linguistic capacity emerges much earlier, at just below age three, and that the change at age four is not in the ability to represent false beliefs so much as to recruit them reliably in the service of explaining human actions. As I have argued, it is not completely clear how long the gap is between successful use of mental verbs with false complements, and the use of such representations in false-belief reasoning. There may well be some additional task demands involved in recruitment of the representations in the service of particular tasks, such as explanation, or narrative. But the gap may be less extreme than the spontaneous speech data suggest.

Second, this strong version of linguistic determinism is seriously discrepant with Leslie's maturational theory of false-belief development. As we shall see below, the data from deaf children calls the maturational account into serious question, so no resolution of the discrepancy is yet evident. However, the early developmental stages of ToMM proposed by Leslie are not called into question at all by this account.

## EMPIRICAL STUDIES OF THE DIRECTION OF RELATIONSHIP

### Normally-developing children

Several researchers have found that mastery of false-belief reasoning tasks is related to measures of language ability, in both normally-developing children and children with autism (Happé 1995; Tager-Flusberg 1996; Tager-Flusberg and Sullivan 1994). Astington and Jenkins (1995) found with normally-developing children that general false-belief understanding assessed by summing across four standard tests of false-belief reasoning, was significantly correlated with measures of syntactic and semantic maturity on the Test of Early Language Development (TELD), even when the effects of age were partialled out. The sophisticated use of sentence forms involving mental-state verbs and their complements coincides roughly in time with the child's successful performance on standard false-belief tasks (Astington and Jenkins 1995; de Villiers 1995a; Tager-Flusberg 1996).

Correlational data of this sort fail to reveal the direction of the relationship between language and theory of mind, so two longitudinal studies have attempted to untangle the relationship between learning the language of the mind and passing false-belief tasks, in normally-developing preschool children.

Astington and Jenkins (1995) studied two cohorts of nursery school children longitudinally over the course of one year in school, using three standard theory of mind tasks (change in location, unexpected contents, and appearance–reality) for a total possible score of 6. In addition, they gave the children a standardized language test, the TELD, that assesses broad syntactic and semantic skills in this age range, using both expressive and receptive formats. In addition, Astington and Jenkins took spontaneous speech samples during pretend play for one of their cohorts, and looked specifically at the use of mental-state verbs. Unfortunately they did not include any measure of complementation with mental verbs, just the overall use of the verbs and the general measure of vocabulary and syntax development. Their findings suggest a clear developmental relationship, with language use predicting theory of mind scores over time: the correlations between *time$_n$ language* and *time$_{n+1}$ theory of mind* were robust and significant, but the reverse, the predictions from *theory of mind at time$_n$* to *language at time$_{n+1}$* were not significant and vanishingly small. Analyzing the spontaneous use of mental-state verbs, they also reach the conclusion that language is 'leading the way', in that the children who were still scoring quite poorly on the standardized tests showed at least occasional use of mental-state verbs, and used apparently appropriately, e.g.

'She'll still think I'm a real person and I'm not a real person. I'll be not a real person.'

Astington and Jenkins's study cannot settle the question of the relative contribution made by the verbs themselves versus their syntactic structures, nor can it decide the directionality of relationship between language and theory of mind. Is the developmental priority of the linguistic use just a function of the difference in task difficulty between occasional, child-controlled spontaneous use, versus experimenter-controlled tasks that require generation and inference? That is the argument familiar from Bartsch and Wellman's work: the spontaneous language may reflect perfectly good false-belief understanding, but only sporadically, compared with the mastery required by experimental tasks.

A study with a similar purpose was conducted by de Villiers and Pyers (1997) who also studied a group of children over the course of one year, from an average age of 3;4 years to 4;4 years, that is, spanning the usual age of mastery of false-belief reasoning. Our goal was to discover the temporal relationships between use of language about the mind, specifically complementation, and the development of false-belief reasoning as indexed by three standard false-belief tasks. The tasks we used were as follows:

*a) Unexpected contents task (Perner et al. 1987)*

On each round of testing we asked about a different familiar container: a Crayola crayon box, a Playdo container, a Cheerios cereal box, and a small milk carton, and asked both about the child's own prior belief (Astington and Gopnik 1988):

When you were sitting over there, what did you think was in the box?

and their friend's likely belief, for a total of two points[1]:

What would (Sally) think is in the box?

*b) Unseen displacement (Wimmer and Perner 1983)*

The child is told a story which is acted out in front of her, and in the story an object is moved without one character's knowledge. The child must then predict where the character will first look for that object.[2] We also asked the question 'why will he look there?', and gave a point for a suitable explanation which did not have to use mentalistic vocabulary, so saying 'because he put it there' counted as a perfectly adequate answer. Thus this task gave a total of two points.[3]

*c) Explaining action (Bartsch and Wellman 1989)*

For the third false-belief task a combination of the above two scenarios was used, in which a puppet is deceived. While the puppet is asleep, the child is shown a familiar box, say an egg carton with eggs, and the eggs are removed from the container and hidden in another unmarked box. The puppet is then woken up and the child is told:

'You know what he likes to do when he wakes up? He likes to eat eggs!'

The puppet is then made to manipulate the (empty) egg box and the child is asked, 'Why is he looking in there?' and 'Why isn't he looking in that (other) box?' Again, mental explanations are not necessary for points on this task: saying, 'because they were in there' is coded as a satisfactory explanation.

These three false-belief tasks thus each had a maximum score of two, for a total of 6 each round. The 'passing' criterion was set at 5 or 6 out of 6.

In addition, in each of three rounds of testing the nineteen children received several tests of language comprehension and elicited production that tapped knowledge of complements with mental and communication verbs, allowing us to develop measures of their complex syntax with and without complements. The comprehension test for complementation was basically trivial in its cognitive demands: could the child hold on to a sentence with a false complement and repeat it as an answer in a story? On each round, children received twelve sets of photographs or drawn pictures of brief stories in which a character was described as making a mistake, telling a lie, or having a false belief. Hence the child had no inferences to make about mental states, as they were provided in the narrative. Half the scenarios involved acts of thinking (verbs *think*, *believe*) and half involved acts of communication (verbs *say* and *tell*). For half of the events, the question asked for a report of the contents of the character's belief/statement, in which a whole sentence or complement+sentence is an appropriate response, e.g.:

He thought he found his ring, but it was really a bottle cap.
What did he think?
Answer: 'that he found his ring'.
*Answer: 'that it was a bottle cap'.

She said she found a monster under her chair, but it was really the neighbour's dog.
What did she say?
Answer.: 'she found a monster'.
*Answer: 'she saw the neighbour's dog'.

For the other half of the questions, the question form required simply a noun rather than the whole propositional content, but the right answer did require integration of the two verbs as discussed earlier:

This girl saw something funny at a tag sale and paid a dollar for it. She thought it was a toy bird but it was really a funny hat.
What did she think she bought?
Answer: 'a toy bird'.
*Answer: 'a funny hat'.

Memory for complements had a total possible score of twelve and the criterion for passing was set at ten or more out of twelve.

The de Villiers and Pyers study also scored the child's spontaneous speech about silent videos, computer games, and stories spontaneously told in the sessions, then analyzed them using the IPSyn: Index of Productive Syntax (Scarborough 1990). The IPSyn basically considers the productivity of different syntactic and morphological forms in the transcript. It demonstrates good reliability for child language corpora of as few as fifty utterances, and is more discriminating of normal syntactic development between the ages of twenty four and forty eight months than is mean length of utterance (MLU).

The IPSyn allowed us to develop two subscores of complex syntax, one reflecting the structures that did not involve that-complementation, i.e. the if-then clauses, relative clauses and other complex forms, and one that reflected propositional complementation (that-complements and wh-complements). We created several sub-totals such as the total Sentence Structure score (SS), the total complex sentences (total complex IPSyn), the total score for complements (IPSyn comps), and the total complex minus complements (IPSyn complex no comps). These measures were entered into regressions to predict false-belief reasoning, and the prediction was that com-plementation, not general syntax productivity, would predict false-belief reasoning. We also tapped syntax sophistication via the traditional MLU measure.

More details of the results and analyses are contained in de Villiers and Pyers (1997) and de Villiers and de Villiers (1999). The score on the 'memory for complements' task turned out to be a very robust predictor of how the children performed on false beliefs, and it also led success on the false-belief tasks. The spontaneous speech measures and the memory for complements score were of course very highly intercorrelated, but we could tease them apart and test the directionality of relationships using a stepwise regression.

We chose Round 2 and Round 3 as our comparison points because they offered the greatest variance in scores. In Round 1, virtually no children passed anything, and by Round 4 almost every child passed the entire battery. The complete set of language measures at Round 2 predicted 55% of the variance in false belief on that round. The most significant predictor variable was production of sentential complements (IPSyn comps) (47% of variance, p<.001). No other language measure added significantly to the variance accounted for by this complement measure. We then performed a step-wise regression to predict 'passing' false belief at Round 3 on the basis of language measures at Round 2. The whole set of language measures at Round 2 predict 38% of the variance in later false belief. Once again, the analysis revealed that the most significant predictor variable was the production of sentential complements (IPSyn comps) at Round 2 (29% of variance, p<.01). Thus the other language measures add only slightly to the predictive power of complements.

So the mastery of complement structures in comprehension and in production turned out to be the best predictor of false-belief reasoning both in a single round of testing (Round 2, chosen for its variability of performance) and across Rounds 2 to 3. The data were asymmetrical in that linguistic complements in Round 2 predicted false-belief reasoning in Round 3, but false-belief reasoning in one round did not predict linguistic complements in the next. The data are certainly in keeping with the model presented above, but correlational and regression studies, even longitudinal ones, are admittedly only weak support for such a case. Especially given the use of verbal false-belief tasks, the correlations with language might reflect only the task requirements of the standard tasks. In addition, it is difficult to assess the direction of developmental influences when everything is changing together in such a short time span, and the possibility arises that differences in task demands could create the developmental orderings that we witness. To subject the hypothesis of linguistic influence to the most stringent test, we need a group of children who demonstrate greater variance in language skill over time, and, ideally, non-verbal tasks of false-belief reasoning should be used.

## Orally-taught deaf children

For these reasons, Peter de Villiers and I have undertaken work with language-delayed deaf children, who provide an important test population in this area of research. Unlike children with autism, deaf children do not have other associated handicaps such as socio-emotional disabilities, social withdrawal, or low intelligence. In all these areas deaf children commonly test in the normal range, though it is obvious that a profoundly deaf child who achieves no functional communication system will eventually demonstrate marked social and intellectual handicaps relative to his hearing peers. However, these effects are considered secondary to language deficiency caused by deafness, unlike the case of children with autism. In this case, the subjects of study are otherwise intellectually and socially normal children with a severe-to-profound hearing loss, congenital or acquired in the first year of life.

As a result of this deafness, the children have markedly reduced access to the spoken language of their caregivers, even with high quality hearing aids. Deaf children attend several kinds of educational institutions, including schools that expose them intensively and early to American Sign Language, but the subjects of concern for the present work attend oral schools for the deaf. In an oral school, the focus is on intensive auditory and speech training, and sometimes training to lip-read, accompanied by increasing use of written text as the children learn to read, as the media for exposure to a first language. Though downplayed as significant by most oral schools, there is also considerable gestural support of speech by hearing people interacting with oral deaf children and by the children themselves. Most deaf children develop a fairly rich repertoire of iconic (pantomimic) gestures, pointing, and simple gesture 'sentences' that they use in the home with hearing parents and siblings, who also use the same 'Home Sign'. A visit to any oral school for the deaf reveals considerable gesturing among the children, particularly out of the formal classroom setting. The nature of this Home Sign has been extensively documented for preschool children by Goldin-Meadow and her colleagues (Goldin-Meadow 1982; Goldin-Meadow and Mylander 1984). A fair assessment of the linguistic sophistication of Home Sign in the preschool years is that it remains at about the equivalent expressive power of the average two-year-old conventional language user (de Villiers *et al.* 1993).

In terms of success in acquiring English, there is a huge range of success among oral deaf children that is not well predicted by their hearing loss or their IQ. However, the average six-year-old deaf child acquiring English as a first language is significantly delayed, both in lexical knowledge and, importantly, in grammar. The inflectional morphology of the language is seriously affected (de Villiers *et al.* 1994; Mogford 1993; Paul and Quigley 1993), with missing plurals, past tense, possessive markers, and so forth, but the overall syntax is also markedly delayed. Even the word order of simple agent–action–patient sentences is less reliably marked by these children compared with hearing children at the same MLU (mean-length-of-utterance and they have particular difficulties with embedded clauses (de Villiers *et al.* 1994). Their narrative ability is impoverished, with much stringing together of simple sentences, and often requiring great leaps of inference by the listener (de Villiers 1990). On average, oral deaf children in the age range of four to nine years perform on standardized tests such as the PPVT (vocabulary) and the CELF (syntax subscale) as being about three to four years delayed compared with hearing children.

At the same time, such children can perform in the normal or superior range on nonverbal tests of ability such as those involving spatial relational patterns, completing visual sequences, or memorizing action sequences. Oral deaf children are usually actively sociable, curious, friendly, and eager to participate in social activities. Emotionally, they are reported to react appropriately to physical and social events. In sum, it is their language skills that are markedly delayed, and the language skills are paramount in predicting other areas of intellectual achievement (e.g. reading, school performance) and social adjustment.

From the point of view of our theory of mind testing, then, oral deaf children provide an excellent test population for theories of the role of language in false-belief reasoning. Because they do not exhibit primary cognitive or socio-emotional problems, any problems that they face in false-belief reasoning must be a function of their language delay. However, these problems could arise in one of three primary ways:

1. They could fail to understand the task, because they do not follow the narrative or the instructions or the questions being asked.

2. They might lack skill in encoding and interpreting events involving false belief because they have had insufficient exposure to situations in which language has highlighted these events. In other words, they have never had language 'invite them to form a category', and nothing else in their environment can do that.

3. They might lack the ability to encode the events in language, hence fail to represent the distinction between the possible world (in someone's mind) and the actual world.

To test the first hypothesis that it is the language required in the standard false-belief tasks that might cause problems for language-delayed children, we have used several non-verbal tests, or at least minimally-verbal tasks, that call upon the same reasoning skills. We test their equivalence against the performance of normally-developing, hearing preschoolers, and check that they call upon the same general reasoning abilities. If deaf children fail these tasks as well as the standard tasks, it is a reasonable claim that their problems lie deeper than the language of the tasks.

Distinguishing between the second two hypotheses is more difficult and ultimately more rewarding for theoretical progress. Herein lies the heart of the Whorfian distinctions: is language weakly or strongly causal in this domain? Does language serve to call attention to certain concepts, highlight them, unite them under a symbol, and hence facilitate access to a mysterious domain, largely invisible and inferential in the case of other minds' contents? Or, it is even more than that: does it provide the representational means without which the very concept would be unattainable?

We cannot yet say that we have found the way to decide between the latter two alternatives, though we are actively researching them. At the very least, our research allows us to distinguish between having the words for mental events, and having the structures of complementation that allow representation of possible worlds. Suppose the real mechanism by which events are tied together and new concepts formed is simply via the words for thinking, knowing, wanting, and so forth, in that they select and label situations requiring reference to hidden states of mind. Then we can check to see if a child with only the labels for mental states is capable of reasoning in nonverbal tasks. Command of the productive vocabulary demonstrates that the child has had 'exposure' potentially sufficient to invite the formation of a concept. However, if the critical aspect is not the vocabulary but the syntactic structure that allows embedded propositions, such a child will not have the ability to reason about false beliefs. Only children who command the vocabulary and the structures should then be able to engage in false-belief reasoning, even when the task itself requires no overt language.

At the time of writing, we have tested around a hundred oral deaf children aged four to nine years of age, on a variety of language, nonverbal IQ, and false-belief tasks. Further details of a subset of these results are reported in Gale *et al.* (1996), and in de Villiers and de Villiers (1999), and we refer here to the results from this published work.

These studies confirm one result very clearly: oral deaf children do experience considerable difficulty with the syntax of English, and the problems are not confined to morphology (de Villiers *et al.* 1993; Paul and Quigley 1993). As in the de Villiers and Pyers (1997) study, we took fairly extensive samples of spontaneous speech, elicited language using silent videotapes of cartoons and enacted events, and then subjected these to analyses of the syntax used. The measures of language were PPVT (for vocabulary), MLU (a rough measure of syntax) and IPSyn: a measure of IPSyn complements, and a measure of IPSyn Sentence Structure without complements, as above. There was enormous variability in the children's linguistic skill, and as usual, the degree of hearing loss was not a very adequate predictor of that variability.

As an indication of the impoverished nature of many deaf children's command of English syntax, consider first their responses to a set of silent videos we have created to try to elicit talk about the mind: instances of intention, desire, and false belief are enacted in these videos. In our ongoing work (de Villiers and de Villiers, 1999; de Villiers and Pyers 1997) we have shown the children silent videos in which events occurred that required positing intentional states to the characters to make sense of the story. Table 5.4 shows a sample of responses to a single such video from six

**Table 5.4.** Elicited language about a mistake

**Typical adult description:**

The girl is reading the newspaper and has her soda on the table next to her. A cleaner comes by and cleans the table, and takes away the soda. A little vase of flowers is now standing where the soda was. The girl wasn't looking so she picks the vase up and tries to drink the flowers!
**Why did she drink the flowers?**
Because she thought it was her soda.
**What was she thinking?**
I guess she thought it was her soda.

**With the children, we prompted using three still pictures from the video to remind them of the event after the spontaneous narrative. We asked staged questions, continuing if we did not elicit a 'mental' explanation:**
1. **what happened?**
2. **why did the girl drink the flowers?**
3. **what was she thinking?**

**Oral deaf subjects**

| *Question* | *Response* |
|---|---|
| **Subject 1**  Age 5;6 | |
| What happened? | Drink drink (gestures drink) (drink what?) drink. |
| E shows pictures: | |
| 1st picture | drink. |
| 2nd picture | clean (gestures wiping table) |
| 3rd picture | drink (screws up face) |
| Why? | yuck. |
| What is she thinking? | think, think, think (mimics) |
| Do the flowers taste yummy? | (shakes head) no. |
| | |
| **Subject 2**  Age 5;10 | |
| What happened? | (gestures drink and makes gulping sound) |
| Drink what? | flower. |
| Why did she drink the flowers? | eew. That's crazy (mimics) |
| What's she doing? (E shows pictures) | |
| 1st picture | juicexxx |
| 2nd picture | wash . . . wash |
| 3rd picture | (gestures drinking) drink flower |
| Why? | flower, flower, wash wash (gestures putting away, drinking, shakes head) uh oh. |
| | wash, wash (gestures picking up) xxx up xx |
| What is she thinking? | flower |
| | |
| **Subject 3**  Age 6;4 | |
| What happened? | Flower. Flower. Flower. |
| What did she do with the flowers? | Flower (unintelligible?) |
| What's happening here? | |
| (E shows pictures) | |

**Table 5.4.** Continued

| | |
|---|---|
| 3rd picture | (gestures drinking flowers) |
| | Flowers. I know. |
| Why is she drinking the flowers? | Flowers. Flowers. (unintelligible) |
| What is she thinking here? | Flowers. Flowers. |

**Subject 4                    Age 6;9**

| | |
|---|---|
| What happened? | She's drinking. She's drinking juice (gestures drinking) |
| What'd she think? | Drink flower. |
| Why was she drinking the flowers? | It's dirty, yuck. |
| What happened here? (1st picture) | She's looking at the paper. |
| What happened here? (2nd picture) | No drinking flowers, dirty. |
| What happened here? (3rd picture) | It's dirty, flower. |
| Why is she drinking the flowers? | Because she drinks it. |
| What is she thinking? | Think flower. |

**Subject 5                    Age 7;2**

| | |
|---|---|
| Spontaneous (during video) | xx xx |
| What happened? | The (a) girl xx drink the flower. |
| Why is she drinking the flowers? | The cup. The cup. |
| What happened? (E show pics) | Drink the flower. |
| What's she doing? (pics) | The cup. |
| Spontaneous (1st picture) | The maid xx clean wipe xx (wash) the table. |
| Spontaneous (3rd picture) | She smell. |
| She smell the flowers? | Yes. |
| Why did she smell the flowers? | The cup. |
| What is she thinking? (3rd picture) | She smell the flower. |

**Subject 6                    Age7;4**

| | |
|---|---|
| What happened? | Boy eat flower. |
| Why'd he eat the flowers? | Because it's yucky. |
| What happened here? (pics) | She drink. |
| Spontaneous (1st picture) | Girl washing table. |
| Spontaneous (3rd picture) | He drink the flower. |
| Why is he drinking the flowers? | Because it's yucky. |
| What is he thinking? (3rd picture) | He thinking get up. |
| He's thinking what? | Get up. |

**Normally-hearing subjects**

**Subject 1                    Age 3;6**

| | |
|---|---|
| What happened? | The . . . her mom took her drink way and she picked up the flowers and she tried to drink that. |
| Why did she drink the flowers? | I dunno. That must be strange. |

**Subject 2                    Age 3;7**

| | |
|---|---|
| What happened? (3rd picture) | She bump into it. |
| Why did she drink the flowers? | Cuz that wasn't her drink. |
| What thinking? | That think is was a drink. |

**Table 5.4.** Continued

| Subject 3 | Age 3;7 | |
|---|---|---|
| What happened? (1st picture) | | She's . . . um . . . wiping it, wiping it. |
| Why did she drink the flowers? (3rd picture) | | (shrug) |
| What is she thinking? | | I don't know. |
| What is she thinking? | | That she wants her soda back. |

| Subject 4 | Age 3;11 | |
|---|---|---|
| What happened? (E shows pictures) | | Mmmmm . . . |
| Why did she drink the flowers? | | I don't know. |
| Why did she drink the flowers? | | Cause she thinks that's still her drink. |

| Subject 5 | Age 4;1 | |
|---|---|---|
| (E shows pictures) What happened? | | She's washing the table. |
| Why did she drink the flowers? | | I don't know. |
| What is she thinking? (3rd picture) | | She thinks, she thought it was soda. |

| Subject 6 | Age 4;2 | |
|---|---|---|
| What happened? | | Umm, he was drinking soda, but then, umm, a lady came and cleaned up the table and she moved the flowers and then he said, 'Hmmm, so I gues I will take a drink,' and then he almost drank the flower. |
| Why did she drink the flowers? | | He thought that the drink was still there. |

low-functioning oral deaf children and six normally-hearing children two or three years younger in age. While it is true that the young normally-hearing children do not give perfectly adult descriptions of the events, it is obvious that their language and narratives contrast dramatically with those from the deaf children. These deaf children's descriptions not only contained markedly impoverished syntax, but also exhibited considerable difficulty in capturing an intentional description of the events. In fact, inspecting these descriptions closely suggests that these children do not conceptualize the events in the same way as the hearing children.

Having established that oral deaf children can have profound delays in the area of syntax, sufficient to delay their acquisition of complementation and other complex forms, the groundwork was partially laid for testing their performance on false-belief reasoning tasks. The second preparatory step was to find nonverbal tests of false-belief reasoning that could be shown to tap the equivalent levels of skill in normally-hearing children as the standard tasks. We have found two such tasks (see de Villiers and de Villiers, 1999) and demonstrated that four-year-old hearing children can pass these tasks, and that their performance on the nonverbal versions is highly correlated with that on the standard false-belief tasks. We should point out that we have found it virtually impossible to test either hearing or deaf children in complete silence, even if the tasks do not require language to present or understand. We use conversational language to encourage, draw attention, and direct the child's responses, and all of the children in the studies have been able to understand this level of language. Language is an inevitable part of human interaction, and it feels highly artificial to engage in silent tasks, especially with the youngest children.

The first task is modelled on the one used by Povinelli and deBlois (1992) in their work with monkeys and chimpanzees, as well as three- and four-year-old children. It is perhaps less categorizable as a false-belief task, but more as one involving the heuristic that seeing leads to knowing, and knowing leads to appropriate advice. In our version of the task, two 'helpers' of the experimenter point to different boxes where a sticker has been hidden, and the child has to decide whose advice to take. One of the helpers saw where the experimenter hid the sticker, and the other helper did not, being blindfolded and in the same vicinity as the child, behind a screen. A sensible choice would be to choose the advice of the seeing-therefore-knowing helper. The child is first taught the basic structure of the game with a sticker hidden in one of four small identical white boxes behind a pull-down screen. At first the experimenter points to the appropriate box for the child to find the sticker, and once this is established as the game, the two helpers join in, one viewing and one blindfolded. After the experimenter hides a sticker, the screen is pulled up and each stooge points to a different box. Ten such trials are run, and the child is credited with 'passing' if he succeeds on eight out of the ten, or six trials correct in a row. The child cannot fix on the choice of a particular individual, as we randomly allocate which helper is blindfolded on each trial by a predetermined random sequence. The helpers give no facial or gestural clues to the child; they just look and point at the boxes.

The results from oral deaf children on this task are clear cut: the average age of passing was 7;3 years, compared with 4;4 years for the hearing control subjects (Gale *et al.* 1996). Furthermore, performance on the task was highly correlated with the performance on standard verbal theory of mind tasks [r (18) = +.60, p < .01], despite the overt language requirement of the standard tasks. Remarkably, in contrast with the intuitive view that it is only the language of the task that might interfere with performance, there were no savings for the deaf subjects by using a nonverbal task. The average age of passers on the standard tasks was 7.41 years (unseen displacement), and 7.25 years (unexpected contents).

The predictions of the current theory were well supported: the best predictor of the deaf children's performance on the nonverbal theory of mind task was their skill at producing the language to explain actions in terms of cognitive states [r = +.61, df = 16, p < .01]. This language-of-the-mind measure was taken from the narratives children produced in responding to silent cartoons and video clips that contained mistakes and misconceptions. The children's spontaneous and prompted explanations of the characters' actions on the video clips were transcribed and scored for their reference to cognitive states such as beliefs, thoughts, knowledge, or ignorance, or desires and emotions. Points were assigned on the basis of the spontaneity and developmental sophistication of the explanations given. Three points were assigned for producing at least one spontaneous explanation referring to the character's cognitive state, two points if cognitive state explanations were only given following prompts, and only one point if reference was made to desires or simple emotions but not to thoughts or knowledge (in keeping with Bartsch and Wellman 1995). A cognitive explanation of action in this task always involved an embedded complement construction.

The second task we have used (de Villiers and de Villiers 1999) requires the child to decide on the appropriate facial expression (surprised or not surprised) for a character in a cartoon story. The character either witnesses or does not witness some unusual object being placed in a familiar container, so it requires similar kinds of inferences to the standard unexpected contents task. For example, a frog gets placed in a Cheerios box. The child is shown the story and with the whole series laid out in front of him, asked to decide whether the character will be surprised or not surprised when the container is opened in the final scene. To succeed, the child must follow the story and figure out the individuals' states of knowledge, aided by the pictorial content and some pretraining that highlights tracking the characters from scene to scene. A pretest guarantees that they know the difference between surprised and not surprised facial expressions. The facial expressions themselves are on small transparencies, so they can be lifted onto the blank face of the character in the final scene—a task all of the children find delight in.

Six such stories constitute the task: three of them involve a character who should not be surprised, three involve a character who should be surprised. The design controls for bias in a particular story by having two sets of equivalent stories, though each child only receives one set of six. Five or six correct answers count as 'passing' this task.

Four-year-old hearing preschoolers find this task moderately difficult, and slightly fewer children pass this 'surprise face' task than pass the standard verbal false-belief tasks (de Villiers and de Villiers 1999). Nevertheless it is well correlated with standard false-belief tasks and the average age of passers of the surprise face task is 4.46 years. Once again, for hearing children, complement syntax predicts performance on the surprise face task, but age makes a significant contribution in addition.

We tested twenty seven moderately to profoundly deaf children in the elementary grades of an oral school for the deaf, none of them formally exposed to sign languages in their education. Their ages varied from 5;2 to 10;1, with a median of 7;0 years. We found that these oral deaf children passed the surprise face task at a slightly older age than for the standard unseen object displacement stories—at about 8;5 years of age—and the tasks are quite highly correlated. Once more, using a relatively non-verbal task did nothing to improve the performance of the deaf subjects who might have been thought to be disadvantaged only by the language of the standard tasks.

Consider the relationship again to language measures, which we further refined for the 'surprise face' study. Measures of the children's syntax production were determined from language samples varying in size from 51 to 111 utterances, with a mean of 67. The Index of Productive Syntax (IPSyn) was used to derive a quantitative measure of the grammatical complexity of the children's language (Scarborough 1990), paralleling the work of de Villiers and Pyers (1997) described above. Our IPSyn scoring of the language samples from the deaf children focused on the Sentence Structure subscale. We derived two separate scores for each deaf child from the Sentence Structure (SS) subscale of the IPSyn: productive use of sentential complements (IPSyn SS-Comps), a score varying from 0 to 4; and the remainder of the Sentence Structure items (IPSyn SS-Other), a score varying from 0 to 36.

Multiple regression analyses allowed us to test the independent effects of the predictor variables on theory of mind performance, carried out for each of two dependent measures: 1) total verbal false-belief reasoning score on three standard unseen displacement stories ('where look?' questions only); and 2) score out of six on the 'surprise face' scenarios. Six predictor variables were entered into each regression: IPSyn SS-Comps, IPSyn SS-Other, PPVT-R verbal mental age (a vocabulary measure), TONI-2 nonverbal IQ, aided hearing loss, and age. As with the hearing preschoolers in de Villiers and Pyers (1997), the deaf children's IPSyn complement score emerged as the only significant independent predictor of performance on the standard false-belief reasoning tasks, separable from the contribution of the more general language measures and background variables like nonverbal IQ, hearing loss and age. For the less verbal 'surprise face' task, both the IPSyn complement score and age made significant independent contributions to the variance in the children's performance on this task.

In summary of these empirical studies, we have evidence suggesting two points about oral deaf children's performance on false-belief reasoning:

a) it is delayed by several years, even with nonverbal tasks

b) performance on any false-belief task, even the nonverbal, is predicted by command of complement syntax.

Together these points suggest that it is specifically the linguistic problems that cause the delay for deaf children, since in all other respects—intelligence, active sociability, attentiveness—they are not initially impaired.

A number of other recent studies are compatible with the results presented on oral deaf subjects showing a strong relationship between language mastery and false-belief understanding. Two other studies have shown a delay in deaf children's false-belief understanding. In the first, Peterson and Siegal (1995) studied twenty six deaf students aged eight to thirteen from Total Communication programmes in Australia. They reported that on a slightly modified version of the standard change-of-location false-belief story, only 35% of the students passed (average age 10;4). There were no significant age effects, nor was nonverbal IQ a predictor of which children passed and which did not. The authors conclude that their study shows that ToM mastery depends on fluent early conversational experience, presumably disrupted in these deaf children. However, Peterson and Siegal did not have any measure of their subjects' language abilities, and there were some shortcomings in their test procedures. The experimenters acted out the scenarios, but the children had to also follow a signed version of the story as well, and it is likely that the procedures seriously taxed the children's attention. The results are compatible with our work, but open to criticism.

A second study of deaf children by Steeds, Rowe, and Dowker (1997) in Britain, used similar standard false-belief tasks—unseen displacement and unexpected contents-translated into British Sign Language. Most of their twenty two subjects were considered to use British Sign Language as their primary language, with some exposure also to Sign-Supported English. The children were in roughly the same age range as in Peterson and Siegal's study, aged five to twelve years, but they performed better, with approximately 70% success rate. Unfortunately there is one oddity: several of the children failed the memory-check control questions, casting their false-belief answers into some doubt. The memory check questions for the unseen displacement task followed the false-belief question, which is not the order in which they are usually asked, and this order allows for no 'correction' of the child's understanding by repeating the story again, with the questions, before the critical question involving false-belief gets asked. The second major disadvantage from our point of view is that no measure of language or syntax was taken from the children, so we cannot gauge their linguistic proficiency in British Sign Language.

There is no reason to believe that deaf children who grow up in a community of supportive signers, and who learn sign language from an early age, should have any deficit in their development of the vocabulary or complex structures necessary for false-belief reasoning. In fact, two of Peterson and Siegal's successful subjects both had deaf parents who used the Australian sign language, Auslan, and Steeds *et al.* credit the greater exposure to British Sign Language, a natural sign system, for the better performance of their group of subjects. In later work, Peterson and Siegal (1997) report that children who grew up with signing family members performed better than other deaf subjects on false-belief tasks, but since their (five) Auslan-signing subjects averaged nine years ten months at the time of the study, that finding can not provide convincing evidence of a normal timetable of development. We are actively researching the signing deaf population in our collaboration with Brenda Schick and Robert Hoffmeister, and intend to explore the relationship of linguistic knowledge of complementation and mental verb usage with false-belief performance in this population.

**Children with Specific Language Impairment**

A second group of children may be expected to show deficits in false-belief reasoning by virtue of their language delay, namely children with Specific Language Impairment. By definition, children with this characterization are not cognitively impaired, nor do they have the associated socio-emotional difficulties of autism, so language delay is the primary disorder. Initial reports suggested that children with SLI show no impairment in false-belief reasoning (Perner *et al.* 1989), but the SLI children had very high PPVT scores (average verbal MA 9.6) and the authors provided no corresponding measure of the children's syntactic mastery. However two other studies have recently suggested a delay in false-belief reasoning in SLI that is concomitant with the children's syntactic development. Iarocci *et al.* (1997) and Cassidy and Ballaraman (1997) have results that suggest that language delay has associated cost in false-belief reasoning. To date, the data from SLI subjects is not completely satisfactory for deciding the role of language in false-belief reasoning, as it is somewhat inconsistent, and, from the point of view taken here, uses inadequate language measures. It is at least possible that some SLI children suffer from only a limited morphological deficit without having associated difficulties in syntax, though this is still a matter of controversy (Rice and Wexler 1996; Van der Lely 1997; Van der Lely and Stollwerck 1997). If so, they may have sufficient syntax to handle complementation with mental verbs and show no particular deficit. Or, for children with SLI, language development may be on a delayed timetable but then show a rapid change around five or six years (Rice and Wexler 1997), in which case there is an explanation for why the studies with younger SLI subjects show deficits, but the ones with older children suggest they have no difficulty. All these possibilities remain open.

It is important to mention again that the delay in false-belief reasoning seen in oral deaf children and possibly also in children with SLI should not be construed as meaning the same thing as the deficits seen in children with autism. Here it is argued that the language of complementation is necessary as a representational tool for false-belief reasoning, which is why the language-delayed children have a deficit. But children with only a language delay, unlike subjects with autism, should not be expected to show deficits in all the other aspects of 'theory of mind' which are less dependent on sophisticated language. So, such important developmental steps as following eye gaze, or interpreting its meaning, or negotiating shared attention, and teasing, and elementary forms of trickery, or emotional empathy, reading other's intentions and responding accordingly—all of these would be expected to proceed on a relatively normal timetable even in a language-delayed child. To the extent that they do not, it might suggest a role for language in also facilitating those aspects, but the case for that has not been made here. It is important to differentiate the more limited problems of the oral deaf child from the more severe and broad deficit in 'theory of mind' commonly seen in autism.

## HOW THEORY OF MIND AFFECTS LANGUAGE

In this final section, I want to acknowledge that the developmental relationship between language and theory of mind is not just one-way. There are many phenomena that reveal the extent to which mature human language depends, critically, on an assessment of point of view—of the speaker, of the subject of a sentence, of a listener. Such concerns do not require us to stray far into pragmatics, into conversational rules, or politeness, or relevance theory. It goes without saying that the skills required for conversation, or narrative, call upon sophisticated understanding and monitoring of the listener. However, considering the appropriate use of sentence structures beyond the very basic forms leads us straight into considerations of mindreading. Once the door to other minds is open (and if we are right, language facilitates that entry), we might find that other linguistic phenomena, that depend on getting certain points of view straight, then come into play in child language.

What is not clear at present is the role of other perspective-taking within language itself, in phenomena that may appear well before the command of mental-state terms and complement structures. For example, deictic terms such as I/you, here/there, this/that are known to appear in children's speech and their comprehension (de Villiers and de Villiers 1974) at an earlier age than complements with mental verbs. Could they be acquired without genuine point-of-view shifts, by means of some simpler heuristic? Or are they the real linguistic precursors? What about the use of definite and indefinite articles, that require the speaker to attend to the listener's state of knowledge, and whether the referent is known or unknown to the listener? Certainly command of articles appears early in language production (Brown 1973), but the subtler tests of comprehension reveal some difficulties even at age four in keeping track of listeners' needs (Cziko 1986; Karmiloff-Smith 1979). Acquisition of these phenomena requires a more detailed examination before we can determine how they interrelate with the results discussed below, and the details promise to be illuminating about the relationship of language, mind, and point of view. Here I give just one example.

One of the fundamental tenets of a hundred years of semantics is that the meaning of sentences is somehow derived from the meaning of their parts, a property called compositionality. Without compositionality, every sentence meaning would be uniquely associated with a situation, and there would be no generativity possible, no way to derive the meaning of a new sentence that had not been spoken before. The basic idea of compositionality is that sentences are linked to situations, that terms in language refer to states of the world, and their truth value is assessed in connection to those states of the world. A sentence is true if the state of the world corresponds, so the meaning of a sentence, on this view, is the set of conditions in the world that make it true. The second fact about language is that we can have multiple terms to refer to the same thing; a particular object may be:

the rose
the flower
my date's corsage
that mess in the sink
some yellow thing down the disposal.

Notice that a sentence containing any such term can be rephrased by substitution of the other terms and the truth value remains unaffected:

Phyllis is extricating the rose with a chopstick.
Phyllis is extricating my date's corsage with a chopstick.
Phyllis is extricating some yellow thing down the disposal with a chopstick.

Hence truth value is maintained under substitution of terms with the same reference, a very desirable property for compositionality.

It has been known for a hundred years that unfortunately the property doesn't work in intentional contexts (Frege 1892; Quine 1960). Consider the same situation as above, but suppose that the character Phyllis is ignorant of the disposal's contents. It might be true that:

Phyllis thinks some yellow thing is down the disposal.

but not that:

Phyllis thinks my date's corsage is down the disposal.

nor:

She thinks a flower is down the disposal.

Why does substitution fail under these circumstances? It fails because to use reference appropriately in an intentional context requires one to calculate the subject's beliefs, not just one's own point of view. In the embedded clause, we enter the subject's point of view, so it no longer matters what we consider co-referential: it matters what Phyllis, the subject, considers coreferential. Notice that this effect is more subtle by far than the truth value switch required by the classic complement case discussed above. There is nothing objectively false about the complement 'a flower is down the disposal' but we cannot attribute that belief to her unless she knows that the yellow thing is a flower! Hence, critically, successful use of intentional sentences involves keeping track of others' knowledge and beliefs, and permitting substitutions of terms only when the inference is warranted by the contents of the subject's beliefs (Larson and Ludlow 1993).

Several recent studies have demonstrated that children do not pay attention at first to the contents of others' beliefs, and thus misjudge the truth value of sentences in which unwarranted substitutions have occurred (Apperley and Robinson, 1998; de Villiers and Fitneva 1995; Russell 1987). In our work we find evidence that mastery of these judgments takes children some months following success on false-belief tasks, which is not too surprising given the complexity and subtlety of the computations that must go on to use substitution appropriately (de Villiers *et al.* 1997). Other examples of phenomena that seem to await command of false-belief understanding can be found in Perez-Leroux (1997) and Hollebrandse (1999), as well as Papafragou (1997).

## WHAT ARE THE IMPLICATIONS FOR CHILDREN WITH AUTISM?

Children with autism have not been the focus here, but the implications for autism should be spelled out. I have proposed a continuum of language influences on cognition, ranging from the largely independent to the highly dependent. To the extent that autism can be seen as simply involving language deficits, we might expect differential problems in cognitive development as a function of the language-dependence of the concept, just as we might expect them for children with SLI, or language delay due to deafness. However, children with autism have problems that extend beyond language, a fact that differentiates these populations. Children with autism might manifest primary and profound problems in the area of 'theory of mind' in general, not just the language-dependent false-belief reasoning. We have no reason to suspect these broader problems with oral deaf children, or children with SLI. The possibility has been suggested that high-functioning subjects with autism who acquire enough language skill might even be able to 'bootstrap' an adequate understanding of people's states of mind, desires, and beliefs to compensate for their primary disability (Tager-Flusberg 1997, and this volume). That is, the language-dependency of false-belief reasoning may turn out to be a boon: it might give certain individuals a way intellectually to represent an understanding of other persons that didn't come naturally.

## Acknowledgements

Preparation of this chapter was supported by NIH grants #R01 HD32442–03 and #R01 DC02872 on which the author is a Principal Investigator.

## Notes

1. We explicitly marked the child's prior belief with the following question form, 'Before, when you were sitting over there, what did you think was in the box?'
2. As suggested by Siegal and Beattie, 1991, we used the form of the question 'where will the boy first look for the cake?'
3. It has since been pointed out to us that the scale created by this analysis has some unfortunate properties, since the child can only gain the second point by gaining the first. We have changed the scoring in our subsequent work to count as 'passing' only if the child gets both points. However, since we wish to report on the earlier work in de Villiers and Pyers (1997) we have left the coding in place for this report. We checked and found that new coding would not in fact affect the coded status (pass/fail) of any of our subjects, because this is a sum across several tasks.

## REFERENCES

Apperly, I. A. and Robinson, E. J. (1998). Children's mental representations of referential relations. *Cognition*, **67(3)** 287–309.

Astington, J. W. and Gopnik, A. (1988). Knowing you've changed your mind: children's understanding of representational change. In Astington, J. W., Harris, P. L., and Olson, D. R. (eds) *Developing Theories of Mind*. Cambridge, UK: Cambridge University Press.

Astington, J. W. and Jenkins, J. M. (1995). Language and theory of mind: a theoretical review and a longitudinal study. Paper presented at the Biennial Meeting of the Society for Research in Child Development, Indianapolis, IN.

Baldwin, D. (1991). Infants' contribution to the achievement of joint reference. *Child Development*, **62**, 875–90.

Baldwin, D. (1993). Infants' ability to consult the speaker for clues to word reference. *Journal of Child Language*, **20**, 395–418.

Baron-Cohen, S. (1991). Precursors to a theory of mind: understanding attention in others. In *Natural theories of mind: evolution, development and simulation of everyday mindreading*, (ed. A. Whiten). Blackwell.

Bartsch, K. and Wellman, H. M. (1989). Young children's attribution of action to beliefs and desires. *Child Development*, **60**, 946–64.

Bartsch, K. and Wellman, H. M. (1995). *Children talk about the mind*. Oxford University Press, New York.

Bornstein, M. H. (1985). Human infant color vision and color perception. *Infant Behavior and Development*, **8**(1), 109–13.

Bowerman, M. (1996). Learning how to structure space for language: a cross-linguistic perspective. In *Language and space*, (ed. P. Bloom, M. Peterson, L. Nadel, and M. Garrett). MIT Press, Cambridge, MA.

Brown, R. (1973). *A first language: the early stages.* Harvard University Press, Cambridge, MA.

Cassidy, K. W. and Ballaraman, G. R. (1997). Theory of mind ability in language delayed children. Poster presented at the Biennial Meeting of the Society for Research in Child Development, Washington, DC.

Cziko, G. (1986). Testing the language bioprogram hypothesis: a review of children's acquisition of articles. *Language*, **67**, 878–98.

Dale, P. (1991). The validity of a parental report measure of vocabulary and syntax at 24 months. *Journal of Speech and Hearing Research*, **34**, 565–71.

Davidson, D. (1993). Thinking causes. In *Mental Causation*, (ed. Heile, J. and Mele, A. R.). Clarendon Press, Oxford.

Dennett, D. (1971). Intentional systems. *Journal of Philosophy*, **68**, 87–106.

de Villiers, J. G. (1995*a*). Steps in the mastery of sentence complements. Paper presented at the biennial meeting of the Society for Research in Child Development, Indianapolis, IN.

de Villiers, J. G. (1995*b*). Questioning minds and answering machines. In *Proceedings of the Boston University Conference on Language Development*, (ed. D. MacLaughlin and S. McEwen). Somerville, MA, Cascadilla Press.

de Villiers, J. G. (1999). On acquiring the structural representations for false complements. In *New perspectives on language acquisition* (ed. B. Hollebrandse). University of Massachusetts Occasional Papers in Linguistics, 22 GLSA, Amherst, MA. pp. 125–36.

de Villiers, J. G. and de Villiers, P. A. (1999). Linguistic determinism and false belief. In *Children's Reasoning and the Mind*, (ed. P. Mitchell and K. Riggs). Psychology Press, Hove, UK.

de Villiers, J. G. and Fitneva, S. (1996, under revision). Referential transparency for opaque containers.

de Villiers, J. G. and Pyers, J. (1997). Complementing cognition: the relationship between language and theory of mind. In *Proceedings of the 21st annual Boston University Conference on Language Development*. Cascadilla Press, Somerville, MA.

de Villiers, J. G., Roeper, T. and Vainikka, A. (1990). The acquisition of long distance rules. In *Language processing and acquisition*, (ed. L. Frazier and J. de Villiers). Kluwer, Dordrecht.

de Villiers, J. G., Bibeau, L., Ramos, E. and Gatty, J. (1993). Gestural communication in oral deaf mother-child pairs. *Journal of Applied Psycholinguistics*, **14**, 319–47.

de Villiers, J. G., de Villiers, P. A., and Hoban, E. (1994). The central problem of functional categories in the English syntax of oral deaf children. In *Theoretical approaches to atypical language*, (ed. H. Tager-Flusberg). Hillsdale, N.J.: Lawrence Erlbaum.

de Villiers, J. G., Pyers, J. and Broderick, K. (1997). A longitudinal study of referential opacity. Paper presented at 22nd annual Boston University Conference on Language Development, November.

de Villiers, P. A. (1990). English literacy development in deaf children: directions for research and intervention. In *Research on Child Language disorders*, (ed. J. Miller). Pro-ed, Austin, TX.

de Villiers, P. A. and de Villiers, J. G. (1974). On this, that and the other: non-egocentrism in very young children. *Journal of Experimental Child Psychology*, **18**, 438–47.

Dunn, J., Brown, J., Slomkowski, C., Tesla, C., and Youngblade, L. (1991). Young children's understanding of other people's feelings and beliefs: individual differences and their antecedents. *Child Development*, **62**, 1352–66.

Eimas, P. and Quinn, P. C. (1994). Studies on the formation of perceptually based basic-level categories in young infants. *Child Development*, **65**(3), 903–17.

Fodor, J. (1975). *The language of thought*. Crowell, New York.

Fodor, J. A. (1983*a*). Imagery and the language of thought. Interview with Johnathon Miller in *States of Mind*, (ed. J. Miller), pp. 84–98. Pantheon Books, New York.

Fodor, J. A. (1983*b*). *The Modularity of Mind*. MIT Press, Cambridge, MA.

Fodor, J. A. (1992). Discussion: a theory of the child's theory of mind. *Cognition*, **44**, 283–96.

Frege, G. (1892/1960). On sense and reference. In *Philosophical writings of Gottlob Frege*, (ed. P. Geach and M. Black), pp. 56–78. Basil Blackwell, Oxford.

Gale, E., de Villiers, P., de Villiers, J. and Pyers, J. (1996). Language and theory of mind in oral deaf children. In *Proceedings of the 20th annual Boston University Conference on Language Development*, Vol. 1 (ed. A. Stringfellow, D. Cahana-Amitay, E. Hughes, and A. Zukowski). Cascadilla Press, Somerville, MA.

Gleitman, L. (1990). The structural sources of verb meanings. *Language Acquisition*, **1**, 3–55.

Goldin-Meadow, S. (1982). The resilience of recursion. In *Language acquisition: the state of the art*, (ed. E. Wanner and L. Gleitman). Cambridge University Press, New York.

Goldin-Meadow, S. and Mylander, C. (1984). Gestural communication in deaf children: the effects and non-effects of parental input on early language development. *Monographs of the Society for Research in Child Development*, **49**, 1–151.

Gopnik, A. and Meltzoff, A. N. (1997). *Words, thoughts, and theories*. MIT Press, Cambridge, MA.

Happé, F. G. (1995). The role of age and verbal ability in the theory of mind task performance of subjects with autism. *Child Development*, **66**, 843–55.

Harris, P. L. (1996). Desires, beliefs and language. In *Theories of theories of mind*, (ed. P. Carruthers and P. K. Smith). Cambridge University Press.

Herrnstein, R. J. (1984). Objects, categories, and discriminative stimuli. In *Animal cognition*, (ed. H. L. Roitblat, T. G. Bever, and H. S. Terrace), pp. 233–61. Lawrence Erlbaum, Hillsdale, NJ.

Hollebrandse, B. (1999). Acquisition of sequence of tense. In *New perspectives on language acquisition*, (ed. B. Hollebrandse). University of Massachusetts Occasional Papers in Linguistics, 22 GLSA, Amherst, MA, pp. 137–54.

Iarocci, G., Della-Cioppa, J., Randolph, B. and Wohl, E. (1997). *Do children with developmental language delay have a theory of mind?* McGill University, Montreal.

Karmiloff-Smith, A. (1979). *A functional approach to child language*. Cambridge University Press.

Karmiloff-Smith, A. (1992). *Beyond Modularity*. Bradford Books, MIT Press, Cambridge, MA.

Kratzer, A. (1997). Course lectures in semantics, University of Massachusetts, Amherst.

Larson, R. K. and Ludlow, P. (1993) Interpreted logical forms. *Synthese*, **95**, 305–55.

Leslie, A. (1987). Pretense and representation: the origins of theory of mind. *Psychological Review*, **94**, 412–26.

Leslie, A. M. (1994). Pretending and believing: issues in the theory of ToMM. *Cognition*, **50**, 211–38.

Mandler, J. and McDonough, L. (1993). Concept formation in infancy. *Cognitive Development*, **8**, 291–318.

Mandler, J. M. and McDonough, L. (1996). Drinking and driving don't mix: inductive generalization in infancy. *Cognition*, **59**, 307–35.

Mandler, J., Bauer, P. and McDonough, L. (1991). Separating the sheep from the goats: differentiating global categories. *Cognitive Psychology*, **23**, 263–98.

Mogford, K. (1993). Oral language acquisition in the prelinguistically deaf. In *Language development in exceptional circumstances*, (ed. D. Bishop and K. Mogford). Lawrence Erlbaum, Hillsdale, NJ.

Nelson, K. (1991) The matter of time: interdependencies between language and thought in development. In *Perspectives on language and thought: interrelations in development*, (ed. S. Gelman and J. Byrnes). Cambridge University Press.

Norris, R. and Millan, S. (1991). Theory of mind: new directions. Social psychology seminar, University of Oxford.

Olson, D. R. (1988). On the origins of beliefs and other intentional states in children. In *Developing theories of mind*, (ed. J. W. Astington, P. L. Harris, and D. R. Olson). Cambridge University Press.

Papafragou, A. (1997). Modality and metarepresentation. Paper presented at the Boston University conference on language development, November.

Paul, P. V. and Quigley, S. P. (1993). *Language and deafness* (2nd ed.). San Diego, CA: Singular Publishing Group.

Perez-Leroux, A. T. (1997). *The acquisition of mood selection in Spanish relative clauses*. The Pennsylvania State University.

Perner, J. (1991a). *Understanding the representational mind*. MIT Press, Cambridge, MA.

Perner, J. (1991b). On representing that: the asymmetry between belief and desire in children's theory of mind. In *Children's theories of mind*, (ed. D. Frye and C. Moore). Hillsdale, N.J.: Lawrence Erlbaum.

Perner, J., Leekam, S. and Wimmer, H. (1987). Three-year-olds' difficulty with false belief: the case for a conceptual deficit. *British Journal of Developmental Psychology*, **5**, 125–37.

Perner, J., Frith, U., Leslie, A. M. and Leekam, S. R. (1989). Exploration of the autistic child's theory of mind: knowledge, belief, and communication. *Child Development*, **60**, 689–700.

Perner, J., Baker, S. and Hutton, D. (1994). Prelief: the conceptual origins of belief and pretence. In *Children's early understanding of mind: origins and development*, (ed. C Lewis and P. Mitchell). LEA, Hove.

Peterson, C. C. and Siegal, M. (1995). Deafness, conversation and theory of mind. *Journal of Child Psychology and Psychiatry*, **36**, 459–74.

Peterson, C. C. and Siegal, M. (1997). Domain-specificity and everyday biological, physical and psychological thinking in normal, autistic and deaf children. In *New Directions for Child Development*, Vol. 75, (ed. H. Wellman and K. Inagnaki), pp. 5570. Jossey Bass, San Francisco.

Povinelli, D. J. and deBlois, S. (1992). Young children's (Homo Sapiens) understanding of knowledge formation in themselves and others. *Journal of Comparative Psychology*, **106**, 228–38.

Premack, D. (1983). The codes of man and beasts. *Behavioral and Brain Sciences*, **6**, 125–67.

Premack, D. and Woodruff, G. (1978). Does the chimpanzee have a theory of mind? *Behavioral and Brain Sciences*, **1**(4), 515–26.

Quine, W. V. O. (1960). *Word and Object*. MIT Press, Cambridge, MA.

Rice, M. and Wexler, K. (1996). A phenotype of specific language impairment: extended optional infinitives. In *Towards a genetics of language*, (ed. M. Rice). Lawrence Erlbaum, Hillsdale, NJ.

Rice, M. and Wexler, K. (1997). Comprehension of an EOI grammar. Paper presented at the Boston University conference on Language Development, November.

Roeper, T. and de Villiers, J. G. (1994). Lexical links in the Wh-chain. In *Syntactic theory and first language acquisition: cross linguistic perspectives*, Vol. 2: Binding, dependencies and learnability, (ed. B. Lust, G. Hermon, and J. Kornfilt). Erlbaum, Hillsdale, NJ.

Rosch, E. and Mervis, C. (19753). Family resemblance: studies in the internal structure of categories. *Cognitive Psychology*, **7**, 573–605.

Russell, J. (1987) 'Can we say..?' Children's understanding of intentionality. *Cognition*, **25**, 289–308.

Ryle, G. (1949). *The concept of mind*. Hutchinson, London.

Scarborough, H. S. (1990). Index of productive syntax. *Applied Psycholinguistics*, **11**, 1–22.

Sellars, W. (1956). Empiricism and the Philosophy of Mind. In H. Feigl and M. Scriven (eds) *Minnesota studies in the Philosophy of Science*, vol 1. Minneapolis: University of Minnesota Press.

Shatz, M. (1994). Theory of mind and the development of social-linguistic intelligence in early childhood. In *Children's early understanding of mind: origins and development*, (ed. C. Lewis and P. Mitchell). Erlbaum, Hillsdale, NJ.

Siegal, M. and Beattie, K. (1991). Where to look first for children's knowledge of false belief. *Cognition*, **38**, 1–12.

Spelke, E. (1998). Core representations and new combinations: language, space, and number. Paper presented at Whither Whorf workshop, May 28–31, Northwestern University.

Steeds, L., Rowe, K. and Dowker, A. (1997). Deaf children's understanding of beliefs and desires. *Journal of Deaf Studies and Deaf Education*, **2**, 185–95.

Tager-Flusberg, H. (1993). What language reveals about the understanding of minds in children with autism. In *Understanding other minds: perspectives from autism*, (ed. S. Baron-Cohen, H. Tager-Flusberg, and D. J. Cohen). Oxford University Press.

Tager-Flusberg, H. (1996). Relationships between language and thought: cognition verbs and theory of mind. Paper presented at the meeting of the International Association for the Study of Child Language, Istanbul, Turkey.

Tager-Flusberg, H. (1997). The role of theory of mind in language acquisition: contributions from the study of autism. In *Research on communication and language disorders: contributions to theories of language development*, (ed. L. Adamson and M. A. Romski), pp. 133–58. Paul Brookes Publishing, Baltimore, MD.

Tager-Flusberg, H. and Sullivan, K. (1994). Predicting and explaining behavior: a comparison of autistic, mentally retarded and normal children. *Journal of Child Psychology and Psychiatry*, **35**, 1059–75.

Tomasello and Kruger (1992). Acquiring verbs in ostensive and non-ostensive contexts. *Journal of Child Language*, **19**, 311–33.

Van der Lely, H. K. J. (1997). Language and cognitive development in a grammatical SLI boy: modularity and innateness. *Journal of Neurolinguistics*, **10**(23), 75–107.

Van der Lely, H. K. J and Stollwerck, L. (1997). Binding theory and grammatical specific language impairment in children. *Cognition*, **62**(3), 245–90.

Wellman, H. M. (1990). *The child's theory of mind*. MIT Press, Cambridge, MA.

Wellman, H. M. and Woolley, J. D. (1990). From simple desires to ordinary beliefs: the early development of everyday psychology. *Cognition*, **35**, 245–75.

Whorf, B. L. (1956). *Language, thought and reality: selected writing of Benjamin Lee Whorf*, (ed. J. B. Carroll). MIT Press, Cambridge, MA.

Wimmer, H. and Perner, J. (1983). Beliefs about beliefs: representation and constraining function of wrong beliefs in young children's understanding of deception. *Cognition*, **13**, 103–28.

# 6

# Language and understanding minds: connections in autism

## HELEN TAGER-FLUSBERG

---

## LANGUAGE AND COMMUNICATION IMPAIRMENTS IN AUTISM

One of the key diagnostic features of autism includes 'qualitative impairments in communication' (APA 1994, p. 70). By definition, children with autism show delays and deficits in the acquisition of language, which range from the almost complete absence of functional communication, to adequate linguistic knowledge but with impairments in the use of that knowledge in conversation or other discourse contexts. Thus autism is considered by most researchers to involve primary impairments in pragmatic aspects of language, or in the ability to use language to communicate effectively in a range of social contexts (Lord and Paul 1997; Tager-Flusberg 1981, 1996; Wilkinson 1998). For the past decade these pragmatic impairments have come to be viewed as intimately linked to deficits in theory of mind, which are considered to be at the core of the disorder (Baron-Cohen 1988; Happé 1993; Tager-Flusberg 1993, 1997), and research on the relationships between pragmatics and theory of mind in autism has been highly productive. This view of autism has provided an important theoretical perspective on the nature of language functioning in autism because it is able to explain the unique and specific pattern of what is relatively spared and what is impaired in this population (Happé 1994a; Tager-Flusberg 1997).

At the same time, this emphasis on the pragmatic language impairment in autism has led to a relative neglect of other linguistic deficits that are found in most individuals with this disorder. While lexical and syntactic knowledge may be *relative* strengths, at least in verbal children with autism, they are, in the majority of cases, significantly delayed in development. Furthermore, it appears that, in a significant number of older children and adolescents with autism, lexical and syntactic knowledge remain delayed relative to other areas of cognitive functioning (Lord and Paul 1997). Thus, these non-pragmatic aspects of linguistic functioning also need to be considered in a comprehensive account of autism, even if they are not deficits that are unique to this syndrome.

To what extent are there important relationships in autism between theory of mind and semantic or syntactic aspects of language? In this chapter I provide an overview of how theory of mind deficits in autism may be intimately related to a broad range of language impairments, including not only pragmatics, but also lexical–semantics, and syntax. Research conducted over the past decade has highlighted some of these latter connections that may be considered at both general and more specific levels. These studies indicate that the relationship between understanding mind and language itself is much deeper than has previously been considered. Furthermore, the direction of this relationship is likely to be more complex when viewed from a developmental perspective. Throughout this chapter I consider the extent to which autism provides a window onto alternative ways in which mind and language may become connected over the course of development.

## PRAGMATICS AND THEORY OF MIND

Toward the end of the first year of life infants come to understand that people are intentional volitional beings whose experience and attention to the world around them may be different from their own view. This conceptual understanding, which may mark the emergence of an early understanding of mind, is manifest in the onset of intentional communication. Indeed, the motivation to communicate with others, and thus to acquire language, is rooted in this view of people as intentional beings with whom to share one's own view of the world and learn about theirs (Baldwin 1995; Locke 1993). From the outset infants' communications express multiple functions: social engagement, protoimperative requesting, and protodeclarative sharing or informing. These communicative patterns, which emerge at around ten to twelve months, reflect developmental connections between communication and social cognition (Carpenter *et al.* 1998).

### Communicative functions

The earliest manifestations of communicative impairment in autism may be found in selective deficits that reflect a lack of understanding of mind. Thus, both naturalistic and experimental studies have shown a selective paucity of proto-declarative communicative gestures in both preverbal and older verbal children with autism (Baron-Cohen 1989; Mundy *et al.* 1986; Wetherby 1986). Unlike protoimperatives, which may only involve an expression of the child's needs, proto-declaratives critically involve joint attention and entail an incipient understanding of intentionality, both of which are profoundly impaired in young children with autism (Loveland and Landry 1986; Mundy *et al.* 1994). When language is acquired in autism, verbal communication continues to be primarily limited to the expression of instrumental functions, or simple labelling (Tager-Flusberg 1996). While autistic children do use language to maintain some social contact (Wetherby and Prutting 1984), they rarely comment on ongoing or past activity, use language to seek or share attention, provide new information, or express intentions, volition or other mental states (Tager-Flusberg 1992, 1993, 1997). Thus, autism is characterized by significant limitations in the range of functions served by language; limitations that can be directly attributed to impaired understanding of other minds.

## CONVERSATIONAL COMPETENCE AND INTENDED MEANING

Children with autism exhibit significant difficulties in conversational contexts. They show impairments in their understanding of the speaker-listener relationship as illustrated, for example, in pronoun reversal errors (Lee *et al.* 1994; Tager-Flusberg 1994). These errors reflect difficulties in conceptualizing notions of self and other, as they are embedded in shifting discourse roles. Children with autism fail to distinguish between given and new information and do not conform to conversational rules (Ball 1978; Baltaxe 1977; Fine *et al.* 1994). They cannot appropriately maintain an ongoing topic of discourse (Tager-Flusberg and Anderson 1991); instead they introduce irrelevant comments or fail to extend a topic by adding new relevant information. One recent study found that there was a significant correlation in children with autism (but not controls) between performance on theory of mind tasks and the ability to respond to a conversational partner with contingent relevant new information (Capps *et al.* 1998). Experimental studies also suggest that children with autism who fail theory of mind tasks do not adhere to Gricean maxims, which are concerned with conversational relevance (Surian *et al.* 1996).

Conversational deficits in autism reflect fundamental problems in understanding that communication is about the expression and interpretation of *intended* rather than literal meaning (Happé 1993; Sperber and Wilson 1986). Several studies have found that even older high-functioning people with autism have great difficulty interpreting non-literal or figurative speech (e.g. Happé 1993, 1994*b*; Minshew *et al.* 1995). Research by Happé (1993) found that there was a close relationship between under-standing metaphor or irony and performance on theory of mind tasks. In a later study Happé (1994*b*) again found a strong relationship between the ability to explain a variety of non-literal messages (e.g. lies, jokes, pretence, irony, sarcasm, double bluff) and theory of mind. Across all the stories in her study, Happé (1994*b*) found that subjects with autistic had great difficulty providing mentalistic explanations for these non-literal utterances compared with matched controls (see also Baron-Cohen 1997). Her findings are taken as strong support for relevance theory (Sperber and Wilson 1986), which is concerned with the central role of intentionality in communication. Using a more structured task, Mitchell *et al.* (1997) also found that children with autism had difficulty interpreting a speaker's intended meaning when presented in a conversational context. Unlike matched controls, the children with autism in their study interpreted utterances in a literal way instead of in relation to the speaker's stated desire.

### Narrative discourse

Communication in other, non-conversational, discourse contexts has also been investigated in children and adolescents with autism. Several studies have explored narrative discourse, particularly storytelling. Telling a good story that focuses on human experience entails the ability to weave together a sequence of events according to a hierarchical organizational structure (the 'landscape of action') with what Bruner (1986) refers to as the 'landscape of consciousness'—the motivations, thoughts and feelings of the main characters in the story. Baron-Cohen *et al.* (1986) were the first to show that, compared with control subjects, children with autism provided fewer mental-state terms in their narratives for a sequence of pictures depicting a simple false-belief scenario. In a more detailed study, Loveland and her colleagues asked their subjects to retell a story presented in the form of a puppet show or video sketch (Loveland *et al.* 1990). The children with autism were less able than controls to consider their listener's needs and produced more bizarre or inappropriate utterances. Some of the children with autism were unable to even understand the story as a representation of meaningful events, suggesting that they lacked a cultural perspective underlying narrative (Bruner and Feldman 1993; Loveland and Tunali 1993). Tager-Flusberg (1995) also found that children with autism told impoverished stories in response to a wordless picture book. Furthermore, none of the children with autism in this study provided any causal explanations for the events in the stories.

In general, these findings on narrative deficits in autism have been interpreted as reflecting deficits in theory of mind (Bruner and Feldman 1993; Loveland and Tunali 1993) However, only one study has directly explored the relationship between narrative and theory of mind performance (Tager-Flusberg and Sullivan 1995). Using another wordless picture book, narratives were elicited from adolescents with autism and matched controls with mental retardation. Only for the subjects with autism was theory of mind performance significantly correlated with a number of different narrative measures including length, number of connectives, emotion, and cognition terms. In addition, in response to probe questions, the subjects with autism gave significantly fewer appropriate explanations for the emotional states of the story characters. These studies all confirm that autism involves particular problems in telling stories; problems that have been closely linked to the capacity to understand other minds (both the listener's and those of the characters within the story).

## Pragmatic impairment in autism

This brief review confirms that pragmatic impairments in autism are found across different discourse contexts. These impairments include: a narrower range of functions served by language; problems understanding that communication is about intended rather than surface meaning; failure to view conversations as a means of modifying and extending the cognitive environment of a conversational partner; and failure to view narratives as a means for communicating about both events and psychological states. What is striking about these impairments in communication is that they occur to some degree across the entire spectrum of autistic disorder. Across all ages, ability levels, and language levels, deficits are found in some or all of these aspects of pragmatics and communication. They are even considered to be one component of the broader autism phenotype, found among some proportion of first degree relatives of individuals with autism (Landa *et al.* 1991; Landa *et al.* 1992; Piven *et al.* 1997). Thus, these deficits have come to be viewed as primary in the diagnosis of autism, and appear to be unique and specific to this disorder (Tager-Flusberg 1996).

Across the studies discussed in this section the close connection between pragmatic knowledge and theory of mind has been highlighted. At both a theoretical (cf. Locke

1993; Sperber and Wilson 1986; Tager-Flusberg 1993) and empirical level these domains seem to be inextricably linked together. Indeed, in some studies, the relationship between specific aspects of communicative competence and theory of mind ability was found to be significantly stronger among subjects with autism than among controls (e.g. Capps *et al.* 1998; Tager-Flusberg and Sullivan 1995). This suggests that there may be a somewhat different developmental relationship between these domains among individuals with autism. At the same time, however, although all researchers agree that pragmatics are closely tied to theory of mind, the direction of this relationship has not been clearly delineated. Some argue that some understanding of mind is a prerequisite for acquiring language (e.g. Locke 1993; Tager-Flusberg 1997) or communication (e.g. Sperber and Wilson 1986). Others suggest that through verbal interactions with others children come to understand that people have minds with contents different from their own (e.g. Dunn *et al.* 1991). These positions may not be incompatible; what is needed is a more detailed *developmental model* of how different components of a theory of mind might be causally related at different points in time to specific aspects of pragmatics, communication, and discourse skills (cf. Charman and Shmueli-Goetz 1998).

At the earliest stages, it is likely that theory of mind is an important precursor to the onset and progress in language acquisition. Research on the relationship between joint attention and language development demonstrates that for children with autism, as well as for other groups of children, there are strong developmental connections between these domains (Carpenter *et al.* 1998; Loveland and Landry 1986; Mundy *et al.* 1994). The clearest evidence comes from Sigman and Ruskin's (1999) longitudinal study, in which they found that responses to bids for joint attention by toddlers and preschoolers with autism predicted language gains several years later, particularly on measures of expressive language (Sigman and Ruskin 1999). This relationship between joint attention and later language was independent of IQ level and provides strong support for the view that joint attention is a crucial precursor of language acquisition in autism. Joint attention, as discussed earlier, is considered to be one of the earliest manifestations of theory of mind development (Baron-Cohen 1995; Tomasello 1995), emerging at the end of the first year. The ability to share attention with others entails the implicit understanding that people are intentional agents. To acquire language the child must interpret the words and communicative gestures of others as intentional acts; indeed early word learning depends on this interpretation, especially in contexts of ostensive definition (cf. Baldwin 1993, 1995). Deficits in joint attention in autism may thus be causally linked to and explain the significant delays in language acquisition that are the hallmark of this disorder (Baron-Cohen *et al.* 1997). The developmental relationship between theory of mind and the acquisition of other aspects of pragmatic and discourse knowledge may not, however, be so clearly unidirectional. More longitudinal studies, of the sort that Sigman and her colleagues (Sigman and Ruskin 1999) have pioneered, will be needed to address these issues in this future.

### Lexical–semantics and theory of mind

Research on the relationship between lexical–semantic knowledge and theory of mind ability has focused more specifically on the acquisition of a representational understanding of mind, marked by performance on false-belief tasks. The majority of children with autism across all the studies that have been conducted fail false-belief and other related tasks (see Baron-Cohen's review, this volume). In most of these studies subjects' lexical knowledge is measured using a standardized test of receptive vocabulary: the Peabody Picture Vocabulary Test (PPVT) or its British counterpart, the BPVT, and, in general, significant correlations have been found between these measures and performance on theory of mind tasks. Happé (1995) conducted the most comprehensive study of this relationship. She pooled the samples of children with autism, children with mental retardation, and normal preschoolers, who had participated in several different studies and found that for both the children with autism and preschoolers (but not the subjects with mental retardation) the correlation between BPVT scores and false-belief performance was statistically significant, independent of age. Several other groups (e.g. Dahlgren and Trillingsgaard 1996; Sparrevohn and Howie 1995) have reported similar findings, though it should be noted that not all studies do (Baron-Cohen *et al.* 1985; Perner *et al.* 1989).

These findings are taken as evidence for a general relationship between lexical development and theory of mind ability, although the level of lexical knowledge needed to pass theory of mind tasks is significantly higher for children with autism than for normal children. Thus, Happé (1995) found that normally-developing children had a fifty per cent chance of passing false-belief tasks at a lexical mental age level of four years, whereas for the autistic children the lexical level was over nine years. Happé (1995) suggests that this difference between children with autism and normal children might be taken as evidence that children with autism rely on language more than other populations to help solve false-belief and other theory of mind tasks. For individuals with autism verbal mediation may be their only way of 'hacking' out a correct solution to these tasks, which other children solve them using non-linguistic cognitive mechanisms. This interpretation implies that language, as measured by lexical–semantic knowledge, may be causally related to theory of mind ability as measured on false-belief tasks in autism, but perhaps not in other populations. We return to the role of language in the acquisition of false-belief understanding in later sections of this chapter.

**Cognition verbs**

At a theoretical level, it is not clear how general vocabulary size (as measured by the PPVT or BPVT) should be conceptually linked to a representational understanding of mind. In contrast, it is more obvious why one might expect specific connections between specific lexical terms, particularly verbs for mental states, and theory of mind ability. Studies of normal preschoolers have found a relationship between comprehension of semantic–pragmatic aspects of cognition verbs (*think, know, guess*) and the ability to pass false-belief tasks (Moore and Davidge 1989; Moore *et al.* 1989). These studies used a task that tapped children's knowledge that these verbs denote different levels of *certainty* on the part of the speaker. In another study of preschoolers, the use of cognition verbs in spontaneous speech was found to be significantly correlated with theory of mind performance (Astington and Jenkins 1995).

Few studies have investigated this more specific link between lexical knowledge of cognition verbs and theory of mind in autism, though Tager-Flusberg (1992) found that young children with autism almost never used these terms in conversations with their mothers. Kazak *et al.* (1997) found that, for children with autism, knowledge of the verbs *know* and *guess* in relation to themselves and other people was related to scores on the BPVT. And in another recent study Ziatas and her colleagues used the same procedures as Moore *et al.* (1989), and found a significant relationship between false-belief performance and certainty judgements for cognition verbs, *think, know,* and *guess* for children with either autism or Asperger's Syndrome (Ziatas *et al.* 1998). While they caution against using their correlational data to infer the causal direction of this relationship, Ziatas *et al.* (1998, p. 762) do state that 'it is theory of mind that acts as a precursor to communicative functions such as belief term development.' Unlike Happé (1995), who argued that language (as measured by general lexical knowledge) was needed for theory of mind development in autism, these authors appear to conclude the opposite, at least for the more specific knowledge of the certainty dimension for cognition verbs.

In an unpublished study we have also explored the relationship between knowledge of cognition verbs and performance on a false-belief task (Tager-Flusberg *et al.* 1995). We gave a group of 16 children and adolescents with autism a modified version of Moore *et al.*'s (1989) certainty task, comparing the verbs *know* and *think* as well as a standard location change false-belief task. The same tasks were given to 34 children with mental retardation who were of similar age and verbal ability as the autistic subjects, and 21 preschoolers. Our main findings replicated those reported by Ziatas *et al.* (1998): there was a significant correlation found between the language and theory of mind tasks for all three groups.

We then analyzed whether the children in each group were more likely to pass the language or the theory of mind task. For both the children with mental retardation and normal preschoolers, the false-belief task was significantly more likely to be passed than the language task (for the mentally retarded group, 24 children either failed or passed both tasks; 10 failed the language task but passed the false-belief task and none failed false-belief and passed language; for the preschoolers, 15 either failed or passed both tasks and 6 failed language but passed false-belief). Thus for these groups it appears that false belief is acquired *before* this aspect of the semantics cognition verbs, as suggested by Ziatas *et al.* (1998). In contrast, for the children with autism the findings were more equivocal: 5 subjects failed both tasks, 10 passed both tasks, and only 1 passed false-belief but failed certainty. We conclude that for our autistic sample, linguistic knowledge of speaker certainty as denoted by cognition verbs is acquired at about the same time as theory of mind, indicating perhaps a more integral developmental connection between these kinds of linguistic and cognitive achievements in autism.

## SYNTAX AND THEORY OF MIND

Until relatively recently, the theoretical and empirical relationships between syntactic knowledge and theory of mind ability have been somewhat neglected (but see chapter by de Villiers, this volume). Tager-Flusberg and Sullivan (1994) were the first to include a standardized measure of syntactic comprehension in addition to IQ and PPVT measures, in a study of theory of mind abilities in subjects with autism and mental retardation. We chose as our measure of syntactic knowledge the Sentence Structure subtest of the Clinical Evaluation of Language Fundamentals (CELF-R), on which about half the test items include complex, multi-clause sentences. One of the main findings in this study was that for the subjects with autism the strongest predictor of performance on both false-belief and explanation-of-action tasks was the measure of syntactic comprehension. Similar findings were obtained for the subjects with mental retardation on the false-belief task but not the explanation-of-action task. These findings were taken as evidence that for individuals with autism there is a strong relationship between syntactic knowledge and overall theory of mind ability; in mental retardation the relationship seemed to be more specific to measures of a representational understanding of mind.

This relationship between theory of mind and language might be a general one, in that false-belief tasks involve complex narratives and often include test questions that include complex syntactic constructions (e.g. *Does X know where Y is? Where does X think Y is?*). Thus one might interpret these findings as showing that children require the 'language of the task' in order to follow the narrative and answer complex test questions. Alternatively, the relationship between syntactic knowledge and theory of mind might be more specific, related to sentential complements.

## Complementation and representing propositional attitudes

De Villiers (de Villiers 1998; de Villiers and de Villiers 1999; de Villiers and Pyers 1997; see also this volume) has pointed out that the cognitive architecture required to represent propositional attitudes, in which the content of the proposition could be marked true or false, is isomorphic to the linguistic representations needed for complement constructions, in which one clause is embedded in a matrix sentence (see also Tager-Flusberg 1997). From an evolutionary perspective, those parts of the grammar (complementation and control) that allow for the embedding of one propositional argument under another proposition seem to be specially designed for the expression of propositional attitudes that are at the heart of a theory of mind (Pinker and Bloom 1990; Tager-Flusberg 1997). Indeed, the two primary classes of verbs that take sentential complements are cognition or mental-state verbs (e.g. *Bobby thought/ forgot/knew that the cake was in the cupboard*), and communication verbs (e.g. *Dad said/argued/whispered that the cake tasted terrible*). Both these verb classes convey the attitude of the person holding the mental state or communicating.

Complementation involves special semantic and syntactic properties that are intimately linked to theory of mind developments (de Villiers 1998; Tager-Flusberg 1997). De Villiers (1998) claims that complementation is uniquely suited for representing false belief because the semantics of complements allow one to talk explicitly about a distinction between the way things are in the world and the way things are represented in the mind. Thus, non-embedded sentences simply represent the world as it is:

(1) Bobby baked a cake and went out to play.

In contrast, sentences containing complements may or may not be based on truth or reality:

(2) Bobby thought that the cake was ready.
(3) Dad said that the cake tasted delicious.

This kind of analysis would apply to any theory of mind task that requires the child to judge the truth content of a mental state against reality, or another person's mental state.

At the syntactic level, the subordinate clause appearing under verbs of cognition or communication is not merely an optional argument or independent clause (called an *adjunct*), but is selected for and embedded under the verb in an obligatory fashion (or as a *complement*). One crucial way in which adjuncts and complements work differently is that wh-questions can only be extracted from complements, not from adjuncts. For example, consider the following sentences:

(4) Why did Bobby think$_t$ that Dad put the cake away$_t$? (complement)[1]
(5) Why did Bobby say$_t$ Dad put the cake away$_t$? (complement)
(6) Why did Bobby leave$_t$ after Dad put the cake away$_t$*? (adjunct)

They can all be interpreted as having the wh-question derive from the initial, or main verb (i.e. why did Bobby *think* (4), *say* (5), *leave* (6)). However, only in the complement constructions could the wh-question also be extracted from the embedded clause (i.e. why Dad put the cake away). For (6), the grammar does not allow the wh-question to be extracted from the adverbial clause, which is a kind of adjunct or optional argument. Thus, at the syntactic level, adjuncts and complements can be distinguished in the way they behave in complex wh-questions.

For both communication and cognition verbs, certain constructions do block the interpretation of the wh-question from the embedded clause. Contrast the following pairs of sentences:

(7) When did Bobby say$_t$ Dad put the cake away$_t$?
(8) When did Bobby say$_t$ where Dad put the cake away$_t$*?

and:

(9) When did Bobby think$_t$ Dad put the cake away$_t$?
(10) When did Bobby know$_t$ Dad put the cake away$_t$*?

Across all these sentences, the question can be about the main verb of communication or cognition: When did Bobby *say*, *think*, or *know* X? This is called the short-distance interpretation. However, for communication verbs a medial wh-question (e.g. *where*) blocks the interpretation that the question is derived from the embedded clause— called the long-distance interpretation. Thus, in (8) the question cannot be interpreted as being about when Dad put the cake away, even though this interpretation is permissible in (7). Similarly for cognition verbs, verbs such as *know* (called factive verbs) block the long-distance interpretation, whereas verbs such as *think* (called non-factive) do not. Thus, (10) can only be interpreted as a question about when Bobby knew Dad put the cake away, whereas (9) can be about either when Bobby thought it, or when Dad put the cake away. Together, the syntax and semantics of complement constructions provide the means for representing propositional attitudes, which lie at the heart of false-belief and other representational theory of mind tasks.

## Experimental studies on complements in autism

In a recent series of studies we have explored the specific connections between performance on false-belief tasks and knowledge of complement constructions for both cognition and communication verbs in subjects with autism and mental retardation. The subject groups, each including 20 older children and adolescents, were matched on age, language (PPVT and Sentence Structure), and IQ. Each subject was given two trials of a standard location change false-belief task that only included a simple test question (*Where will X look for Y?*). We used this simple question to ensure that any relationship found between false-belief performance and knowledge of complements was not simply a confound due to the ability or inability to answer test questions containing cognition verbs with complements on the false-belief task. Among the subjects with autism, 7 passed and 13 failed the false-belief task; among the subjects with mental retardation, 9 passed and 11 failed. There were no significant differences between the groups on the false-belief task, probably because they were closely matched on the standardized language measures (cf. Tager-Flusberg and Sullivan 1994).

## Study 1: extracting complements from complex wh-questions

The first experiment tested the subjects' knowledge of the embedding structure of sentential complements, following the methodology introduced by de Villiers and her colleagues (de Villiers *et al.* 1990). In this study, we told the subjects brief stories accompanied by photographs, followed by a complex wh-question that contained either a communication or cognition verb. Following de Villiers *et al.* (1990), we took the subjects' ability to answer these test questions as evidence of their knowledge of complement constructions.

In one story, for example, a girl was riding home when her radio fell off her bike. On arriving at her house, she found out that the radio was broken after plugging it in a wall socket and seeing that it no longer worked. The story provided temporal information about when the radio broke (when it fell off the bike) and when the girl was convinced that it was broken (when she plugged it in at home). Thus both these pieces of information were available as potential answers to the test question:

(11) When did the girl *think/know* that she broke the radio?

In a different story, a boy went to the movies one afternoon, and left his umbrella there. He realized this after he had returned home that evening, and told his father about his loss. Again information was provided about when the umbrella was lost and when the boy told his father about it. The test question for this story was:

(12) When did the boy *say/say where* he lost his umbrella?

In all, there were eight stories presented in random order: four with cognition verbs (*know* or *think*) and four with communication verbs (*say* or *say where*). As can be seen from the above examples, we systematically varied whether the test wh-question could be extracted from the embedded clause. Thus for two of the stories with cognition verbs, *know* was used (which blocks the extraction of the test question from the embedded clause); for two stories *think* was used (which does not block wh-extraction). Similarly for two of the stories with communication verbs, there was a medial wh-question—*say where* (which also blocks the extraction of the test question from the embedded clause); for two stories there was no medial wh-question (thus permitting extraction of the wh-question). Stories and test questions were counter-balanced across the subjects: half the subjects heard the test questions above in the non-blocked versions (*think* or *say*) and half heard the stories and questions in the blocked versions (*know* or *say where*).

Subjects' responses were coded in the following categories:

*Short*—an answer to the main verb of cognition or communication.

Thus for (11), this would be: *When she plugged it in.* Or for (12): *When he came home that evening.*

*Long*—an answer to a question extracted from the embedded clause.

For (11) this would be: *When it fell off the bike.* For (12): *When he was at the movies.*

*Other*—any other answer.

Note that for the questions containing *know* or *say where* the long responses are blocked and therefore not grammatical, whereas for all the test questions, the short responses are permitted.

We divided each group into those who passed and those who failed the false-belief task. Figure 6.1 presents the number of short and long responses provided by each group. Among both the subjects with autism and mental retardation, those who passed false-belief gave significantly more short responses than did those who failed. For the long responses, among the subjects with autism there were no differences between those who passed and those who failed. In contrast, there was a significant difference for the subjects with mental retardation. There was also a significant interaction effect for the subjects with mental retardation between verb and false-belief status that was due to the subjects with mental retardation who passed false-belief giving significantly more long responses to the cognition verb *think* than to other verbs. This finding suggests that the mentally retarded group was more knowledgeable about cognition verbs than the autistic group, giving more correct responses to them. Finally, for both the autistic and mentally retarded groups, the subjects who failed the false-belief task gave significantly more other responses, indicating that these subjects had difficulty interpreting the complex wh-question. There was a marginally significant group-by-verb type interaction. This was because the subjects with mental retardation

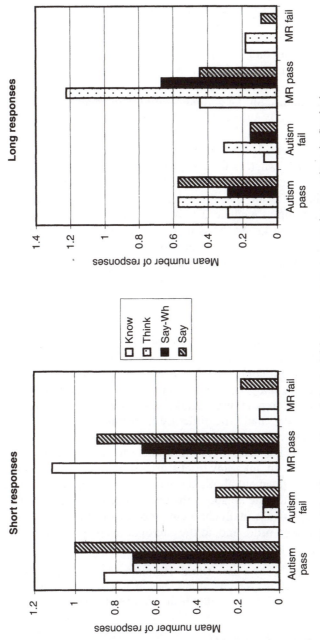

**Fig. 6.1.** Mean number of short and long responses to complex questions in Study 1

gave fewer other responses to the mental verbs than the subjects with autism. The groups were equivalent on the communication verbs.

Taken together, these findings suggest that the subjects with mental retardation were more sensitive to the difference between the communication and cognition verbs, and overall performed better on the test questions with cognition verbs. A regression analysis of the data confirmed this difference between autistic and mentally retarded groups. For both groups performance on the false-belief task was significantly correlated with the two standardized language measures (PPVT and Sentence Structure) and with performance on the communication and cognition verbs in the experimental complementation task. When all these variables were entered into separate regression analyses for the two groups, only one predictor variable was found to be significant. For the mentally retarded group the single significant predictor was performance on the cognition verbs, whereas for the autistic group the single significant predictor was performance on the communication verbs.

These findings indicate that there are strong close connections between knowledge of complementation as evidenced by responses to complex wh-questions, and ability to pass false-belief tasks. At the same time, the findings reported here suggest that the connections may be different for individuals with autism in that they rely on knowledge of the syntax for communication verbs, whereas individuals with mental retardation rely on their knowledge of cognition verbs.

## Study 2: extracting complements from communication verbs

We followed up these findings in a second study, in which we investigated the same subjects' ability to extract the content of a clause embedded under a communication verb (*say*) in different contexts, using a simpler test question. We borrowed a method used by de Villiers and Desjarlais (reported in de Villiers 1998) to investigate preschoolers' ability to report lies, mistakes and true statements. In their study, even the youngest preschoolers had little difficulty reporting true statements, but their ability to report lies was closely linked to their performance on a false-belief task. The children who failed false-belief tasks were more likely to report what really happened rather than what was said. In our study brief stories were told to the subjects, in which a main character made a statement about key events that, depending on the context, was true, a mistake, or a deliberate lie about the event. There were two stories for each context and a photograph of the main character accompanied each story. The six stories were presented in random order and, at the end of each story, the subjects were asked: *What did X say?* Here is an example of one of the lie stories:

This is a story about a boy named David. His mother likes him to read a book every day. But today David isn't reading his book. Mom called up to David and asked him what he was doing. David said, 'I'm reading my book.' But really David was watching television. Later Mom called David down for dinner.

Test Question: *What did David say?*

Responses to the test questions were coded as correct if the subject captured the gist of the statement or gave a verbatim report of the character's utterance. For the lie and mistake stories, incorrect responses were coded as reality responses, if the subject stated what really happened, rather than what was said. Responses that were neither correct nor reports of reality, were coded as other.

We again divided both the autistic and mentally retarded groups into those who passed and those who failed the false-belief task. In Fig. 6.2 the data for the true and lie stories are presented; findings on the mistake stories were essentially the same as for the lie stories but are not shown here. On the lie stories, for both groups, subjects who passed the false-belief task gave significantly more correct responses, thus replicating de Villiers' (1998) findings with preschoolers. The subjects with mental retardation made significantly more reality responses on both lies and mistakes (about 20% of their responses) than did the subjects with autism. Interestingly, almost none of the incorrect responses from the subjects with autism were reports of reality. On the true stories, as expected, for the mentally retarded group there were no differences between those subjects who passed or failed the false-belief task. Their performance was consistently high—about 70% correct. In contrast, the subjects with autism who failed the false-belief task gave fewer correct responses on the true stories. These findings suggest that children with autism who fail false-belief tasks also have problems extracting the complement from a sentence with a communication verb independent of context, suggesting they have greater difficulty with the syntax of complements for communication verbs. This finding on the relationship between the ability to report what someone said in response to a simple wh-question and performance on false-belief tasks appears to be unique to autism. The results of this study confirm that knowledge of complements for communication verbs seems closely tied to theory of mind ability in this population.

### Study 3: referential opacity

The final study to be reported here explored a semantic property of cognition and communication verbs, referred to as referential opacity. Ordinary verbs, such as *move*, are never considered to be opaque; they always allow for substitutions of the main referent. Consider the following example, taken from de Villiers and Fitneva (1996). A mother prepared for her daughter Sarah a surprise birthday gift of a silver box containing candy. Under an ordinary verb like *move*, each of the following statements is equivalent:

(13) Mom moved the silver box. (container)
(14) Mom moved the candy. (contents)
(15) Mom moved the gift. (function)

Thus, we can say that the ordinary verb *move* is referentially transparent, because the term for the referent (box/candy/gift) can always be substituted. In the examples here it would not matter whether Mom or Sarah (who does not know what is in the box or what it's for) moved the object. This is not true for verbs of communication or cognition, depending on the context. Verbs of communication generally do not allow substitution of referential terms (unless one makes an interpretation of *intended* meaning). Continuing with the example introduced here, suppose that Sarah walked

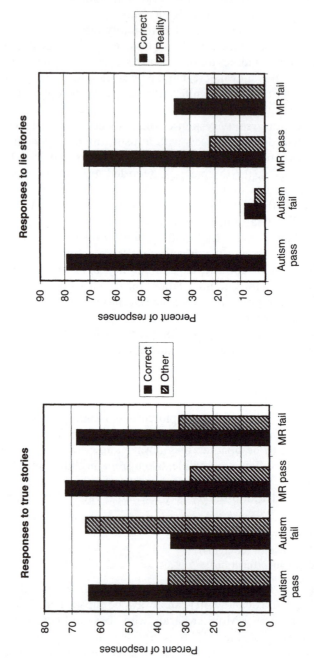

**Fig. 6.2.** Percentage of correct, reality and other responses to the true and lie stories in Study 2

into the room, saw the box, and asked her mother why there was a box on the table. While it would be true to state:

(16) Sarah asked why the box was on the table.

One would not be able to substitute either *candy* or *gift* under the communication verb *ask*:

(17) Sarah asked why the candy/gift was on the table.*

Similarly, if the mother told Sarah not to touch the box, it would be true that

(18) Mom told Sarah not to touch the box.

But one could not substitute under the communication verb *tell*:

(19) Mom told Sarah not to touch the candy/gift.*

The situation is more complex for cognition verbs such as *know*. For Sarah, who is ignorant about the contents and function of the box, the referent (or complement under the verb *know*) is opaque. Thus whereas one could state:

(20) Sarah knew the box was on the table.

One could not state:

(21) Sarah knew the candy/gift was on the table.*

In contrast, because the mother did know about the gift of candy, we could state:

(22) Mom knew the box/candy/gift was on the table.

For the person who has access to the relevant knowledge, cognition verbs are not referentially opaque. This insightful analysis of role of pragmatics or context in the referential opacity of cognition verbs by de Villiers and Fitneva (1996) suggests that there should be close ties between understanding this linguistic property and theory of mind ability. Their work with normal preschoolers confirmed this hypothesis.

Our study with autistic and mentally retarded groups was modelled after the task introduced by de Villiers and Fitneva (1996). We told four stories similar to the one sketched here. Each story was about a container, its contents and function. One person in the story knew the contents and function of the container, one did not. Each of the stories, that were presented in random order, was accompanied by a set of pictures, and included a series of yes/no questions. Half the questions referred to the person who knew (e.g. Mom), half to the ignorant person (e.g. Sarah). For each character in the story there were two questions with ordinary verbs, two with cognition verbs, and two with communication verbs. Half these questions were about the container and half about either the contents or function. In addition two control probe questions were included on each story (e.g. *Does the box have money in it?*) to make sure the subjects were not biased or random in their yes/no responding.

We first examined the responses to the probe questions: 7 subjects with autism and 2 subjects with mental retardation made more than one error across the 8 probes (two per story). These subjects were eliminated from further analyses, and the mentally retarded group was further pruned down to 13 subjects who matched the 13 remaining subjects with autism. We examined the data separately for each type of verb. Following de Villiers and Fitneva (1996) we used a derived score that reflected the *difference* between responses to questions about the container (which were true under all verbs in all conditions) and questions about either the contents or function (which could be true under some verbs and in certain conditions). Using this derived score, a low score (maximum = 4) meant that subjects did allow substitution, treating the verb as transparent, whereas a high score meant that subjects did not allow substitution, treating the verb as opaque.

The data for this experiment are presented in Fig. 6.3. Looking first at the data for ordinary verbs, which should be treated as transparent (low score) for both the person who knows the contents or function and for the ignorant person, it is clear that there are interesting differences between the autistic and mentally retarded groups. The mentally retarded group was, surprisingly, somewhat more resistant than the autistic group to referential substitution even for ordinary verbs. This was especially true for those subjects who passed the false-belief tasks. While it is not entirely clear how to interpret these findings for the subjects with mental retardation, one possibility is that they are treating some of the ordinary verbs (e.g. *take*) as if they had some implicit intentionality. On this view, the subjects with mental retardation are reading psychological causality into some of the ordinary verbs and resisting referential substitution, especially for the ignorant character in the story. De Villiers, Pyers and Broderick (1997) obtained similar findings from young preschoolers in a longitudinal study on the acquisition of referential opacity. In contrast, the subjects with autism were much less likely to make this mentalistic interpretation of ordinary verbs.

The data for the communication verbs show a striking effect of theory of mind ability. For the both the subjects with autism and those with mental retardation, those who passed the false-belief task correctly resisted referential substitution, treating these verbs as opaque, as denoted by their high derived scores. Those who failed the false-belief task did not interpret these verbs as opaque. There was also a significant effect of false-belief performance on the interpretation of cognition verbs. The subjects with autism and mental retardation who failed the false-belief task again treated them as transparent across all contexts. Those who passed false-belief distinguished between the person who knew the contents or function of the container, allowing for referential substitution for this character, and the ignorant person, for whom the cognition verbs were treated as referentially opaque. There was also a significant interaction between group and false-belief status, indicating that the subjects with mental retardation who passed false-belief tasks were more resistant to substitution that the subjects with autism on cognition verbs.

This study demonstrates that a representational understanding of mind is closely linked to knowledge that under certain conditions complements for both communication and cognition verbs are referentially opaque. These findings replicate for autism and mental retardation what de Villiers and Fitneva (1996) found for preschoolers. In addition, this study revealed that subjects with mental retardation were more sensitive than subjects with autism to the referential opacity of cognition verbs, and were more likely to interpret even ordinary verbs in an intentional

**Ordinary verbs**

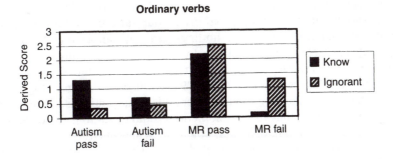

**Communication verbs**

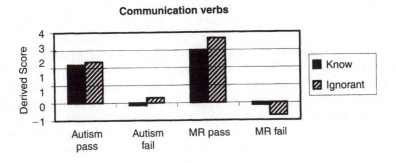

**Cognition verbs**

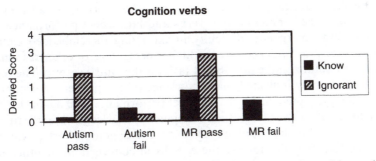

**Fig. 6.3.** Referential opacity scores to ordinary, communication, and cognition verbs in Study 3

or mentalistic way, as was found for normally-developing preschoolers (de Villiers *et al.* 1997).

## Complements and representing beliefs in autism

The three studies summarized here revealed close connections between linguistic knowledge of complement constructions and a representational understanding of mind as evidenced in performance on false-belief tasks. These connections were found not only for individuals with autism, but also for children and adolescents with mental retardation. And because the test questions in our false-belief task contained no complements or cognition verbs, the findings are not simply due to overlapping measures. They replicate similar findings for normally-developing preschoolers as well as for oral deaf children who have normal intellectual and social abilities but limited language (de Villiers and de Villiers 1999, see also this volume; Tager-Flusberg 1997). These specific connections between complements and false belief across so many populations suggest that there is something fundamental in the developmental relationship between these linguistic and cognitive achievements.

At the same time, these studies revealed interesting and potentially important differences between the mentally retarded and autistic groups. For the subjects with mental retardation there was a particular close connection between knowledge of the syntax and semantics of cognition verbs and theory of mind. In the first experiment, the subjects with mental retardation performed better on the cognition verbs than the subjects with autism. Furthermore, the regression analysis showed that their performance on the false-belief tasks was uniquely predicted by knowledge of the syntax for cognition verbs. This analysis suggested that the relationship between language and theory of mind was specific to complements, because neither of the general language measures (vocabulary or general syntax) contributed any additional variance to the regression model. Finally, in the third experiment the subjects with mental retardation were more likely than the subjects with autism to view cognition verbs as referentially opaque and to resist referential substitution for the ordinary verbs, suggesting that they treated at least some of these latter verbs as intentional or including a mentalistic–semantic dimension.

In contrast, the subjects in the autistic group appeared to be less sensitive in these experiments to the linguistic properties of the cognition verbs; instead they showed closer links between the communication verbs and false-belief performance. In both the first and second experiments difficulty in extracting the embedded clause from communication verbs (as evidenced by the higher percentage of other responses) was strongly related to failure on the false-belief task for the autistic group. The regression analysis in the first study indicated that knowledge of complements for communication verbs was uniquely predictive of false-belief performance, and again this relationship was due to specific rather than general linguistic knowledge. Overall, the subjects with autism appeared to be more impaired on the cognition verbs, which is not surprising given that they do not use these verbs in conversation or other forms of discourse (Baron-Cohen *et al.* 1986; Tager-Flusberg 1992). In autism it does not appear that cognition verbs provide a developmental connection to theory of mind. Whereas in other populations such as preschoolers, oral deaf children, and individuals with mental retardation (de Villiers and de Villiers 1999, this volume; Tager-Flusberg 1997), close developmental links are found between a representational understanding of mind and linguistic knowledge of complements of cognition verbs, in autism parallel links are found with communication verbs.

What is the direction of these relationships between theory of mind and sentential complements? Because our studies are all cross-sectional it is not possible to answer this question directly using the findings reported here. Some clues, however, can be taken from de Villiers' longitudinal studies of preschoolers (de Villiers 1998, this volume; de Villiers and Pyers 1997; de Villiers *et al.* 1997) and work by de Villiers and de Villiers (1999) on oral deaf children. These studies suggest that the knowledge of the syntax of complements (treating embedded clauses as complements not adjuncts) as evidenced by use of these constructions to describe the contents of a person's beliefs, or to answer wh-questions containing embedded complements, precedes the ability to pass false-belief tasks. Thus the language of complements appears to be important for the acquisition of a representational understanding of mind, according to de Villiers. At the same time, a representational view of mind appears to develop in children before they know that verbs of communication and cognition are referentially opaque under certain conditions (de Villiers *et al.* 1997), or that factive verbs of cognition block long distance extraction of wh-questions. Thus over the course of the preschool years, knowledge of language (complements) and cognition (representational theory of mind) exhibit mutually influencing developmental constraints, though it is suggested that the structure of complement constructions provides the initial step into representing beliefs in other minds.

In autism, the connections between the knowledge of complements, especially for communication verbs, and theory of mind ability are particularly strong. Because individuals with autism are less sensitive to cognition verbs in language and have less intuitive knowledge of mental states, they are likely to be even more reliant on the structural relationship between complements and propositional attitudes to bootstrap their way into a representational understanding of mind (Happé 1995; Leslie and Roth 1993; Tager-Flusberg 1997). The data presented here indicate that they may depend especially on complements for verbs of communication as their developmental entrance into the ability to represent false beliefs. At the same time, it should be noted that despite the ability of some older children with autism to pass false-belief, which may be a product of their more advanced linguistic knowledge, they still lack mentalistic insight into their own or others' behaviour and remain impaired in their everyday social interactions (Frith *et al.* 1994). Language may help them pass experimental tests of a representational mind, using alternate neurocognitive mechanisms that do not mirror the ways in which other children solve these tasks.

## Connecting minds to language in autism

Autism involves fundamental impairments both in understanding other minds and in language. Together, these cognitive deficits contribute significantly to the social difficulties experienced by all individuals with this devastating disorder. Research on autism has revealed that in this syndrome the development of language is even more closely connected to theory of mind and other aspects of cognitive functioning than for any other population (Lord and Paul 1997; Tager-Flusberg 1993, 1997). The work reviewed in this chapter illustrates how pragmatic, lexical, and grammatical development all show uniquely strong relationships to theory of mind knowledge in children and adolescents in autism across all ages and levels of ability.

The details of many aspects of these relationships have yet to be uncovered. Nevertheless, research on pragmatic aspects of language suggests that they are connected at all developmental points to the child's understanding of mind: from the emergence of communicative functions grounded in joint attention, to the development of advanced social cognitive constructs in middle childhood. These deep, pervasive, and complex connections between theory of mind and pragmatics, not only in autism but also for other children, may be taken as evidence that they are rooted in the same cognitive mechanisms. Connections between lexical and grammatical knowledge and theory of mind appear to be more constrained to a particular developmental stage when the child acquires a representational understanding of mind.

What can we say about the direction of the relationships, and the causal connections between language and theory of mind? The answer to this question is likely to be complex, depending on which components of language and which components of theory of mind we are concerned with at different developmental stages. At this point, we can only begin to sketch out a model of how these two domains may be inter-related over the course of development.

As discussed in a previous section of this chapter, the emergence of language and communication appears to be rooted in early theory of mind understanding, as evidenced in joint attention. Thus, the social-cognitive mechanisms that underlie joint attention, and related conceptual knowledge about the mentalistic nature of people, are crucially tied to the onset of communication and language. In autism, impairments in joint attention explain why language is delayed, and, in the extreme, may account for why a significant number of children with this disorder never acquire language. Deficits in an early understanding of mind account for many other aspects of the pragmatic impairments found in autism. Indeed, the literature on autism suggests that pragmatic development is even more closely tied to theory of mind ability in autism than in other populations, suggesting that in this population (but maybe not others), these two domains may continue to depend on the same underlying neurocognitive mechanisms.

The acquisition of a representational understanding of mind, which takes place at around four years of age in normally-developing children, marks a qualitatively different stage in theory of mind development. The capacity to understand that a person could hold a false belief depends on a more complex cognitive representational system than is needed to support the implicit understanding that people are mental beings. At this stage, language, specifically knowledge of the structure of complement constructions, may play a key role in this aspect of theory of mind development for all children (de Villiers and de Villiers 1999). We suggest that linguistic knowledge of complements may be even more crucial for children with autism for the ability to understand and represent false beliefs. Furthermore, the data presented in this chapter suggest that even though children with autism, like other groups of children, exploit the structural parallels between the language of complements and the representation of other minds, they do so in unique ways. Unlike other children, for children with autism it is linguistic knowledge about *verbs of communication* that provides the crucial link to false belief. Through listening and speaking about acts of communication (what people say), rather than thought (what people think), children with autism come to be able to represent that a person may hold a false belief. For people with autism language is thus causally connected to this aspect of a theory of mind in two ways: through talking about talk, and by using the parallel representational architecture for the syntax of communication verbs and propositional attitudes.

There is still much to be learned about the developmental pathways taken by children with autism and other disorders in their acquisition of language and a theory of mind. We have only begun to outline some segments of these pathways based on the evidence of how closely these domains are connected in different directions, at different developmental stages. Without longitudinal studies, however, we can still only speculate about the causal direction these relationships might take for specific aspects of linguistic and pragmatic knowledge and particular components of theory of mind.

## Acknowledgements

Preparation of this chapter was supported by grants from the National Institute on Deafness and Other Communication Disorders (RO1 DC 01234; PO1 DC 03610) and the National Institute on Neurological Diseases and Stroke (RO1 NS 38668). I am extremely grateful for the help of Robert Joseph in conducting some of the studies reported in this chapter; to Jill de Villiers for her intellectual guidance on many of the issues discussed here; to Anne Lantz Gavin for her help in producing the figures; and to Simon Baron-Cohen, Robert Joseph, and Kate Sullivan for their helpful comments on an earlier draft of this chapter.

## Note

1. In linguistic notation $_t$ denotes a 'trace' left by the moved wh-question; and * marks an ungrammatical interpretation or sentence.

## REFERENCES

American Psychological Association (1994). *Diagnostic and statistical manual of mental disorders*, (4th edn). APA, Washington, DC.

Astington, J. and Jenkins, J. (1995). Theory of mind development and social understanding. *Cognition and Emotion*, **9**, 151–65.

Baldwin, D. (1993). Infants' ability to consult the speaker for clues to word reference. *Journal of Child Language*, **20**, 395–418.

Baldwin, D. (1995). Understanding the link between joint attention and language. In *Joint attention: its origins and role in development*, (ed. C. Moore and P. Dunham). Erlbaum, Hillsdale, NJ.

Ball, J. (1978). A pragmatic analysis of autistic children's language with respect to aphasic and normal language development. Unpublished doctoral dissertation. Melbourne University.

Baltaxe, C. A. M. (1977). Pragmatic deficits in the language of autistic adolescents. *Journal of Pediatric Psychology*, **2**, 176–80.

Baron-Cohen, S. (1988). Social and pragmatic deficits in autism: cognitive or affective? *Journal of Autism and Developmental Disorders*, **18**, 379–402.

Baron-Cohen, S. (1989). Perceptual role-taking and protodeclarative pointing in autism. *British Journal of Developmental Psychology*, **7**, 113–27.

Baron-Cohen, S. (1995). The Eye Direction Detector (EDD) and the Shared Attention Mechanism (SAM): two cases for evolutionary psychology. In *Joint attention: its origins and role in development*, (ed. C. Moore and P. Dunham). Erlbaum, Hillsdale, NJ.

Baron-Cohen, S. (1997). Hey! It was just a joke! Understanding propositions and propositional attitudes by normally developing children and children with autism. *Israel Journal of Psychiatry*, **34**, 174–8.

Baron-Cohen, S., Leslie, A. M. and Frith, U. (1985). Does the autistic child have a 'theory of mind'? *Cognition*, **21**, 37–46.

Baron-Cohen, S., Leslie, A. M., and Frith, U. (1986). Mechanical, behavioral and intentional understanding of picture stories in autistic children. *British Journal of Developmental Psychology*, **4**, 113–25.

Baron-Cohen, S., Baldwin, D. and Crowson, M. (1997). Do children with autism use the speaker's direction of gaze strategy to crack the code of language? *Child Development*, **68**, 48–57.

Bruner, J. (1986). *Actual minds, possible worlds*. Harvard University Press.

Bruner, J. and Feldman, C. (1993). Theories of mind and the problem of autism. In *Understanding other minds: perspectives from autism*, (ed. S. Baron-Cohen, H. Tager-Flusberg, and D. J. Cohen). Oxford University Press.

Capps, L., Kehres, J. and Sigman, M. (1998). Conversational abilities among children with autism and children with developmental delays. *Autism*, **2**, 325–44.

Carpenter, M., Nagell, K. and Tomasello, M. (1998). Social cognition, joint attention, and communicative competence from 9 to 15 months of age. *Monographs of the Society for Research in Child Development*, **63**, Serial No. 255.

Charman, T. and Shmueli-Goetz, Y. (1998). The relationship between theory of mind, language ability and narrative discourse: an experimental study. *Cahiers de Psychologie Cognitive/ Current Psychology of Cognition*, **17**, 245–71.

Dahlgren, S. and Trillingsgaard, A. (1996). Theory of mind in non-retarded children with autism and Asperger's syndrome. A research note. *Journal of Child Psychology and Psychiatry*, **37**, 759–63.

de Villiers, J. (1998). On acquiring the structural representations for false complements. In *New perspectives on language acquisition*, (ed. B. Hollebrandse). University of Massachusetts Occasional Papers in Linguistics, GLSA, Amherst, MA.

de Villiers, J. and de Villiers, P. (1999). Linguistic determinism and false belief. In *Children's reasoning and the mind*, (ed. P. Mitchell and K. Riggs). Psychology Press, Hove, UK.

de Villiers, J. and Fitneva, S. (1996). *Referential transparency for opaque containers*. Unpublished manuscript, Smith College, Northampton, MA.

de Villiers, J. and Pyers, J. (1997). Complementing cognition: the relationship between language and theory of mind. *Proceedings of the 21st Annual Boston University Conference on Language Development*. Cascadilla Press, Somerville, MA.

de Villiers, J., Roeper, T., and Vainikka, A. (1990). The acquisition of long-distance rules. In *Language processing and acquisition*, (ed. L. Frazier and J. de Villiers). Kluwer, Dordrecht, Netherlands.

de Villiers, J., Pyers, J. and Broderick, K. (1997). *A longitudinal study of the emergence of referential opacity*. Paper presented at the 22nd Annual Boston University Conference on Language Development. Boston, MA.

Dunn, J., Brown, J., Slomkowski, C., Tesla, C. and Youngblade, L. (1991). Young children's understanding of other people's feelings and beliefs: individual differences and their antecedents. *Child Development*, **62**, 1352–66.

Fine, J., Bartolucci, G., Szatmari, P. and Ginsberg, G. (1994). Cohesive discourse in pervasive developmental disorders. *Journal of Autism and Developmental Disorders*, **24**, 315–29.

Frith, U., Happé, F., and Siddons, F. (1994). Autism and theory of mind in everyday life. *Social Development*, **3**, 108–24.

Happé, F. (1993). Communicative competence and theory of mind in autism: a test of relevance theory. *Cognition*, **48**, 101–19.

Happé, F. (1994*a*). *Autism: an introduction to psychological theory.* University College Press, London.

Happé, F. (1994*b*). An advanced test of theory of mind: understanding of story characters' thoughts and feelings by able autistic, mentally handicapped and normal children and adults. *Journal of Autism and Developmental Disorders*, **24**, 129–54.

Happé, F. (1995). The role of age and verbal ability in the theory of mind task performance of subjects with autism. *Child Development*, **66**, 843–55.

Kazak, S., Collis, G. and Lewis, V. (1997). Can young people with autism refer to knowledge states? Evidence from their understanding of 'know' and 'guess'. *Journal of Child Psychology and Psychiatry*, **38**, 1001–9.

Landa, R., Folstein, S. and Isaacs, C. (1991). Spontaneous narrative discourse performance of parents of autistic individuals. *Journal of Speech and Hearing Research*, **34**, 1339–45.

Landa, R., Piven, J., Wzorek, M., Gale, O., Chase, G. and Folstein, S. (1992). Social language use in parents of autistic individuals. *Psychological Medicine*, **22**, 245–54.

Lee, A., Hobson, R. P. and Chiat, S. (1994). I, you, me and autism: an experimental study. *Journal of Autism and Developmental Disorders*, **24**, 155–76.

Leslie, A. and Roth, D. (1993). What autism teaches us about metarepresentation. In *Understanding other minds: perspectives from autism*, (ed. S. Baron-Cohen, H. Tager-Flusberg, and D. J. Cohen). Oxford University Press.

Locke, J. (1993). *A child's path to spoken language.* Harvard University Press.

Lord, C. and Paul, R. (1997). Language and communication in autism. In *Handbook of autism and pervasive developmental disorders*, (2nd edn), (ed. D. J. Cohen and F. R. Volkmar). John Wiley and Sons, New York.

Loveland, K. and Landry, S. (1986). Joint attention and language in autism and developmental language delay. *Journal of Autism and Developmental Disorders*, **16**, 335–49.

Loveland, K. and Tunali, B. (1993). Narrative language in autism and the theory of mind hypothesis: a wider perspective. In *Understanding other minds: perspectives from autism*, (ed. S. Baron-Cohen, H. Tager-Flusberg, and D. J. Cohen). Oxford University Press.

Loveland, K., McEvoy, R., Tunali, B. and Kelley, M. L. (1990). Narrative story telling in autism and Down's syndrome. *British Journal of Developmental Psychology*, **8**, 9–23.

Minshew, N., Goldstein, G. and Siegel, D. (1995). Speech and language in high-functioning autistic individuals. *Neuropsychology*, **9**, 255–61.

Mitchell, P. Saltmarsh, R. and Russell, H. (1997). Overly literal interpretations of speech in autism: understanding that messages arise from minds. *Journal of Child Psychology and Psychiatry*, **38**, 685–91.

Moore, C. and Davidge, J. (1989). The development of mental terms: pragmatics or semantics? *Journal of Child Language*, **16**, 633–41.

Moore, C., Bryant, D. and Furrow, D. (1989). Mental terms and the development of certainty. *Child Development*, **60**, 167–71.

Mundy, P., Sigman, M., Ungerer, J. and Sherman, T. (1986). Defining the social deficits in autism: the contribution of nonverbal communication measures. *Journal of Child Psychology and Psychiatry*, **27**, 657–69.

Mundy, P., Sigman, M. and Kasari, C. (1994). Nonverbal communication, developmental level and symptom presentation in autism. *Development and Psychopathology*, **6**, 389–401.

Perner, J., Frith, U., Leslie, A. and Leekam, S. (1989). Exploration of the autistic child's theory of mind: knowledge, belief and communication. *Child Development*, **60**, 689–700.

Pinker, S. and Bloom, P. (1990). Natural language and natural selection. *Behavioral and Brain Sciences*, **13**, 707–84.

Piven, J., Palmer, P., Landa, R., Santangelo, S., Jacobi, D. and Childress, D. (1997). Personality and language characteristics in parents from multiple-incidence autism families. *American Journal of Medical Genetics*, **74**, 398–411.

Sigman, M. and Ruskin, E. (1999). Social competence in children with autism, Down syndrome and developmental delays: a longitudinal study. *Monographs of the Society for Research in Child Development*, **64** Serial No. 256.

Sparrevohn, R. and Howie, P. (1995). Theory of mind children with autistic disorder: evidence of developmental progression and the role of verbal ability. *Journal of Child Psychology and Psychiatry*, **36**, 249–63.

Sperber, D. and Wilson, D. (1986). *Relevance: communication and cognition*. Harvard University Press.

Surian, L., Baron-Cohen, S., and Van der Lely, H. (1996). Are children with autism deaf to Gricean maxims? *Cognitive Neuropsychiatry*, **1**, 55–72.

Tager-Flusberg, H. (1981). On the nature of linguistic functioning in early infantile autism. *Journal of Autism and Developmental Disorders*, **11**, 45–56.

Tager-Flusberg, H. (1992). Autistic children talk about psychological states: deficits in the early acquisition of a theory of mind. *Child Development*, **63**, 161–72.

Tager-Flusberg, H. (1993). What language reveals about the understanding of minds in children with autism. In *Understanding other minds: perspectives from autism*, (ed. S. Baron-Cohen, H. Tager-Flusberg, and D. J. Cohen). Oxford University Press.

Tager-Flusberg, H. (1994). Dissociations in form and function in the acquisition of language by autistic children. In *Constraints on language acquisition: studies of atypical children*, (ed. H. Tager-Flusberg). Erlbaum, Hillsdale, NJ.

Tager-Flusberg, H. (1995). 'Once upon a ribbit': stories narrated by autistic children. *British Journal of Developmental Psychology*, **13**, 45–59.

Tager-Flusberg, H. (1996). Current theory and research on language and communication in autism. *Journal of Autism and Developmental Disorders*, **26**, 169–72.

Tager-Flusberg, H. (1997). Language acquisition and theory of mind: contributions from the study of autism. In *Research on communication and language disorders: contributions to theories of language development*, (ed. L. B. Adamson and M. A. Romski). Paul Brookes Publishing, Baltimore, MD.

Tager-Flusberg, H. and Anderson, M. (1991). The development of contingent discourse ability in autistic children. *Journal of Child Psychology and Psychiatry*, **32**, 1123–34.

Tager-Flusberg, H. and Sullivan, K. (1994). Predicting and explaining behavior: a comparison of autistic, mentally retarded and normal children. *Journal of Child Psychology and Psychiatry*, **35**, 1059–75.

Tager-Flusberg, H. and Sullivan, K. (1995). Attributing mental states to story characters: a comparison of narratives produced by autistic and mentally retarded individuals. *Applied Psycholinguistics*, **16**, 241–56.

Tager-Flusberg, H., Sullivan, K., and Barker, J. (1995). *Semantic knowledge of cognition verbs and theory of mind ability in autistic, mentally retarded, and normal children*. Unpublished manuscript, University of Massachusetts, Boston, MA.

Tomasello, M. (1995). Joint attention as social cognition. In *Joint attention: its origins and role in development*, (ed. C. Moore and P. Dunham). Erlbaum, Hillsdale, NJ.

Wetherby, A. (1986). Ontogeny of communication functions in autism. *Journal of Autism and Developmental Disorders*, **16**, 295–316.

Wetherby, A. and Prutting, C. (1984). Profiles of communicative and cognitive-social abilities in autistic children. *Journal of Speech and Hearing Research*, **27**, 364–77.

Wilkinson, K. (1998). Profiles of language and communication skills in autism. *Mental Retardation and Developmental Disabilities Research Reviews*, **4**, 73–9.

Ziatas, K., Durkin, K. and Pratt, C. (1998). Belief term development in children with autism, Asperger syndrome, specific language impairment, and normal development: links to theory of mind development. *Journal of Child Psychology and Psychiatry*, **39**, 755–63.

# 7

# Theory of mind and executive function: is there a developmental relationship?

JOSEF PERNER AND BIRGIT LANG

## INTRODUCTION

Our main points are that executive function (self control) relates to the development of a theory of mind, in particular around the ages of three to five years, and that a strong contender for explaining this relationship is that a theory of mind is necessary for achieving higher levels of executive control.

## Theory of mind (ToM)

'Theory of mind' is a label for the conceptual system that underlies our folk psychology with which we impute mental states to others and ourselves, that is, what we *know*, *think*, *want*, *feel*, etc. We want to highlight some, for present purposes particularly important, points in children's acquisition of these concepts. A first sign of understanding people's intentions comes from a study by Spelke *et al.* (1995; replicated by Sodian and Thoermer 1998) that by twelve months but not yet at eight months infants infer people's intentions to grasp objects they look at. There is richer evidence that around eighteen months infants infer more complex intentions since they imitate the intention behind failed action attempts (Meltzoff 1995) and they understand differences in food preferences (Repacholi and Gopnik 1997). By eighteen months signs of understanding the mind bloom: children engage in and understand pretence (Leslie 1987; Piaget 1945/1962), they understand distress and engage in empathic comforting behaviour (Bischof-Köhler 1988; Yarrow and Waxler 1975), they understand goals and the standards which they have to live up to (Kagan 1981), etc. These abilities sharpen over the next years; this is also reflected in an increase in their use of corresponding verbs, e.g. *feel*, *want*, *pretend*, *know*, *think* (Bartsch and Wellman 1995).

Not until after the third year do children start to understand that one can mis-conceive of a state of affairs (e.g. believe something false to be true) or that information can misrepresent a state of affairs. This understanding becomes established around the age of four years. Since most of the relevant research for present purposes centres on this transition we describe the test paradigms most frequently used. The most frequently used measure is the false-belief test. The standard version is the *'unexpected transfer'* story (Wimmer and Perner 1983) in which a protagonist puts an object into location *A*. In his absence the object is unexpectedly transferred into location *B*, so that he mistakenly believes that the object is still in location *A*. To assess children's understanding of the protagonist's belief they are asked either where the protagonist thinks the object is, or where the protagonist will look for the object. The typical developmental trend is that at three years almost all children answer wrongly that the protagonist will look in the object's actual location (*B*); in contrast most children older than four, and definitely a clear majority of five-year-olds, answer correctly with location *A*. Another version is the *'deceptive container'* task (Hogrefe *et al.* 1986; Perner *et al.* 1987). For instance, children are shown a Smarties container and asked about its contents. Practically all children say 'Smarties'. They are then shown that it contains a pencil. With the pencil back in the closed container they are asked what another person, who has not yet seen what is inside, would think (or say) was inside. A small but important twist on this procedure turns the task into the *'memory for earlier false belief'* (Gopnik and Astington 1988). The child is simply asked what he or she herself had thought was in the box when first shown. Finally, Flavell *et al.* (1983) pioneered the *appearance–reality* test. For example, children are shown a trick object which they identify reliably as a rock. Manual manipulation reveals that it is just sponge (that looks like a rock). When three-year-olds are asked the reality question about what the object *really is* they tend to answer 'a sponge', and when asked about what the object *looks like* they tend to answer wrongly with 'a sponge' again. Although the retest reliability of a single version of these tests has been questioned (Mayes *et al.* 1996)[1] in many studies even the correlation between the different tests is fairly high (e.g. Gopnik and Astington 1988, average within age cell r = .46; Holmes *et al.* 1996, average age-partialled r = .66).

## Executive function (EF)

*Executive function* (e.g. Duncan 1986; Welsh and Pennington 1988) is a label for those processes in the control of behaviour, like planning, co-ordinating, and controlling sequences of action, that are disrupted upon frontal lobe injury, and which have classically been documented by the work of Bianchi (1922) and Luria (1966). An important realisation is that executive control is not required for all action but only for certain types of problems. We pay, therefore, particular attention to the model by Norman and Shallice (1980/1986; Shallice 1988), who distinguished between two levels of control. At the level of *contention scheduling* the control of action schemas takes place by mutual inhibition and activation. Although this control can be very intricate it is, nevertheless, automatic and ensures coherent execution of action sequences. However there are certain tasks for which a higher level of control is required, which is provided by the *supervisory attentional system (SAS)*. The main specification of this system consists of a list of tasks for which it is necessary—for short, the SAS tasks:

(1) planning/decision making, (2) trouble shooting, (3) novel/ill-learned action sequences (4) dangerous or technically difficult actions, and (5) overcoming strong habitual response tendencies or temptation (e.g. Stroop).

In a different approach, factor analyses of typical executive function tasks (e.g. Welsh *et al.* 1991; Pennington 1997) identified four dimensions:

(1) planning, (2) cognitive flexibility or set shifting, (3) inhibition, and (4) working memory.

Within this analysis (Pennington 1994, p. 248) 'working memory' is supposed to refer to the *central executive* part in Baddeley and Hitch's (1974) model of working memory, which both maintains and inhibits information (Pennington 1994, p. 246), and whose responsibilities Baddeley (1996) illustrates again with a list of tasks: (1) dual task performance, (2) random generation, (3) selective attention, and (4) selective activation of representations in long-term memory.

To summarise these different but similar characterisations one could say that executive functions are needed to maintain a mentally specified goal and to bring it to fruition against distracting alternatives. Our question now is whether there is a developmental link between mastery of executive function tasks and theory of mind development. Before we muster relevant evidence we first introduce several theories that predict and explain such a relationship, so that we can read the presented evidence with an eye on evaluating these theories.

## THEORIES

We start by discussing the two theories that see an essential, functional relationship between the development of greater executive control and the development of theory of mind, that the development of one ability depends functionally on the other.

### (T1) Theory of mind development improves self-control

Wimmer (1989) suggested that with the formation of increasingly sophisticated mental concepts the child gains better understanding of her own mentality and this better understanding gives the child better control of her mental processes. This theory has been elaborated by Perner (1991, Chapter 9) in view of the then available findings on theory of mind development and the development of self control, and it has been applied by Frith (1992) to explain the co-occurrence of self control and theory of mind problems in schizophrenia and by Carruthers (1996) to explain the same coincidence in autism. From this general position it follows that the development of a theory of mind is necessary for executive control. However, no specific predictions are possible about which level of sophistication in a theory of mind is required for particular executive problems.

Recently, Perner (1998) firmed up the theoretical underpinnings of this theory in an attempt to draw more specific predictions about how theory of mind development enables success on particular executive tasks. His analysis is based on the model by Norman and Shallice (1980/1986), outlined above, that posits two levels of control: contention scheduling and the supervisory attentional system (SAS). At the level of contention scheduling, action schemas control each other automatically by mutual inhibition of incompatible sequences and activation of supporting parts in order to ensure coherent action. Since action schemas are mental representations one can ask whether the control is exerted at the level of the representational vehicle or the representational content. Perner (1998) suggested that the hall-mark of contention scheduling is control at the level of the *representational vehicle*, whereas the essence of the SAS consists in control at the level of *representational content*. If we take acquisition of new action schemas as an example, we see that learning (conditioning of stimulus–response associations) can operate at the level of contention scheduling since the reinforcement does not select a schema on the basis of its content but selects that vehicle (regardless of its content) that happened to have been recently activated. In contrast, the following of verbal instructions needs selection by content, e.g. 'put the red card into the left box' needs to strengthen the action schema that serves that purpose: 'red card → put card into left box'. Such control needs to select the schema on the basis of its content and so, by hypothesis, requires control by the SAS.

The example of verbal instructions also illustrates another feature of control by content. In order to represent the content of the instructions one has to represent it as something one might want to obey. This means that one has to represent the intended action sequence *as intended*. Executive control of this kind can therefore be described as 'meta-intentional'. For certain problems, however, boosting the desired action is not sufficient. Inhibition of undesirable action schemas that might interfere is also necessary. This raises first of all the problem of understanding of why inhibition of specific actions is required. This is a problem because in the normal case if I do not intend to act then I won't act that way. So, one needs to understand why absence of an intention to act is not sufficient for omitting certain actions. To understand this one has to grasp the idea that action is caused by action schemas that make one act despite one's lack of intentions to act that way. In other words, one has to understand that the origin of action does not lie directly in the desirability or undesirability of action (the representational content of action schemas) but in the schemas as representational vehicles that cause one to act. Such understanding consists in representing the schemas as representations (i.e. metarepresentation). For that reason, these problems require representation of the schema as a representation. Consequently the control required for problems that ask for inhibition of competing schemas can be called *meta-representational*.

The important aspect of schemas as representational vehicles is that only vehicles (not content) have causal efficacy, i.e. there is something that makes me act or directs my action in a certain way. With this specification we can see a relationship between EF and how Perner (1991) has been characterising the developments leading to an appreciation of false belief: the four-year-old understands that mental states are based on representations (vehicles) that have causal force and make people do things. For instance, in the case of false belief about the location of an object, the belief makes its holder look in the empty place even though the holder has—unlike in pretence—the intention to look in the place where the object is ('the puzzle of false belief', Perner 1991).

A clear developmental prediction follows. The false-belief task as an index of understanding the causal consequence of mental states (representational understanding = metarepresentation) should be mastered at about the same time as and correlate with executive function tasks requiring inhibition of competing schemas (meta-representational control). Although each EF task has to be analysed on its own merits, one could venture the more general classification shown in Table 7.1 of which tasks require meta-intentional and which meta-representational control.

**(T2) Action monitoring is necessary for developing a theory of mind**

Russell (1996, 1998) argues that 'the monitoring of actions and the ability to act at will are necessary ingredients to the development of a 'pretheoretical' form of self-awareness [and] . . . that this form of self-awareness must be in place if the individual is to gain an adequate grasp of mental concepts' (1998, p. 295). The deeper motivation for this claim comes from the conviction that monitoring of action and the ability to act at will (instigation of action) are the bedrock of a pre-theoretical self-awareness, and that such self-awareness is a *sine qua non* for a conceptual grasp of the mind (theory of mind). Or in other words, the concept of an agent is not exhausted by perceptual observation of self-propelled, i.e. animated, objects, but must be founded in the intimate acquaintance with oneself as an agent. Hence, if action-monitoring and the control of action initiation is not fully matured (or impaired as might be the case in children with autism) then theory of mind development is affected. That our theory of mind is grounded in our immediate experience as actors is intuitively quite compelling. But Russell's analysis seems to admit only a very fundamental enabling relationship. It can explain how early problems with action monitoring can be the cause of early and later theory of mind problems. But it is difficult to see on this theory how and why later EF problems, e.g. around the age of four years, should relate to theory of mind development at that age.

A variant by Pacherie (1998) may account for this. Focusing on explaining autism,

**Table 7.1.** Classification of EF-tasks according to requiring meta-intentional or meta-representational control

| Classification | meta-intentional | meta-representational |
|---|---|---|
| SAS-tasks | novel (instruction) dangerous | overcoming habit trouble shooting planning (inhibit overt act) |
| Factor analysis | | planning inhibition cognitive flexibility, set shifting (inhibition of previous set) |
| CE of WM | selective attention retrieve content from LTM | dual task (inhibit other task) random generation (inhibit repetition or other patterns) |

Note:  SAS-task . . .   tasks requiring control by the Supervisory Attentional System (Norman and Shallice 1980/1986)

CE of WM . . . Central Executive component of Working Memory (Baddely and Hitch 1974)

she sees a particular problem in forming motor images as Jeannerod (e.g. 1997) has identified them. Motor images are not required for guiding action, like action monitoring is. They are formed when the execution of motor programs is delayed or blocked and may play a role in trouble shooting and error correction. They also make the intentions in action conscious and are, therefore, prime candidates for building blocks of a theory of mind. Moreover, since they are not needed for basic, trouble-free execution of motor programmes, a failure to form such motor images can be the cause of later-developing EF problems around age four and specifically prevent the theory of mind development at that age.

In any case, even when lacking precise details about which EF problem should be linked to which theory of mind impairment, one can deduce from these positions that a deficit in executive control has knock-on effects on theory of mind development. Although this theory sees the etiology of the ToM-EF link in the opposite direction as the earlier position (T1), the two positions do share the idea that ToM and EF are functionally linked, one of them is an integral part of the other. Position (T1) claimed that to exert executive control one needs mental concepts (ToM), position (T2) claims that to have mental concepts one needs the ability to exert executive control. This distinguishes these positions from the ones to follow, where the correlation between EF and ToM is explained by a common third factor (reasoning strategies, brain structures) or by methodological factors, e.g. executive demands of ToM measuring instruments.

## (T3) Conditional reasoning as a common functional component

Frye, *et al.* (1995) found correlations between theory of mind tasks (e.g. false-belief task) and tasks that require embedded conditionals. These tasks can also be analysed as requiring executive control (e.g. inhibiting a conflicting action schema). For instance, one of the tasks involved a covered ramp inside which a ball could be put at the top into either a left or right hole from where it then rolled down into one of two boxes (left or right). At one setting ($s_1$), visibly marked by a raised flag, the ramp connected upper left hole ($a_1$) with lower left box ($c_1$) and upper right hole ($a_2$) with lower right box ($c_2$), i.e., left-left, right-right. Whereas, at the other setting ($s_2$: lowered flag), the connections were crossed over, i.e. leftright, rightleft. Children were shown the mechanism and then had to predict in which box the ball could be found. To solve this task an understanding of embedded conditionals is required:

IF the *flag is raised* ($s_1$)

THEN    IF ball is put into *left hole* ($a_1$)      THEN point to *left box* ($c_1$),
            IF ball is put into *right hole* ($a_2$)   THEN point to *right box* ($c_2$),

IF the *flag is lowered* ($s_2$)

THEN    IF ball is put into *left hole* ($a_1$)      THEN point to *right box* ($c_2$),
            IF ball is put into *right hole* ($a_2$)   THEN point to *left box* ($c_1$).

Similarly a card sorting task requires the same if-if-then structure, where in one setting ($s_1$: sort by *colour*) the *blue flower* ($a_1$) goes into the box marked with a *blue car* ($c_1$) and the *green car* ($a_2$) into the box with the *green flower* ($c_2$); while under the other setting ($s_2$: sort by *shape*) the *blue flower* ($a_1$) goes into the box marked with a *green flower* ($c_2$) and the *green car* ($a_2$) into the box with the *blue car* ($c_1$).

These two tasks evidently also qualify as executive function tasks (the card sorting is in fact a modification of the WCST often used with frontal lobe patients) since the antecedent condition–consequent action links ($a_1$–$c_1$, $a_2$–$c_2$) established under setting $s_1$ interfere with the links required under $s_2$, i.e. $a_1$–$c_2$, $a_2$–$c_1$. The correlational evidence for a link between these tasks and theory of mind tasks is, therefore, also support for a link between theory of mind and executive control. However, Frye *et al.* (1995) argued that the false-belief task itself requires reasoning with doubly embedded conditionals and, therefore, it is the developing ability to engage in such reasoning that underlies the developmental link between false-belief test performance and performance on executive function tasks like card sorting and the ramp task.

Unfortunately, Frye *et al.* (1995) are not very explicit about how the logical structure of doubly embedded conditionals is supposed to apply to the false-belief task, apart from saying that the different perspectives (self vs. other) constitute the setting conditions and the embedded conditional is to say what each person would say a deceptively looking object is. Recently, Frye (in press) has ventured a concrete proposal for the traditional task, where the chocolate is transferred from here to there and the child is to predict where Maxi will go for his chocolate:

IF me ($s_1$)

THEN    IF looking for chocolate ($a_1$)        THEN there ($c_1$),
        IF . . . ($a_2$)                        THEN here ($c_2$),

IF Maxi ($s_2$)

THEN    IF looking for chocolate ($a_1$)        THEN here ($c_2$),
        IF . . . . ($a_2$)                      THEN there ($c_1$),

The $a_2$ condition has been left out, but could be easily filled in with the assumption that two objects (chocolate and something else) are being switched from here to there and vice versa. This is not the crucial difficulty with this analysis. There are different reasons.

One feature to notice is that this application of the if–if–then structure differs from its application in the card sorting and the ramp problems where the conditionals describe rules that one has to know in order to solve the task. In the case of the false-belief task the stated conditionals surely are not the rules that one brings to bear on the task. At best they are descriptions of what one ends up saying. Moreover, this application highlights a dangerous arbitrariness in how one chooses to describe the problem. For instance, why could I not say:

IF I am looking for chocolate ($a_1$)         THEN there ($c_1$),
IF Maxi is looking for chocolate ($a_2$)      THEN here ($c_2$),

and the task reduces to one with simple conditionals which ought to be within the ability of children one year younger, i.e. three-year-olds (Zelazo and Frye 1996). No principled rule has been stated for why Frye's (in press) analysis of the false-belief task is to be preferred over this alternative one. Even if such a principle could be given then its application would lead to wrong predictions on other tasks. For instance, as early as eighteen months, but not before, infants understand divergent food preferences (Repacholi and Gopnik 1997) which seems to require exactly the very reasoning strategy that Frye applied to the false-belief task:

IF me ($s_1$)

    THEN    IF wanting to eat ($a_1$)        THEN pick crackers ($c_1$),

            IF . . . ($a_2$)                THEN . . . ($c_2$),

IF Other ($s_2$)

    THEN    IF wanting to eat ($a_1$)        THEN pick broccoli ($c_2$),

            IF . . . ($a_2$)                THEN . . . ($c_1$),

In sum, for the stated reasons—arbitrariness of post hoc analyses and contradictory developmental results if a uniform analysis is applied—we think it unlikely that the observed correlation between the false-belief task and executive function tasks (card sorting, ramp task) is due to a common underlying conditional reasoning structure.

## (T4) Common brain regions

Ozonoff *et al.* (1991) and Pennington *et al.* (1998) suggested that the observed association of ToM and EF problems in autism could be due to the fact that both abilities depend on the same or closely interrelated brain structures. Late development of these structures can then also explain why EF and ToM performance are related in normal development. There have been only a few studies investigating the brain region involved in theory of mind. Baron-Cohen *et al.* (1994), using SPECT, identified the right orbitofrontal cortex (Brodmann areas 10–14) as specifically activated when listening to mental words (e.g. *know, want, remember*) in contrast to action words or body parts (e.g. *hand, move, tooth*). Involvement of right frontal cortex is also indicated by the stroke literature reviewed by Brownell *et al.* (Chapter 10, this volume). In a study with PET, Fletcher *et al.* (1995) identified the left medial frontal cortex (Brodmann area 8 and partly 9) as responsible for understanding mentalizing stories (involving misunderstandings, double bluff, etc.) in contrast to stories about physical events. A recent confirmation of this finding (Happé *et al.* 1996) also showed that children with Asperger's Syndrome lacked the pronounced activation of this brain region. The left medial frontal lobe (but mainly identified with Brodmann area 9) was also indicated in another PET study by Goel *et al.* (1995) as being responsible for taking the perspective of a person from a different century (e.g. to judge whether Christopher Columbus would be able to infer the function of a modern artefact) as opposed to inferring the function oneself. This region was also identified in an earlier study on story comprehension (that happened to use stories on deception and other theory of mind relevant material) by Mazoyer *et al.* (1993).

These identified brain regions are part of the prefrontal cortex and/or the border between prefrontal and premotor cortex, i.e. regions that have traditionally been linked with the control of voluntary action. Brodmann area 8 has been implicated in conditional reasoning (Petrides 1982), in particular, ablation studies in macaques show that it is necessary for conditional reasoning that requires a decision on which object to manipulate (Halsband and Passingham 1985; Petrides 1985), i.e. under condition *A* move the round object, under condition *B* move the square object, to find the peanut. This stands in a neat contrast to the lateral premotor cortex (part of area 6) which is necessary for deciding which of two actions to choose on a particular object (e.g. to pull or rotate a lever). This contrast is particularly interesting in view of the finding that understanding of false belief is developmentally correlated with the ability to understand embedded conditionals (Frye *et al.* 1995), since the task for which area 8 is required can be described as a double conditional: if condition *A* then if round then look for peanut there (however, see comments above on arbitrariness of such analyses). Whereas the task dependent on area 6 is a simpler conditional.

Area 9 (which was also implicated in the PET studies by Fletcher *et al.* (1995) and by Goel *et al.* (1995)) has also traditionally, in conjunction with area 46, played a role in the control of delayed responding. Petrides (1991*a*) reported that ablation of areas 9 and 46 destroyed the ability to move an object that hadn't been moved before, i.e. action depending on memory of the object and one's action, but did not impair non-match to sample, i.e., act on that object not seen on the previous trial. In a similar task, the 'subject ordered task' in which subjects can point to objects in any order but never to the same object twice, PET scanning showed areas 9 and 46 bilaterally activated (Petrides *et al.* 1993). Ablation of areas 9 and 46 also impairs memory for presentation order of objects (Petrides 1991*b*). Unfortunately few systematic studies have varied the contribution of area 9 and area 46 systematically. Passingham (1978) found that removal of 9 and 46 impaired monkeys' relearning of the ability to repeat a number of presses on one key on another key, while removal of area 46 alone enabled quick relearning. In sum, area 9 is involved in selecting objects based on one's past response (or order of experience).

The orbital prefrontal cortex found to be activated when reading mental words (Baron-Cohen *et al.* 1994) includes Brodmann areas 10–14 (Baron-Cohen 1995). These areas, in particular area 12, have strong links with the amygdala which is responsible for associating stimuli with rewards. Moreover, ablation of area 12 in monkeys leads again to problems on a series of conditional response tasks that are diagnostic of EF problems: delayed alternation, reversal, and go/no-go tasks (see Passingham (1993) for summary).

So, there is some neuropsychological evidence that the brain regions demonstrably involved in theory of mind also serve executive function tasks. These findings support, on the one hand, the theories of functional relatedness, since it points to common brain regions subserving these common functions. On the other hand, it also opens the possibility that, despite a possible functional independence of ToM and EF, developmental and pathogenic correlations could be observed due to delayed maturation or damage to *accidentally shared* brain regions.

## (T5) Executive component in theory of mind tests

Russell *et al.* (1991) found that the ability to give correct answers in the false-belief task developed together with the ability to suppress pointing to where an object is in favour of pointing to where it is not ('windows task'). The authors argued that the common difficulty is due to executive function problems of younger children and of children with autism since both tasks require inhibiting reference to a salient object or location (e.g. p. 340). Russell *et al.* (1991) tended to emphasise inhibition at a more cognitive level whereas Hughes and Russell (1993) talked of inhibition of action. Similarly Ozonoff *et al.* (1991) considered such a relationship as one possible explanation for their finding that children with autism have more severe executive function difficulties than theory of mind problems as measured, among other tests, with different variations of the false-belief problem. And Harris (1993) pointed out that children with autism tend to have problems with theory of mind tasks in which a mental state conflicts with the state of reality.

This interpretation of children's difficulty with the false-belief task is also reflected in the wide-spread intuition that children fail the false-belief task, even though they do understand belief, because the test response contradicts reality. These intuitions have become known as the *reality masking hypothesis* (Mitchell 1996) indicating the possibility that the attraction to answer in terms of reality may mask children's understanding of belief. This idea was fed by findings that the more salient reality is made (e.g. visually perceived as opposed to just told about) the more difficult the false-belief task becomes (Zaitchik 1991). Conversely, the more support is given to the content of the belief the easier the task becomes (Mitchell and Lacoheé 1991). When the contrast between belief and reality is taken care of by the story and the child has to explain the deviancy of the belief-based behaviour, children show their alleged understanding earlier (Bartsch and Wellman 1989; Robinson and Mitchell 1995). However, these studies are prone to methodological criticism (e.g. Perner 1995; Wimmer and Mayringer 1998) and the originally observed effects are often difficult to replicate and tend to be small. These points are nicely summarised by Mitchell (1996, Chapter 8) who concludes: 'Young children have considerable difficulty with false belief, a difficulty that is not entirely eradicated by protecting them from the salience of current reality' (p. 153).

A possible variant of this theory would be that theory of mind tests require a certain working memory capacity (Davis and Pratt 1995; Gordon and Olson 1998) and, therefore, success tends to emerge at the same time as success with EF tasks which pose similar demands on working memory.

In sum, the main developmental change we see in the false-belief test does probably reflect the development of understanding belief and not merely an increase in executive proficiency. However, executive problems in these tasks may well be responsible for the observed variability in test performance during that larger conceptual development. Consequently, individual differences in executive control can produce substantial correlations between executive function tasks and false-belief tasks (and other comparable theory of mind tasks).

## EVIDENCE

The above discussion of the different theories explaining a relationship between performance on EF and ToM tasks has already given some indication of the original empirical findings that instigated these theories. We now turn to a more systematic review of relevant evidence from pathological development (especially in children with autism) and normal development, and discuss this evidence in the light of the above theories.

### Evidence for an executive component in theory of mind tests?

The notion that theory of mind tasks contain an executive function component was strongly fuelled by the findings on the 'windows task' by Russell *et al.* (1991, 1994). Children were trained to point to one of two opaque containers. One of them contained a sweet but the children didn't know which container that was. The opponent then lifted the container that the child had pointed at. If it contained the sweet the opponent consumed it. If the container was empty the child got to eat the sweet from the other container. This was to teach the child that it is expedient to point to the empty container. Russell *et al.* (1994) also had a condition without opponent. The child had to figure out under which conditions she would obtain the reward and it was tested whether children understood this after ten training trials. Although there was some difficulty understanding the contingencies ('if the container I just pointed at is empty I get the sweet from the other container, if it is full the experimenter gets to keep it') most three-year-olds did succeed. After fifteen such trials containers with windows on the child's side were introduced, so that the child, but not the opponent, could see which container was baited. The remarkable finding speaking for executive problems in this procedure is that, despite understanding of the contingencies after the training, most three-year-olds pointed to the full container when the windows were introduced and children now knew where the sweet was when pointing. Moreover, most of them kept pointing there for up to twenty test trials.

Although Samuels *et al.* (1996) found only a rather weakened tendency among three-year-olds to be so persevering in their unsuccessful strategy, recently Moore *et al.* (in press) replicated the original finding by Russell *et al.* very clearly. A study by Carlson *et al.* (1998) shows directly that at least part of the difficulty that children encounter in deceiving resides in the requirement to point (or verbally refer) to the wrong location, which can be interpreted as a difficulty of suppressing highly routine answer modes. If children were asked to mislead by putting a wrong picture on the box, or by placing an arrow instead of pointing with their finger, three-year-olds improved considerably, though they still found it more difficult than four-year-olds. An important question is whether similar executive problems also affect children's answers in the typical false-belief task. For instance, Russell *et al.* (1994) and Leslie (1994, p. 229) think this to be the case, and there is some evidence of changes to the false-belief test that make it easier and which can be interpreted as reducing the executive demands. However, none of these changes reduces the difficulty to such a degree, that three-year-olds can show a solid understanding of belief. Moreover there are also data that suggest that there is no such executive demand operative.

For instance, it has frequently been argued that Bartsch and Wellman's (1989) alleged finding, that children can explain an erroneous action by referring to the actor's false belief before they can predict such an action on the basis of the actor's false belief, speaks for executive problems in the standard prediction task. In these explanation tasks children observe some character search for band aids in the empty band aids box. Asked simply why he searches there only as many as solve the standard prediction task give an answer in terms of belief or lack of knowledge.[2] There is no difference. Only when prompted with what the actor 'thinks' the difference emerges because some of the children who could not explain before now answer with 'band aids'. Unfortunately, this answer is difficult to interpret as an understanding of belief. For instance, it could mean that children interpreted 'think' in the question as 'want' (Wellman and Bartsch 1988, Experiment 1, provided some evidence for such a tendency in three-year-olds). Moreover, to the degree that higher proportions of three-year-olds can be induced to answer 'he thinks band aids in there' they then also commit errors on a control question (Moses and Flavell 1990, Experiment 2; see Perner, 1995, pp. 253, 254 for an explanation). Wimmer and Gschaider (in press) found that children had, if anything, more difficulty giving a clear explanation for an erroneous act than predicting this action. Robinson and Mitchell (1995) used an ingenious story involving identical twins, one of which witnessed the transfer of the target object whilst the other one had left the room before the transfer. Children were reportedly better able to infer from the one twin's later going to the correct location and the other twin's going to the wrong location which one had been present at the transfer, than they were able to predict where the absent twin would look for the object. However, one needs to compensate observed frequency of correct responses by the baseline incidence of correct answers by children who have no understanding. Assuming a total inability to understand the link between not witnessing the transfer and later behaviour the default prediction for where a twin would look for the object is to name the location where the object is (100% wrong) whereas the default for indicating which twin had been present would be to guess (50% correct). When this compensation is carried out, very little difference between conditions remains (see Perner 1995, p. 253, for details).

Another kind of evidence that seemed to speak for executive problems is the finding that when the displaced object disappears altogether, so that the tendency to point to the object in response to 'where will he look for the object?' becomes difficult, children give more correct answers (i.e. that he will look in the object's original place) (German 1995; Sheffield *et al*. 1993; Wimmer and Perner 1983). Unfortunately, one problem with this finding is that it leaves open whether children give the right answer because they understand false belief and are relieved of executive problems or whether they simply point to the original location because that is the only one where the object and the actor have been together. That this latter explanation might be right is suggested by a version of this task with five locations and where the child is told that the object is relocated from its original box to one of the other four but the child cannot see which one. This should also help suppress the automatic tendency to point to where the object is, since the child simply doesn't know where it is. However, Russell (1996, p. 226) reports that three-year-olds still have severe problems with this version of the false-belief task and Robinson and Beck (in press, Experiment 4) report that no difference between this version and the standard version was found.

In sum, although there is evidence that measures of deceptive ability have a noticeable executive component this is less clear for the false-belief task. It does seem clear that all the difficulty that young children have with the false-belief task cannot be reduced to executive problems. However, there might be enough of an executive problem in these tasks so that the false-belief task correlates with typical executive function measures for that reason.

## Evidence from autism and other developmental disorders

Children afflicted with autism are known to have problems with theory of mind tasks. Early indications of autism are lack of eye gaze following, joint attention behaviours (like pointing out an interesting event) and lack of spontaneous pretend play (Baron-Cohen *et al.* 1996). They seem not particularly impaired in comparison to intelligence-matched controls on the simpler kind of theory of mind tasks, like inferring simple desires and emotions, the kind of task that three-year-old children tend to be quite proficient at (e.g. Baron-Cohen 1991). They tend to be severely and specifically impaired on more demanding theory of mind tasks like the false-belief task (Baron-Cohen *et al.* 1985), although some clinical controls with low IQ (relative to their chronological age) have also shown some impairment on these tasks (Yirmiya *et al.* 1996). Between 15 to 45% of intelligent children with autism (IQ of more than 70) and a mental age of more than four years (the age at which normally-developing children solve these tasks) do also give correct answers. They however fail, despite higher mental age, higher-order belief problems like understanding what John thinks that Mary thinks . . . (Happé 1994). These tasks, and indirect speech acts, like sarcasm and irony, which play on these higher-order mental states, are not appreciated except by very high-functioning patients, sometimes described as Asperger's Syndrome.

Autism has also been linked theoretically to an impairment of frontal lobe tasks (Damasio and Maurer 1978), which comprise tasks measuring executive functioning. Rumsey (1985) found an impairment on the Wisconsin Card Sorting Test in comparison to normally-developing children. Pennington and Ozonoff (1996) review fourteen studies that assessed children with autism on a variety of EF tasks. Of the 32 tasks administered in these studies, 25 showed a significant impairment of children with autism in comparison to intelligence matched controls, with an average effect size of .98 (i.e. a mean of practically one standard deviation below that of the control groups).

Of particular interest are two studies by Ozonoff *et al.* (1991) where twenty three high-functioning children with autism (IQs ranged from 55 to 140) were compared on EF and ToM with a control group of mixed learning problems and mild mental retardation matched for IQ. Among other less established assessments of a theory of mind they used the appearance–reality test and a false-belief test (unexpected contents). For assessing EF they used the Wisconsin Card Sorting Test (WCST) and the Tower of Hanoi. It was found that the autistic impairment was stronger on the EF measures (in particular the Tower of Hanoi) than on the ToM measures and, hence, the EF impairment was a better discriminator for the autistic syndrome. The authors concluded that, therefore, the EF deficit, and not the theory of mind deficit, is more likely to be the primary cause of autism. However, this conclusion seems premature for two reasons. The lack of discriminability of theory of mind measures was mainly due to the first level tasks where the control group was practically at ceiling, which may have prevented the difference showing its true size. Whereas the second-order tasks, where there was no ceiling effect, discriminated almost as well as Tower of Hanoi and better than WCST, both of which had no ceiling effect. Moreover, even if the EF deficit is more severe and provides a better diagnostic discriminator it does not follow that EF is causally primary. In fact, if theory of mind is a *necessary* ingredient for executive control then, under ideal measurement conditions, one would expect no cases that show executive control but fail theory of mind tests, whereas there can be cases of theory of mind competence without executive control. In the world of partial deficits and imperfect measurement this logic translates into saying that the EF impairment should not be less than the ToM impairment as the data by Ozonoff *et al.* (1991) show. In fact, if it can be established that the EF deficit is stronger than the ToM deficit and, in the extreme, that there are cases with no executive control but intact ToM, then that would pose a serious problem for Russell's (1996) and Pacherie's (1998) position—the data by Ozonoff *et al.*, however, do not make that case yet.

However, some recent data on preschool-aged samples of children with autism do indicate that, at the early age of three and a half years (Wehner and Rogers 1994, as cited by Griffith *et al.* 1998) or four and a half years (Griffith *et al.* 1998) children with autism are not particularly EF-impaired in relation to an age- and IQ-matched control group. It appears that over the next years (Griffith *et al.* 1998) the control group gets better at EF while the children with autism do not improve, so that by five and a half years (McEvoy *et al.* 1993) there is a clearly identifiable EF gap between controls and children with autism. If this finding can be firmed up, then it poses a serious problem to Russell's (1998) theory that the theory of mind deficit in autism is due to a prior deficit in executive function and self monitoring. It could be compatible with Pacherie's (1998) theory that autism reflects a failure to form motor images, because motor images may only be required for these later-developing EF problems.

Another problem for the theory that executive dysfunction is at the heart of autism is, as Baron-Cohen and Swettenham (1997, p. 886) point out, that there are many other clinical disorders that are associated with executive dysfunction, e.g. obsessive compulsive disorder (OCD), Tourette's Syndrome (TS), attention deficit with hyperactivity disorder (ADHD), and others, but which do not result in autism. The review by Pennington and Ozonoff (1996) shows ADHD particularly clearly associated with problems on a series of executive function tasks in fifteen of the eighteen reviewed studies. Although effect sizes are not as strong as in the autism studies, they do come close. For instance, on the three tasks that have been used on both disorders, the average effect size was .45 for WCST perseverations (autism studies: .90), .75 for time on Trails B (autism: .62), and 1.08 for Tower of Hanoi (autism: 2.08). Unfortunately we know of no studies comparing executive function with theory of mind in ADHD children.

Baron-Cohen *et al.* (1997) tested high-functioning people with Asperger's Syndrome and, as a control group, ten adults with Tourette's Syndrome for their theory of mind ability to infer mental states from the eyes in a photograph. Subjects had to make a forced choice between two mental adjectives, e.g. is this person reflective or unreflective, concerned or unconcerned? etc. The children with Asperger's Syndrome found this clearly more difficult than the normal controls, whereas the group with Tourette's Syndrome showed no impairment whatsoever. Unfortunately, there was no EF task administered, and EF performance by people with Tourette's Syndrome is too variable (Pennington and Ozonoff 1996) for one to blindly trust that this particular group must have been seriously impaired on EF. We, therefore, cannot conclude convincingly that there are individuals (those with Tourette's Syndrome) with fully functioning theory of mind who have a serious EF impairment.

There are two other studies that do provide the needed data. Baron-Cohen and Robertson (1995) tested three single cases. A child with autism, a child with Tourette's Syndrome (TS), and a child with both. They were tested on three theory of mind tests (false-belief and deception), three inhibition tests (referred to as intention-editing tasks) and one cognitive flexibility task (word fluency). The child with autism failed all three ToM tasks but succeeded on the inhibition tasks, and the child with Tourette's Syndrome succeeded on all ToM tasks but failed two of the three inhibition tasks. It is difficult, however, to evaluate the force of such single case evidence as existence proof of a dissociation between EF and ToM unless each case had been studied extensively to rule out conclusively any ToM or EF competence. Evaluation of the autistic case is especially difficult since it goes against the general trend that autistic children are more—or at least as—severely impaired on EF than on ToM problems (Ozonoff *et al.* 1991).

Tager-Flusberg *et al.* (1997) tested 14 children with Williams syndrome (WMS) and 10 children with Prader–Willi syndrome (PWS) on two false-belief tasks and two EF tasks (day–night Stroop and finger tapping; pass criterion = 13 of 15 trials correct). If we look at the clearest cases indicating a dissociation, namely those children who pass both tasks of one kind and fail both tasks of the other kind, then we find 6 children (3 with Williams and 3 with Prader–Willi syndrome) who passed both ToM tasks and failed both EF tasks. No child passed both EF tasks when failing both ToM tasks.[3]

As it stands, this result speaks strongly against the position T2 that EF competence is a prerequisite for theory of mind (Russell 1996; Pacherie 1998), against T5 that the difficulty of the false-belief task resides in an executive component, and against an extension of T3 that impaired performance on EF and ToM is due to problems with embedded conditionals. It is compatible with T1 that theory of mind is a prerequisite for EF, and it is also compatible with T4 (common brain regions) unless one wanted to claim that ToM and EF use *exactly the same* regions. Furthermore, if we also look at weaker cases of dissociation (children who only pass one of the two tasks of a kind) then we get four more cases where children did better on false-belief than on EF (further weak evidence against EF being a prerequisite for ToM) but also three cases where children did better on EF than on false belief (weak evidence against T1 that ToM is a prerequisite for EF). Overall, these data look like they support the view (T1) that ToM is a prerequisite for EF over its rivals. However, one should point out some problems of interpretation.

The problems centre around the question of how to compare severity of impairment on the basis of task performance. In particular, one could argue that the criterion for passing EF tasks was too restrictive; in the extreme even a single correct trial (1 of 15) indicates executive control. With that scoring criterion all or most critical cases of passing FB but failing EF would vanish and there would be no evidence against the view that EF is a prerequisite for ToM. Of course, one could also defend the stricter pass criterion actually used. Since children realise that they act wrongly (they just can't help their wrong responses), one cannot exclude behavioural changes through learning by negative feedback which does not require executive control. Hence, only immediate switches to the new strategy producing minimal errors would be indicative of executive control.

For these reasons, the presented evidence is no knock-down evidence for any of the alternative theories but provides only a greater challenge to some theories than to others. We now turn to normal development for further evidence that, hopefully, will confirm the pattern of theoretical challenges gained from pathological development.

### Evidence from normal development

There are several studies that show a direct relationship between the development of theory of mind and increasing executive control. Most of these studies concern the development around the age of three to five years. Earlier developmental parallels can only be extrapolated from the age at which developments occur.

### Infants and toddlers

There are few direct tests of children's understanding of mind in this period. Spelke *et al.* (1995) reported that between nine and twelve months children expect a person looking at an object to manipulate that object and not another object. This result was recently replicated by Sodian and Thoermer (1998). One can speculate that this development might be related to the fact that in this period the sustainable delay in the *A–notB* task increases systematically (Diamond 1985; Harris 1973) and the ability for detour reaching (retrieval of an object from a transparent box with entry at the side) develops. Both these developments have been linked to dorsolateral prefrontal cortex (Diamond 1991; Diamond *et al.* 1997). Diamond (1991) emphasised that these tasks require inhibition of a predominant response, e.g. to avoid the *A–notB* error one needs to suppress the reaching to *A* which was practised on previous trials. This raises the question why inhibition of a prepotent response becomes an obstacle again at the age of three to six years. One can avoid this question and question Diamond's interpretation instead. This critical stance finds support in demonstrations of the *A–notB* error occurring even when the infant had never reached for the object at *A* but simply had observed someone else to do so (Evans 1973; Landers 1971; see meta-analysis by Wellman *et al.* 1987). What may develop is working memory ability to retain the intention of wanting to look under *B* after the tedium of being restrained from doing so brings other possibilities to the infant's mind (see Harris (1989) for discussion of this attention-shifting explanation). Under this interpretation one can now speculate that the increase in sustainable delay on the *A–notB* task relates to the finding by Spelke *et al.* (1995) in that the infant around nine months acquires the *meta-intentional* ability of representing the possession of a goal and that such representation of the infant's own goal allows the infant to reinstate this goal after some delay.

Children's ability to understand intentions has clearly been demonstrated by the age of eighteen months. They infer an actor's intention from her failed action (Meltzoff 1995) and they understand differences in food preferences (Repacholi and Gopnik 1997). Progress in children's theory of mind for the next two years consists mainly in better understanding of desires, intentions, and pretend play which is also reflected in their uses of mental verbs (e.g. Bartsch and Wellman 1995). There is some, but no very marked, improvement in that period on more complex versions of, e.g. the *A–notB* task with invisible displacement (Diamond *et al.* 1997, Section VI). What does clearly emerge and further improve in that period is children's ability to follow verbal action instructions (Zelazo and Frye 1996) to implement a novel action schema (e.g. card sorting). By the age of two and a half years children can sort according to a single criterion, e.g. put each card to the identical-looking target. However, they have problems sorting according to two rules, e.g. 'put the car to target *A* and the flowers to target *B*'. By about three years children can do that (e.g. Zelazo and Reznick 1991). But not until about four years can they switch sorting rules (e.g. Zelazo *et al.* 1996). This problem and other EF problems that are mastered around four years have been directly investigated in relation with ToM tasks.

### The four year shift

There are several studies that have used theory of mind tasks, in particular various versions of the false-belief task, and executive function tasks. Russell *et al.* (1991) used their 'windows task' and the false-belief task. Children found them of similar difficulty: 48% passed the windows task (17 of 20 test trials correct) and 62% passed the false-belief task, and the correlation between the two tasks was significant. As mentioned earlier, Samuels *et al.* (1996) did not find the difficulty reported by Russell *et al.* (1991). Across three different versions of the task that required suppression of pointing to the baited box (their Table 2) three-year-olds were successful 79% of the time, whereas they gave only around 30% correct responses on the false-belief, appearance–reality, and memory-for-own-false-belief tasks. Correspondingly, correlations between these theory of mind tasks and the windows task were low, and, when age was partialled out, practically zero (reported correlations also include two further variations of the windows task where pointing was not required). Moore *et al.* (in press), however, clearly replicated the severe problems of three-year-olds with the windows task.

Frye *et al.* (1995) used four theory of mind tasks (appearance–reality, false-belief, memory of earlier false belief, and the pretence–reality distinction) and two set-shifting tasks (described earlier): sorting cards according to a new dimension that conflicted with the old dimension and a physical causality task involving a bead rolling down ramps that could cross over or go straight down. All tasks showed similar increases in correct performance within this age range in three experiments. Theory of mind tasks ranged from 26% to 37% among three-, and from 66% to 90% among five-year olds. Performance on the card-sorting task ranged from 20% to 45% among three- and from

72% to 80% among five-year olds. The ramp task was used only in Experiment 1 where three-year-olds gave 40% and five-year-olds 90% correct answers. Correlations between these tasks are illustrated for the false-belief task: It correlated significantly with the ramp task, but the significance was lost after age had been partialled out. For the three experiments correlations with the card-sorting task were .40**, .53**, and .37**, and with age partialled out: .18 n.s., .40**, and .31*. In sum, even with age partialled out a relationship was still detectable.

Carlson (1997) tested 107 three- to five-year-olds on a set of inhibitory control tasks consisting of two sub-batteries. The conflict battery consisted of three Stroop-like tasks, e.g. 'Say 'day' when a card depicting night is shown and 'night' when day is shown', (Gerstadt *et al.* 1994), two action-suppression tasks, e.g. perform actions the bear tells you to do but do not perform actions the dragon tells you to do (Reed *et al.* 1984), and the card-sort task after Frye *et al.* (1995). The delay battery consisted of four tasks where the child, ready to act, had to wait for a signal, e.g. the child must not release the pinball before the experimenter says 'go!' (Reed *et al.* 1984). The ToM-battery consisted of an appearance–reality task, three false-belief tasks, memory for earlier false belief, and deceptive pointing. The conflict battery correlated somewhat better with the ToM battery than the delay battery, and when age, sex, and verbal intelligence had been partialled out these coefficients were significant but reduced. Since the ToM battery contains deceptive pointing, which by itself might require significant executive control, it is interesting that it did not correlate substantially better with the complete inhibitory battery than either the standard false-belief or the appearancereality test. Moreover, the standard false-belief task by itself correlated with the complete inhibitory battery after age, sex, and verbal intelligence had been partialled out.

Hughes (1998) tested 50 three- and four-year-olds thoroughly for their verbal ability with the British Picture Vocabulary Scale (BPVS) and by analysing their retelling of a story and their verbalisations in free play sessions in terms of length of utterance, information content and grammatical complexity. Also their non-verbal intelligence was assessed with McCarthy's Intelligence Scales. A ToM battery consisted of two false-belief prediction and two explanation tasks (Bartsch and Wellman 1989), a deception game, and a penny-hiding game (Gratch 1964; Oswald and Ollendick 1989). Three executive components were assessed with two tasks each: (1) *working memory* with an auditory sequencing task and a visual search task, where children had to remember the pot they had already emptied; (2) *inhibitory control* with detour reaching (a switch had to be operated in order to reach through an electronically secured opening) and with Luria's hand game (after imitating the experimenter's hand shape they had to switch to doing the opposite shape); (3) *attentional flexibility* with a card-sorting task (however no rule was given, but children had to detect which cards a teddy liked) and a pattern-matching task (children had to copy a repeating pattern, e.g. six times blue–blue–red).

The results showed the theory of mind tasks and EF tasks to be of comparable difficulty; between 52% and 55% of children passed each of the three types of ToM tasks. Performance on the inhibitory control tasks and the repeat-pattern task was between 49% and 52% correct, but performance on the simple set-shifting task was

74% and on the two working memory tasks between 63% and 76% correct. Correlations between the three types of ToM and EF were significant. The correlation between inhibitory control and deception was particularly high, while the correlations between attentional flexibility and FB-prediction as well as FB-explanation failed to be significant. With age partialled out, these correlations drop by .10 to .20 points with a notable exception that FB-prediction and inhibitory control drops to .02. With age, verbal intelligence, and non-verbal ability partialled out, all correlations except one stay positive, but drop below significance except for deception correlated with inhibitory control and attentional flexibility. That at this stage most correlations drop below the level of significance is, perhaps, not too surprising, since these intelligence measures are quite extensive and probably contain some sizeable executive component themselves, especially since low general intelligence (Spearman's *g*) tends to be linked to EF problems (Duncan 1995).

One especially notable feature of these results is that children did not find *belief explanation* easier (53% passed) than *belief prediction* (55% passed) as Bartsch and Wellman (1989) had claimed. Moreover, belief prediction does not show any stronger relationship with inhibitory control than belief explanation, which supports the argument against the need for suppressing a reality-oriented response in the prediction task. Another interesting feature is the correlation of ToM tasks with auditory working memory. This raises the question whether the relationship between ToM and EF comes about due to a capacity increase in working memory with development, as postulated by Pascual-Leone (1970) and Case (1985), or whether the central executive component in working memory (Baddeley 1996) profits from theory of mind development. This is difficult to judge from Hughes's data, since it is not clear to what degree her tasks assess auditory loop capacity or the functioning of the central executive. Other studies have more explicitly addressed this question.

Davis and Pratt (1995) tested three- to five and a half-year-olds on false belief, forward digit span (mostly taxing the auditory loop) and backward digit span (taxing the central executive). Backward digit span was a significant predictor of false-belief understanding even after age and verbal intelligence had been partialled out, whereas forward digit span was not. This indicates that the developmental relationship between false-belief understanding and working memory hinges, in particular, on the central executive component of working memory. This relationship was also confirmed in a study by Gordon and Olson (1998), who tested three- to six-year-olds on theory of mind (false belief, appearance–reality, and memory for earlier false belief) and dual task performance (naming three objects while counting them, e.g. 'one is a doll, two is a car, three is a spoon', or naming the objects while finger tapping). ToM measures correlated with counting-and-labelling, and with naming-while-tapping. After controlling for age (within year correlations) these correlations dropped by about .10 but stayed highly significant.

To investigate planning ability the test most frequently used with frontal lobe patients is the Tower of Hanoi task or some variation of it (Tower of London, Shallice 1988). Unfortunately, this has not been used on the, for us, relevant age group. However, Bischof-Köhler (1998) has developed a planning test in which children must plan a shopping trip and decide which objects to bring along. Their performance is evaluated as to whether they decide on appropriate objects (e.g. carrier bag, wallet) or are distracted by irrelevant but attractive objects (e.g. flash light, Smarties). 'Incompetent shoppers' were children who started to actually shop, 'seducibles' were children who understood that they had to prepare for a shopping trip but nevertheless took mostly attractive objects, and the 'competent shoppers' were those who took only the relevant objects. One hundred and eleven children between 3;2 and 4;7 years were tested on this task and, among other tasks, on a standard false-belief task. Table 7.2 shows the relationship between passing the false-belief test and shopping competence. The data suggest that understanding of false belief is a prerequisite for the ability to plan, since hardly any children who had failed false belief were competent planners.

The reviewed experiments show that there is a reliable developmental relationship between theory of mind acquisition and increasing executive control that remains resistant to partialling out age and, to some degree, partialling out differences in intelligence (though if the intelligence measures are extensive, as in Hughes' case, the remaining relationship my be very small). Table 7.3 provides an overview of all studies by simply averaging correlation coefficients for different measures. There was also some indication that the observed relationships are not just due to executive demands in the false-belief tasks. This is shown particularly clearly in the finding by Hughes that correlations between EF tasks and false-belief tasks were as strong for the explanation task—with no direct executive problem of suppressing a prepotent response—as for the prediction task—where such a danger had been proposed. To investigate this issue further, we introduced a task which, at least at face value, poses minimal executive demands, but requires understanding of one's own intentions as causally effective.

Shultz *et al.* (1980) reported that three-year-olds, who are otherwise quite proficient in judging accidents as unintentional, had a hard time to realise that their reflexive knee movement is involuntary. Perner (1991, pp. 217–20) speculated that the onset of this realisation should relate to children's mastery of false belief since both tasks require an understanding of mental states as causally effective representational states: the belief makes the actor look in the wrong place even though he doesn't want to look in an empty place (unlike in pretend play), and in the case of the knee-jerk reflex the knee moves in the absence of an intention to move it. To test this Lang (1997) assessed 54 three-, four-, and five-year-olds[4] on a false-belief test, assessed their understanding of the knee-jerk reflex, and administered the card-sorting test (Frye *et al.* 1995). Lang's version of the card-sorting test involved the dimensions of colour and size (and not

**Table 7.2.** Contingency between understanding false belief and planning competence, after Bischof-Köhler (1998)

| False belief performance | Planning competence | | |
| --- | --- | --- | --- |
| | incompetent | seducible | competent |
| fail | 24 | 4 | 3 |
| pass | 22 | 17 | 42 |

**Table 7.3.** EF-ToM link: averaged correlations (with age partialled out)

| Studies | FB-Tasks | WM | Inh.-Bat. | CS | Cog.Flex. |
|---|---|---|---|---|---|
| **Hughes** (1998)<br>N=45<br>Age: 3;3–4;7 | FB explanation<br>FB prediction<br>deception, | .42<br>(.25) | .49<br>(.30) | | .25<br>(.18) |
| **Frye et al.** (1995)<br>Exp. 1, N=60<br>Age: 3;1–5;5 | pretend-reality,<br>A-R,<br>FB (self, other) | | | .38<br>(.16) | |
| **Frye et al.** (1995)<br>Exp. 2, N=40<br>Age: 2;8–5;4 | A-R,<br>FB (self, other) | | | .50<br>(.37) | |
| **Frye et al.** (1995)<br>Exp. 3, N=60<br>Age: 2;9–6;1 | A-R,<br>FB (self, other) | | | .33<br>(.25) | |
| **Carlson** (1997)<br>N=107<br>Age: 3;3–4;11 | A-R, deception<br>FB explanation,<br>FB (self, other) | | .66<br>(.34)[a] | .40<br>(.15)[a] | |
| **Lang** (1997)<br>N=28,<br>Age: 3;0–5;11 | FB prediction | | | .26<br>(.01) | |
| **Perner et al.**<br>(1998), N=57<br>Age: 3;0–5;11 | FB prediction | | .39<br>(.35) | .59<br>(.48) | |
| **Davis & Pratt**<br>(1995), N=54<br>Age: 3;3–5;4 | A-R,<br>FB (self, other) | .46 | | | |
| **Gordon & Olson**<br>(1998), N=72<br>Age: 3;0–6;4 | A-R,<br>FB (self, other) | .56<br>(.46) | | | |

[a] these correlations include only one FB task

Legend:　WM　Working Memory　　　Inh. Bat.　Inhibitory Test Battery
　　　　　CS　Cardsorting　　　　　　Cog. Flex.　Cognitive Flexibility
　　　　　FB　False Belief　　　　　　A-R　　　　Appearance–Reality

colour and form as in the original version), which led to the unexpected effect that colour dominated, so that children who switched from first sorting according to size had no, or just a little, difficulty switching to colour. Hence, only for that half that had to switch from colour to size did the test pose a serious executive challenge. For that half of the sample there was the expected correlation between false belief and card sorting, however due to the halving of the sample this was not significant. There was a stronger correlation between false belief and the knee-jerk test. For the halved sample who had to sort first by colour then size (n = 17) this happened to be even stronger, and the result remained significant even after partialling out the performance on the card-sorting test.

In a follow-up study (Perner *et al.* 1998) 57 children (12 children whose knee-jerk reflex could not be elicited) from three to six years were given the same tests as in the first study. However, the traditional card-sorting task with colour and form was used and an inhibition test after Luria's hand game was added (after mimicking the experimenter's sequence of flat hand–fist–flat hand– . . . etc. the children were instructed to always produce the opposite hand shape, i.e. make a fist when the experimenter puts the flat hand down, etc.). When scoring children as passing if they performed perfectly (five of five trials) on the EF tasks then all four tasks were of comparable difficulty: between 52% to 59% of children passed.

Table 7.4 presents the analysis of the relationship between tasks in terms of how much variance of false-belief performance is explained by the various other tasks. The first two rows of Table 7.4 show a (by now) familiar picture, namely that all these tasks are strong predictors of performance on the false-belief task: age and verbal intelligence (the KABC test) explains a quarter of the variance. Also the two EF tasks explain both highly significant amounts of variance. The knee-jerk reflex test, however, explains a good half of all the variance, considerably more than the EF tasks. The second row shows that after introducing age and verbal intelligence into the model each of the two EF tasks and the knee-jerk reflex still explain a significant amount of additional variance. The third row now enters new terrain. When the knee-jerk reflex is introduced into the model then the additional variance explained by the EF tasks sinks to below 10%, whereas if the two EF tasks are introduced first, understanding the knee-jerk reflex still explains a respectable 14% of the variance of false-belief test performance.

This pattern of results clearly suggests that the conceptual advance of understanding the causal significance of mental states reflected in the relationship between false-belief task and knee-jerk reflex task cannot be explained with executive components. For why would this relationship survive when all variance due to executive problems has been accounted for? Moreover, since the knee-jerk reflex task does not contain any obvious executive component or any conditional reasoning requirements, it is likely

**Table 7.4.** Percent of Variance of false-belief performance explained by last factor in model. SPSS logistic regression with Nagelkerke's $R^2$. Data from Perner *et al.* (1998)

| Initial factors in model | Last factor added to model | | | |
|---|---|---|---|---|
| | age + KABC | KR | CS | HG |
| none | 25.5** | 55.8** | 41.4** | 20.3** |
| Age + KABC | — | 30.4** | 21.6** | 12.3* |
| + KneeReflex | — | — | 8.4* | 5.2* |
| + CardSort | — | 17.0** | — | 6.5* |
| + HandGame | — | 23.3** | 15.8* | — |
| + HG + CS | — | 14.0** | — | — |

Legend:  KABC   verbal intelligence test        CS   card sorting (Zelazo *et al.* 1996)
              KR      knee-jerk reflex test              HG   Luria's handgame

that the conceptual advance (after age and verbal intelligence) accounts for 30% of the FB variance and most of the covariance of FB with EF tasks. Less than 10% might be attributable to problems of executive control or conditional reasoning that the knee-jerk reflex task cannot account for. Consequently, these data speak clearly against T5 (executive components in ToM tests) and T3 (doubly embedded conditionals) as accounts of the observed developmental relationship between ToM and EF performance. At best, these theories can account for a minor part of the relationship.

## EVALUATION OF THEORIES

Since substantial data on the relationship between ToM and EF are available only for the kind of tasks (e.g. false-belief, inhibitory control) that develop around the age of four years we restrict our evaluation to this aspect. Overall, the evidence from pathology suggests that there is a clear link between ToM deficits and EF problems (e.g. autism) and that in normal development progress on ToM is paralleled by increases in executive control. In short, the theories clearly have a subject matter to explain.

### (T1) Theory of mind development improves self-control

Pros:  • There is a principled explanation for why ToM development at the level of false-belief understanding should link to inhibitory executive control (Perner 1998).

• Most children with known ToM deficit (autism) are also severely impaired on EF (Ozonoff *et al.* 1991)

• Normal ToM development and EF development correlate, and this correlation is largely explained by understanding the knee-jerk reflex which, by hypothesis, taps the relevant understanding of the causal efficacy of mental states (Perner *et al.* 1998).

• Simple planning seems to depend on false-belief understanding (Bischof-Köhler 1998).

Cons:  • The theory needs to be made more specific about particular EF tests and their precise executive demands.

• A single autistic child (Baron-Cohen and Robertson 1995) has been documented to have failed several ToM tasks but succeeded on EF tasks. Three children with Williams or Prader–Willi Syndrome had more problems on ToM tasks than on EF tasks (Tager-Flusberg *et al.* 1997).

Defence: Single cases are difficult to evaluate as to whether they provide an existence proof that EF is possible in the absence of ToM or whether there were problems assessing the presence of a ToM. In general, arguments based on relative difficulty suffer from a lack of absolute standards of difficulty.

## (T2) Action monitoring is necessary for developing a theory of mind

Pros: • There are principled and plausible considerations of how EF deficits should lead to ToM deficits (Russell 1996; Pacherie 1998).

• The available findings on normal development are compatible with this position.

Cons: • The theory needs to be made more specific about which EF deficits lead to which ToM deficits.

• Clinical groups known for their EF problems, e.g. Tourette's Syndrome, do not show any ToM deficit (Baron-Cohen *et al.* 1997).

• Six children with Williams or Prader–Willi Syndrome had clear problems on EF without any problems on ToM tasks (Tager-Flusberg *et al.* 1997).

• Children understand false belief before they can engage in simple planning (Bischof-Köhler 1998).

Defence: There are no studies showing EF problems without ToM deficit on the same sample of people with Tourette's Syndrome. Arguments based on relative difficulty suffer from lack of absolute standards for comparing difficulty.

## (T3) Conditional reasoning as a common functional component

Pros: • Physiological evidence shows that brain structures involved in ToM and EF are also involved in conditional reasoning problems.

Cons: • Structural analysis of tasks (especially ToM tasks) is too unconstrained so that contradictory analyses are easily possible (see 'Theories').

• If a particular analysis is chosen by stipulation then there are grossly divergent developmental schedules for tasks of the same structure (e.g. false belief at four years, Repacholi and Gopnik's (1997) task at eighteen months).

• Dissociation of EF and ToM in children with Williams or Prader-Willi Syndrome (Tager-Flusberg *et al.* 1997).

• Performance on knee-jerk reflex task (no evident if-if-then structure) accounts for most of the correlation between false-belief and EF tasks (Perner *et al.* 1998).

## (T4) Common brain regions

Pros: • All the recent brain imaging evidence that there is on ToM points to regions that are also involved in EF.

Cons: • There are no real data speaking against the possibility that developmental and psychopathological correlations between EF and ToM are due to common brain structures. Rather, the problem lies in a weakness of behaviourally testable predictions. Unless the theory is restricted to claiming '*identical* brain structures', and not just partially overlapping, then any kind of task dissociation remains compatible with this theory. Only firmer and more complete physiological evidence would help.

## (T5) Executive component in theory of mind tests

Pros:  • There is a sizeable executive demand in deceptive pointing (Carlson *et al.* in press; Russell *et al.* 1991).

  • There may be a small EF component in the false-belief task (Perner *et al.* 1998).

Cons:  • The possible EF component in the false-belief task can only be minor since the knee-jerk reflex task accounts for most of the common variance between FB and EF (Perner *et al.* 1998).

  • The FB-prediction task (which has been claimed to have a particularly strong EF demand) is not more difficult and does not show any greater correlation with inhibition tasks than the FB-explanation task (Hughes 1998).

  • When children do not know the object's real location in the FB-prediction task the executive demand should be considerably reduced but performance is still not better (Robinson and Beck, in press).

## CONCLUSIONS

The position (T1) that ToM is a prerequisite for executive control (EF) should be taken seriously. It provides the best fit to existing data.

It seems difficult, though, and counterintuitive, to accept this conclusion. We think that this is so, because it is natural to assume that EF is a more basic ability, something that characterises the workings of our cognitive machinery which is prerequisite for the more esoteric enterprises like building a theory of mind. This argument reminds us of memory, where it has seemed evident that storage and retrieval of single events are basic and abstraction to general regularities requires higher cognitive capacities. It now looks like reality is upside-down (a point we owe to Bob Lockhart many years ago): the more basic process is to generalise over single instances and the memory of specific episodes requires more abstract processes including, perhaps, something as esoteric as a theory of mind (Perner, in press). Executive functioning may be similar: executive control, too, may require a theory of mind.

By and large, the reviewed data provide good evidence that there is a substantial and direct relationship between ToM and EF development (T1 and T2). It is not mediated to any substantial degree by conditional reasoning ability (T3) or methodological features of ToM assessment techniques (T5). Perhaps the data are somewhat more favourable for T1 (EF requires a ToM) than T2 (ToM depends on EF). However, unless one wants to follow Leslie (1987, 1994) in assuming that a maturing module provides us with a ready made ToM, then it would be but natural that a developing ToM needs the data of one's own intentions to succeed. Hence, any EF impairment in editing one's own intentions should develop into a ToM deficit (T2) as much as a ToM deficit should result in executive dysfunction (T1).

## Acknowledgements

Our deepest gratitude goes to Simon Baron-Cohen, Doris Bischof-Köhler, Claire Hughes, Francesca Happé, Lou Moses, Jim Russell, Kate Sullivan, and Helen Tager-Flusberg for directing us to and providing us with relevant literature.

## Notes

1. Mayes *et al.* (1996) tested children twice on three different false-belief tasks, asking three questions on each test. Retest reliability was assessed within age group for each individual question and task separately, yielding an average $\Phi = .35$, for n = 12 per group. That is, for each reliability test children were classified either as passing or failing. There was no possibility for a child to score as transitional, i.e. as giving correct answers only occasionally. This opportunity might lead to higher reliability measures.
2. This claim rests on an extrapolation from their reported data in their Experiment 2. Each child had several prediction and explanation tasks of which 30 (of 79) were spontaneous and 49 came after prompting. Sixteen children were classified as passing explanation. Extrapolating from the above 30/79 ratio, about 6 children (of 16 correct explainers) would have been classified as *spontaneous* explainers. Assuming that these would also be able to predict correctly, this would leave one child (since only 5 children actually did give correct predictions) who might have explained spontaneously but did not predict correctly. This one child would balance the one classified as predicting correctly without explaining correctly, leaving NO evidence that children are better at spontaneous explanation than at prediction.
3. Courtesy of Kate Sullivan, who provided us with more detail on their data than was available in their publication, we could reconstruct these clear cases of dissociation.
4. We want to point out that the knee-jerk reflex is sometimes difficult to elicit in children of this age. Hence only in 37 of the 54 cases was it possible to get data on understanding the knee-jerk reflex.

## REFERENCES

Baddeley, A. (1996). Exploring the central executive. *The Quarterly Journal of Experimental Psychology*, **49A**(1), 5–28.

Baddeley, A., and Hitch, G. J. (1974). Working memory. In *The psychology of learning and motivation*, Vol. 8, (ed. G. H. Bower), pp. 47–89. Academic Press, New York.

Baron-Cohen, S. (1991). Do people with autism understand what causes emotion? *Child Development*, **62**, 385–95.

Baron-Cohen, S. (1995). *Mindblindness: an essay on autism and theory of mind*. MIT Press, Cambridge, MA.

Baron-Cohen, S. and Robertson, M. (1995). Children with either autism, Gilles de la Tourette syndrome or both: mapping cognition to specific syndromes. *Neurocase*, **1**, 101–104.

Baron-Cohen, S. and Swettenham, J. (1997). Theory of mind in autism: its relationship to executive function and central coherence. In *Handbook of autism*, (ed. D. J. Cohen and F. Volkma), pp. 88093. Wiley.

Baron-Cohen, S., Leslie, A. M. and Frith, U. (1985). Does the autistic child have a 'theory of mind'? *Cognition*, **21**, 37–46.

Baron-Cohen, S., Ring, H., Moriarty, J., Schmitz, B., Costa, D. and Ell, P. (1994). The brain basis of the theory of mind: the role of the orbitofrontal region. *British Journal of Psychiatry*, **165**, 640–9.

Baron-Cohen, S., Cox, A., Baird, G., Swettenham, J., Nightingale, N., Morgan, K., Drew, A. and Charman, T. (1996). Psychological markers in the detection of autism in infancy in a large population. *British Journal of Psychiatry*, **168**, 158–63.

Baron-Cohen, S., Jolliffe, T., Mortimore, C. and Robertson, M. (1997). Another advanced test of theory of mind: evidence from very high functioning adults with autism or asperger syndrome. *Journal of Child Psychology and Psychiatry*, **38**(7), 813–22.

Bartsch, K. and Wellman, H. M. (1989). Young children's attribution of action to beliefs and desires. *Child Development*, **60**, 946–64.

Bartsch, K. and Wellman, H. M. (1995). *Children talk about the mind*. Oxford University Press.

Bianchi, L. (1922). *The mechanism of the brain and the function of the frontal lobes*. Livingstone, Edinburgh.

Bischof-Köhler, D. (1988). Über den Zusammenhang von Empathie und der Fähigkeit, sich im Spiegel zu erkennen. *Schweizerische Zeitschrift für Psychologie*, **47**, 147–59.

Bischof-Köhler, D. (1998). *Projekt zur Untersuchung der spezifischen menschlichen Verhaltens-organisation: Zeitrepräsentation, theory of mind und Motivationsmanagement bei vierjährigen*. Unpublished manuscript, University of Munich.

Carlson, S. M. (1997). Individual Differences in Inhibitory Control and Children's Theory of Mind. Poster presented at the Biennial Meeting of the Society for Research in Child Development. Washington, DC, April.

Carlson, S. M., Moses, L. J. and Hix, H. R. (1998). The role of inhibitory processes in young children's difficulties with deception and false belief. *Developmental Psychology*.

Carruthers, P. (1996). *Language, thought and consciousness. An essay in philosophical psychology*. Cambridge University Press.

Case, R. (1985). *Intellectual development: birth to adulthood*. Academic Press, Orlando, Florida.

Damasio, A. R. and Maurer, R. G. (1978). A neurological model for childhood autism. *Archives of Neurology*, **35**, 777–86.

Davis, H. L. and Pratt, C. (1995). The development of children's theory of mind: the working memory explanation. Special issue: cognitive development. *Australian Journal of Psychology*, **47**(1), 25–31.

Diamond, A. (1985). Development of the ability to use recall to guide action, as indicated by infants' performance on AB. *Child Development*, **56**, 868–83.

Diamond, A. (1991). Frontal lobe involvement in cognitive changes during the first year of life. In *Brain maturation and cognitive development*, (ed. K. R. Gibson and A. C. Peterson), pp. 127–80. Aldine De Gruyter, New York.

Diamond, A., Prevor, M. B., Callender, G., and Druin, D. P. (1997). Prefrontal cortex cognitive deficits in children treated early and continuously for PKU. *Monographs of the Society for Research in Child Development*, **62**, (Serial No. 4).

Duncan, J. (1986). Disorganisation of behaviour after frontal lobe damage. *Cognitive Neuro-psychology*, **3**, 271–90.

Duncan, J. (1995). Attention, intelligence, and the frontal lobe. In *The cognitive neurosciences*, (ed. M. S. Gazzaniga), pp. 721–33. MIT Press, Cambridge, MA.

Evans, W. F. (1973). *The stage IV error in Piaget's theory of object concept development: an investigation of the role of activity.* Unpublished dissertation proposal, University of Huston.

Flavell, J. H., Flavell, E. R., and Green, F. L. (1983). Development of the appearance–reality distinction. *Cognitive Psychology*, **15**, 95–120.

Fletcher, P. A., Happé, F., Frith, U., Baker, S., Dolan, R., Frakowiak, R. S. J., *et al.* (1995). Other minds in the brain: a functional imaging study of the 'theory of mind'. *Cognition*, **57**, 109–28.

Frith, C. D. (1992). *The cognitive neuropsychology of schizophrenia.* Lawrence Erlbaum Associates, Hillsdale, NJ.

Frye, D. Theory of mind, domain specificity, and reasoning. In *Children's reasoning and the mind*, (ed. P. Mitchell and K. J. Riggs). Psychology Press, Hove. (In press.)

Frye, D., Zelazo, P. D. and Palfai, T. (1995). Theory of mind and rule-based reasoning. *Cognitive Development*, **10**, 483–527.

German, T. P. (1995). Children's explanation of action: desires versus beliefs in theory of mind. Unpublished doctoral dissertation. University of London.

Gerstad, C. L., Hong, Y. J. and Diamond, A. (1994). The relationship between cognition and action: performance of children three-and-a-half to seven years on a Stroop-like day-night task. *Cognition*, **53**, 129–53.

Goel, V., Grafman, J., Sadato, N. and Hallett, M. (1995). Modelling other minds. *NeuroReport*, **6**, 1741–6.

Gopnik, A. and Astington, J. W. (1988). Children's understanding of representational change and its relation to the understanding of false belief and the appearance–reality distinction. *Child Development*, **59**, 26–37.

Gordon, A. C. L. and Olson, D. R. (1998). The relation between acquisition of a theory of mind and the capacity to hold in mind. *Journal of Experimental Child Psychology*, **68**(1), 70–83.

Gratch, G. (1964). Response alternation in children: a developmental study of orientations to uncertainty. *Vita Humana*, **7**, 49–60.

Griffith, E. M., Pennington, B. F., Wehner, E., and Rogers, S. (1998). *Executive functions in young children with autism.* Unpublished manuscript, University of Denver.

Hadwin, J. and Perner, J. (1991). Pleased and surprised: children's cognitive theory of emotion. *British Journal of Developmental Psychology*, **9**, 215–34.

Halsband, U. and Passingham, R. (1985). Premotor cortex and the conditions for movements in monkeys (*Macaca mulatta*). *Behavioral Brain Research*, **240**, 368–72.

Happé, F. (1994). *Autism: an introduction to psychological theory.* Harvard University Press, Cambridge, MA.

Happé, F., Ehlers, S., Fletcher, P., Frith, U., Johansson, M., Gillberg, C., Dolan, R., Frackowiak, R. and Frith, C. (1996). 'Theory of mind' in the brain. Evidence from a PET scan study of Asperger syndrome. *NeuroReport*, **8**, 197–201.

Harris, P. L. (1973). Perseverative errors in search by young infants. *Child Development*, **44**, 28–33.

Harris, P. L. (1989). Object permanence in infancy. In *Infant development*, (ed. A. Slater and G. Bremner), pp. 103–21. Lawrence Erlbaum Associates, Hove, UK.

Harris, P. L. (1993). Pretending and planning. In *Understanding other minds: perspectives from autism*, (ed. S. Baron-Cohen, H. Tager-Flusberg, and D. J. Cohen), pp. 283–304. Oxford University Press.

Hogrefe, J., Wimmer, H., and Perner, J. (1986). Ignorance versus false belief: a developmental lag in attribution of epistemic states. *Child Development*, **57**, 567–82.

Holmes, H. A., Black, C., and Miller, S. A. (1996). A cross-task comparison of false belief understanding in a head start population. *Journal of Experimental Child Psychology*, **63**, 263–85.

178   *Understanding other minds*

Hughes, C. (1998). Executive functions in preschoolers: links with theory of mind and verbal ability. *British Journal of Developmental Psychology*, **16**, 233–53.

Hughes, C. and Russell, J. (1993). Autistic children's difficulty with mental disengagement from an object: its implication for theories of autism. *Developmental Psychology*, **29**, 498–510.

Jeannerod, M. (1997). *The cognitive neuroscience in action*. Blackwell Publishers Ltd., Oxford.

Kagan, J. (1981). *The second year*. Harvard University Press, Cambridge, MA.

Landers, W. F. (1971). Effects of differential experience on infant's performance in a Piagetian stage IV object–concept task. *Developmental Psychology*, **5**, 48–54.

Lang, B. (1997). *Das kindliche Verständnis von Intentionen und Selbstkontrolle. Eine Untersuchung über die Zusammenhänge spezieller menschlicher Reifungsprozesse.* Unpublished thesis. University of Salzburg.

Leslie, A. M. (1987). Pretense and representation: the origins of 'theory of mind'. *Psychological Review*, **94**, 412–26.

Leslie, A. M. (1994). Pretending and believing: issues in the theory of ToMM. *Cognition*, **50**, 211–38.

Luria, A. (1966). *Higher cortical functions in man*. Basic Books, New York.

Mayes, L. C., Klin, A., Tercyak, K. P., Cicchetti D. V. and Cohen, D. J. (1996). Testretest reliability for false-belief tasks. *Journal of Child Psychology and Psychiatry*, **37**(3), 313–9.

Mazoyer, B. M., Tzourio, N., Frak, V., Syrota, A., Murayama, N., Levier, O., *et al.* (1993). The cortical representation of speech. *Journal of Cognitive Neuroscience*, **5**, 467–79.

McEvoy, R. E., Rogers, S. J. and Pennington, B. F. (1993). Executive function and social communication deficits in young autistic children. *Journal of Child Psychology and Psychiatry*, **34**, 563–78.

Meltzoff, A. N. (1995). Understanding the intentions of others: re-enactment of intended acts by eighteen-month-old children. *Developmental Psychology*, **31**, 838–50.

Mitchell, P. (1996). *Acquiring a conception of mind: a review of psychological research and theory.* Psychology Press, East Sussex.

Mitchell, P. and Lacohée, R. (1991). Children's early understanding of false belief. *Cognition*, **39**, 107–27.

Moore, C., Angelopoulos, M., and Bennett, P. The role of movement in the development of joint visual attention. *Infant Behavior and Development.* (In press.)

Moses, L. J. and Flavell, J. H. (1990). Inferring false beliefs from actions and reactions. *Child Development*, **61**, 929–45.

Norman, D. A. and Shallice, T. (1980). Attention to Action. Willed and automatic control of behavior. Centre for Human Information Processing Technical Report No. 99. Reprinted in revised form in *Consciousness and self-regulation*, Vol. 4, (ed. R. J. Davidson, G. E. Schwartz, and D. Shapiro), pp. 1–18. Plenum, New York, 1986.

Oswald, D. P. and Ollendick, T. (1989). Role taking and social competence in autism and mental retardation. *Journal of Autism and Developmental Disorders*, **19**, 119–28.

Ozonoff, S., Pennington, B. F., and Rogers, S. J. (1991). Executive function deficits in high-functioning autistic children: relationship to theory of mind. *Journal of Child Psychology and Psychiatry*, **32**, 1081–105.

Pacherie, E. (1998). Motor-images, self consciousness and autism. In *Autism as an executive disorder*, (ed. J. Russell), pp. 215–55. Oxford University Press.

Pascual-Leone, J. (1970). A mathematical model for the transition rule in Piaget's developmental stages. *Acta Psychologica* , **32**, 301–45.

Passingham, R. (1978). Information about movements in monkeys (Macaca mulatta) with lesions of dorsal prefrontal cortex. *Brain Research*, **152**, 313–28.

Passingham, R. (1993). *The frontal lobes and voluntary action.* Oxford University Press, New York.

Pennington, B. F. (1994). The working memory function of the prefrontal cortices: implications for developmental and individual differences in cognition. In *The development of future oriented processes,* (ed. M. M. Haith, J. Benson, R. Roberts, and B. F. Pennington), pp. 243–89. University of Chicago Press.

Pennington, B. F. (1997). Dimensions of executive functions in normal and abnormal development. In *Development of the prefrontal cortex: evolution neurobiology, and behaviour,* (ed. N. Krasnegor, R. Lyon, and P. Goldman-Rakic). Brooks Publishing Co., Baltimore, MD.

Pennington, B. F. and Ozonoff, S. (1996). Executive Functions and developmental psychopathology. *Journal of Child Psychology and Psychiatry,* **37**(1), 51–87.

Pennington, B. F., Rogers, S., Bennetto, L., Griffith, E. M., Reed, D. T. and Shyu V. (1998). Validity tests of the executive dysfunction hypothesis of autism. In *Autism as an executive disorder,* (ed. J. Russell). Oxford University Press.

Perner, J. (1991). *Understanding the representational mind.* Bradford Books, MIT Press, Cambridge, MA.

Perner, J. (1995). The many faces of belief: reflections on Fodor's and the child's theory of mind. *Cognition,* **57**, 241–69.

Perner, J. (1998). The meta-intentional nature of executive functions and theory of mind. In *Language and Thought,* (ed. P. Carruthers and J. Boucher), pp. 270–83. Cambridge University Press.

Perner, J. Memory and theory of mind. In *The Oxford Handbook of memory,* (ed. E. Tulving and F. I. M. Craik). Oxford University Press. (In press.)

Perner, J., Leekam, S. R. and Wimmer, H. (1987). Three-year olds' difficulty with false belief: the case for a conceptual deficit. *British Journal of Developmental Psychology,* **5**, 125–37.

Perner, J., Lang, B. and Stummer, S. (1998). *Theory of mind and executive function: which depends on which.* Unpublished manuscript, University of Salzburg.

Petrides, M. (1982). Motor conditional associative-learning after selective prefrontal lesion in the monkey. *Behavioral Brain Research,* **5**, 407–13.

Petrides, M. (1985). Deficits in nonspatial conditional associative learning after periarcuate lesions in the monkey. *Behavioral Brain Research,* **16**, 95–101.

Petrides, M. (1991*a*). Monitoring of selections of visual stimuli and the primate frontal cortex. *Proceedings of the Royal Social London B,* **246**, 293–8.

Petrides, M. (1991*b*). Functional specialisation within the dorsolateral frontal cortex for serial order memory. *Proceedings of the Royal Social London B,* **246**, 299–306.

Petrides, M., Alivisatos, B., Evans, A. C. and Meyer, E. (1993). Dissociation of human mid-dorsolateral from posterior dorsolateral frontal cortex in memory processing. *Proceedings of the National Academy of Science,* **90**, 873–7.

Piaget, J. (1945/1962). *Play, dreams, and imitation in childhood.* W. W. Norton, New York.

Reed, M., Pien, D. L. and Rothbart, M. K. (1984). Inhibitory self-control in preschool children. *Merrill Palmer Quarterly,* **30**, 131–47.

Repacholi, B. M. and Gopnik, A. (1997). Early reasoning about desires: evidence from fourteen- and eighteen-month-olds. *Developmental Psychology,* **33**(1), 12–21.

Robinson, E. J. and Beck. What is difficult about counterfactual reasoning. In *Children's reasoning and the mind,* (ed. P. Mitchell and K. J. Riggs). Psychology Press, Hove, UK. (In press.)

Robinson, E. J. and Mitchell, P. (1995). Masking of children's early understanding of the representational mind: backwards explanation versus prediction. *Child Development,* **66**, 1022–39.

Rumsey, J. M. (1985). Conceptual problem-solving in highly verbal, nonretarded autistic men. *Journal of Autism and Developmental Disorders*, **15**, 23–36.

Russell, J. (1996). *Agency. Its role in mental development*. Erlbaum (UK) Taylor and Francis Ltd, Hove, UK.

Russell, J. (1998). How executive disorders can bring about an inadequate 'theory of mind'. In *Autism as an executive disorder*, (ed. J. Russell), pp. 256–99. Oxford University Press, Oxford.

Russell, J., Mauthner, N., Sharpe, S. and Tidswell, T. (1991). The 'windows task' as a measure of strategic deception in preschoolers and autistic subjects. *British Journal of Developmental Psychology*, **9**, 331–49.

Russell, J., Jarrold, C. and Potel, D. (1994). What makes strategic deception difficult for children the deception or the strategy? *British Journal of Developmental Psychology*, **12**, 301–14.

Samuels, M. C., Brooks, P. J. and Frye, D. (1996). Strategic game playing in children through the windows task. *British Journal of Developmental Psychology*, **14**, 159–72.

Shallice, T. (1988). *From neuropsychology to mental structure*. Cambridge University Press.

Sheffield, E. G., Sosa, B. B. and Hudson J. A. (1993). Narrative complexity and two- and three-year-olds' understanding of false belief. Paper presented at the 60th Anniversary Meeting of the Society for Research in Child Development, New Orleans, March.

Shultz, T. R., Wells, D., and Sarda, M. (1980). The development of the ability to distinguish intended actions from mistakes, reflexes, and passive movements. *The British Journal of Social and Clinical Psychology*, **19**, 301–10.

Sodian, B. and Thoermer, C. (1998). Do one-year-old infants represent human actions as guided by perception? Poster presented at the XIth International Conference on Infant Studies, Atlanta, GA, April 2–5.

Spelke, E. S., Phillips, A. and Woodward, A. L. (1995). Infant's knowledge of object motion and human action. In *Causal cognition. A multidisciplinary debate* (ed. D. Sperber, D. Premack, and A. J. Premack), pp. 44–78. Oxford.

Tager-Flusberg, H., Sullivan, K. and Boshart, J. (1997). Executive functions and performance on false belief tasks. *Developmental Neuropsychology*, **13**, 487–93.

Wehner, E. and Rogers, S. (1994). Attachment relationships of autistic and developmentally delayed children. Paper presented at the bi-monthly meeting of the Developmental Psycho-biology Research Group, Denver, CO.

Wellman, H. M. (1990). *The child's theory of mind*. Bradford Books, MIT Press, Cambridge, MA.

Wellman, H. M. and Bartsch, K. (1988). Young children's reasoning about beliefs. *Cognition*, **30**, 239–77.

Wellman, H. M. and Woolley, J. D. (1990). From simple desires to ordinary beliefs: the early development of everyday psychology. *Cognition*, **35**, 245–75.

Wellman, H. M., Cross, D. and Bartsch, K. (1987). Infant search and object permanence: a meta-analysis of the A-not-B error. *Monographs of the Society for Research in Child Development*, **51**, (Serial No. 214).

Welsh, M. C. and Pennington, B. F. (1988). Assessing frontal lobe functioning in children: views from developmental psychology. *Developmental Neuropsychology*, **4**, 199–230.

Welsh, M. C., Pennington, B. F., and Groisser, D. B. (1991). A normative-developmental study of executive function: A window on prefrontal function in children. *Developmental Neuropsychology*, **7**, 131–49.

Wimmer, H. (1989). Common-sense Mentalismus und Emotion: einige entwicklungs-psychologische Implikationen. In *Denken und Fühlen*, (ed. E. Roth), pp. 56–66. Springer Verlag, Berlin.

Wimmer, H. and Gschaider, A. Children's understanding of belief: Why it is important to understand what happened. In *Children's reasoning and the mind*, (ed. P. Mitchell and K. J. Riggs). Psychology Press, Hove, UK. (In press.)

Wimmer, H. and Mayringer, H. (1998) False belief understanding in young children: explanations do not develop before predictions. *International Journal of Behavioral Development.*

Wimmer, H. and Perner, J. (1983). Beliefs about beliefs: representation and constraining function of wrong beliefs in young children's understanding of deception. *Cognition,* 13, 103–28.

Yarrow, M. R. and Waxler, C. Z. (1975). The emergence and functions of prosocial behavior in young children. Paper presented at the Biennial Meeting of the Society for Research in Child Development, Denver, CO.

Yirmiya, N., Solomonica-Levi, D., Shulman, C. and Pilowsky, T. (1996). Theory of mind abilities in individuals with autism, Down syndrome, and mental retardation of unknown etiology: the role of age and intelligence. *Journal of Child Psychology and Psychiatry and Allied Disciplines,* 37, 1003–14.

Yuill, N. (1984). Young children's coordination of motive and outcome in judgements of satisfaction and morality. *British Journal of Developmental Psychology,* 2, 73–81.

Yuill, N., Perner, J., Pearson, A., Peerbhoy, D. and van den Ende, J. (1996). Children's changing understanding of wicked desires: from objective to subjective and moral. *British Journal of Developmental Psychology,* 14, 457–75.

Zaitchik, D. (1991). Is only seeing really believing? Sources of the true belief in the false belief task. *Cognitive Development,* 6, 91–103.

Zelazo, P. D. and Frye, D. (1996). Cognitive complexity and control: a theory of the development of deliberate reasoning and intentional action. In *Language structure, discourse and access to consciousness*, (ed. M. Stamenov). John Benjamins, Amsterdam and Philadelphia.

Zelazo, P. D. and Reznick, J. S. (1991). Age-related asynchrony of knowledge and action. *Child Development,* 62, 719–35.

Zelazo, P. D., Frye, D., and Rapus, T. (1996). An age-related dissociation between knowing rules and using them. *Cognitive Development,* 11, 37–63.

# 8

# Pretending, imagery, and self-awareness in autism

PAUL L. HARRIS AND HILARY J. LEEVERS

In this chapter, we examine the idea that children with autism suffer from an impoverished imagination and lack awareness of their own mental states. Our starting point is the deficit in pretend play that Kanner included in his original description of the syndrome (Kanner 1943). We review evidence showing that although children with autism can engage in pretence and appear to understand its special logic, they do play in a restricted or stereotypic fashion. We then consider recent, longitudinal studies that have focused on the development of pretend play in the second year of life. When pretend play has not emerged by eighteen months, and is combined with social difficulties, notably problems in establishing joint attention, a subsequent diagnosis of autism is likely. However, evidence from older children shows that the problem with pretend play is not just a by-product of the social difficulties of children with autism. It is part of a deficit in generating or executing ideas. We go on to ask whether that deficit reflects: (i) a specific problem with ideas that involve the unreal or the impossible; or (ii) a more widespread problem of generating or executing even relatively prosaic ideas. We argue that children with autism are especially handicapped, not in dealing with the unreal images, but in dealing with novelty, especially when they must compose a sequence of actions with little guidance from the external environment or from previous habits. We then examine recent first person reports by adults with autistic symptoms in order to gain further clues into their inner life. We speculate that individuals with autism may experience a mental life that is primarily visual rather than verbal, and may therefore be helped to acknowledge that mental life if they are provided with pictorial rather than verbal indices. We consider the implications of this speculation for the development and education of children with autism.

## RESTRICTED PRETEND PLAY

When children with autism are left to their own devices to play with toys, they are less likely to engage in pretend play than relevant control groups—impaired or normally-developing children of the same verbal ability (Baron-Cohen 1987; Lewis and Boucher 1988; Sigman and Ungerer 1984). This restriction in pretend play should not be seen as an incapacity. If children with autism are given either a general prompt (e.g. the

experimenter presents some props, such as a car and a sho
these do? Show me what you can do with these?') or a more sp
the car in the garage'), they are likely to produce an appropriat
Indeed, when such prompts are provided, group differences betw
autism and controls decrease (Jarrold *et al.* 1996, Riguet *et al.* 19
Ungerer 1984; Experiment 1) and can even be eliminated (Charman and
1997; Gould 1986; Jarrold *et al.* 1996; Lewis and Boucher 1988, Experim
ability to engage in pretend play following prompting undermines Leslie
hypothesis that children with autism are incapable of understanding the peculia
of pretence (e.g. the use of object substitutes and the introduction of imaginary en
and properties). In hindsight, this intact capacity was already suggested by a pionee.
ing, epidemiological survey of early autistic behaviour. Wing (1978) found that
children who displayed two of Kanner's symptoms of autism—a lack of affective
social contact, and repetitive activities—also engaged in less pretend play than a
comparison group of mentally retarded children. Nevertheless, most of the children
with autistic symptoms were capable of at least 'stereotypic' pretend play once they
had attained a verbal age of twenty months.

In summary, experimental and epidemiological evidence shows that children with
autism engage in spontaneous pretend play less than normal children or children with
developmental delays. This difference reflects a restriction on their pretend play and
not an incapacity to pretend. Although their pretence remains limited, they are
capable of such imaginative behaviour when prompted. Below, we enquire more
carefully into the nature of that limitation. First, however, we review longitudinal
evidence showing that a delay in the emergence of pretend play can be an early
indicator of autism.

## LONGITUDINAL RESEARCH

A longitudinal study initiated by Baron-Cohen and his colleagues provides data on the
early emergence of pretend play (Baron-Cohen *et al.* 1992). Among a population of 41
children with an elevated risk of autism (i.e. children with an older, autistic sibling),
they identified 4 children who displayed three deficits at eighteen months: a lack of
pretend play, no protodeclarative pointing, and a failure to monitor other people's
gaze. All four children and no others later received a firm diagnosis of autism. By
contrast, none of the toddlers in a control group of children with developmental delay
showed a deficit on more than one of these items and none of these children went on
to receive a diagnosis of autism.

In a further longitudinal study, with a much larger sample (16 000 children), 12
infants were identified at eighteen months with the same triad of deficits (Baron-
Cohen *et al.* 1996). Again, there proved to be a link between that triad and a later
diagnosis of autism: 10 of the 12 infants were subsequently diagnosed as having autism
(and the remaining 2 were diagnosed as showing a developmental delay). On the other
hand, children who lacked pretend play, or protodeclarative pointing, or both, but did

show any difficulty in gaze monitoring, were likely to receive a diagnosis of ᵥelopmental delay but not of autism.

A sub-set of this large sample was followed up at twenty months (Charman *et al.* ₁997). The children comprised three groups: an autistic group who had displayed the characteristic triad of deficits at eighteen months and who were subsequently diagnosed as having autism (N = 10); a group who had a deficit in play, pointing, or both, but not in gaze-monitoring, at eighteen months and who were developmentally delayed at twenty months, but did not have autism (N = 9); and a no-risk group of children without clinical problems (N = 19). In the testing session at twenty months, differences between the autistic group and the two comparison groups were evident for pretence involving object substitution. In addition, the children with autism were much less likely than the other children to turn to look at an adult, both when an interesting object arrived on the scene and when the adult feigned distress.

Taken together, these three studies indicate that when a deficit in gaze monitoring at eighteen months is linked to a deficit in pointing and a delay in the onset of pretend play, there is a very high probability of a later diagnosis of autism. That probability is dramatically reduced among those eighteen-month-olds that have not yet displayed any pretend play but are nonetheless able to engage in joint attention (see Charman, this volume). In the next section, we consider in more detail the relationship between pretend play and sensitivity to social signals such as visual attention.

## FAILURE TO ATTEND TO SOCIAL SIGNALS OR FAILURE TO PRODUCE A PLAN?

Among normal children, pretend play is often a social activity. Toddlers engage in more sustained and more complex pretence when they play with an attachment figure such as the mother (Slade 1987). This is probably not because they mimic her pretend actions but because they make sense of what she is up to and respond appropriately. For example, when a play partner spills or pours pretend liquid, two-year-olds can engage in pretend wiping of the relevant 'wet' spot (Harris and Kavanaugh 1993, Experiment 5). They appear to grasp that a partner's pretend actions transform the make-believe situation and they 'reply' with a make-believe transformation of their own. In the course of the third year, children begin to engage in collaborative make-believe not just with adults but also with peers and siblings (Dunn and Dale 1984; Howes *et al.* 1989).

Granted that pretend play includes a social and collaborative element in the normal course of development, it is possible that the delayed emergence of pretence among children with autism, and its later impoverishment when it does eventually emerge, is simply a by-product of their social difficulties. Recall the evidence just reviewed: an early feature of the autistic syndrome is a tendency not to look at an adult. In so far as early pretend play is often scaffolded by a play partner who provides props, enacts various pretend gestures, and invites a pretend response, children who are less attentive to the social cues provided by a partner might produce few pretend responses. This speculation is consistent with the findings of Charman *et al.* (1997): None of the children with autism engaged in object substitution even after the adult had shown the child what to do (e.g. had 'fed' the doll with a brick and said: 'Let's pretend. Give the doll something to eat'). Indeed, a similar pattern emerged on an imitation task in which the experimenter modelled an action on an object: the children with autism often failed to pick up the object or failed to do what the adult had demonstrated. The neglect of social signals by children with autism might also explain why their pretend play remains stereotypic even when it does emerge. Perhaps they rarely attend to, and therefore do not gain from, the ideas supplied by other people, especially older siblings and parents. Alternatively, they may be less sensitive to the negative or uncooperative reactions that such stereotypic routines may arouse in other people, especially other children.

However, it is equally possible that the delayed and restricted pretend play of children with autism is not just a by-product of their tendency to ignore social signals, but a problem in its own right. More specifically, it can be construed as a problem in planning. As pretence develops in the normal child, it increasingly displays two related characteristics. First, any given act of pretend, such as pretend sleeping, is carried out with more and more independence from its usual context. The child pretends to go to sleep not just on the bed, but on a cushion, or in an imaginary castle (Piaget 1951). Thus, the child's pretend actions are guided by a plan that is internally generated; the actions are not triggered by cues in the environment. Second, episodes of pretence become more extended as a given theme is sustained in a consequential fashion. Thus, the planning that guides any given pretend episode becomes more autonomous and more elaborate. Arguably, children with autism are poor at this type of planning (Harris 1993). On this interpretation, although they can take up other people's suggestions, or engage in routine pretence with a given prop, they will have difficulty in producing or executing ideas for pretence on their own initiative.

How can we distinguish between these two possibilities? The first suggestion—that the limited pretend play of children with autism is only a by-product of their social difficulties—implies that if they were thrown back on their own resources, and asked to enact their own independent ideas for pretence, differences between children with autism and appropriate controls ought to be eliminated. In such a solitary environment, the tendency of children with autism to neglect or resist social signals ought not to handicap them any more than children in appropriate control groups. The second account, by contrast, implies that the limited initiative of children with autism would be especially obvious if they were asked to enact their own autonomous ideas for pretence, unaided by any form of social support. A simple but compelling experiment carried out by Jarrold *et al.* (1996) provides support for this second interpretation rather than the first. The experimenter started off by modelling some simple pretend actions, for example 'brushing' his teeth. Children were then asked what they could pretend to do. The number of different pretend actions that they managed to carry out over the six-minute test period was counted. The key finding was that children with autism produced such actions at a slower rate than either of the other two groups. On average, the children with autism produced 10 different actions over the test period whereas children in the normal group and a group with moderate learning difficulties managed around 16 and 18 respectively.[1] Because social interaction between experimenter and child was minimal in this test, the most plausible conclusion is that children with autism—independent of the social situation—are less fluent in either generating or executing ideas for pretence than the two control groups—notwithstanding an intact ability to engage in pretend as such. Admittedly, one might insist that the dysfluency of children with autism, even in this asocial situation, is a consequence of a long history of ignoring or failing to benefit from the support that is found in more routine, social situations. However, as we shall see below, children also display problems in less obviously collaborative activities such as drawing.

In sum, the evidence so far suggests that children with autism understand the logic of pretence, and can engage in pretend play, albeit with a delay in its emergence relative to normal children and even relative to impaired children matched for mental ability. Nonetheless, they are less fluent at generating or executing pretend plans. Granted that conclusion, we may try to dissect their lack of fertility in more detail. In particular, we may ask whether children with autism have a specific difficulty in generating or executing ideas of a given class or genre. For example, do they have a special difficulty with ideas that involve a radical departure from what is routinely the case? Alternatively, does their limited fertility extend to any type of idea, whether pedestrian or exotic? To assess these two possibilities, we examine recent research on children's drawings in some detail.

## DRAWING AND THE IMAGINATION

Because children with autism often have poor verbal ability, their drawings can provide a particularly helpful window on their imagination. Until recently, however, most research into the drawings of children and adults with autism has focused on the small minority who are exceptionally skilled artists (Mottron and Belleville 1993 1995; O'Connor and Hermelin 1987; Selfe 1983). The drawings that they produce are often highly accurate depictions based on immediate or recalled observation. Nevertheless, their drawings can also be more creative in content, and go beyond either observation or recollection. Nadia, a young girl with autism, drew many pictures based upon illustrations previously observed in a book but she also elaborated upon the originals and introduced a novel perspective (Selfe 1983). Thus, children with autism who have an exceptional drawing ability can visualise scenes or entities different from anything that they have seen. Is there evidence for such skills in autistic individuals with no special talent for drawing?

Recent evidence shows that the drawing abilities of most children with autism (i.e. those who have no outstanding talent for drawing) are similar to those of controls matched for non-verbal mental age (Charman and Baron-Cohen 1993; Eames and Cox 1994). Children with autism, like their ability-matched controls, are not limited to depicting a concurrently observed scene; they can also draw objects that are absent or occluded (Lewis and Boucher 1991). Indeed, their drawings are comparable to those of controls on a wide range of criteria: the overall spatial arrangement of the various objects depicted, the number of objects depicted, and the amount of detail included in a given drawing (Lewis and Boucher 1991). Thus, in terms of their ability to handle the drawing medium, children with autism, taken as a group, display a normal developmental profile. This is important because it means that if their drawings do turn out to be unusual in other respects, we can reasonably conclude that it is not because of any limitation in their drawing skills.

Scott and Baron-Cohen (1996) argue that despite their relatively intact drawing skills, the drawings of children with autism do differ in important ways from those of normally-developing or developmentally delayed children. In a provocative series of experiments, they asked children with autism to draw a picture of a real man or house and subsequently to draw a picture of an impossible man or house, one 'that does not exist'. In comparison to normal children and mentally handicapped children, children with autism were not impaired in drawing the real pictures—as we would expect from the evidence reviewed so far. On the other hand, although the majority of children in the control groups were successful in drawing an impossible man or house (e.g. a man with two heads or a house with a door in the roof), only one child in the autistic group was successful.[2] Subsequent questioning showed that all children, including those with autism, were able to identify the impossible picture from pairs composed of a possible and an impossible picture (e.g. a two- and a four-legged woman). Thus, the children with autism appeared to understand what a drawing of an impossible object might look like but could not produce such a picture themselves.

Scott and Baron-Cohen (1996) conclude that the difficulty shown by children with autism in drawing impossible entities can be traced back to a limitation in the process by which children initially generate or entertain an idea for such a drawing. They consider two different restrictions on that initial process. First, to visualise an impossible object, children might need to adopt an attitude of pretence towards the content of the image. An impairment in the capacity to adopt that attitude would render them unable to visualise images of unreal objects. Alternatively, children with autism might have difficulty in fusing or combining images in order to create a novel synthesis. Notwithstanding differences in their formulation, both of these proposed restrictions imply that children with autism have difficulty with a particular type of content, namely the generation of images of unreal or novel objects.

Nevertheless, Scott and Baron-Cohen (1996) appropriately point out that difficulty in drawing an impossible entity might arise at a later stage in the drawing process. Children might be able to visualise an impossible man or house but then have difficulty in constructing or executing the appropriate drawing plan. Even among normal children, drawing is restricted by the sometimes complex requirements of planning (Kosslyn *et al.* 1977; Thomas and Silk 1990) especially when the pictures are of novel objects (Berti and Freeman 1997). Thus, children with autism might have difficulty drawing impossible entities not because of an inability to create images of impossible entities but because of planning limitations. Scott and Baron-Cohen (1996) tested and rejected this latter hypothesis in a second experiment. They report that although children with autism were able to follow explicit instructions from the experimenter about how to draw a real object (e.g. a spider or a snake) they were not able to follow instructions about how to draw an unreal object (a two-headed monster with horns and big teeth). The children with autism either drew nothing, or resorted to drawing a normal person while apparently attempting the two-headed monster. Thus, even when the planning of the drawing was effectively in the hands of the experimenter, the children with autism still displayed an inability to draw an impossible entity. By implication, their difficulties are not based on planning limitations.

These findings are not definitive, however. Verbal instructions might have to be quite detailed to guide the drawing of a two-headed monster (certainly, more detailed than those for drawing a snake) and we have no reason to assume that children with autism are good at following detailed, verbal instructions. Indeed, because scoring was based only on children's finished drawings, we cannot be sure that execution was actually guided by the experimenter's instructions even when it was successful. Prior and Hoffman (1990) report that children with autism take a different approach to drawing from normal children: they copied a complex abstract figure (The Rey–Osterrieth Complex Figure) as quickly and accurately as controls, but they completed the elements of the figure in a different order, showing a less global approach. Different instructions may therefore be more appropriate for different children. To the extent that children ignored, or did not need, the experimenter's guidance in drawing the snake and the spider, but at the same time could not take advantage of that guidance in drawing the two-headed monster, a planning explanation remains viable.

We conducted an experiment to test whether children with autism would manage to draw impossible entities if planning demands were minimised, and indeed equivalent in many respects to those needed for drawing a possible entity (Leevers and Harris 1998). Three groups of sixteen children were given a series of drawing tasks: children with autism, children with moderate learning disabilities, and normal four-year-olds (the groups were matched to have a mean receptive verbal mental age of five years and the clinical groups were also matched for chronological age). First, children identified either the real or the impossible version from eight pairs of pictures differing in colour or pattern (e.g. a yellow versus a blue banana; a spotty versus a stripy bee). This was a test of their understanding of the terms 'real' and 'impossible'. It was also intended to clarify the meaning of the terms, if necessary, through corrective feedback. All three groups were equally accurate at selecting the designated picture from the pairs of real and impossible pictures. Indeed, overall performance was very high: 93% correct for the real pictures and 82% for the impossible pictures. Thus, there was no indication that the children required corrective feedback—performance was accurate from the outset in all three groups.

The children then completed four pairs of drawings, by adding a pattern or a colour, to make one real and one impossible version in every pair. For example, they were given two plain white zebras and asked to complete each by choosing between stripes or spots so as to make one real zebra and one impossible zebra. Before each completion, children answered a forced-choice question about how they were going to finish the drawing (e.g. they said whether they would draw spots or stripes). Children were very accurate at answering these forced-choice questions. In addition, all the children who answered a given forced-choice question correctly proceeded to complete the pictures as they had said that they would. Children who gave an incorrect answer to the forced-choice question were given corrective feedback, after which performance was at ceiling levels. Again, there were no group effects. In summary, on this admittedly simple drawing completion task, children were competent at selectively producing pictures of impossible entities as well as possible entities.

Thus, we found no signs of the deficit noted by Scott and Baron-Cohen (1996). However, they had asked children to produce impossible shapes (following the procedure of Karmiloff-Smith (1990)). By contrast, we had asked for impossible patterns or colours. Accordingly, to extend our findings, we asked children to complete pairs of drawings of a house without a door and a man without a head so that one looked real and one impossible. Completion of these pictures gave children an opportunity to introduce structural deviations in the impossible versions. Children unable to finish an impossible picture appropriately were given a specific suggestion of what to do (draw a door in the roof of the house or a two-headed man) but not detailed procedural instructions. Picture completions were judged, by two judges, to be real, impossible, or unsuccessful, using criteria roughly based on those of Karmiloff-Smith (1990) and Scott and Baron-Cohen (1996).

Performance was similar for the pictures of the man and the house, so the data were combined. Children were at ceiling in finishing off the real drawings by adding a door or head. They were also quite good at inventing their own solution for completing an impossible picture. There were 17 successful pictures in the normal group 19 in the MLD group, and 14 in the autistic group (out of a possible maximum of 32 in each group). If the pictures completed after specific instructions are included, these numbers increase to 30 in the normal group, 27 in the MLD group, and 22 in the autistic group. The majority of failures to complete the impossible pictures (75%) resulted in real pictures, especially prior to specific instruction. Again, there were no significant group effects on any aspects of this task. Indeed, some of the children with autism spontaneously implemented highly imaginative solutions to make the pictures look impossible. For example, spontaneous depictions of the impossible house included a house with the door projecting down onto the garden, a house with no door and a huge bed along the bottom, and a house with a clearly misshapen door. In making 'an impossible man' one child added an enlarged and stretched head, another child added many heads that spread down the man's arms, and another added just two detailed heads, facing each other. Figures 1 and 2 show two additional examples of real and impossible men drawn by two autistic boys. In the case of the impossible men, each boy offered a relevant gloss on what they had done. Thus, L. said, 'Two heads' and R. said, 'What about this man, this funny headed man. Is this the impossiblest man that has ever been?'

Taken together, these results appear to rule out the two proposals made by Scott and Baron-Cohen (1996). To the extent that the completion of an impossible drawing requires that children adopt a make-believe or pretend stance to the image that guides their completion, or fuse together otherwise possible images (zebra + spots) into an impossible hybrid (a spotted zebra), children with autism appear to be as competent as normal or learning-delayed children of the same mental age.

How then should we explain the difference in performance between the two sets of findings? We consider two alternative explanations of the discrepancy. First, recall that Scott and Baron-Cohen (1996) gave children examples of impossible pictures to

**Fig. 8.1.** Drawings of a real and an impossible man by L. aged thirteen years six months (receptive VMA = 5.0 years)

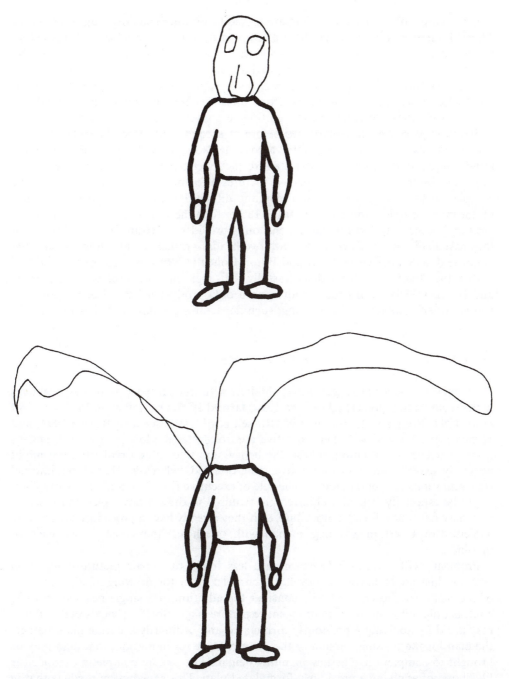

**Fig. 8.2.** Drawings of a real and an impossible man by R. aged nine years ten months (receptive VMA = 5.5 years)

recognise only after the children had attempted to produce such drawings themselves. Thus, children with autism may have attempted to draw 'impossible' pictures before having received any clarification of what was meant by an 'impossible' picture. By contrast, Leevers and Harris (1998) provided such clarification before the children attempted to draw. However, this argument only applies to the first experiment carried out by Scott and Baron-Cohen. By Experiment 2, children should have gained any necessary clarification from the recognition test given at the end of Experiment 1, which took place only a week or two before. A second, and more plausible, explanation is that planning demands differed across the two studies. Scott and Baron-Cohen (1996) required children to draw an entire picture from the beginning, whereas we required children only to complete a picture. The improved performance on the completion tasks suggests that it is planning difficulties that disrupted performance on the more complex whole-picture tasks, rather than the ability to imagine impossible entities. Further support for this conclusion is provided by Craig *et al.* (1998). When they asked children to draw 'a man with two heads'—rather than to draw 'a man that is not real' as requested by Scott and Baron-Cohen (1996)—the majority of children with autism (66.6%) performed successfully. This task, like the tasks used by Leevers and Harris (1998), means that children need only produce a limited departure from routine when completing the drawing; such departures are not needed at the outset.

DRAWING AND EXECUTIVE PROBLEMS

Accumulating evidence suggests that children with autism have particular problems with executive function (Hughes *et al.* 1994; Jarrold 1997; Ozonoff *et al.* 1991; Ozonoff *et al.* 1994; Prior and Hoffman 1990; Russell *et al.* 1991; see also Bishop 1993, and Happé 1994, for reviews). The executive control systems allow people to disengage from their current situation, inhibit the behaviours that the current situation might normally evoke, and plan alternative, goal-directed behaviours based on internal representations or mental models. The role of executive function in planning drawings might be especially critical if children are required to draw a novel picture for which they have never developed a procedure, or if they already have a procedure for drawing a picture in a certain way (e.g. a man with one head) that must be set aside or modified.

Problems with executive functions are less likely to impair picture completion because, instead of having to develop a complex plan for drawing all the elements of the picture, children need only consider the addition of a single new element. By contrast, planning the drawing of an entire picture is an effortful process that children may avoid by applying a previously-formulated and ordinarily accurate plan, namely the plan for the possible version of the picture. Once set in motion, that plan may be brought to completion. The low planning demands of picture completion reduce the likelihood of applying a previously-formulated plan. This explanation predicts that in so far as children with autism are limited by planning problems they will perform less effectively than normal children whether they are asked to draw a picture of a novel but possible entity or a picture of an impossible entity. To the extent that both entities are unfamiliar and have never been drawn before, they should reveal planning difficulties among children with autism to the same extent. Note that this proposal is consistent with the observation that under ordinary circumstances—when producing a familiar picture—the drawing skills of children with autism are comparable to those of normal children of the same mental age. It is also consistent with the repetitive quality noted in the artwork of some children with autism. Selfe (1983) conveys this quality, commenting on a group of high-functioning autistic artists, by stating that 'where the imagination is indicated, it is often used in a distorted or obsessive manner' (p. 153). Rather than resulting from obsession, the production of a series of highly repetitive drawings may reflect a limitation in the formulation of novel drawing plans.

In summary, although all the relevant evidence has not yet been gathered, we suspect that Scott and Baron-Cohen (1996) may be partially correct: the difficulties of children with autism are likely to be especially evident on certain types of drawing task and not others. At the same time, we offer a different analysis of those difficulties. Although the drawing skills of children with autism are usually in line with their mental age, they are likely have special difficulties if they must produce a *novel* sequence of actions, a sequence that has not been brought together previously so as to form a habit, and cannot be triggered currently by a succession of external cues. As described earlier, Jarrold *et al.* (1996) appear to have taxed this restricted capacity by asking children with autism to produce a novel sequence of pretend actions. Similarly, Scott and Baron-Cohen (1996) taxed that same restricted capacity by asking children with autism to produce a novel sequence of drawing actions from scratch. By contrast, in our drawing experiments, we minimised the problem of producing a novel sequence by asking children with autism to finish off a largely intact drawing. Similarly, Craig *et al.* (1998) asked children to add a single novel element to an otherwise routine drawing. If our analysis of the experimental results is correct, a further important conclusion follows: children with autism have an intact capacity for visualising familiar scenes or entities, and for re-combining elements to form a new image.

## IMAGINING NOVEL COMBINATIONS

Further evidence for the above conclusion is provided by psychometric analysis of the pattern of cognitive abilities displayed by children with autism. Reviewing this literature, Frith (1989) notes that whereas children with autism usually display a performance trough on subtests that demand a high degree of communicative competence, they display a performance peak on certain so-called spatial tasks. Notable among these is the Block Design task in which children must look at a two-dimensional pattern (e.g. a black diamond on a white square background) and use small black and white cubes to compose a three-dimensional match. It is difficult to see how any child could do well on this task if they lacked the ability to visualise how the two-dimensional target pattern might be broken down into fragments, and the blocks then used as stand-ins for the fragments in order to re-constitute the whole.

In a more direct test of the ability to visualise novel combinations, Craig *et al.*

(1998) showed children geometric shapes, and asked them to imagine one being positioned in relation to another (e.g. to imagine a triangle on top of a square) so as to make a novel composite. Children were asked to name the ensuing composite (e.g. 'house'). Children with autism performed just as well on this task as normal controls and children with moderate learning difficulties.

Finally, research on the comprehension of pretence by children with autism lends further support to the conclusion that they can visualise novel combinations. Kavanaugh and Harris (1994) acted out various pretend transformations for a group of children with autism (with a mean chronological age of almost ten years, and a verbal mental age of six and a half years). For example, the children watched as the experimenter picked up a blue pen and in a pretend fashion 'drew' stripes on the body of a toy pig. They were then offered three pictures: one of the pig in its pristine state, one depicting the relevant pretend change (a pig with blue stripes on its body), and one depicting an irrelevant change (a pig with yellow spots on its body), and asked to select the picture showing how the pig would look as a result of the make-believe change. The children performed quite well: over 70% of their choices were directed at the picture showing the relevant pretend change although by chance only 33% would be correct.

In summary, the evidence strongly suggests that children with autism can construct a novel composite visual image by re-combining fragments. Evidence for that ability is provided by their drawings of impossible entities, by their performance on the Block Design task, by their accurate naming of imagined, geometrical composites, and by their ability to visualise a novel, pretend transformation (e.g. a pig with blue stripes). In the next section, we examine the first-person reports of people with autism to provide an additional check on this conclusion and to examine the more general question of whether or not autism prevents people from having insight into their own mental processes.

## FIRST-PERSON REPORTS

Although it is generally acknowledged that adults have limited access to their mental processes, certain processes are open to relatively accurate introspection. Indeed, the development in childhood of the ability to introspect accurately is worthy of study in its own right (Flavell *et al.* 1995; Harris 1995). Recent evidence indicates that visual imagery is one key mental process that is open to accurate introspection given the concordance between adults' self-report and behavioural indices. On the one hand, adults report that they use dynamic visual imagery to solve certain visuo-spatial problems. On the other hand, a large body of experimental evidence based on subjects' reaction times indicates that adults do indeed imagine objects and shapes rotating or inverting (Shepard and Cooper 1982).

Research on the child's theory of mind has frequently led investigators to conclude that young children have limited insight into their mental processes (Gopnik 1993). However, there is evidence that young children do understand the nature of visual imagery and can monitor their use of it. For example, even three- and four-year-olds understand that mental images exist, are not publicly visible, and differ in important ways from their real counterparts (Estes *et al.* 1989; Harris *et al.* 1991). In addition, among those four-year-olds who report using visual imagery, reaction times and error patterns are consistent with the use of mental rotation (Estes 1998). In short, it is likely that the use of visual imagery is open to introspection by adults and even by young children. To what extent are people with autism capable of such introspection?

A systematic examination of the introspective abilities of three men diagnosed with Asperger's syndrome (one of whom had been diagnosed with autism in childhood) was conducted by Hurlburt *et al.* (1994). Over a number of days, the men were asked to note down the thoughts and ideas going through their mind whenever they heard a signal from a beep that sounded at random intervals. In a follow-up interview, they were asked in more detail about these and other internal experiences. All three men reported their private experience almost exclusively in terms of visual imagery. By contrast, normal subjects report their private experience not just in terms of visual imagery but also in terms of silent verbalisation and pure thinking, unaccompanied by images or words (Hurlburt 1990). The visual images described by the three men were not necessarily derived from, or consistent with, their concurrent perceptual experience. One man reported that whilst waiting for a train, he had been thinking about a key being inserted into a lock. His visual image included the levers inside the lock being moved by the blades of the key. In the course of the follow-up interview (which took place in a research unit), another man reported on his visual image of a railway carriage that he was involved in restoring. The third even provided clear evidence of being able understand the generation of a novel, visual image from hitherto separate images. When asked to explain why someone might remark of a woman with very short hair, 'She must have been in a fight with a lawnmower', he suggested that in offering this description, the speaker was: '. . . visualising, not too seriously, in his mind, not in reality, a lawnmower going over her head.' Taken together, these three cases raise the possibility that adults with a history of autistic symptoms are (i) capable of reporting on their mental processes; and (ii) may be accurately reporting an interior life that is dominated by visual imagery to a much greater extent than that of normal adults.

Support for both of these suggestions is provided by Temple Grandin, an intelligent and relatively articulate adult who was diagnosed as autistic as a child. Her descriptions of the visual nature of her childhood memories is vividly captured in her earlier writings in which she reports that 'Memories play like a movie on the big screen of my mind.' (p. 19, Grandin and Scariano 1986). She has also described the way that she can visualise the structure and operation of non-existent as well as actual entities with precision, as shown by her successful career in the design of livestock equipment: 'I create new images all the time by taking many little parts of images I have in the video library in my imagination and piecing them together.' (Grandin 1996, p.21). She gives a concrete example from her professional work. In this particular case, her task was to design a dip vat–a long, narrow swimming pool through which cattle move in single file, to rid them of ticks, lice and other parasites: 'Three images merged to form the final design: a memory of a dip vat–in Yuma, Arizona, a portable vat I had seen in a magazine, and an entrance ramp I had seen on a restraint device at the Swift meat-packing plant in Tolleson, Arizona' (Grandin 1996, p.23). It is likely that this capacity for visualising a new object by bringing together hitherto separate images was also available to Grandin in her childhood. She describes an incident from her boarding school days when she had deliberately misled her schoolmates into thinking that they had seen a flying saucer. In fact, she had simply swung a cardboard saucer containing a flashlight in front of another girl's window (Grandin 1996, p.136). Grandin does not explicitly say so, but we may presume that this novel design—involving a planful combination of separate elements—was her own, and called for some ability to visualise a novel combination.

The richness of Grandin's introspective reports is inconsistent with the routine assumption of much recent experimental work on children with autism, namely that they lack the ability to think about or report on mental states. Of course, one plausible explanation is that Grandin is exceptional in her introspective abilities, and this sets her apart from ordinary people with autism, and especially from children with autism. However, careful scrutiny of Grandin's document suggests that this explanation may not be fully accurate. She acknowledges a long-standing and persisting difficulty in making sense of other people. Interestingly, she is inclined to emphasise her difficulties in making sense of other people's emotional lives, and her tendency to neglect relatively subtle emotional signals. For example, she notes that, unlike her sister, she was unaware of any emotional tension between her parents. Because they were not overtly arguing, she assumed that all was well between them. Even as an adult, she comments on the problems that her emotional insensitivity can cause her in her professional dealings.

Thus, in many respects, Temple Grandin is *not* exceptional in relation to other people with autism. Like them, she has an enduring problem in grasping the mental states of other people. We are therefore led to the conclusion that it is possible to display a classic symptom of autism—namely a difficulty in making sense of other people—while at the same time having relatively rich and informative introspective awareness of visual imagery. This disjunction is theoretically important. The dominant approach to the understanding of mental states, whether in the normal child or the child with autism, has assumed that most propositional attitudes are grasped via the same theoretical machinery. Hence, in the case of autism, it has been assumed that any damage to the ability to understand propositional attitudes would have a wide-ranging impact. In particular, it would make it difficult for children with autism to understand the nature of mental processes, including those that can involve visual images, such as thoughts or dreams (Baron-Cohen 1989).

The case of Temple Grandin, however, opens up a different prospect. It is conceivable that autism does not prevent the attainment of relatively normal awareness of certain mental states, notably those involving visual imagery. Thus, children with autism might be able to achieve an understanding of their own visual imagery and they might be able to understand other people's mental imagery, provided a means could be found to signal its existence. Before considering evidence for or against these proposals, we speculate in more detail as follows.

Normal children engage in a good deal of thinking that is in either a silent verbal format or is privately voiced but not directed to other listeners (Berk and Landau

1993; Bivens and Berk 1990; Vygotsky 1962). Accordingly, they are well-placed to detect resemblances between such private thinking, couched as it is in a verbal format, and the thoughts that they overtly voice to other people. Indeed, the two may display a verbatim equivalence. When children detect that equivalence, it is a short step to the possibility of accurate report on their own thought processes. Moreover, it is also likely that they will assume a comparable equivalence in the case of other people. More specifically, on hearing what another person says out loud, normal children can readily take that utterance to be consistent with what that person privately thinks. On this hypothesis, then, language, and more generally participation in conversation, provides a royal road to an understanding of one's own mental life and that of other people (Harris 1996).

The child's passage along that road might be hindered in various ways. First, suppose that children are delayed in their ability to join in conversation. In that case, they would be severely deprived of overt indices of their own private thoughts, and overt indices of the thoughts of other people. Consistent with that expectation, Peterson and Siegal (1995; 1998) have found that deaf children are delayed in their understanding of false beliefs particularly if they grow up in a non-signing as opposed to a signing family (Peterson and Siegal 1997) so that their opportunities to join in conversation are restricted. Second, consider the case of children with autism. If we assume that they are relatively competent at visual imagery, but are less likely to think in a verbal format, then it will be more difficult for them to recognise the potential equivalence between external manifestations of thinking, such as speech, and thought itself because, as far as they are concerned, the two modes of representation are carried out in different media.

However, there is an optimistic implication of this argument. It might be possible to narrow the gap between the two forms of representation in order to help children with autism. More specifically, it might be possible to provide them with an external index of thinking that is pictorial rather than linguistic. In that case, children with autism might find it easier to make a connection between that external format and the private process of thinking, be it in their own case or in the case of another person. McGregor *et al.* (1998) provide relevant evidence. They sought to teach a group of children with autism and adults to understand beliefs and to assess the extent to which normal three-year-olds might also benefit from such tuition. Especially relevant to the present speculation is the fact that one component of the teaching programme consisted in the provision of an external, pictorial index of thinking. Specifically, children were taught using a 'picture-in-the-head' technique. As a given false-belief story was acted out for example a doll placed an item in a given container—children were told: 'When we see something, we have a thought in our heads, like a picture of what we see.' They were then asked to select a picture of the relevant container and to place it into a slit cut in the doll's head. It was further explained that the picture was like a thought, telling the doll where she saw the item in question.

Exposure to the training programme, and particularly exposure to the component involving the 'picture-in-the-head' technique, led to improvements on the training story, and indeed generalisation to an own false-belief task. These data, then, provide encouraging evidence that children with autism can attain some awareness of their own mental processes when they are offered a pictorial index of thought.

Two further studies point to a similar conclusion. Swettenham *et al.* (1996) taught participants that when people see something, they take a 'photo' in their heads, and this guides their actions. This analogy was made more concrete by having children insert relevant photos into the head of a mannequin, akin to the technique used by McGregor *et al.* (1998). Children with autism learned to pass a false-belief task with the help of this 'photo-in-the-head' technique. They also generalised that success to another theory-of-mind task, that focused on the link between seeing and knowing. Similarly, Wellman *et al.* (1997) undertook a small-scale but intensive training study with seven children with autism using thought-bubbles rather than pictures- or photos-in-the-head. Children were told that when a doll looks at something it gets a thought-bubble. They were then shown a thought bubble with the relevant content (e.g. if the doll was looking at a ball then a picture of a ball appeared in her thought-bubble). As training progressed, children were introduced to the idea that people can retain a thought bubble of an object that they are no longer looking at, even if that object is moved or replaced and that such a thought bubble will guide actions and thoughts. This training led to good performance on a standard false-belief task.[3]

Summarising across these various studies, there is a clear promise that the use of an external pictorial representation can help children with autism to develop an understanding of thinking. As yet, training does not yield wide-ranging generalisation, but it does yield some generalisation. An important task for future research is to assess exactly why the training is effective. If our interpretation is correct, it is because it offers the children an external and understandable analogue of their primary mode of thinking, namely visual imagery. A testable prediction of our position is that speech bubbles would be a less effective prosthetic device. In so far as children with autism may engage in less verbal thought, they are less likely to grasp the analogy.


CONCLUSIONS

We have explored the possibility that children with autism have a limited imagination. Our review suggests that they have difficulties on tasks that call for sustained planning of novel actions. At the same time, we have presented various lines of evidence suggesting that children with autism can visualise a new composite in their imagination. Indeed, we speculate that the ability of children with autism to engage in visual imagery, and the likelihood that they rarely think in a verbal format, may provide clues to their well-known difficulties in understanding mental states. Specifically, in the case of normal children the most obvious external analogue of thinking is speaking. That analogy is likely to be less evident to children with autism. Nevertheless, there are encouraging signs that they can benefit from being introduced to what for them is a more accessible analogy, namely between 'pictures in the head' and external images, be they pictures, drawing, or photographs.

## Acknowledgements

The preparation of this chapter was supported by a postgraduate award from the Medical Research Council, UK and by a grant (R01–HD29419) from NIH/NICHD to HJL; and by a grant (R000 22 1174) from the Economic and Social Research Council, UK, to PLH.

## Notes

1. A minority of children did not continue to produce novel pretend actions throughout the test period. Conclusions about group differences across the test period were appropriately based on only those children who continued until the end of the test period, with due allowance being made for slight variation among the groups in verbal mental age.
2. The percentage figures supplied by the authors are 8.3% and 7.7%; we assume that these percentages differ slightly because they represent 1 out of 12 and 1 out of 13 respectively, but the authors offer no explanation of why the sample size varied from one task to the next.
3. Children did well on an unexpected displacement task, but not on a test of own false belief (Smarties task).

## REFERENCES

Baron-Cohen, S. (1987). Autism and symbolic play. *British Journal of Developmental Psychology,* **5**, 139–48.

Baron-Cohen, S. (1989). Are autistic children 'behaviorists'? An examination of their mental–physical and appearance–reality distinctions. *Journal of Autism and Developmental Disorders,* **19**, 579–600.

Baron-Cohen, S., Allen, J. and Gillberg, C. (1992). Can autism be detected at eighteen months? The needle, the haystack, and the CHAT. *British Journal of Psychiatry,* **161**, 839–43.

Baron-Cohen, S., Cox, A., Baird, G., Swettenham, J., Drew, A., Nightingale, N., Morgan, K. and Charman, T. (1996). Psychological markers of autism at eighteen months of age in a large population. *British Journal of Psychiatry,* **168**, 158–63.

Berk, L. and Landau, S. (1993). Private speech of learning disabled and normally achieving children in classroom, academic and laboratory contexts. *Child Development,* **64**, 556–71.

Berti, A. E. and Freeman. N. H. (1997). Representational change in resources for pictorial innovation: a three-component analysis. *Cognitive Development,* **12**, 405–26.

Bishop, D. V. M. (1993). Annotation: autism, executive functions and theory of mind: a neuropsychological perspective. *Journal of Child Psychology and Psychiatry,* **34**, 279–93.

Bivens, J. A. and Berk, L. E. (1990). A longitudinal study of the development of elementary school children's private speech. *Merrill-Palmer Quarterly,* **36**, 443–63.

Charman, T. and Baron-Cohen, S. (1993). Drawing development in autism: the intellectual to visual realism shift. *British Journal of Developmental Psychology,* **11**, 171–85.

Charman, T. and Baron-Cohen, S. (1997). Prompted pretend play in autism. *Journal of Autism and Developmental Disorders,* **27**, 325–32.

Charman, T., Swettenham, J., Baron-Cohen, S., Cox, A., Baird, G. and Drew, A. (1997). Infants with autism: an investigation of empathy, pretend play, joint attention, and imitation. *Developmental Psychology,* **33**, 781–9.

Craig, J., Baron-Cohen, S. and Scott, F. (1998). Drawing ability in autism: a window on the imagination. Unpublished paper. Department of Experimental Psychology and Psychiatry, University of Cambridge.

Dunn, J. and Dale, N. (1984). I a Daddy: two-year-olds' collaboration in joint pretend with sibling and with mother. In *Symbolic play: the development of social understanding* (ed. I. Bretherton), pp. 131–58. Academic Press, Orlando.

Eames, K. and Cox, M. V. (1994). Visual realism in the drawings of autistic, Down's syndrome and normal children. *British Journal of Developmental Psychology*, **12**, 235–9.

Estes, D. (1998). Young children's awareness of their mental activity: the case of mental rotation. *Child Development*, **69**, 1345–60.

Estes, D., Wellman, H. M. and Woolley, J. D. (1989). Children's understanding of mental phenomena. In *Advances in child development and behavior* (ed. H. W. Reese), pp. 41–87, Academic Press, San Diego, CA.

Flavell, J. H., Green, F. L. and Flavell, E. R. (1995). Young children's knowledge about thinking. *Monographs of the Society for Research in Child Development*, **60** (1, Serial No. 243).

Frith, U. (1989). *Autism: understanding the enigma*. Blackwell, Oxford.

Gopnik, A. (1993). How we know our own minds: the illusion of first-person knowledge of intentionality. *Brain and Behavioral Sciences*, **16**, 1–14.

Gould, J. (1986). The Lowe and Costello symbolic play test in socially impaired children. *Journal of Autism and Developmental Disorders*, **16**, 199–213.

Grandin, T. (1996). *Thinking in pictures*. Vintage, New York.

Grandin, T. and Scariano, M. M. (1986). *Emergence: labeled autistic*. Arena Press, Novato, CA.

Happé, F. G. E. (1994). Annotation: current psychological theories of autism: the 'Theory of Mind' account and rival theories. *Journal of Child Psychology and Psychiatry*, **35**, 215–29.

Harris, P. L. (1993). Pretending and planning. In *Understanding other minds* (ed. S. Baron-Cohen, H. Tager-Flusberg, and D. Cohen). Oxford University Press, Oxford.

Harris, P. L. (1995). The rise of introspection. Commentary in Flavell, J. H., Green, F. L., and Flavell, E. R. (1995). Young children's knowledge about thinking. *Monographs of the Society for Research in Child Development*, **60** (1, Serial No. 243).

Harris, P. L. (1996). Desires, beliefs and language. In *Theories of theories of mind* (ed. P. Carruthers and P. K. Smith), pp. 200–20. Cambridge University Press.

Harris, P. L., Brown, E., Marriott, C., Whittall, S. and Harmer, S. (1991). Monsters, ghosts and witches: testing the limits of the fantasy–reality distinction in young children. *British Journal of Developmental Psychology*, **9**, 105–23.

Harris, P. L. and Kavanaugh, R. D. (1993). Young children's understanding of pretense. *Monographs of the Society for Research in Child Development*, **58**, Serial No. 231.

Howes, C., Unger, O. and Seidner, L. B. (1989). Social pretend play in toddlers: parallels with social play and with solitary pretend. *Child Development*, **60**, 77–84.

Hughes, C., Russell, J. and Robbins, T. W. (1994). Evidence for executive dysfunction in autism. *Neuropsychologia*, **32**, 477–92.

Hurlburt, R. T. (1990). *Sampling normal and schizophrenic inner experience*. Plenum Press, New York.

Hurlburt, R. T., Happé, F. G. E. and Frith, U. (1994). Sampling the form of inner experience in three adults with Asperger syndrome. *Psychological Medicine*, **24**, 385–95.

Jarrold, C. (1997). Pretend play in autism: executive explanations. In *Autism as an executive disorder* (ed. J. Russell). Oxford University Press.

Jarrold, C., Boucher, J. and Smith, P. K. (1996). Generativity deficits in pretend play in autism. *British Journal of Developmental Psychology*, **14**, 275–300.

Kanner, L. (1943). Autistic disturbances of affective contact. *Nervous Child*, **2**, 217–50.

Karmiloff-Smith, A. (1990). Constraints on representational chance: evidence from children's drawing. *Cognition*, **34**, 57–83.

Kavanaugh, R. D. and Harris, P. L. (1994). Imagining the outcome of pretend transformations: assessing the competence of normal children and children with autism. *Developmental Psychology*, **30**, 847–54.

Kosslyn, S. M., Heldmeyer, K. H. and Locklear, E. P. (1977). Children's drawings as data about internal representations. *Journal of Experimental Child Psychology*, **23**, 191–211.

Leevers, H. J. and Harris, P. L. (1998). Drawing impossible entities: a measure of the imagination in children with autism, children with learning disabilities, and normal four-year-olds. *Journal of Child Psychology and Psychiatry*, **39**, 399–410.

Leslie, A. M. (1987). Pretense and representation: the origins of 'theory of mind'. *Psychological Review*, **94**, 412–26.

Lewis, V. and Boucher, J. (1988). Spontaneous, instructed and elicited play in relatively able autistic children. *British Journal of Developmental Psychology*, **6**, 325–39.

Lewis, V. and Boucher, J. (1991). Skill, content and generative strategies in autistic children's drawings. *British Journal of Developmental Psychology*, **9**, 393–416.

McGregor, E., Whiten, A. and Blackburn, P. (1998). Teaching theory of mind by highlighting intention and illustrating thoughts: a comparison of their effectiveness with three-year-olds and autistic individuals. *British Journal of Developmental Psychology*, **16**, 281–300.

Mottron, L. and Belleville, S. (1993). A study of perceptual analysis in a high-level autistic subject with exceptional graphic abilities. *Brain and Cognition*, **23**, 279–309.

Mottron, L. and Belleville, S. (1995). Perspective production in a savant autistic draughtsman. *Psychological Medicine*, **25**, 639–48.

O'Connor, N. and Hermelin, B. (1987). Visual and graphic abilities of the idiot savant artist. *Psychological medicine*, **17**, 79–90.

Ozonoff, S., Pennington, B. F. and Rogers, S. J. (1991). Executive function deficits in high-functioning autistic individuals: relationship to theory of mind. *Journal of Child Psychology and Psychiatry*, **32**, 1081–105.

Ozonoff, S., Strayer, D. S., McMahon, W. M. and Filloux, F. (1994). Executive function abilities in autism and Tourette Syndrome: an information processing approach. *Journal of Child Psychology and Psychiatry*, **35**, 1015–32.

Peterson, C. C. and Siegal, M. (1995). Deafness, conversation and theory of mind. *Journal of Child Psychology and Psychiatry*, **36**, 459–74.

Peterson, C. and Siegal, M. (1997). Psychological, biological and physical thinking in normal, autistic, and deaf children. In *The emergence of core domains of thought* (ed. H. M. Wellman and K. Inagaki), pp.55–70, (New Directions for Child Development Series, W. Damon, Gen. Ed.) Jossey Bass, San Francisco.

Peterson, C. C. and Siegal, M. (1998). Changing focus on the representational mind: deaf, autistic and normal children's concepts of false photos, false drawings and false beliefs. *British Journal of Developmental Psychology*, **16**, 301–20.

Piaget, J. (1951). *Play, dreams and imitation*. Heinemann, London.

Prior, M. and Hoffman, W. (1990). Brief Report: neuropsychological testing of autistic children through an exploration with frontal lobe tests. *Journal of Autism and Developmental Disorders*, **20**, 581–90.

Riguet, C. B., Taylor, N. D., Benaroya, S. and Klein, L. S. (1981). Symbolic play in autistic, Down's, and normal children of equivalent mental age. *Journal of Autism and Developmental Disorders*, **11**, 439–48.

Russell, J., Mauthner, N., Sharpe, S. and Tidswell, T. (1991). The 'windows' task as a measure of strategic deception in preschoolers and autistic subjects. *British Journal of Developmental Psychology*, **9**, 331–49.

Scott, F. J. and Baron-Cohen, S. (1996). Imagining real and unreal things: evidence of a dissociation in autism. *Journal of Cognitive Neuroscience*, **8**, 371–82.

Selfe, L. (1983). *Normal and anomalous representational drawing ability in children*. Academic Press, London.

Shepard, R. N. and Cooper, L. (1982). Mental images and their transformations. MIT Press, Cambridge, MA.

Sigman, M. and Ungerer, J. A. (1984). Cognitive and language skills in autistic, mentally retarded and normal children. *Developmental Psychology*, **20**, 293–302.

Slade, A. (1987). A longitudinal study of maternal involvement and symbolic play during the toddler period. *Child Development*, **58**, 367–75.

Swettenham, J. G, Baron-Cohen, S., Gomez, J.-C. and Walsh, S. (1996). What's inside someone's head? Conceiving of the mind as a camera helps children with autism acquire an alternative to a theory of mind. *Cognitive Neuropsychiatry*, **1**, 73–88.

Thomas, G. V. and Silk, A. M. J. (1990). *An introduction to the psychology of children's drawings*. Harvester, Wheatsheaf, London.

Vygotsky, L. S. (1962). *Thought and language*. MIT Press, Cambridge, MA.

Wellman, H. M., Baron-Cohen, S., Gomez, J.-C., Swettenham, J. and Toye, E. (1997). Using thought-bubbles helps children with autism acquire an alternative to a theory of mind. Unpublished paper. Department of Experimental Psychology and Psychiatry, University of Cambridge.

Wing, L. (1978). Social, behavioral and cognitive characteristics: an epidemiological approach. In *Autism: a reappraisal of concepts and treatment* (ed. M. Rutter and E. Schopler). Plenum, London.

# 9

# Parts and wholes, meaning and minds: central coherence and its relation to theory of mind

## FRANCESCA HAPPÉ

This chapter reviews research suggesting that people with autism show a detail-focused processing style, 'weak central coherence', and examines current evidence concerning the relation of this cognitive style to deficits in theory of mind. Kanner (1943) described, as a universal feature of autism, the 'inability to experience wholes without full attention to the constituent parts'. How does this fragmented experience of the world relate to understanding other minds?

## DOMAIN–SPECIFIC AND DOMAIN–GENERAL ACCOUNTS OF AUTISM

Autism has defied all simple explanations. Perhaps in response to such a complex reality, our theories tend to attempt a simplification, leaving aside those features or symptoms for which they cannot account. This is reflected in the pendulum swing in the focus of psychological accounts of autism, from social to non-social facets of the disorder. While the 1980s, for example, saw a vital move towards explanation of the social handicap in autism, these theories skipped over the many non-social aspects of autism. The 1990s have seen a move back to consideration of these non-social features, with the proposal of a number of domain–general accounts. Some of these are represented in the other contributions to this volume (e.g. executive dysfunction, Chapter 7). Each addresses part of the puzzle of autism, none would claim to have the complete story, and it may be that autism is the result of abnormalities in the development of several distinct systems.

Now, while the specifically social deficit accounts of autism, such as theory of mind, find their limitations when faced with the puzzling non-social features of the disorder (see Chapter 10), the new breed of domain–general account also face a challenge, though of a rather different sort. The challenge to these accounts, as Uta Frith (1989) has pointed out, is not to explain too much. That is, any theory must allow people with autism the many things they are good at. A domain–general theory, such as that people with autism are unable to shift attention rapidly, is in danger of predicting too much—a blanket deficit across all tasks. Autism, however, is not a blanket deficit, but a fine landscape of peaks and troughs—parents, teachers, and clinicians are all unsurprised when a child with autism shows remarkable ability in a specific area out of line with his/her usual level of functioning.

## NON-SOCIAL ASPECTS OF AUTISM

Some of the non-social aspects of autism for which an account is needed are shown in Table 9.1 (see Chapter 10 for more detailed discussion). Some of these features are not specific to autism, for example stereotypies are common in general mental retardation without autism, but they are strikingly present even in intelligent individuals on the autism spectrum (Turner 1996). Other features are far more common in autism than in other disorders; savant skills in the classic areas of memory, drawing, music, and maths are perhaps ten times as common in people with autism as in people with other types of mental handicap (Rimland and Hill 1984). Still other features are, if not specific to autism, at least universal—indeed the presence of a restricted repertoire of interests is a diagnostic criterion (DSM-IV; APA 1994).

Accounts of autism as an executive disorder are able to explain some of these non-social difficulties (see Chapter 7). Much harder for such accounts—and indeed for all deficit accounts—is to explain findings of superior performance by individuals with autism. Some of these findings, which suggest that people with autism perform well on tasks which the rest of us find hard (e.g. remembering nonsense) and are not greatly aided by conditions which improve normal individuals' performance (e.g. adding meaning), are summarised in Table 9.2. Theory of mind

**Table 9.1.** Non-social features of autism

- Restricted repertoire of interests
- Obsessive desire for sameness
- Stereotypies
- Savant abilities
- Lack of generalisation
- Excellent rote memory
- Preoccupation with parts of objects
- Fragmented sensory perception

**Table 9.2.** Experimental findings not accounted for by mind-blindness

| ASSETS | DEFICITS | |
|---|---|---|
| memory for word strings | memory for sentences | (e.g. Hermelin and O'Connor 1967) |
| memory for unrelated items | memory for related items | (e.g. Tager-Flusberg 1991) |
| echoing nonsense | echoing with repair | (e.g. Aurnhammer-Frith 1969) |
| pattern imposition | pattern detection | (e.g. Frith 1970) |
| jigsaw by shape | jigsaw by picture | (e.g. Frith and Hermelin 1969) |
| sorting faces by accessories | sorting faces by person | (e.g. Hobson 1983) |

accounts, and other social deficit accounts, cannot provide a full explanation for these types of finding.

## CENTRAL COHERENCE

Motivated by the strong belief that assets and the deficits in autism spring from a single cognitive characteristic, Frith (1989) proposed that autism is characterised by a specific imbalance in integration of information at different levels. A characteristic of normal information-processing appears to be the tendency to draw together diverse information to construct higher-level meaning in context; 'central coherence' in Frith's words. For example, the gist of a story is easily recalled, while the actual surface form is quickly lost, and is effortful to retain (e.g. Bartlett 1932). Central coherence is also demonstrated in the ease with which we recognise the contextually-appropriate sense of the many ambiguous words used in everyday speech (e.g. son–sun, meet–meat, sew–so, pear–pair). The tendency to process information in context for global meaning is seen, too, with nonverbal material—for example, the tendency to misinterpret details in a jigsaw piece according to the expected position in the whole picture. It is likely that this preference for higher levels of meaning also characterises young children and individuals with (non-autistic) mental handicap—who appear, for example, to be sensitive to the advantage of recalling organized versus jumbled material (e.g. Hermelin and O'Connor 1967).

Frith suggested that this feature of human information processing is disturbed in autism, and that weak central coherence could explain very parsimoniously the assets and deficits, as shown in Table 9.2. Frith predicted that individuals with autism would be relatively good at tasks where attention to local information (i.e. relatively piece-meal processing) is advantageous, but poor at tasks requiring the recognition of global meaning or integration of stimuli in context. One of the most positive aspects of Frith's notion of central coherence was this ability to explain patterns of excellent and poor performance with one cognitive postulate. An elegant demonstration was given by Shah and Frith (1993), who focused on the typical autistic peak of performance on the Wechsler scales; the Block Design subtest. Shah and Frith showed that people with autism were unusually good at the standard Block Design task, and that this facility has specifically to do with segmentation abilities; on a modified task using pre-segmented designs, controls performed as well as the autism group. A sizeable advant-age gained from pre-segmentation was shown by normal and mentally handicapped (MH) controls, but not by people with autism—suggesting that the latter group already saw the design in terms of its constituent parts. So while the Block Design task may be hard for the rest of us because we cannot overcome the gestalt of the whole design (for example, we see a typical design as a black diamond, rather than the four triangles of which it is composed)—people with autism have no such difficulty. They do not succumb to the gestalt, and instead easily see the design in terms of its constituent blocks.

The central coherence account of autism, then, predicts skills as well as failures, and as such can best be characterised not as a deficit account, but in terms of cognitive style. As such it is better able than most accounts to explain the many things that people with autism are good at—indeed it has taken much of its evidence from just such findings of success. Success, after all, is more interesting than task failure, since it is less open to alternative explanations, such as low motivation.

## EMPIRICAL WORK RELATING TO CENTRAL COHERENCE

In reviewing the work to date exploring weak central coherence, it is useful to divide studies broadly into those dealing with fairly low-level perceptual processes, those using more complex visuospatial constructional tasks, and those addressing coherence at higher levels involving the semantic system. This is by no means a perfect division, and an interesting issue for future research concerns possible high-level or top-down effects on even apparently peripheral perceptual processes (e.g. Coren and Enns 1993).

### Perceptual coherence

The notion that people with autism fail to integrate information has a number of different implications. Taken to its extreme, it would appear to predict difficulty in perceiving the environment in terms of coherent objects in context. This seems implausible: surely people with autism, who after all negotiate their way around the physical world without difficulty, must see this world as we do in terms of whole objects, rather than disjointed surfaces, lines and angles? To explore coherence at a low, perceptual level I asked individuals with autism (who ranged in age from 8 to 16, and in IQ from 40 to 92) to make simple judgements about standard textbook visual illusions. The logic behind the choice of materials was that at least some illusions can be analysed into a 'to-be-judged' figure and an inducing context or ground (Gregory 1967). In the Titchner circles illusion, for example, it is the presence of the surrounding small or big circles which induces the mis-perception of the inner circles as being of different sizes. If people with autism have a tendency towards fragmented perception, and focus on the to-be-judged parts without integrating them with the surrounding illusion-inducing context, one might expect them to succumb less to the typical mis-perceptions. And this was exactly what happened—the people with autism were better able than normal or MH controls to make accurate judgements of the illusions. This superior ability seemed to be related to disembedding skill, since when the figures were artificially disembedded (by highlighting the to-be-judged parts with raised coloured lines) control groups performed as accurately as the autism group. The autism group, however, were little helped by this artificial disembedding—just as in Shah and Frith's (1993) pre-segmented Block Design task.

Another finding relating to low-level coherence is reported by Jarrold and Russell (1997), who found that people with autism were less aided by canonical presentation of dots in a counting task; while verbal mental age (VMA)-matched mentally handicapped and young normal participants were faster to name the number of dots when these appeared in the familiar patterns (as appear on dice), people with autism were equally good at naming randomly distributed arrays. Although Jarrold and Russell interpret these findings as suggesting that the autism group did indeed process the array analytically (counting each dot separately) and without attention to global configuration, they did not find significant differences in numbers of participants in each group showing a predominantly 'global' or 'local' processing style. Plaisted *et al.* (1998) also explored processing of visual arrays, using visual search paradigms which provoke parallel or serial search processes in normal individuals. Their findings, that people with autism show pop-out in conditions where normal participants show serial search, are striking. This work, and its relation to central coherence, is described in more detail in Chapter 10.

Mottron and Belleville (1993), who have proposed an alternative account of local-global processing anomalies in autism (see Mottron *et al.*, in press), present a case study of a thirty four-year-old man with autism who showed savant drawing skills. On a number of tasks, this man showed fragmented perception and a bias toward local processing. These results have generalised with varying success to the general population with autism (see below). Mottron *et al.* (submitted) found piecemeal drawing in a group of ten adolescents with high-functioning autism. In particular, in an ingenious study using impossible figures, these authors found that normal controls were less good at copying 'impossible' (that is, globally incompatible) figures than possible figures, while the adolescents with autism were less disturbed by the global incoherence of the figures, as reflected in copying time.

Other savant skills may also reflect weak coherence in autism. An interesting example is absolute pitch, which Heaton *et al.* (1998) found to be unusually common in (musically-naive) children with autism. Takeuchi and Hulse (1993) suggest, based on a review of research to date, that absolute pitch can be learnt by most children before about age six, after which 'a general developmental shift from perceiving individual features to perceiving relations among features makes [absolute pitch] difficult or impossible to acquire' (p. 345). If people with autism show a pervasive and persistent local processing bias, this would explain the high frequency of absolute pitch and the superior ability to learn note-name mappings at later ages.

A number of other studies of autism, though not intended to test the notion of central coherence, may relate to failures of integration in low-level processing. Hobson *et al.* (1988) replicated Langdell's (1978) finding that children with autism are less affected by inversion of faces in a recognition task. Since inversion decrements are thought to reflect disruption of the configural aspects of face processing, this finding may indicate a feature-based processing style for faces in autism—which in turn may account for deficits in processing emotional (versus identity) information (McKelvie 1995). Gepner *et al.* (1995) report that five children with autism (aged four to seven years) were not susceptible to visually-induced movement, showing little postural instability (compared with age-matched controls) in response to visually presented environmental motion. Whether individuals with autism would differ significantly in this respect from mental-age or IQ-matched control groups remains to be seen. Another finding suggesting that children with autism may not integrate information from difference sense modalities, comes from DeGelder *et al.* (1991). These authors found that although a group of children with autism (aged six to sixteen years) were as good as MA-matched children on a lip-reading task, they showed little influence in their auditory speech perception from visual speech. The children with autism in this study were less susceptible than controls to the McGurk effect (the blend of visually- and auditorally-perceived sounds). These results may be seen as suggestive of abnormalities in integration of information in low level perceptual systems.

Whether such integration can reasonably be called 'central' is an important matter for future research. On the face of it, fragmentary processing in perceptual tasks would appear to reflect a disruption of low-level, peripheral coherence. It is worth noting, however, that some such tasks may tap surprisingly high-level processes. An example comes from the work of Coren on visual illusions, showing that the semantic content of visual forms can affect the strength of illusions that are normally considered to involve only low-level perceptual systems (Coren and Enns 1993). Another example comes from a comparative study using the Navon task, in which large letters composed of small letters are presented. Subjects are required to report either the local or global letter, in conditions where these are congruous (matching) or incongruous (non-matching). There is now a large literature on this task and several variations (and controversies), however the usual finding is that normal subjects show a global advantage (they are faster to name the big letters than the small) and global precedence (asymmetric effects of incongruity such that mismatch affects local judgement more than global judgement). Fagot and Deruelle (1997) found the usual global advantage in humans, but found a local advantage in baboons—from which they conclude that global precedence does not have a purely perceptual or sensory basis.

Set against the above studies supporting the idea of weak coherence in perceptual tasks, are at least two negative findings. Ozonoff *et al.* (1994) used the Navon hierarchical figure paradigm to test the predicted local bias. A straightforward prediction from the hypothesis of weak central coherence would be that people with autism will show reduced or reversed advantage and precedence effects. Ozonoff *et al.* did not find this, and instead found no group differences on accuracy or response time in either congruent or incongruent conditions. However, as Jolliffe (Jolliffe and Baron-Cohen 1997) and others have pointed out, this finding may be due to the unusually long exposure times used—global advantage and precedence effects are sensitive to small methodological changes (Kimchi 1992). However, Mottron *et al.* (in press) also failed to find a local advantage or precedence effect in autism, using brief presentations, and instead found an autism–specific global advantage on their hierarchical figure task.

## Visuospatial constructional coherence

The skill shown by many people with autism on the Wechsler Block Design subtest, and its apparent grounding in superior segmentation abilities, has already been discussed. A similar skill is often seen on the Embedded Figures Test, in which a small shape must be found within a larger design. Shah and Frith (1983) found superior performance by low-functioning individuals with autism using the children's version of the EFT (in which the pictures are meaningful), and Jolliffe and Baron-Cohen (1997) found superior performance by high-functioning individuals with autism/Asperger's Syndrome using the adult version of the test (abstract geometric designs). Other work on strategic visuospatial tasks includes innovative studies by

Jolliffe (1997). She modified the Hooper test, which requires participants to recognise objects from jumbled fragments, and demonstrated that people with autism and Asperger's Syndrome were good at recognising objects from details, but poor on items requiring integration of parts. A second task devised by Jolliffe required participants to choose which three of four objects should go together to form a coherent scene (e.g. a man, a bucket, a window, a ladder, and a suitcase). Her autism spectrum participants, who were all of normal or superior IQ, were significantly impaired on this, and on a test of spotting an incongruous object in a picture of a scene (e.g. a squirrel in a beach scene).

Pring *et al.* (1995) tested part-whole processing in people with autism and normal children, divided into those showing striking artistic talent (A-level standard) and those not gifted in drawing. They found that artistic talent predicted speed to copy the picture scenes using the blocks, that normal artistically talented children were faster than artists with autism, but that normal and autism subjects in the 'non-talented' group did not differ. On the standard, geometrical block design task the artistically talented subjects (normal and autism groups) were faster than the non-talented groups, and group interacted with this talent factor—the two artistically talented groups did not differ, but in the non-talented groups the participants with autism performed significantly faster than the young normal children. The authors conclude that these results support the notion of a facility in autism for seeing wholes in terms of their parts, rather than as unified gestalts—but that this ability may also be characteristic of individuals with an aptitude for drawing, whether or not they have autism. They suggest that the different results for the two tasks support the notion that while artistic individuals (with or without autism) show superior segmentation ability, the normal subjects were additionally able to use meaning in the picture task—and propose that 'effort after meaning' and 'segmentation decomposition' ability may be distinct processes. They conclude that weak coherence may underlie many of the 'modular talents' found in autism (cf. absolute pitch).

Other work by Pring and Hermelin (1993) suggests that visuospatial processing for meaning does take place in autism—at least at the level of single objects. These authors examined structural and semantic aspects of picture processing in ten mentally handicapped savant artists (six of whom had a diagnosis of autism) and ten children judged in the top 2% for artistic ability (MA-matched to each savant by Ravens Matrices). Participants were shown a set of four drawings and asked to copy these from memory. Target drawings in a set were alike in either structure (same shape) or meaning (e.g. all musical instruments), with one of the four in each case differing on the other dimension (e.g. a light bulb alongside similarly shaped fruits). Both groups found semantically-related targets easier to remember than structurally-related targets. A second study showed that the two participant groups also did not differ in tendency to sort pictures of items from the same semantic category together rather than with structurally similar pictures (e.g. banjo is judged to 'go with' piano not tennis racquet). The authors conclude that, within the domain of expertise, savant artists (like savants in other domains) give evidence of representations similar to those underlying exceptional skill by normal subjects. These findings, which show intact processing of meaning at the single object level, fit well with data from Ameli *et al.*

(1988) who found that bright adults with autism showed a normal advantage in recognition memory for pictures of meaningful (and nameable) objects versus meaningless doodle-like abstract figures. While the use of meaning-generating strategies by normal participants cannot be ruled out, it seems plausible that people with autism can process single objects for meaning but have greater difficulty making meaningful connections between objects (cf. Jolliffe's scene integration studies).

One study, to date, has reported findings directly counter to the idea of weak central coherence at the visuospatial level. Brian and Bryson (1996) used experimental versions of an embedded figures task, contrasting meaningful (objects), meaningless (geometric forms), and fragmented figures within which the target shape was hidden. They found no group by task interaction, comparing individuals with autism (mean age 19, Raven's percentile 34, vocabulary standard score 77) and young normal children (CA 12, Raven's centile 55, VIQ 103) matched on verbal or nonverbal raw scores. Individuals with autism, like normal children, in this study were slower to find a hidden shape in a meaningful versus meaningless drawing, and recognised meaningful figures better than meaningless ones. These findings are challenging for the central coherence account, although it remains to be seen whether groups matched on performance IQ would yield similar results.

## VERBAL-SEMANTIC COHERENCE

Some of the earliest research influential to the central coherence account of autism was by Hermelin and O'Connor, who founded the tradition of cognitive assessment of assets/deficits in autism and well-matched mentally handicapped comparison groups (see Hermelin and O'Connor 1970). Hermelin and O'Connor (1967) showed that people with autism did not derive the usual benefit from meaning in memory; while control subjects recalled sentences far better than unconnected word strings, this advantage from meaning was greatly diminished in the autism group. This work, subsequently replicated by a number of authors (see review and extension by Tager-Flusberg 1991), suggested that people with autism did not make use of either semantic relations (e.g. words from the same category versus assorted words) or grammatical relations (e.g. sentences versus word lists) in memory.

Frith and Snowling (1983; Snowling and Frith 1986) compared comprehension at word, sentence and text level in children with autism and children with dyslexia. They concluded from a battery of tasks (including speed of reading advantage for concrete versus abstract words, and Stroop task interference of word meaning with ink colour) that processing of meaning at the single word level was intact in autism. This conclusion is supported by later work by Eskes *et al.* (1990), who found normal interference in a Stroop task using concrete and abstract words. These results mirror those found in the visual domain—single object/word meaning is intact while connections between items are weakened. In the verbal domain, however, Frith and Snowling (1983) found use of syntactic constraints from sentence context to be intact; children with autism chose words of the right grammatical class to fill gaps in sentences. In contrast, on two innovative tasks tapping integration of words and use of semantic context the autism group was significantly impaired. On a gaps test, in which children had to choose words to fill gaps in a story, children with autism performed significantly worse than those with dyslexia. The second task involved reading out sentences including ambiguous words. Frith and Snowling (1983) used homographs (words with one spelling, two meanings, and two pronunciations) to check whether children with autism would use preceding sentence context to derive meaning and determine pronunciation; e.g. 'In her eye there was a big tear', 'In her dress there was a big tear'. If people with autism have weak central coherence at this level, then reading a sentence may, for them, be akin to reading a list of unconnected words—and sentence context will not be built up to allow meaning-driven disambiguation. In the original studies (Frith and Snowling 1983; Snowling and Frith 1986), and a subsequent replication with higher-functioning children and adults (Happé 1997), individuals with autism failed to use preceding sentence context to determine the pronunciation of homographs. This finding is interesting in that people with autism (at these levels of intelligence) clearly are able in some tasks to read sentences for meaning. Indeed, when instructed in reading for meaning (Snowling and Frith 1986) group differences on the homograph task disappeared. It seems, then, that weak central coherence characterises the spontaneous approach or processing preference of people with autism, and for this reason is best captured in open-ended tasks.

Jolliffe (1997) assessed coherence at the semantic level with an inference task and an ambiguous sentences task (e.g. 'The man wiped his glasses carefully'). In both these tasks participants with autism and those with Asperger's Syndrome showed weak coherence; failing to select the most coherent bridging inference from a set of alternatives, and failing to use context to interpret an ambiguous sentence. Discourse level tasks also revealed piecemeal processing, with poorer ability to arrange sentences to tell a coherent story, or use context to infer reasons for a character's action. Scheuffgen (1998) also found failure to use meaning at story level in a task assessing both verbatim memory through sentence recognition, and gist memory through recall. Individuals with autism (mean CA 12, VIQ 84) were better than MH and normal control groups at recognition of surface form, and this was especially true of children showing decoding–comprehension discrepancies on the WORD (who might be considered hyperlexic). In contrast, the autism group recalled fewer story events (gist recall) from a meaningful, ordered story—and this group difference disappeared on scrambled (meaningless) stories, suggesting that benefit from meaning was accounting for the controls' superior gist recall. These findings bring to mind Kanner's (1943) description of his original cases: '. . . the children read monotonously, and a story . . . is experienced in unrelated portions rather than in its coherent totality'.

## CENTRAL COHERENCE AND THE EXTENDED PHENOTYPE

Since weak central coherence gives both advantages and disadvantages (as would strong central coherence), it is possible to think of this balance (between preference for parts versus wholes) as akin to a cognitive style—a style which may vary in the normal population. The wide range of scores commonly attained in normal samples on the Embedded Figures Test and Wechsler Block Design subtest supports this idea, as does the existence of individual differences in global–local processing in infancy (Colombo *et al.* 1995). As a cognitive style, rather than deficit, weak central coherence is an interesting contender for the aspect of autism which may be transmitted genetically and which may characterise the relatives of individuals with autism. Happé *et al.* (submitted) compared cognitive style in parents and siblings of children with autism, families in whom a son had dyslexia, and families without developmental disorder. They found that parents, and especially fathers, of children with autism showed significantly superior performance on tasks favouring piecemeal, local processing. So fathers of boys with autism were especially good at the EFT, at block design (and little aided by pre-segmentation), and at accurately judging visual illusion figures. They were also more likely than other fathers to give local sentence completions (e.g. 'The sea tastes of salt and . . . ?' 'pepper'). In all these respects they resembled individuals with autism, but, importantly, for these fathers their detail-focused cognitive style was an asset not a deficit.

These results fit well with work by Baron-Cohen and Hammer (1997*a*), which has shown that parents of children with autism are faster on the EFT, and the finding by Baron-Cohen *et al.* (1997) that engineering is over-represented as a profession for fathers of children with autism. While Baron-Cohen *et al.* have described fast EFT and Block Design performance and engineering talent as markers of superior 'folk physics', an alternative explanation would be in terms of weak central coherence. On this account, people with autism and their relatives will be characterised by expertise not with all mechanical systems, but only with systems where detail focus is an advantage. Weak central coherence, unlike 'folk physics', also stretches beyond the visuospatial domain, and predicts piecemeal processing in verbal tasks (e.g. homographs and sentence completion) which is not easily accounted for by the 'folk physics' hypothesis.

## CENTRAL COHERENCE AND THEORY OF MIND

In Frith's (1989) original formulation, deficits in theory of mind were conceptualised as just one consequence of weak central coherence. Understanding social interaction, and extracting the higher-level representation of thoughts underlying behaviour, was seen as the pinnacle of coherent processing and gist extraction. Thus, on this account, people with autism were socially impaired because they were unable to derive high-level meaning. Subsequently, Frith and Happé (1994) modified this view, and proposed as a working hypothesis that the two aspects of autism, weak central coherence and impaired theory of mind, were independent (though interacting) facets of the disorder. The work that led to this revision included a study by Happé (1997) which showed that failure to use preceding sentence context in Snowling and Frith's homograph task was as marked among individuals with autism who passed an array of (first- and second-order) theory of mind tasks as among those who (like most people with autism) failed such tasks. In a larger sample, Happé (1994*a*) also showed that while theory of mind task performance was related to performance on the

Comprehension subtest of the Wechsler scales (commonly thought to require pragmatic and social skill), it was not related to superior performance on the Block Design subtest—the latter being taken as a marker of weak central coherence. Specifically, 76% of theory of mind 'failers' but only 28% of 'passers' showed a personal dip on the Comprehension subtest, while 85% of failers and 86% of passers showed a personal peak on the Block Design subtest. Thus, weak coherence (as reflected in relatively good Block Design) seems to characterise people with autism regardless of their theory of mind ability. Similarly, theory of mind performance had no effect on ability to judge visual illusions in the Happé (1996) study.

There is evidence, too, that the non-social features of autism persist even in the minority of people with autism who do develop some theory of mind ability (albeit with a significant delay). Frith *et al.* (1994), for example, compared everyday life adaptation (as rated by teachers) in children with autism who passed theory of mind tests and those who failed. They found significant advantages in the passing group on socially insightful behaviours, both positive (e.g. taking hints) and negative (e.g. lying, cheating). Interestingly, however, 'passers' were no less impaired in terms of non-social maladaptive behaviours such as self-injury and peculiar mannerisms. In fact, the group who passed theory of mind tests, who had higher verbal ability than those who failed, were more likely to be rated by teachers as showing tics and twitches (75% of passers versus 6% of failers) and preoccupations (75% versus 50%)—features which Frith (1989) has linked to weak central coherence. Turner (1996), in a detailed study of repetitive behaviour in autism, also found equally high levels of insistence on sameness, circumscribed interests, and repetitive movement and language, in those individuals with autism who passed a battery of theory of mind tasks as in those who failed.

These studies, then, suggest that central coherence may be weak in all individuals with autism regardless of their theory of mind ability. As a working hypothesis, Frith and Happé (1994; Happé 1994*b*) therefore proposed that people with autism be conceptualised as lying at the extreme of a normal continuum for central coherence, and having suffered an additional impairment to a dedicated cognitive mechanism (module?) for attribution of mental states. Without doubt these two aspects of autism will interact, but the existence of people with autism who later in life develop some theory of mind ability but remain detail-focused in their processing, suggests that these two aspects of autism are distinct. It should be said however, that these data are by no means conclusive. It may be that we have not yet devised measures of central coherence and theory of mind sensitive enough to degree of abnormality to reveal a true relation between the two.

Indirect evidence about the relation between theory of mind and coherence may come from studies of the extended phenotype of autism. In Briskman *et al.*'s (submitted) family study, scores on questionnaire items tapping social (in particular theory of mind) and non-social (especially weak central coherence) traits and preferences were not significantly correlated in autism probands or relatives. Baron-Cohen has discussed the extended phenotype of autism in terms of superior 'folk physics' and inferior 'folk psychology'. He has found good EFT performance and poor performance on a test of reading expression in the eyes, in separate groups of parents of children with autism. Baron-Cohen and Hammer (1997*a*) have related these findings to normal sex differences on visuospatial tasks (a relative strength in males) and social tasks (a relative strength in females), and propose that autism is an extreme form of the 'male brain'. Although the exact relation between the strength in mechanical processing and weakness in psychological processing is not explicitly discussed, the implication appears to be that these two facets are reciprocal, with relative strength and weakness balancing one another.

Jarrold *et al.* (1998) have preliminary evidence that may support the idea of reciprocal and inverse abilities in segmentation ability (whether interpreted as weak coherence or 'folk physics') and theory of mind. They found that speed on the EFT and performance on Baron-Cohen's 'eyes task' were significantly negatively correlated in a sample of 60 undergraduates (30 men, 30 women). In addition, in a group of 17 children with autism, EFT performance was negatively correlated with theory of mind task performance, with the correlation reaching significance once verbal mental age was partialled out.

Another indirect source of information on the relation between central coherence and theory of mind may be work on field dependence–independence (FD/FI). The EFT, on which people with autism generally excel, was used by Witkin and colleagues as a measure of field independence (Witkin and Goodenough 1981; Witkin *et al.* 1962). It might be a mistake, however, to equate field independence with weak central coherence; while field independent people are conceptualised as succeeding on EFT because of their ability to see but overcome the gestalt, people with autism (according to the weak central coherence account) are good at this test precisely because they fail to see the gestalt, and see the figure instead in terms of its parts. It is this characterisation of FI individuals, as possessing the same contextualising capacity as FD individuals plus the ability to overcome context, which in all likelihood gave rise to the criticism that this so-called cognitive style was in fact a matter of cognitive ability. Whether the suggested distinction between FI and weak central coherence holds up is a matter for empirical inquiry. However, it is possible to derive distinct predictions from FI and weak central coherence; for example, when people with weak central coherence do make errors on the Wechsler Block Design (BD) subtest, these should be of the type that preserve design details and violate configuration. When FI people make errors on the BD, however, they (like FD people) would be expected to make errors reflecting their relative failure to overcome gestalt—i.e. configuration-preserving, detail-violating errors.

The FI/D literature may be relevant, however, for its findings on the relation between cognitive style and social orientation. In the early literature, FD individuals are described as more socially oriented, sensitive, and successful (Witkin and Goodenough 1977). What competence or preference differences lie behind this generalisation remains unclear. However, a number of more recent studies do suggest an intriguing inverse relation between field independence (as measured by success on tasks such as the EFT) and social skills. A study by Saracho (1991), for example, found that FI children were less able than FD children to assume a role or solve a social problem, and teachers perceived FD children as more socially competent.

Saracho (1995) also found that, among 1 276 three- to five-year-olds, FD children showed more social play, while FI children showed more non-social play.

On the one hand, then, there is evidence for weak central coherence in people with autism regardless of their theory of mind success, while on the other hand there is some evidence for an inverse relation between social skills and disembedding ability in normal, and perhaps also autistic, groups. What should we conclude about the relation between theory of mind and central coherence? The answer to this question probably rests on what we mean by 'theory of mind'. Briefly, it is useful to distinguish between two meanings. First, there is the basic ability to form representations capable of capturing propositional attitudes (m-representations in Leslie's current terminology; Leslie 1994)—an ability which is necessary (but perhaps not sufficient) for passing false-belief tests. This ability is conceptualised as species-typical, under high evolutionary pressure, and probably invariant in the normal population (although variation in e.g. speed of operation, is a possibility). Second, there is the individual's emergent social understanding, which is based on the ability to form m-representations in order to attribute mental states, but which is clearly also a function of many other characteristics including personality, motivation, empathy, intelligence, and environmental and experiential factors (e.g. Dunn *et al.* 1991).

In Happé and Frith's current conceptualization, central coherence is independent from theory of mind in its former, but not its latter, meaning. The individual with autism is considered to lie at the extreme end of a normal continuum for central coherence, while having also suffered specific damage to the mechanism for forming m-representations—the theory of mind mechanism, or ToMM. In this sense ToMM is independent of central coherence—the autistic impairment in forming m-representations is not the cause or result of weak central coherence. However, when we consider theory of mind in its second (and broader) sense, then social understanding cannot be considered independent of coherence—because in order to appreciate people's thoughts and feelings in real life one needs to take into account context and to integrate diverse information. So when we measure social understanding in a more naturalistic or context-sensitive way, we are likely to find a contribution from central coherence—and that individuals with weak central coherence and detail-focused processing are less successful in putting together the information necessary for sensitive social inference.

This distinction between the representational mechanism necessary *for* theory of mind and the social understanding springing *from* theory of mind may go some way toward clarifying the relation between coherence and theory of mind in autism. We know that some people with autism pass even complex second-order false-belief tasks, and do so consistently in a way that suggests they are indeed capable of representing mental states (although usually years or decades later than in normal development; Happé 1995). These individuals still show weak coherence—suggesting that the presence or absence of the ToMM is not causally related to this piecemeal processing style. Note that, while these individuals are somewhat better adapted socially, they are still markedly impaired, and often unable to use their apparent understanding of mental states in real life contexts. According to the account given here, this is because of their persisting weak central coherence—which, for example, makes them relatively poor at inferring mental states in stories in which utterances must be interpreted in context (Happé 1994c). So while they can demonstrate their late-acquired m-representational ability in Sally-Ann type false-belief tasks (which are stripped of context and in which each relevant piece of information is fed to the participant), they are limited in their application of this ability in everyday life due to their weak coherence. To the degree that people with autism vary among themselves in how weakly coherent their processing style is, it would be expected that degree of weak coherence would relate inversely to social understanding in everyday life. Individual differences in social ability among the general population may also reflect the operation of central coherence in the use of an intact ToMM in context.

If this account is right, then a number of bold predictions follow. First, it should be possible to find individuals who have weak central coherence but intact ToMM, and vice versa. Where might such groups be found? The fathers in our family study (Happé *et al.*, submitted) might be said to show weak central coherence without a ToMM impairment. More speculatively, one might suggest that Williams Syndrome represents a case of weak central coherence with intact theory of mind (Karmiloff-Smith *et al.* 1995). People with Williams Syndrome show some evidence of piecemeal processing (Bihrle *et al.* 1989), although interestingly they are poor at visuospatial tasks such as Block Design, perhaps due to additional visuospatial deficits. What of the reverse—can we find individuals with strong central coherence but a ToMM impairment? This picture might be hard to spot, because strong coherence may allow fairly good compensation for deficits, but might be reflected in poor false-belief test performance (where facilitatory context is stripped away) in the presence of fairly good social adaptation (e.g. Frith *et al.* 1994).

The alternative is that the ability to attribute mental states (theory of mind) and to integrate information (central coherence) are causally connected, not merely interacting, aspects of autism and possibly of normal development. It is conceivable that integrative processing of environment provides the inputs necessary for the maturation of the theory of mind mechanism. It is also conceivable that our tendency for extraction of higher-level meaning is socially-mediated, although apparently global processing in non-human animals (Jitsumori and Matsuzawa 1991) and infants (Bhatt *et al.* 1994; Freeseman *et al.* 1993) renders this less likely.

## FUTURE DIRECTIONS

Many challenges remain to the central coherence account, not least to specify the mechanism for central coherence. Should we think of a central mechanism taking information from several modules and systems and integrating these for higher-level meaning? Or should central coherence be thought of as a property of each subsystem, in which one might think of a setting for the relative precedence of global versus local processing? This might be resolved through explorations of individuals' central coherence across and within a number of domains—does degree of central coherence in a verbal task predict degree of coherence in a visuospatial task, or are these somewhat independent? Functional imaging work may help to shed light on the unitary or distributed neuro-anatomic substrate(s) for coherence. Neuropsychological studies may also give clues; research on the effects of brain damage suggests a special role for the right hemisphere in the processing of information in context (Robertson and Lamb 1991). Indeed, there is some evidence that deficits in integrative processing in the visuospatial domain correlate with integrative deficits in the verbal-semantic domain, in patients with right hemisphere damage (Benowitz *et al.* 1990; Moya *et al.* 1986).

It is unlikely, however, that autism will prove to be the result of damage confined to one brain region—and the very notion of central coherence conjures up images of diffuse differences in brain organisation. One intriguing finding, in this respect, is that some people with autism have larger or heavier brains than do comparison groups (Bailey *et al.* 1993; Piven *et al.* 1995). It is possible that this reflects an abnormal number or density of neurons, perhaps due to failure of pruning in brain development. In turn, processing with excessive neurons may result in a failure to process information for gist—a lack of drive for cognitive economy, as a result of cognitive capacity for exemplar-based (large memory store) processing. Cohen (1994) has presented a computational model of autism, in which lack of generalisation results from an increase in units (see also Gustafsson 1997)—an intriguing example of how computational analyses may interact with neuroanatomical data and psychological theory to help solve the puzzle of autism.

Just as the idea of a deficit in theory of mind has taken several years and considerable (and continuing) work to be empirically established, so the idea of a weakness in central coherence will require a systematic programme of research. It is to be hoped that, whether right or wrong, the central coherence theory will form a useful framework for thinking about autism, and help us to understand how our need to make sense of those around us, through 'mind-reading', relates to our tendency to integrate details in order to see the bigger picture.

## REFERENCES

Ameli, R., Courchesne, E., Lincoln, A., Kaufman, A. S. and Grillon, C. (1988). Visual memory processes in high-functioning individuals with autism. *Journal of Autism and Developmental Disorders*, **18**, 601–15.

APA (1994). *Diagnostic and statistical manual of mental disorders*, (4th edn), (DSM-IV). American Psychiatric Association, Washington, DC.

Aurnhammer-Frith, U. (1969). Emphasis and meaning in recall in normal and autistic children. *Language and Speech*, **12**, 29–38.

Bailey, A., Luthert, P., Bolton, P., LeCouteur, A., Rutter, M. and Harding, B. (1993). Autism and megalencephaly [letter]. *Lancet*, **341**, 1225–6.

Baron-Cohen, S. and Hammer, J. (1997a). Parents of children with Asperger syndrome: what is the cognitive phenotype? *Journal of Cognitive Neuroscience*, **9**, 548–54.

Baron-Cohen, S. and Hammer, J. (1997b). Is autism an extreme form of the male brain? *Advances in Infancy Research*, **11**, 193–217.

Baron-Cohen, S., Wheelwright, S., Stott, C., Bolton, P., and Goodyer, I. (1997). Is there a link between engineering and autism? *Autism*, **1**, 101–9.

Bartlett, F. C. (1932). Remembering: a study in experimental and social psychology. Cambridge University Press.

Bartlett, J. C. and Searcy, J. (1993). Inversion and configuration of faces. *Cognitive Psychology*, **25**, 281–316.

Benowitz, L. I., Moya, K. L. and Levine, D. N. (1990). Impaired verbal reasoning and constructional apraxia in subjects with right hemisphere damage. *Neuropsychologia*, **23**, 231–41.

Bhatt, R. S., Rovee-Collier, C. and Shyi, G. C. W. (1994). Global and local processing of incidental information and memory retrieval at six months. *Journal of Experimental Child Psychology*, **57**, 141–62.

Bihrle, A. M., Bellugi, U., Delis, D. C. and Marks, S. (1989). Seeing either the forest or the trees: dissociation in visuospatial processing. *Brain and Cognition*, **11**, 37–49.

Brian, J. A. and Bryson, S. E. (1996). Disembedding performance and recognition memory in autism/PDD. *Journal of Child Psychology and Psychiatry*, **37**, 865–72.

Briskman, J., Happé, F., and Frith, U. Exploring the cognitive phenotype of autism: weak 'central coherence' in parents and siblings of children with autism. II: questionnaire measures. (Submitted.)

Cohen, I. L. (1994). An artificial neural network analogue of learning in autism. *Biological Psychiatry*, **36**, 5–20.

Colombo, J., Freeseman, L. J., Coldren, J. T. and Frick, J. E. (1995). Individual differences in infant fixation duration: dominance of global versus local stimulus properties. *Cognitive Development*, **10**, 271–85.

Coren, S. and Enns, J. T. (1993). Size contrast as a function of conceptual similarity between test and inducers. *Perception and Psychophysics*, **54**, 579–88.

DeGelder, B., Vroomen, J. and Van der Heide, L. (1991). Face recognition and lip-reading in autism. *European Journal of Cognitive Psychology*, pp. 69–86.

Dunn, J., Brown, J., Slomkowski, C., Tesla, C. (1991). Young children's understanding of other people's feelings and beliefs: individual differences and their antecedents. *Child Development*, **62**, 1352–66.

Eskes, G. A., Bryson, S. E. and McCormick, T. A. (1990). Comprehension of concrete and abstract words in autistic children. *Journal of Autism and Developmental Disorders*, **20**, 61–73.

Fagot, J. and Deruelle, C. (1997). Processing of global and local visual information and hemispheric specialization in humans (*Homo Sapiens*) and baboons (*Papio papio*). *Journal of Experimental Psychology: Human Perception and Performance*, **23**, 429–42.

Freeseman, L. J., Colombo, J. and Coldren, J. T. (1993). Individual differences in infant visual attention: four-month-olds' discrimination and generalization of global and local stimulus properties. *Child Development*, **64**, 1191–203.

Frith, U. (1970a). Studies in pattern detection in normal and autistic children. I: immediate recall of auditory sequences. *Journal of Abnormal Psychology*, **76**, 413–20.

Frith, U. (1970b). Studies in pattern detection in normal and autistic children. II: reproduction and production of color sequences. *Journal of Experimental Child Psychology*, **10**, 120–35.

Frith, U. (1989). Autism: explaining the enigma. Blackwell, Oxford.

Frith, U. and Happé, F. (1994). Autism: beyond 'theory of mind'. *Cognition*, **50**, 115–32.

Frith, U. and Hermelin, B. (1969). The role of visual and motor cues for normal, subnormal and autistic children. *Journal of Child Psychology and Psychiatry*, **10**, 153–63.

Frith, U. and Snowling, M. (1983). Reading for meaning and reading for sound in autistic and dyslexic children. *Journal of Developmental Psychology*, **1**, 329–42.

Frith, U., Happé, F. and Siddons, F. (1994). Autism and theory of mind in everyday life. *Social Development*, **3**, 108–24.

Fyffe, C. and Prior, M. (1978). Evidence for language recoding in autistic, retarded and normal children: a re-examination. *British Journal of Psychology*, **69**, 393–402.

Gepner, B., Mestre, D., Masson, G. and de Schonen, S. (1995). Postural effects of motion vision in young autistic children. *Neuroreport*, **6**, 1211–4.

Gregory, R. L. (1967). *Eye and brain*. World University Library, New York.

Gustafsson, L. (1997). Inadequate cortical feature maps: a neural circuit theory of autism. *Biological Psychiatry*, **42**, 1138–47.

Happé, F. G. E. (1994a). Wechsler IQ profile and theory of mind in autism: a research note. *Journal of Child Psychology and Psychiatry*, **35**, 1461–71.

Happé, F. (1994b). Autism: an introduction to psychological theory. UCL Press, London.

Happé, F. G. E. (1994c). An advanced test of theory of mind: understanding of story characters' thoughts and feelings by able autistic, mentally handicapped and normal children and adults. *Journal of Autism and Developmental Disorders*, **24**, 129–54.

Happé, F. G. E. (1995). The role of age and verbal ability in the theory of mind task performance of subjects with autism. *Child Development*, **66**, 843–55.

Happé, F. G. E. (1996). Studying weak central coherence at low levels: children with autism do not succumb to visual illusions. A research note. *Journal of Child Psychology and Psychiatry*, **37**, 873–7.

Happé, F. G. E. (1997). Central coherence and theory of mind in autism: reading homographs in context. *British Journal of Developmental Psychology*, **15**, 1–12.

Happé, F., Briskman, J. and Frith, U. Exploring the cognitive phenotype of autism: weak 'central coherence' in parents and siblings of children with autism. I: experimental tests. (Submitted.)

Heaton, P., Hermelin, B. and Pring, L. (1998). Autism and pitch processing: a precursor for savant musical ability. *Music Perception*, **15**, 291–305.

Hermelin, B. and O'Connor, N. (1967). Remembering of words by psychotic and subnormal children. *British Journal of Psychology*, **58**, 213–8.

Hermelin, B. and O'Connor, N. (1970). *Psychological experiments with autistic children*. Pergamon, Oxford.

Hobson, R. P., Ouston, J. and Lee, T. (1988). What's in a face? The case of autism. *British Journal of Psychology*, **79**, 441–53.

Jarrold, C. and Russell, J. (1997). Counting abilities in autism: possible implications for central coherence theory. *Journal of Autism and Developmental Disorders*, **27**, 25–37.

Jarrold, C., Jimenez, F. and Butler, D. (1998). Evidence for a link between weak central coherence and theory of mind deficits in autism. Paper presented at BPS Developmental Section Conference, September 1998, Lancaster.

Jitsumori, M. and Matsuzawa, T. (1991). Picture perception in monkeys and pigeons: transfer of rightside-up versus upside-down discrimination of photographic objects across conceptual categories. *Primates*, **32**, 473–82.

Jolliffe, T. (1997). Central coherence dysfunction in autistic spectrum disorder. Unpublished PhD thesis. University of Cambridge.

Jolliffe, T. and Baron-Cohen, S. (1997). Are people with autism and Asperger syndrome faster than normal on the Embedded Figures Test? *Journal of Child Psychology and Psychiatry*, **38**, 527–34.

Kanner, L. (1943). Autistic disturbances of affective contact. *Nervous Child*, **2**, 217–50.

Karmiloff-Smith, A., Klima, E., Bellugi, U., Grant, J. and Baron-Cohen, S. (1995). Is there a social module? Language, face processing and theory of mind in individuals with Williams Syndrome. *Journal of Cognitive Neuroscience*, **7**, 196–208.

Kimchi, R. (1992). Primacy of wholistic processing and the global/local paradigm: a critical review. *Psychological Bulletin*, **112**, 24–38.

Langdell, T. (1978). Recognition of faces: an approach to the study of autism. *Journal of Child Psychology and Psychiatry*, **19**, 255–68.

Leslie, A. M. (1994). Pretending and believing: issues in the theory of ToMM. *Cognition*, **50**, 211–38.

McKelvie, S. J. (1995). Emotional expression in upside-down faces: evidence for configurational and componential processing. *British Journal of Social Psychology*, **34**, 325–34.

Mottron, L. and Belleville, S. (1993). A study of perceptual analysis in a high-level autistic subject with exceptional graphic abilities. *Brain and Cognition*, **23**, 279–309.

Mottron, L., Belleville, S. and Ménard, A. (1999). Local bias in autistic subjects as evidenced by graphic tasks: perceptual hierarchization or working memory deficit? **40**, 743–55.

Mottron, L., Burack, J. A., Stauder, J. E. A. and Robaey, P. Perceptual processing and autism. *Journal of Child Psychology and Psychiatry*. (In press.)

Moya, K. L., Benowitz, L. T., Levine, D. N. and Finklestein, S. (1986). Covariant defects in visuospatial abilities and recall of verbal narrative after right hemisphere stroke. *Cortex*, **22**, 381–97.

Navon, D. (1977). Forest before trees: the precedence of global features in visual perception. *Cognitive Psychology*, **9**, 353–83.

Navon, D. (1981). The forest revisited: more on global precedence. *Psychological Research*, **43**, 1–32.

Ozonoff, S., Rogers, S. J. and Pennington, B. F. (1991). Asperger's syndrome: evidence of an empirical distinction from high-functioning autism. *Journal of Child Psychology and Psychiatry*, **32**, 1107–22.

Ozonoff, S., Strayer, D. L., McMahon, W. M. and Filloux, F. (1994). Executive function abilities in autism and Tourette syndrome: An information processsing approach. *Journal of Child Psychology and Psychiatry*, **35**, 1015–32.

Piven, J., Arndt, S., Bailey, J., Havercamp, S., Andreasen, N. C. and Palmer, P. (1995). An MRI study of brain size in autism. *American Journal of Psychiatry*, **152**, 1145–9.

Plaisted, K., O'Riordan, M., and Baron-Cohen, S. (1998). Enhanced visual search for a conjunctive target in autism: a research note. *Journal of Child Psychology and Psychiatry*, **39**, 777–83.

Pring, L. and Hermelin, B. (1993). Bottle, tulip and wineglass: semantic and structural picture processing by savant artists. *Journal of Child Psychology and Psychiatry*, **34**, 1365–85.

Pring, L., Hermelin, B. and Heavey, L. (1995). Savants, segments, art and autism. *Journal of Child Psychology and Psychiatry*, **36**, 1065–76.

Rhodes, G., Brake, S., and Atkinson, A. P. (1993). What's lost in inverted faces? *Cognition*, **47**, 25–57.

Rimland, B. and Hill, A. L. (1984). Idiot savants. In *Mental retardation and developmental disabilities*, Vol. 13, (ed. J. Wortis), pp. 155–69. Plenum Press, New York.

Robertson, L. C. and Lamb, M. R. (1991). Neuropsychological contribution to theories of part/whole organization. *Cognitive Psychology*, **23**, 299–330.

Saracho, O. N. (1991). Social correlates of cognitive style in young children. *Early Development and Care*, **76**, 117–34.

Saracho, O. N. (1995). The relationship between the cognitive styles and play behaviours of pre-school children. *Educational Psychology*, **15**, 405–15.

Scheuffgen, K. (1998). Domain general and domain specific deficits in autism and dyslexia. Unpublished PhD thesis. University of London.

Shah, A. and Frith, U. (1983). An islet of ability in autistic children: a research note. *Journal of Child Psychology and Psychiatry*, **24**, 613–20.

Shah, A. and Frith, U. (1993). Why do autistic individuals show superior performance on the Block Design task? *Journal of Child Psychology and Psychiatry*, **34**, 1351–64.

Snowling, M. and Frith, U. (1986). Comprehension in 'hyperlexic' readers. *Journal of Experimental Child Psychology*, **42**, 392–415.

Tager-Flusberg, H. (1991). Semantic processing in the free recall of autistic children: further evidence for a cognitive deficit. *British Journal of Developmental Psychology*, **9**, 417–30.

Takeuchi, A. H. and Hulse, S. H. (1993). Absolute pitch. *Psychological Bulletin*, **113**, 345–61.

Turner, M. (1996). Repetitive behaviour and cognitive functioning in autism. Unpublished PhD thesis. University of Cambridge.

Weeks, S. J. and Hobson, R. P. (1987). The salience of facial expression for autistic children. *Journal of Child Psychology and Psychiatry*, **28**, 137–52.

Witkin, H. A. and Goodenough, D. R. (1977). Field dependence and interpersonal behaviour. *Psychological Bulletin*, **84**, 661–89.

Witkin, H. A. and Goodenough, D. R. (1981). *Cognitive styles: essence and origins.* International University Press, New York.

Witkin, H. A., Lewis, H. B., Hertzman, M., Machover, K., Meissner, P. B. and Wapner, S. (1954). *Personality through perception: an experimental and clinical study.* Harper and Brothers, New York.

Witkin, H. A., Dyk, R. B., Faterson, H. F., Goodenough, D. R. and Karp, S. K. (1962). *Psychological differentiation.* Wiley, New York.

Witkin, H. A., Oltman, P. K., Raskin, E. and Karp, S. (1971). *A manual for the Embedded Figures Test.* Consulting Psychologists Press, California.

# 10

# Aspects of autism that theory of mind cannot explain

KATE C. PLAISTED

It goes without saying that over the last fifteen years a great deal of research in autism has been generated by the hypothesis that children with autism lack theory of mind skills. But running in parallel with the theory of mind research has been a line of research examining the so-called 'asocial' abnormalities in autism. This research can be considered to fall broadly into two camps—that which studies visuospatial process-ing in autism and that which considers object and pattern processing. The aim of this chapter will not be to provide comprehensive review of that literature on the asocial aspects of autism but to highlight the major theoretical ideas. Attempts will be made to consider how far those ideas complement or contradict one another, and where possible to suggest alternative interpretations which might lead to future research. I will then consider how far these ideas can be related to theories concerned with the social and communicative deficits in autism. Could, for example, the theory of mind deficit theory of autism explain the asocial aspects of individuals with autism? Probably not, but equally the study of asocial abnormalities in autism is a long way from explaining theory of mind deficits. There are a few studies which have attempted to relate attentional processing to social behaviours which will be reviewed, and I shall finish with some speculations about how the asocial abnormalities previously high-lighted might relate to deficits in face processing in autism.

## OVER-SELECTIVE ATTENTION

A great number of clinical and anecdotal observations have documented the fascina-tion of children with autism with small details of objects in the environment. Although some common themes emerge concerning the type of stimulation which provides this interest, such as spinning the wheels of a toy car, children with autism are fairly idiosyncratic with respect to the particular stimuli they focus upon. Furthermore, once engaged, children with autism appear to process very little outside the object of interest. Features of autism such as this have led researchers to suggest that children with autism have a general tendency to process only a limited part of the information available in the environment. A number of early hypotheses posited to explain these aspects of autism were later discounted for lack of experimental support and lack of specificity to autism (see Frith and Baron-Cohen 1987, for a review). Nonetheless, some of these ideas have persisted and, with some modification and refinement, continue to inspire current research.

For example, several researchers ascribed to the view that autism was characterised by sensory over- and under-arousal (Hutt *et al.* 1964; Ornitz and Ritvo 1968; Rimland 1964) leading to preferences for or avoidance of certain environmental stimuli, insistence on sameness, and other repetitive behaviours. These aspects of autism were therefore seen as behavioural strategies adopted to reduce unstable sensory experiences. However, it was emphasised by Lovaas and his colleagues (Lovaas *et al.* 1971) that children with autism show wide variability in their responses to particular stimuli on different occasions. For example, a particular noise may provoke extreme distress on one occasion but be entirely ignored on another. Lovaas therefore proposed that the underlying cause of these behaviours was an attentional rather than sensory deficit. Specifically, he proposed that children with autism exhibited stimulus over-selectivity, with the result that they often responded to minor and irrelevant cues in the environment. Not only did this suggestion provide an explanation for inconsistent abnormal responding to environmental stimuli but also for the great difficulty children with autism have in generalizing knowledge or skills learned in one environment to another.

Experimental analysis of Lovaas's hypothesis, however, failed to discriminate between children with autism and children with low IQ. Nonetheless, it was noted by Rincover and colleagues (e.g. Anderson and Rincover 1982) that stimulus over-selectivity in autism was particularly apparent when stimulus cues were spatially separated. For example, Rincover and Ducharme (1987) compared children with autism and typically-developing children matched for mental age, on two discrimination tasks. Each task involved different shapes and different colours; in one task the shapes were filled with colours, so that shape and colour occupied the same location, while in the other, shapes and bars of colour were spatially separated. Once children had learned these discriminations, they were given generalisation tests in order to assess whether both cues (shape and colour) or only one cue (shape or colour) controlled responding. It was found that both cues controlled responding equally in both groups of children in the task where shape and colour appeared in the same location. However, the group with autism, unlike the typically-developing children, responded disproportionately to the two cues in the task where shapes and colours were spatially separated. On the basis of such results, Rincover and colleagues suggested that the primary deficit in autism is overselective visuospatial attention, or 'tunnel vision', as it was dubbed.

## VISUOSPATIAL ATTENTION

This idea subsequently provoked a number of studies examining spatial attention in autism. One procedure used by a number of researchers is a spatial attention cueing task, originally designed by Posner (1980; Posner *et al.* 1984). In this task, participants are required to respond as quickly as possible when they detect a target on a screen which can appear to the left or right of a central fixation point. Prior to the appearance of the target, a cue is presented which provides either valid or invalid information regarding the imminent location of the target—in other words, the cue either directs the participant to the correct location in which the target will appear or incorrectly directs the participant to the wrong location. A robust finding in normal participants is that RT for detecting the target is slower when the cue provides invalid information compared to RT when the target has been validly cued, indicating that the cue serves to orient the participant's attention to a location in space in which the target may or may not appear.

The Posner cueing task can be modified with respect to the type of cue which can be used to orient attention. In one version of the task, a symbolic cue such as an arrow is placed in the centre of the screen, replacing the fixation point. It is assumed that such cues orient attention endogenously and that endogenous attention is under the subject's voluntary control. In the other version, exogenous cues are placed either to the left or right of fixation point, at the same location in which the target will subsequently appear (valid trials) or in a different location (invalid trials). A common form of exogenous cue used in the Posner cueing task is an illuminated box, and such cues are assumed to capture attention automatically at the location in which they occur.

One other factor which is manipulated in the Posner cueing task is the temporal interval between the appearance of the cue and the onset of the target, commonly referred to as stimulus onset asynchrony (SOA). At long SOAs (e.g. 800 ms), subjects are able to make overt eye movements to the cued location, whereas at short SOAs (e.g. 100 ms) it is assumed that they cannot. Nevertheless, the fact that response times to the target are slower on invalid trials compared to valid trials at short SOAs suggests that attention is covertly oriented towards the location of the cue in this condition. Covert orienting of attention is therefore thought of as orienting attention to a spatial location 'in the mind's eye' as opposed to overt orienting which is accompanied by overt behaviours such as eye and head movements. (See Klein *et al.* 1992, for a discussion about the relationships between endogenous and exogenous cueing and overt and covert orienting in normal individuals.)

Posner has argued that spatial cueing tasks of this kind assess the ability to disengage attention from one location, to shift attention to a new location and to engage attention at a location. Such a functional distinction of attentional processing is based on the idea that selective attention can be conceptualised as a 'spotlight' which can be moved through space. Spotlight models of attention assume that only information within the attentional 'beam' is processed so that when it leaves one location (disengagement), that location is left in darkness; that when attention is shifted to a new location, it moves in a continuous way, so that RT for detecting targets far away from the disengaged location is slower than RT for detecting targets which are closer; that attentional processing at a location begins only once the beam has arrived at that location (engaging attention); and that the size and intensity of the beam can be altered. Mapping the spotlight model onto Rincover and Ducharme's (1987) hypothesis that children with autism exhibit 'tunnel vision' raises several possibilities. They may fail to process information outside the current focus of attention due to difficulties in initiating a movement of the beam away from the focus (deficit in disengagement). Another possibility is that the velocity with which the beam is moved from one location to another may be reduced in autism (slowed attention shifting), with the end result that overall less information is processed within a given time window than in the normal case. Alternatively, less information may be processed at a location, because the size and intensity of the beam may be reduced in autism.

These possibilities have been assessed in both endogenous and exogenous versions of the Posner cueing task. Townsend, Courchesne and Egaas (1996), for example, compared a group of normal adults with a group of individuals with autism using an exogenous version of the task. All of the group with autism had cerebellar abnormalities and a subgroup had additional parietal abnormalities. The exogenous cue was the illumination of a box to the left or right of fixation, followed either 800 ms later (overt orienting condition) or 100 ms later (covert orienting) by the target, which appeared in the same or a different location. Townsend *et al.* (1996) found validity effects (faster responding to validly than invalidly cued targets) in the group with autism not only at long but also at short SOAs. Additionally, the subgroup with autism who had both cerebellar and parietal abnormalities showed greater validity effects compared with control individuals at both long and short SOAs, while the remaining individuals with autism (with cerebellar abnormality only) showed comparable validity effects to the control group.

Townsend *et al.* (1996) also measured the speed with which each group responded to a correctly cued target at each SOA and found that all individuals with autism, regardless of brain abnormality, were slower than control individuals at 100 ms, but not 800 ms, SOA. These data are important with respect to interpreting the enhanced validity effect found in the subgroup of individuals with autism who had both cerebellar and posterior parietal damage. If the enhanced validity effect resulted from faster responding to validly cued targets but equal responding to invalidly cued targets compared with the other groups, this would suggest that these individuals were faster to engage attention at the validly cued location. But the slower responding to validly cued targets in all individuals with autism at 100 ms SOA suggests that the subgroup with cerebellar and parietal abnormalities showed an enhanced validity effect because they were even slower than other groups to respond to invalidly cued targets. According to Posner's attentional framework, this suggests that the autistic group with cerebellar and posterior parietal damage found difficulty in disengaging attention from an incorrectly cued location.

This is not a surprising result given that individuals without autism but with posterior parietal damage show enhanced validity effects due to slowed responding to invalidly, but not validly, cued targets compared with normal individuals (Posner *et al.* 1984). Further evidence of involvement of the posterior parietal cortex in spatial attention comes from ERP studies of normal individuals (see, for example, Eimer 1998). This study of individuals with autism on the Posner cueing task therefore suggests that those individuals with autism with parietal abnormalities exhibit similar difficulties in spatial attention as individuals with parietal lesions.

Another study conducted by Townsend and Courchesne (1994) provides further evidence that individuals with autism and parietal abnormalities show abnormal spatial attention effects. Unlike the Posner cueing task, in which attention has to be shifted from trial to trial, this was a sustained attention task in which subjects attended to one location for a block of trials. In this study, five boxes were presented on a screen, one of which was coloured red. The subject's task was to respond to a target circle if it appeared in the red box and to refrain from responding if it appeared in any of the other four boxes.

Three groups of individuals were compared; a group of individuals with autism with additional parietal damage, another autistic group with no parietal damage, and a control group of normal individuals. Both groups of individuals with autism had additional cerebellar abnormalities. The study measured both behavioural responses to the targets and electrophysiological recordings of brain activity during the task. The group of individuals with autism and parietal damage responded more quickly to targets appearing in the attended location compared with the other two groups. Furthermore, this group showed a significantly greater P1 peak amplitude at the attended location (amplitude modulations of the P1 component of an event-related potential are thought to be related to mechanisms of spatial attentional selectivity), and lower P1 peak amplitudes across the remaining four unattended locations compared with the other group with autism (with no parietal abnormalities[1]) and the normal control group.

Townsend and Courchesne (1994) interpreted these results as evidence that individuals with autism with additional parietal damage show a narrowed distribution (or spotlight) of attention around an attended location. They argued that these results suggest that, in some individuals with autism, not only can attention be enhanced at a particular location compared with normal performance, but also areas around the focus of attention may be inhibited to a greater extent than in the normal case. This is certainly consistent with Rincover and Ducharme's (1987) description of 'tunnel vision' in autism, and raises the possibility that autism may be associated with parietal abnormalities which produce deficits in spatial attention (see Bryson *et al.* 1990, for the argument that autism can be conceptualised as a developmental spatial neglect syndrome). However, whether such an effect in the group with autism actually arose as a result of their parietal abnormalities remains to be established because the study did not include a comparison group of individuals with parietal damage but no autism.

Furthermore, it is unclear how the hypothesis of a narrow spotlight of attention by itself can explain the entire pattern of results shown by the groups with autism in Townsend *et al.*'s (1996) study. The idea that enhanced activity at an attended location, which may reduce the speed at which attention can be disengaged from one (e.g. miscued) location in order to be relocated at another (e.g. target) location (LaBerge 1974), may explain the enhanced validity effect in the group with both cerebellar and parietal abnormalities. But it does not predict the finding that at 100 ms SOA, both groups of individuals with autism (i.e. those with and without parietal abnormality) showed slower responding to validly cued targets. If anything, enhanced processing at a validly cued location predicts faster responses to validly cued targets in the Posner cueing task, compared with normal control groups.[2] Clearly an additional reason, which does not appeal solely to parietal mediation, is required to explain this effect.

The explanation advanced by Townsend *et al.* (1996) relates to the cerebellar abnormalities which were present in both groups of autistic individuals. Courchesne and his colleagues (Akshoomoff and Courchesne 1992; Courchesne *et al.* 1994*a,b*) have argued that the cerebellum plays a key role in the control and co-ordination of attention. More specifically, their hypothesis is that the cerebellum is ultimately responsible for the co-ordination of the patterns of excitation required to enhance processing of a stimulus (engaging) and inhibition required to decrease processing (disengaging) when an alternative stimulus requires attention. This hypothesis there-fore predicts that cerebellar abnormality will affect an individual's ability to shift attention from one stimulus to another, or from one spatial location to another. This should be particularly apparent in situations which require attention shifts to be made rapidly.

It is certainly the case that an impressive number of studies have reported cerebellar abnormality in autism (Courchesne *et al.* 1994*a*), and this therefore may be a core neurological deficit in the disorder (but see Robbins 1997 for a critical review of this hypothesis). Furthermore, individuals with autism and cerebellar abnormality have been found to be impaired on a non-spatial attention-cueing task. In this task, participants are required to monitor one stream of information for infrequent targets and, once encountered, to shift attention to another stream of information to monitor for other infrequent targets. Individuals with autism and cerebellar abnormalities have been found to perform in a similar way to patients with cerebellar damage in that they also show impairments on this task when rapid shifts of attention are required (Courchesne *et al.* 1994*a*). Thus, it may be the case that the cerebellar abnormalities of these individuals prevented rapid attention shifts from the fixation point to the cued location in the 100 ms SOA condition, resulting in slowed orienting to validly cued targets.

However, this hypothesis also predicts that validity effects at 100 ms SOA should be reduced or absent in groups of individuals with cerebellar abnormalities, because this time interval should be too short for attention to be oriented from the fixation point to the invalidly cued location; thus, attention would not need to be disengaged from the invalidly cued location and could instead be allocated directly to the target at the time of its appearance. Yet, both group of individuals with autism in Townsend *et al.*'s (1996) study showed significant validity effects—in fact, the group with both cerebellar and parietal abnormalities showed an *enhanced* validity effect at 100 ms SOA and the group with autism with cerebellar abnormalities showed a slightly smaller numerical but statistically comparable validity effect to that of control subjects. Furthermore, it is unlikely that the cerebellar abnormality in the group with autism and parietal damage was responsible for their enhanced validity effect at 800 ms SOA, because this effect was not observed in the autistic group with cerebellar but without parietal damage.

It may be wise at this point to recap the problems in interpreting the pattern of data in the attention-cueing tasks reviewed so far. The idea that autistic individuals with additional parietal damage have a narrow 'spotlight' of attention (Townsend and Courchesne 1994), or 'tunnel vision' (Rincover and Ducharme 1987) predicts enhanced validity effects, which were observed in individuals with autism and parietal damage at both 800 and 100 ms SOA. But the enhanced processing at a location suggested by a narrow spotlight of attention also predicts the complementary effect of quicker responses to validly cued targets, yet both groups of autistic individuals, regardless of parietal abnormality, showed slower responses at 100 ms SOA. Although this effect might be explained instead by slow attention shifting from the fixation point to the valid cue due to cerebellar abnormality, slow attention shifting also predicts the absence of a validity effect at 100 ms SOA. This was found in neither groups of individuals with autism.

Given these difficulties of interpretation, it may be the case the theories of the attentional spotlight and slowed attention shifting are inappropriate ones to apply to this data. In fact, several recent experiments conducted with normal individuals have produced data which challenges the spotlight metaphor of attention.[3] In the light of these challenges, LaBerge and colleagues (LaBerge 1995; LaBerge and Brown 1989; LaBerge *et al.* 1997) have suggested a new model of attentional orienting, and it is worth considering whether it might usefully be applied to the data from visuospatial orienting studies in autism. In brief, this model postulates two processes in visuo-spatial orienting. The first, attentional preparation (triggered by a warning signal or cue), activates a broad, relatively flat, distribution of activity in posterior parietal cortex (PPC), corresponding to the memory of the locations of recently presented stimuli (represented by the thin line in Fig. 10.1a). More importantly, preparatory attention additionally produces a Gaussian curve of activation around the location of a cue, in which the peak of the distribution represents a peak of activity at the centre of the cued area with the amount of activity decreasing gradually either side of the peak (represented by the thick line in Fig. 10.1a). The second process, selective attention (triggered by the onset of the target), produces activity at the point along the Gaussian curve corresponding to the location of the target. This 'injection' of activity is postulated to be determined by inputs from the dorsolateral prefrontal cortex (DLPFC). If the target appears at the cued location, selective attention will add slightly to the activity at the central point of the Gaussian distribution set up by preparatory attention (represented by the dashed line in Fig. 10.1a). In this case, selective attention need only raise activity slightly at the centre of the curve in order to distinguish that precise area from the immediately surrounding area and responding at that location will be fast. However, if an attentional shift is required (e.g. on invalidly cued trials) because the target appears at one of the tail ends of the Gaussian distribution of preparatory attention, selective attention needs to raise activity to a far greater degree than if it had appeared at the central location, in order for activity at the peripheral location to exceed the level of activity at any other point along the curve (Fig. 10.1b). Thus, the model states that the additional time required to raise activity at the peripheral point results in an increase in RT to an invalidly cued target compared to a validly cued one and in this way accounts for the cue validity effect.

This model suggests a number of different ways in which the processes involved in visuospatial orienting may be disrupted in the abnormal brain. For example, the rate at which preparatory attention sets up the Gaussian curve of activity in the PPC may be slower, so that the height of the curve at the time of stimulus events such as cueing or target presentation, may be lower than in the normal case (Fig. 10.2a). Another possibility is that the spread of activity may be different compared with the normal case. For example, activity may be concentrated at the centre and fall steeply on either

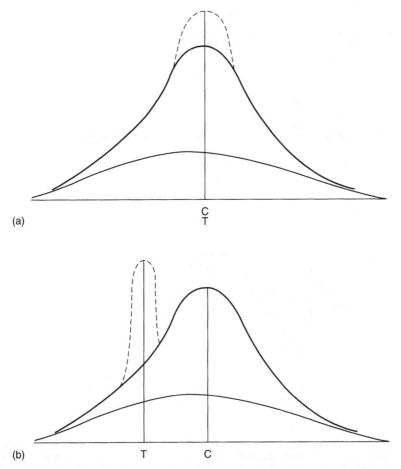

**Fig. 10.1.** Hypothesised distribution of activity corresponding to spatial attention produced in the posterior parietal cortex, adapted from LaBerge (1995; LaBerge and Brown 1989; LaBerge *et al.* 1997). The solid thick line in each case represents preparatory attention following the onset of a cue. The dashed thin line represents selective attention. C and T indicate the location of the cue and target, respectively. Thus, the top panel (a) represents the case where the cue and target are placed at the same location; and the bottom panel (b) represents the case when the target is presented peripherally to the cue.

side (Fig. 10.2b). Or, selective attention could be affected by reduced or slower rates of input from the DLPFC to the PPC, or by inefficient processing of those inputs by the PPC, again resulting in less activity at the point of target presentation.

How far do these possibilities account for the patterns of data for the two groups of individuals with autism on the Posner cueing task obtained by Townsend *et al.* (1996)? A retardation of the rate at which the activity curve corresponding to preparatory attention is established in the PPC can account for the slowed responses to validly cued targets at short SOAs in both autistic groups, because less activity would be

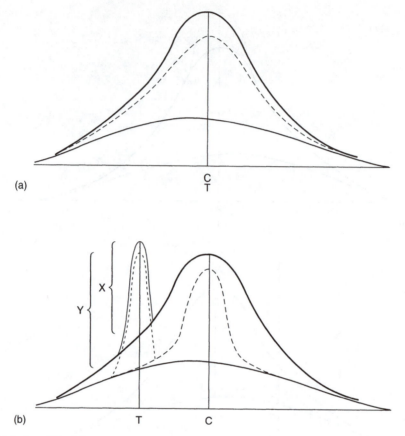

(a)

$$\begin{array}{c} C \\ T \end{array}$$

(b)

T          C

**Fig. 10.2.** Possible differences in preparatory attention between normal individuals (solid thick line) and individuals with autism (dashed thick line). C and T indicate the location of the cue and target respectively. The top panel (a) represents the possibility that the rate of preparatory attention is slowed in autism, with the effect that, at the onset of the target at a validly cued location, there will be less activity at the cued location than in the normal case. The bottom panel (b) represents the possibility that the distribution of activity corresponding to preparatory attention in individuals with autism and parietal damage may additionally show a narrower distribution. When the target appears at a location peripheral to the cue, selective attention will therefore need to raise activity to a greater extent (by value $y$) in the case of autism compared with the normal case (where activity would be raised to value $x$). Distribution of selective attention is represented here as a thin solid line around T for normal individuals and a thin dashed line around T for individuals with autism.

available at the central location at target onset compared with the normal case. However, this deficit would also result in a reduced (or even absent) validity effect at 100 ms SOA, because the invalidly cued target location would require less 'boosting' of activity (from DLPFC projections) by the selective attention process, in order to raise activity at that point above the level of activity at the miscued location, compared with the normal case. Interestingly, the group with autism with cerebellar but without parietal damage showed a numerically smaller validity effect at 100 ms SOA compared with the normal control group, and the hypothesis of reduced rate of preparatory attention may therefore be sufficient to explain the pattern of performance in this group.

It is not sufficient to explain the pattern of performance of the group with autism with both cerebellar and parietal damage. However, if it is additionally assumed that the distribution of activity produced by preparatory attention in the PPC was different in this group (perhaps as a result of their parietal abnormality), with activity falling steeply away from the centre of the curve (see Fig. 10.2b), then this predicts that the validity effect would be enhanced compared with a normal group. This is because activity at the target location would need to be raised to a greater extent (to the value $y$ in Fig. 10.2b) than in the normal case (value $x$ in Fig. 10.2b), thus lengthening the time before a response could be made.

This hypothesis of a narrowing of the distribution of activity in the PPC also predicts the results from the group with cerebellar and parietal abnormalities obtained by Townsend and Courchesne (1994) using a sustained attention task. One effect of activity declining steeply at the central location (which would be constantly primed by the red box cue) is that discrimination of that location from immediately surrounding locations would be enhanced as a result of the enhanced differential levels of activity at those locations. Enhanced discrimination of the target location from non-target locations in a sustained attention task therefore predicts the faster responding to the validly cued target observed in the autistic group with parietal damage compared with the normal control group.[4] These speculations made on the basis of LaBerge's model (1995) may therefore provide a more fruitful means of assessing and interpreting the effects of visuospatial orienting in autism than the spotlight model of attention.

An additional concern to the problem of interpreting the pattern of data from various attentional orienting tasks is whether the attention shifting task designed by Courchesne *et al.* (1994*a*,*b*) taps the same attentional processes as the exogenous version of the Posner cueing task. There are a number of reasons for thinking that it does not. For example, in the attention shifting task, subjects are required to monitor a stream of information for an infrequent target, to respond to the target, and then to use the target as a signal to switch attention to another stream of information. Thus the task requires holding the rules of the task in mind, continuous on-line monitoring of information within a dimension and updating of the switch rule ('if last least frequent target was dimension A then switch to dimension B, if last target was dimension B then switch to dimension A') as well as inhibition of responding to the irrelevant dimension. Such processes are generally considered to be under executive control and thus requiring effortful control of attentional resources and are also thought to be involved in many other neuropsychological tasks such as the Wisconsin Card Sorting Task and intra- and extra-dimensional shift tasks, on which individuals with autism also show impaired performance (see Russell 1997 for a recent review of the executive dysfunction hypothesis of autism). By contrast, in the exogenous version of the Posner cueing task, attention is considered to be drawn involuntarily by the exogenous cues.

The endogenous version of the Posner cueing task and the attention shifting task, however, may be more likely to tap similar attentional processes. After all, the endogenous task is assumed to involve voluntary attentional orienting based on the subject's expectations and intentions (Klein *et al.* 1992). An endogenous Posner cueing task has been employed by Wainwright-Sharpe and Bryson (1993) to compare a group of adults with autism with a group of normal individuals, using the endogenous cue of an arrow placed at the central fixation point followed by the target at short (100 ms) and long (800 ms) SOAs. At 800 ms SOA, both groups showed a cue validity effect. However, the group with autism showed a greater validity effect at 800 ms SOA compared with the control group. In contrast, at 100 ms SOA the group with autism showed no validity effect, responding at the same rate to the target regardless of whether it had been validly or invalidly cued. Furthermore, the autistic group was slower to orient to validly cued targets at both 800 and 100 ms SOA. Unlike the results of Townsend *et al.*'s study (1996) employing exogenous cues, this entire pattern of results is indeed predicted by Courchesne *et al.*'s hypothesis (Courchesne 1994*a,b*) that individuals with autism are slower to shift attention and consistent with the performance of individuals with autism on the attention shifting task.

However, a further issue to be considered is the role that level of cognitive functioning may play in determining the pattern of results of visuospatial cueing tasks. As Burack has pointed out (Burack 1997; Burack and Iarocci 1995), the group with autism in Wainwright-Sharpe and Bryson's study were of lower mean IQ than the control group. Furthermore, in Townsend *et al.*'s study (1996), although the mean IQ of each of the two autistic groups was similar to that of control group, the standard deviations around each mean in the autistic groups were far greater than that of the control group, suggesting that the autistic groups may have contained some individuals with IQs well below the normal range. It is therefore possible that slowed responding on visuospatial cueing tasks may relate to level of intellectual functioning rather than to any aspect of autism.

Burack and Iarocci (1995) addressed whether the results obtained in Wainwright-Sharpe and Bryson's (1993) study related to level of cognitive functioning, by comparing a group of children with autism with a group of children with organic mental retardation, matched for mental age on an exogenous version of the Posner-cueing task, assessing just covert orienting (150 ms SOA). Although they found that the children with autism were overall slower to respond to both validly and invalidly cued targets, both groups of children responded more slowly on invalid than valid trials. Furthermore, there were no differences between the groups in the magnitude of this validity effect. They therefore suggested that individuals with autism may perform on exogenous tasks in accordance with their level of cognitive functioning rather than their autism. They further proposed that the presence of the validity effect at a short SOA in their study and its absence in Wainwright-Sharpe and Bryson's (1993) study might be explained by the fact that the endogenous task taps an impairment in voluntary or controlled processing which is specific to autism, whereas exogenous covert orienting is intact in autism.

This study raises the possibility that the deficits in visuospatial orienting in the two groups with autism in Townsend *et al.*'s (1996) study were also related to level of cognitive functioning. However, the two studies cannot be directly compared because

Burack and Iarocci (1995) introduced two modifications of the exogenous cueing task that were not present in the task used by Townsend *et al.* (1996). First, Burack and Iarocci's task used an identification procedure—participants were required to indicate whether the target was a zero or a cross, and second, on some trials distracters were placed either side of target, as a means of addressing attentional filtering in autism and mental retardation. By contrast, Townsend *et al.*'s (1996) study used a simple target detection procedure and involved no distracters. (It is also difficult to directly compare Burack and Iarocci's study with Wainwright-Sharpe and Bryson's (1993) study for exactly the same reasons.) Furthermore, it cannot be known from Burack and Iarocci's (1995) study whether the enhanced validity effect observed at 800 ms SOA in some individuals with autism in Townsend *et al.*'s (1996) study, and in the autistic group in Wainwright-Sharpe and Bryson's (1993) study, relates to level of cognitive functioning, because Burack and Iarocci's (1995) study did not include a typically-developing control group.

Although the issues of identification processes and filtering irrelevant distracters in autism are interesting ones (Burack 1994; Plaisted *et al.* 1998*a*,*b*), a new study is now required which directly addresses the issue of the role of level of cognitive functioning in visuospatial orienting tasks. That is, a comparison is needed between individuals with autism, individuals with mental retardation, and typically-developing individuals on each version of the Posner cueing task, one using the task parameters employed in Wainwright-Sharpe and Bryson's (1993) endogenous task, and the other using the task parameters employed in Townsend *et al.*'s (1996) exogenous task. Using the same individuals in both versions of the Posner cueing task will allow inferences to made about the degree to which performance in each task is determined by level of cognitive functioning. This would also provide a means of assessing whether individuals with autism perform differently on the endogenous task compared to the exogenous task. That is, the hypothesis that individuals with autism experience executive control difficulties which impede the voluntary control of attention predicts a selective impairment on the endogenous version only. By contrast, the hypothesis that individuals with autism experience difficulties in attention shifting predicts impairments on both tasks, regardless of whether attention is voluntarily or automatically allocated to the potential target location.

In summary, the hypothesis that individuals with autism show over-selective attention (Lovaas *et al.* 1971) or 'tunnel vision' (Rincover and Ducharme 1987) has received some support from studies employing visuospatial orienting tasks. These studies have raised further interesting questions about the mechanisms underpinning visuospatial abnormalities in autism. One key question is how far the spotlight metaphor of selective attention captures the pattern of performance of individuals with autism on these tasks and whether alternative models of normal attention may provide better accounts. Another question is whether visuospatial orienting abnormalities in autism are primarily influenced by an impairment in controlled voluntary processing. If the answer to this question is yes, then differences in performance between individuals with and without autism on tasks which cue attention automatically may be more related to level of cognitive functioning than to autism. This possibility remains to be tested directly.

## STIMULUS DETECTION AND IDENTIFICATION

In contrast to their performance on tasks of visuospatial orienting, individuals with autism often show superior performance on tasks which require processing of patterns and shapes. It is now well established that individuals with autism can be faster and/or more accurate in detecting a small target figure embedded within a larger figure than control groups matched for mental age (Jolliffe and Baron-Cohen 1997; Shah and Frith 1983) and show superior performance on the block design task (Shah and Frith 1993). These are puzzling results considered in the light of the performance of individuals with autism on the visuospatial orienting tasks outlined above, because both the embedded figures task and the block design task require the participant to rapidly scan the stimulus array and therefore presumably involve shifts of attention from one location to another in the array. How are we to account for the discrepancy in performance of autistic individuals on different visuospatial tasks?

One possibility is to deny that the discrepancy exists by postulating that, unlike tasks such as endogenous Posner cueing tasks, performance on tasks such as the embedded figures and block design task does not involve processes such as controlled attention shifts but is instead determined by perceptual processes. The weak central coherence hypothesis (Frith 1989), put forward to explain the performance of autistic children on these tasks, is consistent with this view. This hypothesis draws on the ideas of the Gestalt psychologists by stating that, in normal children, there is a 'drive' to process the holistic properties of a stimulus prior to its constituent parts, and that this drive must be overcome in order to detect a part which is embedded within the holistic percept (Koffka 1935; Kohler 1929). The classic view is that accessing the local properties embedded in a holistic percept is therefore effortful and impedes the detection of an embedded figure. If, however, the drive to process holistic properties (or for central coherence—Frith 1989) is weakened in autism, resulting in a deficit in the perception of the global level of a stimulus, then detection of local information can occur relatively rapidly. According to the weak central coherence hypothesis, autistic children can therefore immediately access the constituent parts of a stimulus, and it is at this level that the solution to the embedded figures and block design tasks lies.

There are a number of studies which have demonstrated that normal individuals respond more rapidly to the global structure of a stimulus (see Kimchi 1992 for a review). Many of these studies have employed a task originally designed by Navon (1977), in which participants are presented with a large figure, such as a letter made up of smaller figures or letters of either the same kind (compatible condition) or a different kind (incompatible condition), and are required to identify the stimuli at the global and/or local level. Global advantage has been observed in two ways. First, normal individuals make fewer errors and are quicker to identify stimuli at the global than at the local level. Second, in incompatible conditions, normal individuals are slower to detect the target letter when it is at the local level compared with when it is at the global level, suggesting that global processing interferes with local processing.

This task therefore provides an excellent test of the weak central coherence hypothesis which predicts that, due to a deficit in global processing, individuals with autism would not be quicker to detect global stimuli and would not show global interference.

However, studies assessing this prediction have produced equivocal results. Ozonoff *et al.* (1994) compared a group of individuals with autism, individuals with Tourette's Syndrome, and normal individuals on a task in which a large global letter was composed of smaller letters. Within a block of trials the participants were required to identify the letter either at the local or at the global level. Participants could therefore selectively attend to either the global or the local level of all stimuli appearing within a block of trials. Contrary to the weak central coherence hypothesis, all individuals including the group with autism were quicker to identify global letters and showed global interference. Another study, conducted by Mottron and Belleville (1993), assessed an individual with autism, E. C., on a version of the task which required letters at both the global level and the local level to be named on each trial. The task therefore required E. C. to attend to both the global and the local level on each trial. In contrast to Ozonoff *et al.*'s (1994) result, E. C. showed a reversal of global interference to local interference by making far more global errors when stimuli were incompatible.

Because the difference in procedures used in each study made it difficult to assess the reasons for the difference in results, we decided to compare the same groups of children with autism and typically-developing children (matched for mental age) on two versions of the Navon task (Plaisted *et al.* 1999). One version was of the same kind used by Ozonoff *et al.* (1994) and the other was of the same kind used by Mottron and Belleville (1993). Thus in one task, the 'selective attention' task, children were told to identify a letter at either the global or the local level within a block of trials and in the other children were required to indicate the presence or absence of a target letter which could appear on any trial at the local or the global level. This 'divided attention' task, like Mottron and Belleville's task, therefore required attention to both the global and the local level on each trial.

Consistent with Ozonoff *et al.*'s (1994) results, we found that children with autism performed like typically-developing children in the selective attention task, by showing global interference and identifying global letters more rapidly than local letters. However, in the divided attention task, like E. C., the children with autism showed a local interference effect and, additionally, detected local targets more rapidly. The fact that the same group of children were assessed on each task means that the reason for this discrepancy must lie in the difference in the requirements for each task. That is, it would appear that when children with autism are primed to attend to the global level, as in selective attention tasks, they experience no difficulties in global perception. This casts some doubt on the idea that children with autism have a deficit in global processing, such that they do not show the primacy of holistic processing typical of normal individuals.

However, when children with autism are not primed to attend to the global level, as in divided attention tasks, they exhibit a preference to process the local level. In the light of the results from the selective attention tasks, we suggested that this weak central coherence effect might be better understood as a difference in the inhibition of irrelevant local information, under conditions which require global information processing in the absence of overt (or covert) priming of the global level, rather than a deficit in central coherence mechanisms responsible for holistic processing.

One assumption made by the weak central coherence hypothesis is that, in the normal case, the perception of the whole results from the integration of its component parts. Thus, weak central coherence in autism may result less from a difference in relative speed of processing the global and local levels of stimuli than from the inability to integrate otherwise separate pieces of information. It is by no means clear that the Navon task taps processes of integration in this sense, a number of studies employing the Navon procedure suggesting instead that the global and local levels are processed by dissociable systems (Badcock *et al.* 1990; Lamb *et al.* 1989, 1990; Shulman *et al.* 1986). A better test of the claim of the weak central coherence hypothesis, that there is a deficit in the ability to integrate information in autism, would be to assess the ability of children with autism on a task which explicitly requires the integration of information for successful performance. One direct test of integration is a visual search task in which participants are required to search a visual array for the presence or absence of a conjunctive target presented among a number of distracters.[5] The target is termed 'conjunctive' because it is a unique combination of two or more features held in common with the surrounding sets of distracters. For example, a red X target placed among red T and green X distracters is uniquely defined by the conjunction of the feature 'red' from one set of distracters and the shape 'X' from the other set. A conjunctive target can be contrasted with a feature target, which differs from all other distracters by possessing a unique feature, such as a red S target among red T and green X distracters.

While a feature target can be detected on the basis of its unique feature, the detection of such a conjunctive target requires the integration of different features, and it has further been argued that this process of integration requires focal attention (Treisman and Gelade 1980). This argument is supported by the fact that RT for the detection of a feature target remains constant regardless of how many surrounding distracters it appears among, while detecting a conjunctive target increases linearly with increases in the number of simultaneously presented distracters. Furthermore, in conjunctive search tasks there is generally a 2:1 ratio between the steepness of the search slopes for target absent and target present trials. These effects have been taken to reflect the operation of a serial, controlled attentional process in which a spotlight of attention is applied to each item in order to integrate its component features and identify it (Treisman and Gelade 1980). Thus, RT will be longer when there are more items in the array to be inspected, and search will be terminated on average in approximately half the time on target present trials than on target absent trials in which all items need to be inspected.

In a series of studies, we have compared the performance of children with autism and typically-developing children, matched for mental age, on feature and conjunctive search tasks, reasoning that the weak central coherence hypothesis would predict that, due to a deficit in the ability to integrate features, the performance of children with autism would be slower in conjunctive tasks than that of the control group (Plaisted *et al.* 1998a; O'Riordan *et al.*, submitted; O'Riordan and Plaisted, submitted). Similarly, the hypothesis that individuals with autism are slower to shift attention (Courchesne *et al.* 1994a,b) makes the same predictions, because it is assumed that, in the conjunctive task, the spotlight of attention is shifted from the location of one item to the next. Neither the weak central coherence hypothesis or the attention shifting hypothesis makes the prediction that children with autism would be impaired on a feature task, and this task therefore provides a nice control condition for any non-specific slowing of responding in groups with autism.

In contrast to the expectations of the weak central coherence hypothesis, we have consistently found that high-functioning children with autism show superior RT performance on conjunctive search tasks than normal children and, where ceiling effects do not mask a difference between groups, are also often faster on feature search tasks. Furthermore, although they are quicker to respond on both target present and target absent trials, children with autism, like normal children, show a 2:1 ratio in their search slopes on target absent and target present trials. This suggests, contrary to the attention shifting hypothesis, that children with autism show no deficit in shifting visuospatial attention from the location of one item to the next.

Thus, the results of studies in autism using the Navon task (Plaisted *et al.* 1999) provide no evidence that individuals with autism have a deficit in the ability to perceive a gestalt, and the visual search studies demonstrate that there is not a deficit in autism in the integration of features into a coherent whole. The visual search tasks also suggest, contrary to the impression given by studies looking at performance on visuospatial orienting tasks in autism, that controlled attentional processing of spatial location is also intact. However, more recent models of the processes involved in conjunctive visual search tasks in normal individuals, which lay less emphasis on the role of the application of an attentional spotlight in the detection of a conjunctive target and more emphasis on other processes, raise the possibility that visual search tasks may not tax attentional processes to a degree sufficient to reveal any visuospatial orienting deficit that may be present in an autistic group.

For example, Wolfe *et al.* (1989) have argued that automatic preattentive processes are critically involved in the detection of conjunctive targets. In line with Treisman's feature integration theory (Treisman and Gelade 1980), they propose that the features of the target and the distracters are represented in feature maps. They further propose that each feature map becomes divided into items which could be the target and items which could not, as a result of excitation of potential target features and/or inhibition of potential distracter features. They propose that the excitation in each feature map is then transmitted to a master map of the spatial locations of each item, raising the activity of the locations of potential targets. The spotlight of attention is then thought to be guided to those points of maximum excitation, where it applies the process of feature integration. Guidance of the spotlight by preattentive processes thus effectively reduces the total area or number of items which need to be searched. If preattentive processing is intact in autism, then attention would be guided to only a small area of the array and under these circumstances we might not expect to observe any attention shifting deficit which may exist in autism.

More important, however, are the questions of what gives rise to the superiority of visual search in autistic children compared with normal children, and whether the same reason underpins their superior performance in visual search tasks and tasks such as the embedded figures task. Recent models of visual search in normal individuals are again useful for assessing these questions. In contrast to Treisman's feature integration theory, which specifies feature integration as the factor which determines the rate at which subjects can detect targets in visual search tasks models, more recent models specify the degree of discriminability between targets and distracters as the rate determining factor (e.g. Duncan and Humphreys 1989). For example, Wolfe *et al.* (1989) argued that the transmission of information from feature maps to the location map is rarely perfect (if it were, the model predicts that attention would be immediately directed to the target with the effect that there would be no increase in RT with increases in the number of items in the array), and that there is noise in the signal from the parallel to the serial stage which arises from other activated features which do not belong to the target. Thus, the more noise that is present, the more potential locations the serial stage will inspect and RT for detection of the target will increase. One of the conditions which the model identifies as likely to result in an increase in noise is where targets and distracters share several features in common or where features of targets and distracters are similar along a dimension (such as a pink target among red distracters). And in many conjunctive search tasks, targets and distracters do share many common features, with the effect that search is guided to more locations than in the case of feature search tasks, where the target possesses a feature which is entirely discriminable from all features held by the distracters. With the reduction in discriminability between distracter and target features, the model predicts an increase in noise in the signal, which will be further enhanced by increased numbers of items in the array. Thus, there is a linear increase in RT with increases in array size in conjunctive tasks where the target and distracters share features in common.

Of course, this predicts that if discriminability between targets and distracters is increased in a conjunctive search task, there should be a corresponding reduction in the steepness of the RT slope across display sizes. This has been demonstrated in several studies. For example, Wolfe *et al.* (1989) gave subjects two conjunctive search tasks. In the first, a standard simple conjunction task, the target was uniquely defined by the conjunction of two features—a large red O target among large red X and large green O distracters. Thus, the target differed from each distracter by only one feature. In the second, the target was uniquely defined by the conjunction of three features—a large red O among small red X, small green O, and big green X distracters. Thus, the target differed from each distracter type by two features. Discriminability between target and distracters was therefore greater in the second than in the first task. In accordance with Wolfe *et al.*'s (1989) model, search slopes were significantly steeper in the first task compared with the second.

Models such as this raise the possibility that the superior performance of children with autism in search tasks results from more efficient processing of the distinguishing features of targets and distracters. As a test of this, we conducted a series of experiments comparing high-functioning children with autism with matched typically-developing children on tasks in which target–distracter discriminability was manipulated both between and within dimensions (O'Riordan and Plaisted, submitted). In all experiments, we contrasted performance on a task in which target–distracter discriminability was low with another in which target–distracter discriminability was high. Regardless of whether discriminability was manipulated between or within dimensions, we replicated the effect in normal children which had previously been observed in normal adults—that is, search was slowed in conditions where target–distracter discriminability was decreased compared with conditions in which targetdistracter discriminability was increased. Furthermore, children with autism showed faster performance compared with normal children and were not slowed to the same extent as normal children in conditions where target–distracter discriminability was decreased.[6]

These results strongly suggest that processes of discrimination operate differently in autism compared with the normal case—that is, children with autism appear to see less similarity between objects which hold features in common than do normal children. Another way of putting this is to say that children with autism process features which are held in common between objects poorly and, by implication, process features which are unique to an object (i.e. those features which differentiate that item from all others) extremely well. And this enhanced ability to discriminate may well underlie the superior performance of children with autism on the embedded figures task. The task is, after all, a discrimination task and a difficult one at that because the target is very similar to many other shapes which go to make up the entire pattern or picture. Detecting the target therefore requires discriminating the target shape from the remaining shapes on the basis of its unique features, and ignoring those aspects of its shape which are held in common with other shapes. If features unique to a stimulus are processed well and features held in common with other stimuli are processed poorly, as we are suggesting is the case in autism, then children with autism should show superior performance on the embedded figures task.

We have assessed this discrimination hypothesis directly by comparing the performance of high-functioning adults and children with autism, with that of normal individuals matched for general cognitive level, on their ability to solve difficult discriminations. What is meant by difficult is that the stimuli to be discriminated shared many features in common and each stimulus possessed very few features unique to itself. Our prediction was that groups with autism would show superior discrimination learning to the normal group, and by using such highly confusable stimuli we hoped to avoid ceiling effects, which would mask a possible difference between groups. This prediction has been confirmed in experiments with both adults and children with autism (Plaisted and O'Riordan, in preparation; Plaisted *et al.* 1998*b*).

A more powerful test of our hypothesis, however, would be to assess performance in a task that is the complementary opposite of a discrimination task. If individuals with autism show enhanced discrimination skills as a result of processing features unique to a stimulus well, but other features of that stimulus held in common with other stimuli poorly, then they should show poor performance on a task whose solution requires preferential processing of the features held in common between a set of stimuli. Such a task is, of course, a categorisation task. Of those studies which have been conducted on the ability of autistic children to categorise, the results of some demonstrate categorisation skills that would be expected given the level of mental age, while other studies demonstrate deficits in categorisation which seem specific to autism. Many of these studies employ matching procedures, such as sorting a set of simultaneously presented items along a dimension or matching one of two simultaneously presented stimuli to a sample stimulus (Shulman *et al.* 1995; Tager-Flusberg 1985; Ungerer and Sigman 1987).

It has been suggested that successful categorisation in autism is determined by the dimension along which the child is required to categorise. That is, autistic children appear to perform as well as comparison groups if they are allowed to sort or match items on the basis of perceptual cues, but can be significantly worse if the task requires categorisation across some other dimension in which perceptual cues are irrelevant (Shulman *et al.* 1995). Thus, it would appear that autistic children are very good at matching features in these sorts of tasks but rather poor in understanding that objects go together based on some other dimension. However, it could be argued that matching and sorting procedures are very limited tests of categorisation skills—when the categorisation can be conducted on the basis of perceptual features, they are assessments of a simultaneous comparison process, and when the stimuli cannot be categorised by physical features, they are assessments of a child's pre-existing concepts. What they are not are tests of an individual's ability to abstract a category and to form concepts.

The procedure that is required for assessing concept formation is one in which each stimulus or exemplar of a category is presented separately, so that there is no opportunity to compare exemplars simultaneously on the basis of perceptual features. This procedure has been extensively employed in prototype abstraction tasks using normal individuals (e.g. Homa *et al.* 1981). Participants are initially trained to categorise two sets of exemplars until they show reliable categorisation, and are then presented for the first time with the prototype of each set and other novel but non-prototypical exemplars, and required to categorise them. A robust finding in normal individuals is that the prototypes of each set of exemplars are categorised more accurately than the non-prototypical exemplars, even though prototypes and exemplars are equally novel.

All models of this prototype effect appeal to a mechanism of generalisation or similarity estimation between the exemplars or between their elements. For example, one of the simpler models, an elemental associative model, explains such prototype effects as follows: during categorisation training, the features or elements of an exemplar become associated with one category so that responding to new exemplars is determined by the associative value of the features which they share with previously trained exemplars. And the prototype, being the central tendency of each set of training exemplars, will acquire more generalised associative strength than another new exemplar, and will therefore be categorised more accurately. Categorisation and prototype abstraction is therefore a phenomenon of generalisation of associative strength between features held in common between a set of exemplars (Mackintosh 1995). Given our hypothesis that autistic individuals process common features poorly, we therefore predicted that autistic individuals would show a deficit in category learning in the initial categorization phase of a prototype experiment and would show a reduced prototype effect in comparison with normal individuals. This has been assessed in experiments involving high-functioning adults with autism (Plaisted *et al.*, submitted) and high-functioning children with autism (Plaisted and O'Riordan, in preparation).

Our prediction was confirmed in both studies, and, because the participants with autism had no associated mental handicap and were matched for general cognitive level with the control group, we concluded that a reduced ability to abstract a proto-type is specific to autism and is not related to general level of cognitive functioning. However, in one other study which has assessed prototype abstraction in autism, conducted by Klinger and Dawson (1995), the children with autism were relatively low-functioning and were therefore compared with a group of children with learning disabilities and normal children matched for mental age. Klinger and Dawson (1995) found that both children with autism and children with learning disabilities were impaired (and to the same extent), compared with typically-developing children. Far from concluding that children with autism can categorise to a level which would be expected of their mental age, Klinger and Dawson (1995) argued that the group with autism and the group with learning disabilities may show this deficit for different reasons.

We agree with this view on an empirical basis. All individuals with autism who participated in our prototype abstraction tasks had also participated in our experiments assessing discrimination, and all the participants with autism showed enhanced abilities to solve difficult discriminations on the one hand and reduced abilities to abstract prototypes on the other. Our suggestion is that this is because these two tasks are complementary opposites and that the pattern of strength and weakness exhibited by autistic individuals in our experiments results from the same underlying mechanism. We propose that this mechanism is one of reduced generalisation of responding between similar stimuli, in which individuals with autism process features held in common among a set of stimuli poorly, and features unique to a stimulus well, compared with non-autistic individuals. By contrast, we predict that individuals with learning disabilities would show a different pattern of performance on discrimination and categorisation tasks compared with normal children by being impaired on *both* tasks. Thus, unlike the case of children with autism, their impairment in categorisation tasks is likely to be the result of general and non-specific difficulties with the task requirements. This prediction remains to be assessed empirically.

We now have a number of converging pieces of evidence to suggest that there is a fundamental difference in the way in which autistic children process stimulus features compared with control children. It appears to be the unique aspects of stimuli which are particularly salient to an individual with autism, while similarities between stimuli are relatively ignored. There are a number of candidate reasons why individuals with autism should find the uniqueness of a stimulus salient and therefore process similarities rather poorly. One possibility is that this difference in stimulus processing lies at the level of perception. That is, individuals with autism may perceive stimuli with greater acuity, such that the features and parts of stimuli are more greatly differentiated than in the normal case. This may affect the initial representation of stimuli in multidimensional psychological space. More specifically, it has been suggested by a number of individuals that the extent to which one stimulus is considered similar to another relates to their distance in this space (e.g. Nosofsky 1992; Shepard 1958). Thus, stimuli may be treated as less similar in autism as a result of a greater disparity between their points of representation in psychological space.

Another possibility is that the salience of the unique aspects of stimuli for individuals with autism lies at the level of attention. Some theories of selective attention assume that selection can occur both on the basis of the location of the stimulus in space and on the basis of the object itself. This assumption is based on the observation that visual information is processed by two visual pathways, known as the dorsal and ventral streams. The dorsal stream connects occipital areas (V1 and V2) with area V5 and visual areas of the posterior parietal cortex (PPC), and is involved in processing the spatial attributes of objects. The ventral stream connects areas V1 to V4 with visual areas within the inferotemporal cortex (IT), and is involved in the discrimination, identification, and recognition of objects (Ungerleider and Mishkin 1982). We have already discussed the processes which may be conducted by the PPC with respect to spatial location, and it is assumed by LaBerge (1995) that the output of those processes is projected to the V1–IT pathway of the ventral stream which contains activity corresponding to shape information. One possible result of the input of spatial information from the PPC is to assist discrimination of one shape from another, by raising activity within the ventral stream regarding one object, relative to activity regarding another, less attended object (LaBerge 1995). But LaBerge also proposes that shape discrimination can be enhanced by inputs from the ventrolateral prefrontal cortex (VLPFC) to identification areas of IT. Specifically, he suggests that an expectation of a particular object, in the form of priming an image of the object in working memory located in the VLPFC, modulates identification processes in area IT, such that an expected object is discriminated from and identified more rapidly than an unexpected one. If this process of preparatory attention operates with greater efficiency in autism, then this could amount to an attentional bias towards features which distinguish stimuli from one another (i.e. the unique features), and impact on discrimination learning and categorisation in the way we have observed in our experiments.

## 'ASOCIAL' VERSUS 'SOCIAL' PROCESSING IN AUTISM

It is a long-standing question whether the social deficits in autism are caused by what are often called 'primary deficits' in perception, attention, and learning. Indeed, the hypothesis that children with autism lack a theory of mind was originally inspired by the intuition that the performance of individuals with autism on so-called asocial tasks made little or no direct connection to the pervasive social oddness or aloofness that is characteristic of the disorder. This has lead to a dominant view that there are asocial abnormalities in autism, such as poor visuospatial orienting and superior local processing, which are mechanistically distinct from the social abnormalities, such as lacking theory of mind skills. Nonetheless, throughout the history of autism research, a number of individuals have maintained that early disruption of those primary processes can impact severely on the later emergence of the social abilities exhibited by normal children (Bryson *et al.* 1990; Courchesne *et al.* 1994*a,b*; Dawson and Lewy 1989; Kinsbourne 1987; Lovaas *et al.* 1979; Ornitz and Ritvo 1968; Rimland 1964).

From this perspective, it therefore makes little sense to argue that there are social versus asocial aspects of autism, because these are regarded to be causally related.

In fact, this perspective makes the stronger claim that social information processing relies on precisely those mechanisms involved in processing non-social information, and views the idea that there are selective processes (or brain areas) responsible for social information processing, which are distinct from processes responsible for asocial information processing, as untenable. According to this view, theory of mind skills develop as a result of a number of early experiences, such as exposure to and categorisation of stimuli involved in social situations, engagement in critical experiences such as joint attention episodes, appropriate generalisation of rules between different social situations, learning to inhibit responses to inappropriate stimuli, and so on. The success of these experiences in the development of a theory of mind is considered to rely on the integrity of the primary processes of perception, learning, and attention. Any impairment in any or all of these processes could therefore lead to a deficit in the acquisition of a theory of mind.

This view makes the prediction that deficits in the primary processes are apparent from a very early age and possibly from birth. This is, of course, a difficult prediction to test because autism cannot be diagnosed until at least eighteen months of age. However, Gillberg and Coleman (1992) have highlighted retrospective and prospective studies of autism which have addressed this question by documenting early symptoms of autism, many of which document abnormalities of perception in autistic infants. For example, in a prospective study, Gillberg et al. (1990) found that seven out ten items in a list of perceptual abnormalities discriminated autism from mental retardation and normality in infants under three years of age.

An alternative approach to the question would be to directly assess perception, attention, and learning processes in very young autistic children. Data of this kind is not yet available. There are, however, a few studies which have recently begun to assess the quality of attentional processing in social contexts exhibited by children with autism. Joseph and Tager-Flusberg (1997), for example, recently conducted an observational study of children with autism and Down's Syndrome, aged five to six years old, assessing the amount of attention children directed at their mothers' faces, researchers present in the room, and objects (either supported by the mothers or not supported). There were no group differences in the amount of attention directed in each of these categories and both groups showed more attention towards objects than to either their mothers' faces or the researchers. However, children with autism showed lower mean duration of attention to their mother's face compared with the children with Down's Syndrome, and far more mothers of autistic children directed their children's gaze towards them.

In another observational study, Swettenham et al. (1998) compared infants with autism of twenty months, infants with developmental delay, and normal twenty-month-old infants on the amount of attention directed towards objects and people. They also measured the frequency of shifts of gaze between different objects, between objects and people present in the room, and between one person and another during a play episode. The study therefore assessed what kinds of stimuli infants with autism attend to and whether infants with autism made the sorts of attentional shifts that would be required for joint attention. The hypothesis that there is a fundamental and early deficit in attention shifting or visuospatial orienting in autism would predict fewer attention shifts overall in the group with autism, regardless of whether the shift involved a social or non-social object. By contrast, theories which posit specialised mechanisms for social information processing which operate from an early age (e.g. Baron-Cohen 1995) would predict fewer attention shifts in infants with autism only in cases involving people.

In fact, evidence was found for both hypotheses. Like the children in Joseph and Tager-Flusberg's (1997) study, the infants with autism showed a shorter mean duration of look at people than the other two groups. They also showed a longer duration of look at objects than the other two groups, both results being consistent with the hypothesis that there are early specific abnormalities in social processing in autism. Also in line with this hypothesis was the finding that infants with autism showed a different pattern of frequency of attention shifting between different categories compared with the other two groups, by showing fewer shifts of attention between object and people and between different people. Furthermore, there were no group differences in frequency of attention shifting between different objects, suggesting no general abnormality in the ability to move attention around a visual array of non-social objects.

However, this conclusion was mitigated by the fact that, in terms of overall frequency of attention shifts regardless of category, infants with autism shifted attention less frequently compared with the other two groups, a finding consistent with the hypothesis that attention shifting is slower in autism (Courchesne *et al.* 1994a,b). And, as Swettenham *et al.* (1998) pointed out, a difference between groups in frequency of attention shifts between non-social objects might have emerged in a situation where there were no adults present, so that the developmental delay and normal groups would not have spent a proportion of the total time attending to adults.

Overall, however, the impression given by these two studies repeats a familiar story, that children with autism show abnormalities in their attention to faces, and Swettenham *et al.*'s study (1998) is important in establishing that this is present from a very early age. The question still remains, however, whether this abnormality results from deficits in processes specialised for face processing or from a more general abnormality in stimulus processing. One possibility is that faces belong to a category of complex stimuli with spatial configurations and that the deficit in autism lies at the level of processing complex spatial configurations. Some evidence for this was found by Davies *et al.* (1994), who compared children with autism and matched control groups on their ability to match random dot patterns on the basis of their spatial configurations. The sample and appropriate test stimuli differed with respect to the absolute positions of the dots, but maintained similar relative positions. They were in this way analogous to a face whose features change in relative position. High-functioning children with autism were impaired on this task.

This, of course, is a result which is predicted by the weak central coherence hypothesis (which posits a deficit in autism in holistic or configural processing), and ostensibly contradicts our findings that individuals with autism process spatial configurations normally in the selective attention version of the Navon task (Plaisted *et al.*, submitted) and simple configurations, such as a red X, in visual search tasks (Plaisted *et al.* 1998*a*). This raises the possibility that normal configural processing was observed in our tests because we used simple highly familiar configural stimuli, and that a deficit in configural processing would be apparent for novel configural stimuli. This question could be addressed by further direct tests of configural processing which manipulate stimulus parameters such as novelty/familiarity and simplicity/complexity.

A further reason why children with autism fail to attend to faces normally may be because of the categorisation problem that faces pose. In normal face processing, it is assumed that learning about a new face involves the formation of a prototype of that face across differences in expression and orientation (Valentine and Bruce 1986). Given that faces change regularly, this can be regarded as quite a difficult categorisation problem, requiring fairly extensive exposure to a new face in order to learn about it and encode it. If, as our experiments suggest, there is a bias towards processing the unique aspects of stimuli rather than similarities across different stimuli, children with autism may fail, or take considerably longer, to form such face prototypes and therefore find faces unworthy of attention because they contain little meaning. Of course, there is a problem of cause and effect here—children with autism may fail to attend to faces because they cannot form face prototypes or may fail to form prototypes because, from an early age, they do not attend to faces! However, experimental assessments of whether it is faces in particular which pose a problem in autism, or whether there are classes of stimuli (such as complex configurations) of which faces are a part which are problematic, will help to elucidate the causal direction.

In summary, research into the performance of autistic individuals on so-called asocial tasks continues to reveal interesting differences in stimulus processing. There is a major debate in autism research as to whether the symptoms of autism are best understood as deficits in specialised social processing systems, or whether they result from abnormalities in general processes of perception, learning, and attention. Furthermore, in the same way that there is considerable debate amongst researchers examining theory of mind deficits in autism over the precise nature of that deficit, there is also considerable debate concerning the mechanisms underpinning the performance of individuals with autism on asocial tasks. It may therefore be rather premature to speculate how far abnormal performance on asocial tasks can be considered to be responsible for the social deficits in autism. Equally, it may be premature to conclude that the social deficits in autism are explained solely by a theory of mind deficit, until asocial abnormalities have been elucidated and it is understood to what extent (if any) they impact on social understanding in autism.

## Notes

1. In fact, this group with autism but no parietal abnormalities showed no differences in P1 peak amplitude across the attended and unattended locations, suggesting an abnormally broad distribution of attention or 'wide' attentional beam. Burack (1994) has also presented data showing that children with autism performed more poorly on a target identification task when the target appeared close to distracters, and showed faster RTs when the target was

surrounded by a 'window' than when it was not, which, Burack argued, reflected a deficit in the ability to voluntarily alter the width of an attentional beam. Whether the results from these two studies are related remains to be established. One difference between the studies which makes them difficult to compare is that Townsend and Courchesne's study involved a simple target detection task at a prespecified location, whereas Burack's involved target identification.

2. It might be argued that a narrow spotlight of attention results in enhanced attentional processing at the location of the fixation point, thus predicting slowed responding to validly cued targets. However, there are both empirical and conceptual reasons for doubting this hypothesis. The empirical reason is that, if there is enhanced processing at the fixation point, this should reduce attentional orienting to an invalid cue as much as to a valid cue, and the outcome of this would be a validity effect of the same magnitude as in control individuals. This was not found in the group of autistic individuals with both cerebellar and parietal abnormalities. The conceptual reason concerns the issue of whether a fixation point has the capacity to engage a spotlight of attention in the same way as a cue. Unlike a cue, which, even if it is inconsistent, has predictive value regarding the location of the target, a fixation point has no predictive value in a Posner cueing task and is therefore unlikely to have any attentional salience.

3. For example, contrary to what would be predicted by the spotlight model, Juola *et al.* (1991) found that uncued targets presented at the centre circle of three concentric rings were not processed as efficiently as cued targets presented in the outer ring.

4. It might be objected that the facilitation in responding due to enhanced discrimination of location would be offset by a slower rate of preparatory attention, which would reduce the height of activity at the central location, predicting little or no difference between the autistic group and the normal group in Townsend and Courchesne's study. However, LaBerge's model (1995) assumes that the distribution of activity in the PPC represents not only preparatory attention but also the stored effects of recent trials. Thus, in a sustained attention task, where within a block of trials attention is cued to the same location (i.e. the red box in Townsend and Courchesne's study), activity at that location will build up over a series of trials. We might expect that the trade-off between enhanced discrimination of location and the slower rate of preparatory attention in the autistic group with parietal abnormalities occurred only over the initial trials of a block, until the point at which activity at the cued location had built up to a normal level. At this point, responding by the autistic group would be faster than the control group, due to the effects of enhanced discrimination of location.

5. By 'integration' I mean putting together the separate features of a stimulus. Integration alternatively could mean the apprehension of the relations that hold between features. Our visual search tasks do not assess the processes implied by this alternative.

6. Duncan and Humphreys (1989) have emphasised that search slopes are affected not only by target–distracter similarity but also distracter–distractor similarity. Their model accounts for such effects as follows: after initial processes of perceptual segmentation and analysis, items in the visual array which correspond to an attentional template of the target compete for access into visual short term memory (VSTM), where the successful item then guides responding. Target–distracter similarity can therefore reduce search rate because the weight (or activity) of a distracter will be similar to that of a target and be more successful in the competition for VSTM. The model also states that similar items become grouped together, and that the entire group will be suppressed to the degree that items within it do not correspond to a target description. Thus distracter–distractor similarity works in opposition to target–distracter similarity—the more similar distracters are to one another, the more will

they be suppressed as a group in the competition for VSTM. Decreasing distracter–distracter similarity can therefore slow search rate by leaving a greater number of ungrouped distracters competing with target items. Our hypothesis suggests that children with autism would be less likely than control children to group distracters on the basis of similarity, and therefore predicts that increasing distracter similarity would enhance the performance of control children but not children with autism.

# REFERENCES

Akshoomoff, N. A. and Courchesne, E. (1992). A new role for the cerebellum in cognitive operations. *Behavioural Neuroscience*, **106**, 731–8.

Anderson, N. B. and Rincover, A. (1982). The generality of overselectivity in developmentally disabled children, *Journal of Experimental Child Psychology*, **34**, 217–30.

Badcock, J. C., Whitworth, F. A., Badcock, D. R. and Lovegrove, W. J. (1990). Low-frequency filtering and the processing of local-global stimuli. *Perception*, **19**, 617–29.

Baron-Cohen, S. (1995). *Mindblindness: an essay on autism and theory of mind*. Bradford Books, MIT Press, Cambridge, MA.

Bryson, S. E., Wainwright-Sharpe, J. A. and Smith, I. M. (1990). Autism: a developmental spatial neglect syndrome? In *The development of attention: research and theory*, (ed. J. T. Enns), pp. 405–27. Elsevier Science Publishers B. V., North Holland.

Burack, J. (1994). Selective attention deficits in persons with autism: preliminary evidence of an inefficient attentional lens. *Journal of Abnormal Psychology*, **103**, 535–43.

Burack, J. (1997). Attention and autism: behavioural and electrophysiological evidence. In *Handbook of autism and pervasive developmental disorders*, (2nd edn), (ed. D. J. Cohen, A. M. Donnellan and R. Paul), pp. 226–47). John Wiley and Sons, New York.

Burack, J. and Iarocci, G. (1995, April). Visual filtering and covert orienting in developmentally disordered persons with and without autism. Paper presented at the meeting of the Society for Research in Child Development, Indianapolis, IN.

Courchesne, E., Townsend, J., Akshoomoff, N. A., Yeung-Courchesne, R., Press, G., Murakami, J., Lincoln, A., James, H., Saitoh, O., Haas, R. and Schreibman, L. A. (1994*a*). A new finding in autism: impairments in shifting attention. In *Atypical cognitive deficits in developmental disorders: implications for brain function*, (ed. S. H. Broman and J. Grafman), pp. 101–37. Lawrence Erlbaum, Hillsdale, NJ.

Courchesne, E., Townsend, J., Akshoomoff, N. A., Saitoh, O., Yeung-Courchesne, R., Lincoln, A., James, H., Haas, R., Schreibman, L. A. and Lau, L. (1994*b*). Impairment in shifting attention in autistic and cerebellar patients. *Behavioural Neuroscience*, **108**, 848–65.

Davies, S., Bishop, D., Manstead, A. S., and Tantam, D. (1994). Face perception in children with autism and Asperger's syndrome. *Journal of Child Psychology and Psychiatry*, **35**, 1033–57.

Dawson, G. and Lewy, A. (1989). Arousal, attention and the socioemotional impairments of individuals with autism. In *Autism: nature, diagnosis and treatment*, (ed. G. Dawson), pp. 49–74. Guilford, New York.

Duncan, J. and Humphreys, G. (1989). Visual search and stimulus similarity. *Psychological Review*, **96**, 433–58.

Eimer, M. (1998). Mechanisms of visual-spatial attention: evidence from event-related brain potential studies. *Visual Cognition*, **5**, 257–86.

Frith, U. (1989). *Autism: explaining the enigma*. Blackwell, Oxford.

Frith, U. and Baron-Cohen, S. (1987). Perception in autistic children. In *Handbook of autism and pervasive developmental disorders*, (ed. D. J. Cohen, A. M. Donnellan, and R. Paul), pp. 85–102. John Wiley and Sons, New York.

Gillberg, C. and Coleman, M. (1992). *The biology of the autistic syndromes*, (2nd edn). Mac Keith Press, London.

Gillberg, C., Ehlers, S., Schaumann, H., Jakobsson, G., Dahlgren, S. O., Lindblom, R., Bagenholm, A., Tjuust, T. and Blidner, E. (1990). Autism under age three years: a clinical study of twenty eight cases referred for autistic symptoms in infancy. *Journal of Child Psychology and Psychiatry*, **31**, 921–34.

Homa, D., Sterling, S., and Trepel, L. (1981). Limitations of exemplar-based generalization and the abstraction of categorical information. *Journal of Experimental Psychology: Human Learning and Memory*, **7**, 418–39.

Hutt, S. J., Hutt, C., Lee, D., and Ounsted, C. (1964). Arousal and childhood autism. *Nature*, **204**, 908–9.

Jolliffe, T. and Baron-Cohen, S. (1997). Are people with autism and Asperger's Syndrome faster than normal on the embedded figures test? *Journal of Child Psychology and Psychiatry*, **38**, 527–34.

Joseph, R. M. and Tager-Flusberg, H. (1997). An investigation of attention and affect in children with autism and Down syndrome. *Journal of Autism and Developmental Disorders*, **27**, 385–96.

Juola, J. F., Bouwhuis, D. G., Cooper, E. E. and Warner, C. B. (1991). Control of attention around the fovea. *Journal of Experimental Psychology: Human Perception and Performance*, **17**, 125–41.

Kimchi, R. (1992). Primacy of holistic processing and global/local paradigm: a critical review. *Psychological Bulletin*, **112**, 24–38.

Kinsbourne, M. (1987). Cerebral-brainstem relations in infantile autism. In *Learning and Cognition in Autism*, (ed. E. Schopler and G. B. Mesibov), pp. 107–25. Plenum Press, New York.

Klein, R., Kingstone, A. and Pontefract, A. (1992). Orienting of visual attention. In *Eye movements and visual cognition: scene perception and reading*, (ed. K. Rayner). Springer-Verlag, New York.

Klinger, L. G. and Dawson, G. (1995). A fresh look at categorization abilities in persons with autism. In *Learning and cognition in autism*, (ed. E. Schopler and G. B. Mesibov), pp. 119–36. Plenum Press, New York.

Koffka, K. (1935). *Principles of Gestalt psychology*. Harcourt Brace, New York.

Kohler, W. (1929). *Gestalt Psychology*. Liveright, New York.

LaBerge, D. (1974). Identification of two components of the time to switch attention: a test of a serial and a parallel model of attention. In *Attention and performance*, Vol. 9, (ed. S. Kornblum), pp. 71–85. Lawrence Erlbaum Associates, Hillsdale, NJ.

LaBerge, D. (1995). *Attentional processing: the brain's art of mindfulness*. Harvard University Press, Cambridge, MA.

LaBerge, D. and Brown, V. (1989). Theory of attentional operations in shape identification. *Psychological Review*, **96**, 101–24.

LaBerge, D., Carlson, R., Williams, J. K. and Bunney, B. G. (1997). Shifting attention in visual space: tests of moving-spotlight models versus an activity distribution model. *Journal of Experimental Psychology: Human Perception and Performance*, **23**, 1380–92.

Lamb, M. R., Robertson, L. C., and Knight, R. T. (1989). Attention and interference in the processing of global and local information: effects of unilateral temporal-parietal junction lesions. *Neuropsychologia*, **27**, 471–83.

Lamb, M. R., Robertson, L. C. and Knight, R. T. (1990). Component mechanisms underlying the processing of hierarchically organised patterns: inferences from patients with unilateral cortical lesions. *Journal of Experimental Psychology: Learning, Memory and Cognition*, **16**, 471–83.

Lovaas, O. I., Schreibman, L., Koegal, R. L. and Rhem, R. (1971). Selective responding by autistic children to multiple sensory output. *Journal of Abnormal Psychology*, **77**, 211–22.

Lovaas, O. I., Koegel, R. L. and Shreibman, L. (1979). Stimulus overselectivity in autism: a review of research. *Psychological Bulletin*, **86**, 1236–54.

Mackintosh, N. J. (1995). Categorization by people and pigeons: the twenty-second Bartlett Memorial Lecture. *The Quarterly Journal of Experimental Psychology*, **48B**, 193–214.

Mottron, L. and Belleville, S. (1993). A study of perceptual analysis in a high-level autistic subject with exceptional graphic abilities. *Brain and Cognition*, **23**, 279–309.

Navon, D. (1977). Forest before trees: the precedence of global features in visual perception. *Cognitive Psychology*, **9**, 353–83.

Nosofsky, R. M. (1992). Similarity scaling and cognitive process models. *Annual Review of Psychology*, **43**, 25–53.

O'Riordan, M. A. and Plaisted, K. C. Differential perception of similarity in autism and typical development. (Submitted.)

O'Riordan, M. A., Plaisted, K. C., Driver, J. and Baron-Cohen, S. Superior visual search in autism. (Submitted.)

Ornitz, E. M. and Ritvo, E. (1968). Perceptual inconstancy in early infantile autism. *Archives of General Psychiatry*, **18**, 76–98.

Ozonoff, S., Strayer, D. L., McMahon, W. M. and Filloux, F. (1994). Executive function abilities in autism and Tourette's syndrome: an information processing approach. *Journal of Child Psychology and Psychiatry*, **35**, 1015–32.

Plaisted, K. C., O'Riordan, M. A. and Baron-Cohen, S. (1998*a*). Enhanced visual search for a conjunctive target in autism: a research note. *Journal of Child Psychology and Psychiatry*, **39**, 777–83.

Plaisted, K. C., O'Riordan, M. A. and Baron-Cohen, S. (1998*b*). Enhanced discrimination of novel, highly similar stimuli by adults with autism during a perceptual learning task. *Journal of Child Psychology and Psychiatry*, **39**, 765–75.

Plaisted, K. C., Swettenham J. G. and Rees, E. Children with autism show local precedence in a divided attention task and global precedence in a selective attention task. (Submitted.)

Plaisted, K. C. and O'Riordan, M. A. Children with autism show enhanced perceptions learning and reduced prototype effects—further evidence of reduced generalization. (In preparation.)

Plaisted, K. C., O'Riordan, M. A., Aitken, M. R. F. and Killcross, A. S. Categorisation in autism: evidence of a reduced prototype effect. (Submitted.)

Posner, M. I. (1980). Orienting of attention. *Quarterly Journal of Experimental Psychology*, **32**, 3–25.

Posner, M. I., Walker, J. A., Friedrich, F. J. and Rafal, R. D. (1984). Effects of parietal injury on covert orienting of attention. *The Journal of Neuroscience*, **4**, 1863–74.

Rimland, B. (1964). *Infantile autism*. Appleton-Century-Crofts, New York.

Rincover, A. and Ducharme, J. M. (1987). Variables influencing stimulus overselectivity and 'tunnel vision' in developmentally delayed children. *American Journal of Mental Deficiency*, **91**, 422–30.

Robbins, T. W. (1997). Integrating the neurobiological and neuropsychological dimensions of autism. In *Autism as an executive disorder*, (ed. J. Russell), pp. 21–53. Oxford University Press.

Russell, J. (1997). How executive disorders can bring about an inadequate 'theory of mind'. In *Autism as an executive disorder*, (ed. J. Russell), pp. 256–304. Oxford University Press.

Shah, A. and Frith, U. (1983). An islet of ability in autistic children: a research note. *Journal of Child Psychology and Psychiatry*, **24**, 613–20.

Shah, A. and Frith, U. (1993). Why do autistic individuals show superior performance on the block design task? *Journal of Child Psychology and Psychiatry*, **34**, 1351–64.

Shepard, R. N. (1958). Stimulus and response generalization: tests of a model relating generalization to distance in psychological space. *Journal of Experimental Psychology*, **55**, 509–23.

Shulman, G. L., Sullivan, M. A., Gish, K., and Sakoda, W. J. (1986). The role of spatial frequency channels in the perception of local and global structure. *Perception*, **15**, 259–73.

Shulman, C., Yirmiya, N. and Greenbaum, C. W. (1995). From categorisation to classification: a comparison among individuals with autism, mental retardation and normal development. *Journal of Abnormal Psychology*, **104**, 601–9.

Swettenham, J., Baron-Cohen, S., Charman, T., Cox, A., Baird, G., Drew, A., Rees, E. and Wheelwright, S. (1998). The frequency and distribution of spontaneous attention shifts between social and nonsocial stimuli in autistic, typically developing and nonautistic developmentally delayed infants. *Journal of Child Psychology and Psychiatry*, **39**, 747–53.

Tager-Flusberg, H. (1985). Basic level and superordinate level categorization by autistic, mentally retarded and normal children. *Journal of Experimental Child Psychology*, **40** 450–69.

Townsend, J. and Courchesne, E. (1994). Parietal damage and narrow 'spotlight' spatial attention. *Journal of Cognitive Neuroscience*, **6**, 220–32.

Townsend, J., Courchesne E. and Egaas, B. (1996). Slowed orienting of covert visual-spatial attention in autism: specific deficits associated with cerebellar and parietal abnormality. *Development and psychopathology*, **8**, 563–84.

Treisman, A. and Gelade, G. (1980). A feature integration theory of attention. *Cognitive Psychology*, **12**, 97–136.

Ungerer, J. A. and Sigman, M. (1987). Categorization skills and receptive language development in autistic children. *Journal of Autism and Developmental Disorders*, **17**, 3–16.

Ungerleider, L. G. and Mishkin, M. (1982). Two cortical visual systems. In D. J. Ingle, M. A. Goodale, and R. J. W. Mansfield (Eds.) *Analysis of visual behaviour*, pp. 549–85. Cambridge MA, MIT Press.

Valentine, T. and Bruce, V. (1986). The effects of distinctiveness in recognising and classifying faces. *Perception*, **15**, 525–35.

Wainwright-Sharpe, J. A. and Bryson, S. E. (1993). Visual orienting deficits in high-functioning people with autism. *Journal of Autism and Developmental Disorders*, **23**, 1–13.

Wolfe, J. M., Cave, K. R. and Franzel, S. L. (1989). Guided search: an alternative to the feature integration model for visual search. *Journal of Experimental Psychology: Human Perception and Performance*, **15**, 419–33.

# Part 2  Theory of mind: neurobiological aspects

# 11

# The role of the frontal lobes and the amygdala in theory of mind

VALERIE E. STONE

## INTRODUCTION

One male macaque approaches another who is next to a food source. The one approaching moves his head forward, raises his brows, and opens his mouth in a threat display. The other monkey withdraws from the food source, signalling his submission by smacking his lips.

A graduate student is at a Society for Neuroscience conference, talking to a relatively well-known researcher at a poster, when the president of the society comes up. The president greets the researcher. The graduate student excuses himself, ducks his head and discreetly withdraws.

In both cases, a subordinate withdraws when a dominant animal approaches a valuable resource. The subordinate macaque, however, may simply respond to the dominant macaque's approach, without explicitly representing the dominant animal's mental state. He recognizes which other individual he is interacting with, remembers that this male is dominant to him, recognizes the facial gesture, and has a physiological and emotional response which leads him to withdraw and signal submission. The graduate student's response doubtless also includes this kind of emotional and physiological component, but he may also represent the researcher's and the president's mental states 'They want to talk to each other; she would probably rather talk to the president,' in order to compute the appropriate response.

This example illustrates some parallels between social cognition in humans and in other primates. Our social behaviour is similar in many ways to other primates'. We negotiate social hierarchies, keep track of kin members, compete over limited resources, and encode past histories of interaction with specific individuals. Humans, however, appear to have more complex abilities to represent others' mental states and to use these mental states as the basis of social computations. The term 'theory of mind' is used to refer to humans' ability to make inferences about others' mental states (e.g. beliefs, desires, intentions) and to predict others' behaviour based on those mental states. This ability forms an important basis for negotiating the large social groups and the complex social world in which humans live and have lived throughout their evolutionary history. Whether or not theory of mind is unique to humans among primates, evolution must build on structures that already exist, so theory of mind would have evolved by building on other social information-processing systems in the brains of our ancestors. Thus, whatever brain systems are involved in theory of mind probably include those systems used for social information-processing in other primates (Brothers and Ring 1992).

Theory of mind involves both 'cold cognition'—inferences about others' *epistemic* states such as beliefs, knowledge, focus of attention—and 'hot cognition'—inferences about others' *affective* states such as emotions, preferences, beneficent or hostile intentions. Because it involves such a diverse set of high-level inferences, theory of mind is unlikely to be localized in a single brain region. Baron-Cohen and Ring (1994) have suggested that it would be more accurate to think of theory of mind inferences as being computed by a distributed neural circuit, with different regions contributing different types of computations. This chapter expands on their model, discussing several different brain regions that might play a role in theory of mind. At this point, there is only a small amount of empirical evidence relating to the brain basis of theory of mind, so any account must be speculative. This chapter reviews the evidence for the role of the amygdala, orbitofrontal cortex, medial frontal cortex, and dorsolateral frontal cortex. Focusing on the role that specific regions might play leaves out several important factors in a thorough account of the neural basis of theory of mind. This chapter does not explore processing differences between the right and left hemispheres; a thorough review of that literature is provided in the chapter by Brownell *et al.* in this volume. It also does not discuss the role of specific neurotransmitters, such as serotonin or oxytocin, that are thought to play a role in social behaviour (Raleigh and Brammer 1993; Raleigh *et al.* 1991; reviewed in Brothers 1994; Carter and Altemus 1997; Insel 1997; Nelson and Panksepp 1998). Furthermore, it does not discuss the role of particular patterns of connectivity between these areas. However, evidence for the role of the amygdala and frontal regions in theory of mind provides a starting point for further investigation into these other questions.

## THE FRONTAL LOBES AND THEORY OF MIND

Because the frontal lobes seem to be involved in 'higher' cognition, it may be most profitable to look for structures that underlie social cognitive abilities, such as theory of mind, in frontal cortex. 'Prefrontal cortex', a term used to refer to cortex anterior to the premotor area, can be divided into somewhat functionally distinct subregions, with different consequences for damage to each area. There is agreement on two functionally important subregions.

1. dorsolateral frontal cortex, the upper (dorsal) and outer (lateral) surface of the frontal lobes including Brodmann's areas 6, lateral portions of 8–10, 44–46, regions that receive their blood supply from the middle cerebral artery; and

2. orbitofrontal cortex, primarily Brodmann's area 11, the ventral surface of the frontal lobes that sits above the eyes (the orbits) (Benson and Miller 1997; Bowen 1989; Kaczmarek 1984; Mattson and Levin, 1990). (See Fig. 11.1.)

Damage to dorsolateral frontal cortex produces a variety of general cognitive

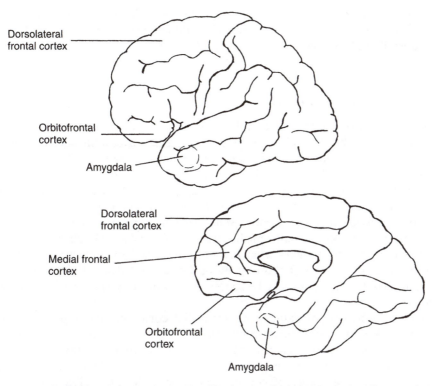

**Fig. 11.1.** Brain regions that may be involved in theory of mind. The upper diagram shows the outer surface of the left hemisphere. The lower diagram is of the medial surface of the right hemisphere, shown from a slice made between the two hemispheres. Only the approximate position of the amygdala is shown, as it is located inside the anterior temporal lobes, just in front of the hippocampus.

deficits, both low-level and high-level functions, such as novelty detection, inhibition of irrelevant sensory stimuli, temporal sequencing of events in memory, planning, executive function, task-switching, and working memory (Benson and Stuss 1986; Kimberg *et al.* 1997; Knight and Grabowecky 1995; Mattson and Levin 1990). Damage to orbitofrontal cortex, in contrast, produces primarily social and emotional changes: inappropriate humour, socially inappropriate behaviour (particularly verbal behaviour), self-centred behaviour, and a tendency to rambling, digressive speech (Alexander *et al.* 1989; Benson and Miller 1997; Bowen 1989; Damasio and VanHoesen 1983; Kaczmarek 1984; Mattson and Levin 1990).

There is less agreement on the functional importance of other subdivisions of prefrontal cortex. Medial frontal cortex is the inside surface of the frontal lobes between the two hemispheres, including Brodmann's areas 32, 12, and the medial portions of 8–10. Medial frontal cortex receives its blood supply from the anterior cerebral artery. Consequences of damage to this area may include apathy, akinesia, difficulties with language, and some inappropriate behaviour, depending on whether the damage is more ventral or more dorsomedial (Alexander *et al*. 1989; Bowen 1989). Also, the term *dorso*lateral excludes areas of lateral frontal cortex that are not dorsal, such as area 47 and the lower parts of areas 10 and 45.


### Orbitofrontal cortex and theory of mind

Each of the subregions of the frontal lobes may have its own contribution to make to theory of mind. Orbitofrontal cortex seems to be important in social cognition, because, of all the regions of the frontal lobes, damage there seems to most directly affect social behaviour. This discussion of the consequences of orbitofrontal damage includes patients with ventromedial cortex damage, that is, damage that includes both orbitofrontal cortex and the lower portion of medial frontal cortex. The two patient groups are discussed together because ventromedial damage includes orbitofrontal cortex damage, and because ventromedial frontal patients' social behaviour has been well characterized, and matches what has been described for patients with damage only to orbitofrontal cortex. Following Baron-Cohen and Ring (1994), this chapter argues that these problems in social behaviour arise from subtle impairments in theory of mind.

After damage to orbitofrontal or ventromedial cortex occurs, a person may go through a marked change in social behaviour. Patients with orbitofrontal or ventro-medial damage often make inappropriate comments, particularly sexual comments, make inappropriate jokes, make poor choices in personal relationships, and have difficulty with the pragmatics of conversation (Alexander *et al*. 1989; Benson and Miller 1997; Damasio and VanHoesen 1983; Eslinger and Damasio 1985; Gronwall *et al*. 1998; Kaczmarek 1984; Mattson and Levin 1990; Saver and Damasio 1991). I have witnessed several examples of inappropriate behaviour while testing orbitofrontal patients. One patient opened the conversation when we went into a testing room by saying, 'OK, let's take our clothes off now.' Another patient, apropos of nothing we had been talking about, launched into a description of the pornographic novels he had been reading lately, and how he hoped that reading them would help save his marriage. (He and his wife were later separated.) None of these patients gave any indication that they thought they were saying anything inappropriate.

Though striking, such incidents do not occur during every social interaction. Difficulties with conversational pragmatics, however, are evident in any interaction with patients of this type. Orbitofrontal patients exhibit poor use of relevance, tending to drift from topic to topic, without giving the listener a clear sense of connection between topics (Alexander *et al*. 1989; Kaczmarek 1984). They do not appear to check whether the listener is interested in what they are saying. It is often difficult to get a word in edgewise, because they seem insensitive to signs that their conversational partner is trying to say something (Alexander *et al*. 1989). They will sometimes refer to something as if the listener knew what they were talking about, without having ever mentioned it; for example, a patient might say, 'It just wasn't the right job for him', without ever having mentioned what the job was. If the graduate student in the example at the beginning of the chapter had orbitofrontal damage, he probably would have continued his conversation with the researcher when the president approached, insensitive to cues that the president was trying to enter the conversation.

Because of these social difficulties, patients with orbitofrontal or ventromedial damage often have difficulty maintaining friendships and intimate relationships. Furthermore, they are often taken advantage of by others. One patient that I tested told me about marrying a woman he had not known for very long. After the ceremony, she told him that she had married him only so that she could get a green card, and had no intention of having a relationship with him. He was genuinely surprised, and said that, up until that moment, he had no idea she was using him. Another patient had divorced his wife when his family discovered that she was stealing money from him. Eslinger and Damasio (1985) report that E.V.R., a patient with ventromedial damage, lost money by getting involved in several questionable business relationships.

The personality changes following orbitofrontal cortex damage have been described as 'pseudopsychopathic' or as 'acquired sociopathy' because of patients' relative lack of concern for how they affect others (Benson and Stuss 1986; Eslinger and Damasio 1985; Mattson and Levin 1990; Saver and Damasio 1991; Tranel 1994). However, these terms may be inappropriate. True psychopaths or sociopaths are characterized not only by their lack of concern for others, but also by their skill at manipulating or exploiting others. Patients with orbitofrontal damage do not have the necessary social skills to manipulate others; on the contrary, they are themselves vulnerable to being exploited. 'Socially impaired' would be a more accurate term. These patients' difficulty in reading the social information around them makes them appear unconcerned, but this difficulty also makes them vulnerable to others.

In contrast to their social skills, patients with damage to orbitofrontal cortex or ventromedial frontal cortex can (though do not always) perform normally on many tests of executive function and other cognitive functions, such as the Wisconsin Card Sorting Test, tests of verbal fluency, and some reasoning tasks (Mattson and Levin 1990). They are aware of their surroundings, know the place and time, and can be quite knowledgeable about current events. They may be somewhat distractible, but this appears primarily to affect preparation and execution of a response, rather than cognitive processing *per se* (Mattson and Levin 1990; Whyte *et al.* 1998). Thus, the pattern of symptoms following these types of damage is a pattern of notably impaired social cognition with general cognitive functioning relatively preserved.

Could this pattern reflect impairments in theory of mind? Theory of mind is certainly implicated in the pragmatics of language: the use of relevance and proper reference (Baron-Cohen 1995; Frith 1996; Happé 1994a,b; Tager-Flusberg 1993). Patients with damage to orbitofrontal cortex may not pay attention to what their conversational partner is interested in or knows about because they are not able to model others' minds easily. Theory of mind impairments could also result in inappropriate behaviour. Deciding whether or not to take a particular action involves having some model of what other people would think about it. From before their brain damage, these patients have a lifetime of experience knowing what is socially appropriate. Thus, they behave inappropriately not because they do not know from experience what is appropriate, but because they have difficulty computing 'on-line' during an interaction what would seem to others to be appropriate:

Social rule-breaking is common . . . and it comes about *because the person no longer has the ability to judge how things [he/she] does are affecting other people.* (Gronwall *et al.* 1998, p. 65; emphasis added.)

Impairments in modelling others' mental states could make it difficult for someone to infer what others' reactions to certain actions would be.

If, as Baron-Cohen and Ring (1994) proposed, orbitofrontal cortex is part of a theory of mind circuit, then damage to orbitofrontal cortex would produce subtle impairments in theory of mind rather than the complete loss of mentalizing abilities. Orbitofrontal patients might be slower to make theory of mind inferences or might have difficulty integrating mental state inferences with other information. In real interactions, decisions have to be made rapidly and integrated with other information that is constantly changing, so real-time social interaction should pose the greatest challenge to a moderately impaired theory of mind mechanism.

Both neuroimaging studies and tests with lesion patients indicate that orbitofrontal cortex may be involved in theory of mind. Baron-Cohen *et al.* (1994), using SPECT, looked at areas that were activated during the recognition of mental state terms, such as 'remember', 'think', 'imagine'. Subjects listened to a list of words containing mental state terms and distractor terms matched for frequency, such as 'tape', 'district', or 'park', and were asked, for each word, to indicate whether it had to do with the mind or not. In the control condition, subjects listened to a different list of words, including words like 'shoulder' and 'teeth', as well as distractor terms, and were asked to indicate whether each word had to do with the body or not. They found that right orbitofrontal cortex relative to left frontal polar cortex was active during the mental state terms task.

Systematic tests of theory of mind in patients with orbitofrontal lesions have only been undertaken recently. If orbitofrontal cortex is part of a theory of mind circuit, then we would predict that patients with orbitofrontal cortex damage would not have difficulty on the most basic theory of mind tasks, but that it would take more difficult tasks to reveal their deficits. First order false-belief tasks can be passed by four-year-old children (Gopnik and Astington 1988; Wellman 1990; Wimmer and Perner 1983), second order false-belief tasks can be passed by five- to six-year-old children (Perner and Wimmer 1985), and adults are at ceiling on both types of tasks (Stone *et al.* 1998*a*). Thus, false-belief tasks test a very basic level of theory of mind inferences.

In order to test adults, we have devised a more developmentally advanced theory of mind task, a test of *faux pas* recognition (Stone *et al.* 1998). A *faux pas* occurs when someone says something awkward, hurtful, or insulting to another person, not knowing or not realizing that it should not have been said. For example, one of the items in the test gave the following story:

Jeanette bought her friend Anne a crystal bowl for a wedding gift. Anne had a big wedding and there were a lot of presents to keep track of. About a year later, Jeanette was over one night at Anne's for dinner. Jeanette dropped a wine bottle by accident on the crystal bowl, and the bowl shattered. 'I'm really sorry, I've broken the bowl,' said Jeanette. 'Don't worry,' said Anne, 'I never liked it anyway. Someone gave it to me for my wedding.'

Recognizing a *faux pas* requires both an understanding of false or mistaken belief and an empathic inference about how the statement would affect someone. Seven-year-old children who could pass first and second order false-belief tasks did poorly on the *faux pas* task, but a larger proportion of children performed correctly on the task by age eleven; furthermore, twelve-year-olds with Asperger's syndrome were significantly impaired on the *faux pas* task, but not on compehension of control stories (Baron-Cohen *et al.* submitted). IQ was not correlated with performance on *faux pas* recognition in either the control subjects or the subjects with Asperger's syndrome.

Stone *et al.* (1998*a*) gave five patients with bilateral orbitofrontal cortex damage and five controls a series of theory of mind tasks that varied in difficulty: first-order false-belief tasks, second-order false-belief tasks, and the *faux pas* task. These patients scored at ceiling on the Mini Mental State Exam, a quick measure of basic cognitive functioning. The orbitofrontal patients performed well on first- and second-order false-belief tasks, indicating that their theory of mind abilities were intact at the seven-year-old level. They were impaired on the *faux pas* task, however (Stone *et al.* 1998*a*). (See Fig. 11.2.) Just as they often say inappropriate things in their own lives, they also have difficulty recognizing when someone says something inappropriate. Furthermore, we ran an additional 'empathy' condition where subjects were read the *faux pas* stories and asked 'How would [for example] Jeanette feel?' Even those patients who had failed to recognize *faux pas* had occurred could make the empathic inference that the character in the story would have felt hurt or insulted. However, they did not conclude from that fact that anything inappropriate had been said. Since we know from their performance on the false-belief tasks that their ability to represent 'cold' cognitive states like belief and knowledge is intact, and since they seem to have a basic level of empathic understanding, these results may indicate that they have difficulty combining information about mental states with affective information.

The *faux pas* task is a highly verbal task. However, theory of mind impairments in orbitofrontal patients are evident on less verbal tasks as well. We gave these same patients a series of face-processing tasks varying in difficulty that required them to infer someone else's internal state from information in the face. The more basic tasks tested whether they could recognize facial expressions of basic emotions (fear, anger, sadness, happiness, disgust, and surprise) from photographs of the full face. The more difficult task, 'Reading the Mind in the Eyes', tested their ability to read complex mental states from photographs of the eyes only (Baron-Cohen *et al.* 1997*b*). The orbitofrontal patients performed as well as or better than the controls did on recognizing basic facial experessions, but were significantly impaired on inferring mental states from information around the eyes (Stone *et al.* 1998*a*). (See Fig. 11.3.) A vocabulary test showed that they had full comprehension of the mental state terms used in this task, so their impairment cannot be accounted for by verbal comprehension difficulties.

These results from two different theory of mind tasks, one highly verbal and one more visual, indicate that orbitofrontal cortex may well be involved in theory of mind. In the future, how these patients and ventromedial patients perform on other advanced theory of mind tests should clarify the role of this region of the frontal lobes in theory of mind.

## Alternative explanations of orbitofrontal patients' social deficits

Other theories have been proposed to account for the deficits in social behaviour that follow damage to orbitofrontal cortex. One theory that is commonly advanced to explain orbitofrontal patients' social deficits is that they are disinhibited. Thus, their inappropriate behaviour reflects what anyone would do without inhibition. Once a possibility for action comes to mind, these patients take the action, unable to inhibit the behaviour on the basis of possible consequences. While it may be true that orbitofrontal patients have some disinhibition, this is not a sufficient explanation for their social behaviour. Although they may say inappropriate things, they do not act on what they say. An orbitofrontal patient may make a verbal advance or lewd comment, but will not engage in lewd behaviour. If disinhibition is to be invoked as an explanation for what these patients say, then we are left without an explanation for what they do or rather, what they do not do. In addition, disinhibition does not provide a good account of their difficulties with conversational pragmatics. Inappropriate use of reference, failure to take account of common ground, and poor use of relevance do not follow in a straightforward way from disinhibition. Finally, it is not clear why being disinhibited would lead to failures of *faux pas* recognition or difficulties reading mental states from subtle expressions around the eyes. Thus, the hypothesis that orbitofrontal damage causes a partial impairment of the theory of mind mechanism provides a more concise explanation for the entire spectrum of social deficits exhibited by these patients than does the theory of disinhibition.

Another theory that has been proposed to account for the social and decision making deficits[1] of patients with ventromedial frontal damage is Damasio's 'Somatic Marker Hypothesis' (Damasio 1994). This theory postulates that the ventromedial region of the frontal lobes is critical for processing information about how emotional reactions are associated with particular imagined outcomes. These reactions are stored as memories of physiological emotional reactions, and when deciding which action to take, people rely on these 'gut feelings', or somatic markers, in choosing what to do.

> . . . *somatic markers are a special instance of feelings . . . [that] have been connected, by learning, to predicted future outcomes of certain scenarios* . . . Somatic markers . . . assist deliberation by highlighting some options (either dangerous or favorable) and eliminating them rapidly from subsequent consideration. (Damasio 1994, p. 174; emphasis in the original.)

People avoid bad outcomes because they have a physiological reaction to imagining the course of action leading to that outcome. Damasio hypothesizes that ventromedial cortex is crucial for processing information about these somatic markers. Ventromedial frontal patients have been found to lack autonomic responses to anticipated negative outcomes (Bechara *et al.* 1993). The somatic marker hypothesis can certainly account for inappropriate soical behaviour. Lacking the physiological response of imagined shame or embarrassment, a person would not have any reason to avoid inappropriate behaviour. This hypothesis could also possibly account for results on the *faux pas* test. Normally, upon hearing about another person's social gaffe, one experiences an emotional reaction of vicarious shame or embarrassment. It is possible that, without this somatic response to reading about a *faux pas*, orbitofrontal patients cannot tell that something has been said that should not have been said. However, the 'Reading the Mind in the Eyes Task' does not depend on emotional responses in the same way, so the somatic marker hypothesis cannot account for both sets of results on theory of mind tests. It is also not clear how the somatic marker hypothesis could explain deficits in conversational pragmatics, such as inappropriate use of reference, and failure to take account of common ground.

Rolls (1996) has proposed that one of the major functions of orbitofrontal cortex is to represent changing reward values in the environment. There is strong evidence for this account, showing that orbitofrontal cortex is active in macaques when reversal learning or extinction occurs, and that earlier synapses in the temporal lobes are not involved (Rolls 1996). Studies of patients with orbitofrontal cortex lesions show that such patients have difficulty with reversal learning and extinction (Rolls *et al.* 1994). Rolls's theory by itself can explain some, but not all, of patients' inappropriate social behaviour and deficits in conversational pragmatics. However, this theory dovetails with the hypothesis that orbitofrontal cortex is involved in theory of mind. Orbito-frontal cortex is a large region, and is therefore likely to carry out several functions. It may be that in normal subjects, appropriate behaviour is maintained by punishment, such as disapproval, or by withholding of a reward, such as approval from the social environment. According to Rolls's theory, orbitofrontal patients would have difficulty learning from others' changing reactions to their behaviour. However, a theory of mind inference would be necessary to know whether another person approves or disapproves of one's behaviour. A combination of Rolls's theory and the 'theory of mind theory' could also explain some deficits in pragmatics. If a conversational partner initially seemed interested in a topic, and then lost interest, a patient with orbitofrontal damage would not be able to adjust behaviour based on this change in the social environment. A more cognitive explanation than Rolls's theory may be needed to account for other pragmatic deficits exhibited by patients with orbitofrontal damage. Relevance and common ground depend not on reward values in the environment, but on the semantic relatedness of different topics or on representing what someone else knows.

The fact that orbitofrontal cortex represents changing reward values also does not, by itself, account for the performance of patients with orbitofrontal damage on theory of mind tests. The *faux pas* task requires judgments about other people, and does not involve reward or punishment for one's own behaviour. Furthermore, in none of the *faux pas* stories is there information about a story character's reaction to the other character's *faux pas*, so there is no punishment or reward. The 'Reading the Mind in the Eyes Task' also does not involve any rewards or punishments, merely a choice between two mental state terms. The evidence is strong that orbitofrontal cortex does represent changing reward values. This account, combined with some theory of mind capacity in orbitofrontal cortex, can explain many of the social impairments of patients with orbitofrontal damage.

In short, while orbitofrontal patients may have some deficits in inhibition and in encoding 'somatic markers', neither of these theories gives a complete account of their social deficits. Rolls's theory provides a good account of how orbitofrontal damage disrupts affective responses. The theory that orbitofrontal damage also disrupts theory of mind is able to explain the whole pattern of social problems suffered by orbitofrontal patients: inappropriate social behaviour, deficits in conversational pragmatics, and impairments on theory of mind tests. It is a parsimonious explanation for the social deficits (though not the nonsocial deficits) of patients with orbitofrontal cortex damage.

## Medial frontal cortex and theory of mind

Just as with orbitofrontal patients, some patients with damage to medial frontal cortex may also exhibit social inappropriateness and problems with discourse. The literature on consequences of medial frontal damage leads to few firm conclusions, because the consequences of medial frontal damage can vary substantially, and correlations between type of symptom and location of lesion are not clear. Medial frontal damage can produce akinesia, particularly acutely, and difficulty initiating action (Alexander *et al.* 1989). Patients may say or do little, appearing apathetic and moving slowly, symptoms which may occur because of damage to the supplementary motor area (Alexander *et al.* 1989; Bowen 1989). Patients with medial frontal damage may also have some executive function deficits, showing impairment on the Wisconsin Card Sorting Test (Mattson and Levin 1990). Deficits in social behaviour and social cognition are not their most salient symptoms. However, patients with either right or left hemisphere lesions in medial frontal cortex have been noted to say inappropriate things or use humour inappropriately (Alexander *et al.* 1989). Left medial frontal lesions can also impair patients' ability to understand nonliteral language, such as metaphors and proverbs (Alexander *et al.* 1989). Benson and Stuss (1986) and Benson and Miller (1997) caution that there may not be a close mapping between exact symptoms and exact regions of the frontal lobes. Tentatively, one can say that socially inappropriate behaviour may result from medial frontal lesions that are more ventral; akinesia may result from more dorso-medial lesions, but the distinction between these two types of medial frontal damage is far from clear (Bowen 1989).

The socially inappropriate behaviour of medial frontal patients could be due to subtle deficits in theory of mind. Their pragmatic language difficulties could also arise from theory of mind deficits. Happé has noted that understanding the nonliteral use of language may often depend on theory of mind, so left medial frontal damage could well impair medial frontal patients' abilities in this domain because of a theory of mind deficit (Alexander *et al.* 1989; Happé 1994*a,b*).

Empirical support for the role of medial frontal cortex in theory of mind comes primarily from neuroimaging studies that have demonstrated left medial frontal activity during theory of mind tasks. Goel *et al.* (1995) found selective activation of left medial frontal cortex and left temporal cortex during a task requiring subjects to model another person's mental state about a target object. Control tasks required only a visual description of the object, memory retrieval or inferring the function of an object from its form. Fletcher *et al.* (1995) also found left medial frontal activation, in the medial portion of Brodmann's areas 8 and 9, during a task requiring mental state inferences compared with tasks requiring subtle physical inferences. They did not find any orbitofrontal cortex activation. Happé *et al.* (1996) further pinpointed left medial frontal cortex, area 8, as important for theory of mind by showing that five individuals with Asperger's Syndrome did not show activity in area 8 during the same tasks.

The role of medial frontal cortex in theory of mind remains a puzzle to be sorted out. These neuroimaging studies found dorsal medial activation during theory of mind tasks, yet as noted above, it seems that social difficulties occur after medial damage that is more ventral than dorsomedial (Bowen 1989). Patients with medial frontal damage are relatively rare, because strokes are much more common in the middle cerebral artery than in the anterior cerebral artery, which supplies medial frontal cortex. Theory of mind has so far been tested in only one patient with medial frontal damage, an elderly patient with a prefrontal leucotomy whose damage included medial frontal regions (Bach *et al.* 1998). However, although the patient was impaired on second-order false-belief tests and advanced versions of Happé's Strange Stories, these deficits probably resulted from impairments in executive function, as the patient also had severe deficits on measures of executive function (Bach *et al.* 1998). No selective theory of mind deficits have yet been found in patients with selective medial frontal damage. In the next few years, systematic tests of theory of mind and executive function in patients with medial frontal damage should do much to illuminate these issues.

**Dorsolateral frontal cortex and theory of mind**

Dorsolateral frontal cortex may also be involved in theory of mind, if only because the general cognitive functions of dorsolateral frontal cortex are necessary in carrying out some theory of mind computations. False-belief tasks, for example, place strong demands on inhibitory control, sequencing and working memory (Ozonoff *et al.* 1991; Pennington *et al.* 1997; Stone *et al.* 1998a). To solve a first- or second-order false-belief task, a subject must keep all the elements of the story in working memory before the questions are asked—the original location of the object, where the object was moved, where each character was when object was moved—and must remember them in the proper sequence. Furthermore, answering the 'belief' question correctly requires inhibiting what the subject knows to be true in order to answer with what one of the story characters believes to be true. Reality may be more salient than a story character's beliefs, and executive control may be required to inhibit responses based on the real location of the object.

When Stone *et al.* (1998a) tested orbitofrontal patients on theory of mind tasks, five patients with left dorsolateral frontal damage were also tested on the same tasks. We manipulated the working memory demands of the false-belief tasks by running them in two conditions: with and without a memory load. For example, one of the stories was about Tony, who came into the kitchen and put a bottle of Coke in a cabinet. After he left the room, a woman named Maria came in and moved the Coke into the refrigerator. Later, Tony came back in. In the 'memory load' condition, subjects watched the action of this story on videotape as the experimenter told the story, and had to keep the elements of the story in working memory in proper sequence to answer the questions. For the 'no memory load' condition, we printed out video stills of the action in the story, and laid them out in front of the subjects as the experimenter told the story. All the pictures were visible while subjects answered the questions. Thus, the subjects did not have to remember the story elements or sequence them. This manipulation had no effect on orbitofrontal patients' performance.

Dorsolateral frontal patients, in contrast, performed much better in the 'no memory load' condition (see Fig. 11.2). Working memory load significantly impaired their performance on false-belief tasks. However, even when they made errors in the 'memory load' condition, they were not more likely to make errors on the belief questions as opposed to the other questions (Stone *et al.* 1998*a*). Thus their performance overall gave us no reason to conclude that they have any deficits in making mentalistic inferences *per se*. On the *faux pas* task, they made errors only when they got confused about the details of the stories, even though the stories were always right in front of them (Stone *et al.* 1998*a*). These patients with dorsolateral frontal damage had lower scores than the orbitofrontal patients on the Mini Mental State Exam. Thus, for these two groups, performance on this test of general cognitive functioning does not predict performance on the *faux pas* task.

One weakness of this study is that it compared patients with bilateral orbitofrontal damage with patients with unilateral dorsolateral frontal damage. We can conclude from the results that left dorsolateral cortex alone does not seem to be critical for making mental state inferences. However, it is still possible that bilateral damage to dorsolateral frontal cortex would produce theory of mind deficits. Price *et al.* (1990) report two adult patients with bilateral dorsolateral frontal damage acquired early in life. They tested these patients on a perspective-taking task, which does require a

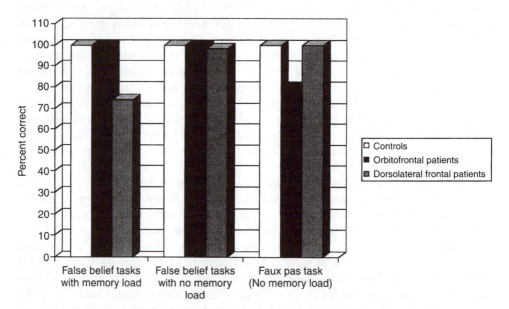

**Fig. 11.2.** Performance of frontal patients and controls on theory of mind tasks. N = 5 in each group of subjects. Because there were no strong differences in performance between first- and second-order false-belief tasks in any groups, performance on false-belief tasks in this graph was averaged over first- and second-order tasks.

theory of mind. The subject looked at a map of a town and was told that someone at a certain location on the map was lost and needed to get to a particular house on the map. The experimenter then read a set of directions for getting from where the lost person was to the house. The directions contained four different ambiguities such that a person could make mistakes and end up at the wrong house. After reading the directions, the subjects were asked to say which parts of the directions were ambiguous and could have led the lost person to make a mistake. These two patients failed this task.

The task could be seen as a theory of mind task, because it depends on understanding false-belief. However, it also places demands on working memory, because the subject has to keep all of the directions in memory to answer the question. Thus, these patients could have failed on this task because of working memory limitations rather than because their theory of mind was impaired. Further studies, investigating how bilateral dorsolateral frontal patients perform on theory of mind tasks that are controlled for executive function demands, are needed.

## THE AMYGDALA AND THEORY OF MIND

The finely tuned links between the meanings of social stimuli on the one hand, and the patterns of physiologic activity set into play on the other, presumably are embodied in the network of intrinsic connections in the amygdala. (Kling and Brothers 1992, p. 356.)

The amygdala is a small almond-shaped structure that is located in the medial temporal lobes, just anterior to the hippocampus. It receives polysensory connections from many cortical areas, and sends projections to the hypothalamus, which serve to initiate autonomic responses, ventro–striatal areas, which provide a pathway to initiate motor responses, and to temporal, orbitofrontal, and insular cortex, which may provide a cognitive output (Everitt and Robbins 1992; Halgren 1992; Rolls 1992). The amygdala serves several general functions within the domain of emotion and social behaviour. While it cannot be specific to theory of mind, it forms an important input system to the theory of mind circuit.

The amygdala processes emotional responses and information about reward (Aggleton 1992; Gaffan 1992; Halgren 1992; Kling and Brothers 1992; LaBar and LeDoux 1997; Rolls 1992). In particular, the lateral and central nuclei of the amygdala have been implicated in fear responses (LeDoux 1988, 1990). Natural selection has designed us so that those activities that enhance fitness are rewarding, and elicit positive emotions to draw us towards those activities, while those that are deleterious to fitness elicit negative emotions to push us away from those activities. The amygdala, therefore, should be involved in any highly fitness-relevant situation. It will be activated in recognizing the situation, and in producing the adaptive response, for example, recognizing a dangerous predator and initiating a fear response: freezing or flight (Kling and Brothers 1992; LeDoux *et al.* 1988, 1990). The set of stimuli that activate the amygdala should vary from species to species, as what is adaptive also varies.

Many types of information in the social environment are fitness-relevant. Direct eye contact signifies that one is the object of a conspecific's attention. It may be the first signal in an attack, a mating attempt, or an initiation of social exchange, any of which could affect one's fitness. Being the object of another's attention is unlikely to be fitness-neutral. Accordingly, people respond to direct eye contact autonomically, and even young infants respond strongly to eye contact (Baron-Cohen 1995). Young *et al.* (1995) note that the amygdala is strongly interconnected with the superior temporal sulcus, which, in macaques, has been found to be critical to determining gaze direction. In human subjects, bilateral amygdalotomy impairs the ability to judge gaze direction, and in particular, to judge direct eye contact (Young *et al.* 1995). It is unknown whether this impairment results from a geometric problem computing gaze direction or from a lack of the usual emotional response to eye contact. However, we can speculate that recognizing and responding affectively to the socially significant state 'looking at me' may be one of the important soical functions of the amygdala.

Information about others' eye gaze direction is a central building block for theory of mind. Joint attention, understanding reference, and knowing what someone else knows based on what they have seen, all depend on information about gaze direction (Baron-Cohen 1995; Baron-Cohen *et al.* 1997*a*). Thus, if the amygdala is involved in marking information about others' gaze direction as significant, then the amygdala must form a crucial input to the theory of mind mechanism.

Because others' emotional states can have a significant impact, information about others' emotions is also fitness-relevant. The amygdala appears to be involved in recognizing emotional displays. In monkeys, cells in the amygdala can be selectively activated in response to facial expressions of threat, predator warning vocalizations, infants' vocalizations on being separated from the mother, and displays of a conspecific approaching (Brothers and Ring 1992; Kling and Brothers 1992). In humans, fMRI studies have shown that the amygdala is active during presentation of the facial expression of fear (Morris *et al.* 1996; Phillips *et al.* 1997). People who have suffered bilateral amygdala damage have difficulty recognizing facial and vocal expressions of emotion, particularly fear and anger (Adolphs *et al.* 1994; Broks *et al.* 1998; Calder *et al.* 1996; Scott *et al.* 1997; Young *et al.* 1995). Of course, the significance of another's affect may depend on who he or she is, so information about identity can also be important in determining the response to another's affective signal. Cells in the amygdala have been found to respond to the individual identity of conspecifics (Kling and Brothers 1992; Rolls 1992). Information about others' affective mental states may also be an important input to the theory of mind mechanism.

Halgren (1992) notes that, in humans, the amygdala receives information from the cortex that is already highly processed, and can generate an emotional response not just to concrete percepts, but also to words, thoughts, mental images, and 'other meaningful stimuli that have previously been associated with visceral upset' (p. 213). Thus, even complex situations or abstract ideas (such as a belief about another person's mental state) may cause emotional reactions. The graduate student in the example at the beginning of the chapter could have an emotional reaction, generated in the amygdala, to the thought, 'Maybe that researcher was relieved that the president came up, because she really didn't want to talk to me.' Thus, the amygdala may be interwoven with the other parts of the theory of mind mechanism, involved in generating emotional reactions on the basis of others' mental states. Consistent with this, stimulation of the amygdala may produce complex social emotions: the impression of being criticized, socially isolated, or threatened, or the impression that another person is demanding (Brothers 1994; Brothers and Ring 1992; Kling and Brothers 1992).

There is some empirical support for a role for the amygdala in theory of mind. Baron-Cohen *et al.* (1999) have found amygdala activation in normal subjects during an fMRI scan while subjects are doing the 'Reading the Mind in the Eyes Task', inferring complex mental states from images of the eyes, relative to a control task. Furthermore, they found that the amygdala was not active during this task when they scanned individuals with Asperger's Syndrome. Stone *et al.* (1998*b*) also found that two patients with bilateral amygdala damage were impaired on this task, relative to controls. (See Fig. 11.3.) In addition, one bilateral amygdalotomy patient was significantly impaired on the *faux pas* test (Stone *et al.* 1998*b*).

Baumann and Kemper (1985) reported that the brains of autistic subjects studied on autopsy showed that cells in the amygdala were unusually densely packed. If the amygdala is a critical input system to the theory of mind mechanism, and that input system is not functioning properly in individuals with autism because of abnormal cell growth patterns, this could be an important factor in their abnormal development of a theory of mind.

CONCLUSIONS

Scholars have started collecting direct empirical evidence on the role of each of these brain regions in theory of mind only in the past few years. Based on the curently available evidence, there is reason to conclude that orbitofrontal cortex, medial frontal cortex, dorsolateral frontal cortex, and the amygdala are all involved in theory of mind computations. Research in coming years can provide information about the

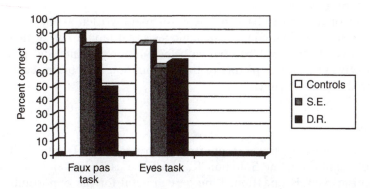

**Fig. 11.3.** Performance of two patients with bilateral amygdala damage, S. E. and D. R., on two theory of mind tasks.

precise role of each region. Brothers and Ring (1992) have talked about the distinction between 'cold' and 'hot' aspects of theory of mind, that is, between representations of the purely cognitive states of others, such as belief and knowledge, and representations of their affective and motivational states, such as emotions or hostile intentions. One possible area of inquiry is the role of each region in 'hot' and 'cold' mental-state inferences. The amygdala seems to form an important input to one of the earliest-developing and purely cognitive aspects of theory of mind, joint attention, by getting the developing brain to pay attention to others' eye gaze. It may be productive to investigate the role of the amygdala specifically in joint attention. Another important question is the nature of the contribution of each cerebral hemisphere. Fletcher *et al.* (1995) and Goel *et al.*, (1995) found selective left medial frontal activation during theory of mind tasks, whereas Happé *et al.* (1999) and Winner *et al.* (1998) have found theory of mind deficits in patients with right hemisphere damage. These results are not inconsistent, but the exact role of each hemisphere can be clarified in the future. Stone *et al.* (1998*a*) and Stone *et al.* (1998*b*) found theory of mind deficits in patients with bilateral orbitofrontal damage, but not in patients with unilateral left dorsolateral frontal damage. Price *et al.* (1990) also found a possible theory of mind deficit in patients with bilateral dorsolateral frontal damage. The deficits in theory of mind and in recognition of gaze direction that have been found in amygdala patients have been reported for patients with bilateral amygdala damage (Stone *et al.* 1998*b*; Young *et al.* 1995). More study is needed to determine if bilateral damage to particular brain structures is necessary to disrupt theory of mind.

Neuroimaging and lesion studies have different and complementary contributions to make to future research into theory of mind. Neuroimaging studies can reveal whether an area is involved in a particular task, but not whether that area is critical for that task. Studies with lesion patients can supplement neuroimaging studies by revealing whether a particular region is critical for a particular function. However, because lesion location varies within patient groups and because often a large area with more than one structure is damaged in lesion patients, it can be difficult to get a high degree of anatomical specificity from lesion studies. Neuroimaging studies may provide a more precise picture of the exact regions involved. The two methods should work in concert in future research.

Any account of the neural basis of theory of mind written at this point must be speculative. In the years that come, systematic tests that tap into all of these different aspects of theory of mind can be used with focal lesion patients and neuroimaging paradigms to give us a clearer picture of the contribution each brain region makes to this vital social cognitive ability.

## Ackowledgements

Preparation of this chapter was supported by grants from Trinity College at the University of Cambridge, the Solomon R. and Rebecca D. Baker Foundation, and the Cure Autism Now Foundation. I am very grateful for the opportunity I had to spend time in the Department of Experimental Psychology at the University of Cambridge as a visiting scholar in 1997–1998 when I began writing this chapter. I thank Simon Baron-Cohen, Bruce Pennington, Melissa Rutherford, and Piotr Winkielman for thoughtful comments on early drafts of this chapter. Finally, without the rich intellectual environment provided by discussions with my collaborators and colleagues, Andy Calder, Jill Keane, Bob Knight, Michele O'Riordan, Kate Plaisted, and Andy Young, the ideas presented here could not have taken shape. Special thanks go to Simon Baron-Cohen for his tremendous colleagueship over the past five years. His collaboration has been essential and invaluable in everything presented in this chapter.

## Note

1. Both ventromedial patients and patients with pure orbitofrontal damage may show inappropriate social behaviour. In addition, Damasio describes ventromedial patients as going through endless deliberations to make even simple decisions, such as when to schedule an appointment or what to wear. The patients I have examined with only orbitofrontal damage and no medial frontal damage do not have these difficulties with decision making. Thus, these difficulties in ventromedial patients may be caused specifically by medial frontal damage, and could have to do with deficits in response selection, rather than a lack of somatic markers.

## REFERENCES

Adolphs, R., Tranel, D., Damasio, H. and Damasio, A. R. (1994). Impaired recogniton of emotion in facial expressions following bilateral damage to the human amygdala. *Nature*, **372**, 669–72.

Aggleton, J. P. (1992). The functional effects of amygdala lesions in humans: a comparison with findings from monkeys. In *The amygdala: neurobiological aspects of emotion, memory and mental dysfucntion* (ed. J. P. Aggleton), pp. 485–503. Wiley-Liss, New York.

Alexander, M. P., Benson, D. F. and Stuss, D. T. (1989). Frontal lobes and language. *Brain and Language*, **37**, 656–91.

Bach, L., Davies, S., Colvin, C., Wijeratne, C., Happé, F. and Howard, R. (1998). A neuropsychological investigation of theory of mind in an elderly lady with frontal leucotomy. *Cognitive Neuropsychiatry*, **3**(2), 139–59.

Baron-Cohen, S. (1995). *Mindblindness: an essay on autism and theory of mind*. MIT Press, Cambridge, MA.

Baron-Cohen, S. and Ring, H. (1994). A model of the mindreading system: neuropsychological and neurobiological perspectives. In *Origins of an understanding of mind* (ed. P. Mitchell and C. Lewis). Erlbaum, Hillsdale, NJ.

Baron-Cohen, S., Ring, H., Moriarty, J., Shmitz, P., Costa, D. and Ell, P. (1994). Recognition of mental state terms: clinical findings in children with autism and a functional neuroimaging study of normal adults. *British Journal of Psychiatry*, **165**, 640–9.

Baron-Cohen, S., Ring, H., Wheelwright, S., Bullmore, E., Brammer, M., Simmons, A. and Williams. S. (1999). Social intelligence in the normal and autistic brain: an fMRI study. *European Journal of Neuroscience*, **11**, 1891–8.

Baron-Cohen, S., Baldwin, D. A. and Crowson, M. (1997*a*). Do children with autism use the speaker's direction of gaze strategy to crack the code of language? *Child Development*, **68**(1), 48–57.

Baron-Cohen, S., Joliffe, T., Mortimore, C. and Robertson, M. (1997*b*). Another advanced test of the theory of mind: evidence from very high functioning adults with autism or Asperger syndrome. *Journal of Child Psychology and Psychiatry*, **38**(7), 813–22.

Baron-Cohen, S., O'Riordan, M., Stone, V. E., Jones, R. and Plaisted, K. (in press). Recognition of faux pas by normally developing children and children with Asperger Syndrome. *Journal of Autism and Developmental Disorders*.

Baumann, M. L. and Kemper, T. (1985). Histoanatomic observations of the brain in early infantile autism. *Neurology*, **35**, 866–74.

Bechara, A., Tranel, D., Damasio, H. and Damasio, A. R. (1993). Failure to respond autonomically in anticipation of future outcomes following damage to human prefrontal cortex. *Society for Neuroscience Abstracts*, **19**, 791.

Benson, D. F. and Miller, B. L. (1997). Frontal lobes: clinical and anatomic aspects. In *Behavioral neurology and neuropsychology* (ed. T. E. Feinberg and M. J. Farah), pp. 401–8. McGraw Hill, New York.

Benson, D. F. and Stuss, D. T. (1986) *The frontal lobes*. Raven Press, New York.

Bowen, M. (1989). Frontal lobe function. *Brain Injury*, **3**, 109–28.

Broks, P., Young, A. W., Maratos, E. J., Coffey, P. J., Calder, A. J., Isaac, C. L., Mayes, A. R., Hodges, J. R., Montaldi, D., Cezayirli, E., Roberts, N. and Hadley, D. (1998). Face processing impairments after encephalitis: amygdala damage and recognition of fear. *Neuropsychologia*, **36**(1), 59–70.

Brothers, L. (1997). *Friday's footprint: how society shapes the human mind*. Oxford University Press, New York.

Brothers, L. and Ring, B. (1992). A neuroethological framework for the representation of minds. *Journal of Cognitive Neuroscience*, **4**(2), 107–18.

Calder, A. J., Young, A. W., Rowland, D., Perrett, D. I., Hodges, J. R. and Etcoff, N. L. (1996). Facial emotion recognition after bilateral amygdala damage: differentially severe impairment of fear. *Cognitive Neuropsychology*, **13**(5), 699–745.

Carter, C. S. and Altemus, M. (1997). Integrative functions of lactational hormones in social behavior and stress management. *Annals of the New York Academy of Science*, **807**, 164–74.

Damasio, A. R. (1994). *Descartes' error: emotion, reason and the human brain*. Avon Books, New York.

Damasio, A. R. and VanHoesen, G. W. (1983). Emotional disorders associated with focal lesions of the limbic frontal lobe. In *Neuropsychology of human emotion* (ed. K. M. Heilman and P. Satz), pp. 85–110. Guilford Press, New York.

Eslinger, P. J. and Damasio, A. R. (1985). Severe disturbance of higher cognition after bilateral frontal lobe ablation: patient EVR. *Neurology*, **35**, 1731–41.

Everitt, B. J. and Robbins, T. W. (1992). Amygdala-ventral striatal interactions and reward-related processes. In *The amygdala: neurobiological aspects of emotion, memory and mental dysfunction* (ed. J. P. Aggleton), pp. 401–29. Wiley–Liss, New York.

Fletcher, P. C., Happé, F., Frith, U., Baker, S. C., Dolan, R. J., Frackowiak, R. S. J. and Frith, C. (1995). Other minds in the brain: a functional imaging study of 'theory of mind' in story comprehension. *Cognition*, **57**, 109–28.

Frith, C. (1996). Brain mechanisms for 'having a theory of mind'. *Journal of Psychopharmacology*, **10**(1), 9–15.

Gaffan, D. (1992). Amygdala and the memory of reward. In *The amygdala: neurobiological aspects of emotion, memory and mental dysfunction* (ed. J. P. Aggleton), pp. 471–83. Wiley–Liss, New York.

Goel, V., Grafman, J., Sadato, N. and Hallett, M. (1995). Modeling other minds. *Neuroreport*, **6**, 1741–6.

Gopnik, A. and Astington, J. W. (1988). Children's understanding of representational change and its relation to the understanding of false belief and the appareance–reality distinction. *Child Development*, **59**, 26–37.

Gronwall, D., Wrightson, P. and Waddel, P. (1998). *Head injury: the facts*. Oxford University Press.

Halgren, E. (1992). Electrophysiological responses in the human amygdala. In *The amygdala: neurobiological aspects of emotion, memory and mental dysfunction* (ed. J. P. Aggleton), pp. 191–228. Wiley–Liss, New York.

Happé, F. (1994*a*). An advanced test of theory of mind: understanding of story characters' thoughts and feelings by able autistic, mentally handicapped and normal children and adults. *Journal of Autism and Developmental Disorders*, **24**(2), 129–54.

Happé, F. (1994*b*). Communicative competence and theory of mind in autism: a test of Relevance Theory. *Cognition*, **48**, 101–19.

Happé, F., Ehlers, S., Fletcher, P. C., Frith, U., Johansson, M., Gillberg, C., Dolan, R., Frackowiak, R. and Frith, C. (1996). 'Theory of mind' in the brain: evidence from a PET scan study of Asperger syndrome. *Neuroreport*, **8**(1), 197–201.

Happé, F., Brownell, H. and Winner, E. (1999). Acquired theory of mind impairments following right hemisphere stroke. *Cognition*, **70**, 211–40.

Insel, T. R. (1997). A neurobiological basis of social attachment. *American Journal of Psychiatry*, **154**(6), 726–35.

Kaczmarek, B. L. J. (1984). Neurolinguistic analysis of verbal utterances in patients with focal lesions of frontal lobes. *Brain and Language*, **21**, 52–8.

Kimberg, D. Y., D'Esposito, M. and Farah, M. J. (1997). Frontal lobes: cognitive neuropsychological aspects. In *Behavioral neurology and neuropsychology* (ed. T. E. Feinberg and M. J. Farah), pp. 409–18. McGraw-Hill, New York.

Kling A. S. and Brothers, L. A. (1992). The amygdala and social behavior. In *The amygdala: neurobiological aspects of emotion, memory and mental dysfunction* (ed. J. P. Aggleton), pp. 353–77. Wiley–Liss, New York.

Knight, R. T. and Grabowecky, M. (1995). Escape from linear time: prefrontal cortex and conscious experience. In *The cognitive neurosciences* (ed. M. S. Gazzaniga). MIT Press, Cambridge, MA.

LaBar, K. S. and LeDoux, J. E. (1997). Emotion and the brain: an overview. In *Behavioral neurology and neuropsychology* (ed. T. E. Feinberg and M. J. Farah), pp. 675–89. McGraw-Hill, New York.

LeDoux, J. E., Iwata, J., Cicchetti, P. and Reis, D. J. (1988). Different projections of the central amygdaloid nucleus mediate autonomic and behavioral correlates of conditioned fear. *Journal of Neuroscience*, **8**, 2517–29.

LeDoux, J. E., Cicchetti, P., Xagoraris, A. and Romanski, L. M. (1990). The lateral amygdaloid nucleus: sensory interface of the amygdala in fear conditioning. *Journal of Neuroscience*, **10**, 1062–9.

Mattson, A. J. and Levin, H. S. (1990). Frontal lobe dysfunction following closed head injury. *Journal of Nervous and Mental Disease*, **178**(5), 282–91.

Morris, J. S., Frith, C. D., Perrett, D. I., Rowland, D., Young, A. W., Calder, A. J. and Dolan, R. J. (1996). A differential neural response in the human amygdala to fearful and happy facial expressions. *Nature*, **383**, 812–5.

Nelson, E. E. and Panksepp, J. (1998). Brain substrates of infant-mother attachement:

contributions of opioids, oxytocin and norepinephrine. *Neuroscience and Biobehavioral Research*, **22**(3), 437–52.

Ozonoff, S., Rogers, S. J. and Pennington, B. F. (1991). Executive function deficits in high-functioning autistic individuals: relationship to theory of mind. *Journal of Child Psychology and Psychiatry*, **32**, 1107–22.

Pennington, B. F., Rogers, S. J., Bennetto, L., Griffin, E. M., Reed, D. T. and Shyu, V. (1997). Validity tests of the executive dysfunction hypothesis of autism. In *Autism as an executive disorder* (ed. J. Russell), pp. 143–73. Oxford University Press.

Perner, J. and Wimmer, H. (1985). 'John thinks that Mary think that . . .': attribution of second-order false beliefs by five to ten year old children. *Journal of Experimental Child Psychology*, **39**, 437–71.

Phillips, M. L., Young, A. W., Senior, C., Brammer, M., Andrews, C., Calder, A. J., Bullmore, E. T., Perrett, D. I., Rowland, D., Williams, S. C. R., Gray, J. A. and David, A. S. (1997). A specific neural substrate for perceiving facial expressions of disgust. *Nature*, **389**, 495–8.

Price, B., Daffner, K., Stowe, R. and Mesulam, M. (1990). The comportmental learning disabilities of early frontal lobe damage. *Brain*, **113**, 1383–93.

Raleigh, M. J. and Brammer, G. L. (1993). Individual differences in serotonin-2 receptors in social behavior in monkeys. *Society for Neuroscience Abstracts*, **19** 592.

Raleigh, M. J., McGuire, M., Brammer, G. L., Pollack, D. and Yuwiler, A. (1991). Serotonergic mechanisms promote dominance acquisition in adult male vervet monkeys. *Brain Research*, **559**, 181–90.

Rolls, E. T. (1992). Neurophysiology and functions of the primate amygdala. In *The amygdala: neurobiological aspects of emotion, memory and mental dysfunction* (ed. J. P. Aggleton), pp. 143–65. Wiley–Liss, New York.

Rolls, E. T. (1996). The orbitofrontal cortex. *Philosophical Transactions of the Royal Society*, **351**, 1433–43.

Rolls, E. T., Hornak, J., Wade, D. and McGrath, J. (1994). Emotion-related learning in patients with social and emotional changes associated with frontal lobe damage. *Journal of Neurology, Neurosurgery and Psychiatry*, **57**(12), 1518–24.

Saver, J. L. and Damasio, A. R. (1991). Preserved access and processing of social knowledge in a patient with acquired sociopathy due to ventromedial frontal damage. *Neuropsychologia*, **29**, 1241–9.

Scott, S. K., Young, A. W., Calder, A. J. and Hellawell, D. J. (1997). Impaired auditory recognition of fear and anger following bilateral amygdala lesions. *Nature*, **385**, 254–7.

Stone, V. E., Baron-Cohen, S. and Knight, R. T. (1998a). Frontal lobe contributions to theory of mind. *Journal of Cognitive Neuroscience*, **10**(5), 640–56.

Stone, V. E., Baron-Cohen, S., Young, A. W., Calder, A. and Keane, J. (1998b). Impairments in social cognition following orbitofrontal or amygdala damage. *Society for Neuroscience Abstracts*, **24**, 1176.

Tager-Flusberg, H. (1993). What language reveals about the understanding of minds in children with autism. In *Understanding other minds: perspectives from autism* (1st Edn) (ed. S. Baron-Cohen, H. Tager-Flusberg, and D. Cohen). Oxford University Press.

Tranel, D. (1994). 'Acquired sociopathy': the development of sociopathic behavior following focal brain damage. *Progress in Experimental Personality and Psychopathology Research*, 285–311.

Wellman, H. M. (1990). *The Child's Theory of Mind*. MiT Press, Cambridge, MA.

Whyte, J., Fleming, M., Cavallucci, C. and Coslett, H. B. (1998). The effects of visual distraction following traumatic brain injury. *Journal of the International Neuropsychological Society*, **4**(2), 127–36.

Wimmer, H. and Perner, J. (1983). Beliefs about beliefs: representation and constraining function of wrong beliefs in young children's understanding of deception. *Cognition*, **13**, 103–28.

Winner, E., Brownell, H., Happé, F., Blum, A. and Pincus, D. (1998). Distinguishing lies from jokes: theory of mind deficits and discourse interpretation in right hemisphere brain-damaged patients. *Brain and Language*, **62**, 89–106.

Young, A. W., Aggleton, J. P., Hellawell, D. J., Johnson, M., Broks, P. and Hanley, J. R. (1995). Face processing impairments after amygdalotomy. *Brain*, **118**, 15–24.

# 12

# How can studies of the monkey brain help us understand 'theory of mind' and autism in humans?

NATHAN J. EMERY AND DAVID I. PERRETT

## INTRODUCTION

The first edition of *Understanding other minds* discussed the ability of human and non-human primates to read the mental states of others from non-verbal signals. This ability or 'theory of mind' is apparent in three- to four-year-old children and possibly some of the great apes (Tomasello and Call 1997; however, see Heyes 1998). Some authors have argued that a theory of mind is dependent on language (e.g. Sparrevohn and Howie 1995). If so, then no non-human primate has the capacity for a theory of mind.

Baron-Cohen's (1994) account of a human mind-reading system is amenable to study in non-human primates because it envisages a theory of mind mechanism dependent on the interactions between separate brain modules for detecting eye direction, intentionality and sharing attention. These latter capacities may well be present in non-human primates and even be apparent in neuronal responses (Perrett and Emery 1994).

Tomasello *et al.* (1993) propose three levels of social understanding that are also appropriate for neuroscientific analysis. The first level would support the perception of behaviour of an animate being and allow prediction of the consequences of that behaviour. The second level would allow understanding that another's behaviour is intentional or goal-directed, by conceiving of the other individual as an 'intentional agent' whose behaviour and attention are purposive. The third level of understanding would be compatible with theory of mind, where another individual is conceived of as an agent whose thoughts and beliefs may differ from those directly inferred from overt behaviour and actions. Certainly, the first two levels of understanding are appropriate for study at the cellular level (see section B).

A related approach to 'mind-reading' was formulated by Leslie Brothers (1990) in her 'social brain hypothesis'. Brothers suggested that the ability to process the 'dispositions and intentions of other individuals' (1990, p. 27) was sufficiently developed in primates to warrant a 'separate module of cognition', and that such a module should be apparent at the neural level (see Brothers and Ring 1993; Brothers *et al.* 1990; and section B).

It is the purpose of this chapter to document the neural mechanisms in the non-human primate which may underlie the evolution of social understanding in the way envisaged by Brothers (1990), Baron-Cohen (1994) and Tomasello *et al.* (1993). The review focuses on neuroanatomical, neurophysiological, and neuropsychological studies of the non-human primate brain. The chapter may help cognitive and developmental psychologists understand a theory of mind in a more mechanistic fashion.

A principal theme throughout this review is that high-level visual processing puts both human and non-human primates in a position to understand the intentions and emotions of other animals and the purpose of their behaviour. We recognise the emotions of others by identifying their facial expressions. Similarly we recognise the purpose of behavioural actions by identifying the component movements and the relation of those movements to a goal. Part of this recognition involves matching up the sight of the behaviour and expressions of others to our own actions and emotions. Through this matching we reap the social benefits of the skills and experience of others. Thus visual recognition includes both the analysis of the visual image and the associations between what we see, what we feel, and what we do. Social recognition goes one step further than a visual definition of edges, features, or faces; it is performed in a functional context whereby the information revealed has utility in guiding our actions and shaping our survival.

It should be noted that the intended use of the phrases 'understanding others' and 'reading their minds' is more behavioural than mentalistic. Behaviourism describes the formation of learned associations between stimuli and responses without recourse or reference to intervening mental events or conscious awareness. It is a moot point as to whether an individual needs to empathise with the feelings of a second individual in order to behave in a way that benefits from the feelings of the other. On the other hand, possessing the capacity to recognise the symptoms of feelings in others both offers behavioural benefits and provides the potential for empathy (Brothers 1989).

## A. COMPARATIVE NEUROANATOMY OF PRIMATE SOCIAL COGNITION

What can the neuroanatomy of the primate brain reveal about social cognition and theory of mind? The brain is an extremely complex biological structure, with many subdivisions contributing to different behavioural and cognitive functions, such as perception, memory, decision-making, planning, motor control, and emotions. The visual system alone is comprised of over thirty cortical regions (Felleman and Van Essen 1991) and there are many subcortical nuclei which also contribute to visual function.

The complexity of the brain's structure reflects the complexity of its functions. A relatively simple piece of behaviour, such as a motor reflex, only requires a relatively simple neuroanatomical circuit: sensory neuron to dorsal horn of the spinal cord to motor neuron. The simplicity of this circuit is mainly dependent on the function of the circuit; the detection of a noxious stimulus and the generation of a motor response to move the endangered limb and therefore protect the limb from damage. A more complex operation, such as recognition of an object, requires additional neural circuitry.

It will be argued in this section that the everyday social cognition of monkeys and apes requires a particular neuroanatomy to process and evaluate social signals and make appropriate social decisions. The pressure to evolve an ability to 'mind read' is also a pressure to evolve a particular advanced neuroanatomical architecture to interpret the behaviour of others within a mentalistic framework.

Three brain regions have been the focus for neurophysiological and neuro-behavioural analyses of non-human primate social cognition. These are the anterior temporal cortex (especially the cortex of the anterior section of the superior temporal sulcus; STS), the amygdala (in particular the basolateral nuclei group) and the different areas which comprise the orbitofrontal cortex. Kling and Steklis (1976) suggested that these three regions were crucial for forms of affiliative behaviour. Recent neurobiological studies in macaques (Brothers *et al.* 1990; Emery *et al.* 1998) and humans (Adolphs *et al.* 1998; Damasio 1994) have provided evidence that these regions may be essential for more than just affiliative behaviour. The anatomy of these three regions also suggests a role in social cognition.

Two anatomical approaches will be discussed, each utilising published anatomical data and statistical techniques to determine the possible role of different brain structures in social cognition and 'mind-reading'. The first approach uses data on anatomical connections (Area A connects to Area B but not to Area C, etc.) to establish a connectivity matrix of the entire cortex and amygdala, then uses non-metric multidimensional scaling (NMDS) to evaluate the relationships between brain areas from the overall connectivity patterns. Unfortunately, this approach can only be used in those species in which the brain connections are well studied, such as the rat, cat, and macaque.

The second anatomical approach to be discussed is less constrained by the actual species studied, but depends on the availability of volumetric brain data and socio–ecological profiles for a large number of closely related species. Fortunately, Stephan and colleagues (e.g. Stephan *et al.* 1981) have completed the painstaking measurement of the volumes of individual brain regions for a large number of primate and non-primate species. The volume of individual brain components from a large number of species is then correlated with socio–ecological factors, such as social group size and percentage of fruit in the diet. A significant positive correlation implicates a given brain component in computations that are critical for social life or for acquisition of a particular food type. The results of this method can then help us formulate hypotheses about the proposed socio–ecological pressures on primate brain evolution.

Both of these methods are useful for deriving hypotheses about the function of a particular brain region, especially when there are no direct studies of the region's function. More traditional methods, such as electrophysiology, lesions, and neuro-imaging can then be utilised to determine the region's precise behavioural function.

### i. Non-metric multidimensional scaling (NMDS) analysis

NMDS analysis has only recently been incorporated into the tools used by neuro-scientists to evaluate a brain area's contribution to a particular behaviour. Although on the surface NMDS appears to be useful only for bringing some sort of order to the complexity of neuroanatomical connectivity, when coupled with a knowledge of the function of different brain regions it becomes a powerful analytic and predictive tool. Briefly, the NMDS technique requires that a matrix of anatomical connections is produced for all brain regions to be analysed (i.e. area X connects with areas Y and Z, but not areas V and W). In the analyses to be discussed here, a matrix was constructed where a 0 was designated for no known connection between areas X and Y, a 1 for a unidirectional connection, and a 2 for a reciprocal connection. These input data were transformed to reduce the effects of large numbers of zeros in the connection matrices, which may distort output configurations (for details see Young *et al.* 1995).

NMDS analysis of this matrix of connections produces an output that makes apparent the similarity between different brain areas based on their connection patterns. Areas that have similar connections are grouped close to one another in the NMDS output, whereas brain areas with different connections are placed far apart. Although an NMDS output can be computed in many dimensions, 2D outputs are the most easily interpreted.

NMDS was initially used in studies of brain connectivity by Young and colleagues (Young 1992, 1993; Young *et al.* 1995) to determine whether models of the primate visual system were correct in their assumption that there are two processing streams of visual information; a ventral stream responsible for the recognition of objects and a dorsal stream responsible for the analysis of object position, motion, and visual control motor behaviour (Goodale and Milner 1992; Ungerleider and Mishkin 1982). Using NMDS analysis of the connections of cortical areas, Young (1992) found that the dorsal visual areas were grouped together in a two-dimensional NMDS output plot, as were the ventral visual areas. This objective analysis of connections provided support for the notion of two cortical visual systems. Young also noted that the two processing streams converge within the anterior STS. This brain area has been shown to contain neurons that seem to combine both dorsal and ventral functions. Some STS cells code not only for the form of objects (such as face) but also their motion and location (Baker *et al.* 1998; Oram and Perrett 1996). Young therefore argues that NMDS can be useful in predicting the function of brain areas.

Young (1993) extended his analysis to include the documented connections of the entire cerebral cortex. He included the connections to the hippocampus and amygdala, due to their extensive cortical connectivity and their proposed relationships with the cortex in functions such as memory and emotion. The amygdala was treated as a single entity in Young's analysis. A connection of a cortical region to one component nucleus within the amygdala was treated the same as a connection to a different component nucleus. Yet the amygdala is an extremely complex structure; a collection of thirteen nuclei located in the medial temporal lobe (Amaral *et al.* 1992). The lateral and basolateral nuclei of the amygdala receive many projections from sensory cortex and project back to sensory, motor, cingulate, hippocampal, and prefrontal cortices. By contrast, the central and medial nuclei of the amygdala project to subcortical nuclei and appear to be involved primarily in regulating blood pressure, heart rate, breathing, and the hormones controlling sexual and feeding behaviour and response to stress (see Emery and Amaral 1999, for review).

Emery (1997) extended the matrix of data for NMDS to include all documented interconnections between cortical areas and the component nuclei of the amygdala. Figure 12.1 gives the output of NMDS applied to this extended database. In this new plot, the amygdala nuclei grouped together in three clusters; the basolateral group (lateral, lateral basal, medial basal, and accessory basal nuclei), the centromedial group (central, medial, and cortical nuclei, and periamygdaloid cortex) and the peripheral nuclei group (cortical transition area, anterior amygdaloid area, and amygdalo–hippocampal area).

With similar results to Young's (1993) analysis, the different cortical areas processing the same sensory modality are positioned together in the NMDS output. A number of results are important to the present chapter. First, the basolateral group of nuclei is separated from the centromedial group and peripheral nuclei. Investigators performing comparative analyses of the mammalian amygdaloid complex have stressed previously that the basolateral and centromedial groups are distinct entities with different functions (Humphrey 1936; Johnson 1923). The NMDS analysis provides objective support for this separation. Neurons responsive to faces in the amygdala, and those (Leonard et al. 1985; Rolls 1984, 1992) responsive to the actions of others (Brothers and Ring 1993; Brothers et al. 1990) have been found in the basolateral nuclei, but not in the centromedial or peripheral nuclei. The basolateral group of nuclei are located close to the cortical association areas with direct input into the amygdala, such as the inferotemporal cortex, insula, superior temporal gyrus, temporal pole, and the polysensory perirhinal and entorhinal cortices. The centromedial nuclei are located close to the cortical regions which receive major outputs from the amygdala, such as the frontal cortex (including orbito- and medial frontal cortex) and the cingulate cortex.

Second, all brain regions which have been attributed a possible role in primate social cognition (from neurobehavioural and neurophysiological studies of monkeys) are closely grouped together. These include the temporal cortex (CITd, AITd, AITv), temporal pole (TGv), superior temporal sulcus (STPa, TS2), basolateral amygdala (LB, L, MB, AB), cingulate cortex (A23, A24), prefrontal cortex (A9, A10), and orbitofrontal cortex (A10, A12, A13). The ananatomical analysis suggests that further studies of the neural basis of primate social cognition, and ultimately theory of mind, should concentrate on these areas.

Interestingly, medial orbitofrontal cortex (A14) groups more with the centromedial nuclei than with the basolateral nuclei. The exact homology between this area and the medial frontal areas in humans that are activated theory of mind tasks (Fletcher et al. 1995; Frith and Frith 1999) is unclear.

As stated earlier, one limitation of the NMDS technique is that its application is limited to species for which anatomical connections are already defined. The NMDS analysis performed for Fig. 12.1 is based on species of primates limited to the macaque genus. How can the relationship between a brain area and proposed function be examined in a larger number of related species, such as the anthropoid primates? The next section details an appropriate comparative technique that builds upon the results of the NMDS analysis.

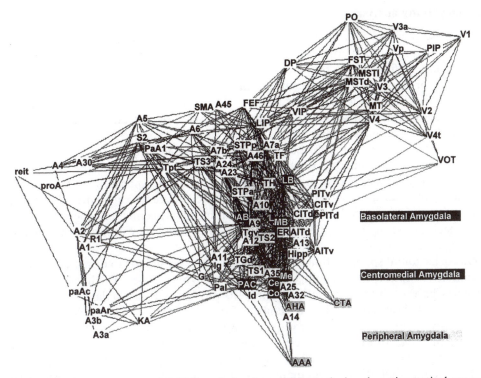

**Fig. 12.1.** 2–D solution to a NMDS analysis of amygdalocortical and corticocortical connections of the macaque brain. Brain regions are abbreviated by text, lines record the 951 reported connections between these brain regions. Brain regions that lie close to one another in this illustration have similar connections. Note that the centromedial nuclei of the amygdala (Ce Me Co and PAC) are grouped separately from the basolateral nuclei (AB, L, LB, MB) and the peripheral nuclei (CTA, AAA and AHA). Abbreviations: Anterior amygdaloid area (AAA); accessory basal nucleus (AB); amygdalohippocampal area (AHA); dorsal anterior inferotemporal cortex (AITd); ventral anterior inferotemporal cortex (AITv); sensorimotor area 1 (A1); sensorimotor area 2 (A2); sensorimotor area 3a (A3a); sensorimotor area 3b (A3b); primary motor cortex (A4); somatosensory area 5 (A5); premotor cortex (A6); posterior parietal area (A7a); parietal area 7b (A7b); dorsal prefrontal cortex (A9); frontal pole (A10); rostral orbital frontal cortex (A11); lateral orbital frontal cortex (A12); central orbital frontal cortex (A13); medial orbital frontal cortex (A14); cingulate gyrus, posterior (A23); cingulate gyrus, anterior (A24); medial prefrontal cortex (A25); prefrontal motor area (A30); cingulate gyrus, rostral (infralimbic cortex, A32); perirhinal cortex (A35); prefrontal cortex, area 45 (A45); frontal cortex, principal sulcus (A46); central nucleus (Ce); dorsal caudal inferotemporal cortex (CITd); ventral caudal inferotemporal cortex (CITv); cortical nucleus (Co); cortical Transition Area (CTA); dorsal prelunate area (DP); entorhinal cortex, A28 (ER); frontal eye field; A8 (FEF); floor of the superior temporal cortex (FST); gustatory cortex (G); hippocampal formation including the hippocampus and subicular cortices (Hipp); insular cortex; dysgranular layer (Id); insular cortex, granular layer (Ig); primary auditory cortex (KA); lateral nucleus (L); lateral basal nucleus (LB); lateral intraparietal area (LIP); medial basal nucleus (MB); medial nucleus (Me); dorsal medial superior temporal cortex (MSTd); lateral medial superior temporal cortex (MSTl); middle temporal area (MT); caudalparakaniocortical auditory area (paAc); lateral parakanio cortical auditory area (paAl); rostral parakaniocortical auditory area (paAr);

## ii. Comparative analysis

The precise environmental pressures that have shaped the anatomy and increased the size of the primate brain are relatively unknown. A number of theories have been put forward to explain why the primate, and especially human, brain is larger and more complexly organised than that of other mammalian species. Tool making, hunting, extractive foraging and food processing, and the use of mental maps for locating food have all been proposed as cognitive capacities that required an expansion of the primate brain and mind (Barton and Dunbar 1997; Dunbar 1998). A problem for some of these theories is that the particular capacity is unique to humans or restricted to great apes (e.g. tool making and hunting). It is difficult to argue that the progressive evolution of brain size across primate species is due to the appearance of an ability that develops so abruptly. Other theories do not differentiate the capacities of primates and non-primate mammals. Many mammalian and non-mammalian species require the capacity to acquire food through extractive foraging or may utilise 'mental maps' to navigate territories.

One behavioural specialisation, which appears relatively unique to primates, is social cognition or Machiavellian intelligence (Byrne and Whiten 1988). The hypothesis that primates have evolved a specialised ability to predict and manipulate conspecifics' behaviour has been proposed by a number of investigators (Byrne and Whiten 1988; Humphrey 1976). The primate brain may have become larger and more complex to provide the extra processing capacities required for this increased social intelligence (e.g. an extensive memory to recall social relationships, a capacity for forward planning and predicting what others might do in given situations). Therefore, it is suggested that the ability to 'mind read' is ultimately the product of the expansion of the primate brain, especially the neocortex and limbic system including the amygdala.

A number of investigators (Barton 1996; Dunbar 1992, 1995; Sawaguchi 1990, 1992) have attempted to show a relationship between overall brain size (or size of a brain component) and a crude measure of social cognition, mean social group size. Mean group size may represent the possible number of relationships that an individual may be required to process. This measurement presumes that the species being studied has some capacity for social intelligence. A number of animal species live in large social groups (ants, termites, bees) but it is assumed that these animals do not possess the

---

periamygdaloid cortex (PAC); parainsula cortex (PaI); posterior intraparietal area (PIP); dorsal posterior inferotemporal cortex (PITd); ventral posterior inferotemporal cortex (PITv); prokaniocortical auditory area (proA); parieto-occipital area (PO); circular sulcus, area reIt (reit); retroinsular area (RI); somatosensory area 2 (S2); supplementary motor area (SMA); anterior superior temporal polysensory area (STPa); posterior superior temporal polysensory area (STPp); parahippocampal gyrus (TF); dorsal temporal pole (TGd); ventral temporal pole (Tgv); parahippocampal gyrus (TH); auditory area Tpt (Tpt); auditory area in rostral portion of superior temporal gyrus (TS1); auditory area in mid-portion of STG and adjacent cortex in superior temporal sulcus (TS2); auditory area within caudal part of STG and adjacent cortex in STS (TS3); primary visual cortex, A17 (V1); secondary visual cortex, A18 (V2); visual area 3, A19 (V3); visual area 3a (V3a); visual area 4 (V4); visual area 4, transitional (V4t); ventral intraparietal area (VIP); ventral occipitotemporal visual area (VOT).

level of social intelligence that is displayed by primates. Yet social complexity in different taxonomic groups (including insects) may have led to brain development analogous to that described below.

Dunbar (1992) found a significant correlation between the ratio of neocortex to rest of brain (brain minus neocortex) and mean group size for a large number of prosimians, Old and New World monkeys, and apes including *Homo Sapiens*. This relationship has been found to hold for prosimians and anthropoids when analysed separately (Barton 1996; Dunbar and Joffe, in press). The whole of the neocortex, however, does not process social information. Evidence to date suggests that the anterior temporal cortex, the orbitofrontal cortex, and possibly the cingulate cortex are the regions of cortex which contribute most significantly to primate social behaviour. Large regions of neocortex including the sensory and motor cortices probably do not contribute in any unique way to social behaviour. Joffe and Dunbar (1997) re-analysed the cortex-group size relations, using volume of neocortex minus the volume of primary visual cortex (area V1), and found the relationship was still significant. Although V1 is a large component of neocortex, there are more than thirty visual areas (Felleman and Van Essen 1991) and many auditory, somatosensory, gustatory, olfactory, and motor areas which are included in Joffe and Dunbar's (1997) 'non-V1 neocortical areas'. Unfortunately, Stephan *et al.*'s (1981) database of brain component volume does not separate the sensory or motor cortical areas further. Joffe and Dunbar's (1997) analysis of the cortical regions that relate in size to measures of social complexity cannot be extended. Only a further painstaking analysis of separate brain regions of a range of primate species will help determine the contributions of individual brain regions to social cognition.

The NMDS analysis discussed in the previous section indicates the importance of the amygdala in the brain circuitry involved in macaque social behaviour. Recent studies of the effect of ibotenic acid lesions of the amygdala on the social behaviour of adult rhesus macaques also stress this point (Emery *et al.* 1998). Barton and Dunbar (1997) and Joffe and Dunbar (1997) analysed the relationship between the size of the amygdala (or component amygdala nuclei) and social group size but did not find a significant correlation.

For unknown reasons, Joffe and Dunbar (1997), however, did not use data for amygdala volume for all species available (Stephan *et al.* 1981, 1987). When all available data is analysed a different picture emerges (see Fig. 12.2). Larger animals tend to have larger brains with larger amygdala. If small primates tend to live in small groups, and large primates tend to live in large groups, then size of the brain and size of the amygdala would correlate with social group size. Such correlations are relatively uninteresting as they would mean that social evolution triggered or depended on increased body mass, rather than depending on particular brain structures. A more sophisticated comparative analysis first partials out any general increase in body or overall brain size with social group size and then looks for residual relationship between the volume of a given brain component and social group size.

Emery (1997) analysed the way that social evolution affected the volume of the amygdala, basolateral and centromedial groups, and lateral basal nucleus (removing

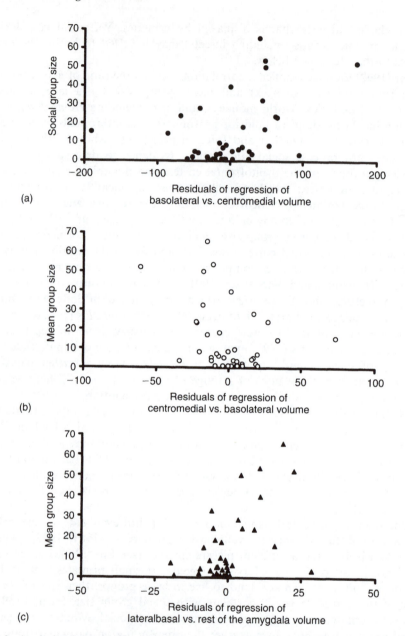

**Fig. 12.2.** Analysis of the relationship between brain component volume and social group size for forty four strepsirhine and haplorhine primate species.

(a) Residuals of the regression of basolateral and centromedial nuclear complex volumes are plotted against social group size.

(b) Residuals of the regression of lateral basal nucleus volume against volume of the rest of amygdala are plotted against social group size.

(c) Residuals of the regression of centromedial volume against basolateral volume are plotted against social group size.

the possible effects of rest of brain, centromedial group, basolateral group, and rest of amygdala accordingly). Thus, to analyse the relationship between the volume of the amygdala and social group size, the following steps were taken. For forty four primate species (excluding *Homo sapiens*), the volume of amygdala was first regressed against the volume of the rest of the brain. The residuals of this regression represent the interesting variation of amygdala size that is unrelated to the overall variation in brain size. These residuals were then correlated with social group size. The result showed no significant relationship. There was, however, a significant positive relationship between basolateral nucleus volume and social group size when the relation between baso-lateral and centromedial nuclear size had been partialled out. The lateral basal nucleus is a major component of the basolateral complex and its volume correlated positively with social group size, after removing the effect of the volume of the rest of the amygdala). There was a significant negative relationship between centromedial nucleus volume and social group size when the relation between centromedial and basolateral nuclear size had been partialled out.

The analysis also confirms the importance of differentiating the components of the amygdala, rather than treating the structure as unified whole. The amygdala as a whole may not have increased in size with evolution of social complexity in primates but particular components of the amygdala have developed at the expense of other amygdala components. The basolateral nuclear complex within the amygdala increases in volume as social group size increases. The centromedial nuclear complex by contrast shows the opposite relation and decreases in size as social group size increases. The comparative analysis thus confirms the separation of the two nuclear groups that was revealed from NMDS analysis of anatomical connections.

The findings of this analysis were replicated when data were subjected to the method of Comparative Analysis of Independent Contrasts (Purvis and Rumbaut 1995) which controls for the fact that a trait (such as social group size) may be similar in closely related species because of common ancestry rather than because of convergent evolution and adaptation to a similar evolutionary pressure.

This result also suggests that, during the evolution of primates, the role of the amygdala in behaviour may have changed. Old World monkeys and apes became more reliant on visual and auditory forms of communication, compared with the predominantly olfactory communication of prosimians and the predominantly auditory communication of New World monkeys (Allman 1982). During evolution the visual areas of the neocortex increased in number (Kaas and Krubitzer 1991). With increasingly complex social life this may have produced a requirement for more amygdalo–cortical connections to allow attributions of socioemotional significance to be made to visual stimuli (such as particular facial expressions and gestures; Emery and Amaral, 1999).

Evidence for the involvement of the human amygdala in decoding signals of social importance comes from the activation of this region by facial expressions (Morris *et al.* 1996) and body movements (Bonda *et al.* 1996). Recent fMRI studies also implicate the human amygdala in interpretation of mental states of others from their faces and eyes. Adults with high-functioning autism or Asperger's Syndrome show problems in interpreting mental states of others. They perform poorly in a task that presents close up images of the eye region of faces and requires observers to make attributions of the mental state to the owner of the eyes. Unlike control subjects, adults with Asperger's Syndrome show no activation of the amygdala when engaged in this 'reading the mind in the eyes' task (Baron-Cohen *et al.* 1999).

Dunbar (1998) has suggested that 'apes appear to be capable of the additional cognitive processing associated with mind-reading' because the volume of the neo-cortex is not constrained by the volume of the sensory processing areas. Once a 'crucial threshold' for neocortex volume has been reached (enabling sufficient sophistication in sensory processing and motor control), additional neocortex can be used for more specialised functions, such as would be essential for a theory of mind. This is a promising thesis but is difficult to reconcile with Semendeferi *et al.*'s (1997) recent analysis of magnetic resonance images (MRI) of chimpanzee, gorilla, orang-utan, gibbon, macaque, and human frontal lobes. The frontal lobes and, in particular, the prefrontal cortex, have long been associated with social behaviour in monkeys (Brody and Rosvold 1952; Myers *et al.* 1973) and social decision-making in humans (Damasio 1994). Recent neuroimaging studies have also implicated the orbitofrontal (Baron-Cohen *et al.* 1994), and medial frontal cortex in theory of mind in humans (Fletcher *et al.* 1995; see also Frith and Frith, this volume). Semendeferi *et al.* (1997), on the other hand, found that although the human frontal lobes were larger than those of the other species studied, the relative size of the human frontal lobes was not larger than expected for a primate brain of human size. They also found that the individual sectors of the frontal lobe (dorsal, medial, and orbital) were similar in relative size (i.e. percentage of frontal cortex) in all the species studied. Semendeferi *et al.* (1997) suggested that 'aspects other than relative volume of the frontal lobe have to be responsible for the cognitive specialisations of the hominids'.

Thus, while there is a clear relationship between the volume of the neocortex as a whole and social group size, comparative anatomy does not yet reveal which cortical areas outside the primary visual cortex are the most critical for social cognition and a theory of mind. Further study in this area warrants more complex measures of brain volume (including architectonic analyses of the borders between brain regions) and more complex measures of social cognition. Byrne (1993), for example, analysed Dunbar's (1992) neocortex ratio with the number of instances of 'tactical deception' reported per genus. Tactical deception, or the intentional deception of a second party to influence the second party's behaviour, has been proposed to be an essential component of theory of mind (Byrne and Whiten 1988; although see Heyes 1998). Social network size (Kudo *et al.* 1998) and mating parameters (Pawlowski *et al.* 1998) have also been used as indices of social complexity, and correlate with the neocortex ratio. Although the evidence that non-human primates use theory of mind is rather limited (Heyes 1998; Tomasello and Call 1997), there is substantial evidence that non-human primates have excellent social skills. Further studies to determine the nature of social skills manifest in a large number of primate species can help us understand the evolution of theory of mind in primates.

To summarise the anatomical review in this section, NMDS analysis of the connections between brain regions within the macaque distinguishes between two groups of nuclei within the amygdala: the basolateral and corticomedial nuclear complexes. The NMDS analysis also identifies the basolateral nuclear group as being closely related to a circuit of brain regions involving the frontal cortex and anterior temporal cortex. These other brain regions are already implicated in social cognition from neuropsychological studies and from single cell recordings (see next sections). Hence the analysis of anatomical connections implicates the basolateral nuclear group as being related to the brain circuitry supporting social cognition. Comparative anatomy across different primate species demonstrates that the basolateral nuclear group increases in volume as species adopt larger group sizes. By contrast the centromedial group decreases in volume with increasing social complexity.

The basolateral nuclear complex within the primate amygdala is in an important anatomical position for processing socially relevant information about the behaviour of group members. Such information processing is a probable precursor to 'mind-reading' (Whiten 1996). The next section will discuss the processing of socially relevant information in the STS, which is one of the main cortical areas providing input to the basolateral region of the amygdala.

## B. NEUROPHYSIOLOGY OF MONKEY SOCIAL COGNITION

In the macaque monkey, one brain region has been implicated as a focus for the perceptual processing of the visual appearance of the face and body. Within the temporal lobe, the cortex in the anterior section of the superior temporal sulcus (STS) contains a variety of anatomical sub-regions and a number of distinct cell populations which may contribute to the visual recognition and understanding of actions (Perrett and Emery 1994). In one region (the anterior superior temporal polysensory area, STPa, Felleman and Van Essen 1991) within the upper bank of the STS, there are several types of neurones relevant to understanding actions. One type of cell encodes the visual appearance of the face and body while they are static or in motion (Gross *et al.* 1972; Perrett *et al.* 1984, 1985a, 1990a, 1992; Wachsmuth *et al.* 1994). A second type codes particular face and body movements but is unresponsive to static images or still frames of the face and body (Bruce *et al.* 1981; Oram and Perrett 1994a,b, 1996; Oram, *et al.* 1998; Perrett *et al.* 1985b, 1990b,c). A third type of cell in the temporal lobe codes face and body movement as goal directed action. This type of cell responds only to particular body movements made in relation to particular objects or positions in space (e.g. a hand reaching for an object, but not hand movements alone). This type of cell occurs throughout the STS but is most frequently found in the lower bank of the sulcus, particularly in area TEa (Oram *et al.* 1998; Perrett *et al.* 1989, 1990c,d; Seltzer and Pandya 1978). A further type of cell codes any movement which is not a predictable consequence of the monkey's own actions (Hietanen and Perrett 1993a,b, 1996a,b; Perrett *et al.* 1990d). Each individual cell type will be discussed in separate sub-sections.

### i. Body posture

Cells selectively responsive to visual information about the form of static or moving animal bodies show generalisation, in that they respond to the sight of monkeys, humans, and other mammals. They could therefore contribute to understanding the posture and actions of conspecifics and other animals. Sub-populations of these cells are selectively responsive to the sight of particular parts of the body, including the eyes, mouth, whole head, fingers, hand, arms, legs, torso, and whole body. The majority of the cells are sensitive to the perspective view and orientation of body components (Ashbridge *et al.* 1998; Wachsmuth *et al.* 1994). (Note here that view and orientation are distinguished because changes in perspective view lead to changes in the visibility of surface details and component of an object, whereas changes in orientation do not.) For example, particular cells will respond only to the palm side of the hand pointing upwards, other cells will respond only to the open hand with fingers splayed, other cells will respond only to the leg bent at the knee and pointing to left of the observing subject, and yet other cells will respond only to the eyes or face pointing up (Carey *et al.* 1997; Gross *et al.* 1972; Perrett *et al.* 1985a, 1990a, 1992; Tanaka *et al.* 1991; Tanaka 1993).

Sensitivity to the orientation and perspective view of the head and body enables the cells to code specific postures that are components of novel actions (for example, those associated with newly acquired food processing skills; Byrne 1995; Byrne and Byrne 1991, 1993) or some particular social signals (e.g. threat postures in which the head is lowered, jaw lowered, and eyebrows raised; Hinde and Rowell 1961). The cells also specify how the posture of another individual is oriented with respect to the observer. Without such specification, interactions between individuals would be impossible. When one individual presents an arm for grooming, a social partner must perceive the position, orientation, and distance of the arm in order to begin grooming it.

It is not usual to think of the visual processing of static form as underlying comprehension of actions. This, however, overlooks the ability of individuals to understand momentary postures during an action sequence and to infer how an action was performed. The performance of dextrous manual tasks (e.g. tying a knot or performing a magic trick with sleight of hand) can easily be specified as a series of static pictures, each demonstrating particular sub-goals or stages in the action sequence.

### ii. Direction of attention

The initial coding of body components in a view- and orientation-specific manner does not prevent subsequent encoding that generalises for the same posture across different views. Generalisation across view can be achieved by combining the outputs of a number of view-specific cells, each sensitive to the same posture seen from a specific vantage-point (Perrett *et al.* 1992).

Figure 12.3 illustrates the responses of a cell type selective for one component head view and orientation. The cell in Fig. 12.3 responds to the right profile view facing down but is unresponsive to the face view head down (not shown) or the left profile

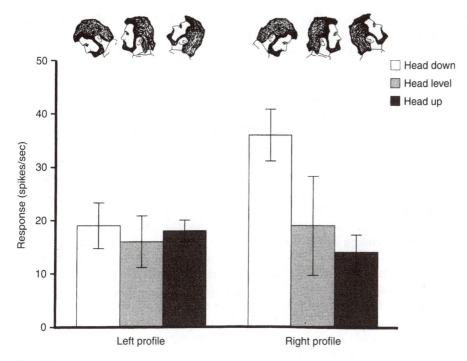

**Fig. 12.3.**

The responses of one cell selective for head view and orientation. The mean ($\pm$ 1 S.E., n = 5) response to left and right profile head in different orientations is illustrated together with a representation of the stimuli. Response to the right profile view facing down was greater than response to profile head views and orientations. The cell was also unresponsive to the face view head down (not shown).

head down. The responses of this cell illustrate the specifity of information processed and may be signalling 'attention down and right', whereas other cells have more general responses, such as signalling 'attention down'.

Note that to code postures that might signify attention down or attention up, the visual system needs to discriminate between different orientations of the same head view (e.g. left profile head down vs. left profile head level). Hence it is not surprising that coding of body parts takes place (at least initially) in an orientation- and view-specific manner. Invariance across viewing circumstance, which can include partial occlusion or change in perspective, can be achieved by combining the outputs of cells sensitive to particular body components from different views and orientations. The extensive and sophisticated coding of attention direction is indicative of its importance for primate social interaction. Observing threatening gestures and recognising them as threats is insufficient; knowing whether the gesture is being made in your direction is a crucial determinant of an appropriate response (Perrett and Mistlin 1990; Perrett *et al.* 1989; Walsh and Perrett 1994).

The outputs of cells coding components of the face and body from one view and orientation appear to be combined hierarchically so that a collection of components can specify a particular meaningful posture or action (Perrett *et al.* 1994, 1995). Evidence for hierarchical combination of signals is limited but is apparent in increased response latency of cells higher up given putative hierarchies (Perrett *et al.* 1992). Cells higher up in one hierarchy combine outputs from three cell types, one sensitive only to eye direction, a second sensitive to head direction, and a third coding body direction. Thus higher level cells can respond to the eyes pointing left, or the face pointing left, or the body pointing left (Perrett *et al.* 1985*a*, 1992; Wachsmuth *et al.* 1994). Such a convergence of visual information can signal a conceptually unified action, such as 'animal attending left'. Note that the response to multiple components allows coding of actions when particular body regions are obscured from sight. The cells may code the face direction if the eyes are obscured by shadow, too distant to be discerned clearly, or occluded from sight, and may code the body direction if the head is occluded from sight.

The responses to individual body components for the cells coding meaningful actions (such as 'attending left') usually have a hierarchy of importance, with the eyes being more important than the head, and the head in turn being more important than the body. For example, if the eyes are visible and aimed not left but at the viewer, this can prevent cells from responding to the rest of the face pointing left. Similarly, if the head is pointing at the viewer, this can prevent response to the left profile view of the body (Perrett *et al.* 1992, 1995). This hierarchy of importance coupled with the independent sensitivity to the eyes, face, and body cues means that the cells can signal direction of attention under differing viewing conditions (where the eyes or face are occluded from sight). Moreover the cells appear to respond on the basis of the best evidence available since the eyes may be more informative than the face and the face more informative than the body (see below).

The direction of eye gaze, head and body posture, and the direction of an individual's movements in relation to objects may provide a 'window into the mind' of others. These cues can help assess where or what another individual is attending to and why they are performing particular actions. Human infants, in the first year of life, follow the direction of gaze of their mother. This 'joint attention' appears crucial to social development in humans and is impaired in autism (Baron-Cohen 1994; Leekam *et al.* 1997). The capacity to follow gaze is manifest in the chimpanzee (Povinelli and Preuss 1995) but the evolutionary origins of gaze-following and shared attention and their underlying neural mechanisms are not understood. Following gaze is a necessary, but not sufficient condition for shared attention. For the latter, there may need to be an additional requirement where two individuals share the knowledge that each is following the gaze of the other (Emery *et al.* 1997; Perrett and Emery 1994).

Despite the neurophysiological findings of cellular sensitivity to attention direction in macaque monkeys, behavioural evidence for gaze-following in Old World monkeys has so far been lacking. Indeed, Anderson *et al.* (1996) report that rhesus macaques cannot be trained to use human gaze to locate hidden food. To investigate this discrepancy, we measured eye movements of macaque monkey subjects during presentation of films displaying a conspecific directing attention towards a 'target' object and ignoring an identical 'distracter' object. Results show that a subject shown the films makes more frequent inspections of the target than the distracter. Thus rhesus macaques do spontaneously utilise the direction of attention of conspecifics to orient their own attention (Emery *et al.* 1997). When an observing monkey sees a stimulus monkey attending in one direction, the observer modifies its own gaze direction to inspect the region of space that the stimulus monkey is attending to, even if there is no target object present in that space (Emery *et al.* 1997). Thus it appears that monkeys search out what others are attending to.

More recently Tomasello *et al.* (1998) have also found that five different primate species (rhesus, stumptail, pigtail macaques, sooty mangebeys, and chimpanzees) follow the attention cues of conspecifics. Further studies with static slides of stimulus monkeys show that the direction of head and gaze is more salient in capturing attention than body orientation (Lorincz *et al.* 1998), as would be predicted from the results of neuronal responses described earlier.

### iii. Linking the perception of expressions to emotions

Particular populations of cells in the temporal cortex are selective for certain facial expressions (Hasselmo *et al.* 1989; Perrett and Mistlin 1990; Perrett *et al.* 1984). Some cells code angry or threatening expressions, others code frightened grimaces. For macaque monkeys, threats include a rounded open mouth without the teeth displayed, head lowered, vertical contraction of the skin of the forehead (equivalent to raising of eyebrows for humans), and direct eye contact (Hauser 1996; Hinde and Rowell 1961). Individual cells code expressions through the conjoint sensitivity to these multiple facial cues. Indeed, without combined sensitivity to several facial cues, expressions would be ambiguous. For example, an open mouth could signify a threat or it could signify that an individual is yawning or eating, for example. This cellular coding can provide the basis for recognising expressions and comprehending the emotions of others.

One of the functions of the amygdala appears to lie in linking sensory stimuli to particular emotional responses such as fear (Aggleton 1993). Indeed, the amygdala has been implicated in the formation of conditioned fear responses to auditory stimuli (Le Doux 1995). The neuroanatomy and latency of cell responses are both consistent with a flow of visual information about faces from the temporal cortex to the amygdala. The interplay between the amygdala and temporal cortex in the analysis of emotional visual stimuli remains speculative. Within the amygdala the particular visual configurations of faces arriving from the temporal cortex may come to be associated with negative emotional states (particularly fear). This association may feed back to the cortex to consolidate the visual sensitivity of the particular cell groups in the temporal cortex sending information to the amygdala. This feedback may allow long term visual representations of important stimuli to get laid down within the cortex. The limbic system remains responsible for the formation of new emotional associations and the link between what is seen and the feeling or knowledge of fear, but the cortex comes to hold the 'look-up table' of important visual patterns (e.g. expressions).

Visual analysis of the emotions of others allows vicarious learning: an animal can acquire a fearful response to potentially dangerous objects through associating the sight of objects with the expression of fear in others (Mineka *et al.* 1984; Wiener and Levine 1992). Through first-order classical conditioning, an infant might come to associate the sight of the fearful expression of a parent with its own startle response (unconditioned response) to a loud noise (unconditioned stimulus). This could easily happen if a loud noise startles both the infant and its parent. After such conditioning, if the infant subsequently witnesses an adult showing fear responses to snakes, for example, then the infant may acquire the fear response to snakes through second-order conditioning without the negative experience of being bitten. The infant simply has to witness the parent's fearful face in conjunction with the sight of a snake.

Note here that a second essential part of the 'tool kit' for such vicarious learning (or social referencing) is proper comprehension of the attention direction of others. The infant needs to attend to the object that is causing the parent to exhibit fear. In any environment there will be many objects in the field of view, but following the parent's attention direction (using head or gaze direction, or more subtle body posture cues) will allow the infant to experience the object causing the parent's fear.

As reviewed above, the temporal cortex provides two sources of information that are vital in this context. First, many of the cells are sensitive to the direction of attention as specified by the gaze direction, head view and orientation, and body posture. Second, particular cells are sensitive to the facial posture, mouth configuration, and expression (Perrett and Mistlin 1990). The temporal cortex can thus provide a description of facial expressions that an individual can learn to associate with emotional responses. The emotional associations need not be restricted to facial expressions. The temporal cortex can provide a visual specification of a wealth of gestures that can be associated with the personal experience of positive or negative emotions.

The visual analysis of expressions in the temporal lobe provides a direct window into the feelings of others. Links between the visual appearance of expression and systems engaged in particular patterns of emotional response are an inevitable consequence of learning. Even if the emotions of others are not realised in an empathic sense, there is no doubt that the emotional reactions of others have profound effects on our own learning and attitudes.

### iv. Body movements

A further type of cell in the STS is selectively responsive to particular types of body movement and remains inactive to static images of the body. The function of such cells may lie in their capacity to provide a description of how bodies are moving. From this information it is possible, with subsequent processing, to work out what individuals are doing in terms of meaningful 'goal-directed' actions (see below). The cells also provide a basis for guiding social interactions. Social contact involves numerous actions and reactions: one individual extends an arm, a second individual may flinch or may accept this as a grooming gesture. To react, each individual must first recognise the nature of the movements of the other.

Cells that respond to body movement combine information about the form of body components with information about the type of movement they are executing (Oram and Perrett 1994a,b, 1996; Oram et al. 1998). Different sub-populations of cells code the sight of movements of the eyes, mouth, whole head, torso, legs, arms, and fingers or whole hands (Mistlin and Perrett 1990; Oram et al. 1998; Perrett et al. 1985b, 1990c, 1994, 1995). The movements of body components are specified relative to the viewer, such that some cells respond to the head rotation from right profile to facing the viewer and others to the opposite direction. Other populations code rotations of the head in the vertical plane (i.e. head turning up or bowing down).

The components of movements appear to be combined to produce descriptions of coherent whole body actions such as walking (Perrett et al. 1985b, 1989, 1990b), crouching (Perrett et al. 1984), climbing (Brothers and Ring 1993), and turning (Oram and Perrett 1994a; Oram et al. 1998). The combination of information about the movement of different body parts appears to proceed in an exactly analogous way to that described for cells responsive to static postures. That is, cells responsive to whole body movements code specific directions of motion (e.g. left profile body view walking left) and may respond to several body components moving left (e.g. head alone, torso and arms alone, or legs alone). This convergence again allows the specification of simple whole body actions even when parts of the body are obscured from sight.

### v. Goal-directed actions

The coding described above can be understood with sole reference to the movements of a body within the visual image. Actions, however, are more than simple movements; they can involve goal-directed behaviour. To understand actions it is necessary to realise the purpose or the cause of the movement. Inanimate objects may move (when acted upon by animate objects), but by definition only animate objects complete actions with goals and purpose.

There is one way that visual information can be used, not only to classify the details of the movement, but also to specify the goal-directed nature of the movement. This can be achieved by relating body movements to other aspects of the visual environment. Movement coding becomes action coding when visual events are specified in such a way as to clarify both the nature of the movements (of an agent) performing the motion and how these movements relate to their goal. The goal may be the viewer, an object, another individual, or a place in the environment. This type of coding provides a basis for understanding and imitating the specific actions of others, for understanding the purpose of their behaviour, or for communicative signals.

This type of coding is apparent in several groups of cells within the STS. Some cells code whole body movements such as walking but only when they are directed to reach a particular position in the environment (Perrett et al. 1990b,c). The most extensively studied cells that can be described as coding actions are those in the ventral bank of the STS (area TEa) that are selectively responsive to hand actions (Perrett et al. 1989,

1990*c,d*). Different sub-populations of these cells show selectivity for specific hand–object interactions, such as reaching for, retrieving, manipulating, picking, tearing, and holding (Perrett *et al.* 1989).

The responses of such cells are elicited when both the appropriate hand movements and the appropriate movements of the object acted upon are visible. Hand movements alone miming an action without an object fail to elicit a response. Studies of cells sensitive to the act of object manipulation reveal that the relation between hand and object movements can be specified even more exactly. Cells responsive to object manipulation would not respond to the sight of the appropriate hand movements combined with object movements when the hand and object were spatially separated by a few centimetres (Perrett *et al.* 1989). In this way the cells were sensitive to the causal relation between the agent performing the action and the object acted upon; the cells responded to causally related actions and not to hand–object movements that were not causally related.

The cells generalised across several different instances of the same action, including the sight of the action from different perspectives, at different distances or speeds, or even performed on different objects. The majority of cells responded well to the sight of the optimal hand actions performed by a human or another monkey, although the exact visual characteristics of what constitutes a hand remain to be specified. One interesting finding is that these cells respond to the sight of the monkey's own hands performing the action (Perrett *et al.* 1989). Here the cells would respond to videotapes of actions performed by the monkey and to the direct sight of the monkey's hands performing the action in real time. This equivalence between the sight of the monkey's own hand performing an action and the sight of other hands performing the same action may well be essential for imitation or shaping one's own actions to match those witnessed (see 'monkey see—monkey do' below).

### vi. Linking the sight of actions to the production of actions—'monkey see—monkey do'

Neural activity in a variety of areas in the frontal lobe is associated with the execution of motor acts. Recently it has become apparent that visual information about motor acts is also encoded in particular premotor areas. Neuronal responses to the sight of hand actions identical to those described in the STS have been found in area F5 of premotor cortex (di Pellegrino *et al.* 1992; see also Tanila *et al.* 1992). Some F5 cells respond to the sight of particular hand actions (e.g. grasping, picking, or reaching) made by the experimenter. The same cells respond to the equivalent actions performed by the monkey in the light or dark. Such prefrontal cells thus code both the motor components of hand actions (independent of vision) and the visual appearance of the hand actions. The critical difference between the coding of actions in the frontal and temporal areas is that the frontal cortex appears to code the 'general concept' of an action. The frontal cells are activated during the execution of an action (e.g. grasping). The frontal cells are also activated by the sight of an action performed by another (i.e. the experimenter grasping an object). The cells respond to the sight of an object that can form the goal of an action (i.e. an object that is to be grasped). Moreover, following the presentation of an object which the monkey must act upon after a short delay, the cells will remain responsive during the delay even in the dark; presumably while the monkey holds in mind the upcoming action that must be performed at the end of the delay. By contrast, the cells in the temporal cortex code only the visual form of the action when performed by the monkey or another. It is quite likely that the visual analysis of actions is performed initially in the temporal cortex and that the visual selectivity for actions in premotor areas depends on input from the action coding cells in temporal cortex (although the precise anatomical pathways through which this could occur are not known).

The cells in the prefrontal cortex respond selectively both to the performance of a specific action by the monkey and to the sight of the same specific action performed by another. With this dual capacity one neural system can enable the motor performance of an action to be matched to an action witnessed visually. Such a matching capacity can support the visual imitation of simple familiar actions.

The 'monkey see—monkey do' prefrontal cells share some of the features of visual selectivity of STS units described above. Neurones in both areas show sensitivity to the interaction between the agent performing the action (the hand) and the object or goal of the action. Neither group of cells responds to the sight of the objects alone, which might afford particular actions (tearing, picking, etc.), nor do the cells respond to the sight of appropriate hand movements pantomiming the action in the absence of the objects. Di Pellegrino *et al.* (1992) argue that the existence of such cells in premotor cortex provides some evidence for the theory that substrates of perception and action are, at least to some extent, overlapping.

Functional imaging techniques have begun to be used to examine the neural substrates of movement production, perception, and imagery. Decety *et al.* (1994) examined brain activity during motor perception and imagery in the same human subjects. Activation patterns associated with watching a computer graphic 'hand' move to pick up objects were compared with the activation patterns associated with imagining hand movements needed to pick up static objects. Decety *et al.* report that the motor imagery task produces greater activation of brain regions associated with movement production than regions associated with visual analysis of motion (see also Parsons *et al.* 1995). Recent studies indicate that witnessing real hand movements activates the human brain in pre-motor cortex and in left superior temporal sulcus: presumably in areas that are homologous to those described in the brain of the macaque monkey (Grafton *et al.* 1996; Rizzolatti *et al.* 1996). Thus the populations of visual neurones in the temporal cortex of the macaque monkey reviewed here appear to have homologues in the human brain. Functional imaging studies appear to be showing that the sight of actions produces activity changes at the same prefrontal areas that are involved in control of the execution of corresponding actions. Recent studies of humans instructed to watch action sequences with a view to reproducing them indicate that premotor areas are activated by the sight of familiar actions but not novel, meaningless actions which must also be remembered and imitated (Decety *et al.* 1997).

The premotor cortex has been implicated in tasks requiring visual memory but is rarely connected to any perceptual function *per se*. The experimental investigation of Fadiga *et al.* (1995) suggests, however, that perception and action share some neural substrates. They stimulated the motor cortex of subjects while they watched actions, such as grasping and drawing, and in comparable control conditions (i.e. looking at the objects that were grasped). The evoked potentials recorded in the hand muscles that resulted following magnetic stimulation were larger in the two conditions where the subjects observed the experimenter making movements. The authors concluded that there is a system which 'matches' observations of actions and their execution (Fadiga *et al.* 1995).

There are several reasons why the neural substrates for action production and action perception could be largely shared. For example, the capacity to copy elaborate manual skills necessary for food processing would seem to confer an advantage by obviating the need for learning by trial and error in situations that may be painful (gorilla processing stinging nettles leaves, Byrne and Byrne 1991, 1993) or dangerous (e.g. chimpanzees catching and eating scorpions). While it is clear that great apes and even parrots do show evidence for the capacity to imitate actions demonstrated visually by humans (Custance *et al.* 1995), most reviews conclude that there is little or no good behavioural evidence from observational studies or laboratory experiments that monkeys imitate or comprehend the goals of others (Byrne 1995; Galef 1988; Heyes 1998; Visalberghi and Fragaszy 1990; Whiten and Ham 1992; though see Bugnyar and Huber 1997). Many instances of so-called 'imitative' behaviour made by non-human animals can be dismissed as simple instances of 'response facilitation' or 'stimulus enhancement' with trial and error learning (Heyes 1998).

Nevertheless, the physiological recordings from frontal and temporal neocortex provide perhaps the most convincing evidence that there are brain processes in monkeys that can provide a detailed understanding of the actions of conspecifics, and that the sight of these actions can be matched to the motor commands for the individual to reproduce the actions that it sees (Perrett and Emery 1994). The same apparatus may well support imitation of a series of novel actions to produce a specific goal.

### vii. Consequences of self-produced actions

The above descriptions review cells which are selective for body postures and body movements. A different type of cell in area STPa codes movement more generally and responds to the type of movement independent of form. These cells may respond to movement left whether the item moving is a body or an object, and will respond to objects that are small or large, dark or light (Bruce *et al.* 1981; Oram and Perrett 1994). Superficially this last group of cells appears the least likely to contribute to an understanding of others' actions, but this conclusion overlooks one important property of the cells; their ability to respond selectively to unexpected movements. Unexpected motions arise almost exclusively from other animals. The cells remain silent when the monkey itself creates movement in the world as a direct consequence of its own actions. For example, the cells respond to the sight of an object moved by an experimenter but do not respond when the same object is moved by the monkey itself (Hietanen and Perrett 1993*b*, 1996*a*). This property appears quite common within the

STS cell populations and has also been found in the processing of somatosensory information (Mistlin and Perrett 1990).

The critical variable for these cells seems to be the distinction between the 'self-generated' and 'generated by others' dimension of the stimuli rather than the arousal such stimuli generated by others might produce. This is partly evident in the lack of habituation to visual and tactile events under the control of the experimenter (Hietanen and Perrett 1993*b*; Mistlin and Perrett 1990). The cells fire over and over again to actions repeated by the experimenter. Repeated actions of others even when executed in a rhythmic (predictable) manner do not cause habituation. It is interesting in this context that several authors have noted the importance of identifying movements that are self-propelled for building up an understanding of intentionality in children (for review see Baron-Cohen 1994).

The properties of such cells may contribute to monitoring the consequences of the monkey's own actions (Hietanen and Perrett 1993*a,b*, 1996*a,b*; Mistlin and Perrett 1990). The cells are sensitive to experience and lock on to new consequences of actions. In one experiment a monkey subject was trained to move a grating by rotating a striped drum (using a video image of the drum projected onto a screen with a fixation spot located at the centre). This mechanical arrangement allowed the experimenter and the monkey to produce equivalent grating movements. When the subject rotated the drum many of the STPa movement sensitive cells remained silent. However, when the experimenter rotated the same drum at comparable speeds, the cells responded. In this situation the link between the monkey's actions and the changes in the world were correlated. After a period of training the nervous system registered the correlation in such a way that the world changes no longer activated the STPa neurones.

Realisation of the external/self-generated nature of changes in the world may be important more generally for the psychological health of the individual. Frith (1992) has argued that schizophrenic individuals suffer hallucinations, in part because they fail to attribute the production of stimuli to themselves. Thus a schizophrenic may hear voices because they wrongly attribute self-produced subvocal speech to others. More generally, schizophrenic patients may be impaired in understanding the behaviour of others, particularly in terms of how the behaviour of others relates to the patient's own behaviour (see Penn *et al.* 1997).

It is interesting to speculate on the development of the STS system that discriminates unpredictable sensory events from events consistent with the expectations of one's own actions. In social interactions, specific acts of one individual have a high probability of triggering retaliatory or reciprocal acts in a second individual. Motor plans for a threat lunge are likely to produce a retreating motion of the threatened individual. Predicting where the other will be after a threat will be essential for pressing home an attack or completing an intended defence. Predicting the behaviour of others is equally important for affiliative interactions. The didactic arrangement of behaviour can build in complexity provided social partners know what to expect from each other. Sensing the relationship between what one does and the consequent changes in the world is one thing, but realising how one's own actions affect the behaviour of others opens up a whole spectrum of social understanding. Others can be seen not only as autonomous entities but also as reactive social partners. Such perceptions will rely on the visual apparatus for recognising postures, gestures, and actions as well as the apparatus for making predictions as to what others are likely to do (and therefore what we expect to see them do) as a consequence of our own behaviour. The rudiments of this last ability can be seen in the sensitivity of STS cells to expectations about simple visual changes that are self-produced.

## C. NEUROPSYCHOLOGICAL MODELS OF AUTISM

From the results described in the previous two sections, we would predict that lesions of the amygdala and/or STS would result in difficulties in processing aspects of another individual's behaviour or representing the mental state of others in relation to intentions towards objects and goals. The early studies of Kluver and Bucy (1939) revealed that large lesions of the anterior temporal lobe (including the amygdala, hippocampal formation, and temporal cortex) produced a syndrome of abnormal behaviour which included a tendency to overreact to all objects, hypoemotionality and loss of fear, hypersexuality, hyperorality, and an inability to recognise objects. The so-called 'Kluver–Bucy syndrome' has been fractionated into distinct components; the amygdala was found to be responsible for the emotional, oral, and sexual deficits (Horel *et al.* 1975; Weiskrantz 1956) and the temporal cortex for the visual deficits (Akert *et al.* 1961; Horel *et al.* 1975). Aggleton and Mishkin (1990) showed that combined lesions of the STS and inferior temporal cortex produced the visual and emotional deficits of the Kluver–Bucy syndrome.

A relationship between the amygdala and social cognition was further indicated through the studies of Kling and colleagues (Kling and Brothers 1992; Kling and Steklis 1976). The amygdala-lesioned monkeys were socially isolated, failing to initiate social interactions or to react appropriately to social gestures or signals from other group members. These deficits in social behaviour were very similar to those seen in autistic individuals.

It would therefore seem reasonable to suggest that lesions of the amygdala in infancy would also produce some of the social deficits seen in childhood autism. Thompson and Towfighi (1976), Thompson *et al.* (1977) found that amygdala lesions in infant rhesus monkeys produced socio–emotional deficits that lasted into adulthood. Bachevalier (1991, 1994) lesioned either the medial temporal lobe (including amygdala, periamygdaloid cortex, hippocampus, and entorhinal and perirhinal cortices) or the hippocampal formation and amygdala separately. The lesioned infants were raised and paired with an age-matched control animal. At two months, the infants with medial temporal lobe lesions were more passive (i.e. displayed increased inactivity and decreased object manipulation) and displayed increased temper tantrums and initiated less social contact than controls. At six months, they interacted very little with the control animal, actively withdrawing from all approaches made by the normal animals. The infants with medial temporal lobe lesions also displayed expressionless faces and body movements and showed increased self-directed behaviour and motor stereotypy. When these animals were tested later in adulthood, the same behaviours were displayed (Bachevalier 1994). Malkova *et al.* (1997) found that the socio–emotional deficits displayed by the adult monkeys who received medial temporal lobe lesions as infants were more pronounced than the deficits displayed by adult monkeys who sustained medial temporal lobe lesions as adults.

When the amygdala alone was lesioned, a similar pattern of social abnormalities was seen, but to a lesser extent (Bachevalier 1994). Social deficits following selective lesions to the hippocampal formation were less marked and less durable with no deficits apparent at six months (Beauregard *et al.* 1995).

These results suggest that in macaques early lesions to the amygdala and, to a lesser extent, the hippocampus result in social behaviour deficits similar to those seen in young autistic children. Such a conclusion is in line with the findings of recent fMRI studies (Baron-Cohen *et al.* 1999, discussed earlier), which suggest that the difficulties that autistic individuals have in reading mental states from the faces of others is in part due to abnormal amygdala function. These neuropsychological studies of macaques begin to provide a model for studying autism. Further research may clarify the role of particular nuclear groups within the amygdala in the production of social deficits and the effect of amygdala lesions on mother–infant interaction (the first true social bond) or what knock-on effect changes to mother–infant interaction have on subsequent social behaviour.

## SUMMARY

This review has focused on three areas of neuroscience research in non-human primates. This research collectively identifies neural mechanisms which, when functioning normally, could contribute to 'mind-reading' in humans and which, when pathological, could contribute to autism. The first section provided statistical analyses of neuroanatomical data which were used to demonstrate a likely role of the amygdala (in particular the lateral basal and basolateral nuclear regions within the amygdala) in social cognition.

The second section reviewed neurophysiological studies of cells in temporal cortical regions, which provide the visual specification of face and body signals to the amygdala through the basolateral nuclear complex. Such signals from body movements and facial expressions are turning out to be potent stimuli for activating the amygdala in humans (Bonda *et al.* 1996; Morris *et al.* 1996). Collectively, the temporal cortex cells reviewed, can provide a window into the minds of others. They can, in principal, support an understanding of what other individuals are attending to, what they feel emotionally, what aspects of the environment cause these feelings, how others are interacting, and the goals of these interactions. Of course an observer may not explicitly realise the feelings and plans of others; nonetheless the visual specification supplied by the temporal cortex allows the observer to capitalise on the minds and behaviour of others and to react in the most appropriate way. Provided the visual system can specify what others are doing, one need not understand intentions or be able to mind read (Baron-Cohen 1994) in order to come up with appropriate behavioural reactions.

The third section reviewed neuropsychological studies of infant macaques with medial temporal lobe or selective amygdala lesions. These studies have begun to show how damage to discrete neural systems leads to behavioural abnormalities that are strikingly similar to those displayed by autistic children.

## Acknowledgements

We thank Malcolm Young, Jack Scannell, and Gully Burns for help with the NMDS transformations, and Rob Barton for advice about comparative analysis of brain component volume.

## REFERENCES

Adolphs. R., Tranel, D., Damasio, H. and Damasio, A. (1994). Impaired recognition of emotion in facial expressions following bilateral damage to the human amygdala. *Nature*, **372**, 669–72.

Adolphs, R., Tranel, D. and Damasio, A. R. (1998). The human amygdala in social judgement. *Nature*, **393**, 470–74.

Aggelton, J. P. (1993). The contribution of the amygdala to normal and abnormal emotional states. *Trends in Neurosciences*, **16**, 328–33.

Aggelton, J. P., Burton, M. J. and Passingham, R. E. (1980). Cortical and subcortical afferents to the amygdala of the rhesus monkey (Macaca mulatta). *Brain Research*, **190**, 347–68.

Aggleton, J. P. and Mishkin, M. (1990). Visual impairments in macaques following inferior temporal lesions are exacerbated selectively by additional damage to superior temporal sulcus. *Behavioural Brain Research*, **39**, 262–74.

Akert, K., Gruesen, R. A., Woolsey, C. N. and Meyer, D. R. (1961). KluverBucy syndrome in monkeys with neocortical ablations of the temporal lobe. *Brain*, **84**, 480–97.

Allman, J. (1982). Reconstructing the evolution of the brain in primates through the use of comparative neurophysiological and neuroanatomical data. In *Primate brain evolution: methods and concepts*, (ed. E. Armstrong and D. Falk), pp. 13–28. Plenum Press, New York.

Amaral, D. G., Price, J. L., Pitkanen, A. and Carmichael, S. T. (1992). Anatomical organisation of the primate amygdaloid complex. In *The amygdala: neurobiological aspects of emotion, memory and mental dysfunction*, (ed. J. P. Aggleton), pp. 1–66. WileyLiss, New York.

Anderson, J. R., Montant, M. and Schmitt, D. (1996). Rhesus monkeys fail to use gaze direction as an experimenter—given cue in an object—choice task. *Behavioral Processes*, **37**, 47–55.

Ashbridge, E., Perrett, D. I. and Oram, M. W. (1998). Effect of image rotation and size change on object recognition: responses of single units in the macaque monkey temporal cortex. (Submitted.)

Bachevalier, J. (1991). An animal model for childhood autism: memory loss and sociopathic disturbances following neonatal damage to the limbic system in monkeys. In *Advances in neuropsychiatry and psychopharmacology*, (Vol. 1: Schizophrenia Research), (ed. C. A. Tamminga and S. C. Schultz), pp. 129–140. Raven Press Ltd, New York.

Bachevalier, J. (1994). Medial temporal lobe structures and autism: a review of clinical and experimental findings. *Neuropsychologia*, **32**, 627–48.

Baker, C. I., Keysers, C. and Perrett, D. I. (1998). Temporal cortex and object permanence: cells responsive to visual stimuli occluded from sight. *European Journal of Neuroscience*, **10**, S10, 235.

Baron-Cohen, S. (1994). How to build a baby that reads minds: cognitive mechanisms in mindreading. *Current Psychology of Cognition*, **13**, 513–52.

Baron-Cohen, S., Ring, H., Moriarty. J., Schmitz, B., Costa, D. and Ell, P. (1994). Recognition of mental state terms: clinical findings in children with autism and a functional imaging study of normal adults. *British Journal of Psychiatry*, **165**, 640–9.

Baron-Cohen, S., Ring, H., Wheelwright, S., Bullmore, E., Brammer, M., Simmons, A., and Williams, S. (1999). Social intelligence in the normal and autistic brain: an fMRI study. *European Journal of Neuroscience*, **11**, 1891–8.

Barton, R. A. (1996). Neocortex size and behavioural ecology. *Proceedings of the Royal Society London Biological Sciences*, **263**, 173–7.

Barton, R. A. and Dunbar, R. I. M. (1997). Evolution of the social brain. In *Machiavellian intelligence 2: evaluations and extensions*, (ed. A. Whiten and R. W. Byrne). Cambridge University Press.

Beauregard, M., Malkova, L. and Bachevalier, J. (1995). Stereotypies and loss of social affiliation after early hippocampectomy in primates. *NeuroReport*, **6**, 2521–6.

Bonda, E., Petrides, M., Ostry, D. and Evans, A. (1996). Specific involvement of human parietal cortex in the perception of biological motion. *Journal of Neuroscience*, **16**, 3737–44.

Brody, E. B. and Rosvold, H. E. (1952). Influence of prefrontal lobotomy on social interaction in a monkey group. *Psychosomatic Medicine*, **14**, 406–15.

Brothers, L. (1989). A biological perspective on empathy. *American Journal of Psychiatry*, **146**, 10–9.

Brothers, L. (1990). The social brain: a project for integrating primate behavior and neurophysiology in a new domain. *Concepts in Neuroscience*, **1**, 27–51.

Brothers, L. and Ring, B. (1993). Mesial temporal neurons in the macaque monkey with responses selective for aspects of social stimuli. *Behavioural Brain Research*, **57**, 53–61.

Brothers, L., Ring, B. and Kling, A. (1990). Response of neurons in the macaque amygdala to complex social stimuli. *Behavioural Brain Research*, **41**, 199–213.

Bruce, C. J., Desimone, R. and Gross, C. G. (1981). Visual properties of neurons in a polysensory area in superior temporal sulcus of the macaque. *Journal of Neurophysiology*, **46**, 369–84.

Bugnyar, T. and Huber, L. (1997). Push or pull: an experimental study on imitation in marmosets. *Animal Behaviour*, **54**, 817–31.

Byrne, R. W. (1993). Do larger brains mean greater intelligence? *Behavioral and Brain Sciences*, **16**, 696–7.

Byrne, R. W. (1995). *The thinking ape: evolutionary origins of intelligence*. Oxford University Press.

Byrne, R. W. (1996). Relating brain size to intelligence in primates. In *Modelling the early human mind*, (ed. P. Mellars and K. R. Gibson), pp. 49–56. MacDonald Institute for Archaeological Research, Cambridge.

Byrne, R. W. and Byrne, J. M. E. (1991). Complex leaf-gathering skills of mountain gorillas (*Gorilla g. beringei*): variability and standardization. *Cortex*, **27**, 521–46.

Byrne, R. W. and Byrne, J. M. E. (1993). Hand preferences in the skilled gathering tasks of mountain gorillas (Gorilla g. beringei). *American Journal of Primatology*, **31**, 241–61.

Byrne, R. W. and Whiten, A. (1988). *Machiavellian intelligence: social expertise and the evolution of intellect in monkeys, apes and humans*. Oxford University Press.

Carey, D. P., Perrett, D. I. and Oram, M. W. (1997). Recognizing, understanding and reproducing action. In *Handbook of neuropsychology*, (series ed. F. Boller and J. Grafman), Vol. 11: Action and cognition, (ed. M. Jeannerod), pp. 111–29. Elsevier.

Cusick, C. G., Seltzer, B., Cola, M. and Griggs, E. (1995). The myloarchitectonics and corti-cocortical terminations within the superior temporal sulcus of the monkey: evidence for subdivisions of superior temporal polysensory cortex. *Journal of Comparative Neurology*, **260**, 513–35.

Custance, D. M., Whiten, A. and Bard, K. A. (1995). Can young chimpanzees (Pan troglodytes) imitate arbitrary actions? Hayes and Hayes (1952) revisited. *Behaviour*, **132**, 837–59

Damasio, A. R. (1994). *Descartes' error: emotion, reason and the human brain*. Picador, London.

Decety, J., Perani, D., Jeannerod, M., Bettinardi, V., Tadary, B., Woods, R., Mazziotta, J. C. and Fazio, F. (1994). Mapping motor representations with positron emission tomography. *Nature*, **371**, 600–2.

Decety, J., Grezes, J., Costes, N., Perani, D., Jeannerod, M., Procyk, E., Grassi, F. and Fazio, F. (1997). Brain activity during observation of actions: influence of action content and subject's strategy. *Brain*, **120**, 1763–77.

di Pellegrino, G., Fadiga, L., Fogassi, V., Gallese, V. and Rizzolatti, G. (1992). Understanding motor events: a neurophysiological study. *Experimental Brain Research*, **91**, 176–80.

Dunbar, R. I. M. (1992). Neocortex size as a constraint on group size in primates. *Journal of Human Evolution*, **20**, 469–93.

Dunbar, R. I. M. (1995). Neocortex size and group size in primates: a test of the hypothesis. *Journal of Human Evolution*, **28**, 287–96.

Dunbar, R. I. M. (1998). The social brain hypothesis. *Evolutionary Anthropology*.

Dunbar, R. I. M. and Joffe, T. H. Neocortex size and social group size in prosimians. *Primates*. (In press.)

Emery, N. J. (1997). Neuroethological studies of primate social perception. Unpublished doctoral thesis. University of St Andrews.

Emery, N. J. and Amaral, D. G. (1999). The role of the amygdala in primate social cognition. In *Cognitive Neuroscience of Emotion*, (eds. R. D. Lane, and L. Nadel). Oxford University Press, New York.

Emery, N. J., Lorincz, E. N., Perrett, D. I., Oram, M. W. and Baker, C. I. (1997). Gaze following and joint attention in rhesus monkeys (Macaca mulatta). *Journal of Comparative Psychology*, **111**, 1–8.

Emery, N. J., Machado, C. J., Capitanio, J. P., Mendoza, S. P., Mason, W. A. and Amaral, D. G. (1998). The role of the amygdala in dyadic social interaction and the stress response in monkeys. *Society for Neuroscience Abstracts*, **24**, 312.4

Fadiga, L., Fogassi, L., Pavesi, G. and Rizzolatti, G. (1995). Motor facilitation during action observation—a magnetic stimulation study. *Journal of Neurophysiology*, **73**, 2608–11.

Felleman, D. J. and Van Essen, D. C. (1991). Distributed hierarchical processing in the primate cerebral cortex. *Cerebral Cortex*, **1**, 1–47.

Fletcher, P. C., Happé, F., Frith, U., Baker, S. C., Dolan, R. J., Frackowiak. R. S. J. and Frith, C. D. (1995). Other minds in the brain—a functional imaging study of theory of mind in story comprehension. *Cognition*, **57**, 109–28.

Frith, C. D. (1992). *The cognitive neuropsychology of schizophrenia*. Lawrence Erlbaum Associ-ates, Hillsdale, NJ.

Frith, C. D. and Frith, U. (1999). In *Understanding other minds 2: perspectives from autism and cognitive neuroscience*, (ed. S. Baron-Cohen, H. Tager-Flusberg and D. Cohen). Oxford University Press.

Galef, B. G. (1988). Imitation in animals: field and laboratory analysis. In *Social learning: psychological and biological perspectives*, (ed. T. Zentall and B. G. Galef), pp. 1–28. Lawrence Erlbaum Associates, Hillsdale, New Jersey.

Goodale, M. A. and Milner, A. D. (1992). Two separate visual pathways for perception and action. *Trends in Neurosciences*, **15**, 20–5.

Grafton, S. T., Arbib, M. A., Fagdiga, L. and Rizzolatti, G. (1996). Localization of grasp representations in humans by positron emission tomography. 2: observation compared with imagination. *Experimental Brain Research*, **112**, 103–11.

Gross, C. G., Rocha-Miranda, C. E. and Bender, D. B. (1972). Visual properties of neurons in inferotemporal cortex of the monkey. *Journal of Neurophysiology*, **35**, 96–111.

Harries, M. H. and Perrett, D. I. (1991). Modular organization of face processing in temporal cortex: physiological evidence and possible anatomical correlates. *Journal of Cognitive Neuro-science*, **3**, 9–24.

Hasselmo, M. E., Rolls, E. T. and Baylis, G. C. (1989). The role of expression and identity in the face—selective responses of neurons in the temporal visual cortex of the monkey. *Behavioural Brain Research*, **32**, 203–18.

Hauser, M. D. (1996). *The evolution of communication*. MIT Press, Cambridge, MA.

Heyes, C. M. (1998). Theory of mind in nonhuman primates. *Behavioral and Brain Sciences*, **21**, 101–48.

Hietanen, J. K. and Perrett, D. I. (1993a). Motion sensitive cells in the macaque superior temporal polysensory area: I. lack of response to the sight of the monkey's own hand. *Experimental Brain Research*, **93**, 117–28.

Hietanen, J. K. and Perrett, D. I. (1993b). The role of expectation in visual and tactile processing within temporal cortex. In *Brain mechanisms for perception and memory: from neuron to behaviour*, (ed. T. Ono, L. Squire, M. Raichle, D. I. Perrett and M. Fukuda), pp. 83–103. Oxford University Press.

Hietanen, J. K. and Perrett, D. I. (1996a). A comparison of visual responses to object- and ego-motion in the macaque superior temporal polysensory area. *Experimental Brain Research*, **108**, 341–5.

Hietanen, J. K. and Perrett, D. I. (1996b). Motion sensitive cells in the macaque superior temporal polysensory area: Response discrimination between self- and externally generated pattern motion. *Behavioural Brain Research*, **76**, 155–167.

Hinde, R. A. and Rowell, T. E. (1961). Communication by postures and facial expressions in the rhesus monkey (Macaca mulatta). *Proceedings of the Zoological Society of London*, **138**, 1–21.

Horel, J. A., Keating, E. G. and Misantone, L. J. (1975). Partial KluverBucy syndrome produced by destroying temporal neocortex or amygdala. *Brain Research*, **94**, 347–59.

Humphrey, N. K. (1976). The social function of intellect. In *Growing points in ethology*, (ed. P. P. G. Bateson and R. A. Hinde), pp. 303–17. Cambridge University Press.

Humphrey, T. (1936). The telencephalon of the bat. I: the non-cortical nuclear masses and certain pertinent fibre connections. *Journal of Comparative Neurology*, **65**, 603–711.

Joffe, T. H. and Dunbar, R. I. M. (1997). Visual and socio–cognitive information processing in primate brain evolution. *Proceedings of the Royal Society of London: Biological Sciences*, **264**, 1303–7.

Johnson, J. B. (1923). Further contributions to the study of the evolution of the forebrain. *Journal of Comparative Neurology*, **35**, 337–481.

Jones, E. G. and Burton, H. (1976). Area 1 differences in the laminar distribution of thalamic afferents in cortical fields of the insular, parietal and temporal regions of primates. *Journal of Neurology*, **168**, 197–248.

Kaas, J. H. and Krubitzer, L. A. (1991). The organization of extrastriate visual areas. In *Neuroanatomy of the visual pathways and their development*, (ed. B. Dreher and S. R. Robinson), pp. 302–23. MacMillan Press Ltd, London.

Kling, A. and Green, P. C. (1967). Effects of neonatal amygdalectomy in the maternally reared and maternally deprived macaque. *Nature*, **213**, 742–3.

Kling, A. and Steklis, H. D. (1976). A neural substrate for affiliative behaviour in non-human primates. *Brain, Behavior and Evolution*, **13**, 216–38.

Kling, A. S. and Brothers, L. (1992). The amygdala and social behaviour. In *The amygdala: neurobiological aspects of emotion, memory and mental dysfunction*, (ed. J. P. Aggleton), pp. 353–78. Wiley–Liss, New York.

Kluver, H. and Bucy, P. C. (1939). Preliminary analysis of functions of the temporal lobes in monkeys. *Archives of Neurology and Psychiatry*, **42**, 979–1000.

Kudo, H., Lowen, S. and Dunbar, R. I. M. (1998). Neocortex size and social network size in primates. *Behaviour*. (In press.)

Le Doux, J. E. (1995). Emotion: clues from the brain. *Annual Review of Psychology*, **46**, 209–35.

Leekam, S., Baron-Cohen, S., Perrett, D. I., Milders, M. and Brown, S. (1997). Eye-direction detection: a dissociation between geometric and joint attention skills in autism. *British Journal of Developmental Psychology*, **15**, 77–95.

Leonard, C. M., Rolls, E. T., Wilson, F. A. W. and Baylis, G. C. (1985). Neurons in the amygdala of the monkey with responses selective for faces. *Behavioural Brain Research*, **15**, 159–76.

Lorincz, E. N., Baker, C. I., Perrett, D. I. and Miall, R. C. (1998). Which visual cues do monkeys use to follow attention: a study of social communication. *Society for Neuroscience Abstracts*, **24**, 658–10.

Malkova, L., Mishkin, M., Suomi, S. J. and Bachevalier, J. (1997). Socioemotional behavior in adult rhesus monkeys after early versus late lesions of the medial temporal lobe. *Annals of the New York Academy of Sciences*, **807**, 538–40.

Mineka, S., Davidson, M., Cook, M. and Keir, R. (1984). Observational conditioning of snake fear in rhesus monkeys. *Journal of Abnormal Psychology*, **93**, 355–72.

Mistlin, A. J. and Perrett, D. I. (1990). Visual and somatosensory processing in the macaque temporal cortex: the role of 'expectation'. *Experimental Brain Research*, **82**, 437–50.

Morris, J. S., Frith, C. D., Perrett, D. I., Rowland, D., Young, A. W., Calder, A. J. and Dolan, R. J. (1996). A neural response within human amygdala differentiates between fearful and happy facial expressions. *Nature*, **383**, 812–15.

Myers, R. E., Swett, C. and Miller, M. (1973). Loss of social group affinity following prefrontal lesions in free-ranging macaques. *Brain Research*, **64**, 257–69.

Oram, M. W. and Perrett, D. I. (1994a). Responses of anterior superior temporal polysensory (STPa) neurons to 'biological motion' stimuli. *Journal of Cognitive Neuroscience*, **6**, 99–116.

Oram, M. W. and Perrett, D. I. (1994b). Neural processing of biological motion in the macaque temporal cortex. In Computational vision based on neurobiology, (ed. T. B. Lawton). *SPIE Proceedings*, **2054**, 155–65.

Oram, M. W. and Perrett, D. I. (1996). Integration of form and motion in the anterior superior temporal polysensory area (STPa) of the macaque monkey. *Journal of Neurophysiology*, **76**, 109–29.

Oram, M. W., Perrett, D. I., Wachsmuth, E. and Emery, N. J. (1998). Coding of limb, body-articulation and whole body motion in the anterior superior temporal polysensory area (STPa) of the macaque monkey. (Submitted.)

Parsons, L. M., Fox, P. T., Downs, J. H., Glass, T., Hirsch, T. B., Martin, C. C., Jerabek, P. A. and Lancaster, J. L. (1995). Use of implicit motor imagery for visual shape discrimination as revealed by PET. *Nature*, **375**, 54–8.

Pawlowski, B., Dunbar, R. I. M. and Lowen, S.. Neocortex size, social skills and mating success in primates. *Behaviour*. (In press.)

Penn, D. L., Corrigan, P. W., Bentall, R. P., Racenstein, J. M. and Newman, L. (1997). Social cognition in schizophrenia. *Psychological Bulletin*, **121**, 114–32.

Perrett, D. I. (1996). View-dependent coding in the ventral stream and its consequences for recognition. In *Vision and movement mechanisms in the cerebral cortex*, (ed. R. Caminiti, K.-P. Hoffmann, F. Lacquaniti and J. Altman), pp. 142–51. HFSP, Strasbourg.

Perrett, D. I. and Emery, N. J. (1994). Understanding the intentions of others from visual signals: neurophysiological evidence. *Current Psychology of Cognition*, **13**, 683–94.

Perrett, D. I. and Mistlin, A. J. (1990). Perception of facial attributes. In *Comparative perception*, (ed. W. C. Stebbins and M. A. Berkley), (Vol. 2: complex signals), pp. 187–215. John Wiley, New York.

Perrett, D. I., Smith, P. A. J., Potter, D. D., Mistlin, A. J., Head, A. S., Milner, A. D. and Jeeves, M. A. (1984). Neurons responsive to faces in the temporal cortex: studies of functional organization, sensitivity to identity and relation to perception. *Human Neurobiology*, **3**, 197–208.

Perrett, D. I., Smith, P. A. J., Potter, D. D., Mistlin, A. J., Head, A. S., Milner, A. D. and Jeeves, M. A. (1985*a*). Visual cells in the temporal cortex sensitive to face view and gaze direction. *Proceedings of the Royal Society of London Biological Sciences*, **223**, 293–317.

Perrett, D. I., Smith, P. A. J., Mistlin, A. J., Chitty, A. J., Head, A. S., Potter, D. D., Broennimann, R., Milner, A. D. and Jeeves, M. A. (1985*b*). Visual analysis of body movements by neurons in the temporal cortex of the macaque monkey: a preliminary report. *Behavioural Brain Research*, **16**, 153–70.

Perrett, D. I., Harries, M. H., Bevan, R., Thomas, S., Benson, P. J., Mistlin, A. J., Chitty, A. J., Hietanen, J. K. and Ortega, J. E. (1989). Frameworks of analysis for the neural representation of animate objects and actions. *Journal Experimental Biology*, **146**, 87–114.

Perrett, D. I., Harries, M. H., Mistlin, A. J., Hietanen, J. K., Benson, P. J., Bevan, R., Thomas, S., Ortega, J., Oram, M. W. and Brierly, K. (1990*a*). Social signals analysed at the single cell level: someone's looking at me, something touched me, something moved. *International Journal of Comparative Psychology*, **4**, 25–50.

Perrett, D. I., Harries, M. H., Benson, P. J., Chitty, A. J. and Mistlin, A. J. (1990*b*). Retrieval of structure from rigid and biological motion; an analysis of the visual response of neurons in the macaque temporal cortex. In *AI and the eye*, (ed. T. Troscianko and A. Blake), pp. 181–201. J. Wiley, Chichester.

Perrett, D. I., Harries, M. H., Chitty, A. J. and Mistlin, A. J. (1990*c*). Three stages in the classification of body movements by visual neurons. In *Images and understanding*, (ed. H. B. Barlow, C. Blakemore and M. Weston-Smith), pp. 94–108. Cambridge University Press.

Perrett, D. I., Mistlin, A. J., Harries, M. H. and Chitty, A. J. (1990*d*). Understanding the visual appearance and consequences of hand actions. In *Vision and action: the control of grasping*, (ed. M. A. Goodale), pp. 163–80. Ablex Pub.

Perrett, D. I., Hietanen, J. K., Oram, M. W. and Benson, P. J. (1992). Organization and functions of cells responsive to faces in the temporal cortex. *Philosophical Transactions of the Royal Society of London*, **335**, 23–30.

Perrett, D. I., Oram, M. W. and Wachsmuth, E. (1994). Understanding minds and expression from facial signals: studies at the brain cell level. Proceedings of the 2nd IEEE International Workshop on Robot and Human Communication, Supplement, pp. 3–12.

Perrett, D. I., Oram, M. W., Wachsmuth, E. and Emery, N. J. (1995). Understanding the behaviour and 'minds' of others from their facial and body signals: studies of visual processing within the temporal cortex. In Emotion, memory and behaviour: studies on human and non-human primates, (ed. T. Nakajima and T. Ono). *Taniguchi Symposia on Brain Sciences*, **18**, 155–67. Japan Scientific Societies Press, Tokyo.

Petrides, M. and Iversen, S. D. (1978). The effect of selective anterior and posterior association cortex lesions in the monkey on performance of a visual–auditory compound discrimination test. *Neuropsychologia*, **16**, 527–37.

Petrides, M. and Iversen, S. D. (1979). Restricted posterior parietal lesions in the rhesus monkey and the performance on visuospatial tasks. *Brain Research*, **161**, 63–77.

Povinelli, D. J. and Preuss, T. M. (1995). Theory of mind. Evolutionary history of a cognitive specialization. *Trends in Neuroscience*, **18**, 418–24.

Purvis, A. and Rambaut, A. (1995). Comparative analysis by independent contrasts (CAIC): an Apple Macintosh application for analysing comparative data. *Computer Applications in Biosciences*, **11**, 247–51.

Rizzolatti, G. and Arbib, M. (1998). Language within our grasp. *Trends in Neurosciences*, **21**, 188–94.

Rizzolatti, G., Fadiga, L., Matelli, M., Bettinardi, V., Paulesu, G., Perani, D. and Fazio, F. (1996). Localization of grasp representations in humans by PET. 1: observation vs. execution. *Experimental Brain Research*, **111**, 246–53.

Rolls, E. T. (1984). Neurons in the cortex of the temporal lobe and in the amygdala of the monkey with responses selective for faces. *Human Neurobiology*, **3**, 209–22.

Rolls, E. T. (1992). Neurophysiological mechanisms underlying face processing within and beyond the temporal cortical visual areas. *Philosophical Transactions of the Royal Society of London: Biological Sciences*, **335**, 11–21.

Sawaguchi, T. (1990). Relative brain size, stratification and social structure in anthropoids. *Primates*, **31**, 257–72.

Sawaguchi, T. (1992). The size of the neocortex in relation to ecology and social structure in monkeys and apes. *Folia Primatologia*, **58**, 131–45.

Seltzer, B. and Pandya, D. N. (1978). Afferent cortical connections and architectonics of the superior temporal sulcus and surrounding cortex in the rhesus monkey. *Brain Research*, **149**, 1–24.

Seltzer, B. and Pandya, D. N. (1984). Further observations on parietotemporal connections in the rhesus monkey. *Experimental Brain Research*, **55**, 301–12.

Semendeferi, K., Damasio, H., Frank, R. and Van Hoesen, G. W. (1997). The evolution of the frontal lobes: a volumetric analysis based on three-dimensional reconstructions of magnetic resonance scans of human and ape brains. *Journal of Human Evolution*, **32**, 375–88.

Sparrevohn, R. and Howie, P. H. (1995). Theory of mind in children with autistic disorder: evidence of developmental progression and the role of verbal ability. *Journal of Child Psychology and Psychiatry*, **36**, 249–63.

Stephan, H., Frahm, H. and Baron, G. (1981). New and revised data on volumes of brain structures in insectivores and primates. *Folia Primatologia*, **35**, 1–29.

Stephan, H., Frahm, H. and Baron, G. (1987). Comparison of brain structure volumes in insectivora and primates VII: amygdaloid components. *Journal of Hirnforsch*, **5**, 571–84.

Tanaka, K. (1993). Neuronal mechanisms of object recognition. *Science*, **262**, 685–88.

Tanaka, K., Saito, H., Fukada, Y. and Moriya, M. (1991). Coding visual images of objects in the inferotemporal cortex of the macaque monkey. *Journal of Neurophysiology*, **66**, 170–89.

Tanila, H., Carlson, S., Linnnankoski, I., Lindroos, F. and Kahila, H. (1992). Functional properties of dorsolateral prefrontal cortical neurons in awake monkey. *Behavioural Brain Research*, **47**, 169–80.

Thompson, C. I. and Towfighi, J. T. (1976). Social behavior of juvenile rhesus monkeys after amygdalectomy. *Physiology and Behaviour*, **17**, 831–6.

Thompson, C. I., Bergland, R. M. and Towfighi, J. T. (1977). Social and nonsocial behaviours of adult rhesus monkeys after amygdalectomy in infancy or adulthood. *Journal of Comparative and Physiological Psychology*, **91**, 533–48.

Tomasello, M. and Call, J. (1997). *Primate cognition*. Oxford University Press, New York.

Tomasello, M., Kruger, A. C. and Ratner, H. H. (1993). Cultural learning. *Behavioral and Brain Sciences*, **16**, 495–511.

Tomasello, M., Call, J. and Hare, B. (1998). Five primate species follow the visual gaze of conspecifics. *Animal Behaviour*, **55**, 1063–9.

Ungerleider, L. and Mishkin, M. (1982). Two cortical visual systems. In *Aspects of visual behavior*, (ed. D. G. Ingle, M. A. Goodale and R. J. W. Mansfield), pp. 549–86. MIT Press, Cambridge, MA.

Visalberghi, E. and Fragaszy, D. (1990). Do monkeys ape? In *'Language' and intelligence in monkeys and apes*, (ed. S. T. Parker and K. R. Gibson), pp. 247–73. Cambridge University Press.

Walsh, V. and Perrett, D. I. (1994). Visual attention in the occipitotemporal processing stream of the macaque. *Cognitive Neuropsychology*, **11**, 243–63.

Wachsmuth, E., Oram, M. W. and Perrett, D. I. (1994). Recognition of objects and their component parts: responses of single units in the temporal cortex of the macaque. *Cerebral Cortex*, **5**, 509–22.

Wiener, S. G. and Levine, S. (1992). Behavioral and physiological responses of mother and infant squirrel monkeys to fearful stimuli. *Developmental Psychobiology*, **25**, 127–36.

Weiskrantz, L. (1956). Behavioral changes associated with ablations of the amygdaloid complex in monkeys. *Journal of Comparative and Physiological Psychology*, **49**, 381–91.

Whiten, A. (1996). When does smart behaviour-reading become mind-reading? In *Theories of theories of mind*, (ed. P. Carruthers and P. K. Smith), pp. 277–92. Cambridge University Press.

Whiten, A. and Byrne, R. W. (1997). *Machiavellian intelligence 2: evaluations and extensions*. Cambridge University Press.

Whiten, A. and Ham, R. (1992). On the nature and evolution of imitation in the animal kingdom: Reappraisal of a century of Research. In *Advances in the study of behaviour*, Vol. 21, (ed. P. J. B. Slater, J. S. Rosenblatt, C. Beer and M. Miliski), pp. 239–83. Academic Press, New York.

Young, M. P. (1992). Objective analysis of the topological organization of the primate cortical visual system. *Nature*, **358**, 152–5.

Young, M. P. (1993). The organization of neural systems in the primate cerebral cortex. *Proceedings of the Royal Society of London: Biological Sciences*, **252**, 13–8.

Young, M. P., Scannell, J. W., O'Neil, M. A., Hilgetag, C. C., Burns, G. and Blakemore, C. (1995). Non-metric multidimensional scaling in the analysis of neuroanatomical connection data and the organization of the primate cortical visual system. *Philosophical Transactions of the Royal Society of London: Biological Sciences*, **348**, 281–308.

# 13

# Cerebral lateralization and theory of mind

HIRAM BROWNELL, RICHARD GRIFFIN, ELLEN WINNER,
ORI FRIEDMAN, AND FRANCESCA HAPPÉ

## INTRODUCTION

Theory of mind (ToM), predicting and explaining behaviour in terms of mental states, represents a crucial human ability that is best understood from several perspectives. In this chapter, we focus on neuropsychological investigations of ToM capacities that may be lateralized to one cerebral hemisphere; however, we locate these claims for lateralized components of ToM in an overview that includes many themes and that draws on several literatures. Our goal is to integrate ToM capacity into a general framework that incorporates philosophical, neuropsychological, and cognitive principles. We start with a brief statement of how ToM fits within current views on evolutionary psychology and developmental psychology to highlight a few critical features of ToM. Next, we provide background on localization and, in particular, lateralization of function. This selective review draws on work with monkeys as well as with humans. We emphasize the importance of the right hemisphere in ToM and related domains, but also discuss the role of bilateral prefrontal regions in ToM computations. Finally, and most importantly, we outline a neuropsychological model for ToM that incorporates contributions of prefrontal and limbic regions as well as the two hemispheres. The core ideas include the maintaince 'decoupled' or alternative representations, selecting from among alternatives, and the relative salience of competing representations.

## EVOLUTION AND THE SOCIAL BRAIN

Proposals citing evolutionary pressure for social cognitive abilities have a long history (e.g. Chance and Mead 1953; Jolly 1966; Kummer 1968). In one influential paper, Humphrey (1976) portrayed nonhuman primate social networks as riddled with complex computational problems, far outweighing those found in predator-prey relations or those required for learning and reasoning about the physical world. Humphrey depicted primates as *homo psychologicus* or 'natural psychologists', social tacticians who must take into account detailed knowledge of conspecifics who are likely opponents and possible allies. Survival and reproductive success seem likely to depend on being able to predict—reliably—the behaviour of conspecifics. Such complex problems, moreover, necessitate considerable neural resources, and thus offer a plausible evolutionary explanation for the huge brain-to-body ratio in the higher primates. Related work in evolutionary biology, such as Trivers's (1971) 'reciprocal altruism' and Axelrod and Hamilton's (1981) 'Tit for Tat', proposed explanatory principles for survival strategies and behaviours in such networks. Dawkins and Krebs (1978; Krebs and Dawkins 1984) suggested that communication should evolve to be manipulative, and to serve the genetic benefit of the sender. These theories began to merge into a unified picture. Byrne and Whiten (1988), with mounting evidence of tactical deception in primate social networks, coined the phrase 'Machiavellian intelligence' as an apt if not so flattering characterization of the evolution of human intelligence. In short, the extraordinary problem-solving capacities of the human brain appear to be fundamentally social in nature and, arguably, appear qualitatively similar in function to the problem-solving abilities of related species. The similarity of social intelligence across different primates stands in contrast to the striking discontinuity between human and non-human generative language ability.

In addition to proposals about the evolutionary origins of ToM in humans, primate work has also stimulated methodological statements bearing on how best to characterize and test for ToM ability. When Premack and Woodruff (1978) first asked 'Does the chimpanzee have a theory of mind?' they sought to show that our closest primate relatives predict behaviour in very much the same way we do; that is, by inferring the intentions and motivations of another. The extensive peer commentary on this paper, most notably by the philosophers Dennett (1978), Pylyshyn (1978), Bennett (1978), and Harman (1978), not only addressed a number of interesting epistemological and ontological issues regarding the Premack and Woodruff analysis, but put forth a number of suggestions carrying methodological weight as well. The now widely-accepted criterion for having a fully representational theory of mind, or 'beliefs about beliefs', was set: predicting behaviour based on the notion of a *false* belief.

## THE CHILD'S DEVELOPING ONTOLOGY OF INTENTIONAL STATES

The watershed task—the prediction of behaviour based on a *false* belief—is passed by children at roughly four years of age (e.g. Wimmer and Perner 1983; Perner *et al.* 1987). This ability appears to emerge rather late when compared with children's everyday behaviours. Sullivan and Winner (1991), for example, relate the case of a two-year-old boy who, when asked by his grandmother *not* to touch the dials on the radio, immediately did so as soon as she left the room. Upon the grandmother's return the child said, 'You didn't know this, but I was fixing it' (p. 160). While many utterances by young children concerning mental states may be dismissed as imitation or merely conversational (e.g. 'know what?'), many are not so easily dismissed. Three-year-old children's spontaneous speech is riddled with talk of mental states *as representations* (Bartsch and Wellman 1995). Yet, despite such ostensibly complex language, three-year-olds appear to be unable to appreciate, and employ in the prediction of behaviour, false beliefs as causal entities.

Yet beliefs themselves, even false beliefs, are indeed items in three-year-olds' ontology, however fleeting and context-specific. Wellman and Bartsch (1988) have shown that three-year-olds can assign a causal role to a belief if that belief does not conflict with what the child knows to be true. For example, if the child does not know the location of an object, or if an object is in two locations, only one of which was seen by the character, the child will then be able to predict where the character will look. It is important to note that there is no conflicting belief in this case as both are concordant with what the child believes to be real. Moreover, three-year-old children who fail the false-belief task are sometimes able to invoke false beliefs as causal in their explanations (Bartsch and Wellman 1989).

A critical developmental milestone appears to be linked specifically to what can be termed *decoupled* representation, that is, the young child's ability to entertain simultaneous, alternative, or conflicting beliefs. There are clear developmental precursors to a fully realized ability to manipulate alternative representations. In his developmental model of ToM, Leslie (1987, 1994; Leslie and Roth 1993) posits a 'decoupler' mechanism which matures between eighteen to twenty four months and facilitates the ability to represent representations; he calls this 'metarepresentation' or 'M-representation.'[1] The first evidence of the M-representation system in action, according to Leslie, is observed in the pretence and shared pretence of young children. Shared pretence not only requires that the child hold in mind two contradictory representations concurrently (e.g. the banana is a telephone *and* the banana is a banana), but also that the child appreciate that a partner's behaviour is caused by a fictional attitude (pretending) and relates to a fictional state of affairs (the banana is a phone). Because the child must disregard the literal meaning of a pretending speaker's utterance, and instead infer the speaker's intention, shared pretence may be considered an instance of Gricean communication (Grice 1975; Leslie and Happé 1989).[2] Based on such a formulation, the two-year-old child could be said to have a theory of mind, despite not being able to pass the false-belief task for another two years. (See also Baron-Cohen 1995; Fodor 1992; Premack 1990; and Whiten 1996, for similar conclusions.)

Another key feature of the child's emerging ToM capabilities rests on the salience of the stimulus items used. Zaitchik (1991) has shown that three-year-old children are able to predict behaviour based on a false belief if the salience of the stimulus is diminished. If children are not shown the location of an object, but merely told of its existence, they are able to make successful false-belief predictions. The same has been shown for other, less salient, representations such as values (Flavell *et al.* 1990) and intentions (Moses 1990, as cited in Astington and Gopnik 1991).

In sum, the prediction of behaviour based on a false belief rests on at least two components: the ability to decouple representations and the ability to mark the salience of certain stimuli, either by inhibition or amplification. There is debate on when in the course of normal development these components first appear and when they are fully functional, but there is no disagreement involving their place in the adult ToM. There is likewise no disagreement that a person's proficiency using false beliefs to understand the behaviour of others provides a good index of ToM ability. These components of ToM will figure prominently in our discussion.

## LOCALIZATION OF FUNCTION WITHIN AND ACROSS THE CEREBRAL HEMISPHERES

Because of the gross anatomical symmetry of the two hemispheres, their functional differences received relatively little discussion until the latter half of the nineteenth century (Springer and Deutsch 1998). The notion of hemispheric specialization is due in large part to the influence of Broca. Broca's appreciation of the relationship between left hemisphere damage and speech abnormalities, as well as a correlation between handedness and speech, set the stage for the battles of cerebral dominance. Wernicke's work on the role of the left temporal lobe in speech comprehension and Leipmann's studies in apraxia fuelled the distinction and led to the proposal that the left hemisphere directed higher cognitive functions, such as language and purposeful movement, and played the 'leading' role to the subdominant and unspecialized right hemisphere. For the next several decades, until the early twentieth century, researchers concentrated on the localization of function within the left hemisphere, leaving the 'minor' right largely ignored.

One obvious reason for this emphasis on the left hemisphere is the importance of language functions. Another, less obvious reason for this neglect may be due to the extent of damage needed for clinical symptoms to emerge; while even a small lesion to the left hemisphere may produce an aphasia or some other symptom, a similarly-sized lesion to the right hemisphere may not result in any detectable functional deficits (Semmes 1968). There is as yet no definitive account for this difference between the hemispheres; however, there are several threads that can be woven together. It is now known that there are significant differences in the distribution of white and grey matter between the hemispheres. The appearance of 'white' matter is due to glial sheaths that surround axons and obscure—to visual inspection—the blood in capillaries. Myelination of an axon increases the speed of transmission and is characteristic of neurons involved in long distance processing. The appearance of 'grey' matter is due to the absence of myelination, that is, due to blood visible through the walls of capillaries. A higher proportion of grey matter is associated with relatively more cell bodies that send and receive information over short distances, that is, local processing. The left hemisphere is described as containing greater cell density, as having relatively more nonmyelinated fibres, especially in the frontal and precentral regions, and as having more areas devoted to motor and specific sensory functions. The right hemisphere, in contrast, is described as having more areas of 'associative' (higher level, integrative) cortex. (Galaburda 1995; Gur *et al.* 1980; Kertesz *et al.* 1990. See Best (1988) for a comprehensive account of cerebral asymmetries based on different growth gradients in neural development.)

These characteristics of the left hemisphere implicate its role in focused computations requiring faster, more localized processing involving collections of cells working together in close spatial proximity. Closely interconnected circuitry has the benefit of carrying out subtle alterations of a serial schematic action sequence, allowing for 'many possible variations on any one cognitive theme' (Kinsbourne 1982, p. 412). Moreover, proximal circuitry is ideal for fast, routinized processes such as syntactic analysis or speech production. Such small and quick variations are necessary for fine motor control performances such as speech production (e.g., the short delay in the onset of voicing between 'pa' and 'ba') and corresponding aspects of speech comprehension. Regarding comprehension, consider the difference between the consonant-vowel syllables 'ba', 'da', and 'ga': the primary distinctions among these are frequency changes occurring within the first 50 milliseconds. The left hemisphere has shown a clear advantage on such tasks (Kimura 1967, 1993; Mattingly and Studdert-Kennedy 1991). On this view, a lesion to the left hemisphere can affect a large proportion of the tissue employed in fast-acting, concerted processing and, as such, produce an obvious impairment.

In contrast, the right hemisphere possesses relatively more myelinated axons that, presumably, link different brain regions which, together, carry out functions that (1) do not require the same degree of localized, sequential processing or (2) require integration of different types of input initially processed in different parts of the brain. In this way, the integrative nature of the functions supported by the right hemisphere may require more extensive damage for clinical presentation in right hemisphere damaged (RHD) patients, at least insofar as concerns comprehension of propositional knowledge and language. Relatedly, patients with small, purely cortical right-sided strokes often recover quickly and well enough to resume their normal lives and, as a result, are not often seen by researchers.

## FUNCTIONS ASSOCIATED WITH THE RIGHT HEMISPHERE

Before starting this selective review, we emphasize that the patients tested are, with few exceptions, stroke patients who have suffered unilateral brain damage somewhere in the territory of the middle cerebral artery. This area includes posterior portions of the frontal lobe, and portions of the temporal and parietal lobes as well. Localization within the right hemisphere is typically not discussed in detail in these papers. In what follows, we use the term 'right hemisphere' as it has been used in the literature—to refer to regions anywhere within the hemisphere, though usually regions served by the middle cerebral artery and excluding the prefrontal regions.

### History and overview of interpretations of right hemisphere functions

The right hemisphere has been assigned a major role in some domains. The dominance of the right hemisphere in spatial reasoning became evident in the early part of this century, as RHD patients exhibited particular difficulty on visuospatial tasks. Similarly, RHD patients exhibited deficits in the production and perception of emotion. The left hemisphere came to be stereotyped as analytic, logical, local, and rational, while the right hemisphere as synthetic, Gestalt, holistic, global, and intuitive with respect to processing in several domains (Kolb and Whishaw 1996). These characterizations, however, do not adequately capture the phenomenon of lateralization; computations carried out within the right hemisphere require the same degree of precision as those in the left. Moreover, cerebral lateralization and specialization should not be viewed as a battle for dominance between the hemispheres, but more as a developmental streamlining of complementary functioning, much of which occurs in ontogeny and may not be specified in the genome (Deacon 1997). Nevertheless, a sufficient number of regularities emerge to make lateralization of function a useful perspective for cognitive neuroscience.

The RHD literature on language impairment is wide-ranging and complex. Deficits include problems with integration of verbal as well as spatial material (Benowitz *et al.* 1990), and also include verbosity, tangentiality, confabulation, concrete and fragmentary performance, difficulty with pragmatic inference, aberrant production and comprehension of humour, lack of self-monitoring in verbal responses, and difficulty in the interpretation and production of the prosodic and emotional dimensions of language (Beeman and Chiarello 1998; Brownell and Gardner 1988; Brownell and Martino 1998; Brownell *et al.* 1995; Code 1987; Gardner *et al.* 1983; Joanette *et al.* 1990; Myers 1999; Tompkins 1994). We illustrate that ToM impairments fit easily within the range of deficits associated with right-sided brain injury. We will argue that a common feature of many reported deficits is that RHD patients exhibit difficulty processing decoupled or alternative interpretations of a stimulus, specifically with regard to the generation, synchronization, and marking of multiple representational sets.

## The role of the right hemisphere in ToM

Our first question is whether or not RHD affects a person's ToM. A set of recent studies (Brownell *et al.* 1997; Happé *et al.* 1999; Winner *et al.* 1998) establishes the nature of the deficit: RHD patients retain a basic ability to understand that people may harbour different beliefs about the world, but nonetheless have difficulty applying ToM to support comprehension.

A sample stimulus item used by Winner *et al.* (1998) serves to illustrate the deficit and how it has been tested with RHD patients and non brain-damaged control participants. The critical items all had the same structure built around a speaker's literally false statement concerning an awkward, potentially embarrassing situation ranging from cheating on a diet to cheating on one's spouse. The scenarios were designed to favour either of two interpretations: a deceitful lie uttered in self protection or an ironic joke uttered to lighten an awkward moment after one has been found out. In all scenarios, the addressee knows the truth of the situation. The critical distinction is that in joke scenarios, the speaker is *aware* of the addressee's knowledge while in lie scenarios the speaker is *unaware* of the addressee's knowledge. Questions posed during presentation of an item are presented below, along with their purpose. Additional factual questions were posed during presentation of the scenario to ensure that participants maintained their focus on the task. If a participant answered the factual questions incorrectly, the vignette was presented again from the beginning. Items were presented to participants using a tape recorder and, simultaneously, in written form. A sample item is shown below:

Sue smoked two packs of cigarettes a day. Zelda had been begging her to quit for years. Zelda promised that she would buy Sue dinner one night after work if Sue quit smoking for one week. Sue agreed to try.

After two miserable days of not smoking, Sue began to sneak cigarettes in the bathroom. She told one friend, but she didn't tell Zelda.

One day, Zelda came into the bathroom and saw smoke coming from one of the stalls. She recognized Sue's shoes and could tell that it was Sue who was in the stall smoking.

QUESTION: Did Zelda realize that Sue was still smoking? Yes/No

This question measured a participant's sensitivity to a character's true first-order belief. Because all items included a true first-order belief, this question does not provide a sensitive index of first-order ability, but does guarantee that participants understand the content of a stimulus item.

Zelda turned and left the bathroom before Sue could see her. Just then, Sue's friend, who was in the next stall, asked Sue, 'Does Zelda know that you are still smoking?'

QUESTION: What do you think Sue told her friend?

(a) 'Yes, Zelda knows that I am still smoking.'

(b) 'No, Zelda does not know that I am still smoking.'

This and the following question measure a participant's understanding of the characters' second-order beliefs which could be true or false in different scenarios.

QUESTION: Did Sue think that what she said was really true? Yes/No

Sue returned to her desk. Zelda asked Sue, 'Are you having trouble keeping your no-smoking promise?'

Sue replied, 'I haven't touched a cigarette all week.'

QUESTION: When Sue said that to Zelda, did she think that Zelda would believe her? Yes/No

This question measures a participant's ability to chart the implications of second-order beliefs.

QUESTION: When Sue said, 'I haven't touched a cigarette all week', was she:

(a) lying to avoid getting caught

(b) joking to cover up her embarrassment

This question taps a participant's ability to apply ToM to discourse interpretation, that Sue is lying.

In other comparable items, Zelda and Sue might confront one another in the women's room such that knowledge of the truth is clearly shared between the two:

Sue opened the stall door with a lit cigarette in her hand and saw Zelda staring at her. Zelda turned and left the bathroom. Sue returned to her desk. Zelda asked Sue, 'Are you having trouble keeping your no-smoking promise?'

Sue replied, 'I haven't touched a cigarette all week.'

Here, of course, Sue has been caught and must try to mend the effects of her behaviour.

The most relevant results include a selective deficit in that the RHD patients were able to answer fact questions correctly but, on average, had more difficulty with discourse interpretation than the controls. Patients were less consistent in identifying second-order belief questions and less consistent in interpreting the final utterance as a joke or lie. In addition, the results confirm the link between second-order belief capacity and discourse interpretation. For both the RHD patients and the controls, a participant's degree of success distinguishing jokes from lies could be predicted very well (r = approximately +.7) from his or her facility with second-order beliefs.

Thus, second-order belief ability was shown to be reduced subsequent to RHD, and this reduction may well underlie these patients' poor discourse performance separating ironic jokes from lies. This study was designed specifically to test patients' sophistication with second-order belief and not first-order belief; first-order belief test questions *always* tapped true beliefs, which left unsettled the extent to which patients would also demonstrate impaired first-order belief deficits. Also left unsettled was the extent to which RHD patients' difficulties with ToM could be separated from general problems of inference.

The selectivity of the ToM deficit is supported by results from another study that examined the extent to which people consider the knowledge of an addressee as well as other features of a conversation. Brownell *et al.* (1997) used terms of personal reference as a measure of discourse performance that is sensitive to what conversational partners know or do not know. Specifically, the task used in a pair of highly similar studies was to follow a conversation and, in that context, to choose an appropriate term to refer to someone not physically present. As illustrated below, in all stimulus conversations, the speaker and addressee were described as having equal, and relatively low, status, white collar jobs in which politeness would be the norm. The speaker and addressee were always described as having just met and having a conversation in the work environment about someone else, the referent. The referent was always male. In some items the referent was described as having an equal status (that is, the same occupation, for example, another clerk or museum guard) as the people talking, and in other items as having a clearly higher status (for example, a new vice president or director). The stimulus items also varied in terms of whether the speaker, the addressee, or both were well acquainted with the referent. For example:

You have just met Fran Hill, who, like you, is about to start working as a reservations clerk for American Airlines. You are describing your hopes about the job, when she says to you: 'I heard that the other clerk who works in the reservations office is getting a big prize for having broken the reservations record this month.' It then comes out in conversation between you and Fran Hill that neither of you has met Oliver Harding, the other clerk she is referring to.

The choices varied in terms of formality. We asked:

Which of the following would you choose to respond to Fran Hill?
(a) 'Well, Oliver must be a really hard worker.'
(b) 'Well, Mr. Harding must be a really hard worker.'

A moment's reflection serves to identify the conventionally polite choices. In general, higher status people are referred to more formally. Beyond that static element of conversational context, an appropriate choice of a term of reference requires simultaneous consideration of both the speaker's and addressee's familiarity with the referent. Informality ('. . . Oliver . . .') is appropriate only in the one case in which both the speaker and referent are well acquainted with the referent. In all other cases, the more formal ('. . . Mr. Harding . . .') is canonically preferred. If only the speaker knows the referent, using the informal first name alone constitutes flaunting one's familiarity. If only the addressee knows the referent well, or if neither the speaker nor the addressee knows the referent, a speaker's use of the informal first name reflects presumptuousness. And, lastly, if both the speaker and addressee know the referent well, use of the formal title and last name seems a little odd, as if the speaker is trying to deny familiarity and to insert social distance from the referent.

Stimulus conversations were presented to RHD patients and to non brain-damaged control participants using a tape recorder and, simultaneously, on a typed script. In addition, simple outline drawings representing the referent, the speaker, and the addressee were kept in view to help patients maintain attention to the relevant characters. After a stimulus was presented, and before choosing a term of reference, the participant was asked factual questions about how well the speaker and listener knew the referent and about the status of the referent's job relative to the speaker and listener (that is, either higher or equal). Only after answering these factual questions correctly (which very rarely required repetition of the stimulus vignette) was the participant asked to choose an appropriate utterance to continue the conversation.

The dependent measure was a 'formality score', defined as the proportion of times a participant selected the formal term of reference. Statistical analysis focused on two critical comparisons: (1) the consistency with which participants restricted their use of informal terms of reference to the one situation in which both the speaker and addressee knew the referent; and (2) the consistency with which participants used formal terms for high status referents.

The results were quite clear and equivalent across two highly similar studies. The RHD patients showed no deficit whatsoever in their use of status as a conversational variable. Both the patients and the non brain-damaged control participants consistently—and to the same degree—used more formal terms to refer to high status people. However, the patients were far less consistent than the controls in incorporating knowledge states into their responses, even though in all cases the participants had answered the factual information correctly. (Specifically, there was a reliable group difference in contrast scores representing this critical comparison across the four combinations of speaker and addressee knowledge.) In these two studies, then, the RHD patients showed a deficit in restricting their use of informal terms to just the one, canonically appropriate context. Thus, the RHD patients exhibited a selective impairment in application of mental states that distinguished their decreased competence in ToM from their ability to incorporate other conversational elements into their responses.

Further documentation of the functional selectivity and—for the first time—the anatomical specificity of ToM deficits is provided by a recent study by Happé *et al.* (1999). These authors tested the effects of right-sided damage on patients' understanding of first-order false belief using verbal stories involving mental states and pictorial cartoons whose humour rested on mental states. Happé *et al.* were also able to test left-hemisphere damaged (LHD) aphasic patients using modified procedures on ToM tasks. And, most importantly, on one of their cartoon tasks, Happé *et al.* were able to use exactly the same procedure to test all groups (non brain-damaged controls, RHD patients, LHD patients) and were thus able to document the anatomical specificity of a ToM impairment.

The first task compared patients' comprehension of stories based in large part on ToM and, for comparison, control stories that required inference for understanding but did not require ToM. The items were those used in a functional imaging study carried out by Fletcher *et al.* (1995). A sample ToM story follows:

*Example ToM story*

A burglar who has just robbed a shop is making his getaway. As he is running home, a policeman on his beat sees him drop his glove. He doesn't know the man is a burglar; he just wants to tell him he dropped his glove. But when the policeman shouts out to the burglar, 'Hey, you! Stop!', the burglar turns around, sees the policeman and gives himself up. He puts his hands up and admits that he did the break-in at the local shop.
*Test question*: Why did the burglar do that?

*Example control story*

A burglar is about to break into a jeweller's shop. He skilfully picks the lock on the shop door. Carefully he crawls under the electronic detector beam. If he breaks this beam, it will set off the alarm. Quietly he opens the door of the store-room and sees the gems glittering. As he reaches out, however, he steps on something soft. He hears a screech and something small and furry runs past him, towards the shop door. Immediately the alarm sounds.
*Test question*: Why did the alarm go off?

Participants were timed as they read each story silently. When finished, participants turned the page over and latency was recorded. Participants then answered the test question. Their responses were later scored for accuracy and completeness, which, in the case of the ToM items, included the success with which a response appropriately characterized a character's mental state.

The pattern of results across this and other tasks argues strongly for a selective ToM deficit in RHD patients. The control participants performed equivalently on the ToM stories and the control stories, or they performed better on the ToM items. The RHD patients consistently performed worse (both in terms of latency to finish reading and in quality of explanation) on the ToM stories.

Happé *et al.* replicated and extended this finding using a cartoon task. Participants viewed a set of captionless cartoon pairs. Each pair consisted of an original cartoon and a cartoon identical in all respects but one: the humour element had been removed. The humour in half of the original cartoons was based on a person's ignorance or false belief. We refer to these as ToM cartoons. The humour in the other half was based on violation of either a physical or social norm. We refer to these as nonToM cartoons. The participant's task was to view each pair of items (one original and one altered, not funny version of the same cartoon) and to select the correct, funny item. Time to choose was recorded, as was the number of correct choices.

On this task, non brain-damaged controls, RHD patients, and LHD aphasic patients were tested. The LHD group was small (n = 5) but homogeneous. All were diagnosed as having Broca's aphasia subsequent to lesions that included Broca's area and a variety of other structures in the left hemisphere. As is typical for patients with lasting Broca's aphasia, this group of Broca's patients had left frontal lesions that extended beyond Broca's area per se and that often included subcortical pathways. The overall pattern was clear and the same as observed for the stories. The non brain-damaged controls and the LHD patients performed equivalently on the two kinds of items while the RHD patients performed reliably worse on the ToM items.

A ToM deficit is the most parsimonious explanation for these patients' performances across different measures. The RHD patients performed consistently poorly on ToM items while the non brain-damaged controls and LHD patients showed no such selective deficit. Alternative accounts based on overall difficulty of inference demands are simply not consistent with these results. The findings obtained with the LHD Broca's patients, though preliminary due to the small sample size, argue for the anatomical specificity of ToM problems associated with RHD. Further corroboration comes from a recent study by Stone *et al.* (1998) who report no ToM deficits in patients with unilateral left dorsolateral damage. Viewed in aggregate, this work argues for a consistent link between ToM deficits and right-sided damage.

Based on these results, it would be reasonable to expect increased right hemisphere activation during brain imaging studies of ToM tasks. However, the findings to date force a more complicated account. Of particular interest in this regard is the study by Fletcher *et al.* (1995), who used some of the same stimulus items as Happé *et al.* (1999; see also Goel *et al.* 1995). While heightened right-sided activity was measured during ToM tasks, especially in medial frontal regions (see Fig. 3 and Table 4) and the anterior cingulate, increased activity was more consistently observed in the left medial prefrontal cortex (Brodmann's areas 8 and 9) relative to a control condition. In the direct comparison between the ToM and physical story conditions, the Fletcher *et al.* study also indicates heightened right hemisphere activity in the posterior cingulate cortex and in the inferior right parietal cortex. Fletcher *et al.* did not interpret these as right hemisphere effects because the same areas did not show heightened activation in comparison to another control condition consisting of unrelated sentences, which undermined the conclusion that these right hemisphere areas had a specific link to ToM (p. 121). We agree with Fletcher *et al.*'s reasons for emphasizing those areas whose specific links to ToM were supported most convincingly by their data. We note, though, that their results do not provide a strong argument against right hemisphere involvement. Specifically, the demands of trying to integrate and thus remember the unrelated sentences may have required extra right hemisphere participation (Joanette *et al.* 1990; Schacter *et al.* 1996). Given the subtraction methodology used in PET studies, the extra task demands of the unrelated sentence condition could possibly explain the apparent inconsistency of right hemisphere involvement in ToM tasks. We are not surprised by the implications of left medial prefrontal involvement given the left hemisphere's superiority in linguistic operations and the role of the prefrontal cortex in working memory, planning, and other so-called 'executive' functions. (We discuss these functions in more detail below, paying special attention to issues of laterality.)

In other imaging work, Baron-Cohen *et al.* (1994) found the right orbitofrontal cortex to be selectively activated when participants identified words having to do with the mind (e.g. 'think') as opposed to the body (e.g. 'hand'). We are intrigued by this finding but are as yet unsure exactly how to fit this work in with the extant literature. Baron-Cohen *et al.* carried out a region-of-interest hypothesis, examining only bilateral orbitofrontal and frontal polar regions but not the more posterior prefrontal regions; nor did the task have an inferential component. It is therefore difficult to directly compare this work to the Fletcher *et al.* study or with the findings from the semantic accessing literature, which also focuses on the activity in more posterior prefrontal regions (Warburton *et al.* 1996).

Because the study of intentional attribution is relatively new to cognitive neuroscience, and there have only been a handful of lesion and imaging studies directly concerned with this topic, we should not expect a clear picture of this complex human ability to have emerged. Predicting the behaviour of conspecifics or, for that matter, any intentional system (Dennett 1987) is arguably our most exercised form of cognition, with novel problems occurring on a daily, even moment to moment, basis. Needless to say, the processing demands are multifarious and often quite extensive. The lack of direct evidence on this topic necessitates an appeal to the literature outside ToM, where regional processing biases are becoming clearer. Such an appeal may provide us with framework to predict, on both structural and functional dimensions, where and how ToM problems are being solved in the brain.

## The role of the right hemisphere in domains related to ToM

The ToM studies on RHD subjects can be viewed as an extension of a substantial body of work that both provides empirical support for the nature of the impairments and indicates how ToM fits into a larger view of cognition and communication that emphasizes the importance of alternative representations or interpretations. (See Beeman 1998; Brownell *et al.* 1995; Burgess and Chiarello 1996, for discussion.) Humour, for example, is an area of deficit for RHD patients. Verbal jokes often rest on reinterpretation of a punch line, that is, on appreciation of revised interpretations that reflect ToM. Consider the following joke that, in different forms. has served as a stimulus item in three studies (Bihrle *et al.* 1986; Brownell *et al.* 1983; Shammi and Stuss 1999).

The neighbourhood borrower approached Mr. Smith one Sunday afternoon and said, 'Say, Smith, are you using your lawnmower this afternoon?'
'Yes, I am,' Mr. Smith replied warily.
*Punch line*: The neighbourhood borrower replied, 'Fine, then you won't be using your golf clubs. I'll just borrow them.'

In Brownell *et al.* (1983), RHD patients were presented with the beginning of a joke and asked to select the correct, funny punch line among from alternatives that included non sequitur endings that were simply incongruent ('The grass is greener on the other side of the fence'), correct punchlines that were incongruent but that could be reinterpreted to fit with the joke, and straightforward continuations of the story that did not have any element of incongruity ('Gee, do you think I could borrow it when you're done?'). The major finding, which was replicated in later studies, was that RHD patients were prone to selecting the incongruous endings whether or not they could be reinterpreted to fit with a joke's beginning; RHD patients were not fooled by the straightforward endings but were drawn to the non sequitur endings. The patients apparently had an intact sense of the primary narrative requirement of verbal humour—that a punch line violates expectancies generated during the body of the joke. Yet, they had trouble processing the secondary meaning of a punch line that distinguished it from other candidate endings that were also incongruous. This study was designed and carried out without any consideration of ToM. However, the jokes used as the basis for stimuli all required reinterpretation of the punch line, and fully half of the items involved elements of mistaken beliefs, ignorance, or fooling a victim.

The Brownell *et al.* (1983) study included only RHD patients and non brain-damaged control participants. However, Shammi and Stuss (1999) used the same items as part of a comprehensive study of humour in patients with different lesion sites. Her results underscored the anatomical specificity of the deficit: right pre-frontally damaged patients were impaired in punch line selection while non aphasic, left prefrontally damaged patients were not. Also, Bihrle *et al.* (1986) tested a group of aphasic patients with lesions distributed across the left hemisphere on a pictorial humour task and found that RHD but not LHD was associated with this inability to apprehend alternative meanings of humour. In addition, Bihrle *et al.* found that RHD patients were drawn to slapstick humour that did not require the same sophisticated appreciation of mental states or integration of disparate elements.

Our review suggests that ToM deficits contribute to RHD patients' problems comprehending some types of humour and, in addition, that ToM impairments represent one manifestation of a broader problem that extends beyond humour and beyond humour based on ToM. Brownell *et al.* (1986), for example, reported that RHD patients had analogous impairments when adequate comprehension required revising interpretations of non-humorous discourse. A typical, two-sentence, stimulus item follows.

Sally became too bored to finish the history book.
She had already spent five years writing it.

Most listeners generate an inference upon hearing the first sentence that Sally was reading a dull book. After the second sentence, however, normal listeners abandon their initial inference in order to incorporate both sentences under a single interpretation, that Sally is an author running out of enthusiasm for a long project. The RHD patients tested in this study seemed 'normal' insofar as they generated the same initial inference as the controls, but the patients became stuck on the initial inference and often failed to abandon their initial interpretation in favour of an alternative that was, in the end, more consonant with both sentences. Comprehension was tested by presenting fact questions to ensure that they had understood and retained the material in individual sentences and inference questions that tapped whether or not participants could revise their initial inferences. As suggested above, the RHD patients were distinguished from the control participants in their heightened tendency to respond 'true' to test statements such as 'Reading the history book bored Sally' that were based on the first sentence in isolation, and in their decreased tendency to respond 'true' to appropriate, unifying inferences such as 'Sally became bored writing a history book'.

The deficit uncovered in this study was not simply one of an inability to integrate information across sentence boundaries. RHD patients were not distinguished from controls in their interpretation of sentence pairs in which the overall gist followed naturally from the order in which information was presented, as in the following example.

Johnny missed the wild pitch.
The windshield was shattered.

Here, patients and controls tended, appropriately, to endorse test sentences such as 'A baseball broke the windshield' and to reject items such as 'The car was in an automobile accident'. (See Brownell *et al.* 1992; Leonard *et al.* 1997, for other examples of RHD patients' successful integration of information across sentence boundaries.) The deficit can be characterized as trouble moving flexibly from one interpretation to another, a cognitive rigidity. More recent work by Tompkins and her colleagues (Tompkins *et al.* 1997) suggests that RHD patients' comprehension deficits reflect an inability to construct alternative readings. Under either description of the deficit, RHD patients are limited by their decreased prowess with alternative interpretations, even when those interpretations do not rest clearly on mistaken beliefs, ignorance, or efforts to fool someone.

The characterization of RHD patients' deficit in terms of processing alternative meanings has also often been demonstrated using phrasal and lexical materials in a series of 'off-line' (that is, unspeeded) tasks. For example, Winner and Gardner (1977; see also Myers and Linebaugh 1981; VanLancker and Kempler 1987, for similar studies) have shown that RHD patients' comprehension of phrasal metaphors such as 'he has a heavy heart' is surprisingly poor, even compared with that of LHD patients with aphasia. RHD patients tended to use literal interpretations and to have trouble acknowledging the nonliteral, alternative meaning of even these over learned phrases. Analogous results have been reported for single-word, polysemous stimuli such as 'warm' which can refer literally to temperature or, more metaphorically, to one's personality (e.g. Brownell *et al.* 1984; Brownell *et al.* 1990). These early studies reinforce the asymmetry between the respective roles of the left and right hemispheres in processing stimuli defined in terms of having more than a single interpretation.

More recent work has used 'on-line' experimental techniques to examine processing of different types of meaning relations by LHD and RHD brain-damaged patients and by the left and right hemispheres of neurologically intact control participants. For example, Bottini *et al.* (1994) reported PET data corroborating the special role of the right hemisphere for processing of metaphoric alternative meaning in neurologically intact adults.

Another approach has been to use a variation on the semantic priming paradigm (e.g. Neely 1991). The experimental task is to decide whether or not a string of letters (the 'target') presented on a computer screen is a real word. A 'prime' word is presented prior to the target. The prime may or may not be related to the target, and, more specifically, the prime can be related in different ways to the target. The interesting result is that participants respond more quickly to real word targets when they are preceded by a prime that is semantically related in particular ways. Recent work by several researchers has used lateralized field presentation in conjunction with priming paradigms with neurologically intact young adults to explore the different responses of the two hemispheres to semantic associations. In most of these studies, a prime word or words is presented at fixation, which results in the word being viewed in both the left visual field, which projects to the right hemisphere, and the right visual field, which projects to the left hemisphere. The target word is then presented to one side of the central fixation point, that is, to just one visual field, thereby isolating the contralateral hemisphere's processing of that target.

A large body of work provides solid support for differences in how the two hemispheres process meaning. (See Burgess and Chiarello 1996; Burgess and Simpson 1988; Chiarello 1998, for reviews.) The right hemisphere is more likely than the left to process weak or diffuse associations and low frequency alternative meanings, and the right hemisphere maintains activation over longer prime—target intervals. The left hemisphere actively dampens or inhibits activation of alternatives and focuses on the contextually most dominant reading. Nakagawa (1991), for example, examined the effects of strong and weak associations (e.g. 'pound' provides a strong association to 'hammer', whereas 'drop' provides a weak association to 'hammer') on subsequent recognition of words presented to the right and left visual fields. Nakagawa found very different priming effects for each hemisphere. The left hemisphere performance benefited only from strong, frequent associations, whereas even the weakest associations benefited right hemisphere performance. Beeman and his colleagues (Beeman *et al.* 1994; see Beeman 1998, for a review) has reported analogous results described in terms of a right hemisphere predilection for 'coarse grained' semantic coding. For example, when three distantly related primes ('foot', 'cry', and 'glass') are presented to both hemispheres using central presentation, target words ('cut') show more facilitation when presented to the right hemisphere than to the left hemisphere. In contrast, the left hemisphere shows greater response to a single direct prime ('scissors') than it did to a set of distantly related primes. The right hemisphere showed as much facilitation for a set of weakly associated primes as for a single direct prime.

The recurring theme in the work by several researchers is that the right hemisphere's contribution to semantic processing includes long lasting facilitation effects from even weakly associated primes. These same researchers have interpreted their work as providing an account for the discourse-level impairments of RHD patients and have in some cases performed parallel studies using brain-damaged patients and non brain-damaged controls (Beeman 1993, 1998; Burgess and Chiarello 1996; Burgess and Simpson 1988; Chiarello 1998). The left hemisphere excels at selecting and processing a single, dominant interpretation while inhibiting the others. In many linguistic and social contexts, the left hemisphere's focused approach works well. However, whenever there is not a single appropriate, highly activated interpretation, the right hemisphere will play a larger role: when several considerations must be integrated or when an initially attractive interpretation must be abandoned in favour of another.

## FUNCTIONS ASSOCIATED WITH PREFRONTAL REGIONS

The relevance of prefrontal regions to ToM is well established. Activation studies, such as reviewed in other chapters in this volume, provide strong support for prefrontal component of ToM. In addition, lesion studies document deficits in ToM tasks (see Stone, Chapter 11, this volume). What bears closer examination is how functions associated with prefrontal regions relate to those attributed to the right hemisphere. It is not always possible to draw a clear distinction between the functions of the prefrontal regions and those of the right hemisphere. The catalogue of linguistic and cognitive impairments observed in RHD patients could be substituted, virtually without notice, into any review article on prefrontal impairments (McDonald 1993). McDonald (1993) provides an important perspective on how this could be. One reason is that the literatures on RHD and frontal lobe disorders have remained largely independent of one another. Moreover, as one might suspect, the majority of RHD patients tested have most likely had damage to the frontal lobes. Additionally, studies on the prefrontal lobe have faced difficulties similar to those common to RHD studies. Prefrontal lesions, like RH lesions, are often difficult to notice, as they do not affect motor control or standard measures of intelligence (Shallice and Burgess 1991). A small lesion may have no noticeable affect on behaviour. For classic behavioural pathology, such as uncontrolled and maladaptive behaviour, apathy, perseveration, etc. (Luria 1973), frontal damage may have to be quite extensive. It has been argued that many of these so-called classic symptoms may require global cerebral dysfunction (Canavan *et al.* 1985). Finally, it is often difficult to distinguish left- from right-hemispheric locus in the medial prefrontal areas, due largely to their proximity. Consequently, most treatments of prefrontal function do not emphasize lateralization of function. We will emphasize lateralization within the prefrontal regions when possible, although we acknowledge that these functional asymmetries are not as universally accepted as is the case for more posterior functions. In addition, we cite reports detailing the effects of well-specified lesions in monkeys to provide clues to the functional differences and similarities of the various frontal regions in humans.

Tasks sensitive to prefrontal lesions involve tests of working memory, behavioural suppression, directed attention, and sensitivity to context. In monkeys, for example, lesions to the dorsolateral regions produce deficits in delayed response or delayed alternation tasks, where monkeys have difficulty inhibiting their tendency to search where they first found food, instead of searching where they just saw it hidden (Jacobsen 1936). Likewise, on a task involving sampling food wells, Passingham (1985) found monkeys with dorsolateral lesions to perseverate, that is, to return to previously sampled wells while neglecting many unsampled ones. Monkeys with lesions to the ventromedial aspects of the prefrontal cortices are able to pass the above tasks, though they are unable to pass the delayed non-match to sample task which requires them to connect a reward (food) to the newer of two stimuli (Mishkin and Manning 1978). Finally, posterior prefrontal lesions produce deficits in multipart tasks requiring conditional associations between two stimuli in order to find a reward. These tasks require the monkeys to reverse their expectations (e.g. if $x$ then $z$; if $y$ then not-$z$). Unlike the previous tasks, only the stimulus relationship of the reward—but not its location—changes (Petrides 1986). Prefrontal tasks specific to humans show the same patterns. For instance, the classic 'executive function' task, the Wisconsin Card Sort, requires marking the relevance of previous stimuli or responses with regard to the current context (e.g. Kolb and Whishaw 1996).

One noticeable characteristic of the above tasks is that they all involve marking the relevance of previously learned information to a novel context, and more specifically, they all involve a negative marking (e.g. not-*x*) of previous information. The ability to assign 'not-*x*' to a representation in memory is necessary for shifting attention to alternative or opposite choices.[3] Deacon (1997) writes:

. . . tasks sensitive to prefrontal damage . . . involve shifting between alternatives or opposites, alternating place from trial to trial, shifting from one stimulus to a new one, or from one pairwise association to another depending on . . . different cues . . . They all have to do with using information about something you've just done or seen *against itself*, so to speak, to inhibit the tendency to follow up that correlation and instead shift attention and direct action to alternative associations. Precisely because one association works in one context or trial, it is specifically excluded in the next trial or under different stimulus conditions (p. 263).

The appreciation of the role of the prefrontal cortices in attention, planning, inhibition, and working memory across domains has led researchers to deem these regions the brain's 'senior executive' or locus of 'executive function' (Goldman-Rakic 1987; Joseph 1996; Shimamura 1995). The term 'senior executive' is perhaps misleading in that it implies that there is a general decision-maker in the brain. It is important to note that the notion of a neural control structure need not be equated with decision making. Clark (1996) provides a useful softening of the notion of control structures, considering them 'any neural substrate whose primary role is to modulate the activity of other neural circuits, structures, or processes—that is to say, any items or processes whose role is to control the inner economy rather than to track external states of affairs or to directly control bodily activity' (p. 136). The prefrontal cortex appears to be such a structure. Clark's treatment dispenses with the tacit homunculus in 'executive' accounts, and it is the treatment we prefer.

With respect to lateralization of function, Milner *et al.* (1991) have shown that the right prefrontal cortex in humans is associated with memory for the temporal placement and frequency of events. Schacter *et al.* (1996) argue that right prefrontal regions are crucial for item-specific recognition as opposed to recognition based on the general characteristics of previously studied objects. Such activations may reflect effortful or intentional retrieval processes (see also Kapur *et al.* 1995). Other studies on memory retrieval have invited researchers to make similar left-right distinctions, such as 'general event knowledge' vs. 'event-specific knowledge' (Conway and Rubin 1993), 'familiarity' vs. 'recall or recollection' (Hintzman and Curran 1994) or 'gist' vs. 'verbatim' (Brainerd *et al.* 1995). Consistent activation of the right frontal lobe during episodic retrieval tasks has been confirmed by recent PET studies (Tulving *et al.* 1994). Similarly, Deglin and Kinsbourne (1996), in a task requiring subjects to solve syllogisms, found that electroconvulsive suppression of the left hemisphere resulted in a marked sensitivity to the plausibility of the content of certain premises. Rather than focusing on the logical relations of the syllogism, subjects attempted to specify the details of the contents of the dubious propositions. Suppression of the right hemisphere did not produce the same reliance on personal experience or detailed knowledge of the propositions.

This work is consistent with our claims that the right hemisphere is necessary for the activation of extensive representational sets and, in this vein, for meaning that is implied or novel rather than explicit and based on existing routines. We should not expect a meaningful representation to be located in a single isolable substrate. Meaning, of course, consists in relationships. Implied meaning, moreover, requires a larger set of relationships or component parts than does manifest or literal meaning, thus increasing the demands of synchronization. We have already argued that the right hemisphere shows superiority in the realm of integrated or implied meaning, and the work of Schacter *et al.* (1996), among others, suggests the same is true for episodic and item-specific recognition memory.

The selection of an appropriate response to an ambiguous or multistep task requires the maintenance of heterogeneous representational sets for an extended period of time. The high degree of connectivity between the prefrontal regions to other, more posterior and subcortical, brain regions make this region architectonically well-suited for the maintenance of the extensive network necessary for such computations (Goldman-Rakic 1987; Pandya and Barnes 1987).

The multiple representations putatively maintained through the participation of association areas must be tagged or somehow made distinctive. Damasio (1989, 1994) has proposed such a mechanism regarding social decision making which he calls the 'somatic marker' hypothesis: a circuit of neural mechanisms and substrates underlying the marking of values of past and potential behavioural schemas. Damasio suggests that the ventromedial and orbitofrontal cortices, with their extensive connections to the amygdala and various limbic regions, act as 'convergence' zones, using the state of the soma (a combination of the state of viscera, internal milieu, and skeletal musculature) to mark the value of anticipated consequences and possible responses. A convergence zone contains a record (or, 'set') of simultaneous activity throughout cortical and subcortical structures, the output of which goes to the amygdala and other various autonomic effectors, which in turn activate somatic states pertinent to the set. The distribution and signal intensity of a newly enacted state is perceived by the somatosensory cortices in conjunction with the original set. Patients with damage to ventromedial and orbital regions may lose the ability to use the state of the soma as a value marker for potential outcomes, resulting in the odd and often inappropriate social behaviour observed in patients with prefrontal damage. Damasio further suggests that right frontal regions have an advantage in the maintenance of this biasing and winnowing network, specifically regarding the marking of punishing consequences.

There is substantial evidence that right (as opposed to left) frontal regions have a greater involvement in negative emotions such as are linked to withdrawal behaviour. Davidson *et al.* (1994), Gray (1994), and others have proposed that the right frontal lobe is concerned with marking negative consequences while the left frontal regions guide approach-related behaviour. EEG measures of resting anterior brain activity have found greater left-frontal activity to correlate with measures of approach-related behaviour and greater right-frontal activity to correlate with withdrawal (Sutton and Davidson 1997). Similarly, in laboratory studies designed to manipulate emotion through various means (e.g. films, monetary reward, and punishment, etc.), pleasant states were associated with greater left activation while unpleasant states showed increased right-sided anterior activation. Similar results have been obtained in nonhuman primate studies, where abnormally fearful monkeys show greater EEG activation in the right frontal lobes (Kalin *et al*. 1998). Davidson speculates that, regarding the prefrontal modulation of the amygdala and other limbic regions, the left prefrontal cortex has an advantage in shutting down negative stimuli more quickly. Damage to these regions may present with pathological amplification of this distinction: right frontal lesions are associated with manic-like excitement, with confabulatory and prosodically abnormal speech, while left frontal lesions are more often associated with apathy, depression, schizophrenic-like behaviours, and, especially with damage in medial areas, reduced speech, mutism, and catatonia (Gainotti 1972; Robinson and Downhill 1995).

Interestingly, as suggested by Kinsbourne (1982), the affectively charged approach-withdrawal distinction may relate to the lateralization of sensorimotor function and also to lateralization of higher cognitive functions including focal attention. To appreciate our interpretation of Kinsbourne's model, it is important to note that all vertebrates, and motile organisms in general, possess lateralized sensorimotor functions that support an essentially free range of motion during approach and withdrawal behaviours. The successful detection of predator or prey requires bilateral peripheral pre-attentive monitoring. Even simple organisms, whose behaviour is largely driven by external stimuli, must be able to represent an object in a specific location in space, which in humans is typically associated with right parietal regions. However, simple organisms may lack the cognitive resources to bring attention, anticipation, and many features of past experiences to bear on decision-making processes, which in humans are associated with the prefrontal regions and, perhaps, with left more than right prefrontal regions. Kinsbourne writes:

. . . behaviourally more elaborately equipped species can cost account their decision making more exactly. Having oriented to a stimulus perceived in meager detail in the peripheral sensory field, they bring focal attention to bear to make finer distinctions before committing themselves to action. As the object is scrutinized . . . two processes proceed in parallel: information is extracted serially, feature by feature; and concurrently, the location of each feature is registered on a centrally represented spatial framework, relative to the feature locations already represented (p.412).

Kinsbourne acknowledges that information processing with regard to feature extraction or directed focal attention is typically mediated by the left hemisphere, while relational information is typically lateralized to the right. (See also work by Arguin *et al*. 1993; Treisman and Gelade 1980.) Once focal attention begins, such as in approach behaviours, the need to maintain relational information between the organism and the object is relaxed because the need to effectively spatially orient to the object, by this point, is past. Likewise, withdrawal behaviours do not necessitate, or even allow for, the same kind of serial feature-extraction processing as approach behaviours. During avoidance behaviours, information about the relation between the organism and the object must be maintained over time and constantly updated for successful withdrawal to occur. Thus, we are drawn to the notion that the lateralized roles of prefrontal and posterior regions we have discussed in terms of symbolic and emotional processing have quite simple and fundamental phylogenetic roots.

## OUTLINE OF A NEUROPSYCHOLOGICAL ACCOUNT OF THEORY OF MIND

The neuropsychological literature on ToM has focused on two large regions of the human brain; the prefrontal cortex and the right hemisphere. Both areas have been implicated in reports on working memory, executive function, comprehension of discourse including humour, insight, and interpersonal skills, as well as ToM (e.g. Alexander *et al.* 1989; McDonald 1993). We believe that a large portion of the observations in the literature can be incorporated into a framework that includes, but is not limited to, ToM. We note also that many of the functional features that we have attributed to right hemisphere and prefrontal regions appear to be absent or diminished in autistic patients. The Wisconsin Card Sort, Tower of Hanoi, and other classic tests of prefrontal function have proven difficult for autistic patients, even for those who are able to pass first- and second-order false-belief tasks (Ozonoff *et al.* 1991; Russell *et al.* 1991; see in particular chapters by Perner and by Happé, this volume). Difficulty with the interpretation of non-literal speech is also symptomatic of autism and has been implicated as playing a role in their ToM deficits (Mitchell and Isaacs 1994). Language pragmatic factors have also been suggested to underlie normal children's and RHD patients' ToM deficits (Siegal *et al.* 1996).

The prefrontal regions are critical for ToM in that they support a person's ability to select from among representations that are divorced from sensory input. The literature identifies the prefrontal regions as relevant to working memory, aspects of attention, marking for salience, and selection. Social decision making, including ToM, rests on conflicting information that must be maintained and evaluated; the most relevant information must be highlighted, and the less relevant information must be inhibited, for successful interpretation to occur. The architectonic changes in the human brain over the course of recent evolution are such that the prefrontal cortex, with its extensive connections with both cortical and subcortical regions, is well suited for this role. These structural and functional attributes are entirely consistent with work by Damasio (1994) as well as others, and consistently point to the prefrontal regions' contributions to multi-step decision-making processes, and to how the right prefrontal regions may have a larger role for 'hot' or more affectively-laden ToM problems. (See Brothers and Ring 1992.) The many connections to and from the prefrontal areas make these regions the obvious choice for modulating information from different sources and modalities, and implicate their role in the winnowing and amplification of possible behavioural options.

The second core idea is that the right cerebral hemisphere is vital for humans' ability to maintain multiple representational sets. ToM, and competence in a host of other cognitive domains, depends crucially on a person's ability to refer to alternative, often conflicting, interpretations of the same topic. While the left hemisphere inhibits or dampens alternatives, the right hemisphere, we argue, is critical for people's ability to maintain access to alternative representations including those involved in figurative language, jokes, and stories as well as mental states. They may be weak semantic associates as examined by Beeman (1998), alternative readings of a punch line as examined by Shammi and Stuss (1999) or Bihrle *et al.* (1986), or different mental states as examined by Happé *et al.* (1999) or Winner *et al.* (1998).

Taken together, evidence from the many literatures addressed above presents a compelling case for lateralized information-processing biases. Much of the time, the mechanisms underlying our ToM, or our 'folk psychology' in general, appear to operate effortlessly; we simply 'know' what another is thinking, how he or she is feeling, and consequently, what that person is about to do. At other times, however, the process is not so automatic; we belabour possible scenarios, perhaps wondering what we would do if faced with the same situation, or perhaps relying on our past experience with that person or with people in general. As Dennett (1987, 1998) has repeatedly stressed, our ability to predict behaviour successfully through ToM (what he calls the 'intentional stance') relies on the *rationality* of behaviour. Our well-crafted tools of mental-state attribution would be rendered useless if behaviour did not, for the most part, fit our folk psychological stereotypes. Yet daily life presents us with a variety of social scenarios, many stereotypical, even script-like, and many of which are novel, and quite complicated indeed. Thus the neural substrates underlying the process of inferring the content of mental states, on our view, will vary depending on the demands of the task at hand. Novel tasks that require maintaining and updating relational and ambiguous information will necessitate right-hemisphere involvement, while requirements of the more routine, script-like ToM tasks may be processed largely by left hemisphere regions. Moreover, as suggested by Kinsbourne (1982), Deglin and Kinsbourne (1996), and Arguin *et al.* (1993), we can expect more left activation for tasks requiring focal attention or non-conflicting syllogistic reasoning.

As detailed in other chapters in this volume, research on the neural substrates underlying ToM has been informed by studies with lesion populations, abnormal phenotypes, and various *in vivo* imaging techniques. It is important to note that what ties these paradigms together in the present context is a functional analysis, which is extrinsic to the anatomy. The same problems may be solved using different neural mechanisms, even in the same brain, and a complex problem will have many component parts, each of which may implicate a different brain region or structure. Nonetheless, converging research from many areas has contributed to our under-standing of the working brain, and the heterogeneous processes that underlie our folk psychology.

In sum, though the literatures on RHD, frontal pathology, and activation in intact brains are at times difficult to interpret, some reliable generalizations emerge. We argue that the right hemisphere and prefrontal regions both are required for normal ToM; impairment in either can disrupt task performance. The importance of the right hemisphere's contribution to these aspects of social cognition seems to depend on several factors. The need to maintain alternative readings or tangential associations for longer periods of time, the novelty of the situation (that is, the absence of an appropriate decision-making algorithm), and the affective marking of an alternative are all features that will increase the potential contribution of the right hemisphere.

We note in conclusion some implications that invite empirical test. It should be possible to amplify right hemisphere contributions to ToM by using scenarios which require affective marking by the participant. Similarly, right hemisphere involvement should be heightened when an inference about a person's mental state requires integrating conflicting or ambiguous information, or information that requires detailed episodic memory. In contrast, right hemisphere involvement should be minimized when mental states can be inferred on the basis of highly salient, non contradictory information. In general, the right hemisphere helps preserve the raw material from which the prefrontal and limbic regions draw in decision-making processes. Theory of mind thus provides a rich framework for understanding social cognition from a neuroscientific perspective.

## Acknowledgements

The order of the first two authors is alphabetical and reflects equal contributions. Preparation of this chapter was supported in part by grants 2R01 NS 27894 and DC 00081.

We thank Daniel Dennett, Marcel Kinsbourne, Jeff Stewart, Andrew Stringfellow, and Chris Westbury for many suggestions and discussions that have improved this chapter greatly.

## Notes

1. Leslie changed his terminology from meta- to M-representation after Perner (1991) took issue with his usage. Perner prefers to save the term 'metarepresentation' to signify representations of representations *as* representations. The issue of what constitutes meta-representation is currently the centre of a lively and important debate. (See Sperber, forthcoming.)
2. Genuine communication in the Gricean sense requires at least three orders of intentionality, e.g. I *intend* you to *recognize* that I *intend* you to do *x*. While this argument has been extensively worked out, it is a less parsimonious treatment of intentional attribution than is generally seen in developmental psychology. (See also Bennett, 1976.)
3. The degree to which this marking necessitates a strong, episodic-like representation to be held on-line for comparison is an open question. Depending on the task, the mechanism may require far fewer processing demands, such as a subtle weight change or attention shift. Thus resulting as a functional equivalent of marking 'not-*x*' to the current context.

## REFERENCES

Alexander, M. P., Benson, F. D. and Stuss, D. T. (1989). Frontal lobes and language. *Brain and Language*, **37**, 656–91.

Arguin, M. Joanette, Y. and Cavanagh, P. (1993). Visual search for feature and conjunction targets with an attention deficit. *Journal of Cognitive Neuroscience*, **5**, 436–52.

Astington, J. W. and Gopnik, A. (1991). Theoretical explanations of children's understanding of the mind. *British Journal of Developmental Psychology*, **9**, 7–31.

Axelrod, R. and Hamilton, W. D. (1981). The evolution of cooperation. *Science*, **211**, 1390–6.

Baron-Cohen, S. (1995). *Mindblindness*. MIT Press, Cambridge, MA.

Baron-Cohen, S., Leslie, A. M. and Frith, U. (1985). Does the autistic child have a 'theory of mind'? *Cognition*, **21**, 37–46.

Baron-Cohen, S., Ring, H., Moriarty, J., Schmitz, B., Costa, D. and Ell, P. (1994). The brain basis of theory of mind: the role of the orbitofrontal region. *British Journal of Psychiatry*, **165**, 640–9.

Bartsch, K. and Wellman, H. M. (1989). Young children's attribution of action to beliefs and desires. *Child Development*, **60**, 946–64.

Bartsch, K. and Wellman, H. M. (1995). *Children talk about the mind*. Oxford University Press, New York.

Beeman, M. (1993). Semantic processing in the right hemisphere may contribute to drawing inferences during comprehension. *Brain and Language*, **44**, 80–120.

Beeman, M. (1998). Coarse semantic coding and discourse comprehension. In *Right hemisphere language comprehension: perspectives from cognitive neuroscience*, (ed. M. Beeman and C. Chiarello) pp. 255–84. Lawrence Erlbaum Associates, Mahwah, NJ.

Beeman, M. and Chiarello, C. (1998). *Right hemisphere language comprehension: perspectives from cognitive neuroscience*. Lawrence Erlbaum, Mahwah, NJ.

Beeman, M., Friedman, R. B., Grafman, J. and Perez, E. (1994). Summation priming and coarse semantic coding in the right hemisphere. *Journal of Cognitive Neuroscience*, **6**, 26–45.

Bennett, J. (1976). *Linguistic Behavior*. Cambridge University Press.

Bennett, J. (1978). Some remarks about concepts. *The Behavioral and Brain Sciences*, **1**, 557–60.

Benowitz, L. I., Moya, K. L. and Levine, D. N. (1990). Impaired verbal reasoning and constructional apraxia in subjects with right hemisphere damage. *Neuropsychologia*, **28**, 231–41.

Best, C. T. (1988). The emergence of cerebral asymmetries in early human development: a literature review and a neuroembryological model. In *Brain lateralization in children: developmental implications*, (ed. D. L. Molfese and S. J. Segalowitz), pp. 5–34. Guilford Press, New York.

Bihrle, A. M., Brownell, H. H., Powelson, J. A. and Gardner, H. (1986). Comprehension of humorous and non-humorous materials by left and right brain damaged patients. *Brain and Cognition*, **5**, 399–412.

Bottini, G., Corcoran, R., Sterzi, R., Paulesu, E., Schenone, P., Scarpa, P., Frackowiak, R. S. and Frith, C. D. (1994). The role of the right hemisphere in the interpretation of figurative aspects of language: a positron emission tomography activation study. *Brain*, **117**, 1241–53.

Brainerd, C. J., Reyna, V. F. and Kneer, R. (1995). False-recognition reversal: when similarity is distinctive. *Journal of Memory and Language*, **34**, 157–85.

Brothers, L. and Ring, B. (1992). A neuroethological framework for the representation of minds. *Journal of Cognitive Neuroscience*, **4**, 107–18.

Brownell, H. H. and Gardner, H. (1988). Neuropsychological insights into humour. In *Laughing matters: a serious look at humour*, (ed. J. Durant and J. Miller), pp. 17–34. Longman Technical, London.

Brownell, H. H. and Martino, G. (1998). Deficits in inference and social cognition: the effects of right hemisphere brain damage on discourse. In *Right hemisphere language comprehension: perspectives from cognitive neuroscience*, (ed. M. Beeman and C. Chiarello), pp. 309–28. Erlbaum, Mahwah, NJ.

Brownell, H. H., Michel, D., Powelson, J. and Gardner, H. (1983). Surprise but not coherence: sensitivity to verbal humor in right-hemisphere patients. *Brain and Language*, **18**, 20–7.

Brownell, H. H., Potter, H. H., Michelow, D. and Gardner, H. (1984). Sensitivity to lexical denotation and connotation in brain-damaged patients: a double dissociation? *Brain and Language*, **22**, 253–65.

Brownell, H., Potter, H. H., Birhle, A. M. and Gardner, H. (1986). Inference deficits in right brain damaged patients. *Brain and Language*, **27**, 310–21.

Brownell, H. H., Simpson, T. L., Bihrle, A. M., Potter, H. H. and Gardner, H. (1990). Appreciation of metaphoric alternative word meanings by left and right brain-damaged patients. *Neuropsychologia*, **28**, 375–83.

Brownell, H. H., Carroll, J. J., Rehak, A. and Wingfield, A. (1992). The use of pronoun anaphora and speaker mood in the interpretation of conversational utterances by right hemisphere brain-damaged patients. *Brain and Language*, **43**, 121–47.

Brownell, H., Gardner, H., Prather, P. and Martino, G. (1995). Language, communication and the right hemisphere. In *Handbook of neurological speech and language disorders*, (ed. H. S. Kirshner), pp. 325–49. Marcel Dekker, Inc., New York.

Brownell, H., Pincus, D., Blum, A., Rehak, A. and Winner, E. (1997). The effects of right-hemisphere brain damage on patients' use of terms of personal reference. *Brain and Language*, **57**, 60–79.

Burgess, C. and Chiarello, C. (1996). Neurocognitive mechanisms underlying metaphor comprehension and other figurative language. *Metaphor and Symbolic Activity*, **111**, 67–84.

Burgess, C. and Simpson, G. B. (1988). Cerebral hemispheric mechanisms in the retrieval of ambiguous word meanings. *Brain and Language*, **33**, 86–103.

Byrne, R. and Whiten, A. (1988). The Machiavellian intelligence hypotheses: editorial. In *Machiavellian intelligence: social expertise and the evolution of intellect in monkeys, apes and humans*, (ed. R. Byrne and A. Whiten) pp. 1–9. Clarendon Press, Oxford.

Canavan, A., Janota, I. and Schura, P. H. (1985). Luria's frontal lobe syndrome: psychological and anatomical considerations. *Journal of Neurology, Neurosurgery and Psychiatry*, **48**, 1049–53.

Chance, M. R. A. and Mead, A. P. (1953). Social behavior and primate evolution. *Symposia of the Society for Experimental Biology*, 7, 395–439.

Chiarello, C. (1998). On codes of meaning and the meaning of codes: semantic access and retrieval within and between hemispheres. In *Right hemisphere language comprehension: perspectives from cognitive neuroscience*, (ed. M. Beeman and C. Chiarello), pp. 141–160. Lawrence Erlbaum Associates, Mahwah, NJ.

Clark, A. (1996) *Being there: putting brain, body and world back together again*. MIT Press, Cambridge, MA.

Code, C. (1987). *Language, aphasia and the right hemisphere*. Wiley, New York.

Conway, M. A. and Rubin, D. C. (1993). The structure of autobiographical memory. In *Theories of memory*, (ed. A. F. Collins, S. E. Gathercole, M. A. Conway and P. E. Morris) pp. 103–37. Lawrence Erlbaum, Hillsdale, NJ.

Damasio, A. R. (1989). The brain binds entities and events by multiregional activation from convergence zones. *Neural Computation*, **1**, 123–32.

Damasio, A. R. (1994). *Descartes' error: emotion, reason and the human brain*. Grosset/Putnam, New York.

Davidson, R. J. (1992). Anterior cerebral asymmetry and the nature of emotion. *Brain and Cognition*, **20**, 125–51.

Davidson, R., Gray, J., Le Doux, J., Levenson, R., Panksepp, J. and Ekman, P. (1994). Is there emotion-specific physiology? In *The nature of emotion: fundamental questions*, (ed. P. Ekman and R. Davidson), pp. 235–62. Oxford University Press, New York.

Dawkins, R. and Krebs, J. R. (1978). Animal signals: information or manipulation? In *Behavioral ecology: an evolutionary approach*, (ed. J. R. Krebs and N. B. Davies), pp. 282–314. Blackwell, Oxford.

Deacon, T. W. (1997). *The symbolic species: the co-evolution of language and the brain.* W. W. Norton and Company, New York.

Deglin, V. L. and Kinsbourne, M. (1996) Divergent thinking styles of the hemispheres: how syllogisms are solved during transitory hemisphere suppression. *Brain and Cognition*, **31**, 285–307.

Dennett, D. C. (1978). Beliefs about beliefs. *The Behavioral and Brain Sciences*, **1**, 568–70.

Dennett, D. C. (1987). *The intentional stance.* MIT Press, Cambridge, MA.

Dennett, D. C. (1998). *Brainchildren: essays on designing minds.* MIT Press, Cambridge, MA.

Flavell, J. H., Flavell, E. R., Green, F. L. and Moses, L. J. (1990). Young children's understanding of fact beliefs versus value beliefs. *Child Development*, **61**, 915–28.

Fletcher, P. C., Happé, F., Frith, U., Baker, S. C., Dolan, R., Frackowiak, R. S. J. and Frith, C. (1995). Other minds and the brain: a functional imaging study of theory of mind in story comprehension. *Cognition*, **57**, 109–28.

Fodor, J. (1992). A theory of the child's theory of mind. *Cognition*, **44**, 283–96.

Gainotti, G. (1972). Emotional behavior and hemisphere side of lesion. *Cortex*, **8**, 41–55.

Galaburda, A. (1995). Anatomic basis of cerebral dominance. In *Brain asymmetry*, (ed. R. J. Davidson and K. Hughdahl), pp. 51–73. MIT Press, Cambridge, MA.

Gardner, H., Brownell, H., Wapner, W. and Michelow, D. (1983). Missing the point: the role of the right hemisphere in the processing of complex linguistic materials. In *Cognitive processing in the right hemisphere*, (ed. E. Perecman), pp. 169–91. Academic Press, New York.

Goel, V., Grafman, J., Sadato, N. and Hallett, M. (1995). Modeling other minds. *NeuroReport*, **6**, 1741–6.

Goldman-Rakic, P. S. (1987). Circuitry of primate prefrontal cortex and regulation of behavior by representational memory. In *Handbook of physiology: the nervous system*, Vol. 5, (ed. F. Plum), pp. 373–417. American Physiological Society, Bethesda, MD.

Gray, J. A. (1994). Three fundamental emotion systems. In *The nature of emotion: fundamental questions*, (ed. P. Ekman and R. J. Davidson), pp. 243–7. Oxford University Press, New York.

Grice, H. P. (1975). Logic and conversation. In *Syntax and semantics*, Vol. 3: Speech acts, pp. 41–58. Seminar Press, New York.

Gur, I. K., Packer, J. P., Hungerbuhler, J. P., Reivich, M., Orbist, W. D., Amarnek, W. S. and Sackheim, H. A. (1980). Differences in the distribution of gray and white matter in human cerebral hemispheres. *Science*, **207**, 1226–8.

Happé, F., Brownell, H. and Winner, E. (1999). Acquired theory of mind impairments following right hemisphere stroke. *Cognition*, **70**, 211–40.

Harman, G. (1978). Studying the chimpanzee's theory of mind. *The Behavioral and Brain Sciences*, **1**, 591.

Hintzman, D. L. and Curran, T. (1994). Retrieval dynamics of recognition and frequency judgements: evidence for separate processes of familiarity and recall. *Journal of Memory and Language*, **33**, 1–18.

Humphrey, N. (1976). The social function of the intellect. In *Growing points in ethology*, (ed. P. P. G. Bateson and R. A. Hinde) pp. 303–17. Cambridge University Press.

Jacobsen, C. (1936). Studies of cerebral functions in primates. *Comparative Psychology Monographs*, **13**, 1–68.

Joanette, Y., Goulet, P. and Hannequin, D. (1990). *Right hemisphere and verbal communication.* Springer–Verlag, New York.

Jolly, A. (1966). Lemur social behaviour and primate intelligence. *Science*, **153**, 501–6.

Joseph, R. (1996). *Neuropsychiatry, neuropsychology and clinical neuroscience: emotion, evolution, cognition, language, memory, brain damage and abnormal behavior*, (2nd edn). Williams and Wilkins Co., Baltimore, MD.

Kalin, N. H., Shelton, S. E., Rickman, M. and Davidson, R. (1998). Individual differences in freezing and cortisol in infant and mother rhesus monkey. *Behavioral Neuroscience*, **112**, 251–4.

Kapur, N., Friston, K. J., Young, A. and Frith, C. D. (1995) Activation of human hippocampal formation during memory of faces: a PET study. *Cortex*, **31**, 99–108.

Kertesz, A., Polk, M., Black, S. E. and Howell, J. A. (1990). Sex, handedness and the morphometry of cerebral asymmetries on magnetic resonance imaging. *Brain Research*, **530**, 40–8.

Kimura, D. (1967). Functional asymmetry of the brain in dichotic listening. *Cortex*, **3**, 163–8.

Kimura, D. (1993). *Neuromotor mechanisms in human communication*. Oxford University Press, New York.

Kinsbourne, M. (1982). Hemispheric specialization and the growth of human understanding. *American Psychologist*, **37**, 411–20.

Kolb, B. and Wishaw, I. Q. (1996). *Fundamentals of human neuropsychology*, (4th edn). W. H. Freeman, New York.

Krebs, J. R. and Dawkins, R. (1984). Animal signals: mind reading and manipulation. In *Behavioural ecology: an evolutionary approach*, (ed. J. R. Krebs and R. Dawkins), pp. 380–401. Blackwell.

Kummer, H. (1968). *Social organization of hamadryas baboons*. University of Chicago Press.

Leonard, C. L., Waters, G. S. and Caplan, D. (1997). The use of contextual information by right brain-damaged individuals in the resolution of ambiguous pronouns. *Brain and Language*, **57**, 309–42.

Leslie, A. M. (1987). Pretense and representation: the origins of 'theory of mind'. *Psychological Review*, **94**, 412–26.

Leslie, A. (1994). ToMM, ToBy and agency: core architecture and domain specificity. In *Mapping the mind: domain specificity in cognition and culture*, (ed. L. Hirschfeld and S. Gelman), pp. 119–48. Cambridge University Press, New York.

Leslie, A. M. and Happé, F. (1989). Autism and ostensive communication: the relevance of metarepresentation. *Development and Psychopathology*, **1**, 205–12.

Leslie, A. M. and Roth, D. (1993). What autism teaches us about metarepresentation. In *Understanding other minds: perspectives from autism*, (ed. S. Baron-Cohen, H. Tager-Flusberg and D. Cohen) pp. 83–111. Oxford University Press, New York.

Luria, A. R. (1973). The frontal lobes and the regulation of behavior. In *Psychophysiology of the frontal lobes*, (ed. K. H. Pribram and A. R. Luria), pp. 3–26. Academic Press, New York.

Mattingly, I. and Studdert-Kennedy, M. (1991). *Modularity and the motor theory of speech perception*. Erlbaum, Hillsdale, NJ.

McDonald, S. (1993). Viewing the brain sideways? Frontal versus right hemisphere explanations of non-aphasic language disorders. *Aphasiology*, **7**, 535–49.

Milner, B., Corsi, P. and Leonard, G. (1991). Frontal lobe contributions to recency judgements. *Neuropsychology*, **29**, 601–18.

Mishkin, M. and Manning, F. (1978). Nonspatial memory after selective prefrontal lesions in monkeys. *Brain Research*, **143**, 313–23.

Mitchell, P. and Isaacs, J. E. (1994). Understanding of verbal representation in children with autism: the case of referential opacity. *British Journal of Developmental Psychology*, **12**, 439–54.

Moses, L. J. (1990). Young children's understanding of intention and belief. Unpublished doctoral dissertation. Stanford University.

Myers, P. S. (1999). *Right hemisphere damage: disorders of communication and cognition*. Singular Publishing Group, San Diego.

Myers, P. S. and Linebaugh, C. W. (1981). Comprehension of idiomatic expressions by right-hemisphere damaged adults. In *Clinical aphasiology: conference proceedings*, (ed. R. H. Brookshire), pp. 254–61. BRK Publishers, Minneapolis.

Nakagawa, A. (1991). Role of anterior and posterior attention networks in hemispheric asymmetries during lexical decisions. *Journal of Cognitive Neuroscience*, **3**, 315–21.

Neely, J. H. (1991). Semantic priming effects in visual word recognition: a selective review of current findings and theories. In *Basic processes in reading: visual word recognition*, (ed. D. Besner and G. Humphreys), pp. 264–336. Lawrence Erlbaum, Hillsdale, NJ.

Ozonoff, S., Pennington, B. F. and Rogers (1991). Executive function deficits in high-functioning autistic individuals: relationship to theory of mind. *Journal of Child Psychology and Psychiatry*, **32**, 1081–105.

Pandya, D. and Barnes, C. (1987). Architecture and connections of the frontal lobe. In *The frontal lobes revisited*, (ed. E. Perecman), pp. 41–72. IRBN Press, New York.

Passingham, R. E. (1985). Memory of monkeys (Macaca mulatta) with lesions in prefrontal cortex. *Behavioral Neuroscience*, **99**, 3–21.

Perner, J. (1991). *Understanding the representational mind*. MIT Press, Cambridge, MA.

Perner, J., Leekam, S. R. and Wimmer, H. (1987). Three-year-olds' difficulty with false belief. *British Journal of Developmental Psychology*, **5**, 125–37.

Petrides, M. (1986). The effect of periarcuate lesions in the monkey on the performance of symmetrically and asymmetrically reinforced visual and auditory go, no-go tasks. *Journal of Neuroscience*, **6**, 2054–63.

Premack, D. (1990). The infant's theory of self-propelled objects. *Cognition*, **36**, 1–16.

Premack, D. and Woodruff, G. (1978). Does the chimpanzee have a theory of mind? *The Behavioral and Brain Sciences*, **1**, 515–26.

Pylyshyn, Z. W. (1978). When is attribution of beliefs justified? *The Behavioral and Brain Sciences*, **1**, 592–3.

Robinson, R. G. and Downhill, J. F. (1995). Lateralization of psychopathology in response to focal brain injury. In *Brain asymmetry*, (ed. R. J. Davidson and K. Hugdahl), pp. 693–711. MIT Press, Cambridge, MA.

Russell, J., Mauthner, N., Sharpe, S. and Tidswell, T. (1991). The 'windows task' as a measure of strategic deception in preschoolers and autistic subjects. *British Journal of Developmental Psychology*, **9**, 331–50.

Sackheim, H., Greenberg, M. S., Weiman, A. L., Gur, R. C., Hungerbuhler, J. P. and Geshwind, N. (1982). Hemispheric asymmetry in the expression of positive and negative emotions: neurological evidence. *Archives of Neurology*, **39**, 210–8.

Schacter, D. L., Curran, T., Galluccio, L., Milberg, W. P. and Bates, J. (1996). False recognition and the right frontal lobe: a case study. *Neurospsycholgia*, **34**, 793–808.

Semmes, J. (1968). Hemispheric specialization: a possible clue to mechanism. *Neuropsycholgia*, **6**, 11–26.

Shallice, T. and Burgess, P. (1991). Higher-order cognitive impairments and frontal lobe lesions in man. In *Frontal lobe function and dysfunction*, (ed. H. S. Levin, H. M. Eisenberg and A. L. Benton), pp. 125–38. Oxford University Press, New York.

Shammi, P. and Stuss, D. T. (1999). Humour Appreciation: a role of the right frontal lobe. *Brain*, **122**, 657–66.

Shimamura, A. P. (1995). Memory and frontal lobe function. In *The cognitive neurosciences*, (ed. M. Gazzaniga) pp. 803–13. MIT Press, Cambridge, MA.

Siegal, M., Carrington, J. and Radel, M. (1996). Theory of mind and pragmatic understanding following right hemisphere damage. *Brain and Language*, **53**, 40–50.

Sperber, D. (ed.). *Metarepresentation: proceedings of the tenth Vancouver Cognitive Science Conference*. Oxford University Press, New York. (Forthcoming.)

Springer, S. and Deutsch, G. (1998). *Left brain, right brain: perspectives from cognitive neuroscience*, (5th edn). W. H. Freeman and Company, New York.

Stone, V., Baron-Cohen, S. and Knight, R. (1998). Frontal lobe contributions to theory of mind. *Journal of Cognitive Neuroscience*, **10**, 640–56.

Sullivan, K. and Winner, E. (1991). When three-year-olds understand ignorance, false belief and representational change. *British Journal of Developmental Psychology*, **9**, 159–71.

Sutton, S. K. and Davidson, R. J. (1997). Prefrontal brain asymmetry: a biological substrate of the behavioral approach and inhibition systems. *Psychological Science*, **8**, 204–10.

Tompkins, C. A. (1994). *Right hemisphere communication disorders*. Singular Publishing Group, San Diego.

Tompkins, C. A., Baumgaertner, A., Lehman, M. T. and Fossett, T. R. D. (1997). Suppression and discourse comprehension in right brain-damaged adults: a preliminary report. *Aphasiology*, **11**, 505–19.

Treisman, A. and Gelade, G. (1980). A feature integration theory of attention. *Cognitive Psychology*, **12**, 97–136.

Trivers, R. (1971). The evolution of reciprocal altruism. *Quarterly Review of Biology*, **46**, 35–57.

Tulving, E., Kapur, S., Craik, F. I. M., Moscovitch, M. and Houle, S. (1994). Hemispheric encoding/retrieval asymmetry in episodic memory: positron emission tomography findings. *Proceedings of the National Academy of Sciences*, **9**, 2016–20.

VanLancker, D. R. and Kempler, D. (1987). Comprehension of familiar phrases by left but not by right hemisphere damaged patients. *Brain and Language*, **32**, 265–77.

Warburton, E., Wise, R. J., Price, C. J., Weiller, C., Hadar, U., Ramsay, S. and Frackowiak, R. S. (1996). Noun and verb retrieval by normal subjects: studies with PET. *Brain*, **119**, 157–79.

Wellman, H. and Bartsch, K. (1988). Young children's reasoning about beliefs. *Cognition*, **30**, 239–77.

Whiten, A. (1996). When does smart behaviour-reading become mind-reading? In *Theories of theories of mind*, (ed. P. Carruthers and P. K. Smith), pp. 277–92. Cambridge University Press.

Wimmer, H. and Perner, J. (1983). Beliefs about beliefs: representation and constraining function of wrong beliefs in young children's understanding of deception. *Cognition*, **13**, 103–28.

Winner, E. and Gardner, H. (1977). The comprehension of metaphor in brain damaged patients. *Brain*, **100**, 717–29.

Winner, E., Brownell, H., Happé, F., Blum, A. and Pincus, D. (1998). Distinguishing lies from jokes: theory of mind deficits and discourse interpretation in right hemisphere brain-damaged patients. *Brain and Language*, **62**, 89–106.

Zaitchik, D. (1991) Is only seeing really believing? Sources of the true belief in the false belief task. *Cognitive Development*, **62**, 91–103.

# 14

# The physiological basis of theory of mind: functional neuroimaging studies

## CHRIS FRITH AND UTA FRITH

---

## INTRODUCTION

There are several chapters in this book which address theory of mind and the brain. There are other chapters which deal in depth with other topics we touch on here, especially the distinctions between behaviour which presupposes theory of mind and superficially similar behaviour which does not. Finally, elsewhere in this volume there are extensive discussions about the terms 'theory of mind', 'mentalising' and 'mind-blindness'. We have decided to include some observations on these topics which are highly relevant to the design and interpretation of neuroimaging studies. We believe that such studies would be uninterpretable or misleading without being set in the context of the broader research questions.

## THREE USES OF THE TERM 'THEORY OF MIND'

The term 'theory of mind' has become a useful, but often misleading, shorthand. As in Premack and Woodruff (1978), the first paper on this topic, the term refers to the attribution of mental states and the prediction of other people's behaviour on the basis of their mental states. This is a pervasive human tendency. People implicitly assume that other people's behaviour can be predicted on the basis of their knowledge, beliefs and, desires, rather than on the basis of real states of affairs in the world (Leslie 1987). This assumption does not depend upon any particular theory of how to interpret the behaviour of others.

There is another way of using the term theory of mind: here it refers to an implicit, but potentially conscious, everyday theory. Just like any other theory, theory of mind guides interpretation of often noisy and distorted input in making best guesses and in going beyond the information given. Such a theory would be influenced by the social and cultural context of the individual. For instance, folk psychologies have very different and sometimes institutionalised views on social and psychological causes, and these profoundly affect the interpretation of everyday behaviour (Lillard 1997).

In this chapter we will use the term theory of mind (ToM for short) in a more restricted way, namely to refer to a specific cognitive mechanism that is a prerequisite for the attribution of mental states and a prerequisite (necessary, but not sufficient) for an implicitly held theory of mind. This 'mentalising mechanism' is presumed to be universally present in all human beings, but appears to be faulty to varying degrees in individuals with autism (Frith *et al.* 1991).

This chapter explores the physiological basis of such a mechanism in the brain. It appears, at least at first glance, that what the mechanism does is relevant to a very high level and characteristically human function, namely awareness of own and others' mental states, in other words, self-consciousness. If so, then it might be difficult to locate this function in the animal brain: experimental lesion studies would be ruled out. We have to rely on studies of patients who show impairments in mentalising and on brain imaging studies of normal volunteers.

## THEORY OF MIND AND EVOLUTION

Studies of monkeys, apes, and humans suggest that only humans, and possibly some apes, have theory of mind abilities, while monkeys do not (Cheney and Seyfarth 1990; Heyes 1998). It is therefore reasonable to assume that new brain regions or systems have evolved, which underpin these abilities. Studies of people with autism also suggest that there is a circumscribed brain system associated with theory of mind abilities. These studies, especially those of autistic people with normal intelligence, show that theory of mind abilities can be impaired while other aspects of social cognition remain intact (e.g. Baron-Cohen *et al.* 1997).

A complete understanding of theory of mind in the brain requires that we should also understand the roots of theory of mind and the precursor abilities from which it evolved. There seem to be at least two distinct possibilities. First, mentalising may be a domain-specific ability. In this case mentalising has evolved from more basic, but specialised forms of social cognition. Second, theory of mind may not be domain-specific, but may depend on the appearance of a special form of representation (e.g. metarepresentation) which is necessary for representing mental states, but can be used outside the social domain. In this case ToM has evolved in the context of more general problem-solving abilities.

Evidence from autism can be seen to support both of these possibilities. On the one hand there is the observation that people with autism can perform well on a false photograph task while at the same time being impaired on a false-belief task (Leekam and Perner 1991; Leslie and Thaiss 1992). This suggests that ToM is domain-specific since these two tasks appear to be formally identical. On the other hand, the observation that even high-functioning people with autism perform badly on executive tasks suggests that difficulties with ToM tasks may reflect a more general difficulty with processing certain types of problem (Russell 1998).

## SOCIAL INTERACTION WITH AND WITHOUT THEORY OF MIND

Mentalising ability plays a major role in human social interactions. Nevertheless complex social interactions can occur in the absence of theory of mind. For example, monkeys such as the vervet choose allies on the basis of the rank and power that they bring to the alliance; they will attempt to 'reconcile' conflicts by grooming and they will redirect aggression towards a subordinate who is the kin of their persecutor (see Byrne 1998 for a review). Yet intensive studies of these monkeys have provided no evidence that they compute mental states (Cheney and Seyfarth 1990). Thus it is important to distinguish between theory of mind and other aspects of social cognition. In this chapter we shall try to distinguish between brain regions implicated in theory of mind and those implicated in social cognition more generally.

## FINE CUTS METHODOLOGY

The distinction between intact and impaired social and communication abilities in autism has led to a categorisation of behaviours that do and do not necessitate mentalising ability (Frith and Happé 1994; Happé and Frith 1995, 1996). The possibility of making a fine cut between otherwise very similar behaviours is attractive as it suggests that 'nature is being carved at its joints'. Normal development is mostly a seamless and apparently homogeneous progress. Increases in different skills go together, such as learning to talk and to comprehend, learning to read and to write, learning to solve verbal reasoning problems, and learning to navigate in space. And yet, in all these examples, it is well known that individual differences exist and that there can be discrepant abilities in any combination of these skills. To name but one example, there are hopeless spatial navigators who are excellent verbal problem solvers. There are pairs of abilities that are closer still and yet dissociations can be observed. In the case of autism, one striking example is the ability to use instrumental gestures coexisting with an inability to use expressive gestures (Attwood *et al.* 1988).

Autism provides a systematic way of contrasting types of social and communicative behaviour that normally develop together, and reveal very different cognitive prerequisites for each. A review of the experimental literature on ToM deficits in autism suggests that there are distinct deficits in those aspects of social communication that are dependent on mentalising. In contrast there are often assets in other aspects that appear to be independent of mentalising. Table 14.1 shows examples of such assets and deficits.

In real life behaviour too, contrasts can be found between assets and deficits that follow the same fault line. In interview based studies (Fombonne *et al.* 1994; Frith *et al.* 1994) informants were asked about examples of everyday behaviour in individuals with autism. A distinction could be made between 'socially active' behaviour, not requiring mentalising ability, and 'socially interactive' behaviour, requiring the ability to mentalise. Examples are shown in Table 14.2.

There were consistent deficits in so-called interactive behaviour, which was often reported as absent or rare. This was in contrast to socially active behaviour which was reported as present to varying degrees. The amount of interactive behaviour shown was related to performance on standard false-belief tasks. Passing false-belief tasks was associated with a higher frequency of socially interactive behaviours. Such an association was also found by Hughes *et al.* (1994) in a sample of young French children with autism.

**Table 14.1.** Assets and deficits in social communication in autism

| Assets | Deficits |
| --- | --- |
| Understanding false pictures, photographs (Charman and Baron-Cohen 1992; Leekham and Perner 1991; Leslie and Thaiss 1992) | vs. false beliefs |
| Understanding behavioural picture sequences using descriptive language (Baron-Cohen *et al.* 1986) | vs. mentalistic picture sequences vs. mental state language |
| Using instrumental gestures (Attwood *et al.* 1988) | vs. expressive gestures |
| Understanding see (Perner *et al.* 1989) | vs. know |
| Protoimperative pointing (Baron-Cohen 1989) | vs. protodeclarative pointing |
| Understanding occluded objects (Baron-Cohen 1992) | vs. occluded information |
| Recognising happiness, sadness (Baron-Cohen *et al.* 1993) | vs. surprise |
| Engaging in sabotage (Sodian and Frith 1992) | vs. deception |
| Understanding literal expressions (Happé 1993) | vs. metaphorical expressions |
| Enjoying mastery of a skill (Capps *et al.* 1996) | vs. taking pride in mastery |

**Table 14.2.** Examples of everyday behaviour reported in structured interviews with informants (Frith *et al.* 1994)

| Behaviour not requiring mentalising usually rated as present in autism | Behaviour requiring mentalising usually rated as absent in autism |
| --- | --- |
| Showing desire to please | Choosing appropriate gifts |
| Taking turns in conversation | Responding to hints in conversation |
| Engaging in fixed small talk | Flexible small talk |
| Delivering message | Supplying missing information |
| Using person as tool | Using person as recipient of information |
| Elicited play | Spontaneous pretend play |
| Giving honest answer to question | Keeping secrets and confidences |
| Reading up on facts | Enjoying fiction |
| Manipulating behaviour | Manipulating attitudes |
| Forming obsessive attachments | Reciprocal friendships/relationships |

THEORY OF MIND IN THE BRAIN

What regions of the brain should we suppose to be particularly involved in mentalising? Autism research over the last ten to fifteen years has strengthened the hypothesis that the mentalising function has an innate component which is modular and which can be damaged (see other chapters). What is the neural substrate of this component? How does damage affect it? The tried and trusted approaches to this sort of question are unfortunately inappropriate for this purpose. Animal models where lesions and their repair can be controlled experimentally are inappropriate because mentalising appears to be a specifically human accomplishment. Although it is obvious that any specifically human brain function has to have evolved from some pre-existing function, no plausible precursor has been proposed as yet.

**Social cognition**

What functions—and what brain regions—would it be promising to look at? General social and emotional behaviour seems a good starting point. However, the fine cuts analysis gives ample demonstration that not all of this behaviour necessitates ToM. A more focused explanation of social behaviour that does necessitate mentalising would seem to be a more promising strategy. Nevertheless, it is true that individuals with autism often also show impoverished general social affiliative behaviour. Klin *et al.* (1992), in particular, have argued that simple social behaviour without a mentalising component is impaired in children with autism, and this is discernible early in childhood, well before even normally-developing children show unequivocal evidence of attributing beliefs. Brain regions that subserve social behaviour may therefore be a reasonable starting point. Brothers (1990) drew together data from a range of animal studies which showed overlapping evidence for a social brain. This social brain involves primarily the limbic system (in particular the amygdala, the orbital frontal cortex, and the anterior cingulate cortex) and the superior temporal cortex. The limbic system undoubtedly has a major role in the experience and expression of emotion. Lesions to parts of this system in monkeys lead to major impairments of social interaction (Kling and Brothers 1992; Raleigh and Stelkis 1981). Superior temporal cortex contains cells which are specifically responsive to items that are important in social interactions such as faces and facial expressions. Bilateral removal of the temporal lobe, including the amygdala and most of the hippocampus produces the Kluver–Bucy syndrome which has long been considered to have certain similarities with autism (e.g. Hetzler and Griffin 1981). For instance, lesioned monkeys with this syndrome show unusual movement patterns, absence of vocalisations in response to other monkeys, and absence of emotional behaviour.

If a region that is part of the social brain is the locus of the hypothetical mentalising component of theory of mind, which region, among the many, is this likely to be? Bachevalier and Merjanian (1993) described impairments in the social behaviour of rhesus monkeys who were lesioned as infants in the amygdaloid and hippocampal cortex. These monkeys behaved in a manner that was suggestive of social inactivity and lack of social interest. Their peers avoided interacting with them, while they themselves showed much aimless activity. Does this picture resemble autism? Not necessarily, according to our previous analysis. But, given Klin *et al.*'s (1992) study, impairment on social behaviour which does not require ToM ability may capture an important aspect of the development of autism.

One behaviour that is seen as emerging very early from a mentalising capacity is joint attention (Mundy and Sigman 1989). A convincing demonstration of theory of mind ability in a non-human primate would be joint attention (Gomez 1996). It follows that, if a lesion could be identified that abolished joint attention, then this might enable the systematic search for the anatomical basis of theory of mind capacity. This is yet to be done. Likewise no brain imaging study of joint attention in humans exists as yet.

## Language

Like theory of mind, language in its fullest manifestation is observed only in humans. The brain basis of language has been studied extensively in patients with lesions and using brain imaging. From these studies we know that language depends largely on an extended brain system which is concentrated in the left hemisphere in regions of the frontal, temporal, and parietal cortex around the sylvian fissure. We also know that language involves many components which, at least in the adult, can be damaged independently. They are associated with discrete areas within the language system (McCarthy and Warrington 1990, chapters 6–9). The major traditional anatomical components are Broca's area (inferior frontal gyrus; pars opercularis and pars triangularis, Brodmann's areas 44 and 45) and Wernicke's area (regions of the temporal and parietal cortex around the sylvian fissure, Brodmann's areas 21, 22, and 40). Broca's area is part of the premotor system and is concerned with speech production (and possibly grammar), while Wernicke's area is concerned with speech perception including phonological analysis, and aspects of the meaning of heard words. These are all components of language which are necessary for what has been called 'coded communication' (as opposed to 'ostensive–inferential' communication; Sperber and Wilson 1986). With such components it is possible to name objects, to echo words, and to convert print to sound. Even when other aspects of communication are severely impaired, people with autism can be quite successful at precisely these aspects of language. They can show echolalia, hyperlexia, and naming abilities.

The language components supported by the traditional language area of the brain are not sufficient for truly human ostensive-inferential communication, in which ideas and intentions are transferred between speakers. This aspect of communication is reflected in pragmatics and is intimately connected with theory of mind. For example, Happé (1993) has shown that the ability to understand metaphors is related to the ability to pass explicit theory of mind tasks. The brain basis of this aspect of language is far less well understood.

Right hemisphere patients show pragmatic difficulties in verbal and non-verbal communication. They are said not to understand humour, metaphors, or irony. All of this points to theory of mind problems. They show some impairments in social communication which are strongly reminiscent of similar failure in high-functioning individuals with autism. In particular, right hemisphere patients fail to understand the following: metaphorical remarks (Brownell *et al.* 1990), inferred meaning (Bryan 1988), nonconventional meaning (Hirst *et al.* 1984), indirectly stated material (Brookshire and Nicholas 1984), indirect requests (Foldi 1987; Weylman *et al.* 1989), and the emotional-prosodic quality of utterances (Ross 1981). Despite the common report of social and emotional problems following right hemisphere damage (e.g. in two cases reported by Ross and Mesulam 1979), these patients' problems with pragmatics have not been investigated in terms of a breakdown of the understanding of speakers' intentions. (But see Brownell *et al.*, Chapter 13, this volume).

We are aware of only one brain imaging study of pragmatic aspects of language. Bottini *et al.* (1994) scanned volunteers while they checked the plausibility of literal or metaphorical sentences, with presentation of strings of unrelated words as a control condition. In comparison with the word strings the sentences activated the traditional language areas in the left hemisphere extending to the temporal pole and some prefrontal areas. In comparison with the literal sentences, the extra areas activated by the metaphorical sentences were confined to the right hemisphere and some medial areas. Areas on the right included the middle temporal gyrus and right DLPFC, while the medial areas included the precuneus and the anterior cingulate cortex.

## Gestures

A limited form of social communication is also possible with gestures using a system that is quite independent of that underlying language. Gestures frequently involve limb movements such as shrugs or beckoning movements. Evidence of the independence of gestures from language comes from observations of brain-damaged patients. After dominant hemisphere damage a patient may lose the use of language while still being able to use gestures. This is particularly striking in the deaf who normally use limb movements for language (sign language) as well as for gestures. Even though the output system is the same in both cases, damage to the dominant hemisphere can eliminate the use of limb movements for language while still allowing the same limb movements for gestures (Poizner *et al.* 1984).

The apraxia observed in some brain-damaged patients after damage to the frontal or parietal lobes is a form of impairment of gesture (see, for example, Halsband 1998). However, the term often refers to the ability to make limb movements when using objects or when miming the use of objects. While this overlaps with our interest, studies of apraxia used in this sense do not directly concern communicative gestures. There have been a number of imaging studies in which normal volunteers watch limb movements in order to identify or imitate them (Grèzes *et al.* 1998). These studies also activate regions in the frontal and parietal cortex. However, here also, the limb movements employed have not been specifically associated with communication. Specific studies of communicative gestures have yet to be performed.

Studies of the use of gesture by autistic people suggest that it is possible to distinguish gestures that involve mentalising from those that do not. Autistic people use 'instrumental' gestures (signs indicating commands such as, 'come here', 'go away', 'give me food') normally. However, they fail to use gestures aimed at changing the mental state of the observer, e.g., gestures indicating compassion or triumph (Attwood *et al.* 1988). They also use protoimperative, but not protodeclarative gestures (Baron-Cohen 1989). Brain imaging methodology would be well suited to investigating the brain systems underlying these different classes of gesture.

## Emotions

The expression and recognition of emotion are widely considered to have a major role in social cognition. By identifying the emotions expressed by others we get clues about their mental state. Recent neuropsychological studies have demonstrated that there are many systems dedicated to detecting emotions, rather than a single one. For example, damage to the amygdala can impair the recognition of fear without affecting the ability to recognise other emotions (Calder *et al.* 1996). This result is confirmed by brain imaging studies which have shown that presentation of a fearful face activates the amygdala, while presentation of happy, angry, or disgusted faces does not (Morris *et al.* 1996). Disgust seems to activate a part of the insula also concerned with gustatory sensation (Phillips *et al.* 1997). Anger activates regions in orbital frontal cortex (Blair *et al.* 1999). That different emotions are associated with different brain systems probably reflects the fact that different behaviour is appropriate when we detect different emotions in others. When someone expresses fear, we look for the source of their fear. When someone expresses anger we avoid them, or stop doing what we were doing.

Studies of the recognition of emotions in people with autism also suggest fractionation between different emotions. In particular, recognition of some emotions depends upon mentalising ability while recognition of others does not. Thus, emotions such as happiness are identified normally, while emotions such as surprise, embarrassment, and jubilation are not (Baron-Cohen *et al.* 1993). To recognise these latter emotions, it is necessary to understand the mental states of those experiencing the emotion. For example, surprise occurs when we discover that our belief about a situation is false. It would be interesting to examine the recognition of such emotions in brain-damaged patients or in normal volunteers while they are being scanned, but such studies have yet to be carried out.

The studies reviewed above have concerned the identification of emotion from facial expressions. However, it is possible to respond to an emotion without identifying it. Some patients who cannot identify emotions will still show autonomic responses to these emotions, and normal volunteers will show autonomic responses and conditioning to facial expressions which they have not recognised because the expressive face has been masked by a neutral one (Esteves *et al.* 1994). These observations are consistent with LeDoux's work on fear responses. He has proposed that there are two routes involved in processing emotions; a 'fast and dirty' route which leads to autonomic responses and rapid action without recognition, and a slow, accurate route which involves recognition. Either route can be impaired independently, leading either to emotional responses without recognition, or to recognition without an emotional response (LeDoux 1996). Work has started identifying the brain systems associated with these two routes in humans (Morris *et al.* 1998; Whalen *et al.* 1998). In addition, while both these routes have relevance to social interactions, neither may relate to theory of mind.

It appears that the presentation of faces displaying different emotions elicits activity in different brain systems. However, it is still possible that there is a single brain system which is involved in the recognition of one's own emotions so that they can be reported. This system may be a component of ToM, specifically self-awareness. Activation of anterior cingulate cortex is observed in studies of different kinds of emotion. It is activated when volunteers are asked to report what emotion they experience in response to visual stimuli (Lane *et al.* 1997*a*). The ability to give introspective reports appears to depend upon theory of mind (Hurlburt *et al.* 1994). The ability to 'mind-read' others' feelings is a direct result of mentalising. It is not clear whether the anterior cingulate is also activated when emotions in others have to be reported. There are people who have a specific difficulty in recognising their own emotions, alexithymics, (Lane *et al.* 1997*b*). However, these people do not appear to manifest other features of autism.

## Studies of mentalising

So far we have discussed abilities which are important features of social cognition, but which do not necessarily involve mentalising or theory of mind. Although the ability to mentalise (to read the mental states of others) has been studied extensively in children (Astington *et al.* 1988), there have been surprisingly few attempts to study this ability explicitly in patients with brain damage (for studies of mentalising in schizophrenia see R. Corcoran, Chapter 16, this volume). (See also V. Stone, Chapter 11, this volume.)

Happé *et al.* (1999) have shown that RH lesioned patients are impaired on theory of mind tasks relative to left hemisphere patients, but were not able to pinpoint the brain systems involved more precisely. Stone *et al.* (1998) have reported performance of patients with lesions of orbital frontal cortex or dorsolateral prefrontal cortex on a series of theory of mind tasks. The patients with orbital lesions had no problems with first- or second-order theory of mind tasks or with empathising with the feelings of others. However, they did have difficulty recognising social *faux pas*. In contrast the patients with dorsolateral prefrontal lesions had difficulties with most of the tasks, but this seemed to reflect problems with remembering and understanding the material rather than a specific difficulty with mentalising.

There is clearly a need for more studies of patients with circumscribed lesions and for the development of test material for which difficulties with mentalising can be distinguished from more general problems of understanding.

## Imaging studies

Can *in vivo* brain imaging in humans help to establish which regions of the social and/or non-social brain are active during tasks that require mentalising and those that do not? As we have indicated above, the research on autism has already categorised and validated such tasks. It is now a matter for systematic research to establish the critical regions. The important aim is to show convergence of many different tasks in different modalities. The convergent region clearly would then be a target for further search of cellular abnormalities.

A start has been made in this programme. At present, the results are rather mixed. However, we will review the few studies that have been carried out and that purport to pinpoint a specific brain region as the neural substrate of mentalising.

A PET study by Fletcher *et al.* (1995) required volunteers to read stories which involved mental state attribution, and comparison physical stories without a mental state element, as well as a base line control involving unrelated sentences (see Table 14.3 for examples). The mentalising stories (concerning double bluff, white lie, misunderstanding, etc.) had been used previously with high-functioning children and adults with autism, and proved sensitive to even quite subtle difficulties in mental state attribution (Happé 1994). In this brain scan study the standard subtraction method of functional brain imaging was used and statistical parametric mapping, rather than a regions-of-interest approach. A number of regions active when reading stories were even more active when reading stories requiring mentalising, including the posterior cingulate cortex and the right temporoparietal junction. However, an area of left medial frontal cortex was observed to be active only when reading the stories requiring mentalising. According to the Talairach atlas the activation was centred in Brodmann's area 8 and extended into the adjacent area 9. This region is also close to

**Table 14.3.** Examples of conditions used in the study of Fletcher *et al.* 1995

---

Theory of mind story

---

A burglar who has just robbed a shop is making his getaway. As he is running home, a policeman on his beat sees him drop his glove. He doesn't know the man is a burglar, he just wants to tell him he dropped his glove. But when the policeman shouts out to the burglar, 'Hey, you! Stop!', the burglar turns round, sees the policeman and gives himself up. He puts his hands up and admits that he did the break-in at the local shop.

Question: Why did the burglar do this?

---

Physical story

---

A burglar is about to break into a jeweller's shop. He skilfully picks the lock on the shop door. Carefully he crawls under the electronic detector beam. If he breaks this beam it will set off the alarm. Quietly he opens the door of the store-room and sees the gems glittering. As he reaches out, however, he steps on something soft. He hears a screech and something small and furry runs out past him, towards the shop door. Immediately the alarm sounds.

Question: Why did the alarm go off?

---

Unlinked sentences

---

The four brothers stood aside to make room for their sister, Stella. Jill repeated the experiment several times. The name of the airport had changed. Louise uncorked a little bottle of oil. The two children had to abandon their daily walk. She took a suite in a grand hotel. It was already twenty years since the operation.

Question: Did the children take their walk?

---

anterior cingulate cortex, Brodmann's area 32. There was also a separate peak of activation in anterior cingulate cortex, but this reached significance in only one of the relevant comparisons. The medial prefrontal cortex is much enlarged in man compared with other animals (Passingham, R. W., personal communication). Furthermore it is not easy to distinguish medial frontal regions from cingulate cortex proper since there are considerable individual differences in the morphology of this area. Examination of the structural images for individual volunteers suggested that the region where the activations associated with mentalising were observed lay in the paracingulate sulcus. For convenience we shall also continue to identify these regions in terms of Brodmann areas, since this is the terminology used in most publications. These results back the idea that a separable brain system may underlie the innate capacity to mentalise, damage to which would lead to autism. The area pinpointed in this study was also activated in an independent study which aimed to investigate processes involved in story comprehension (Mazoyer *et al.* 1993)—stories which, in fact, had a strong theory of mind component (e.g. deception).

The same paradigm was also used to study people with Asperger's Syndrome (Happé *et al.* 1996). The subjects were five right-handed males, mean age 24 (range 20–27). All had been diagnosed with Asperger's Syndrome on the basis of developmental history and current presentation (marked social abnormality, good language in the presence of verbal and nonverbal communication difficulties, presence of circumscribed special interests, resistance to change). A history of clumsiness was present in four out of five cases. The mean WAIS Full Scale IQ for the group was 100 (range 87–112), the mean VIQ was 110 (93–125), mean PIQ 92 (83–100). MRI scans showed no evidence of gross morphological abnormalities, and all volunteers were free from epilepsy and were not currently taking any medication. Performance on the tasks used during scanning was at a similar level for the clinical and the normal control group for the physical stories and the unlinked sentences. The performance on ToM stories was less good for the Asperger's group, a result which is expected from the theory of mind deficit hypothesis of autism. Nevertheless it should be noted that all Asperger's subjects correctly answered most of the test questions of the mentalising stories and read these stories slightly faster than the physical stories.

The comparison of story reading and unlinked sentences highlights areas involved in story integration and in the drawing of inferences to create an overall meaning. The major difference between story and non-story conditions involved the temporal poles bilaterally and the left superior temporal gyrus. These same areas were also activated in the Asperger's volunteers, but for this group the difference between stories and sentences was significantly less pronounced in all regions. This suggests that subjects with Asperger's Syndrome process meaningful connected narrative and meaningless jumbled sentences in a more similar way than do controls. Interestingly, the Asperger's subjects were at least as good as previously scanned controls with unlinked sentences, but performed slightly worse on both story conditions. These findings fit a current theory suggesting that autism is characterised by a cognitive style of weak central coherence, a failure to integrate information in context to extract higher level meaning or gist (Frith 1989). Piecemeal processing of stories, as of unlinked sentences, would be predicted by this account (Jolliffe 1997).

The most important comparison, mentalising vs. non-mentalising stories, indicated a critical difference between the clinical and normal groups: the Asperger's group did not activate the same region of paracingulate cortex (area 8/9) during ToM stories. A direct comparison of the groups (the group by condition interaction) confirmed that there was a significant difference in this region. However, the Asperger's group significantly activated a neighbouring area of left paracingulate cortex (Brodmann's area 9/10) when processing ToM stories. Controls also activated this area, but to a far lesser extent than area 8/9. This lack of overlap between the results from the two groups suggests that the Asperger's subjects' mentalising performance was subserved by a brain system in which one key component was missing.

One explanation for this abnormal pattern of activation is that the Asperger's subjects were using a more general-purpose reasoning mechanism in order to infer mental states. Area 9, which covers a large expanse of cortex, has been implicated in a number of brain imaging studies of problem solving and general cognitive ability. However, the medial frontal area activated in the present study has not previously been linked to any specific cognitive function. No macroscopic structural abnormalities of medial prefrontal cortex were present in the MRI scans of the five Asperger's volunteers. This suggests the possibility that the abnormal activation in this critical region resulted from structural damage in another part of an extended system. Alternatively there may be microscopic abnormalities in inter-cellular connections.

The same set of stories were used in a second study in which brain activity was assessed by fMRI rather than PET (Gallagher *et al.* in press). In addition, the same volunteers were shown a series of cartoons in which incidents were presented in pictures, rather than words. Essentially, even though the cartoons are single pictures, they are also narratives in the sense that they tell a story. Cartoons are humorous because usually more than one interpretation is possible, but the more surprising—i.e. funny—solution, is the one that fits best. Depending on the cartoon, some of these surprising solutions involved taking into account the mental states of the characters depicted, while others did not. By contrasting these two types of cartoons, mentalising areas were again isolated. The control task in this study consisted of pictures of a number of unrelated objects which the volunteers passively observed.

A very similar pattern of activity was observed for both stories and cartoons when ToM narratives were compared with non-ToM narratives, largely replicating the findings of Fletcher *et al.* (1995). Activity was seen in the temporal poles and the temporoparietal junction bilaterally, the right middle frontal gyrus, and medially in the precuneus and the medial prefrontal cortex (paracingulate sulcus). Apart from the medial prefrontal region, all these areas were activated, but to a lesser extent, when the non-ToM narratives were compared with the control tasks. Only activity in the medial prefrontal region was specific to the ToM narratives. With the greater resolution of fMRI it was possible to distinguish a number of peaks in the medial prefrontal region (Brodmann's areas 8, 9 and the border of 10 and 32) lying along the paracingulate sulcus.

Goel *et al.* (1995) used a novel mentalising task which involved taking into account another person's knowledge. They asked volunteers to judge whether someone living in the fifteenth century (e.g. Christopher Columbus) would have known the use of a series of objects that were presented during the scan. In the control condition subjects simply judged whether the objects were old or new from their own perspective. The argument is that taking another person's point of view, distant in time, involves mentalising. A number of areas were more active when the mentalising task was contrasted with the control task, including medial prefrontal cortex (Brodmann's area 8).

In a very different type of study, Baron-Cohen *et al.* (1994), using SPECT and a regions of interest approach, asked adult volunteers to listen to a list of words and decide which of these words 'described the mind or things the mind can do' (e.g. think, remember). The comparison task involved picking out those words which 'described the body or what the body can do'. The relevance of the task is underpinned by the finding that children with autism performed poorly on a similar mental word judgement task (and well in judging body terms). The argument is that mentalising is involved in the comprehension of the mental state verbs which was required for making correct judgements about these verbs, in contrast to the comprehension of physical state verbs. Looking at the difference between the two types of verbs thus could reveal brain areas dedicated to mentalising. During the mind–word task there was increased blood flow in the right orbito–frontal cortex relative to the left frontal polar region. However, data concerning other brain regions was not available.

Baron-Cohen *et al.* (1999) used another type of mentalising task, previously validated with autistic groups, involving the interpretation of eye gaze as depicted in photographs. This involved both verbal and nonverbal processing of information with mental state content. Volunteers had to look at pairs of eyes and at the same time select one of two descriptive adjectives, e.g. 'concerned' vs. 'unconcerned'. The contrasting task was a judgement of the same stimuli in terms of whether they were the eyes of male or female individuals. In normal subjects the theory of mind task activated a number of areas, including the left dorsolateral prefrontal cortex and Broca's area, the medial prefrontal cortex, and bilateral temporo–parietal areas. Of particular note was the observation that the left amygdala was activated in the normal controls, but not in a group of patients with Asperger's Syndrome. There are, however, some problems with the interpretation of this study. First, the choice between descriptors always involved a selection between a negative and a positive value. Thus, the contrast between mentalising and physical judgement could also be said to involve a value or emotive judgement. Second, the experimental task required understanding of complex words while the control task did not. This difference could account for the similarity of the regions activated with those seen in studies of word meaning (Vandenberghe *et al.* 1996). As will be discussed below, there may well be an overlap between brain areas concerned with meaning and those concerned with mentalising. For this reason it is particularly important to use tasks which clearly distinguish between these processes.

Heider and Simmel (1944) first drew attention to the fact that people readily attribute intentions to geometric shapes moving on a surface, such as in animated films. This observation provided the basis for an imaging study of mentalising in which volunteers observed two triangles moving on a screen (Castelli *et al.*, in preparation). Three conditions were contrasted which reliably elicited descriptions of the movements as a) random movement; b) goal-directed interactions (following, fighting, chasing); and c) mentalising actions (surprising, mocking, bluffing). This task was validated with autistic groups who showed fewer mental state attributions to ToM animations than controls (Abell *et al.*, submitted). In contrast with the other two conditions, observation of mentalising movement elicited more activity in several areas; temporal–parietal junction, fusiform gyrus and occipital gyrus (bilaterally, but with more activity on the right), and medial frontal cortex (Brodmann's area 9). Two of these areas (temporal–parietal junction and medial frontal cortex) were observed in the previous studies of mentalising, while the other regions may be concerned with aspects of visual processing specific to the interpretation of moving objects.

## THE SIGNIFICANCE OF THE AREAS ACTIVATED BY MENTALISING TASKS

Since mentalising cannot be studied in animals, and has been, as yet, little studied in patients with lesions, there have been no prior expectations about which brain regions would be activated or what the broader function of these regions might be. On the basis of the results of the imaging studies reviewed above we now have some data with which to start developing hypotheses about the physiological basis of mentalising abilities. Overall the results suggest that a distributed system is involved, of which the major components are a medial frontal region bordering the anterior cingulate cortex and the temporo–parietal junction predominantly on the right. The involvement of this latter component may relate to the observation that pragmatic aspects of language are particularly sensitive to right hemisphere damage.

### The role of medial prefrontal cortex (paracingulate sulcus)

In as far as accurate location is possible, activation associated with mentalising has been reported in the paracingulate sulcus (Brodmann's area 8, and also in the immediately adjacent area 9 and the anterior cingulate cortex). In monkeys the frontal eye fields are located in Brodmann's area 8. However, in humans the frontal eye fields are more posterior and more lateral (Paus 1996) and located in Brodmann's area 6. Thus, it is not clear what the monkey homologue of human area 8 may be. There is much evidence that the anterior cingulate cortex is an important component of the motor system. In both monkeys and humans there is evidence for a cingulate motor area which contains representations of body parts (Dum and Strick 1993). However, this region is in the posterior part of the anterior cingulate cortex (called the caudal cingulate by Paus *et al.* 1998). The activations associated with mentalising are all more anterior (see Fig. 14.1). There is little information from animal and lesion studies about the role of the rostral part of the anterior cingulate. There are, however, a number of brain imaging studies which have activated these regions of medial frontal cortex.

In addition to the studies of explicit mentalising, activations of medial prefrontal areas (Brodmann's areas 8, 9, and 10) have been reported during conditional responding (Petrides *et al.*, 1993), while watching complex biological motion (Bonda *et al.*

1996; Castelli *et al.*, in preparation), when monitoring whether the speech we hear is our own or someone else's (McGuire *et al.*, 1996*a*), and when having 'stimulus-independent thoughts' (McGuire *et al.*, 1996*b*).

There is a general consensus that the ACC is involved in the monitoring of action (Posner and Dehaene 1994). A recent study (Carter *et al.* 1998) implicated the caudal anterior cingulate more specifically in monitoring responses in situations where errors are likely due to response competition, rather than simply responding to errors. However the rostral anterior cingulate has also been activated when reporting emotions elicited by pictures (Lane *et al.* 1997*a*), when experiencing pain (e.g. Rainville *et al.* 1997), and when experiencing a 'ticklish' tactile sensation (Blakemore *et al.* 1998).

Figure 14.1 shows the location of these various activations plotted on the medial surface of a standard brain in Talairach space. It is apparent from this plot that the regions listed as being in 'medial frontal' or 'anterior cingulate' cortex are all very close to each other, with the exception of responses to biological motion which are more anterior. They seem to lie along the border of the anterior cingulate cortex and may well all be in the paracingulate sulcus. With a few exceptions most of the tasks that produced these activations can be characterised as requiring subjects to attend to their own thoughts (stimulus-independent thoughts), feelings (emotion, tickle, pain)

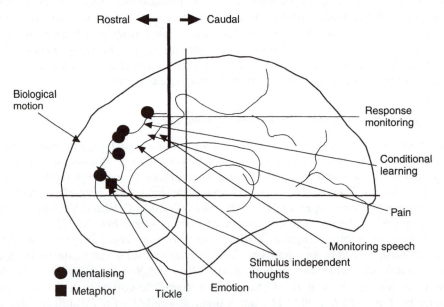

**Fig. 14.1.** A medial view of the brain in Talairach space showing the position of activations associated with mentalising and understanding metaphors (filled shapes) lying on the border of the medial prefrontal cortex and the rostral anterior cingulate cortex (the paracingulate sulcus). The arrows indicate the location of activations associated with a number of other tasks that have activated the same region. The bold vertical line indicates the division between rostral and caudal anterior cingulate proposed by Paus *et al.* (1998). The studies from which these locations are derived are listed in the text.

and actions (speech, responses). We might tentatively conclude from this observation that the mentalising tasks activate areas involved in monitoring one's own inner states. However, the allocation of this role to medial frontal cortex needs to be confirmed, firstly by carefully considering other studies which have activated this area, but are not listed here (see Grady, in press; Paus *et al.* 1998) and, secondly, through replication of the studies that are listed here.

### The role of temporo–parietal cortex

(See also N. Emery and D. Perrett, Chapter 12, this volume.)

### Biological motion

The term 'biological motion' refers to the characteristic movement of living things. Johansson (1973) was the first to demonstrate that human actions (such as walking or dancing) can be recognised when all that can be observed is the movement of a few points of light attached to the joints of the person moving. This shows that there is something characteristic and recognisable about the movements of humans, and the same applies to other living things (Premack 1990). Perrett *et al.* (1989) have found that there are cells in the superior temporal sulcus (STS) of the monkey which respond to moving hands and faces. There have also been a number of brain imaging studies implicating the same region in humans. Puce *et al.* (1998) found activation in this area elicited by moving eyes or mouth (within a face), but not by movement in general. General movement elicited activity in a region more ventral and posterior, previously identified as the human analogue of V5 (Watson *et al.* 1993). Bonda *et al.* (1996) used the Johansson technique with moving spots of light to show volunteers a grasping hand or a dancing figure, and activated a similar region. (The medial activation referred to in the previous section appeared in the comparison of dancing with grasping.) The same general region was also activated by lip movements (Calvert *et al.* 1997) and hand gestures (Grèzes *et al.* 1998). In all these studies the activity was predominantly in the right hemisphere (see Fig. 14.2). We might have expected to find the same area activated in the study in which subjects observed and interpreted the behaviour of moving triangles. However, it is interesting that this was only the case when subjects were observing mentalising, but not merely goal-directed movement. Less expected is the observation that activity occurred in this region also in the studies in which subjects read stories or looked at drawings, since in these studies no movement was presented. We can speculate that what makes biological motion 'biological' is that we perceive an intention behind the movement, so this region might be concerned more generally with the recognition of intentions. It is possible that this ability to recognise intentions evolved from an ability to interpret movements of other living creatures.

A related phenomenon has been observed by Rizzolatti and his colleagues (Gallese *et al.* 1996) in relation to reaching movements. Cells in inferior frontal cortex are active when the monkey makes a particular grasping movement. However, the same cells are also active when the monkey observes someone else making the same grasping

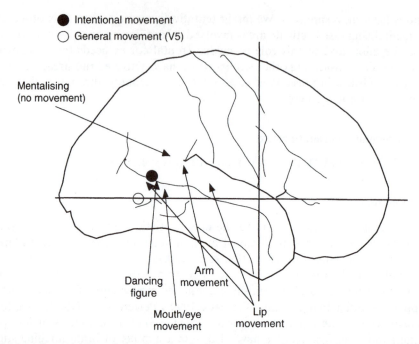

**Fig. 14.2.** A lateral view of the right hemisphere of the brain in Talairach space showing the positions of activations associated with biological motion. The black circle locates the peak activation elicited by intentional motion and the grey circle indicates V5, the general motion area. The location of activation from a mentalising task in which no motion occurred is also indicated. The studies from which these locations are derived are listed in the text.

movement. In consequence these cells have been labelled 'mirror neurons'. Like those that detect biological motion, these mirror neurons could also be involved in the recognition of intentions, perhaps on the basis of imitation (Rizzolatti and Arbib 1998). However, activity in inferior frontal cortex was not observed in the various studies of mentalising reviewed above. Imaging studies in which human volunteers make or observe grasping movements have yet to give definitive results. Grafton *et al.* (1996) observed activity in inferior frontal cortex when volunteers observed grasping movements or when they imagined making grasping movements, but not when they actually made grasping movements. In this study activity was also observed in the temporal cortex, as would be expected, since grasping is a form of biological motion. However, this activity was more anterior than in other studies of biological motion and also restricted to the left hemisphere. One possible important difference between the mirror neurons in inferior frontal cortex and the 'biological motion' neurons in STS is hinted at by a study from Perrett's group which indicates that some temporal lobe neurons distinguish between self-generated movement and externally generated movements (Hietanen and Perrett 1993). These neurons respond when something moves through the visual field, but not when the monkey moves its own limb through the visual field. Ability to infer the intentions of others from their movements might require information from both the mirror neurons and the neurons that respond specifically to the movements of others.

## Meaning

Brain imaging studies of meaning or semantics have mostly been concerned with the meaning of single words or the identity of objects. These studies (e.g. Vandenberghe *et al.* 1996) indicate that activity associated with meaning is largely restricted to the left hemisphere, with activation in inferior frontal cortex and middle and inferior temporal gyrus. Activity is also seen in the region of the temporo–parietal junction close to the region activated in the mentalising studies. When the meaning of sentences rather than single words is involved, a similar pattern of left side activation is seen extending forward into the temporal pole (Bottini *et al.* 1994). However, when narratives rather than sentences are involved, homologous areas in the right hemisphere are activated to an even greater extent than those on the left (Happé *et al.*, in preparation). Thus, concern with meaning, especially meaning of narratives, activates regions of the temporo–parietal junction similar to those associated with tasks specifically concerned with mentalising. This is consistent with our discussion of language at the beginning of this chapter. Understanding language depends in a large part on understanding the intentions of the speaker. This will apply especially to lengthy communications such as narratives, but will play a small role even in the understanding of single words.

## CONCLUSIONS

Few studies have yet been undertaken to elucidate the brain basis of theory of mind in humans. However, clues are now available to develop hypotheses which can guide future experiments. Brain imaging studies in which volunteers have to make inferences about the mental states of others activate a number of brain areas, most notably the medial frontal cortex and the temporo–parietal junction. Other areas are also involved which we have not discussed here. On the basis of a range of imaging studies we speculate that this region of the medial frontal cortex (the paracingulate sulcus) is also involved in monitoring our own thoughts, actions, and feelings. While grammar and phonology are well known to depend on the left hemisphere, studies of patients with lesions suggest that pragmatic aspects of language depend largely upon the right hemisphere. Brain imaging studies suggest that attention to the meaning of narratives also elicits right hemisphere activity concentrated in the temporal lobe and extending from the temporo–parietal junction to the temporal pole. When volunteers have to make inferences about the mental states of characters in stories or cartoons a similar pattern of activation is seen, with additional activity in medial frontal cortex. The area of the temporo–parietal junction at the end of the STS is also activated by biological motion. We speculate that one aspect of the human ability to make inferences about the intentions of others evolved from a system concerned with analysing the movements of other creatures. This information about the behaviour of others is combined with the information about own mental states represented in medial prefrontal areas. We propose that the critical mechanism that allows humans to develop a theory of own and other minds results from the development of introspection (monitoring one's own mind) and an adaptation of a much older social brain concerned with monitoring the behaviour of others.

# REFERENCES

Abell, A., Happé, F. and Frith, U. Do triangles play tricks? Attribution of mental states to animated shapes in normal and abnormal development (submitted).

Astington, J. W., Harris, P. L. and Olson, D. R. (ed.) (1988). *Developing theories of mind.* Cambridge University Press, New York.

Attwood, A. H., Frith, U. and Hermelin, B. (1988). The understanding and use of interpersonal gestures by autistic and Down's syndrome children. *Journal of Autism and Developmental Disorders*, **18**, 241–57.

Bachevalier, J. and Merjanian, P. M. (1993). The contribution of medial temporal lobe structures in infantile autism: a neurobehavioural study in primates. In *The neurobiology of autism*, (ed. M. L. Bauman and T. L. Kemper), pp. 146–69. Johns Hopkins University Press, Baltimore.

Baron-Cohen, S. (1989). Perceptual role taking and protodeclarative pointing in autism. *British Journal of Developmental Psychology*, **7**, 113–27.

Baron-Cohen, S. (1992). Out of sight or out of mind—another look at deception in autism. *Journal of Child Psychology and Psychiatry*, **33**, 1141–55.

Baron-Cohen, S., Jolliffe, T., Mortimore, C. and Robertson, M. (1997). Another advanced test of theory of mind: evidence from very high functioning adults with autism or Asperger Syndrome. *Journal of Child Psychology and Psychiatry*, **38**, 813–22.

Baron-Cohen, S., Leslie, A. M. and Frith, U. (1986). Mechanical, behavioural and intentional understanding of picture stories in autistic children. *British Journal of Developmental Psychology*, **4**, 113–25.

Baron-Cohen, S., Spitz, A and Cross, P. (1993). Do children with autism recognize surprise—a research note. *Cognition and Emotion*, **7**, 507–16.

Baron-Cohen, S., Ring, H., Moriarty, J., Schmidt, C., Costa, D. and Ell, P. (1994). Recognition of mental state words: a functional neuroimaging study of normal adults and a clinical study of children with autism. *British Journal of Psychiatry*, **165**, 640–9.

Baron-Cohen, S., Ring, H. A., Wheelright, S. Bullmore, E. T., Brammer, M. J., Simmons, A. and Williams, S. C. R. (1999). Social intelligence in the normal and autistic brain: an fMRI study. *European Journal of Neuroscience*, **11**, 1891–8.

Blair, R. J. R., Morris, J. S., Frith, C. D., Perrett, D. I. and Dolan, R. J. Dissociable neural responses to facial expressions of sadness and anger. *Brain*, **122**, 883–93.

Blakemore, S-J., Wolpert, D. M. and Frith, C. D. (1998). Central cancellation of self-produced tickle sensation. *Nature Neuroscience*, **1**, 635–40.

Bonda, E., Petrides, M., Ostry, D. and Evans, A. (1996). Specific involvement of human parietal systems and the amygdala in the perception of biological motion. *Journal of Neuroscience*, **16**, 3737–44.

Bottini, G., Corcoran, R., Sterzi, R., Paulesu, E., Schenone, P., Scarpa, P., Frackowiak, R. S. J. and Frith, C. D. (1994). The role of the right hemisphere in the interpretation of figurative aspects of language. *Brain*, **117**, 1241–53.

Brookshire, R. H. and Nicholas, C. E. (1984). Comprehension of directly and indirectly stated main ideas and details in discourse by brain-damaged and non-brain-damaged listeners. *Brain and Language*, **21**, 21–36.

Brothers, L. (1990). The social brain: a project for integrating primate behaviour and neuro-psychology in a new domain. *Concepts in Neuroscience*, **1**, 27–51.

Brownell, H. H., Simpson, T. L., Bihrle, A. M., Potter, H. H. and Gardner, H. (1990). Appreciation of metaphorical alternative word meanings by left and right brain-damaged patients. *Neuropsychologia*, **28**, 375–83.

Bryan, K. L. (1988). Assessment of language disorders after right hemisphere damage. *British Journal of Disorders of Communication*, **23**, 111–25.

Byrne, R. W.(1998). Cognition in great apes. In *Comparative neuropsychology*, (ed. A. D. Milner), pp. 228–44. Oxford University Press.

Calder, A. J., Young, A. W., Rowland, D., Perrett, D. I., Hodges, J. R. and Etcoff, N. L. (1996). Facial emotion recognition after bilateral amygdala damage: differentially severe impairment of fear. *Cognitive Neuropsychology*, **13**, 699–745.

Calvert, G. A., Bullmore, E. T., Brammer, M. J., Campbell, R., Williams, S. R. C., McGuire, P. K., Woodruff, P. W. R., Iversen, S. D. and David, A. S. (1997). Activation of auditory cortex during silent lip reading. *Science*, **276**, 593–96.

Capps, L., Sigman, M. and Yirmiya, N. (1996). Self-competence and emotional understanding in high-functioning children with autism. *Annual Progress in Child Psychiatry and Child Development*, **1996**, 260–79.

Carter, C. S., Braver, T. S., Barch, D. M., Botvinick, M. M., Noll, D. and Cohen, J. D. (1998). Anterior cingulate cortex, error detection and the online monitoring of performance. *Science*, **280**, 747–9.

Castelli, F., Abell, A., Happé, F., Frith, C. D. and Frith, U. The brain activity elicited by intentional vs non-intentional movement: inferring minds from motion. (In preparation.)

Charman, T. and Baron-Cohen, S. (1992). Understanding drawings and beliefs: a further test of the metarepresentation theory of autism. *Journal of Child Psychology and Psychiatry*, **33**, 877–93.

Cheney, D. and Seyfarth, R. (1990). *How monkeys see the world*. University of Chicago Press.

Dum, R. P. and Strick, P. L. (1993). Cingulate motor areas. In *Neurobiology of cingulate cortex and limbic thalamus*, (ed. B. A. Vogt and M. Gabriel), pp. 415–41. Birkhauser, Boston, USA.

Esteves, F., Dimberg, U. and Öhman, A. (1994). Automatically elicited fear; conditioned skin conductance responses to masked facial expressions. *Cognition and Emotion*, **9**, 99–108.

Fletcher, P., Happé, F., Frith, U., Baker, S. C., Dolan, D. J., Frackowiak, R. S. J. and Frith, C. D. (1995). Other minds in the brain: a functional imaging study of 'theory of mind' in story comprehension. *Cognition*, **57**, 109–28.

Foldi, N. S. (1987). Appreciation of pragmatic interpretation of indirect commands: comparison of right and left hemisphere brain-damaged patients. *Brain and Language*, **31**, 88–108.

Fombonne, E., Siddons, F., Achard, S., Frith, U. and Happé, F. (1994). Adaptive-behaviour and theory of mind in autism. *European Child and Adolescent Psychiatry*, **3**, 176–86.

Frith, U. (1989). *Autism: explaining the enigma*. Blackwell, Oxford.

Frith, U. and Happé, F. (1994). Autism: beyond 'theory of mind'. *Cognition*, **50**, 115–32.

Frith, U., Morton, J. and Leslie, A. M. (1991). The cognitive basis of a biological disorder: autism. *Trends in Neuroscience*, **14**, 433–8.

Frith, U., Happé, F. and Siddons, F. (1994). Autism and theory of mind in everyday life. *Social Development*, **3**, 108–24.

Gallese, V., Fadiga, L., Fogassi, L. and Rizzolatti, G. (1996). Action recognition in the premotor cortex. *Brain*, **119**, 593–609.

Gallagher, H. L., Happé, F., Brunswick, N., Fletcher, P. C., Frith U. and Frith, C. D. Reading the mind in cartoons and stories: an fMRI study of 'theory of mind' in verbal and non-verbal tasks. *Neuropsychologia* (in press).

Goel, V., Grafman, J., Sadato, N. and Hallett, M. (1995). Modelling other minds. *Neuroreport*, **6**, 1741–6.

Gomez, J. C. (1996). Mutual awareness in primate communication: a Gricean approach. In *Self-awareness in humans and animals*, (ed. S. T. Parket, R. W. Mitchell and M. L. Boccia), pp. 61–80. Cambridge University Press.

Grady, C. L. Neuroimaging and activation of the frontal lobes. In *The human frontal lobes: function and disorders*, (ed. B. L. Miller and J. L. Cummings). Guilford Press, New York. (In press.)

Grafton, S. T., Arbib, M. A., Fadiga, L. and Rizzolatti, G. (1996). Localization of grasp representations in humans by positron emission tomography. 2: observation compared with imagination. *Experimental Brain Research*, **112**, 103–11.

Grèzes, J., Costes, N. and Decety, J. (1998). Top down effect of strategy on the perception of human biological motion. *Cognitive Neuropsychology*, **15**, 553–82.

Halsband, U. (1998). Brain mechanisms of apraxia. In *Comparative neuropsychology*, (ed. A. D. Milner), pp. 184–212. Oxford University Press.

Happé, F. G. E. (1993). Communicative competence and theory of mind in autism: a test of relevance theory. *Cognition*, **48**, 101–19.

Happé, F. G. E. (1994). An advanced test of theory of mind: understanding of story characters' thoughts and feelings by able autistic, mentally handicapped and normal children and adults. *Journal of Autism and Developmental Disorders*, **24**, 129–54.

Happé, F. and Frith, U. (1995). Theory of mind in Autism. In *Learning and cognition in autism*, (ed. E. Schopler and G. B. Mesibov), pp. 177–97. Plenum Press, New York.

Happé, F. and Frith, U. (1996). The neuropsychology of autism. *Brain*, **119**, 1377–400.

Happé, F., Ehlers, S., Fletcher, P., Frith, U., Johansson, M., Gillberg, C., Dolan, R., Frackowiak, R. and Frith, C. (1996). 'Theory of mind' in the brain. Evidence from a PET scan study of Asperger syndrome. *NeuroReport*, **8**, 197–201.

Happé, F., Gallagher, H. L., Brunswick, N., Fletcher, P. C., Frith U. and Frith, C. D. Brain activity associated with extracting the meaning from verbal and non-verbal narratives. (In preparation).

Happé, F., Brownell, H. and Winner, E. (1999). Acquired 'theory of mind' impairments following stroke. *Cognition*, **70**, 211–40.

Heider, F. and Simmel, M. (1944). An experimental study of apparent behaviour. *American Journal of Psychology*, **57**, 243–59.

Hetzler, B. E. and Griffin, J. L. (1981). Infantile autism and the temporal lobe of the brain. *Journal of Autism and Developmental Disorders*, **11**, 317–30.

Heyes, C. M. (1998). Theory of mind in nonhuman primates. *Behaviour and Brain Sciences*, **21**, 101–34.

Hietanen, J. K. and Perrett, D. I. (1993). Motion sensitive cells in the macaque superior temporal polysensory area. I: lack of response to the sight of the animal's own limb movement. *Experimental Brain Research*, **93**, 117–28.

Hirst, W., LeDoux, J. and Stein, S. (1984). Constraints on the processing of indirect speech acts: evidence from aphasiology. *Brain and Language*, **23**, 26–33.

Hughes, C., Russell, J. and Robbins, T. W. (1994). Evidence for executive dysfunction in autism. *Neuropsychologia*, **32**, 477–92.

Hurlburt, R. T., Happé, F. and Frith, U. (1994). Sampling the form of inner experience in three adults with Asperger syndrome. *Psychological Medicine*, **24**, 385–95.

Johansson, G. (1973). Visual perception of biological motion and a model of its analysis. *Perception and Psychophysics*, **14**, 202–11.

Jolliffe, T. (1997). Central coherence in autism. Unpublished PhD thesis, University of Cambridge.

Klin, A., Volkmar, F. R. and Sparrow, S. S. (1992). Autistic social dysfunction: some limitations of the theory of mind hypothesis. *Journal of Child Psychology and Psychiatry*, **33**, 861–76.

Kling, A. and Brothers, L. (1992). The amygdala and social behaviour. In *The amygdala*, (ed. J. Aggleton), pp. 353–77. Wiley, New York.

Lane, R. D., Fink, G. R., Chua, P. M. L. and Dolan, R. J. (1997a). Neural activation during selective attention to subjective emotional responses. *NeuroReport*, **8**, 3969–72.

Lane, R. D., Ahern, G. L., Schwartz, G. E. and Kasznia, A. W. (1997b). Is alexithymia the emotional equivalent of blindsight? *Biological Psychiatry*, **42**, 834–44.

LeDoux, J. E. (1996). *The emotional brain*. Simon and Schuster, New York.

Leekam, S. and Perner, J. (1991). Does the autistic child have a metarepresentational deficit? *Cognition*, **40**, 203–18.

Leslie, A. M. (1987). Pretence and representation: the origins of 'Theory of Mind'. *Psychological Review*, **94**, 412–26.

Leslie, A. M. and Thaiss, L. (1992). Domain specificity in conceptual development: evidence from autism. *Cognition*, **43**, 225–51.

Lillard, A. (1997). Other folks' theories of mind and behaviour. *Psychological Science*, **8**, 268–74.

Mazoyer, B. M., Tzourio, N., Frak, V., Syrota, A., Murayama, N., Levrier, O., Salamon, G., Dehaene, S., Cohen, L. and Mehler, J. (1997). The cortical representation of speech. *Journal of Cognitive Neuroscience*, **5**, 467–79.

McCarthy, R. A. and Warrington, E. K. (1990). *Cognitive Neuropsychology*. Academic Press, London.

McGuire, P. K., Silbersweig, D. A. and Frith, C. D. (1996a). Functional neuroanatomy of verbal self-monitoring. *Brain*, **119**, 907–17.

McGuire, P. K., Paulesu, E., Frackowiak, R. S. J. and Frith, C. D. (1996b). Brain activity during stimulus independent thought. *NeuroReport*, **7**, 2095–99.

Morris, J., Frith, C. D., Perrett, D. I., Rowland, D., Young, A. W., Calder, A. J. and Dolan, R. J. (1996). A differential neural response in the human amygdala to fearful and happy facial expressions. *Nature*, **383**, 812–5.

Morris, J. S., Öhman, A. and Dolan, R. J. (1998). Conscious and unconscious emotional learning in the human amygdala. *Nature*, **393**, 467–70.

Mundy, P. and Sigman, M. (1989). The theoretical implications of joint attention deficits in autism. *Development and Psychopathology*, **1**, 173–83.

Paus, T. (1996). Location and function of the human frontal eye-field: a selective review. *Neuropsychologia*, **34**, 475–83.

Paus, T., Koski, L., Caramanos, Z. and Westbury, C. (1998). Regional differences in the effects of task difficulty and motor output on blood flow response in the human anterior cingulate cortex: a review of 107 PET activation studies. *NeuroReport*, **9**, 235–45.

Perner, J., Frith, U., Leslie, A. M. and Leekam, S. R. (1989). Exploration of the autistic child's theory of mind: knowledge, belief and communication. *Child Development*, **60**, 689–700.

Perrett, D. I., Harries, M. H., Bevan, R., Thomas, S., Benson, P. J., Mistlin, A. J., Chitty, A. J., Hietanen, J. K. and Ortega, J. E. (1989). Frameworks of analysis for the neural representation of animate objects and actions. *Journal of Experimental Biology*, **146**, 87–113.

Petrides, M., Alivisatos, B., Evans, A. C. and Meyer, E. (1993). Dissociation of human mid-dorsolateral from posterior dorsolateral frontal cortex in memory processing. *Proceedings of the National Academy of Sciences USA*, **90**, 873–7.

Phillips, M. L., Young, A. W., Senior, C., Brammer, M., Andrew, C., Calder, A. J., Bullmore, E. T., Perrett, D. I., Rowland, D., Williams, S. C. R., Gray, J. A. and David, A. S. (1997). A specific neural substrate for perceiving disgust. *Nature*, **389**, 495–8.

Poizner, H., Bellugi, U. and Iragui, V. (1984). Apraxia and aphasia for a visualgestural language. *American Journal of Physiology*, **246**, 868–83.

Posner, M. I. and Dehaene, S. (1994). Attentional networks. *Trends in the Neurosciences*, **17**, 75–9.

Premack, D. (1990). The infant's theory of self-propelled objects. *Cognition*, **36**, 1–16.

Premack, D. and Woodruff, G. (1978). Does the chimpanzee have a theory of mind? *The Behavioural and Brain Sciences*, **4**, 515–26.

Puce, A., Allison, T., Bentin, S., Gore, J. C. and McCarthy, G. (1998). Temporal cortex activation in humans viewing eye and mouth movements. *Journal of Neuroscience*, **18**, 2188–99.

Rainville, P., Duncan, G. H., Price, D. D., Carrier, B. and Bushnell, M. C. (1997). Pain effect encoded in human anterior cingulate, but not somatosensory cortex. *Science*, **277**, 968–71.

Raleigh, M. J. and Stelkis, H. D. (1981). Effects of orbital frontal and temporal neocortical lesions on affiliative behaviour of vervet monkeys. *Experimental Neurology*, **73**, 378–89.

Rizzolatti, G. and Arbib, M. A. (1998). Language within our grasp. *Trends in the Neurosciences*, **5**, 188–94.

Ross, E. D. (1981). The aprosodias. Functional-anatomic organization of the affective components of language in the right hemisphere. *Archives of Neurology*, **38**, 561–9.

Ross, E. D. and Mesulam, M. (1979). Dominant language functions of the right hemisphere? Prosody and emotional gesturing. *Archives of Neurology*, **36**, 144–9.

Russell, J. (ed.) (1997). *Autism as an executive disorder*. Oxford University Press

Sodian, B. and Frith, U. (1992). Deception and sabotage in autistic, retarded and normal children. *Journal of Child Psychology and Psychiatry*, **33**, 591–605.

Sperber, D. and Wilson, D. (1986). *Relevance: communication and cognition*. Blackwell, Oxford.

Sprengelmeyer, R., Young, A. W., Sprengelmeyer, A., Calder, A. J., Rowland, D., Perrett, D., Homberg, V. and Lange, H. (1997). Recognition of facial expressions: selective impairment of specific emotions in Huntingdon's disease. *Cognitive Neuropsychology*, **14**, 839–79.

Stone, V. E., Baron-Cohen, S. and Knight, R. E. (1998). Frontal lobe contributions to Theory of Mind. *Journal of Cognitive Neuroscience*, **10**, 640–56.

Vandenberghe, R., Price, C., Wise, R., Josephs, O. and Frackowiak, R. S. J. (1996). Functional anatomy of a common semantic system for words and pictures. *Nature*, **383**, 254–6.

Watson, J. D. G., Myers, R., Frackowiak, R. S. J., Hajnal, J. V., Woods, R. P., Mazziotta, J. C., Shipp, S. and Zeki, S. (1993). Area-V5 of the human brain—evidence form a combined study using positron emission tomography and magnetic-resonance-imaging. *Cerebral Cortex*, **3**, 79–94.

Weylman, S. T., Brownell, H. H., Roman, M. and Gardner, H. (1989). Appreciation of indirect requests by left- and right-brain-damaged patients: The effects of verbal context and conventionality of wording. *Brain and Language*, **36**, 580–91.

Whalen, P. J., Rauch, S. L., Etcoff, N. L., McInerney, S. C., Lee, M. B. and Jenike, M. A. (1998). Masked presentations of emotional facial expressions modulate amygdala activity without explicit knowledge. *Journal of Neuroscience*, **18**, 411–8.

# 15

# Theory of mind in action: developmental perspectives on social neuroscience

AMI KLIN, ROBERT SCHULTZ, AND DONALD J. COHEN

## THE NEED FOR A THEORY OF THEORY OF MIND IN ACTION

'You, the neurotypicals, believe that autistic people have no feelings, no beliefs, not even sexual thoughts. Who are the ones without a theory of mind? Because we don't talk as much about these things, you assume that your beliefs about us are true. Well, this is a false belief, if I am allowed to make a little pun, another thing I am not supposed to be able to do because I am autistic.'[1]

This statement was abstracted from a session of a self-support group for bright adult individuals with autism. The young man, M., made this remark without anger, but in a typically wry, sarcastic style, using his own, personalized reading of the theory of mind literature on autism. On a different day, M. was observed in his sheltered employment placement, an academic institution, where he was responsible for aspects of computer programming and data management. After making a similar sarcastic remark to his supervisor, he turned away without a word indicating the end of the interaction, walked past a colleague brushing shoulders, stopped about ten inches away from a senior adviser's face, and said, without a greeting, and in a loud and mechanical tone of voice, that his computer was 'too slow even for a professor'. He then moved to his open office space, and paced back and forth in front of his computer talking to himself, completely oblivious to the fact that several employees and outsiders were observing him. Another supervisor came to ask M. for help. M. mumbled, under his breath, but clearly audibly, 'and they complain I am not doing my job, if I can't sit in front of my computer . . .' M. acquiesced in following the supervisor, but, as they walked down the hall and the supervisor began to explain the problem, M. walked two steps ahead, facing forward, and marching in complete disregard to what was being said to him.

M. is a very bright college graduate, whose long-standing disability is well documented. In early childhood he had no interest in other children; he was indifferent to his mother's comings and goings, and his gaze was described as blank and never eye to eye. His body would be stiff when held and he never sought comfort. His first words were names for appliances, particularly light fixtures; he reversed pronouns, did not use the words yes and no, but often uttered unusually complex words when by himself. When little, he often flapped his hands and walked on his toes. M.'s educational history included several periods of special and residential education, as well as home school-ing. Thanks to his outstanding intellectual capacity, and his mother's perseverance, M. was able to enroll in a community college, later transferring to a prestigious university, where he graduated in computer science.

In the two brief observations described above, M. made a speech employing mental state terms, perspective-taking, self-attributions, and intentional humour. He also failed to bring his comments to a leave-taking conclusion, inadvertently touched a colleague, failed to greet a senior adviser, came too close to the latter, failed to modulate the volume of his voice given the proximity of his listener, made a complaint that verged on a *faux pas* (which, in different circumstances, could cost him his job), exhibited bizarre behaviours oblivious to the fact that he was in a public space, was unable to suppress his negative thoughts about another supervisor's request, and failed to adjust his gait and posture to that of his conversational partner while walking.

Does M. have a theory of mind? And if so, can he use his theory of mind skills in his daily, real-life social adjustment, so that, for example, he will not lose his job?

## THEORY OF MIND (ToM) SKILLS IN BRIGHT INDIVIDUALS WITH AUTISM.

As described in detail in several chapters in this volume, the ToM model of social development posits that being able to conceive of mental phenomena is the founda-tional base of human social interaction. This capacity is seen as a cognitive mechan-ism with neurofunctional localization, a developmental course of maturation, and possibly, intergenerational transmission. An insult to this mechanism is proposed to be both universal and causative in autism in its various manifestations.

Like M., cognitively bright individuals with autism and related conditions make us think more carefully about this model. For example, despite their pronounced social disability, they have been shown to succeed on ToM tasks at different levels of complexity (e.g. Bowler 1992; Dahlgren and Trillingsgaard 1996). Clearly, there is a ceiling effect on most traditional ToM tasks, which were designed for use with children aged four to six years. New, more advanced tests of ToM (e.g. Baron-Cohen *et al.* 1997) in fact appear to capture the ToM deficits in even these more able individuals, supporting the notion of universality of ToM deficits in the autistic population if developmentally appropriate tasks are utilized. However, the question remains as to whether those individuals who pass four- to six-year level ToM tasks possess the social skills displayed by typical children at that age. If these individuals' ToM capacities do not translate into commensurate social adaptation skills, one might have to qualify the ToM hypothesis of social development in terms of a *necessary but not sufficient* social cognitive faculty fostering social competence.

In a research sample of 58 individuals with higher-functioning autism and Asperger's syndrome followed in our centre, whose mean age is 16 years and whose IQs are in the normative range, the average age-equivalent score on the Interpersonal Relationships subdomain of the *Vineland Adaptive Behavior Scales* (Sparrow *et al.* 1984) is 3.9 years (Klin *et al.* 1997). This number illustrates the magnitude of their social disability. Given these individuals' relatively high standard scores (in the low 80s) on tests of higher language skills such as making inferences from social text, generating appropriate sentences in response to a picture of people interacting, and understanding figures of speech (as included in the *Test of Language Competence*, Wiig and Secord 1989), it is likely that their ToM skills are even higher than the four- to six-year level focus of traditional ToM tasks, which in most cases they have no problem passing. As M., they may in fact show surprising knowledge of mental state phenomena if these are explicitly elicited during clinical interviews. However, they lack the ability to operationalize this understanding into a functional tool that would allow them to adjust better to the demands of real-time, real-life social situations, as their extremely low Vineland scores clearly indicate.

Pondering about this phenomenon, Sigman and colleagues (1995) remarked that 'the only children who achieve metarepresentation and social comprehension without recourse to the nearly automatic emotional understanding that most normal people possess are autistic children' (p. 174). This issue is particularly problematic when the focus of social skills training intervention is on explicit teaching of ToM skills (e.g. Baron-Cohen and Howlin 1999); some studies of this approach have shown that, despite improviement in children's performance on experimental tasks, there is apparently little improvement in general social competence (Ozonoff and Miller 1995) or in communicative competence (Hadwin *et al.* 1997). The acquisition of the ability to reason about mental states would, therefore, appear not to be sufficient to foster generalization and spontaneity in social development. In fact, the acquisition of ToM skills by individuals with autism has been likened to the acquisition of a foreign language: rote memorization, repeated drills, and explicit learning may lead to a modicum of communication competence in that language, which, however, may go unaccompanied by an intuitive feel for its grammar, structure, and cultural roots, resulting in a stilted and less fluent command of the language.

Hence the suggestion that individuals with autism may acquire ToM capacities (i.e. they may pass ToM tasks) in an atypical fashion, via compensatory means, without fully acquiring the benefits accrued from normal ToM skills acquisition (e.g. Happé and Frith 1995). If so, it would be very important to know more about the processes required to make ToM skills fully operational, so that the semblance of ToM competence exhibited by bright individuals with autism is more fully understood.

There are at least two factors likely to be involved in the discrepancy often obtained between ToM competence as shown in experimental tasks and social competence as exhibited in daily social adjustment. First, ToM tasks are typically presented by means of verbal instructions. Given the association between ToM task performance and verbal skills (Eisenmajer and Prior 1991; Prior *et al.* 1990), it is possible that bright individuals with autism are capable of using verbal scaffolding to improve their performance. In fact, most social skills training programmes include the rehearsal of verbal scripts to be used in social situations (e.g. Mesibov 1986). There are important limitations to this approach, however, chief among which is the well-known lack of generalization, particularly in novel situations. This limitation suggests a second factor to be considered, namely the lack of spontaneous use of whatever social cognitive resources are available. In most ToM tasks, the problem to be solved is explicitly defined by the question posed ('Where will Sally look for her marble'), creating the requirement to use knowledge about mental states ('Sally did not see what happened in her absence') and the implications of these to the situation at hand ('Sally believes that the marble is still where it was before she left'). Bright individuals with autism appear to have little difficulty with such tasks. In real life, however, social situations seldom present themselves in this fashion. Before a ToM problem can be solved ('Is this person helping or mocking me?'), it needs to be identified as such as a result of a person's spontaneous predisposition to perceive the relevant social elements of the situation (minimally, who are the relevant people involved and their general characteristics, e.g. peer/adult, their facial, bodily, and voice expressions, and the fast changes thereof). Whether or not a ToM skill is used also depends on the person's ability to combine the various social elements of the situation into a social context, within which the problem can then be defined (e.g. other people's social cues convey concern, I am in a situation that conveys the need for help, thus the utterance 'Can we help you?' is a genuine offer of help; alternatively, the social cues convey teasing, I am in no need of help, thus the utterance 'Can we help you?' is an ironical and potentially aggressive remark). A formal test in which these various social elements were to be verbally and explicitly defined to an individual with autism might produce the correct attribution of intention; a naturalistic occurrence of such a situations, say in a high school cafeteria, might not. This is the reason why social skills training programmes not only include scripts or concrete social problem-solving algorithms, but also provide explicit instructions on how to identify and characterize situations in which such scripts or algorithms apply, particularly novel situations which have not been practiced or rehearsed (e.g. Klin and Volkmar, in press).

One avenue to exploring the gap between experimental ToM findings and clinical measures of real-life social skills would be to minimize the factors which may be promoting the subjects' better performance on ToM tasks and which are often absent in naturalistic settings. In the past two or three years we have developed such an experimental strategy; to reduce the gap between experimental and real-life requirements, we intended the new measure to:

1. Reduce the confound of verbal mediation by minimizing verbal instructions;

2. Reduce explicit definitions of the task by measuring the relative salience of the social elements of the task, and the spontaneity with which subjects employ their social cognitive capacities;

3. Use stimuli that can be interpreted at different levels of social cognitive sophistication, from absence of social attributions to attributions including mental states (e.g. intentions, beliefs, and feelings), as well as interactions thereof (e.g. social relationships). ToM tasks often utilize a dichotomous choice between a ToM and a non-ToM response. Given the likelihood that individuals with autism (and their relatives, when these participate in genetic research) may exhibit variable degrees of ToM capacities, it is important to quantify ToM skills, emphasizing the degree of social understanding rather than adopting an all-or-nothing approach.

The strategy we have adopted to satisfy these requirements has been to study people's ability to attribute social meaning to ambiguous visual stimuli. These stimuli are not explicitly or verbally defined to the subjects, nor are they people or people-like entities (such as dolls). They are geometric shapes, which, however, act like people.

## AN OLD-NEW PARADIGM: ATTRIBUTING SOCIAL MEANING TO AMBIGUOUS VISUAL STIMULI

In a classic study of social attribution, Heider and Simmel (1944) presented a silent movie to female college students in which geometric shapes—a large triangle ($T$), a small triangle ($t$), and a small circle ($c$)—moved in a screen occupied by a stationary rectangle which had a little opening (a door) that opened and closed. The movements of the shapes cannot be easily described without the use of anthropomorphic words because of the compelling impact on the viewer that human actions take place—e.g. the actors chase, fight, entrap, play with one another, get frightened or elated or frustrated. And yet, these are only geometric shapes. The movie was shown in three different conditions: subjects were (1) shown the movie twice and asked to write down what they had seen (Experiment 1); (2) told to interpret the movie in terms of people and then answered specific questions (Experiment 2); and (3) shown the movie in reverse and were asked specific questions as in #2 (Experiment 3). All but one of 34 female college students described the movie in human terms in Experiment 1. In Experiment 2, many scenes were interpreted in the exactly the same way by the students, suggesting that some perceptual configurations (the way the movements occurred in the movie) conveyed specific information that shaped social attributions in a predictable way. In Experiment 3, when the movie was shown in reverse, all subjects interpreted the movements as human action, but there was much more variability in interpretation, presumably because subjects were struggling to 'fit in' a plot that explained or brought together the 'human' movements they saw.

Based on these results, Heider and Simmel were able to define a series of stimulus configurations that appeared to constrain social attribution. When the shapes touched one another successively with only momentary contact, the 'scene' was interpreted as hitting. Interestingly, when the movie was shown in reverse, the aggressor (who was hitting whom) also reversed. If however, the contact was more prolonged, the movements were interpreted as 'more friendly'. But these rules applied only to the shapes that moved by themselves in the movie, i.e. the actors (i.e. $T$, $t$, and $c$). When the interaction was between one of these actors and a geometric shape that did not move by itself (i.e. the rectangle, and its little door), the attributions were different. $T$, $t$, and $c$ were always seen as imparting movement to the door; the door was never seen as imparting movement to them. This suggested that if the shape did not move by itself, it was not viewed as an agent or person. If the 'door' had been moving by itself and then interacted with a previously 'passive' triangle, the attribution was likely to be different.

Attributions were made not only when the shapes touched, but also when simultaneous or successive movements occurred without contact. But the way these movements were interpreted was different: while contact implied some form of physical causation (e.g. hitting), contingent movement with no contact implied psychological causation (e.g. 'trying' to avoid). The interpretation of various interactions, however, whether physical or psychological, often depended on previous interactions that had been seen. In other words, the interpretation of movements became anchored on the subjects' emerging perceptions as to who were the actors and which were the 'props', as well as the characteristics of the actors (e.g. aggressor) and their needs (e.g. being weaker implied the need to escape the stronger aggressor).

Several perceptually-based principles of social attribution were thus defined: (1) if the shapes moved by themselves, they were likely to be people; if not, they were inanimate things or 'props'; (2) when contact occurred between 'people', they could be 'aggressive' or 'friendly' depending on the perceptual characteristics of the contact; however, if contact occurred between a shape that moved by itself with a shape that did not, the interaction was seen as the former operating the latter, never the other way around; (3) when movements of 'people' were contingent but contact did not occur, causation was seen in psychological terms (e.g. a form of communication). Although it did not happen, if the interaction between 'people' and 'props' did not involve contact, the subjects might have interpreted it as some form of magical event (e.g. Ali Baba closing a gate using supernatural powers) or, in our days, somebody using remote control; (4) perceptual configurations were not enough to explain social attributions: they became increasingly more dependent on the subjects' perception of the invariances of the movie; i.e. the characters' attributes (e.g. to determine the origin of the action) and their needs and consequent intentions.

Heider and Simmel concluded that while 'perceptions give rise to anthropomorphic attributions . . . the movements become anchored in a field of objects and persons and interpreted as acts' (p. 256). Movement configurations are not interpreted arbitrarily, but become 'embedded in our picture of [physical and social] reality' (p. 256). And once we consider a movement as the action of a person, 'perception of motive or need is [immediately] involved' (p. 257). But the cues for ascribing motivation or intention cannot be inferred from a movement in isolation (e.g. a circle entering a house); preceding interactions with other actors offer cues for the determination of motives.

The notion that certain kinds of perception elicit social attribution, but that causal attributions based on fundamental elements of social reality—needs and intentions—constrain the interpretation of percepts in predictable ways has become the staple of much current research in causal attribution (see below). Nevertheless, Heider and Simmel's paradigm has been used primarily to explore the content of social attributions (e.g. Shor 1957; Greenberg and Strickland 1973), not the capacity for making attributions. And yet, this cartoon microcosm offers a compelling paradigm to study social cognitive capacities, including the spontaneity with which a given perceiver makes use of whatever social understanding he or she has available to interpret the shapes' movements.

## THE SOCIAL ATTRIBUTION TASK (SAT)

In order to study the capacity for social attributions, we have been using a version of Heider and Simmel's (1944) movie which contains all of the sequences described in their original paper. We adapted the procedure for use with developmentally disabled individuals and created a coding system to examine and quantify different aspects of social attribution. We call the resulting procedure the Social Attribution Task (SAT).

The SAT requires the subject's ability to recognize visual stimuli as social phenomena and then to extract visual cues from the display in order to create a social context (i.e. make social attributions). The SAT is presented as a salient video display that lasts 50 seconds. The 'cast of characters' are a rectangle that has a small opening that opens and closes (like a 'door'), a big triangle, a small triangle, and a small circle or dot. The movements of the shapes are contingent upon one another, in such a way that they move in synchrony, against one another, or as a result of the action of the other shape. The sequence represents the unfolding of a story that is virtually identical to the one used in Heider and Simmel's (1944) cartoon. Data obtained with this procedure are a series of narratives. The first narrative is obtained after the video sequence is shown twice. The sequence is then broken down into six meaningful segments and presented sequentially. We found this necessary in order to avoid placing too much burden on memory and narrative organizational processes, two factors that could place unnecessary demands upon children and on individuals with disabilities. In this way, the task is focused on the subjects' abilities to make attributions at varying levels of sophistication rather than on memory capacities. After each segment is shown, the subjects are asked to state as completely as possible 'what happened there'. Once these various narratives are obtained, the subjects are told (or reinforced) to see the shapes as people, and to answer the questions 'What kind of a person is the big triangle/small triangle/small circle?'

Normally, developing subjects typically create a narrative that depicts a social story involving e.g. the 'teaming' up of the two small shapes against the bigger one. There are scenes of 'bravery', 'elation', 'outbursts of anger', 'trapping', 'threatening', and so forth. Here is one example of a narrative segment provided by a young typically developing adolescent with normative verbal IQ:

What happened was that the larger triangle—which was like a **bigger kid** or a **bully**—and he had **isolated** himself from everything else until **two new kids** come along and the **little one** was a bit more **shy, scared,** and the smaller triangle more **like stood up for himself** and **protected the little one.** The big triangle got **jealous** of them, came out, and **started to pick on the smaller triangle.** The little triangle **got upset** and **said** like 'What's up?' 'Why are you doing this?' . . .

Clearly, this adolescent was able to provide a coherent social story that was filled with social attributions (words in **bold**) of personality invariances (e.g. bully, shy), descriptions of relationships (e.g. stood up for himself, protected the other), and attributions of feelings (e.g. jealous, upset); these attributions built on his implied understanding of the characters' needs, intentions, and even beliefs about the acceptability of certain behaviours. In contrast, narratives obtained from individuals with autism have been typically different. Here is one example of a narrative segment provided by a young adolescent with autism who had a verbal IQ comparable to the typical child above:

The big triangle went into the rectangle. There were a small triangle and a circle. The big triangle went out. The shapes bounce off each other. The small circle went inside the rectangle. The big triangle was in the box with the circle. The small triangle and the circle went around each other a few times. **They were kind of oscillating around each other, maybe because of a magnetic field.** After that, they go off the screen. **The big triangle turned like a star—like a Star of David**—and broke the rectangle.

This adolescent was clearly unable to provide a social narrative. Mostly, the narrative was a geometric description of the movements he had seen. However, his narrative was not devoid of an attempt to ascribe some forms of interpretation ('like a Star of David') and even causation ('a magnetic field') to the display (words in **bold**). For example, in an apparent attempt to understand the contingent movements of the two little shapes (usually described by typical viewers as celebration or happy play, as the little circle had just escaped the pursuit of the larger triangle thanks to the small triangle's help), this subject explained the interaction as governed by a physical form of causation, namely a magnetic field. While the typical child was using the fundamentals of social relationships to attribute meaning to the ambiguous visual display, the child with autism was using the fundamentals of physical relationships to do the same. They were both viewing the same display, but their minds appeared to be searching for different kinds of principles, social and physical, respectively. This mirrors Baron-Cohen's (Chapter 4, this volume) notion that whilst folk psychology may be impaired in autism, folk physics might even be superior.

Several narratives were intially obtained from a number of pilot cases of normally-developing and normative-IQ socially disabled individuals. We were able to verify the compelling social nature of the video (as described by Heider and Simmel) in typically developing individuals, and were impressed with how socially impoverished the narratives were which we obtained for the individuals with autism, many of whom described the video solely in geometric terms.

In order to quantify the sophistication of social attributions contained in the SAT narratives, we developed a detailed coding system, which emerged from a sample of pilot narratives from both typical and socially disabled (normative-IQ) adolescents and adults. Six index scores were derived from the narratives. A summary description is provided in Table 15.1.

These various indices were not meant to measure independent capacities. They are, of course, fundamentally interrelated given that the presence of an underlying social frame within which a subject makes attributions to the ambiguous visual stimuli is likely to result in high scores across these various indices; conversely, the absence thereof is likely to result in low scores across the various indices.

The underlying capacity for imposing a social frame of reference on the movements of the geometric shapes is best summarized by the Animation Index score, which provides an overall summary of the subject's capacity for attributing social meaning to ambiguous visual stimuli. Nevertheless, each index focuses on a given aspect of social attribution that has been given research and/or clinical attention in the literature of autism or early social development.

The Theory of Mind indices, whether focused on cognitive mental states (e.g. knowledge, desire, belief) or affective mental states (particularly the emphasis on emotions that can only exist within a ToM framework such as jealousy,

**Table 15.1.** Social attribution task index scores*

**Pertinence Index**: From our pilot work, it was clear that there was a need to measure the extent to which narratives are pertinent to the task of making social attributions, and the extent to which attributions follow some underlying representation of social reality. Accordingly, the Pertinence Index measures the percentage of propositions that are *vague references* (a physical or social referent is not defined, e.g. 'a lot of odd movements'), *misattributions* (within the wide constraints of the video, the attributions are not possible, e.g. 'the rectangle is a table'), *irrelevant or tangential propositions* (the attribution cannot be related to a social plot, e.g. 'the structure changed its design'), or *inconstant referents* (the referent for a character or prop changes over the course of the narrative). Such propositions would be likely to result in communication breakdown in real life, and would reflect the subject's difficulties in interpreting stimuli meaningfully and in a situation-relevant fashion from a social standpoint. Scoring of this index is derived from the percentage of non-pertinent propositions out of the total number of propositions, and a proposition is defined as a verb plus its argument (Stein and Glenn 1979).

**Salience Index**: Based on Heider and Simmel's (1944) work, and our pilot work with normally-developing adolescents and adults, a number of salient items of social attribution in the video segment which are typically included in the SAT narratives can be identified. These include, for example, the acknowledgment that the rectangle is a human enclosure, there are three (and only three) agents throughout, the two triangles fight, the big triangle is the aggressor, and the little circle escapes the big triangle. Nineteen high frequency attributions can be identified in adult narratives. The Salience Index is calculated in terms of the percentage of such attributions included in the subject's narrative. The index is meant to capture the extent to which typical invariances in SAT attributions are detected by a given subject.

**Theory of Mind/Cognition Index**: This index corresponds to the percentage of propositions containing mental state terms (denoting desire, knowledge, thoughts, motivation/intention, or behaviours intended to alter another person's mental states) from the total number of propositions included in the subject's narratives. This index is derived from Tager-Flusberg's work (e.g. 1992) on autistic children's use of psychological states in their spontaneous narratives.

**Theory of Mind/Affect Index**: This index corresponds to the percentage of propositions containing emotional terms (e.g. happy, sad, alarmed, envious, sulking) attributed to the characters of the video from the total number of propositions made. Guidelines for scoring were partially derived from the work of Bretherton and colleagues (e.g. 1986).

**Animation Index (AI)**: This index corresponds to a summary measure of the narrative's general level of social attribution. It includes (1) *Behaviours*: from those which necessitate intentional actors or agents but do not involve uniquely human or anthropomorphized mental activity (e.g. chasing) to behaviours that reflect the actor's attempt to alter another character's mental state (e.g. intimidating); (2) *Perceptions*: allusions to sensory experiences; (3) *Emotions*: both 'simple' emotions (e.g. happy) and higher order emotions which can only result from social action (e.g. jealous); (4) *Cognitive States*: mental states at a lower developmental level (involving e.g. desire or knowledge) and at a higher developmental level (involving e.g. thoughts or beliefs); (5) *Relationships*: from references to relationships defined by the features of the shapes (e.g. big, small) to those reflecting attribution of personality traits (e.g. a bully); and (6) *Symbolic nature*: allusion to the symbolic nature of a shape or other referent (e.g. 'the rectangle represents a house', 'power may turn against itself'). This index is scored following a hierarchical procedure, based on level achieved within each category, rather than on frequency of scored categories or specific items. This index was intended to grade overall level of social cognitive sophistication without penalizing subjects on the basis of the length of narrative provided.

**Table 15.1.** Continued.

---

**Person Index**: After the spontaneous narratives are collected, subjects are explicitly instructed to see the shapes as people, and then answer the question of what kind of a person they were. This index is intended to measure the subject's ability to derive invariant or stable personality features from the shapes' actions in the video. This ability is graded in ascending level based on the subjects use of the characters' (1) physical properties (descriptions based on the shapes' form, e.g. big, small); (2) relative properties (descriptions of the interrelated social roles of the characters although still based on their form, e.g. adult, dad, child, baby); (3) behaviourally-derived attributes (descriptons based on the characters' actions, e.g. protector, trapping kind of person); and (4) abstracted psychological features (these attributions reflect characterological statements, e.g. curious, timid). Like the Animation Index, this index is scored hierarchically, in terms of level achieved, rather than in terms of frequency of attributes generated for each character.

---

\* Detailed coding instructions based on these principles are available upon request from the first author.

embarrassment), refer to the main body of literature described in the present volume.

The Salience Index refers to the readiness with which a subject imposes a social interpretation to ambiguous visual stimuli. Given our attempt to capture the apparent lack of spontaneous use of whatever social cognitive resources might be available that we informally observed in bright individuals with autism, this index is of particular interest to us.

The Pertinence Index refers not only to the capacity to adhere to an underlying social frame while imposing meaning on the visual display, but also to the ability to inhibit reasoning processes that are not relevant in social attribution. The inability to constrain one's utterances to what is relevant in a social interaction, and to refrain from introducing irrelevant information, are both related deficits often described as conversational skill deficits in bright individuals with autism and related conditions (e.g. Landa, in press).

Finally, the Person Index refers to the normally-developing young child's tendency to quickly create 'personality' attributions (i.e. stable traits and dispositions) in relation to people (e.g. Eder 1989, 1990) and then to often overuse this capacity by applying human attributes to a variety of not necessarily human phenomena (e.g. Carey, 1985; Inagaki and Hatano 1987; Inagaki and Sugiyama 1988). This tendency to 'anthropomorphize' reasoning about the world is thought to be pervasive in children (e.g. Carey 1985), and may remain with us in adulthood in many different forms (e.g. Tversky and Kahneman 1975). To our knowledge, little is known about this interesting phenomenon in autism.

We have recently compiled SAT data on adolescents and adults with autism and Asperger's syndrome with normative verbal IQs, as well as on normally developing subjects with comparable age and verbal IQ (Klin, submitted for publication). The socially disabled subjects had achieved a normative score on the Oral Expression subtest of the *Test of Language Competence* (Wiig and Secord 1989), a test requiring the generation of appropriate utterances to a picture portraying the interaction of people. On this very structured test these individuals were, therefore, able to adhere to the social task constraints. On the SAT, however, their results were strikingly deficient relative to the control group. On the Animation Index their results were on average at the most basic level of attribution, defined as the presence of a proposition containing the description of an intentional behaviour but not uniquely human nor requiring the presence of attribution of mental states (e.g. chasing, fighting, breaking). Individual results were quite telling, however, in that a substantial number of the subjects saw the video sequence entirely in geometric terms. The control group's average was at a level requiring multiple attributions of behaviours implying one character's manipulation of another's mental states, as well as attributions of higher level cognitive and affective mental states. On the Pertinence Index, over one third of the propositions contained in the socially disabled subjects' narratives were non-pertinent, i.e. irrelevant to the task at hand. Given that propositions that faithfully described the geometric movements of the video were not included as 'non-pertinent', it was clear that the subjects tried to comply with the task demands, but their efforts were often not appropriate as social attributions. In the example narrative of the young adolescent with autism (given above), reasoning about magnetic fields or geometric transformations of the stimuli illustrates the effort to make sense of the visual stimuli without resorting to social interpretations. If this index can be seen as an indicator of social reasoning in real-life situations, this result would suggest that one third of these individuals' utterances in a social situation would be irrelevant or otherwise non-pertinent to the constraints imposed by such a situation. This would clearly impact on their ability to adjust to the demands placed by reciprocal conversations. In contrast to the results for the individuals with autism, only a small number of the propositions contained in the controls' narratives were coded as irrelevant.

On the Salience Index, only a quarter of the commonly salient social elements of the video were detected by the socially disabled individuals, relative to 90% in the control group. If this index is an indicator of a subject's predisposition to think socially about visual stimuli, say a situation in which a person enters a busy high school cafeteria and is confronted with a complex array of social visual stimuli, this result would mean that our subjects would on average detect only about a quarter of what was happening. It would hardly be a surprise, therefore, if they formed a very fragmented interpretation of what was actually going on and possibly affecting them.

The Theory of Mind indices, both cognitive and affective, indicated that only a very small number of the socially disabled individuals' propositions contained a mental state term; narratives provided by controls continued 4 to 5 times as many propositions with mental state terms.. This result replicates previous findings of low usage of mental state terms in spontaneous narratives of individuals with autism (see Tager-Flusberg, Chapter 6, this volume). It does seem, therefore, that these individuals' attempts to make sense of social phenomena do not frequently include reasoning based on mental states.

Finally, results on the Person Index indicated that when forced to see the geometric characters as people and then to describe them, the socially disabled individuals on average limited their answers to attributions directly related to the physical properties of the shapes (e.g. 'What kind of a person is the big triangle?' Answer: 'A grown up').

In contrast, controls utilized on average at least two different and non-contrastive (e.g. good–bad) personality attributions to describe the three shapes. This result emphasizes the limitations of the socially disabled individuals to understand the implications of the behaviours displayed by the shapes as determinants of their 'character'.

These results are surprising given the high level of cognitive and linguistic abilities of the subjects with autism and Asperger's Syndrome. To the extent that the SAT results are an indicator of spontaneous social reasoning patterns in these individuals, we can tentatively state that a large proportion of salient social elements of a situation escape their detection; their reasoning about the social environment is often irrelevant to a social understanding of it; when present, social attributions seldom involve considerations of other people's mental states; and the understanding of other people is often limited to their physical attributes. We may help them a great deal by explicitly and verbally defining the social variables and the social cognitive task at hand. If left to their own devices, however, they appear to show a very low readiness to process visual stimuli in socially meaningful ways.

The SAT provides a window into a person's social cognitive capacities. The various indices were created with a view to quantifying and further specifying a profile of global skills that have research and/or clinical interest. By understanding the social attribution mechanisms involved in the SAT, we hope to identify some of the factors that make social attribution second nature to most people, and a major obstacle to individuals with autism. What does it take, then, to construct a social understanding out of the movements of these geometric shapes?

## DEVELOPMENTAL CONSIDERATIONS

The issue of how children discern inanimate from social stimuli, or, more generally, of how children construct their social reality, has been addressed by two very distinct child development literatures. The first group of studies focus on children's perceptions of simple objects such as geometric shapes, and how these shapes gain 'animacy', or agent-like attributes, very much like people. This approach abstracts the minimal requirements for some form of social attribution to take place by utilizing simple experimental stimuli that differ from control stimuli on a single variable of interest, thus allowing for a precise dissection of social attribution. This reductionist approach makes it possible to build a fairly simple, often cognitively-based model of social attribution in which, however, early babyhood social and affective experiences are not considered. The second group of studies begins exactly with what is left out in the first approach, namely with babies' early social, affective, and communicative experiences, with an emphasis on how construction of social reality is embedded in such experiences. Phenomena such as the still-face effect, social referencing, and ritualized communicative gestures are seen as evidence of implicit understanding of social processes, and, by extension, of the distinct nature of social as against inanimate phenomena. The focus on global domains of the baby's experiential reality, however, makes it very difficult to construct simple models of social attribution. Nevertheless, the ubiquity and early emergence of the social, affective, and communicative phenomena studied, and the infant's impressive social capacities that are demonstrated through them, make it impossible to ignore them in any model of early social development. It is unclear to what extent these two groups of studies can meaningfully converge, as they may represent different levels of discourse (Winograd 1975), although important attempts to bring them together have recently been made (e.g. Baron-Cohen 1995).

The stage for this discussion was set by Heider and Simmel's (1944) paper. There was something compellingly person-like about abstract objects moving by themselves, and once they were seen as agents, subjects proceeded immediately to ascribing needs, desires, intentions, feelings, and beliefs to the various characters, which both con-strained, and in turn were constrained by, the interpretations of the relationships among the various characters. With great similarity to this model, Premack and Premack (1995) have more recently proposed that human social competence consists of three hierarchically organized components. The first component—the Intentional System—is peripheral or perceptual in nature: if an object moves by itself (is 'self-propelled') in a goal-directed fashion, it is seen as intentional. Infants are thought to be capable of recognizing a small number of goals, namely escape from confinement, responsiveness to another intentional object (e.g. company of others), and overcoming gravity. By understanding how these goals interrelate, infants develop a motivational theory. Intentionality (in infants and young children, in contrast to adults) is not seen as a separate mental state but as intrinsically part of action, resulting perceptually and automatically from looking at self-propelled and goal-directed objects. The second component—the Social System—is internal or cognitive in nature: while the Intentional System is activated by individual objects, this component is activated by interactions between intentional objects. Its purpose is to assign positive or negative value to these interactions using two criteria, namely 'intensity' and 'sociality'. Intensity defines actions as 'hard' (e.g. hitting) which is valued as negative, and 'soft' (e.g. caressing) which is valued as positive. Sociality refers to the actions of one intentional object as 'helping' another object to achieve its goal, or 'hurting' another object from achieving its goal. Infants are thought to expect the value of the action (soft or hard, helping or hurting) to be reciprocated among intentional objects. The third component—Theory of Mind—is activated by the representations of inter-actions of the intentional objects as produced by the Social System. Its purpose is to explain these interactions. Its output corresponds to basic states of mind, such as perception, desire, and belief.

This model offers an attractively simple diagram of social competence. The fact that infants have been shown to appreciate the special nature of self-propelled objects (Premack 1990) and goal-directed behaviours (Gergely *et al.* 1995; Leslie and Keeble 1987; Mandler 1992) as early as six to twelve months of age has prompted the hypothesis that infants are hardwired to perceive intention depending only on appro-priate stimulation. Different cognitive scientists have seen this mechanism as one of the main triggers of social cognitive development, leading eventually to the emergence of Theory of Mind (Baron-Cohen 1995; Leslie 1994; Premack and Premack 1995). Leslie (1994) in fact extended the perceptual nature of intention and value judgment of simple interactions among agents to include also the phenomena of perception and communication. For example, he describes how children perceive agents as objects involved in 'causation at a distance': the behaviour of an object may be affected by distal stimuli implying the phenomenon of *perception*; and they act to influence another agent from a distance implying *communication*.

Implicit in Premack and Premack's model is the notion that animate and inanimate objects (people and things) can be differentiated on the basis of their movements. For example, inanimate objects can move only if movement is imparted to them, and causative interaction between two inanimate objects can occur only if there is contact. In contrast, agents are self-propelled and can have an impact on another agent from a distance. A set of rules governing animate and inanimate objects is applied to visual stimuli. If the rules for inanimate objects are broken, the perception of an agent results. Departing from this view, Spelke and colleagues (1995) propose that social attribution is a domain-specific case of causation in that children suspend their knowledge of rules guiding inanimate objects altogether when perceiving people. For example, one study compared the reactions of four-month-old infants to a person or an inanimate object disappearing behind a door (Legerstee 1994). The infants responded to the disappearance of the object by touching the door; in contrast, they responded to the disappearance of the person by vocalizing to the person rather than by trying to touch the door. This finding suggests that infants reason differently about the movements of people than about the movements of inanimate objects. Building on this and their own studies, Spelke and colleagues suggest that social attribution is guided by human-specific principles that are accessible to children from very early on in their lives. In other words, people are treated as people by infants not because they are self-propelled and goal-directed; rather, early inborn skills set humans apart from the inanimate world from the outset. And a range of expectations apply to this domain which do not apply to any other domain of their experience. This is not a trivial distinction because according to this model the genesis of social attribution should not be found in perceptual invariances in the visual field; rather it should be found in the various human-specific principles with which infants are endowed, and which they apply to stimuli making up their social experiences. A not exhaustive list includes the notions that humans react to one another (contingency), respond in kind to one another's actions (reciprocity), supply information to one another (communication), perceive and express emotions, and use gaze to indicate engagement with target.

How have these domain-specific 'principles of human action' been experimentally demonstrated? That infants expect that humans react in a contingent fashion to one another has been shown through a series of paradigms (Tarabulsy *et al.* 1996), the most well-known among which is the still-face paradigm (Tronick *et al.* 1978). When mothers who have previously been stimulating their babies in a playful fashion withdraw the smiles and vocalization and assume a still-face, infants as young as two to three months first make attempts to continue the interaction but then stop smiling, avert their gaze, and may protest vigorously (Field *et al.* 1986; Gusella *et al.* 1988). Such studies suggest that very young infants have clear expectations regarding social engagement, and protest if these expectations go unfulfilled. That infants expect that humans reciprocate the actions of one another has been shown in studies of imitative games of infancy such as peek-a-boo (Trevarthen 1979), where babies as young as nine months understand the roles involved in the joint activity and work to maintain their reciprocal structure (Ross and Lollis 1987). If, for example, the adult partner stops playing the game, babies are likely to look back and forth between the adult and objects and repeat their turn or assume the turn of the adult. Such studies suggest that infants expect reciprocity in social contact. Even earlier precursors of reciprocal engagement can be seen in the emergence of imitation in young infants. New-born infants imitate facial and manual gestures (Meltzoff and Moore 1977) and emotional expressions (Field *et al.* 1982) modelled by an adult; they also react with great interest to an adult who imitates their own actions (Field 1977). The notion that early imitation corresponds to an infant's attempt to elicit a response from another person (Meltzoff and Moore 1992) would suggest that infants not only expect reciprocity on the part of the social partner (as in peek-a-boo) but also try to elicit it themselves. That infants expect that humans exchange information is evident in studies of communication skills in young babies. By the age of nine months, pointing gestures are made with the explicit intention of communicating a request; some gestures become ritualized forms of communication (Bates *et al.* 1979). Before that, by the age of six months, it is possible to engage babies in a vocal dialogue that includes turn-taking and emotional communication (e.g. Ricks 1975). Much prior to uttering the first word, therefore, infants exhibit very specific expectations regarding communicative engagement.

Infants' sensitivity to emotional expressions is shown in a host of studies involving both the visual and the auditory modalities. One-day-old infants can discriminate between happy versus sad faces (Field and Walder 1981); five-month-olds can discriminate between happy versus sad vocalizations (Walker-Andrews and Grolnick 1983), and between happy versus angry vocal expressions (Walker-Andrews and Lennon 1991); five-month-olds are also capable of matching facial and vocal expressions on the basis of congruity (Walker 1982). Infants are not only sensitive to the emotional expressions of others, they also react appropriately to emotional signals (Haviland and Lelwica 1981). For example, they react negatively to their mothers' depressed affect (Tronick *et al.* 1986), and appropriately to the emotional content of praise or prohibition (Fernald 1993). An important instance of reactivity to the meaning of emotional expressions is found in the phenomenon of social referencing: between ten and twelve months, infants search for the emotional expression of a significant other to resolve a state of uncertainty and regulate their behaviour accordingly (approaching or avoiding) (Campos and Sternberg 1981). Several studies have shown that an infant's likelihood of interacting with a stranger, of crossing a visual cliff, of touching new toys, and so forth, are considerably influenced by the emotional messages sent by the parents (Feinman and Lewis 1983). Interestingly, humans cannot claim exclusivity over this process, as young chimpanzees have been shown, very much like human infants, to be capable of acquiring information about their complex social and physical environments through social referencing and can use emotional information to alter their own behaviour (Russell *et al.* 1997). Finally, sensitivity to gaze direction is another rich source of social information available to the young infant at least from the age of five months, when, for example, infants are shown to smile less to an adult who is averting his or her eyes (Caron *et al.* 1997); some studies have demonstrated infant sensitivity to the direction of the eyes at even earlier ages (Erlich 1993 in Spelke *et al.* 1995). The information that looking implies attending or engaging is apparently available to infants as young as 3 months: for example, at this age infants will smile considerably less if an adult turns the head or closes the eyes (Caron *et al.* 1997). Sometime between five and nine months, infants follow the gaze of another person towards what becomes an object of shared attention (Scaife and Bruner 1975), and they can use this information to predict the other person's actions (Spelke *et al.* 1995). Whether this results from general learning and social experiences or from the operation of a specific 'shared attention mechanism' (Baron-Cohen 1995) remains to be fully tested.

In summary, two rather distinct approaches to the study of early social development provide us with different perspectives on how children gain an understanding of what are and what are not social phenomena. The first, which can be described as a 'cognitive competency' model, posits that people are different from things because they are intentional objects; the attribution of intentionality is a perceptual phenomenon resulting from self-propelled and goal-directed objects being seen as people. Once objects are perceived as intentional, a motivational theory of social interaction follows (positive/negative, helping/hurting), which eventually leads into an explanatory theory of social interaction (based on mental states or a theory of mind). The second approach, which can be described as a 'social-affective experiential' model, posits that people are treated as different from things because they form a differentiated and preferential domain of experience from the time of birth or soon after. This domain of experience corresponds to social affective exchanges between a baby and an adult or a very small number of adults. In the context of Heider and Simmel's movie, the first approach would state that certain kinds of movement indicate that the objects are intentional beings, and that their interactions are positive/negative, helpful/ hurting; the effort to explain these interactions would promote the use of mental states such as desires, feelings, and thoughts. The second approach would state that the shapes are interpreted as people because their actions map onto the child's expectations and experiences of how people interact. Heider and Simmel combined these two statements in their interpretation of their subjects' responses: the movements of the shapes compelled subjects to see them as people, although the actual plot they narrated was anchored in their interpretations of the attributes of the actors and their relationships, i.e. the subjects' expectations of how people behave. However, the subjects' imagination was not given free rein; rather, their attributions were constrained by the movements themselves, resulting in some responses that were very similar across many subjects (e.g. that the two triangles were fighting). But the movements themselves did not elicit such invariant attributions when the movie was shown in reverse, quite likely because the movie did not then reflect a plausible social situation, i.e. the subjects' expectations of what a readily identified social situation would look like.

Despite the plausibility of Heider and Simmel's account, we are still left without a clear explanation of what happened in the subjects' minds when they watched the movie, i.e. we do not know whether certain perceptual principles of human action captured by the shapes' movements generated the subjects' social attribution, or, alternatively, the movements were seen as human because they mapped so readily on the subjects' social expectations. Was the movie showing us some fundamental laws of human movement, as Premack and Premack might suggest, or was the movie simply an artistic rendering of human movement? In the way we are currently using the movie in the SAT paradigm, this question is not important, given that our goal is simply to measure a subject's readiness to impose social meaning upon the visual display. If, however, our goal is a more ambitious attempt to explain the phenomenon, causally and developmentally, then this question becomes quite central. For example, are we to explain our SAT results in terms of the autistic individuals' inability to detect intentionality in the shapes' movements, or in terms of their lack of readiness in applying social expectations to what they see, a reflection of their impoverished life-long social experiences? In other words, are we to focus our study of social attribution on specific perceptual and cognitive mechanisms or on the global process of social engagement?

Whether or not one is studying a specific social cognitive mechanism or a result of social experiences is, at times, not immediately recognized. For example, our group has recently completed a neuroimaging study of face perception in higher-functioning individuals with autism (Schultz *et al.* in press). We studied face and object perception with functional magnetic resonance imaging (fMRI) and found reduced activation among patients with autism in the right fusiform gyrus (FG) and increased activation of the inferior temporal gyri (ITG) during face perception. The function of FG in face perception is well documented (Haxby *et al.* 1999; Kanwisher *et al.* 1997). The ITG, on the other hand, has been implicated as one of the regions involved in non-face object perception (Gauthier *et al.* 1999; Haxby *et al.* 1999; Kanwisher *et al.* 1997). In the subjects with autism, face perception engaged brain areas that were selectively activated during object perception in our normal control samples. The results indicated that individuals with autism did not rely on the normal neural substrate during face perception but rather engaged brain areas that were more important to non-face, object processing. In summary, rather than treating faces as a special form of visual stimulus they treated faces as ordinary objects.

It would be tempting to hypothesize from these results that a circumscribed area of the brain, namely the FG, and the mechanism it represents, namely perception of face identity, were causatively related to autism. Given the centrality of face perception in interpersonal interactions, this would be a perfectly plausible theory of autism. However, other recent studies (e.g. Gauthier *et al.* 1997, 1999) have suggested that the FG is not necessarily the brain site for face recognition; rather it appears to be a site associated with visual expertise, so that when a person becomes an expert on a given object category (say, tapestry), selective activation of the FG occurs when the person is looking at an instance of that object. How would this alter our interpretation of the fMRI study reported above? The FG was not selectively activated when the individuals with autism were looking at faces because they were not experts on faces. In contrast, normally-developing individuals have a lifetime to develop this expertise, a result of thousands upon thousands of hours of focusing one's attention on other people's faces, beginning as soon as the visual system allows for enough acuity and flexible focus, probably around the first few weeks of life. If the association between the FG and a visual expert system is corroborated, the study of a specific social cognitive mechanism—face perception—will in fact have been a study of early experiences with faces, or, in the case of autism, the study of the lack of social engagement in these individuals.

While the conclusion that individuals with autism treated faces as objects would not be altered, the developmental and neurofunctional accounts of why this was so would move us away from a hypothesis seeing autism as a disorder of face perception, back into what we already know, namely that in autism social engagement is extremely reduced, probably from very early in life. A similar rationale can be made with regard to the hypothesis that a social cognitive mechanism responsible for detecting intentionality—such as the Intentionality Detector (ID) described by Baron-Cohen (1995)—is a major facilitator of social development. On the basis of the discussion above, it would not be possible to determine whether the individuals with autism fail to see the geometric shapes because they cannot detect intentional objects—they do not have the ID, cognitively or neurofunctionally—or because they fail to readily impose social expectations on what they see, a reflection of their impoverished lifelong experiences of social engagement. We can further explore this issue by reviewing some implications of recent neuroimaging studies of the perception of human action.

## NEUROFUNCTIONAL CONSIDERATIONS

To our knowledge, the only study to date that has explored brain systems involved in the perception of human movements was conducted by Bonda and colleagues (1996). These researchers measured cerebral metabolic activity in normal human subjects using positron emission tomography (PET) during a task of perception of 'biological motion', or the movements characteristic of living things. The human movements were simulated in three-dimensional space using point-light displays using a technique pioneered by Johansson (1973), which permits the depiction of human movement by means of a few isolated points of light attached to major joints in the body. Naive observers readily interpret the moving cluster of light points as representing a human figure, despite the complete absence of form cues. The results were quite surprising: while rather mechanical motions (e.g. bringing a cup to one's mouth) implicated the intraparietal sulcus and the caudal part of the superior temporal sulcus in the left hemisphere, the perception of more social human movement (dance-like expressive movements) implicated parts of the right superior temporal sulcus and adjacent temporal cortex, the amygdala, as well as other structures closely interconnected with the amygdala, such as the subcallosal gyrus, the septal area, and the caudal orbitofrontal cortex. Given the involvement of the amygdaloid system in the various emotional states such as fear (Scott *et al.* 1977), social bonds (Steklis and Kling 1985), conspecific communication gestures (Dicks *et al.* 1969), and facial expressions (Young *et al.* 1995), the authors of the study interpreted the activity in the amygdala as an emotional disposition experienced by the perceiver in response to the behaviour perceived. The amygdala activation was restricted predominantly to the right hemisphere, the function of which has been related to emotional processing (Heilman *et al.* 1993). It is of interest to consider that both the mechanical movement (bringing a cup to one's mouth) and the more social movements (dancing expressively) can be considered as forms of self-propelled goal-directed actions; and yet only the latter were associated with affectively-related, prefrontal activation. Therefore, despite the likely attribution of intentionality to both conditions (both were self-propelled and goal-directed), only the more social one selectively activated areas of the brain that we normally associate with social-affective actions. In other words, the attribution of intentionality by itself, if not occurring within a social framework, would appear to be associated with more circumscribed, non-frontal and non-limbic areas.

The fact that the 'expressive dancing' condition in Bonda and colleagues' study mapped on brain systems associated with affective processing suggested to us that our social attribution task would result in a similar pattern of brain activation, given that it also required ideation of social actions. In order to explore this possibility, we recently completed an fMRI study (Schultz *et al.* submitted) of normally-developing individuals using stimuli that were of the same nature as the ones utilized in the behavioural SAT study described above. The fact that individuals with autism did so poorly on that task suggested that if circumscribed brain systems were identified in association with that task in unaffected subjects, the regions identified would be of particular interest for further study in the context of autism.

The study involved a comparison between two tasks: the first required geometric reasoning, whereas the second required social reasoning. On both tasks, the visual stimuli consisted of the movements of geometric shapes. On the first task, the shapes followed geometric trajectories and the movements were not contingent on one another. On the second task, the movements were similar to the ones included in the SAT paradigm, i.e. they were created to represent social situations. On the first task, subjects were asked to answer whether or not at least two of the shapes were moving along a trajectory consistent with its geometric form (e.g. a triangle moving along a triangular trajectory)—the geometric reasoning task—whereas on the second task subjects were asked to answer whether the shapes were 'friends' or 'not friends'— the social reasoning task. The tasks were conducted in this form in order to ensure that the subjects were employing reasoning about geometric trajectories (on the first task) and social relationships (on the second task) as we expected them to do; in our pilot studies, simple passive viewing of the movements of shapes, however random we might construct them to be, appeared to at times generate social reasoning, presum- ably because of a rather prepotent tendency of typical adults to interpret ambiguous movement as social. An effort was made to keep complexity, quantity, and location of movement of the displays in the two tasks as directly comparable as possible, so that the comparison between the two tasks would isolate the variable of social ideation. The results were surprisingly strong, with significant selective brain activation for the social reasoning task in a fairly large area of the medial prefrontal cortex; statistical analyses revealed that the major area of activation, however, was centered in Brodmann's area 9.

It is of interest that this region has been shown to be involved in a small number of ToM imaging studies. For example, in a PET study by Fletcher and colleagues (1995), where subjects were read stories involving (or not) mental state elements, an area of the left medial frontal cortex on the border of Brodmann's areas 8 and 9 was selectively activated during the mentalizing stories. A subsequent study of five individuals with Asperger's syndrome with this task showed reduced medial prefrontal activity in response to ToM task. Moreover, the center of activation was displaced 2 cm below and 8 mm more anterior compared to the controls, in a transitional region between BA 9 and 10 (Happé *et al.* 1996). Another PET study (Goel *et al.* 1995) requiring reasoning about the beliefs and intentions of others revealed overlapping areas of selective activation relative to the study by Fletcher and colleagues, with prominent activation of the left medial frontal lobe (primarily Brodmann's area 9) and left temporal lobe (Brodmann's areas 21, 39/19, 38).

Involvement of Brodmann's area 9 has not been uniformly reported in imaging studies of ToM. One SPECT study (Baron-Cohen *et al.* 1994) in which subjects were asked to imagine what the mind can do (mental states) versus what the body can do (non-mental states) reported increased blood flow in the right orbito-frontal cortex relative to the left frontal poles. However, information about other brain regions was not reported. Although preliminary, one can conclude at this point that Brodmann's area 9 and adjacent areas deserve further exploration in future imaging studies of mentalizing. What is of particular interest is that both the above referenced studies, and our own, overlapped in terms of selective brain regions of activation, and yet the tasks were quite different in terms of verbal mediation and reasoning demands.

Having said that, it would be mistaken to conclude that this region of the brain subserves cognitive mentalizing activities to the exclusion of other related psychological functions. The orbital and medial prefrontal cortices have also been associated with other mental activities, particularly those involved in affective processing. In a series of studies of the neuroanatomic correlates of emotions (Lane *et al.* 1997*a, b*; Reiman *et al.* 1997), these brain regions have been shown to participate in affective processing unrelated to the type of emotion, its valence, or the method used to generate them. It is of interest, however, that the ventral medial prefrontal cortex appeared to be differentially involved in positive and negative emotions (Lane *et al.* 1997*a*) and pleasant and unpleasant emotions (Lane *et al.* 1997*b*). This finding is important because it suggests that emotions are differentially processed in the brain based on whether they can be seen as eliciting approach behaviours or withdrawal behaviours (Davidson *et al.* 1990). This model of brain representation of emotions matches an affective experience with a specific predisposition to respond, a position that can be easily understood in the context of the evolution of adaptive mechanisms important for survival: for example, it would be difficult to conceive of an antelope's emotional reaction to a lion in isolation from the antelope's immediate flight behaviour. The same argument can be made with regard to the function of the orbital and medial frontal cortices. Studies of this brain area in patients (Damasio *et al.* 1990; Hornak *et al.* 1996) and nonhuman primates (Dias *et al.* 1996) suggest that it participates in integrating information about rewards and punishments to bias future behaviour.

One neurofunctional model of social reasoning emerging from this work is Damasio's 'somatic marker hypothesis', according to which the ventromedial prefrontal cortex (medial Bromann's area 11) and the amygdala play an important role in a person's ability to generate and use one's body's emotional cues to guide one's thoughts and behaviours, especially as they concern social and personal decisions for which logical analysis is less pertinent to the task (e.g. Saver and Damasio 1991; Damasio 1994; Adolphs *et al.* 1998). Patients with lesions in this area appear to be insensitive to the future consequences of their actions in that they fail to generate anticipatory autonomic reactions of the same magnitude as controls. Bechara, Damasio and colleagues (1997) attribute this to a lack of feedback from the autonomic system which reacts during the decision-making process but is ignored in the patient with ventromedial prefrontal damage.

Another region of importance in this context is the anterior cingulate, lesions to which also seem to be associated with impaired social functioning (Damasio 1995; Devinsky *et al.* 1995; Saver and Damasio 1991). As a result, regions of the brain comprising of the anterior cingulate, the adjacent medial prefrontal cortices, and the amygdala have been proposed as a functional system for the integration of thought and emotion which 'interact so intimately that they constitute the source for the energy of both external action (movement) and internal action (thought animation, reasoning)' (Damasio 1994, p. 71). In this model the organism's initial autonomic response is driven by actions of the amygdala and quickly sensed at the level of ventral-medial frontal cortex, which in turn feed back into upper regions of the medial prefrontal cortex and anterior cingulate, where affective responses are integrated with additional information, externally or internally generated.

This neurofunctional 'loop' brings together affective and reasoning processes involved in social interaction, and generates a number of empirical hypothesis as to where in this system the breakdown may occur in autism. Given the range of manifestations of autism (in terms of severity and variability of symptom presentation), the breakdown could occur at different points, and maybe in different degrees, giving rise to different syndromes of social disorder. To suggest one example not previously discussed in this chapter (but see Perner and Lang, Chapter 7, this volume), Pennington, Ozonoff, and colleagues (e.g. Pennington and Ozonoff 1996) have argued that deficits in executive functions (EF), including working memory, may play a contributory role in social disorders. As social reasoning appears to involve integration of multiple sources of internal and external information, and given that the EF are thought to be mediated by frontal structures overlapping or contiguous to the prefrontal medial cortices (Duncan 1986), it would be possible that damage to EF could derail the neurofunctional loop proposed by Damasio and others. Another key constituent of this neurofunctional loop is the amygdala, a structure which is a focal point for many contemporary theories of autism (e.g. Schultz *et al.* in press; Bachlevalier 1994).

The tentative picture emerging from these studies is that, from a brain perspective, it might be difficult to dissociate mental state reasoning (as in the ToM studies) from affective processing and related predispositions to respond, and maybe from other important psychological processes (e.g. EF). The findings of our imaging study using the SAT paradigm converge with findings reported both in ToM studies and in emotion-processing studies. One possible way to explain this overlap would be to consider that our subjects' social attributions included both mentalizing about intentions, beliefs, and desires on the one hand, and experiences of emotion and predisposition to respond on the other hand, given that the task required a value judgment as to whether an interaction was 'friendly' or 'not friendly'. Future, more refined studies might be able to further clarify this issue. The exciting new juncture in the study of social cognition is that our interpretations of both behavioural and neurofunctional studies can be mutually constrained by data originating from the two research strategies, which can no longer be pursued in isolation.

Another interpretation of our fMRI SAT findings is that attributing social meaning to visual displays is by necessity affectively mediated, given that the appreciation of interaction between people may involve an evaluative component (good/bad, helpful/ hostile) that is intrinsically associated with a predisposition to respond in certain ways (to approach or to distance oneself). This interpretation would frame mentalizing activities as an outgrowth of social-affective experiences, reversing the current direction proposed by ToM theorists (e.g. Baron-Cohen 1988), according to whom ToM mechanisms, from intentionality detectors to shared-attention mechanisms (Baron-Cohen 1995) are autonomous biocognitive capacities making possible reciprocal social engagement and communication. On the assumption that theory of mind skills are not present in animals of lower phyletic ranking than the higher primates, the view ascribing primacy to ToM skills would signify an unusual evolutionary discontinuity, given that evolution usually assembles jerry-built new mechanisms from old, highly conserved and well-proven ones. In this sense, the view that considers ToM skills as evolving, ontogenetically and phylogenetically, from social–affective experiences, might be more plausible from an evolutionary standpoint. For example, the attribution of intentionality might have evolved from close monitoring of biological motion—not only with one's eyes, but also with one's heart and, at times, with one's legs (to get away from the threatening living object). This speculation would be consistent with Bonda and colleagues' study (1996), in which the visual processing of biological motion was associated with selective activation of amygdaloid structures, including frontal connections.

This speculation would also allow us to broaden the discussion of ToM with a view to encompassing the impressive body of developmental studies reviewed in the previous section, which suggests that social-affective experiences are as early in emerging and at least as important as the ToM mechanisms in social cognitive development; it might even suggest a hypothesis as to why higher-functioning individuals with autism seem to be unable to utilize their ToM skills spontaneously in their real-life social adjustment, the initial clinical puzzle with which we started this chapter.

## SOCIAL COGNITIVE DEVELOPMENT: A FUNCTIONAL APPROACH

To view the development of ToM skills within a broader context of social development represents an attempt to see maturation and emergence of social cognitive mechanisms as means to realising a major function in human adaptation, namely the establishment of social engagement and relationships. This view contrasts with the approach adopted in most chapters of this book, in which specific mechanisms (e.g. intentionality detector, metarepresentational skills) are thought to be both a precondition of social development, and a neurobiologically pre-determined outcome. The shift we propose comes from a consideration of evolutionary principles impinging upon human development: for example, organisms evolve by building on phylogenetically more primitive mechanisms, by channelling maturation and development towards ever more complex ways of realizing the target function, and by allowing for a great deal of plasticity and redundancy to be built in the system so that the probability of breakdowns in the important function is diminished.

This functional approach captures important principles in embryological maturation. For example, the infant's grasping reflex would be an important skill were babies required still to hold on to their mother's body for survival. The functional principle is exemplified here in that the muscles of the infant's hands do not mature at a uniform rate; rather those muscles involved in the grasping reflex mature at an accelerated rate compared with adjacent muscles because they will be involved in a skill which emerges very early (immediately after birth) (Anokhin 1964). Although this functional approach is commonplace in biological research, its relevance to our understanding of social development has been given less attention. What would be the implications of seeing social development in this light?

The first implication is that social engagement and the establishment of relationships should be based on a highly redundant and plastic system, not on single mechanisms. A range of ways of engaging socially are available to babies, through the tactile, visual, and auditory modalities. Social learning occurs by means of imitation, reactions to other people's affective responses, and shared-attention behaviours, and in other ways. Although in the intact child all of these avenues of social engagement are well integrated and interrelated, the redundancy of this system allows for multiple developmental trajectories resulting from the combination of variable endowment and its interaction with environmental factors, including primarily the immediate social responses of caregivers. Redundancy also allows for enough plasticity in the system so that if one avenue of social engagement is blocked or reduced, the function is realized through alternative pathways. Children with sensory impairments will still be socially related, albeit in a way that reflects their impairment and their compensatory mechanisms. The difficulty in positing single mechanisms as preconditions of social development is that, according to the functional view, if a higher level form of social engagement is blocked (e.g. conceiving of other people as intentional beings), the system should fall back on more primitive mechanisms (e.g. people should still be salient targets of attention, imitation behaviours should still occur, and fairly elaborate forms of attachment behaviours should still be observed). The fact that these forms of social engagement are greatly reduced in a large proportion of children with autism raises the question of where the breakdown is occurring, and whether current models of this breakdown go low enough in the hierarchy of social mechanisms to encompass the severity of the social disability evidenced in these children.

The second implication relates to the jerry-built nature of new adaptive mechanisms, in which new accomplishments are not points of discontinuity in evolution but outgrowths of highly conserved behaviours. As outlined in the previous section, regions of the brain that are now being identified as possible neurofunctional representations of mentalizing skills are contiguous with regions associated with affective processing, which, in turn, may be organized in terms of approach/withdrawal responses to stimulus. It would not be surprising, for example, if a higher order social skill, such as the attribution of intentionality to others, was found to be neurofunctionally related to the capacity to process certain kinds of movements as human (or, more, generally, as animate), given that a range of species are required to monitor the movements of others and to respond to them in order to flee or approach, play or fight. The point to be emphasized here is that the human capacity for attribution of intentionality would be unlikely to become dissociated from the more primitive monitoring/response behaviours seen in lower species. Although the former would elevate the latter to a different level of social sophistication and effectiveness (it is more flexible to be able to infer intentions based on multiple elements in the situation than simply to react automatically to a stimulus configuration), the former would also benefit from the automaticity and immediacy of the latter, so that a reaction that is now cognitive could continue to generate immediate responses. Sometimes, these responses are described as intuitive or reflexive, given that a person appears to be reacting without full disclosure of all of the relevant information. But reciprocal social engagement—which includes processing of fast-shifting facial expressions, voice inflections, posture, etc.—would either be impossible without a moment by moment intuitive reaction of one person towards the other, or be extremely mechanical and stilted, if a person had to go through a process of sequential inferences as to what the intentions of another person might be.

It should also be the case that if the capacity for inferring intentionality in others is not available, as is proposed to be the case in autism, the person should be able to fall back on the more primitive mechanism, which can still be associated with elaborate and adaptive forms of social engagement. For example, if a person crosses the path of a squirrel, there is immediate attention to the human intruder, followed by a response which in most cases is flight, but in some cases is approach (to get some food). Clearly, squirrels are able to monitor their environment for animate movements and their possible goal direction, and to assess quickly whether these are threatening or friendly. There are numerous examples in the non-primate animal world of flight/withdrawal, play/competition, attachment/rejection behaviours, and yet these behaviours are not based on ToM skills, for which there is some suggestive evidence of being present only in the higher order primates. Interestingly, many such behaviours are not evidenced in even very able individuals with autism.

The third implication of the functional system is that the mechanisms subserving it are highly integrated, creating a seamless system in which the different parts cannot be fully understood in isolation. For example, although thought and affect have often been studied separately in the laboratory environment, this would probably be an unhelpful and artificial distinction to be made in the context of social engagement. Consider infants' ability to learn about an object in their environment from their parents' emotional reactions to that object, an ability previously described as social referencing. Would it be tenable to precondition it on the basis of the capacity for joint attention? Simply looking at their onset in ontogeny or phylogeny is not helpful, because both phenomena are observed around the same time in infants, and both have been documented in nonhuman primates (Russell *et al.* 1997; Emery *et al.* 1997). In joint attention, the child follows a person's gaze direction toward an object, which now becomes the focus of shared attention. In social referencing, the child seeks affective information in another person in order to evaluate a novel stimulus. Although it is not clear whether more primitive forms of joint attention can be identified in 'lower' or non-primate species, it might not be too far-fetched to see social referencing as a distant relative of 'heard' behaviours in which one animal signals to others to warn off imminent danger. Both involve processing of affective signals (e.g. facial expressions in one, screeches in the other), an emotional response to them (e.g. fright), and a predisposition to respond in a certain way (e.g. cry/avoid, or flee). No doubt the advent of joint attention transforms more primitive forms of social referencing, but it is unlikely to sever them from their more primitive roots, because although more sophisticated, it still serves the same function. It is equally unlikely that joint attention is unrelated to these more primitive reactions. And if one were to search for the neurofunctional representation of joint attention in the brain (a study that may be carried out soon), it is very probable that this cognitive skill, like other mentalizing activities, might also be contiguously located to affect-related, response-predisposing sites.

The fourth implication, closely related to the integrated nature of the system, is the synergy expected in the development and differentiation of the various mechanisms of social engagement. For example, the advent of more sophisticated forms of social interaction, from pointing to language exchange to nonliteral forms of communication, will continue to elevate the social referencing mechanism to qualitatively new levels. While social engagement becomes increasingly more sophisticated as a result of imagination, pretence, teasing, teasing, humour, irony, and metaphor, there is still an evaluative component which is automatic, intuitive or immediate, and which allows for moment-by-moment social adjustment. Were this not to be the case, we would be enchained to an explicit process in which we would understand, say, nonliteral speech, only after we problem-solved the incongruities contained in the communication, which would include an analysis of the semantic value of the utterance, an explicit description of the speaker's voice inflection, other emotional expressions and behaviours, and the setting in which the utterance took place. By the time we completed this process, the speaker might have left the room altogether. In other words, if we followed this process, we would understand other people's minds but in a belaboured, mechanical, computer-like fashion, missing the tempo of the interaction, and thus failing to adjust to the reciprocity and demands of the social situation.

A final implication of the functional approach relates to the fact that any model of social development, in man as in other species, needs to provide an account of social relationships. The gathering together of members of a species carries, in most cases, survival value. Typically, this evolutionary problem is solved by means of relationships. Both instrumental and affiliative forms of relating are found in non-primate species. Although the biological bases of relationships are only now being identified, already certain neuropeptides (Insel 1997) as well as brain circuitry (Brothers 1989, 1996) have been associated with the capacity for forming affective bonds with others.

A functional view of social engagement would require the integration of this powerful system in the process of social development (cf. Bowlby 1973). Although it is plausible to predicate some forms of relationships on metarepresentational abilities, this would still leave out a wide range of possibilities encountered in non-primate species. Many of these possibilities, however, are not available to a large proportion of individuals with autism, who, unfortunately, not only do not appear to have a theory of minds, but also seem not to have a 'theory of people': people are not as uniquely distinct from the surrounding non-social environment as they are for even very young children. In the same way that some forms of relationships might not be predicated on ToM skills, it is also difficult to imagine how, in isolation from social-affective systems, ToM skills would lead to relationships. This is in fact one of the commonest complaints of more able individuals with autism, who, despite an ability to cognitively understand other people, often live lives devoid of close relationships.

## THE NEED FOR A THEORY OF THEORY OF MIND IN ACTION

In light of the previous discussion, we can now return to the issue of how brighter individuals with autism might be unable to translate their social cognitive resources into competent social adaptation. The fact that in autism higher ToM skills appear to be predicated on higher cognitive and language capacities makes it likely that some forms of ToM tasks can be solved by more able individuals with autism because the tasks are presented explicitly and verbally, not unlike a problem-solving task in other psychological domains. Spontaneous social adaptations, however, require a series of additional skills—from seeking and detecting the salient aspects of a social situation to reacting quickly to fast-changing emotional expressions. In normative development, these various facets of social engagement—social cognitive and affective—are well-integrated in a seamless and synergistic fashion. The social cognitive machinery is put in motion because of a need to constantly monitor and evaluate the behaviour of others, because of a desire to engage socially, and because of a drive to develop relationships. In a way, ToM skills are the evolutionary roof top of a house in which the walls are grounded in an evolutionary account of social engagement. Basic social-affective mechanisms prompt us to social action. In brighter individuals with autism, the ToM roof appears to be free-standing.

In summary, the current ToM competency model of social interaction has provided an effective and parsimonious account of the cognitive requirements for intersubjectivity. In order to capture the remaining social phenomena outlined in this chapter, and to explain the social deficits evidenced in bright individuals with autism, it would appear necessary for this model to be expanded in order to provide an account of how ToM skills are put in action. This attempt would be likely to generate a convergence between social cognitive and social affective behavioural studies similar to the one we are now witnessing in functional neuroimaging research of the same psychological processes.

## SUMMARY

In this chapter we have attempted to address the reasons why bright individuals with autism may be unable to spontaneously use their social cognitive resources, including their ability to successfully pass lower-order ToM tasks, in their real-life social adaptation. Findings obtained using a new method, the Social Attribution Task, suggest the possibility that less studied, but early emerging social skills such as attending to, identifying, and monitoring salient social elements in the environment might play an important role in a person's construction of social understanding. We propose that these skills need to be considered in any model of the ontogeny of ToM, and that there are good evolutionary and neurofunctional reasons to do so. Finally, we contextualize the development of social understanding within a functional approach in which the emergence of social cognitive skills occurs as a way of advancing an important adaptive goal, namely social engagement. We conclude by arguing for an expansion of current competency models of social cognitive development in order to address the issue of how ToM skills are put in action in normative social adaptation, and why this mechanism is unavailable to individuals with autism.

The transdisciplinary nature of the current debate on ToM, as reflected in this volume, is likely to advance the field towards being an integrative social neuroscience. The major benefits of this development are likely to be not only cross-fertilization among the various disciplines but also the imposition of constraints on theory building, which can no longer occur in isolation from considerations about brain architectonics, functional neuropathways, and evolutionary considerations. The progress towards a more unified approach to the study of social development is likely to move us much closer to an understanding of the disabilities involved in autism than has hitherto been possible.

## Note

1. M.'s remarks reflect his ability to think about other people's beliefs and to make deliberately sarcastic and humorous statements. Of course his remarks are factually inaccurate, as no 'neurotypical' researcher working within the framework of theory of mind holds the notion that individuals with autism have no beliefs or feelings; rather the current theory of mind hypothesis of autism suggests that the ability to think about thinking, to have beliefs about other people's beliefs, etc., is greatly reduced, delayed, or inflexible, maybe reflecting an unusual or atypical developmental acquisition of these skills. M. is not an expert on the theory of mind literature, but he is an extraordinarily bright individual who is capable of having sophisticated conversations in an explicit setting, and yet exhibits equally extraordinary deficits in spontaneous social adaptation.

## REFERENCES

Adolphs, R., Tranel, D. and Damasio, A. R. (1998). The human amygdala in social judgment. *Nature*, **393**, 470–4.
Anokhin, P. K. (1964). Systemogenesis as a general regulator of brain development. *Progress in Brain Research*, **9**, 54–105.

Bachevalier, J. (1994). Medial temporal lobe structures and autism: A review of clinical and experimental findings. *Neuropsychologia*, **32**, 627–48.

Baron-Cohen, S. (1988). Social and pragmatic deficits in autism: cognitive or affective? *Journal of Autism and Developmental Disorders*, **18**, (3), 379–403.

Baron-Cohen, S. (1995). *Mindblindness: an essay on autism and theory of mind*. MIT Press, Cambridge, MA.

Baron-Cohen, S. and Howlin, P. (1999). *Teaching children with autism to mind-read: a practical guide for teachers and parents*. Wiley, New York.

Baron-Cohen, S., Ring, H., Moriarty, J., Schmitz, B., Costa, D. and Ell., P. (1994). Recognition of mental state terms: clinical findings in children with autism and a functional neuroimaging study of normal adults. *British Journal of Psychiatry*, **165**, (5), 640–9.

Baron-Cohen, S., Wheelwright, S. and Jolliffee, T. (1997). Is there a 'language of the eyes'? Evidence from normal adults and adults with autism or Asperger syndrome. *Visual Cognition*, **4**, 311–31.

Bates, E., Benigni, L., Bretherton, I., Camaioni, L. and Volterra, V. (1979). *The emergence of symbols: cognition and communication in infancy*. Academic Press, New York.

Bechara, A. H., Damasio, H., Tranel, D. and Damasio, A. R. (1997). Deciding advantageously before knowing the advantageous strategy. *Science*, **275**, 1293–5.

Bonda, E., Petrides, M., Ostry, D. and Evans, A. (1996). Specific involvement of human parietal systems and the amygdala in the perception of biological motion. *The Journal of Neuroscience*, **15** (1), 3737–44.

Bowlby, J. (1973). *Attachment and loss, Vol. 2: Separation, anxiety, and anger*. Basic, New York.

Bowler, D. M. (1992). 'Theory of Mind' in Asperger's syndrome. *Journal of Child Psychology and Psychiatry*, **33** (5), 877–93.

Bretherton, I., Fritz, J., Zahn-Waxler, C. and Ridgeway, D. (1986). Learning to talk about emotions: a functionalist perspective. *Child Development*, **57**, 529–48.

Brothers, L. (1989). A biological perspective on empathy. *American Journal of Psychiatry*, **146**, 10–9.

Brothers, L. (1996). Brain mechanisms of social cognition. *Journal of Psychopharmacology*, **10** (1), 2–8.

Campos, J. J. and Sternberg, C. R. (1981). Perception, appraisal and emotions: the onset of social referencing. In *Infant social cognition* (ed. M. E. Lamb and L. R. Sherrod), Erlbaum, Hillsdale, NJ.

Carey, S. (1985). *Conceptual development in childhood*. MIT Press, Cambridge (MA).

Caron, A. J., Caron, R., Roberts, J. and Brooks, R. (1997). Infant sensitivity to deviations in dynamic facial-vocal displays: the role of eye regard. *Developmental Psychology*, **33**, (5), 802–13.

Dahlgren, S. O. and Trillingsgaard, A. (1996). Theory of mind in non-retarded children with autism and Asperger's syndrome: a research note. *Journal of Child Psychology and Psychiatry*, **37**, 759–63.

Damasio, A. R. (1994). *Descartes' error: emotion, reason, and the human brain*. G. P. Putnam's Sons, New York.

Damasio, A. R. (1995). On some functions of the human prefrontal cortex. *Annals of New York Academy of Sciences*, **769**, 241–51.

Damasio, A. R. (1996). The somatic marker hypothesis and the possible functions of the prefrontal cortex. *Philosophical Transactions of the Royal Society of London—Series B: Biological Sciences*, **351**, 1413–20.

Damasio, A. R., Tranel, D. and Damasio, H. (1990). Individuals with sociopathic behavior caused by frontal damage fail to respond autonomically to social stimuli. *Behavioral Brain Research*, **41**, 81–94.

Davidson, R. J., Ekman, P., Saron, C., Senulis, J. and Friesen, W. V. (1990). Approach/withdrawal and cerebral asymmetry: emotional expression and brain physiology. *International Journal of Personality and Social Psychology*, **58**, 330–41.

Davinsky, O., Morrell, M. J. and Vogt, B. A. (1995). Contributions of anterior cingulate cortex to behavior. *Brain*, **118**, 279–306.

Dicks, D., Meyers, R. E. and Kling, A. (1969). Uncus and amygdala lesions: effects on social behavior in the free-ranging rhesus monkey. *Science*, **165**, 69–71.

Duncan, J. (1986). Disorganization of behavior after frontal lobe damage. *Cognitive Neuropsychology*, **3**, 271–90.

Eder, R. (1989). The emergent personologist: the structure and content of 3-, 5- and 7-year-olds' concepts of themselves and other persons. *Child Development*, **60**, 1218–28.

Eder, R. (1990). Uncovering young children's psychological selves: individual and developmental differences. *Child Development*, **61**, 849–63.

Eisenmajer, R. and Prior, M. (1991). Cognitive linguistic correlates of 'theory of mind' ability in autistic children. *British Journal of Developmental Psychology*, **9**, 351–64.

Emery, N. J., Lorincz, E. N., Perrett, D. I. and Oram, M. (1997). Gaze following and joint attention in rhesus monkeys. *Journal of Comparative Psychology*, **111** (3), 286–93.

Feinman, S. and Lewis, M. (1983). Social referencing at ten months: a second-order effect on infants' responses to strangers. *Child Development*, **54**, 878–87.

Fernald, A. (1993). Approval and disapproval: infant responsiveness to vocal affect in familiar and unfamiliar languages. *Child Development*, **64**, 657–74.

Field, T. and Walden, T. (1981). Production and perception of facial expressions in infancy and early childhood. In, *Advances in child development and behavior* (ed. H. W. Reese and L. P. Lipsitt) Academic Press, New York.

Field, T., Goldstein, S., Vega-Lahr, N. and Porter, K. (1982). Discrimination and imitation of facial expressions by neonates. *Science*, **218**, 179–81.

Field, T., Vega-Lahar, N., Scafidi, F. and Goldstein, S. (1986). Effects of maternal unavailability on motion-infant interactions. *Infant Behavior and Development*, **9**, 473–8.

Fletcher, P. C., Happe, F., Frith, U., Baker, S. C., Dolan, R. J., Frackowiak, R. S. and Frith, C. D. (1995). Other minds in the brain: a functional imaging study of 'theory of mind' in story comprehension. *Cognition*, **57** (2), 109–28.

Gauthier, I., Anderson, A. W., Tarr, M. J., Skudlarski, P. and Gore, J. C. (1997). Levels of categorization in visual recognition studies using functional magnetic resonance imaging. *Current Biology*, **7**, (9), 645–51.

Gauthier, I., Tarr, M., Anderson, A., Skudlarski, P. and Gore, J. (1999). Activation of the middle fusiform 'face area' increases with expertise in recognizing novel objects. *Nature Neuroscience*, **2**, 568–73.

Gergely, G., Nádasdy, Z., Csibra, G. and Bíró, S. (1995). Taking the intentional stance at 12 months of age. *Cognition*, **56**, 165–93.

Goel, V., Grafman, J., Sadato, N. and Hallett, M. (1995). Modeling other minds. *NeuroReport*, **6**, 1741–6.

Greenberg, A. M. and Strickland, L. H. (1973). 'Apparent behavior' revisited. *Perceptual and Motor Skills*, **36**, 227–33.

Gusella, J. L., Muir, D. W. and Tronick, E. Z. (1988). The effect of manipulating maternal behavior during an interaction on 3- and 6-month olds' affect and attention. *Child Development*, **59**, 1111–24.

Hadwin, J., Baron-Cohen, S., Howlin, P. and Hill, K. (1997). Does teaching theory of mind have an effect on the ability to develop conversation in children with autism? *Journal of Autism and Developmental Disorders*, **27**, (5), 519–37.

Happé, F. and Frith, U. (1995). Theory of mind in autism. In *Learning and cognition in autism*, (ed. E. Schopler and G. B. Mesibov), pp. 177–97. Plenum Press, New York.

Happé, F., Ehlers, S., Fletcher, P., Frith, U., Johansson, M., Gillberg, C., Doland, R., Frackowiak, R. and Frith, C. (1996). 'Theory of mind' in the brain. Evidence from a PET scan study of Asperger syndrome. *Neuroreport*, **8**(1), 197–201.

Haviland, J. M. and Lelwica, M. (1987). The induced affect response: 10-week-old infants' responses to three emotional expressions. *Developmental Psychology*, **23**, 97–104.

Heider, F. and Simmel, M. (1944). An experimental study of apparent behavior. *The American Journal of Psychology*, **57**(2), 243–59.

Heilman, K. M., Bowers, D. and Valenstein, E. (1993). Emotional disorders in neurological diseases. In *Clinical neuropsychology*, (ed. D. M. Heilman and E. Valenstein), pp. 461–97. Oxford University Press, New York.

Hornak, J., Rolls, E. T. and Wade, D. (1996). Face and voice expression identification in patients with emotional and behavioral changes following ventral frontal lobe damage. *Neuropsychologia*, **34**, 247–61.

Inagaki, K. and Hatano, G. (1987). Young children's spontaneous personification and analogy. *Child Development*, **58**, 1013–20.

Inagaki, K. and Sugiyama, K. (1988). Attributing human characteristics: developmental changes in over- and under-attribution. *Cognitive Development*, **3**, 55–70.

Insel, T. R. (1997). A neurobiological basis of social attachment. *American Journal of Psychiatry*, **154**(6), 726–35.

Johansson, G. (1973). Visual perception of biological motion and a method for its analysis. *Perceptual Psychophysiology*, **14**, 202–11.

Kahneman, D. and Tversky, A. (1973). On the psychology of prediction. *Psychological Review*, **80**, 237–51.

Kanwisher, N., McDermott, J. and Chun, M. M. (1997). The Fusiform face area: A module in human extrastriate cortex specialized for face perception. *Journal of Neuroscience*, **17**, 4302–11.

Klin, A. and Volkmar, F. R. (in press). Treatment and intervention guidelines for individuals with Asperger syndrome. In *Asperger syndrom* (ed. A. Klin, F. R. Volkmar and S. S. Sparrow). Guilford Press, New York.

Klin, A., Volkmar, F. R., Schultz, R., Pauls, D. and Cohen, D. (1997). Asperger syndrome: nosology and phenomenology. Paper presented at the 44[TH] Annual Meeting of the American Academy of Child and Adolescent Psychiatry, Toronto, Canada, October.

Klin, A. (submitted). Attributing social meaning to ambiguous visual stimuli in autism.

Landa, R. (in press). Social language use in Asperger's syndrome and high-functioning autism. In *Asperger's syndrome*, (ed. A. Klin, F. R. Volkmar and S. S. Sparrow). Guilford Press, New York.

Lane, R., Reiman, E., Ahern, G., Schwartz, G. and Davidson, R. (1997). Neuroanatomical correlates of happiness, sadness and disgust. *American Journal of Psychiatry*, **154**(7), 926–33.

Lane, R., Reiman, E., Bradley, M., Lang, P., Ahern, G., Davidson, R. and Schwartz, G. (1997). Neuroanatomical correlates of pleasant and unpleasant emotion. *Neuropsychologia*, **11**, 1437–44.

Legerstee, M. (1994). Patterns of 4-month-old infant responses to hidden silent and sounding people and objects. *Early Development and Parenting*, **3**, 71–80.

Leslie, A. M. (1994). Spatiotemporal continuity and the perception of causality in infants. *Perception*, **13**, 287–305.

Leslie, A. M. and Keeble, S. (1987). Do six-month-old infants perceive causality? *Cognition*, **25**, 265–88.

Mandler, J. M. (1992). How to build a baby. II: conceptual primitives. *Psychological Review*, **99**, 587–604.

Meltzoff, A. N. and Moore, M. K. (1977). Imitation of facial and manual gestures by human neonates. *Science*, **198**, 75–8.

Meltzoff, A. N. and Moore, M. K. (1992). Early imitation within a functional framework: the importance of person identity, movement and development. *Infant Behavior and Development*, **15**, 479–505.

Mesibov, G. B. (1986). A cognitive program for teaching social behaviors to verbal autistic adolescents and adults. In *Social behavior in autism*, (ed. E. Schopter and G. B. Mesibov), pp. 143–56. Plenum, New York.

Ozonoff, S. and Miller, J. N. (1995). Teaching theory of mind: a new approach to social skills training for individuals with autism. *Journal of Autism and Developmental Disorders*, **25** (4), 415–33.

Pennington, B. F. and Ozonoff, S. (1996). Executive functions and developmental psycho-pathology. *Journal of Child Psychology and Psychiatry*, **37** (1), 51–87.

Premack, D. (1990). The infant's theory of self-propelled objects. *Cognition*, **36**, 1–16.

Premack, D. and Premack, A. J. (1995). Intention as psychological causes. In *Cuasal Cognition: a multidisciplinary debate*, (ed. D. Sperber, D. Premack and A. J. Premack), pp. 185–99. Oxford University Press.

Prior, M. R., Dahlstrom, B. and Squires, T. L. (1990). Autistic children's knowledge of thinking and feeling states in other people. *Journal of Child Psychology and Psychiatry*, **31**, 587–602.

Reiman, E. M., Lane, R. D., Ahern, G. L., Schwartz, G. E., Davidson, R. J., Friston, K. J., Yun, L-S. and Chen, K. (1997). Neuroanatomical correlates of externally and internally generated human emotion. *American Journal of Psychiatry*, **154**, 918–25.

Ricks, D. M. (1975). Vocal communication in pre-verbal normal and autistic children. In *Language, cognitive deficits and retardation*, (ed. N. O'Connor), Butterworth, London.

Ross, H. S. and Lollis, S. P. (1987). Communication within infant social games. *Developmental Psychology*, **23**, 241–8.

Russell, C., Bard, K. and Lauren, B. (1997). Social referencing by young chimpanzees. *Journal of Comparative Psychology*, **111** (2), 185–91.

Saver, J. L. and Damasio, A. R. (1991). Preserved access and processing of social knowledge in a patient with acquired sociopathy due to ventromedial frontal damage. *Neuropsychologia*, **29**(12), 1241–9.

Scaife, M. and Bruner, J. S. (1975). The capacity for joint visual attention in the infant. *Nature*, **253**, 265–6.

Schultz, R. T., Gauthier, I., Klin, A., Fulbright, R., Anderson, A., Volkmar, F., Skudlarski, P., Lacadie, C., Cohen, D. J., Gore, J. C. (in press). Abnormal ventral temporal cortical activity among individuals with autism and Asperger syndrome during face discrimination. *Archives of General Psychiatry*.

Schultz, R. T., Klin, A., van der Gaag, C., Skudlarski, P., Herrington, J. and Gore, J. C. (Under review). Medial prefrontal involvement in the process of social attribution: An fMRI study.

Schultz, R. T., Romanski, L., Tsatsanis, K. (in press). Neurofunctional models of Asperger syndrome: clues from neuroimaging. To appear in A. Klin, F. R. Volkmar and S. S. Sparrow (eds.) *Asperger Syndrome*. New York: Plenum Press.

Scott, S. K., Young, A. W., Calder, A. J., Hellawell, D. J., Aggleton, J. P. and Johnson, M. Impaired auditory recognition of fear and anger following bilateral amygdala lesions. *Nature*, **385**, 254–9.

Shor, R. E. (1957). Effect of preinformation upon human characteristics attributed to animated geometric figures. *The Journal of Abnormal and Social Psychology*, **54**, 124–6.

Sigman, M., Yirmiya, N. and Capps, L. (1995). Social and cognitive understanding in high-functioning children with autism. In E. Shopler and G. B. Mesibov (eds.) *Learning and cognition in autism* (pp. 159–76). Plenum Press, New York.

Sparrow, S., Balla, D. and Cicchetti, D. (1984). *Vineland Adaptive Behavior Scales, Expanded Edition*. American Guidance Service, Circle Pines, MN.

Spelke, E. S., Phillips, A. and Woodward, A. L. (1995). Infant's knowledge of object motion and human action. In *Causal Cognition: a multidisciplinary debate*, (ed. D. Sperber, D. Premack and A. J. Premack), Oxford University Press.

Stein, N. and Glenn, C. G. (1979). An analysis of story comprehension in elementary school children. In *New directions in discourse comprehension*, Vol. 2, (ed. R. Freedle). Ablex, Norwood (NJ).

Steklis, H. O. and Kling, A. (1985). Neurobiology of affiliative behavior in non-human primates. In *The psychobiology of attachment and separation*, (ed. M. Reite and T. Field), Academic Press, New York.

Tager-Flusberg, H. (1992). Autistic children's talk about psychological states: deficits in the early acquisition of a Theory of Mind. *Child Development*, **63**, 161–72.

Tarabulsy, G. M., Tessier, R. and Kappas, A. (1996). Contingency detection and the contingent organization of behavior in interactions: implications for socioemotional development in infancy. *Psychological Bulletin*, **120** (1), 25–41.

Trevarthen, C. (1979). Communication and cooperation in early infancy: a description of primary intersubjectivity. In *Before speech: the beginning of interpersonal communication*, (ed. M. Bullowa), pp. 321–47. Cambridge University Press.

Tronick, E., Als, H., Adamson, L., Wise, S. and Brazelton, T. B. (1978). The infant's response to entrapment between contradictory messages in face-to-face interaction. *Journal of the American Academy of Child and Adolescent Psychiatry*, **17**, 1–13.

Tronick, E. Z., Cohn, J. and Shea, E. (1986). The transfer of affect between mothers and infants. In *Affective development in infancy*, (ed. T. B. Brazelton and M. W, Yogman), pp. 11–25. Ablex, Norwood (NL).

Walker, A. S. (1982). Intermodal perception of expressive behaviors by human infants. *Journal of Experimental Child Psychology*, **33**, 514–35.

Walker-Andrews, A. S. and Grolnick, W. (1983). Infants' discrimination of vocal expressions. *Infant Behavior and Development*, **6**, 491–8.

Walker-Andrews, A. S. and Lennon E. (1991). Infants' discrimination of vocal expressions: contributions of auditory and visual information. *Infant Behavior and Development*, **14**, 131–42.

Wiig, E. and Secord, W. (1989). *Test of Language Competence—Expanded Edition*. Psychological Corporation, San Antonio (TX).

Winograd, T. (1975). Frame representations and the procedural-declarative controversy. In *Representation and understanding: Studies in cognitive science*, (ed. D. Bobrow and A. Collins), Academic Press, New York.

Young, A. W., Aggleton, J. P., Hellawell, D. J., Johnson, M., Broks, P. and Hanley, J. (1995). Face processing impairments after amygdalotomy. *Brain*, **118**, 15–24.

# Part 3 Theory of mind: clinical aspects

# 16

# Theory of mind in other clinical conditions: is a selective 'theory of mind' deficit exclusive to autism?

RHIANNON CORCORAN

## 1. INTRODUCTION

### Aim

If this book is testimony to one thing, it is that the majority of specialists who work with people with autism know that these children and adults have enormous problems when they are asked to appreciate, or attend to, the contents of someone else's mind. Fifteen or so years of elegant empirical research, summarised in various chapters of this book and its earlier edition, have left little room for doubt about this. However, controversy still surrounds several issues about the nature and extent of the mind-reading problem and its specificity to autism. It is this latter debate which this chapter addresses. Is it really correct to argue that a 'theory of mind' (ToM) deficiency is exclusive to autism? Phrased in this way the answer has to be one typical in psychology: yes and no. Of course, the problem lies with the question. It lacks definition. If we were to ask instead whether it is justified to argue that autism is the only condition (we know of) in which a failure of neurodevelopment has resulted in an apparently selective inability to think about other's thoughts, then the answer is 'yes'. If, on the other hand, we ask whether theory of mind deficits are only ever seen in association with autism or the autistic spectra, the answer might well veer towards 'no' with interest.

In this chapter my aim is to present the evidence which points to theory of mind deficits in other clinical populations. In doing this, I am going to keep in mind two different questions: 'Is it the case that 'theory of mind' deficits can be seen in other clinical samples?' and; 'Is a selective deficit in 'theory of mind' exclusive to autism?'. Furthermore, I will use these two questions as a filter to focus on the question of how exactly we develop the ability to mind-read in everyday life. To explain: if we find that there are disorders in which theory of mind deficits exist alongside other cognitive or socio–cognitive deficits or biases, then it will be possible to explore whether these are related or unrelated to the mind-reading skill. In this way, this chapter may also speak to the modularity debate which surrounds theory of mind (e.g. Fodor 1983).

## The approach

I will not, in this chapter, be presenting the case of children or adults with Down's Syndrome. Data from this population has most often been collected as comparison data in studies of autism. Most of these studies have shown that people with Down's Syndrome and indeed those with mental retardation of unknown aetiology, perform reasonably well on 'theory of mind' tasks and certainly not less well than would be expected on the basis of either their performance on matched tasks or their mental age. Neither do I intend to review those papers which have found theory of mind difficulties in conditions which are thought to lie on the autistic spectrum. Such conditions include semantic–pragmatic language disorder, disintegrative disorder and Fragile X syndrome (Garner *et al.* unpublished; Militerni *et al.* 1997; Shields *et al.* 1996). My approach will be ,to look at conditions which are clearly distinct from autism in which there is theoretical justification, or where it is empirically reasonable, to explore ToM. Amongst these are psychiatric disorders where social, cognitive, or emotional difficulties predominate in the clinical picture, adult personality disorders in which social functioning plays a major part, developmental disorders associated with antisocial behaviour and neurological disorders in which there is clear evidence of social and/or communicative dysfunction.

I propose to begin with the area in which my own work lies, schizophrenia, because it is here that recent interest has developed.

## 2. THE CASE OF SCHIZOPHRENIA

### Empirical and theoretical justification

Although schizophrenia is an illness which becomes clinically manifest during adolescence or early adult life, accruing evidence from epidemiological studies (e.g. Jones *et al.* 1993; Murray and Lewis 1987) supports a neurodevelopmental aetiology for this illness, at least for the chronic deficit state manifestation. Poor social functioning in childhood in those who later are diagnosed as suffering from chronic schizophrenia is becoming an established finding of considerable theoretical and practical significance.

This empirical evidence underpinned the argument, proposed by Chris Frith in 1992, that schizophrenia can be understood as a disorder of the representation of mental states. Frith argued that the signs and symptoms of schizophrenia reflect underlying cognitive deficits within a system which enables the recognition and monitoring of one's own willed intentions as well as the attribution of intentions, thoughts and beliefs to others.

The single most important feature to appreciate about Frith's model of schizophrenia is its sign/symptom specificity. It is argued that the specific psychotic signs or symptoms reflect the precise nature of the metarepresentational dysfunction. For example, passivity phenomena like delusions of control, thought insertion, thought withdrawal or auditory hallucinations are thought to result from the patient's failure to monitor his/her own intentions to act (Frith and Done 1989; Mlakar *et al.* 1994). Abulia, or lack of will, is held to arise from a complete failure to represent intentional behaviour (Frith 1987). Formal thought disorder is considered to be a manifestation of the patient's inability to consider the knowledge state of the person to whom he/she is talking (Frith 1992). Paranoid delusions, it is argued, arise from a failure to represent the intentions and beliefs of others accurately.

### The original studies

In a series of four studies, Chris Frith and I investigated the notion that certain people with schizophrenia might have difficulty inferring the thoughts, beliefs and intentions of other people (Corcoran and Frith 1996; Corcoran *et al.* 1995, 1997; Frith and Corcoran 1996). Based on the meta-representational model of schizophrenia, we expected to find these problems in patients with negative features and those with formal thought disorder or paranoid delusions. Otherwise we expected to see normal performance on ToM tasks. At the outset we developed a sign/ symptom subgrouping technique which was best able to demonstrate the specificity of the predictions. Thus, we allocated all of our schizophrenic subjects into one of six groups. These can be seen in Table 16.1. The first group consisted of any patient who displayed the negative behavioural signs of abulia, alogia, social withdrawal and/or blunted affect. The second group comprised those patients with positive behavioural signs including formal thought disorder and incongruous affect but without negative signs. Any patient with paranoid type delusions (like delusions of persecution, misidentification, misinterpretation, reference or of thoughts being read) but without behavioural signs was allocated to the third group. Patients with passivity features but no paranoid delusions or behavioural signs comprised the fourth group. Group five consisted of patients with none of the afore mentioned signs or symptoms but who described other, less typical symptoms such as musical hallucinations, sexual or hypochondriacal

**Table 16.1.** The sign/symptom subgrouping technique adopted to examine the predictions of the metarepresentational model of schizophrenia

| The patient subgroup | Signs/symptoms |
| --- | --- |
| 1. Negative signs | Social withdrawal; blunted affect; poverty of speech; abulia. |
| 2. Positive signs | Formal thought disorder (including derailment, neologisms, flight of ideas, incoherence of speech); disorganized behaviour; incongruous affect. |
| 3. Paranoid delusions | Delusions of reference, persecution, misinterpretation, and misidentification, and delusions of thoughts being read; third person and persecutory auditory hallucinations. |
| 4. Passivity features | Delusions of control and influence; thought insertion; thought withdrawal; second person auditory hallucinations. |
| 5. Other symptoms | Musical hallucinations, sexual, hyponchondriacal, and grandiose delusions etc. |
| 6. Remission | Free of signs and symptoms for at least two weeks. |

delusions. The final group was made up of those people with a DSM III-R/IV diagnosis of schizophrenia but who were, at the time of testing and for at least the two preceding weeks, free of overt signs and symptoms.

### Understanding hints

The first test we devised to examine ToM in adults of differing abilities and degrees of illness was called the 'hinting task' (Corcoran *et al.* 1995). The task incorporated ten scenarios involving two characters, one of whom drops a heavy hint at the end of each story. Some examples are given in Table 16.2. The story is read to the subject who is asked what the character really means by the utterance. A correct response involves inferring, from the context in which the speech act takes place, the intention of the speaker, clearly different to what the character actually says.

We tested fifty five people with a DSM III-R diagnosis of schizophrenia (APA 1987) on this task. We also collected data from thirty normal controls and fourteen psychiatric controls who were suffering from anxiety and/or depression but who had no psychotic features to their illness. We found symptom-specific differences in the performance on this very simple ToM task which were independent of overall levels of functioning. Notably, the schizophrenic patients with negative behavioural signs performed significantly poorer than those with passivity features, those in remission and the two control groups. The patients with paranoid delusions performed significantly worse than the two control groups, as did the very small group with positive behavioural signs. It is interesting that the patients with features of passivity and those in remission performed at a level comparable to the control groups. A point of further interest about the findings on this task is that, while we found no correlation between the hinting task and estimated current IQ in the control groups, there was a significant correlation between IQ and hints in the schizophrenic group as a whole. This suggested the possibility that while the controls were using different skills to do the two tasks, the patients with schizophrenia were to some extent having to rely upon generalized cognitive abilities to perform this very simple social task.

**Table 16.2.** Two examples of the hinting task stimuli

| Item 2 | Item 4 |
|---|---|
| Melissa goes to the bathroom for a shower. Anne has just had a bath. Melissa notices the bath is dirty so she calls out to Anne: 'Couldn't you find the Ajax, Anne?' Question – What does Melissa really mean when she says this? (Add: Melissa goes on to say: 'You're very lazy sometimes Anne!' Questions – What does Melissa want Anne to do?) | Paul has to go to an interview and he's running late. While he is cleaning his shoes, he says to his wife Jane: 'I want to wear my blue shirt but it's very creased.' Question – What does Paul really mean when he says this? (Add: Paul goes on to say: 'Its in the ironing basket.' Question – What does Paul want Jane to do?) |

*Understanding false belief and deception*

The second in this series of studies used simple stories and associated cartoon type illustrations to examine the ability of people with schizophrenia to understand false belief and deception (Frith and Corcoran 1996). Forty six people with schizophrenia performed these tasks alongside twenty two normal controls and thirteen psychiatric controls. The pattern of results was clear. Patients with paranoid delusions were impaired on questions which required an inference to be made about one of the character's mental states, at both first- and second-order level. The twelve patients with behavioural signs (mostly negative) had problems with these questions too but they also had problems answering control questions where they had to remember a factual part of the story. So, it seemed that those patients with behavioural signs had ToM difficulties alongside more general cognitive problems. However, those with delusions of a paranoid nature seemed to have specific problems with understanding false belief and deception. Again, patients with passivity symptoms and those in remission performed well on these tasks.

*Understanding jokes*

The third study in this series looked at visual joke appreciation (Corcoran *et al.* 1997). Here two sets of ten cartoons were shown to subjects. One set comprised visual jokes in which one had to infer the mental state of the main character in order to appreciate the jokes. The other set consisted of cartoons in which the content was purely physical or behavioural and in which, therefore, it was not necessary to infer the mental state of the characters. Jokes, it was argued, all require first-order mental state inference given that they all require an understanding of the intention to be funny. However, only the ToM jokes require second-order mentalizing skills. Data was collected from forty four patients with schizophrenia, forty normal controls and a small group of seven psychiatric controls. In this study we found that while for the control groups there was no difference in the understanding of the two sets of jokes, schizophrenic patients found the mental-state jokes more difficult to understand. This effect was most marked in patients with behavioural signs, but patients with paranoid delusions also showed more difficulty with these types of jokes, as did our patients with passivity features (n = 8). Patients in remission again performed as normal.

*Conversational maxims versus the politeness–tact protocol*

The final study looked at the appreciation of the Gricean maxims (Grice 1975) and the politeness convention (Corcoran and Frith 1996). Here it was suggested that while the maxims are 'rules of thumb' which govern across the board, the politeness convention is much more flexible and its precise use depends on certain contextual variables which change from instance to instance. We expected that the ability to choose when to be polite would be impaired in those with paranoid delusions in whom the use of the traditional conversational maxims (i.e. the maxims of quantity, quality, relation and manner) would be intact. In patients with behavioural signs we expected to see an across-the-board problem with conversational language. In other words, an 'on-line' ToM deficit was predicted in patients with paranoid delusions, whilst a general problem relating to knowledge of social rules was predicted in those with behavioural signs. This is what we found. Therefore, using a different paradigm, we demonstrated specific problems with theory of mind in patients with paranoid delusions, but more widespread socio–cognitive difficulties, including theory of mind, were evident in people with negative features.

## Interpreting the findings

When we interpret the finding of this series of studies using the two questions—of exclusivity to autism and selectivity of dysfunction—mentioned in the introduction, we can highlight several interesting issues. Clearly we had demonstrated theory of mind deficits in schizophrenia. As regards the selectivity of the deficit, the argument differs according to signs/symptoms expressed. In those with negative features, the mentalizing problem looks, at face value, to be very similar to that seen in autism, with scores on the simple tasks being generally very poor. Qualitatively, in answering the ToM questions, people with negative feature schizophrenia had a tendency to fail to recognise hidden intentions and false beliefs and tended not to use mental-state language in their explanations. However, while the extent of the problem looked to be the same as that seen in autism, it was clear that, in this group of patients, other cognitive skills were also impaired, probably to a similar extent. Thus, with the theory of mind stories, the patients with negative features failed not only the ToM question but also the memory control question. In the maxims task, the poor performance on the Gricean maxims seen alongside a problem with the more context-dependent politeness convention suggests a broader[1] difficulty of social semantic knowledge. Furthermore, many studies exploring the neuropsychology of schizophrenia have emphasised a broad set of cognitive deficits in this group. In particular, executive skills and memory are thought to be impaired. (e.g. Corcoran and Frith 1993, 1994; Shallice *et al.* 1991; Tamlyn *et al.* 1992). So, with autism it seemed as though this group shared the extent of the problem but not, what some would have, the specificity of the difficulty.[2]

Though we had seen few patients with formal thought disorder who were suitable candidates for testing, those we had seen tended to give bizarre misinterpretations of the experimental tasks which did not appear to lack mental-state terminology, inappropriate though it was. This group's performance on these tasks seemed to improve as the thought disorder remitted. The problem did not therefore appear to be a failure of development, as was argued to be the case for the patients with negative features, but more a temporary malfunction in which reasoning was biased by their psychotic preoccupations. It may be that any task which involves an element of reasoning may have been equally affected. This theory of mind difficulty, then, is unlike that seen in autism. Mental-state language is used but theory of mind is not intact and nor probably are other reasoning skills, because of the state-dependent effects of the psychotic condition. The quantitative extent of the problem may however be as great as that seen with negative signs and in autism. These patients scored very poorly on ToM tasks.

In those with paranoid delusions, where we also saw theory of mind problems, the extent of the problem was clearly not as great as that seen in autism or in negative signs. On all tasks there was evidence of poor performance, but the difficulty was not as grave. When these patients failed, the tendency was to fail to recognise hidden intentions or false beliefs and not to use mental-state language. The form of the dysfunction looked like that seen in relation to negative signs and in some people with autism. Also, the deficit seemed to be fairly specific in these patients. We saw no evidence of memory problems in the theory of mind stories and no general tendency to fail the maxims and thus, we would argue, no evidence of a more widespread social semantic deficit. Neuropsychological studies would, on the whole concur with this picture. Patients with positive symptoms tend to be cognitively intact (Corcoran and Frith 1993, 1994; Frith *et al.* 1991).

The final thing to stress about these findings in schizophrenia is that, at least in those whose signs and symptoms do remit, the mentalizing problem is quite different from that seen in autism. We showed that in those patients in remission—no doubt due to the use of effective neuroleptic treatment—ToM skills were normal. These subjects performed as well as the normal and non-psychotic psychiatric control groups. Since some of these patients had long histories of paranoid thinking or thought disorder, this suggests strongly that the problem was a state-dependent one which lifted with the lifting of the positive psychosis. Thus in both positive signs and positive paranoid symptoms we seemed to be looking at temporary breakdowns or biases. In those with chronic negative feature schizophrenia, whose condition does not remit, there was seemingly a breakdown in the mentalizing ability.

## Further studies

Frith's thesis and the accompanying studies generated a fair amount of interest and several other researchers have since explored theory of mind in schizophrenia. All of these studies have produced findings to support the existence of theory of mind difficulties in the illness. What they do not all agree on is the association to signs and symptoms.

### Mental-state and non-mental-state representation and executive skills in schizophrenia

The most thorough exploration of the theory of mind deficit in schizophrenia which followed on from Frith's (1992) hypothesis and the work presented above was that of Graham Pickup (unpublished doctoral thesis) who explored, in greater depth and with admirable rigour and skill, the theory of mind deficit in schizophrenia and its relationship to signs and symptoms as well as to performance on other cognitive tasks.

In his first study, Pickup compared theory of mind performance using versions of the unexpected transfer task and the Smarties tasks (Perner *et al.* 1989; Wimmer and Perner 1983) with performance on two first-order non-mental representation tasks. The first used a map to represent objects which subsequently move, rendering the map out-of-date. This task paralleled the unexpected transfer task. In the second task, paralleling the Smarties task, an object is drawn in a location, but the drawing becomes an out-of-date representation of reality when the object is swapped for another. Leslie and Thaiss (1992) and Charman and Baron-Cohen (1992) had found children with autism to perform well on these non mental-state tasks while scoring poorly on first-order ToM tasks. Pickup found no indication of mental-state nor non mental-state representational deficits in his groups of people with schizophrenia using these first-order tasks.

The same exploration using second-order tasks revealed no differences between his sample of people with schizophrenia and controls in performance on the non-mental representation task, but highly significant group differences on the second-order false-belief task. It was clear that the behavioural signs subgroup was performing less well than the normal or psychiatric controls (unipolar depression or anxiety) and schizo-phrenics in remission. When he looked at within-group differences across the two tasks, Pickup found that while the two control groups and the group in remission found the tasks equally challenging, those patients with behavioural signs and also those with paranoid symptoms found the mental-state task more difficult. Further corroboration was obtained when the first- and second-order performance was combined to form mental-state and non mental-state composite scores. While no group differences emerged for the non mental-state composite score, there were clear group differences for the mental-state composite score. The patients with behavioural signs obtained lower composite scores than the two control groups and the remitted group, while those with paranoid symptoms obtained lower scores than the normal control group and the remitted group. When a measure of current IQ was considered, the difference between the paranoid group and the other groups was reduced to a trend. However, if a measure of premorbid IQ was covaried, the difference remained significant.

In a second study, Pickup explored the relation of theory of mind to executive function using a two stage spatial discrimination task requiring simple discrimination and simple reversal. On this task, the behavioural signs group was found to make more perseverative errors at the reversal stage than the other groups. However, Pickup showed that no relationship existed between performance on this task and per-formance on ToM as measured by the composite ToM score.

Pickup also used the hinting task in his studies. Of the thirty schizophrenics who performed this task, those who performed more poorly than the normal sample were those with behavioural signs or paranoid symptoms. Contrary to Corcoran *et al.* (1995), no significant difference was found between the behavioural signs group and the remitted group on this task where only a trend in the predicted direction was found.

From his studies, of which only a selection are presented here, Pickup concluded that he could identify no problems with first-order ToM in his sample of people with schizophrenia but that second-order mentalizing is clearly compromised in those with behavioural signs and also in those with paranoid symptoms. Thus, Pickup argued that the extent of the deficit seen in schizophrenia is not comparable to that found in autism. It is worth pointing out that Pickup's findings differ somewhat from the general findings of Corcoran and Frith in failing to identify first-order deficits in those with negative features. Furthermore, his findings on the paranoid patients are not as strong as those demonstrated in our earlier work. It is likely that these discrepancies can be explained by methodological differences between the studies.

Pickup chose an approach in which comprehension was tested in a strict step-by-step fashion. Every time a new piece of information was entered into his stories/settings, the subject was asked a comprehension question about the change. He hoped thus to increase confidence that any results obtained did not reflect comprehension or memory problems. In this he was successful, but in choosing this approach, he necessarily surrendered ecological validity. In real life ToM situations we are not prompted for our comprehension of each added piece of information. It is in this appreciation of context and context-change ('on-line' mentalizing) that Corcoran and Frith argue paranoid patients fail.

### Theory of mind and intellectual functions

One of the important findings to come out of Pickup's work was the role of intellectual level in determining ToM performance in the paranoid subgroup. A recent study by Doody *et al.* (1998) addressed this question very elegantly. The study made use of five experimental groups: schizophrenia, affective disorder (all of whom had a psychotic element to their illness), mild learning disability, schizophrenia with mild learning disability and non-psychiatric controls. All subjects performed the Sally-Anne task (Wimmer and Perner 1983) and the Ice-Cream Van test (Perner and Wimmer 1985). The symptoms and signs of the schizophrenic samples were measured using the Positive and Negative Symptom Scale (Kay *et al.* 1987). These authors demonstrated some evidence of first-order ToM problems in approximately 22% of the co-morbid schizophrenia/learning disabled group. This was comparable to the figure for the mentally retarded group (26%). For second-order ToM, both subjects with schizophrenia and those with mild mental retardation showed impaired ability to understand the task. However, when those patients who failed to answer reality control questions correctly were excluded from the analysis, a specific impairment of ToM was seen only in relation to schizophrenia. Thus, both those subjects with a co-morbid diagnosis of schizophrenia and mild learning disability and those with schizophrenia with a normal premorbid IQ, seemed to fail the second-order ToM task because of a specific impairment. This difficulty related to both negative and positive symptom clusters. The relationship to symptoms held only in the schizophrenic group even though the affective disorder group displayed the same clusters of psychopathology. This study therefore presents strong evidence of a specific second-order theory of mind problem in schizophrenia which is related to symptomatology in this condition. That there was no strong evidence of poor performance on first-order theory of mind agrees with Pickup's conclusions and demonstrates again that the problem seen in schizophrenia is more subtle than that seen in autism.

### False beliefs, intentions and the nature of the aberrant responding

In a paper which looked at differences between the attribution of intention and the attribution of false belief, Sarfati *et al.* (1997a) showed, amongst other things, that while a difficulty in attributing false belief seemed to be exclusive to the schizophrenic group, there was no difference between the schizophrenic group and a group with major depressive disorder in the ability to attribute intention. However, the former group did perform more poorly on this intention task than a normal sample which was well matched for ability levels and demographic variables. The study found no differences in task performance within the schizophrenic group divided according to DSM-III-R subtypes of paranoid, undifferentiated and residual. However, there was a significant tendency for those scoring highest on a measure of thought and language disturbance to perform most poorly on the attribution of intention task. The authors suggested that a deficit in the attribution of intention may be exclusively associated with the presence of thought and language disturbance (i.e. formal thought disorder) and they provided similar evidence using the same experimental paradigm in support of this claim in a subsequent paper (Sarfati *et al*. 1997*b*). On the other hand, they suggest that the deficit which they demonstrate in attributing false beliefs to cartoon comic strip characters characterises schizophrenia across the board, since no differences were seen in performance according to DSM-III-R subtype, or according to scores on schedules assessing the presence of negative signs and positive symptoms. There was a strong indication in the data that the items which involve the attribution of false belief were more difficult than those exploring the attribution of intention, but the findings could not support the claim that the two types of attribution involve independent processes. In fact, the difference in complexity of the two tasks may be the best way to explain the apparent link between the intentions task and thought disorder, rather than arguing that the inability to infer intentions is specific to that group of patients. Since it is precisely these patients who are likely to be the least able to concentrate, it is not surprising that they demonstrate deficits on even the simplest tasks. The exclusivity claim is inconsistent with the results of our study which looked at intentions behind indirect speech where, although we found that thought disorder is associated with problems attributing intention, we also found very clear difficulties in other signs and symptom subgroups as well (Corcoran *et al*. 1995).

Sarfati *et al*. were interested in the failures that were made on the false-belief task. They pointed out that, unlike people with autism, those with schizophrenia who fail this task do not attribute a true belief but rather respond in a random fashion to these stimulus items. In further discussion of the nature of the mistakes made by the schizophrenic sample, Sarfati *et al*. (1997*a*) note 'that the schizophrenic subjects were unable to extract the relevant data which gave meaning and intention to the character's behaviour' (p.12). This lack of the appreciation of, sometimes subtle, contextual cues which can inform one about behaviour is a well established trait of the schizophrenic cognitive profile (for example see Chapman *et al*. 1964 for an early form of this cognitive explanation). Again, this latter finding points to what may be an important difference in the nature of the ToM deficit which exists in schizophrenia compared with that seen in autism. There is a vast difference between arguing that people fail ToM tasks because they do not appreciate that others have minds and the alternative argument that people do poorly on ToM tasks because they cannot extract the relevant contextual cues needed to inform the inference process.

*Characterising the groups with theory of mind problems*

The final study to be reviewed in this section is by Langdon *et al*. (1997).These authors found strong support for the existence of ToM difficulties in schizophrenia using a picture-sequencing paradigm, a study of mental-state language in explanatory narratives and an own mental state recall task. These three methodologies were all adaptations of methods previously used by researchers in autism. The first test was the picture-sequencing task in which subjects had to order four-card cartoon drawings to make a sensible story. These stories were of six kinds: mechanical, social script, pretence, unrealised goal, intention and false belief. It was found, on the basis of overall performance on this task, that the patients could be cast into three subgroups. The first subgroup consisted of patients who correctly ordered all stories. The second subgroup were those who only made errors on the false-belief stories. This second group also took longer to perform both the false-belief and the pretence stories. The third group comprised those who seemed to have general sequencing difficulty.

The narratives produced as explanations of the cartoon sequences by the three subgroups were then examined for use of mental-state language by a 'blind' rater using established scoring procedures. The authors found that those patients with the selective meta-representational deficit on picture sequencing used fewer intentional–cognitive terms than controls or those patients who were error-free on the sequencing task but did not differ in their use of other mental state language. Those patients with general sequencing problems used less mental state language across the board, with the exception of perception terms, which they tended to use more than any of the other groups.

The authors went on to investigate the relationship between awareness of own mental states and appreciation of others' mental states. Procedures were used to look at the ability to remember seen objects, past pretences, finished goals, unrealised intentions, correct beliefs and false beliefs. The authors showed that the group whose sequencing of false-belief scenarios was selectively impaired had problems recalling past intentions and, to a lesser extent, past false beliefs. The group with general sequencing problems had difficulty recalling all of the above mental states but remembered the seen objects without difficulty. Interestingly, there was evidence from the performance of some patients for a double dissociation between the recall of own mental states and the understanding of others' mental states. Some of the patients who performed well on the false-belief sequencing task performed very poorly on the recall of past intentions, while other patients performed well on the recall of past intentions but very poorly on the false-belief sequencing task. This evidence for a double dissociation agrees with our earlier findings where, in general, patients with passivity features seem quite able to infer other people's mental states but have problems monitoring their own intentions to act (e.g. Corcoran *et al.* 1995; Frith and Corcoran 1996; Frith and Done 1989; Mlakar *et al.* 1994).

Symptomatology was then looked at. What Langdon *et al.* found was that those patients with poor meta-representational skills were most likely to have alogia, social withdrawal and, particularly, flat affect. Unlike our own studies, Langdon *et al.* could find no association between paranoia and impaired meta-representation. To what extent this null finding can be explained by the symptom measurement and clustering techniques used is unclear. In their discussion though, the authors propose that in paranoia there may be an inability to critically analyse the social inferences that are drawn. These authors argue that paranoid patients may tackle social inferences in a probabilistic manner instead of a straight forward conditional manner (i.e. 'if . . . then

... or ... then ... or ... then' instead of 'if ... then'). From this inappropriate starting point, the wrong choice may be made and not subsequently analysed for its suitability. This may result in inappropriate mental-state inferences, but these patients have an intact ability to think about others' thoughts and to use mental-state language. Langdon *et al.*'s study was not designed to look at this kind of difficulty but their suggestion seems highly plausible and is similar to the suggestion Chris Frith and I have made about the ToM deficit in paranoia (see section 2.5).

To summarise Langdon *et al.*'s work, these authors identified a group of people with schizophrenia in whom there appeared to be a specific problem with the appreciation of other people's mental states. These were patients with characteristic 'autistic' symptoms. They also identified a group in whom mentalizing was disturbed in association with other more generalised cognitive problems to do with an inability to 'manipulate symbolic representations'. These patients were most likely to display negative symptoms of poverty. Furthermore, they speculated as to the possibility that ToM might go awry in paranoia as a result of inappropriate reasoning and evaluation skills. Thus, Langdon *et al.* would presumably argue that autism is not the only condition in which a specific deficit of mental-state appreciation can be demonstrated.

## *Pragmatic language—the appreciation of ironic utterances*

The ability of people with schizophrenia to appreciate the meaning of ironic utterances has recently been studied by Mitchley *et al.* (1998). It has been argued that to appreciate an ironic statement requires a theory of mind since one must go beyond the literal meaning of the statement to infer intent. However, one could argue, as was done with the original Gricean maxims, that the appreciation of irony only really requires a knowledge of a 'rule of thumb'. If a statement appears to be a blatant reversal of the circumstances to which it refers, it must be ironic. Therefore, to appreciate irony all one must do is simply reverse the meaning of the utterance. This is a hard and fast rule which is context-independent, requiring few if any inferences to be drawn. However we view irony, Mitchley *et al.* showed that people with schizophrenia were more likely to interpret an ironic statement literally than were a non-psychotic psychiatric control group who performed at ceiling. Furthermore, this tendency towards literal interpretation was most prominent in patients with negative signs. The identification of such a severe problem with the comprehension of pragmatic speech in these patients agrees with our study of the Gricean maxims (Corcoran and Frith 1996) and may be interpreted as more evidence of a general socio–cognitive problem in this sample. However, Mitchley *et al.* found the literal interpretation of ironic utterances to be associated with lower current IQ.

## Explaining the theory of mind deficits seen in schizophrenia: a model

Following on from our findings in schizophrenia, Chris Frith and I went on to offer a neuropsychological model of ToM in which it was proposed that people are able to think about other people's thoughts using a mechanism which is, for all intents and purposes, a devoted or specialised one because its use within non-mental-state reasoning situations would be limited simply by the paucity of relevant problems in daily life.

Theoretically, however, the same system could be used to answer non-mental state social material. The beginnings of this model were set out in Corcoran, Mercer and Frith, C. (1995) and it is elaborated in Corcoran and Frith (submitted). The model runs as follows: when people attempt to figure out what another person is thinking, intending, or believing, the initial step is to introspect. We try to determine what we ourselves would think, believe, or intend within the present context. We do this by referring to the contents of our autobiographical memory and any relevant information about ourselves will be retrieved from this source. This retrieved material will be context-specific, because that is how information is stored in autobiographical memory. This retrieved information relating to our own former experiences constitutes a 'best guess' base upon which conditional reasoning skills can operate. Amongst the conditionals which must be considered are: (i) whether our knowledge of ourselves is a good enough base to inform us about this particular other person; (ii) whether the context of the past has enough in common with the current context to make abstraction realistic; and (iii) whether any personal or situational idiosyncrasies might be at work (now or with the retrieved information) which should be considered.

Since the theory of mind problems in schizophrenia appear to be symptom/sign specific, the biases or failures in this system are also proposed to be specific to the psychotic manifestation. Our predictions about autobiographical recall were as follows: those with chronic negative feature schizophrenia will have impaired autobiographical memory. Given the likelihood of a neurodevelopmental aetiology in this type of schizophrenia and the evidence which points to poor premorbid childhood social functioning in this subgroup of patients, we proposed that the ability to recall relevant social events from autobiographical memory might be diminished. The early and long-standing social isolation may have prevented the encoding and storage of relevant material. In those with paranoid delusions, we argued instead for a bias in the retrieval of information from autobiographical memory. Negative or bizarre events would tend to be recalled, thus resulting in an abnormal platform from which to mentalize. Conditional reasoning, it is argued, will be impaired in all groups who display ToM problems. A failure to make use of subtle cues to inform decision making is a classic hallmark of the schizophrenic cognitive profile. The identification of subtle contextual cues is one of the factors important in the conditional reasoning component of mentalizing as set out above. Furthermore, there is good evidence for poor reasoning skills in schizophrenia (see Corcoran and Frith (submitted) for a review of this literature). Some argue that poor reasoning is a particular feature of those with delusions (e.g. Garety *et al.* 1991) whilst others relate it to the illness more generally (Mortimer *et al.* 1996).

Our recent and ongoing work has involved testing this model. Of particular interest are the results we have obtained which demonstrate the existence of parallel deficits in social conditional reasoning and ToM in our subsamples of people with schizophrenia. In this study we examined the performance of thirty one people with schizophrenia on five versions of the thematic selection task which varied according to the social nature and degree of familiarity of the story content. The same patients also performed the hinting task. We found that those patients who performed poorly on the hinting task, that is those with behavioural signs and those with paranoid delusions, also markedly failed to show facilitation of conditional reasoning performance with the stories of a social nature, even when a highly familiar rule was being examined. The facilitation afforded by the social stories was substantial, however, for our normal sample, a finding typical of normal samples (e.g. Cosmides 1989). Furthermore, the facilitation was convincing for our schizophrenic patients with passivity features and for those in remission, at least for the familiar social rule. The associations we found were independent of general intellectual functioning.

We argued that the best explanation of these results is a weakness in the ability to reason by analogy. Our patients seemed to be unable to use analogous experience to initiate the reasoning process required by current tasks. This was a difficulty which extended across social reasoning whether on tasks involving card selection or tasks which involve the inference of meaning from indirect speech acts. To infer the meaning of a hint, we must recollect stored analogous autobiographical experiences on which to build the inferential process. It is in the use, the recollection, or the manipulation of analogous experiences that our patients with behavioural signs or paranoid delusions fail.

We are in the process of examining the relationship between theory of mind test performance and strength and quality of autobiographical memory retrieval. Using the incidents section of the Autobiographical Memory Interview (AMI, Kopelman *et al.* 1993) our data does suggest relationships between the ability to recollect events from past life and the ability to infer meaning from indirect speech. Of note is the parallel nature of the pattern of dysfunction across the schizophrenic sample divided according to symptoms or signs expressed. Again, we see the same groups of patients performing most poorly on the hinting task and the autobiographical memory task.

The quality of the recalled items is also something that we are interested in, since it is capable of providing an explanation of why paranoid patients misinterpret intention in their characteristic negative and self-referential way. There does seem to be a tendency for those with paranoid delusions to remember negative and/or bizarre events from their past life. This may be a particular feature of their recollections from childhood. Responses given to the questions in this section of the AMI by paranoid deluded patients included those which were essentially normal, those which were very negative but probably true (e.g. a first memory of saying goodbye to a mother who never came back; being parted from siblings to go into children's homes) and those which were clearly delusional memories (e.g. having been run over by a truck but getting up unscathed because the body was described as being like rubber, or being shot through the head in primary school). More data on this aspect of the model needs to be collected before we can argue with confidence for a role of quantity and quality of recollected experiences in explaining the ToM deficits in people with schizophrenia.

To what extent this model of adult ToM functioning can explain normal functioning and the abnormal development of ToM in autism is an open issue. In the normal adult sample it is extremely difficult, perhaps impossible, to obtain a wide enough range of scores on theory of mind and autobiographical memory tasks to allow the test of such a model. This is why, in our current work, we are interested in testing people who, as a result of neurological damage, have poor autobiographical memory or poor social reasoning. Examples would include amnesic patients and latter-day Phineas Gages. In autism, it is interesting to note the relative lack of studies of autobiographical memory functioning. An early study by Boucher (1981) examined recent event memory in children with autism and found it to be inferior to the event memory of age-matched controls. Powell and Jordan (1993) had attributed the failure of these children to produce narratives of personal events to the fact that they have failed to establish what they called an 'experiencing self' which is needed to search memory in the absence of relevant episodic cueing. In 1994, they offered an alternative explanation that these children failed to develop a social memory system. To my knowledge, this is the only work to date which has looked at the functioning of autobiographical recall in people with autism, with the exception of those studies exploring the autobiographical writings of very able adults with autism (e.g. Happé 1991). Some researchers in the field of normal development stress the proximity of emergence of the first theory of mind skills to that of the first autobiographical retrieval skills (Howe and Courage 1997; Nelson 1992; Welch and Melissa 1997).

## Schizophrenia and theory of mind—a summary

Perhaps the most important thing to stress about the work on schizophrenia which has been reviewed above is its firm clinical and theoretical grounding. Consider for example the symptoms of the illness. Delusions are idiosyncratic and incorrigible false beliefs usually concerning the self or the functioning of the self within the social world. Of these, paranoid delusions are probably the most widely experienced. Paranoid thinking consists of misinterpretations of people's intentions towards one and firmly held beliefs that people mean one harm. It is clear when speaking to patients with paranoid delusions that there is an aberrant quality to the way they think about other people's thoughts, beliefs and intentions.

In general the studies undertaken to date agree that second-order ToM skills are poor in people with behavioural signs. It is also widely known that these patients have cognitive impairments (see Frith *et al.* 1991). Some studies point to more selective but less severe problems in ToM in people with paranoid delusions. Otherwise these patients seem cognitively intact. Whilst the schizophrenia work argues against the exclusivity-to-autism claim, the theory of mind difficulties seen in association with schizophrenic signs and symptoms are not as severe as those seen in autism and probably have different origins. What is stressed in the schizophrenia literature is that the core deficit may lie in the use of previously acquired information and/or within the reasoning domain. In autism it is generally, though not universally, held that the theory of mind deficit is highly selective and independent of other cognitive skills.

## 3. THEORY OF MIND IN OTHER CLINICAL SAMPLES

**Adult psychiatric disorders**

To my knowledge, the only groups of adult psychiatric patients who have been investigated for ToM skills, other than schizophrenics, are those who formed the control comparisons in the schizophrenia work. In our own and Pickup's work these were people with primary diagnoses of unipolar depression and/or anxiety. In Doody *et al*.'s study (1998) the comparison sample was patients with affective disorder with a strong psychotic component. In none of these studies was there any indication of defective ToM when these groups were compared with a healthy adult sample. Doody *et al*.'s work is particularly significant in this respect since the affective control group had similar symptom profiles to those with schizophrenia and while ToM problems were associated with particular signs and symptoms in schizophrenia, there was no such indication in the affective group. Quite why this should be is unclear and there is obviously a need for more work in this area examining bipolar and unipolar psychotic depression in a symptom-specific way.

The null finding in this group is important for other reasons as well. First, it has implications for those models which specify a primary role for executive functions in theory of mind, since depressed samples tend to show attenuated scores on tests like verbal fluency (Frith 1992) and hypoperfusion of left prefrontal cortex in Positron Emission Tomography studies (Bench *et al*. 1992 1993; Dolan *et al*. 1994). This left prefrontal hypoperfusion at rest is also a characteristic of schizophrenia and Dolan *et al*. (1993) have demonstrated that it is related to psychomotor poverty in both depression and schizophrenia. Using pooled data the regional cerebral blood flow anomaly was shown to be independent of diagnosis. Given that patients with schizophrenia with psychomotor poverty display a ToM deficit while those with depression apparently do not, it is reasonable to argue that the ToM deficit in negative feature schizophrenia is not a consequence of the hypometabolism of the left dorsolateral prefrontal cortex. However, those patients with unipolar depression who have been examined for ToM skills may not have been as seriously ill as those in whom PET evidence demonstrates hypometabolism of left dorsolateral prefrontal cortex. Some functional imaging studies have demonstrated a relationship between the severity of depression and the degree of prefrontal hypometabolism (George *et al*. 1993). Finally, given the tendency in depressed patients to recall negative events from their past lives (e.g. Bower 1981; Fogarty and Hemsley 1983), one might expect biased theory of mind performances in this group if the model of ToM proposed to account for the schizophrenia findings is correct. However, the presence of anosagnosia in paranoia and not depression may be an important factor to consider. Depressed patients might well recall negative experiences in their initial attempts to mentalize but, as they are insightful about their condition, they may reject this first recollection in favour of a more suitable recollection from a second stage search. People with paranoid schizophrenia are typically not insightful about their illness and would therefore not reject negative or bizarre memories, as they would consider these normal.

## Adult personality disorders

*Psychopathy*

In 1995, Linda Mealey argued that primary sociopaths have an abnormal theory of mind. She argues that the psychopath's ToM is different to most other people's because they cannot appreciate the emotional states of others. In other words, Mealey is suggesting a deficit in empathy in these people, not a theory of mind failure as such. In autism, a behavioural empathy deficit exists and it had been assumed that this deficit is attributable to the primary theory of mind impairment. Interestingly, using techniques which measure skin conductance to distressing stimuli, Blair (in press) has shown that children with autism do display an essentially normal empathic physiological response. It is implied that the cognitive ToM deficit precludes empathic display in autism. However, two explanations of the relationship between empathy and ToM exist. First is the argument that, to show empathy, one must be able to appreciate other people's mental states. The second position is that empathy and ToM are in fact dissociable.

James Blair and colleagues (1996) went on to explore this notion in psychopathic men. They were interested to find out if the psychopath, who was clearly shown to lack empathy as measured by skin conductance responses to distressing visual stimuli (see Blair *et al.* 1997), also lacks a ToM. To test ToM functioning in adult subjects, Francesca Happé's advanced test was used (see Fletcher *et al.* 1995). In this test of story comprehension one has to appreciate the mental states of story characters in order to give a correct response about their subsequent behaviour. Blair *et al.* compared twenty five psychopaths with twenty five non-psychopathic controls who were imprisoned for murder or manslaughter and who were matched for age and IQ. No differences in theory of mind skills were identified. Both groups performed in a normal fashion, using appropriate mental-state terminology on this task.

Blair and colleagues concluded that different deficits lie at the root of lack of behavioural empathy in autism and psychopathy. In autism, a primary deficit of social cognition (i.e. ToM) precludes a behavioural empathic display. In psychopathy, it is argued that a primary emotional deficit precludes empathic experiences. Theory of mind is intact in these people but there is no evidence of empathy at the behavioural level and there is attenuated physiological arousal to stimuli that usually give rise to empathic feelings in normal subjects.

Thus, Blair *et al.* consider that a lack of ToM does not provide a suitable explanation for the extreme social deviance displayed by people with psychopathy. In fact, the prototypical features of the psychopath's thinking (exploitative and manipulative of other's mental states) would lead us to the same conclusion. What Blair *et al.* do not consider and this seems to be what Mealey suggests, is that, though intact, as demonstrated by adequate performance on tasks exploring the appreciation of knowledge state and beliefs, the psychopath's theory of mind is abnormal because he is unable to use emotional signals to inform and perhaps short-circuit this cognitive process. Perhaps in the normally-functioning adult, emotional signals and the appropriate physiological responses to these act in a facilitatory way to speed up the cognitive

ToM process. It is interesting to note that the incidence of maternal rejection and abuse reported by psychopaths is extremely high. Such reports include frequent reports of active attempts to terminate pregnancy using essentially violent means (Raine 1997). That childhood abuse and neglect might be factors associated with abnormal mentalizing is considered in the literature, reviewed below, relating to borderline personality disorder and conduct disorder. The recollection of negative events may also characterise patients with schizophrenia who have paranoid delusions (see earlier section which attempts to explain the theory of mind deficits seen in schizophrenia). It is clear that more information needs to be gathered before we can really make a judgement about the state of the psychopath's ToM.

### Borderline personality disorder

Borderline personality disorder is defined in DSM IV (American Psychiatric Association 1994) as a 'pervasive pattern of instability of mood, interpersonal relationships and self-image, beginning by early adulthood and present in a variety of contexts . . .'.

In a series of studies, Peter Fonagy, Mary Target and colleagues report the existence of mentalizing difficulties in people with borderline personality disorder (Fonagy and Target 1998; Fonagy *et al.* 1995, 1996, 1997). A depleted reference to metal states was seen in the narrative language given in response to the questions in a semi-structured interview from which details about the nature of parental attachment can be obtained (Adult Attachment Interview, George *et al.* 1985). The attachment profiles of these individuals are described as being 'entangled' or 'unresolved' and in this respect and given the evidence of impaired mentalizing, it is significant that these people typically report a much higher prevalence of sexual and physical abuse.

Fonagy and colleagues argue that the impoverished mentalizing skills of people with borderline personality disorder result from the very negative aspects of their upbringing. Not only do they report being abused by their parents, they also describe parents as being non-reflective, lacking in empathic display, or extremely inconsistent in their responses to their needs. Several possible reasons are put forward to explain why mentalizing fails to develop, or is actively inhibited, in these people. Amongst these are that, as children, these people did not want to recognise the mental states within their parents which caused them to abuse or that the ambivalent responses (or lack of response) of the parent to the child's needs could not nurture the development of these skills in the children.

This work has a great deal to say about how theory of mind skills develop in normal children and therefore how weaknesses of mentalizing might arise. It is interesting that the authors do not advocate a universal failure of mentalizing in borderline patients. Rather, what is suggested is a breakdown in the skill as it arises within emotionally-laden mentalizing situations. In other words, it is suggested that mentalizing may be intact in, for example, the patient–therapist relationship, but lacking or dysfunctional in parent–child relationships. It is the poor quality of mentalizing within the parent–child relationship which Fonagy and colleagues see as accounting for the transmission of this disorder through generations.

To summarise, the mentalizing deficit seen in borderline personality disorder is different to that seen in autism on two counts. First, in autism a neurodevelopmental failure from birth is the argument favoured to explain the difficulties with theory of mind. In borderline disorder it is argued that the mentalizing problems have their origin in the environmental circumstances of childhood which have hindered the adequate growth of these skills. Furthermore, unlike autism, the theory of mind problems are thought to fractionate in borderline disorder according to the inter-personal nature or emotional load of the social situation.

## Neurological disorders

### Frontal lobe epilepsy

Given the interest that exists in the relationship between mentalizing and other cognitive skills such as executive skills and autobiographical memory, there was bound to be interest in a clinical population with damage to or dysfunction in frontal areas of the brain which can give rise to deficits in these skills (see Valerie Stone, Chapter 11, this volume). This interest is reinforced by the neuroimaging studies which indicated specific activation in circumscribed areas of medial prefrontal or orbital frontal cortex when theory of mind tasks were performed by normal volunteers compared to matched measures requiring behavioural analysis (see Chris Frith and Uta Frith, Chapter 14, this volume).

In an ongoing collaboration with Caroline Harris and Pamela Thompson from the Chalfont Centre for Epilepsy, information from twenty four hour ambulatory EEG monitoring and/or MRI is being used to identify the site of seizure onset in patients with suspected frontal lobe foci. So far we have gathered data from five people with right frontal or fronto–temporal foci (RF/FT), three people with left frontal or fronto–temporal foci (LF/FT) and three people with bilateral frontal foci or damage (BF). Table 16.3 shows the summary statistics of the hinting task, the AMI incidents section total score and intellectual level for these three small groups and a for larger group of normally-functioning adults. Analyses revealed several things of interest, even given these very small numbers. Significant differences existed between the groups on the performance on the Hinting Task. The RF/FT group demonstrated attenuated appreciation of hints compared with the normal sample and this difference was seen to be independent of group differences in IQ. The total score on the incidents section of

**Table 16.3.** Descriptive statistics relating to the performance of the frontal lobe epilepsy groups on the hinting task, the AMI and estimated IQ

| Measure | normal sample | RF/FT group | LF/FT group | BF |
|---|---|---|---|---|
| number | 23 | 5 | 3 | 3 |
| Hinting task ** | 19.04 (0.9) | 16.2 (2.8) | 17.7 (2.1) | 17.7 (1.5) |
| AMI total *** | 26.7 (0.54) | 18.8 (4.1) | 23.3 (3.7) | 22.0 (5.0) |
| estimated IQ* | 113 (11.3) | 90.2 (5.2) | 102.7 (6.1) | 93.7 (7.6) |

* F = 9.18, p<0.001. Normal sample > RF/FT and BF. ** F = 6.05, p<0.01. ANCOVA F = 4.98, p<0.01. Normal sample > RF/FT. *** F = 19.5, p<0.001. Normal sample and LF/FT > RF/FT, normal sample > BF.

the AMI also differed between the groups. Post hoc analysis revealed that the differences lay between the group with RF/FT foci and the LF/FT group and the normal sample, with the former group recalling significantly fewer vivid memories than the latter two. The BF group also performed more poorly on this test of recollection than the normal sample.

This limited data supports the idea of impoverished autobiographical memory retrieval in association with right prefrontal dysfunction, a finding which would be predicted by the PET study of Shallice *et al.* (1994). Furthermore, there is also evidence of attentuated performance on a very simple mentalizing task in the group of patients with right frontal or fronto–temporal foci. Thatcher (1992) links the normal mastery of false belief at age four to the spurt in physical growth of the right prefrontal cortex which occurs at the same age. It was mentioned earlier that several researchers in the domain of normal development have suggested a link between mentalizing and autobiographical memory, which emerge at about the same age (e.g. Howe and Courage 1997). The significance of this finding to the model of mentalizing proposed to explain the dysfunctions seen in schizophrenia is clear.

*Gilles de la Tourette Syndrome*

According to Burd *et al.* (1987) there is a substantial co-morbidity of autism with Gilles de la Tourette Syndrome. Simon Baron-Cohen and Mary Robertson were interested to explore this co-morbidity to see how it related to overlapping cognitive deficits and areas of brain dysfunction. Brain imaging studies have highlighted an area of medial frontal cortex as being particularly involved in mental-state attribution, the cognitive dysfunction regarded as deficient in autism (Fletcher *et al.* 1995). In Tourette's Syndrome, it is the anterior cingulate which appears to be abnormal (Moriarty *et al.* 1993) and this is an area considered crucial for intention-editing, a cognitive failing in Tourette's Syndrome (Baron-Cohen *et al.* 1994). Baron-Cohen and Robertson identified three children to test using three standard ToM tasks, three intention-editing tasks and the verbal fluency task. One child had autism, another had Tourette's Syndrome and a third had autism and Tourette's Syndrome. Their results showed that only the children with autism had problems on the ToM tasks while only the children with Tourette's Syndrome had difficulty on the intention-editing tasks, but all three children had problems on verbal fluency—an independent test of executive functions. The authors stress the significance of the results in casting doubt on the idea that ToM depends upon intact executive skills since the boy with Tourette's Syndrome had deficient verbal fluency performance but intact ToM. As the authors point out, however, only evidence of a double dissociation is really compelling.

*Callosal agenesis*

The two hemispheres of the brain are considered to possess different types of information-processing expertise. Simplistically, the left hemisphere specialises in the logical processing of linguistic material, while the right hemisphere's specialisation is in perceptual, emotional and subjective analysis of information. Given this, it is possible that in a condition where the normal interconnections between the two hemispheres are lacking, as in callosal agenesis, there might be difficulty in the rationalization of other perceptual viewpoints and others' subjective belief states. Such an argument becomes more compelling when we consider that the processing of prosodic aspects of language and non-verbal communication, both invaluable when it comes to understanding others' intentions, are regarded as being specialisms of the right hemisphere. Temple and Vilarroya (1990) looked at this possibility in their investigation of two siblings with callosal agenesis, a girl of nearly seven with a WISC-R IQ of 78 and her five-year-old brother, thought to be of normal intelligence. The Sally-Anne task was used to explore ToM function in these children and both children performed perfectly. From this we can deduce that passing a first-order ToM task does not depend upon the transfer of information between hemispheres. If information exclusively processed by the right hemisphere is needed in mentalizing, this information does not have to be verbally rationalized by the left hemisphere.

## Developmental disorders

### Conduct disorder

According to DSM IV, conduct disorder is characterised by 'a repetitive and persistent pattern of behaviour in which the basic rights of others or major age-appropriate societal norms are violated'.

The problems which these children have within social contexts are thought by some to be due to abnormal or under-developed sociocognitive skills (Dodge 1980; Selman 1980). Others argue that it is the abnormal experiences of these children which disenable the development of appropriate representations of interpersonal behaviour (McKeough *et al.* 1994). Armed with this knowledge, Happé and Frith (1996) undertook an investigation of these children's mentalizing skills. These authors regarded it as entirely possible that 'an environment in which negative attitudes predominate might shape the child's theory of mind'. An intact development of a 'theory of nasty minds' was proposed. This proposal rested upon the assumption that abuse and neglect feature highly in the environments of these children.

The primary tool which these authors used to look at mentalizing in this group was the Vineland Adaptive Behaviour Scales (Sparrow *et al.* 1984). With this instrument they also used the supplementary questions developed by Frith *et al.* (1994) to look at the types of everyday socially-oriented behaviours which either require or do not require an intact ToM. Two standard false-belief tasks were also used. These were passed by all the children in the study who included eighteen children with conduct disorder ranging in age from six to twelve years and eight normal children. Teachers from the special school which the children with conduct disorder attended answered the questions about the types of behaviours the children did or did not display.

The fact that the children with conduct disorder passed the ToM tests demonstrates that these children have a ToM. However, the questions answered by the teachers about the behaviour of the children indicated 'marked and specific' differences between the children with conduct disorder and the normal sample. The most striking differences were displayed in the responses to questions which required the child to use mentalizing skills; for example, the dropping and understanding of hints.[3] The pattern of responses was very much like, though not as marked as, that seen by Frith *et al.* (1994) in their study of the children with autism who pass standard false-belief tasks. Unlike the children with autism, though, the reports of these children's behaviour included high levels of antisocial behaviours such as bullying but low levels of the bizarre behaviours which characterised the autism sample (e.g. odd preoccupations).

In an argument to explain these findings which was, in fact, very similar to that proposed by Fonagy and colleagues in their studies of borderline patients (see section 3.2.2), Happé and Frith (1996) proposed that some children with conduct disorder may indeed have problems understanding complex mental states. This, they suggest, is a delay which is not likely to be damaging in itself, but when it occurs within a generally hostile environment, the effect on the child may be important. The child may assume negative intentions in others by default. Such a universal belief will have behavioural repercussions. The child will behave in an aggressive or hostile manner in return.

One final point about this group is that they too have poor executive skills—particularly poor planning and impulse inhibition (Lueger and Gill 1990; Pennington and Bennetto 1993). The relationship between ToM and executive skills is a recurring theme in this and the autism literature.

### Attention-deficit hyperactivity disorder (ADHD)

Children with attention-deficit hyperactivity disorder often display behaviours which, as well as reflecting their diminished ability to concentrate, also seem to indicate a somewhat diminished appreciation of correct social behaviour. For example, according to DSM IV, they often talk excessively, interrupt people and fail to listen to what others are saying.

In a single case study of a nine-year-old boy with ADHD, Buitelaar *et al.* (1996) noted poor performance in several first-order and all second-order ToM tasks. These problems were accompanied by difficulties of a comparable degree on emotion matching tasks, visuospatial and motor skills, planning, organization and impulse inhibition tasks. The child however was good at verbal comprehension and reasoning tasks. There is a clear need for larger samples of ADHD children to be studied.

Buitelaar *et al.* argue that, in their single case, the ToM difficulties arise as a consequence of the visuospatial and executive skills deficits. They go on to suggest that the boy's intact abilities of comprehension and reasoning shelter him from significant everyday social handicap. This is an extremely interesting notion which may point to the different ways that everyday versus experimental theory of mind scenarios are tackled. The studies of Frith *et al.* (1994) and Dewey (1991) demonstrate that even high-functioning people with autism or Asperger's Syndrome who pass theory of mind tasks show poor appreciation of others' mental states in their day-to-day lives. This dissociation between experimental and everyday tasks is extremely interesting and needs to be addressed in autism and within the samples reviewed in this chapter, where it seems to be quite typical.

*Prelingual hearing loss*

Prelingual hearing loss is another, if somewhat different, developmental disability which could conceivably have repercussions on the normal development of a ToM. Peterson and Siegal (1995) argue that children who lose the ability to hear prior to the onset of adequate receptive linguistic skills will suffer because they have not had access to information about other people's mental states through normal conversation. It is important to appreciate that, in 90% of cases of prelingually deaf children in Australia, sign language is learned not from parents but from other deaf children at school. In other words, in Australia at least, the access which prelingually deaf children have to conversation is extremely limited until school age. Furthermore, the argument is strengthened when we consider that hearing parents of deaf children will find communicating about abstract, non-observable mental states particularly difficult.

The authors wonder whether theory of mind is normally acquired through early conversational experiences within the family. Children may only become aware of others' and indeed their own, mental states by means of verbal references to them by parents and siblings. The development of theory of mind in this manner has been proposed by Dunn (1988) and explored by Perner and colleagues (1994). A lack of early exposure to such conversational topics could explain a theory of mind deficit in prelingually deaf children and, the authors argue, may also be consistent with deficits in autism. The social aloofness of children with autism could preclude exposure to conversations of this nature. It is worth pointing out at this stage that a similar argument could be used to explain the deficit seen in the ADHD child described above, since a clinical feature of these children is a failure to listen to others' conversations. Furthermore, the social isolation of children later to be diagnosed with chronic deficit state schizophrenia has implications too in this respect.

Peterson and Siegal extend this point about the inexperience of young children or those with autism of pragmatic adult conversation, by pointing out the misunderstanding which may develop in the phrasing of the ToM question in the Sally-Anne task. When the inexperienced child is asked 'Where will Sally look for her marble?' he/she might misinterpret this and assume that the experimenter simply wants them to locate the marble. Given their lack of familiarity with complex adult language, this is entirely possible. It is for this reason that in their study they adapted the question asked for a subgroup of their subjects. The question; 'Where will Sally look first for her marble?' was asked of this subgroup in an attempt to stress the interest in Sally's belief state.

The authors tested the performance on the Sally-Anne task in a group of twenty six prelingually deaf Australian children of normal IQ and ranging in age from eight to thirteen. Sixty five per cent of the children failed the task. This failure rate is not significantly different from that found in autistic children. In support of the notion that the poor appreciation of adult intentional language may account for failure on the Sally-Anne task, a trend towards better performance on the task was noted when the adapted version of the question was used as a way of concentrating the child's mind on the belief state of Sally.

Peterson and Seigel's work certainly has important implications for the neuro-developmental model of the ToM deficit in autism. In 1997, the same authors undertook a study in which they explored the functioning of prelingually deaf children in what are considered to be the three core domains of thought; everyday physics, biology and psychology (Wellman and Gelman 1992). It was argued that prelingually deaf children within hearing families and those with autism, would demonstrate problems only on tasks which challenged their skills of folk psychology (i.e. ToM tests), since the development of this domain requires exposure to abstract, mentalistic conversations at an early age. In matched tasks assessing the domains of folk physics and folk biology, these children would perform adequately. It was predicted that normal children and prelingually deaf children who come from families with at least one deaf, fluently signing member would perform the tasks from the three core domains at an equivalent level. These predictions were held out by robust results. The pattern of performance in deaf children from hearing families was the same as that seen in autism, as was the extent of the difficulty experienced on the Sally-Anne task. The deaf children with fluently signing deaf family members did not show this domain-specific under-functioning. These results point very clearly to the negative impact which conversational deprivation has on ToM and the authors stress again that the autism data can be explained in a similar way (see Tager-Flusberg, Chapter 6, this volume for language studies in autism).

### Congenital blindness

Shared visual attention, gestures, facial expressions and body posture have a significant role to play in the understanding of intention and thoughts and one might therefore predict that anyone who has not been exposed to these forms of communication would find the understanding of others' minds very difficult. Children with congenital blindness would, of course, fall into this category. Again, any problems with theory of mind which might exist in these children would indicate the development of theory of mind through experience of interpersonal relations. However, since blind adults function perfectly well in the social world, it is likely that any difficulties of ToM which might arise in these children would best be construed as a developmental delay resulting from a primary impairment of visual perception. Hobson (1990) has detailed the existence of 'autistic-like' features in congenitally blind children. These include delayed emergence of pretend play, confused use of personal pronouns, inflexible use of symbols and impoverished perspective-taking abilities. Hobson (1990) argues that the existence of these autistic-like features in this group supports his thesis that theory of mind develops from innate capacities in the normal infant for perceiving affective expressions in others. More recently, Brown *et al.* (1997) studied twenty four three- to nine-year-old congenitally blind children. Again, an increased prevalence of autistic-like features in this sample was found. The authors continue to stress the implications that these findings have for the development of theory of mind. It is unclear how congenitally blind children perform on experimental ToM tasks, but given the behavioural clues which point to delayed development of 'everyday' theory of mind skills, studies which look at this are necessary.

## 4. OTHER CLINICAL SAMPLES AND THEORY OF MIND—SUMMARY AND IMPLICATIONS

In this chapter I have concentrated on conditions where one might reasonably expect to encounter ToM problems in adults or children. It is clear that problems with mentalizing do exist in disorders other than autism but, generally speaking, these are biases or problems on ToM tasks resulting from other cognitive factors. In most part, the problems are not as severe as those seen in autism; they are more subtle and may be detected only using more naturalistic probes. The gross deficit on the simple first-order experimental tasks seems to be mostly a feature of classic autism. Again, this stresses the difference in severity of the dysfunction seen.

The case for schizophrenia has already been summarised, but the findings gathered from the other samples are largely consistent with the findings on and speculations made about, the ToM dysfunctions seen in schizophrenia. For example, one of the strongest suggestions made in a number of the studies reviewed here is that environmental factors have a strong bearing on the adequate functioning of ToM. Parental neglect and abuse and negative or bizarre recollections are all put forward by several authors as possible causes of deficient mentalizing. On a similar note, a lack of exposure to appropriate information sources at a young age is proposed to play a role in chronic deficit state schizophrenia and prelingual deafness. It is in these two conditions that the greatest problems with theory of mind have in fact been noted. It is these putative causes that distinguish the ToM deficits seen in autism from those of other samples. Autism is a neurodevelopmental condition and one of its consequences is a failure to develop a ToM. What is unclear is whether the failure of neuro-development occurs to a specific module of the brain which is devoted to the appreciation of mental states. One of the things that the studies of other clinical samples has pointed out quite clearly is that mentalizing skills are also acquired as a result of interpersonal interactions within the family setting. Now, the question in autism becomes whether it is necessary to argue for a specific cognitive neurodevelopmental failure, or whether the impaired ToM arises as a consequence of the child's lack of interest in interacting with other people. Alternatively, the failure in neurodevelopment may have caused a relative inability to learn from, generalise, or appropriately manipulate social interactions. An explanation which favours inabilities to generalise or appropriately manipulate situations is consistent with the notion that executive skills are central to the drawing of social inferences. It certainly seems that executive skills deficits are a feature of autism, at least as studied in adults and they seem to predominate in the other clinical samples reviewed here where ToM difficulties are also found. The idea that ToM fails because of an impoverished ability to learn from social interactions is rather different. What is suggested here is that there may be an inability to gather together information from disparate but similar experiences which can be used to form a social heuristic or script. We know that the difficult part about mentalizing lies in the consideration of context-specific information. In other words, each situation is subtly different and should result in subtly different predictions about mental state. It is for this reason that normally-functioning adults can sometimes draw inappropriate mental-state conclusions. These context-specific differences must be appreciated and used, to fine tune the prediction that comes from the consideration of the heuristic alone. The skill of detecting novelty and acting appropriately in the light of it requires executive skills (Shallice 1988).

The study of other samples in which theory of mind difficulties are seen can enable explanations of how we mentalize and how mentalizing can fail, which are plausible alternatives to the notion of a failure of a devoted module. It is for this theoretical reason that the study of theory of mind in clinical samples other than autism should continue. However, more practically, it is certainly true that identifying a problem as crucial to normal functioning as mentalizing is, will promote better understanding of the relevant clinical conditions and may eventually lead to effective psychological treatment options.

## Acknowledgements

As always, I am grateful to Chris Frith for his long-standing collaboration and support and for commenting on an earlier version of this chapter. Thanks also to Graham Pickup and James Blair for their comments. Our work on schizophrenia was supported by a grant from the Medical Research Council and latterly by the Wellcome Trust.

## Notes

1. Surian *et al.* (1996) did find difficulties across the board when they used a similar task in children with autism. These authors argued that the poor performance on all maxims reflected the underlying problem of understanding other minds and they did not differentiate between the maxims and the politeness task as we had done.
2. Note that there are grounds for believing that the ToM deficit in autism may be secondary to executive skills deficits (Hughes *et al.* 1994; Ozonoff *et al.* 1991).
3. Blair (personal communication) argues that the behavioural differences reported to exist between the normal and the conduct disordered sample in this study might be better understood as an indication of an empathic as opposed to a ToM dysfunction.

## REFERENCES

American Psychiatric Association (1987). *Diagnostic and statistical manual of mental disorders*, (3rd edn), (revised), (DSM IIIR). APA, Washington, DC.

American Psychiatric Association (1994). *Diagnostic and statistical manual of mental disorders*, (4th edn), (DSM IV). APA, Washington, DC.

Baron-Cohen, S. and Robertson, M. M. (1995). Children with either autism, Gilles de la Tourette syndrome or both: mapping cognition to specific syndromes. *Neurocase*, 1, 101–4.

Baron-Cohen, S., Cross, P., Crowson, M. and Robertson, M. (1994). Can children with Tourette's Syndrome edit their intentions? *Psychological Medicine*, 24, 29–40.

Bench, C. J., Friston, K. J., Brown, R. G., Scott, L. C., Frackowiak, R. S. and Dolan, R. J. (1992). The anatomy of melancholia—focal abnormalities of cerebral blood flow in major depression. *Psychological Medicine*, 22, 607–15.

Bench, C. J., Friston, K. J., Brown, R. G., Frackowiak, R. S. and Dolan, R. J. (1993). Regional cerebral blood flow in depression measured by positron emission tomography: the relationship with clinical dimensions. *Psychological Medicine*, **23**, 579–90.

Blair, R. J. R. Psychophysiological responsiveness to the distress of others in children with autism. *Journal of Personality and Individual Differences*. (In press.)

Blair, J., Sellars, C., Strickland, I., Clark, F., Williams, A., Smith, M. and Jones, L. (1996). Theory of mind in the psychopath. *The Journal of Forensic Psychiatry*, **7**, 15–25.

Blair, R. J. R., Jones, L., Clark, F. and Smith, M. (1997). The psychopathic individual: a lack of responsiveness to distress cues? *Psychophysiology*, **34**, 192–8.

Boucher, J. (1981). Memory for recent events in autistic children. *Journal of Autism and Developmental Disorders*, **11**, 293–301.

Bower, G. H. (1981). Mood and memory. *American Psychologist*, **36**, 129–48.

Brown, R., Hobson, P. and Lee, A. (1997). Are there 'Autistic-like' features in congenitally blind children? *Journal of Child Psychology and Psychiatry*, **38**, 693–703.

Buitelaar, J. K., Swab, H., Van der Wees, M. and Wildschut, M. (1996). Neuropsychological impairments and deficits in theory of mind and emotion recognition in a non-autistic boy. *European Journal of Child and Adolescent Psychiatry*, **5**, 44–51.

Burd, L., Fisher, W., Kerbeshian, J. and Arnold, M. (1987). Is development of Tourette syndrome a marker for improvement in patients with autism and other pervasive developmental disorders? *Journal of the American Academy of Child and Adolescent Psychiatry*, **26**, 162–5.

Chapman, L. J., Chapman, P. P. and Miller, G. A. (1964). A theory of verbal behavior in schizophrenia. In *Progress in experimental personality research*, (ed. B. A. Maher). Academic Press, New York.

Charman, T. and Baron-Cohen, S. (1992). Understanding drawings and beliefs: a further test of the metarepresentation theory of autism. *Journal of Child Psychology and Psychiatry*, **33**, 1105–12.

Corcoran, R. and Frith, C. D. (1993). Neuropsychology and neurophysiology in schizophrenia. *Current Opinion in Psychiatry*, **6**, 74–9.

Corcoran, R. and Frith, C. D. (1994). Neuropsychology and neurophysiology in schizophrenia. *Current Opinion in Psychiatry*, **7**, 47–50.

Corcoran, R. and Frith, C. D. (1996). Conversational conduct and the symptoms of schizophrenia. *Cognitive Neuropsychiatry*, **1**, 305–18.

Corcoran, R. and Frith, C. D. Conditional reasoning and 'theory of mind'. The case of schizophrenia. *British Journal of Psychology*. (Submitted.)

Corcoran, R., Mercer, G. and Frith, C. D. (1995). Schizophrenia, symptomatology and social inference; investigating theory of mind in people with schizophrenia. *Schizophrenia Research*, **17**, 5–13.

Corcoran, R., Cahill, C. and Frith, C. D. (1997). The appreciation of visual jokes in people with schizophrenia: a study of 'mentalizing' ability. *Schizophrenia Research*, **24**, 319–27.

Cosmides, L. (1989). The logic of social exchange: has natural selection shaped how humans reason? Studies with the Wason selection task. *Cognition*, **31**, 187–276.

Dewey, M. (1991). Living with Asperger's syndrome. In *Autism and Asperger syndrome*, (ed. U. Frith). Cambridge University Press.

Dodge, K. A. (1980). Social cognition and children's aggressive behavior. *Child Development*, **51**, 162–70.

Dolan, R. J., Bench, C. J., Liddle, P. F., Friston, K. J., Frith, C. D., Grasby, P. M. and Frackowiak, R. S. (1993). Dorsolateral prefrontal cortex dysfunction in the major psychoses, symptom or disease specificity? *Journal of Neurology, Neurosurgery and Psychiatry*, **56**, 1290–4.

Dolan, R. J., Bench, C. J., Brown, R. G., Scott, L. C. and Frackowiak, R. S. J. (1994). Neuropsychological dysfunction in depression: the relationship to regional cerebral blood flow. *Psychological Medicine*, **24**, 849–57.

Doody, G. A., Gotz, M., Johnstone, E. C., Frith, C. D. and Cunningham Owens, D. G. (1998). Theory of mind and psychoses. *Psychological Medicine*, **28**, 397–405.

Dunn, J. (1988). *The beginnings of social understanding*. Blackwell, Oxford.

Fletcher, P., Happé, F., Frith, U., Baker, S. C., Dolan, R. J., Frackowiak, R. S. J. and Frith, C. D. (1995). Other minds in the brain; a functional imaging study of 'theory of mind' in story comprehension. *Cognition*, **57**, 109–28.

Fodor, J. (1983). *The modularity of mind*. MIT Press, Cambridge, MA.

Fonagy, P. and Target, M. (1998). Attachment and borderline personality disorder: a theory and some evidence. Paper presented at the University College London Theory of Mind Conference, March 1998.

Fonagy, P., Steele, M., Steele, H., Leogh, T., Kennedy, R., Mattoon, G. and Target, M. (1995). Attachment, the reflective self and borderline states. In *Attachment theory: social development and clinical perspectives*, (ed. S. Goldberg, R. Muir and J. Kerr). Analytic Press, New York.

Fonagy, P., Leigh, T., Steele, M., Steele, H., Kennedy, R., Mattoon, G., Target, M. and Gerber, A. (1996). The relation of attachment status, psychiatric classification and response to psychotherapy. *Journal of Consulting and Clinical Psychology*, **64**, 22–31.

Fonagy, P., Target, M., Steele, M. and Steele, H. (1997). The development of violence and crime as it relates to security of attachment. In *Children in a violent society*, (ed. J. Osojsky). Guildford Press, New York.

Fogarty, S. and Hemsley, D. (1983). Depression and accessibility of memories. A longitudinal study. *British Journal of Psychiatry*, **142**, 232–7.

Frith, C. D. (1987). The positive and negative symptoms of schizophrenia reflect impairments in the perception and initiation of action. *Psychological Medicine*, **17**, 631–48.

Frith, C. D. (1992). *The cognitive neuropsychology of schizophrenia*. Lawrence Erlbaum Associates, Hove.

Frith, C. D. and Corcoran, R. (1996). Exploring theory of mind in people with schizophrenia. *Psychological Medicine*, **26**, 521–30.

Frith, C. D. and Done, D. J. (1989). Experiences of alien control in schizophrenia reflect a disorder in the central monitoring of action. *Psychological Medicine*, **19**, 359–63.

Frith, C. D., Leary, J., Cahill, C. and Johnstone, E. C. (1991). Performance on psychological tests. Demographical and clinical correlates of the results of these tests. *British Journal of Psychiatry*, **159** (supplement 13), 26–9.

Frith, U., Happé. F. and Siddons, F. (1994). Autism and theory of mind in everyday life. *Social Development*, **2**, 108–24.

Garety, P., Hemsley, D. and Wessely, S. (1991). Reasoning in deluded schizophrenic and paranoid patients. *Journal of Nervous and Mental Disease*, **179**, 194–201.

Garner, C., Callias, M. and Turk, J. The executive function and theory of mind performance in boys with Fragile X syndrome. Poster presented at the Society for the Study of Behavioural Phenotypes conference. November 1997

George, C., Kaplan, N. and Main, M. (1985). *The adult attachment interview*. Department of Psychology, University of California at Berkley.

George, M. S., Ketter, T. A. and Post, R. M. (1993). SPECT and PET imaging in mood disorders. Journal of Clinical Psychiatry, **54** (S), 6–13.

Grice, H. P. (1975). Logic and conversation. In *Syntax and semantics*, Vol. 3: Speech acts, (ed. P. Cole and J. L. Morgan). Academic Press, New York.

Happé, F. G. E. (1991). The autobiographical writings of three Asperger Syndrome adults:

problems of interpretation and implications for theory. Chaper 7, In: U. Frith (ed.) Autism and Asperger Syndrome. Cambridge University Press, Cambridge.

Happé, F. G. E. and Frith, U. (1996). Theory of mind and social impairment in children with conduct disorder. *British Journal of Developmental Psychology*, **14**, 385–98.

Hobson, R. P. (1990). On acquiring knowledge about people and the capacity to pretend: Response to Leslie (1987). *Psychological Review*, **97**, 114–21.

Howe, M. L. and Courage, M. L. (1997). The emergence and early development of autobiographical memory. *Psychological Review*, **104**, 499–523.

Hughes, C., Russell, J. and Robbins, T. W. (1994). Evidence for executive dysfunction in autism. *Neuropsychologia*, **32**, 477–92.

Jones, P. B., Bebbington, P., Foester, A., Lewis, S. W., Murray, R. M., Russell, A., Sham, P. C., Toone, B. K. and Wilkins, S. (1993). Premorbid social underachievement in schizophrenia. Results from the Camberwell Collaborative Psychosis Study. *British Journal of Psychiatry*, **162**, 65–71.

Jordan, R. and Powell, S. (1994). Personal episodic memory and narrative ability in children with autism. Paper presented at the British Psychological Society London Conference, 19–20 December.

Kay, S. R., Fisbein, A. and Opler, L. A. (1987). The positive and negative symptoms scale (PANNS) for schizophrenia. *Schizophrenia Bulletin*, **13**, 261–76.

Kopelman, M., Wilson, B. and Baddeley, A. (1993). *The autobiographical memory interview.* Thames Valley Test Company, Bury St Edmonds.

Langdon, R., Michie, P. T., Ward, P. B., McConaghy, N., Catts, S. V. and Coltheart, M. (1997). Defective self and/or other mentalizing in schizophrenia: a cognitive neuropsychological approach. *Cognitive Neuropsychiatry*, **2**, 167–93.

Leslie, A. M. and Thaiss, L. (1992). Domain specificity in conceptual development: neuropsychological evidence. *Cognition*, **43**, 225–51.

Lueger, R. J. and Gill, K. J. (1990). Frontal lobe cognitive dysfunction in conduct disorder adolescence. *Journal of Clinical Psychology*, **46**, 696–706.

McKeough, A., Yates, T. and Marini, A. (1994). Intentional reasoning: a developmental study of behaviourally aggressive and normal boys. *Development and Psychopathology*, **6**, 285–304.

Mealey, L. (1995). The sociobiology of sociopathy: an integrated evolutionary model. *Behavioral and Brain Sciences*, **18**, 523–99.

Militerni, R., Bravaccio, C. and Dantuono, P. S. (1997). Childhood disintegrative disorder: review of cases and pathogenic consideration. *Developmental Brain Dysfunction*, **10**, 67–74.

Mitchley, N. J., Barber, J., Gray, J. M., Brooks, D. N. and Livingstone, M. G. (1998). Comprehension of irony in schizophrenia. *Cognitive Neuropsychiatry*, **3**, 127–38.

Mlakar, J., Jensterle, J. and Frith, C. D. (1994). Central monitoring deficiency and schizophrenic symptoms. *Psychological Medicine*, **24**, 557–64.

Moriarty, J., Costa, D., Schmitz, B., Trimble, M., Robertson, M. and Ell, P. (1993). A study of Gilles de la Tourette syndrome using HMPAO SPECT. *Nuclear Medicine Communications*, **14**, 266–7.

Mortimer, A. M., McKay, I., Quemada, L., Eastwood, C. N. and McKenna, P. J. (1996). Delusions in schizophrenia: a phenomenological and psychological exploration. *Cognitive Neuropsychiatry*, **1**, 289–303.

Murray, R. M. and Lewis, S. W. (1987). Is schizophrenia a developmental disorder? *British Medical Journal*, **295**, 681–2.

Nelson, K. (1992). Emergence of autobiographical memory at age four. *Human Development*, **35**, 172–7.

Ozonoff, S., Pennington, B. F. and Rogers, S. J. (1991). Executive function deficits in high functioning autistic children. Relationship to theory of mind. *Journal of Child Psychology and Psychiatry*, **32**, 1081–106.

Pennington, B. F. and Bennetto, L. (1993). Main effects or transactions in the neuropsychology of conduct disorder? Commentary on: 'The neuropsychology of conduct disorder'. *Development and Psychopathology*, **5**, 153–64.

Perner, J. and Wimmer, H. (1985). 'John thinks that Mary thinks that . . .' Attribution of second-order beliefs by five to ten year old children. *Journal of Experimental Child Psychology*, **39**, 437–71.

Perner, J., Frith, U., Leslie, A. M. and Leekham, S. (1989). Exploration of the autistic child's theory of mind: knowledge, belief and communication. *Child Development*, **60**, 689–700.

Perner, J., Ruffman, T. and Leekham, S. R. (1994). Theory of mind is contagious: you catch it from your sibs. *Child Development*, **65**, 1228–38.

Peterson, C. C. and Seigal, M. (1995). Deafness, conversation and theory of mind. *Journal of Child Psychology and Psychiatry*, **36**, 459–74.

Peterson, C. C. and Siegel, M. (1997). Domain specificity and everyday biological, physical and psychological thinking in normal, autistic and deaf children. *New Directions for Child Development*, **75**, 55–70.

Pickup, G. (1997). The representation of mental states in schizophrenia. Unpublished PhD thesis. University of London.

Powell, S. D. and Jordan, R. R. (1993). Being subjective about autistic thinking and learning to learn. *Educational Psychology*, **13**, 359–70.

Raine, A. (1997). Birth trauma and violence. Paper presented at the British Neuropsychiatry Association Annual Conference. Cambridge, June 1997.

Sarfati, Y., Hardy-Bayle, M-C., Nadel, J., Chevalier, J-F. and Widlocher, D. (1997*a*). Attribution of mental states to others by schizophrenic patients. *Cognitive Neuropsychiatry*, **2**, 1–17.

Sarfati, Y., Hardy-Bayle, M-C., Besche, C. and Widlocher, D. (1997*b*). Attribution of intentions to others in people with schizophrenia: a non-verbal exploration with comic strips. *Schizophrenia Research*, **25**, 199–209.

Selman, R. L. (1980). *The growth of interpersonal understanding: development and clinical analysis.* Academic Press, New York.

Shallice, T. (1988). *From neuropsychology to mental structure.* Cambridge University Press.

Shallice, T., Burgess, P. W. and Frith, C. D. (1991). Can the neuropsychological case study approach be applied to schizophrenia? *Psychological Medicine*, **21**, 661–73.

Shallice, T., Fletcher, P., Frith, C. D., Grasby, P., Frackowiak, R. S. J. and Dolan, R. J. (1994). Brain regions associated with the acquisition and retrieval of verbal episodic memory. *Nature*, **368**, 633–5.

Shields, J., Varley, R., Broks, P. and Simpson, A. (1996). Social cognition in developmental language disorders and high level autism. *Developmental Medicine and Child Neurology*, **38**, 487–5.

Sparrow, S., Balla, D. and Cicchetti, D. (1984). *Vineland adaptive behavior scales.* American Guidance Service, Circle Pines, Maine.

Surian, L., Baron-Cohen, S. and Van der Lely, H. (1996). Are children with autism deaf to Gricean maxims? *Cognitive Neuropsychiatry*, **1**, 55–71.

Tamlyn, D., McKenna, P. J., Mortimer, A. M., Lund, C. E., Hammond, S. and Baddeley, A. D. (1992). Memory impairment in schizophrenia: its extent, affiliations and neuropsychological character. *Psychological Medicine*, **22**, 101–15.

Temple, C. M. and Vilarroya, O. (1990). Perceptual and cognitive perspective taking in two siblings with callosal agenesis. *British Journal of Developmental Psychology*, **8**, 3–8.

Thatcher, R. W. (1992). Cyclic cortical organisation during early childhood. *Brain and Cognition*, **20**, 24–50.

Welch, R. and Melissa, K. (1997). Motherchild participation in conversation about the past: relationship to preschoolers' theory of mind. *Developmental Psychology*, **33**, 618–29.

Wellman, H. M. and Gelman, S. A. (1992). Cognitive development: foundational theories of core domains. Annual Review of Psychology, **43**, 337–75.

Wimmer, H. and Perner, J. (1983). Beliefs about beliefs: representation and constraining function of wrong beliefs in young children's understanding of deception. Cognition, **13**, 103–28.

# 17

# Theory of mind and the early diagnosis of autism

TONY CHARMAN

## WISHFUL THINKING AND FRAMING QUESTIONS

An over-simplistic extension of the 'theory of mind deficit hypothesis' of autism—that individuals with autism show a specific impairment in their theory of mind abilities evidenced by their performance on false-belief tasks (see Baron-Cohen *et al.* 1993; Yirmiya *et al.* 1998, for reviews)—might lead to the conclusion that theory of mind tasks will provide a litmus test or diagnostic marker for autism. Following this erroneous line of thinking for a moment, the proposal might hold true whatever the associations are between the theory of mind and executive function impairments found in individuals with autism (see Ozonoff 1997; Perner and Lang, Chapter 4, this volume). In this simplistic, hypothetical world it may not matter whether theory of mind and executive function deficits in autism are causally related (in one direction or the other) or whether they are independent of each other. If it could be demonstrated that the theory of mind hypothesis of autism was correct at the descriptive level—that individuals with autism show unique and universal impairments on theory of mind tasks that are not shown by individuals with other disorders, regardless of whether these impairments are specific to theory of mind tasks compared with other types of reasoning tasks (Zelazo *et al.* 1996)—then developmentally appropriate theory of mind tasks could act as diagnostic markers.

There is some benefit to indulging temporarily in such over-simplistic thinking. It enables us to frame one set of critical considerations that would need to be addressed if an impairment in any ability is to act as a diagnostic for autism. First, the deficit would have to be unique to individuals with autism. That is, it should not be found in individuals with other clinical disorders, such as general developmental delay or specific language disorder, from whom one would be attempting to make a differential diagnosis. Second, the deficit would have to be universal. It would have to be found in every individual with autism, otherwise our marker or litmus test would lack sensitivity. Third, the measure used to assess the deficit would have to be developmentally appropriate. As this implies, the ability in question may not be an all-or-none developmental accomplishment but rather may proceed through a series of steps, as development is ongoing. We can now generate a set of questions regarding the possible role of theory of mind in the early diagnosis of autism: What theory of mind skills might be developmentally appropriate to aid early diagnosis? How might these (presumably) earlier-developing skills relate to later first-order theory of mind ability, as evidenced by an understanding of false belief (Wimmer and Perner 1983)? What ability do other clinical groups demonstrate in these early theory of mind skills? How should we measure these early theory of mind abilities in clinical practice? How might deficits in early theory of mind abilities in autism be associated with early executive or other information-processing deficits?

In this chapter, I highlight the shortcomings of the over-simplistic notion that false-belief tasks could provide some sort of litmus test for autism. I instead develop an account in which developmentally appropriate theory of mind abilities might be an aid to early diagnosis. Next, I review what we already know about the early diagnosis and early symptoms of autism, and summarize findings from recent prospective and long-itudinal studies into the early diagnosis of autism that are beginning to provide some answers to these questions.

## THE PROBLEM WITH FIRST-ORDER THEORY OF MIND TASKS AS A LITMUS TEST

Although the age at which children with autism are diagnosed by clinical services in a number of countries has decreased over the last few decades, it is still rare for children to receive a diagnosis before the age of three years (Gillberg *et al.* 1990; Howlin and Moore 1997; Siegel *et al.* 1988; Stone and Rosenbaum 1988; see Stone 1997, for a review). Thus, commonly in clinical practice, children are assessed for diagnosis after infancy during the preschool years. This is the time during which typically-developing children begin to demonstrate theory of mind ability, at least at the first-order level of understanding their own and others' desires and beliefs (Astington and Gopnik 1991; Astington *et al.* 1988; Mitchell 1996). This coincidence could fuel the erroneous train of thought entertained above and lead us to conclude that first-order theory of mind tasks, such as false-belief and appearance–reality tasks (Flavell *et al.* 1983; Perner *et al.* 1987; Wimmer and Perner 1983), are candidate diagnostic markers for autism. However, on closer scrutiny several problems are apparent.

The first problem is that 50% to 75% of individuals with autism have mild to severe developmental delay (DeMeyer *et al.* 1974; Wing and Gould 1979) so first-order theory of mind tasks may not be developmentally appropriate at a diagnostic assess-ment conducted between the ages of three and five years. Even for the minority of individuals without developmental delay, the litmus test notion does not stand up to close scrutiny. For false-belief performance to act as a diagnostic marker for autism, the impairment would have to meet the 'universality' and 'uniqueness' requirements (Zelazo *et al.* 1996)—at least to a certain degree—in order for the specificity and sensitivity of the test to be adequate for clinical use. Although there is substantive evidence that group differences have been found between individuals with autism and matched control subjects (see Baron-Cohen *et al.* 1993; Happé 1995, Yirmiya *et al.* 1998 for reviews), a closer examination of the research findings calls into question whether the universality and uniqueness requirements are met to a sufficient degree for theory of mind tests to be clinically useful, even for the minority of individuals with autism for whom they would be developmentally appropriate.

In terms of the universality requirement, which affects the sensitivity of a diagnostic test: most studies have demonstrated that the majority of individuals with autism fail standard false-belief tasks, but performance has not been at floor. All studies have demonstrated some false-belief competence with samples of individuals with autism, with success rates varying from 20% to 40% (see Happé 1995, for a review). In addition, simple manipulations such as the Mitchell and Lacohée (1991) posting procedure have been shown to increase false-belief task performance in individuals with autism to 59% (Charman and Lynggaard 1998). In terms of the uniqueness requirement, which affects the specificity of a diagnostic test, inspection of past studies reveals a wide variation in the theory of mind performance of groups of individuals with a developmental delay without autism. While some studies have replicated Baron-Cohen *et al.*'s (1985) finding of near-ceiling performance on first-order theory of mind tasks, others have found only 50% to 70% of participants passing, and several recent studies have found a success rate of 50% or lower, for individuals with a developmental delay, significantly lower than that of typically-developing mental age-matched children (Benson *et al.* 1993; Charman *et al.* 1998; Yirmiya *et al.* 1996; Zelazo *et al.* 1996; see Yirmiya *et al.* 1998, for a review).

In summary, first-order theory of mind tasks are not diagnostic markers for autism. This is partly because there are many reasons why a child might fail such a test (language, memory, reasoning, executive, or other related factors, rather than mentalizing factors *per se*). They are developmentally inappropriate for many clinical diagnostic assessments, unless the child has a verbal mental age of greater than four years, and the variable evidence for the universality and uniqueness of theory of mind impairments to individuals with autism would give them low sensitivity and specificity as diagnostic markers. In the case of autism, they become important when viewed alongside converging evidence from a number of sources. Importantly, to date this account has been largely non developmental, and adopting a developmental perspective offers more promise, as discussed below. However, the exercise of debunking the over-simplistic premise that first-order theory of mind tasks might act as a diagnostic marker for autism at the typical age for diagnostic assessment has not been without value. It has enabled us to identify the important considerations of the universality, uniqueness, and developmental appropriateness of any other candidate markers. For example, Uta Frith (1989) has proposed that there will not be a single case of autism spectrum disorder in which theory of mind ability is mental age-appropriate. This is an attempt at framing a universalist and specific hypothesis, in terms of specific developmental delay of theory of mind. To date, there is no disconfirming evidence for her claim. The second benefit of considering the simplistic position is to frame both clinical and theoretical questions regarding the association between early markers and later deficits in theory of mind ability, as well as their association with other psychological impairments found in individuals with autism. To answer such questions a more developmental approach is required. This is where we turn next.

## PRECURSORS TO A THEORY OF MIND AS A POSSIBLE SOLUTION

Developmental accomplishments rarely emerge suddenly and fully-formed. Rather, development proceeds via a sequence of stages or phases, each of which may represent an advance in the skill or cognitive process of concern. This is likely to be true for the development of a theory of mind, and its impairment in autism.

Gomez *et al.* (1993) outline two conceptual meanings of the term 'precursor'. First, a precursor might announce the coming of something else. The precursor signals or announces the advent of more complex capacities (which Gomez *et al.* (1993) term the 'John the Baptist' way of being a precursor). An alternative meaning of a precursor is when the former precursor substance can be transformed into the latter (which Gomez *et al.* (1993) term the 'chemical' way of being a precursor). In a cautionary note, Sigman and Mundy (1993) point out that, in both cases, an ontogenic relationship is presumed but the notion of causation avoided.

Angold and Hay (1993) propose a more conservative definition of precursors. They list four types of evidence that can be used to support the claim that one state is a precursor of another: (i) resemblance between the two states; (ii) stability of individual differences from one state to the next; (iii) evidence that emergence of the first state is a prerequisite for the second to occur; and (iv) experimental disruption or manipulation of the first state has predictable consequences for the second. However, evidence which meets just one of these criteria is not sufficient—for example, behavioural isomorphism may indicate homotypic continuity, rather than a precursor relationship.

In terms of the clinical questions regarding early signs or markers for autism, it need not be a requirement that the most conservative definition of a precursor be employed. Early putative theory of mind abilities could still be useful as early diagnostic markers or indicators. Of course, for a proper understanding of the underlying pathogenesis of autism—at either the behavioural or neurodevelopmental level—we would want to know about the status of any precursor abilities. While these questions are not the primary focus of the present chapter, discussion will be given to these ideas where appropriate.

Thus, a developmental account of children with autism should not start with impaired theory of mind ability in individuals of school age, but rather with impairments in putative precursors to a theory of mind in young preschool children. A considerable body of research has demonstrated autism-specific impairments in candidate infant abilities such as empathic response, pretend play, joint attention, and imitation (see Charman *et al.* 1997, 1998, for reviews):

(i)   *Empathic response*: children with autism show poor co-ordination of affective response. They are less likely than controls to combine smiles with eye contact, less likely to smile in response to smiles from their mother (Dawson *et al.* 1990; Kasari *et al.* 1990), and are impaired in their empathic responses (Sigman *et al.* 1992).

(ii)  *Functional and pretend play*: in unstructured or free-play conditions, children with autism produce significantly less pretend play, but intact functional play, compared with chronological or mental age-matched comparison groups (see Jarrold *et al.* 1993, for a review). Under structured, or prompted, conditions some studies have found that children with autism produced fewer functional and symbolic acts than developmentally-delayed controls (e.g. Mundy *et al.* 1986; Wetherby and Prutting 1984), whilst in some studies children with autism produced as many functional and symbolic acts as controls (e.g. Lewis and Boucher 1988).

(iii) *Joint attention*: there is substantial experimental evidence for impairments in both the production and comprehension of joint attention behaviours in children with autism. Many studies have shown, for example, that whilst children with autism are able to use gestures to request objects (protoimperative gestures) or to engage in social action routines, they nevertheless do not use gestures to share interest in objects or their properties (protodeclarative gestures) (e.g. Baron-Cohen 1989; Mundy *et al.* 1986; see Mundy *et al.* 1993, for a review).

(iv) *Imitation*: Whilst some studies have demonstrated impaired imitation—in particular of complex and novel sequences of actions—in children with autism (see Rogers *et al.* 1996; Smith and Bryson 1994, for reviews), other studies have found that school-age children with autism are able to produce basic-level imitation of gestures, actions on objects, and facial expressions (Charman and Baron-Cohen 1994; Loveland *et al.* 1994).

Theoretical accounts based on these findings claim a crucial role for these abilities in normal social and communicative development, specifically in the development of theory of mind abilities, and impairments in these abilities have been linked to the later problems in social understanding and social communication that characterize autism (Baron-Cohen 1993, 1995; Hobson 1993; Leslie 1987, 1994; Meltzoff and Gopnik 1993; Mundy 1995; Mundy *et al.* 1993; Rogers and Pennington 1991). That is, these accounts suggest that these social communicative abilities might be precursors to the development of a theory of mind.

## RETROSPECTIVE EVIDENCE FOR IMPAIRMENTS IN INFANT PRECURSOR ABILITIES

Two sources of information have been studied for evidence that these putative precursor abilities may be impaired in children with autism in the first few years of life: retrospective parental report of early symptoms, and videos taken before the child was diagnosed (see Stone 1997, for a review). The evidence from a series of studies where parents have been asked to report retrospectively on symptoms in the first, or more commonly the second, year of life appears to demonstrate that children with autism do show specific impairments or delays in many aspects of these infant precursor social communicative abilities.

The early studies by Ornitz *et al.* (1977), DeMeyer (1979), and Hoshino *et al.* (1982) compared retrospective parental report of the behaviour of children with autism with that of typically-developing children. These studies found that fewer children with autism were using pointing and fewer of them imitated compared with the comparison group, in the Ornitz *et al.* (1977) study showing an increased incidence of sensory and repetitive abnormalities as well. However, two cautions relevant to the possibility of these behaviours acting as potential diagnostic markers for autism are warranted. First, in the absence of a comparison group matched for level of developmental and language delay, we do not know if the lack of pointing and imitation are specific to autism. Second, not all children with autism were reported to show none of the behaviours in question. In the Hoshino *et al.* (1982) study, 30% of the children with autism with a DQ greater than 70 were reported to point by the age of eighteen months, though only 9% of the children with autism with a DQ below 50 were reported to have done so, with similar figures of 30% and 15%, respectively, for imitation. Thus, the presence (by retrospective report) of these behaviours does not rule out that the child is autistic. One further caution is that the definition of the behaviours employed in these studies lacks precision and does not make the important distinction between communicative function and form (Charman 1997). Proto-declarative pointing (pointing for interest) and protoimperative pointing (pointing to ask) may look like similar behaviours to parents at the surface level, although there is good evidence that the former but not the latter is the communicative function that is specifically impaired in autism (Baron-Cohen 1989; Charman 1997, 1998).

Other studies have identified the symptoms which parents of children with autism report first noticing retrospectively, and compared these with the symptoms first noticed by parents of children with general developmental delay. Gillberg and colleagues (Dahlgren and Gillberg 1989; Gillberg *et al.* 1990) found that peculiarities of gaze, hearing, play, and 'autistic aloneness' differentiated between the two groups. They also found that non-social behaviours—abnormal responses to sensory stimulation, but not insistence on sameness or resistance to change—differentiated between the groups. Ohta *et al.* (1987) found that the majority of parents of children with autism reported first being concerned when their child was between eighteen and thirty months old. The concerns that discriminated them from those reported by parents of children with general developmental delay were social communicative behaviours, including difficulty in forming personal relationships, a poor response to others, poor peer relationships, and ignoring others as if deaf. Importantly, the incidence of reporting of these concerns by the parents of the comparison children was very low. Therefore the behaviours were highly specific to autism. Two other early symptoms, delayed speech and restlessness and hyperactivity, were also reported significantly more commonly by the parents of children with autism; however, they were also commonly reported by the parents of children with developmental delay without autism and thus would not be specific enough to act as markers for autism.

Two other retrospective report studies had no comparison group. Stone *et al.* (1994) found that three quarters of parents reported concerns regarding impaired imitation abilities, abnormal social play and abnormal non-verbal communication, with half of parents also reporting concerns about other social and communicative behaviours, such as lack of awareness of others and impaired peer relationships, as well as stereotyped body movements and a restricted range of interests. Frith *et al.* (1993)

found that while one quarter of parents reported concerns in their child's first year of life, 65% had concerns before the end of the second year, with language problems being the most frequently reported concern.

The authors of many of these studies discuss the possibility that retrospective reporting may be biased by later knowledge and behaviour. However, there is considerable agreement on what types of behaviours are first noted as abnormal by parents of children with autism, and roughly at what age. Social and communicative abnormalities in non-verbal communication and gestures, peer relationships, responses to others, play, and imitation skills, are found across most studies. Abnormalities in terms of repetitive and stereotyped behaviours are found in some but not all studies. In the majority of studies parents report these concerns before the end of the second year of life, but less frequently in the first year.

Another source of information has recently come to light regarding the early development of children with autism—home videos taken before the child was diagnosed. In a retrospective review of home videos taken by parents of children with autism and parents of typically-developing children between birth and two years of age, Adrien *et al.* (1993) found that within the first year children with autism showed impairments in social interaction, lack of social smile, lack of appropriate facial expression, hypotonia, and poor attention. In the second year of life additional impairments characterized the children with autism, including ignoring people, preference for aloneness, lack of eye contact, lack of appropriate gestures, and lack of emotional expression. In a similar study comparing the home videos taken at first birthday parties, Osterling and Dawson (1994) found that children with autism were less likely to look at others, less likely to show an object or point to objects, and less likely to orient to their name, compared with typically-developing controls.

Again, the caution of whether these impairments are specific to autism, rather than to general development delay, needs to be made. However, these enterprising studies consolidate the information elicited from retrospective parental accounts of early symptoms. One further related retrospective study systematically extracted information regarding motor, visual, hearing and social development from health checks at six, twelve, and eighteen months on children later diagnosed with autism (Johnson *et al.* 1992). Johnson and colleagues found that an indication of a problem in these domains did not discriminate children with autism from developmentally-delayed controls at either six or twelve months, but that at eighteen months the children with autism were reported to have more problems in the social, hearing and language domains.

In summary, retrospective evidence suggests that, as early as the first year of life, and certainly by the end of the second year of life, children with autism show a distinctive pattern of impairments, compared with typically-developing and developmentally-delayed children. The abnormalities that most clearly differentiate children with autism from other children are in precursors of theory of mind abilities, in which older already-diagnosed samples have been shown to have specific impairments: emotional or empathic response, joint attention behaviours, such as pointing and use of eye contact to monitor attention, imitation, and imaginative and pretend play. In addition, there is also evidence for the presence of early abnormalities in sensory, motor, and repetitive and stereotyped behaviours, although most studies concur that the best discriminators at this age are likely to be the social and communicative impairments.

Two questions arise from this retrospective work. First, which exact social or communicative behaviours are likely to be the most discriminating, either to aid in the differential diagnosis of young preschool children with autism or even in their early identification? Second, at what age might these behaviours be most discriminating, since as set out above adopting a developmental perspective reminds us that the characteristic behaviour of children with autism changes as they develop? Recent advances in the early detection of autism, both in a prospective epidemiological screening study (Baron-Cohen *et al.* 1992, 1996) and in earlier referral to more informed clinic services (Camaioni *et al.* 1997; Lord 1995; Stone *et al.* 1997), have led to the systematic assessment of younger children with autism than was previously possible. These studies allow us to examine infant and young preschool social communicative behaviours as they emerge, thus enabling us to plot more precisely the 'natural history' of autism. These recent studies have clinical and theoretical implications: they increase our knowledge of which precursor theory of mind, or indeed other, abilities are likely to best aid the clinical diagnosis of young children with autism. They may also provide one strand of evidence to help decide between the competing accounts of pathogenic development in autism. Lastly, tying these two strands of thinking together, they may also inform and direct efforts in the design, content, and evaluation of intervention programmes aimed at ameliorating the social, communicative, and repetitive impairments that characterise autism.

## A PROSPECTIVE SCREENING STUDY

Adopting a perspective from developmental psychology, related to the notion of precursors to a theory of mind set out above, Baron-Cohen and colleagues concluded that there are behaviours that typically develop by eighteen months of age which are noticeably absent even in school-age children with autism, and which therefore should offer clues to improving early detection and diagnosis. As reviewed above, these behaviours include pretend play (Baron-Cohen 1987; Ungerer and Sigman 1981), protodeclarative pointing (Baron-Cohen 1989; Sigman *et al.* 1986), and gaze-monitoring (Leekam *et al.* 1997; Phillips *et al.* 1995). Baron-Cohen and colleagues developed a screening instrument to measure these abilities, with the aim of prospectively indentifying infants with autism at age eighteen months by their impaired development in these skills (Baron-Cohen *et al.* 1992, 1996). The CHAT (CHecklist for Autism in Toddlers) assesses pretend play, protodeclarative pointing, and gaze-monitoring by parental report and Health Visitor observation.

In the first study, the CHAT correctly identified four children with autism at eighteen months of age from a high-risk sample of forty one siblings of children already diagnosed as autistic and fifty typically-developing children (Baron-Cohen *et al.* 1992). The four children later diagnosed as autistic were the only ones who failed all five key items measuring both pretend play and protodeclarative pointing by both parental report and Health Visitor observation, and also the gaze-monitoring item included in the practitioner observation section of the CHAT. Of the remaining eighty seven children, a substantial minority failed one of these behaviours at eighteen months, most commonly pretend play (14%), followed by protodeclarative pointing (8%), but none failed more than one of these, and all were developing normally when reviewed at thirty months of age.

In the second study, a random population of 16 000 children at eighteen months of age was screened by their Health Visitors or family physicians using the CHAT (Baron-Cohen *et al.* 1996). Just twelve children out of 16 000 failed all five key items (as scored by both Health Visitors and parents when administered at age eighteen months and on repeated administration one month later; see Baron-Cohen *et al.* (1996) for details of the screening procedure). On follow-up assessment at age forty two months, eight of these twelve children met ICD-10 (WHO 1993) criteria for childhood autism, two met ICD-10 criteria for atypical autism, and one the criteria for pervasive developmental disorder not otherwise specified, with the remaining child having a language disorder (see Baird *et al.* 1998; Cox *et al.* 1999, for details). In addition, a sample of children who failed the two CHAT items asking about proto-declarative pointing, but who also failed one or two but not three of the other key items (whom at the outset we considered may be at risk for developmental delay rather than autism), were also followed up at age forty two months. Of the twenty one children with this CHAT profile seen at the forty two months follow-up, nine met ICD-10 (1993) criteria for PDD-NOS and two children met criteria for Asperger's Syndrome, seven children had a language disorder, one child was generally develop-mentally delayed, and only two children were considered developmentally normal at this age. Sixteen children who passed all five key CHAT items at the eighteen-month screening were also seen at forty two months of age. Fifteen were considered clinically normal and one child met criteria for an expressive developmental language disorder.

Questions relating to the sensitivity of the CHAT as a population screening instru-ment await the findings of further screens and follow-up of the same 16 000 cohort of children. Preliminary results of a six-year follow-up of the same population using a further parent screening instrument, paediatric and child psychiatric clinic data, special needs registers, and school and Health Visitor records, show that the sensitivity of the CHAT in prospectively identifying autism is only moderate, with nineteen children with childhood autism, three children with atypical autism, and eleven children with PDD-NOS being missed by the initial eighteen-month screen (see Baird *et al.* submitted, for details). Additionally, we expect that cases of Asperger's Syndrome will come to light at an older age, and we are currently attempting to screen the same cohort for this disorder. However, in terms of the focus of the current chapter the CHAT has been shown to have a high specificity for prospectively identifying children with autism and related pervasive developmental disorders, with eleven of the twelve children failing all five key items at eighteen months receiving an autism spectrum diagnosis at age three years.

Thus, as predicted from the notion that developmental precursors to a theory of mind, such as joint attention behaviours and pretend play, may act as diagnostic markers for autism in young preschoolers, children who fail to show protodeclarative pointing, gaze-monitoring, and pretend play at eighteen months of age are at high risk for autism. Even when a child shows impairments in a number but not the whole set of these early-emerging social communication behaviours, they are at risk for a related pervasive developmental disorder or a language disorder. Clearly, some cautions are necessary. Some children with moderate and severe developmental delay were excluded from the screening; the screening instrument relied on children failing to ever show these joint attention and pretend play behaviours, both by parental report and by practitioner observation, on two administrations conducted one month apart; and the network of professionals was trained by the specialist research group leading the project. However, confidence that impairments in joint attention and pretend play are good early diagnostic markers or indicators is enhanced by the fact that there now exists converging evidence from several sources, including retrospective parental report, early home videos and prospective screening, that children with autism and related disorders show impairments in these abilities by the age of eighteen months.

## EXPERIMENTAL WORK WITH INFANTS AND PRESCHOOLERS WITH AUTISM

The CHAT prospective screening study (Baron-Cohen *et al.* 1996) offered an opportunity to study precursor abilities in more detail in infants with autism and related pervasive developmental disorders at the clinical assessments conducted at age twenty months (Charman *et al.* 1997, 1998). Experimental measures of empathy (Sigman *et al.* 1992), functional and pretend play (Baron-Cohen 1987), joint attention and requesting abilities (Butterworth and Adamson-Macedo 1987; Phillips *et al.* 1992), attention shifting (Swettenham *et al.* 1999), and imitation (Charman and Baron-Cohen 1994) were conducted.

The group of infants with autism showed very low production of some behaviours, in contrast to the infants with PDD and language delay. For example, only half the infants with autism looked at the experimenter during the display of feigned distress in the empathy task, and only one was rated as showing facial concern. Similarly, while all but three of the infants with PDD and one infant with language delay produced at least one example of a gaze switch of visual attention in response to ambiguous toys on the joint attention task—and did so consistently with gaze switches occurring on nearly two thirds of trials in both groups—only one third of the infants with autism produced even one example of a gaze switch. In contrast, they produced as many 'non-social' looks at the box that controlled the toys. In another task designed to assess the spontaneous distribution of visual attention between objects and people (Swettenham *et al.* 1998), the infants with autism shifted attention between two objects more than the comparison groups, and shifted attention less between objects and people, and between two people. They also spent less time overall looking at people and more time looking at objects. On the goal-detection tasks—taken as measures of imperative or requesting behaviour—one third of the infants with autism looked at the experimenter following the ambiguous action on at least one trial. Although the infants with PDD and language delay produced more than twice as many looks to the experimenter as the individuals with autism, these differences did not reach statistical significance because at least some of the infants with autism were producing some imperative looks on at least some trials, and because comparatively lower levels of these behaviours were produced by the individuals with language disorder compared with the joint attention task. On the imitation task, the infants with autism imitated on only one fifth of the trials, in contrast to infants with PDD and language delay who imitated on over half the trials. On the spontaneous play task no infants with autism and only three with PDD produced any examples of pretend play, in contrast to half the infants with language delay. However, two-thirds of subjects in all three groups produced some examples of functional play.

One conclusion from this study is that isolated examples of pretend play, gaze switching, and imitative behaviour in clinical diagnostic assessments of infants or preschool children cannot rule out a diagnosis of PDD—nor indeed of autism, since many individuals with PDD, and a few individuals with autism, did produce examples of all the target social communication behaviours (with the exception of spontaneous pretend play). When considering the role of impairments in empathic response, joint attention behaviours, pretend play, and imitation in infants and young preschoolers referred for early diagnostic assessment of autism, it is important to bear in mind that the diagnosis of autism relies on a child showing a number of impairments across at least three domains of behaviours (DSM-IV 1994; ICD-10 1993). An isolated impairment (particularly in a single assessment) is clearly not diagnostic. However, when a child has impairments in a number of these early social communicative abilities that relate to the domains of reciprocal social interaction and communication this may be indicative of autism or a related pervasive developmental disorder. One important consideration, that was also relevant to the findings of the retrospective parental report and home video studies, is the relationship between impairments in these two domains and those in the third domain of repetitive behaviours, stereotyped patterns, and restricted interests, necessary for a diagnosis of autism.

In another aspect of the prospective CHAT study, we assessed parental report of past and present symptoms using the Autism Diagnostic Interview-Revised (ADI-R; Lord *et al.* 1994) in the prospectively identified cohort at age twenty months and forty two months. An unexpected finding was that the age of onset of repetitive abnormalities in children with childhood autism and related PDD was significantly later than the age of onset of social and communication abnormalities (Cox *et al.* 1999). One possibility is that there is a relatively later onset of repetitive and restricted behaviours, at least in a full blown form that warrants a score of definite abnormality on the ADI-R, in comparison to the early onset of social and communicative abnormalities, some of which were apparent in nearly all children with autism by twenty months. This might be because these features have a separate aetiology from the social and communicative difficulties characteristic of the disorder (Bishop 1993); or because they arise secondarily in some way to the other features (Mundy 1995; Mundy and Crowson 1997); or because those children presenting with these features early on represent a subgroup of the disorder. Clarification of the emergence of the social, communicative, and repetitive behaviours in autism is important not only for clinical diagnosis but also potentially as an empirical test of different psychological and neurobiological accounts of the underlying pathology in autism.

Recent advances in the organisation, referral procedures, and expertise of diagnostic centres has enabled other groups to study young preschoolers with autism. Several recent studies have examined the behaviours that discriminate individuals with autism from those with general developmental delay during the preschool years (Camaioni *et al.* 1997; DiLavore and Lord 1995; Lord 1995; Stone *et al.* 1997). Using the Pre-Linguistic Autism Diagnostic Observation Schedule (PL-ADOS; DiLavore *et al.* 1995) at age two, three, and five years, DiLavore and Lord (1995) found that whilst there were no autism-specific impairments in very simple requesting behaviour at age two (e.g. a requesting routine with a balloon where the balloon is passed back-and-from the child to the experimenter—with no eye contact necessary), for more complicated requesting behaviours (e.g. requesting an out-of-reach snack by either vocal, verbal, or gestural means—with no eye contact necessary) there were autism-specific differences at age two, although these had disappeared at age three. For declarative joint attention gestures which involve co-ordination of eye contact with a gesture, there were clear autism-specific impairments at ages two, three, and five for initiating gestures, but only at ages two and three for following, or responding to, such gestures.

Mundy *et al.* (1994) presented data from a cross-sectional study which supports the view that the nature of the joint attention and gestural impairment in autism is related to developmental level. Mundy *et al.* (1994) compared the declarative and imperative joint attention skills (measured on the Early Social Communication Scales: ESCS; Seibert *et al.* 1982) of preschool children with autism with a mental age of around eighteen months with those of preschool children with autism with a mental age of around thirty months. The children with autism with a mental age of eighteen months were impaired relative to controls on both low level (eye contact) and high level (conventional gestures) joint attention behaviours, whilst children with autism with a mental age of thirty months were impaired on the high-level conventional joint attention gestures only. Similarly, whilst children with autism with a mental age of eighteen months were specifically impaired on measures of responding to joint attention gestures produced by the experimenter, the children with autism with a mental age of thirty months were not. For requesting gestures, the only significant group difference was that the children with autism with a mental age of eighteen months produced significantly fewer high-level requesting gestures than the normally-developing children, but not the developmentally-delayed controls. This reflects in part the relatively low frequency of high-level requesting behaviours (e.g. pointing to toys out of reach) produced by the developmentally-delayed control children without autism with a mental age of eighteen months. For the children with a mental age of thirty months, all three groups produced similar levels of low- and high-level requesting gestures.

Stone *et al.* (1997) studied non-verbal communicative behaviour in a sample of children with autism between twenty seven and thirty eight months of age. They found differences in the amount, function, and form of the communications produced by the children with autism, compared with developmentally-delayed controls. The children with autism communicated less often during a structured interaction. When they did communicate they were more likely to request objects or actions and less likely to direct the examiner's attention to an object or activity (i.e. comment) than controls. Further, fewer communicative acts involved eye gaze and fewer involved the combination of gestures with eye contact or vocalizations (Stone *et al.* 1997). However, a greater proportion of acts (including requests) involved the direct manipulation of the examiner's hand towards the object. Stone and colleagues conclude that a two-year-old child whose communicative repertoire reveals an absence of pointing and showing objects, and the presence of manipulating other people's hands, reaching and giving objects, may require a clinical evaluation to rule out autism (Stone *et al.* 1997). In a series of three case studies of children seen at six-monthly intervals between the third and the fifth year of life, Camaioni *et al.* (1997) demonstrated the importance of attention to the individual differences shown by individuals with autism through development. While during the period of study one of the three children showed no examples of either the production or the comprehension of protodeclarative pointing, one child produced examples of both behaviours in later assessments and another produced but appeared not to comprehend declarative pointing.

Lord (1995) reports the results of diagnostic assessments conducted at age two and a half years, and at follow up one year later, in a cohort of children, all referred for possible pervasive developmental delay, using systematic parental report information elicited by the ADI-R at both timepoints. Lord (1995) found that whilst some aspects of communication (including joint attention behaviours such as the production and understanding of pointing declarative gestures), social behaviour (including greeting, sharing enjoyment, use of another's body to communicate, and interest in other children), and repetitive and stereotyped behaviour (hand and finger mannerisms and unusual sensory behaviours) discriminated children with autism from those with general developmental delays at both age two and three, other behaviours were only discriminating at the older timepoint. These included spontaneous imitation and imaginative play, offering comfort, range and appropriateness of facial expression, and unusual preoccupations and whole body mannerisms. Lord (1995) comments that this changing profile of discriminating items between the third and fourth year of life is mostly due to the reduced proportion of developmentally-delayed children without autism who show these behaviours. The relevance of these findings to the present discussion is that the particular nature of both the behaviours that characterize autism by their absence (such as lack of pointing accompanied by eye gaze), and those that characterize autism by their presence (such as unusual preoccupations), may change during the preschool years, and are related to the degree of developmental delay shown by the children with autism and the developmentally-delayed children without autism to whom they are being compared (see also Lord *et al.* 1997, for an analysis of discriminating items on the ADI-R data in a larger sample by developmental level). That is, no behaviour by its presence or its absence is diagnostic of autism at any one age, but a particular profile of behaviours when set against a child's overall developmental level may act as strong indicator or marker for autism.

These findings, in conjunction with those that are emerging from the prospective screening study described above, are potentially of great clinical importance, as they help us to refine the application of the diagnostic criteria for autism to young preschool children. Differentiation of autism from general developmental delay is perhaps most difficult in very young children or those with low mental ages, due to the general absence of directed behaviours in individuals with developmental levels under two years of age (Baird *et al.* 1998; Cox *et al.* 1999; Lord 1995; Lord *et al.* 1997). Refinement of our understanding of the subtleties of characteristic autistic behaviours, particularly early-emerging preverbal social and communicative behaviours, such as putative precursor-to-theory of mind abilities including empathic response, joint attention, requesting behaviours, pretend play, and imitation will increase our ability to make these fine-grain clinical discriminations.

## CONCLUSIONS AND SOME REMARKS ABOUT DEVELOPMENTAL THEORY AND PATHOGENIC PROCESSES IN AUTISM

At the outset of this chapter, I set up a hypothetical world characterized by erroneous and over-simplistic patterns of thinking. The real-world evidence for the potential contribution of the concept of theory of mind to early and accurate diagnosis of autism is beginning to accumulate. Many of the sources of evidence available to us concur that impairments in 'precursor' theory of mind abilities such as empathic response, joint attention behaviours, pretend play, and imitation are suitable early markers for autism, because from a very young age (perhaps the second or third year of life) they are seen in children with developmental and language delays without autism—from whom clinical discriminations are commonly made in clinical practice. The other category of behaviours that are required to make a diagnosis of autism are repetitive patterns, stereotyped behaviours, and restricted interests. Although from some sources of evidence these behaviours are also present and specifically discriminate children with autism from other groups at a young age, there is more equivocal evidence for these being universally present and discriminating in the very youngest children during infancy (Cox *et al.* 1999; Stone 1997; Stone *et al.* 1999).

These findings raise important questions regarding theory of mind development, and further related questions regarding the pathogenic process in autism. In terms of developmental theory, what is the relationship between early-emerging social communicative abilities, such as the putative precursor abilities, and the later acquisition of a theory of mind? The fact that there is some continuity of impairment in autism between the two sets of skills does not really help us. While this meets the requirement for precursor status at its most generous structural level (Gomez *et al.* 1993) it says nothing about how they are related (Angold and Hay 1993). Such evidence can only be provided by longitudinal studies that demonstrate that there is stability of individual differences from one state to the next, that emergence of the first state is a prerequisite for the second to occur, and that experimental disruption or manipulation of the first state has predictable consequences for the second. While there is some limited evidence to this effect both in typically-developing children (see Dunn 1996, for a review of the developmental relationship between pretend play and later theory of mind ability) and in children with autism (Mundy *et al.* 1993), we await the outcome of further longitudinal studies. Another important question concerns the developmental relationship between social and communicative abilities, and other cognitive abilities, such as executive function (Bishop 1993; Ozonoff and McEvoy 1994). Once again, coexistence of these impairments in autism tells us nothing about whether these abilities are functionally related in one direction or the other, or whether they are simply unrelated co-occurring deficits (Pennington 1991).

Such questions are not merely theoretical considerations. A better understanding of the relationship between these two sets of impairments in autism may have important implications for our understanding of the neurodevelopmental disease processes that underlie autism, and for appropriate strategies and modes of intervention at neuro-biological, psychological, and behavioural levels (Mundy and Crowson 1997; Yeung-Courchesne and Courchesne 1997). A developmental approach to identifying and tracking the symptoms that characterise autism in infancy and the preschool years will provide one important source of information to contribute to answering these important theoretical and clinical questions. The research reviewed in this chapter provides encouraging evidence that such research programmes are underway.

## REFERENCES

Adrien, J. L., Lenoir, P., Martineau, J., Perrot, A., Hameury, L., Larmande, C. and Sauvage, D. (1993). Blind ratings of early symptoms of autism based on family home movies. *Journal of the American Academy of Child and Adolescent Psychiatry*, **33**, 617–26.

American Psychiatric Association (1994). *Diagnostic and statistical manual of mental disorders*, (4th edn), (DSM-IV). American Psychiatric Association, Washington, DC.

Angold, A. and Hay, D. F. (1993). Precursors and causes in development and psychopathology: an afterword. In *Precursors and causes in development and psychopathology*, (ed. D. F. Hay and A. Angold), pp. 1–21. Wiley, London.

Astington, J. W. and Gopnik, A. (1991). Theoretical explanations of children's understanding of the mind. *British Journal of Developmental Psychology*, **9**, 7–31.

Astington, J., Harris, P. and Olson, D. (1988). *Developing theories of mind*. Cambridge University Press, New York.

Baird, G., Cox, A., Baron-Cohen, S., Swettenham, J., Charman, T., Drew, A., Wheelwright, S., and Nightingale, N. What are the rates of false positives and negatives in detecting autism at 18 months of age using the CHAT? A six-year follow-up study. (Submitted).

Baron-Cohen, S. (1987). Autism and symbolic play. *British Journal of Developmental Psychology*, **5**, 139–48.

Baron-Cohen, S. (1989). Perceptual role-taking and protodeclarative pointing in autism. *British Journal of Developmental Psychology*, **7**, 113–27.

Baron-Cohen, S. (1993). From attention–goal psychology to belief–desire psychology: the development of a theory of mind and its dysfunction. In *Understanding other minds: perspectives from autism*, (ed. S. Baron-Cohen, H. Tager-Flusberg and D. Cohen), pp. 59–82. Oxford University Press, Oxford.

Baron-Cohen, S. (1995). *Mindblindness: an essay on autism and theory of mind*. MIT Press, Cambridge, MA.

Baron-Cohen, S., Leslie, A. M. and Frith, U. (1985). Does the autistic child have a 'theory of mind'? *Cognition*, **4**, 37–46.

Baron-Cohen, S., Allen, J. and Gillberg, C. (1992). Can autism be detected at 18 months? The needle, the haystack and the CHAT. *British Journal of Psychiatry*, **161**, 839–42.

Baron-Cohen, S., Tager-Flusberg, H. and Cohen, D. (ed.) (1993). *Understanding other minds: perspectives from autism.* Oxford University Press, Oxford.

Baron-Cohen, S., Cox, A., Baird, G., Swettenham, J., Nightingale, N., Morgan, K., Drew, A. and Charman, T. (1996). Psychological markers of autism at 18 months of age in a large population. *British Journal of Psychiatry*, **168**, 158–63.

Benson, G., Abbeduto, L., Short, K., Nuccio, J. and Maas, F. (1993). Development of a theory of mind in individuals with mental retardation. *American Journal on Mental Retardation*, **98**, 427–33.

Bishop, D. (1993). Annotation: Autism, executive functions and theory of mind: a neuro-psychological perspective. *Journal of Child Psychiatry and Psychology*, **34**, 279–93.

Butterworth, G. E. and Adamson-Macedo, E. (1987). The origins of pointing: a pilot study. Paper presented at the annual conference of the Developmental Psychology Section of the British Psychological Society. September 1987, York, UK.

Camaioni, L., Perucchini, P., Muratori, F. and Milone, A. (1997). Brief report: a longitudinal examination of the communicative gestures deficit in young children with autism. *Journal of Autism and Developmental Disorders*, **27**, 715–25.

Charman, T. (1997). The relationship between joint attention and pretend play in autism. *Development and Psychopathology*, **9**, 1–16.

Charman, T. (1998). Specifying the nature and course of the joint attention impairment in autism in the preschool years: implications for diagnosis and intervention. *Autism: The International Journal of Research and Practice*, **2**, 61–79.

Charman, T. and Baron-Cohen, S. (1994). Another look at imitation in autism. *Development and Psychopathology*, **6**, 403–13.

Charman, T. and Lynggaard, H. (1998). Facilitating false belief performance in autism. *Journal of Autism and Developmental Disorders*, **28**, 33–42.

Charman, T., Swettenham, J., Baron-Cohen, S., Cox, A., Baird, G. and Drew, A. (1997). Infants with autism: an investigation of empathy, pretend play, joint attention and imitation. *Developmental Psychology*, **33**, 781–9.

Charman, T., Baron-Cohen, S., Swettenham, J., Cox, A., Baird, G. and Drew, A. (1998). An experimental investigation of socialcognitive abilities in infants with autism: clinical implications. *Infant Mental Health Journal*, **19**, 260–75.

Cox, A., Klein, K., Charman, T., Baird, G., Baron-Cohen, S., Swettenham, J., Wheelwright, S. and Drew, A. (1999). Autism spectrum disorders at 20 and 42 months of age: stability of clinical and ADI-R diagnosis. *Journal of Child Psychology and Psychiatry*, **40**, 719–32.

Dahlgren, S. O. and Gillberg, C. (1989). Symptoms in the first two years of life: a preliminary population study of autism. *Archives of Psychiatry and Neurological Science*, **238**, 169–74.

Dawson, G., Hill, D., Spencer, A., Galpert, L. and Watson, L. (1990). Affective exchanges between young autistic children and their mothers. *Journal of Abnormal Child Psychology*, **18**, 335–45.

DeMyer, M. K. (1979). *Parents and children in autism.* Winston, Washington, DC.

DeMyer, M. K., Barton, S., Alpern, G., Kimberkin, C., Allen, J., Yang, E. and Steele, R. (1974). The measured intelligence of autistic children. *Journal of Autism and Childhood Schizophrenia*, **4**, 42–60.

DiLavore, P. and Lord, C. (1995). Do you see what I see? Requesting and joint attention in young autistic children. Poster presentation at Biennial Conference of the Society for Research in Child Development. Indianapolis, IL.

DiLavore, P., Lord, C. and Rutter, M. (1995). Pre-Linguistic Autism Diagnostic Observation Schedule (PL-ADOS). *Journal of Autism and Developmental Disorders*, **25**, 355–79.

Dunn, J. (1996). Children's relationships: bridging the divide between cognitive and social development (The Emmanuelle Miller Memorial Lecture 1995). *Journal of Child Psychology and Psychiatry*, **37**, 507–18.

Flavell, J., Green, F. and Flavell, E. (1983). The development of appearance–reality distinction. *Cognitive Psychology*, **15**, 95–120.

Frith, U. (1989). *Autism: explaining the enigma*. Blackwells, Oxford.

Frith, U., Soares, I. and Wing, L. (1993). Research into earliest detectable signs of autism: what the parents say. *Communication*, **27**, 17–18.

Gillberg, C., Ehlers, S., Schaumann, H., Jakobsson, G., Dahlgren, S. O., Lindblom, R., Bagenholm, A., Tjuus, T. and Blinder, E. (1990). Autism under age 3 years: a clinical study of 28 cases referred for autistic symptoms in infancy. *Journal of Child Psychology and Psychiatry*, **31**, 921–34.

Gomez, J. C., Sarria, E. and Tamarit, J. (1993). The comparative study of early communication and theories of mind: ontogeny, phylogeny and pathology. In *Understanding other minds: perspectives from autism*, (ed. S. Baron-Cohen, H. Tager-Flusberg and D. Cohen), pp. 397–426. Oxford University Press.

Happé, F. G. E. (1995). The role of age and verbal ability in the theory of mind task performance of subjects with autism. *Child Development*, **66**, 843–55.

Hobson, R. P. (1993). *Autism and the development of mind*. Lawrence Erlbaum, Hove.

Hoshino, Y., Kumashiro, H., Yashima, Y., Tachibana, R., Watanabe, M. and Furukawa, H. (1982). Early symptoms of autistic children and its diagnostic significance. *Folia Psychiatrica et Neurologica*, **36**, 267–374.

Howlin, P. and Moore, A. (1997). Diagnosis in autism: a survey of over 1200 patients in the UK. *Autism: The International Journal of Research and Practice*, **1**, 135–62.

Jarrold, C., Boucher, J. and Smith, P. (1993). Symbolic play in autism: a review. *Journal of Autism and Developmental Disorders*, **23**, 281–308.

Johnson, M. H., Siddons, F., Frith, U. and Morton, J. (1992). Can autism be predicted on the basis of infant screening tests? *Developmental Medicine and Child Neurology*, **34**, 316–20.

Kasari, C., Sigman, M., Mundy, P. and Yirmiya, N. (1990). Affective sharing in the context of joint attention interactions of normal, autistic and mentally-retarded children. *Journal of Autism and Developmental Disorders*, **20**, 87–100.

Leekam, S., Baron-Cohen, S., Perrett, D., Milders, M. and Brown, S. (1997). Eye-direction detection: a dissociation between geometric and joint-attention skills in autism. *British Journal of Developmental Psychology*, **15**, 77–95.

Leslie, A. M. (1987). Pretence and representation: the origins of 'theory of mind'. *Psychological Review*, **94**, 412–26.

Leslie, A. M. (1994). Pretending and believing: issues in the theory of ToMM. *Cognition*, **50**, 211–38.

Lewis, V. and Boucher, J. (1988). Spontaneous, instructed and elicited play in relatively able autistic children. *British Journal of Developmental Psychology*, **6**, 325–39.

Loveland, K., Tunali-Kotoski, B., Pearson, D. A., Brelsford, K. A., Ortegon, J. and Chen, R. (1994). Imitation and expression of facial affect in autism. *Development and Psychopathology*, **6**, 433–43.

Lord, C. (1995). Follow-up of two-year-olds referred for possible autism. *Journal of Child Psychology and Psychiatry*, **36**, 1365–82.

Lord, C., Rutter, M. and Le Couteur, A. (1994). Autism Diagnostic Interview–Revised. *Journal of Autism and Developmental Disorders*, **24**, 659–86.

Lord, C., Pickles, A., McLennan, J., Rutter, M., Bregman, J., Folsten, S., Fombonne, E., Libya, M. and Minshew, N. (1997). Diagnosing autism: analysis of data from the Autism Diagnostic Interview. *Journal of Autism and Developmental Disorders*, **27**, 501–17.

Meltzoff, A. N. and Gopnik, A. (1993). The role of imitation in understanding persons and developing theories of mind. In *Understanding other minds: perspectives from autism*, (ed. S. Baron-Cohen, H. Tager-Flusberg and D. Cohen),. pp. 335–66. Oxford University Press.

Mitchell, P. (1996). *Acquiring a conception of mind: a review of psychological research and theory.* Erlbaum, Hove.

Mitchell, P. and Lacohée, H. (1991). Children's early understanding of false belief. *Cognition*, **39**, 107–27.

Mundy, P. (1995). Joint attention and social-emotional approach behavior in children with autism. *Development and Psychopathology*, **7**, 63–82.

Mundy, P. and Crowson, M. (1997). Joint attention and early social communication: implications for research on intervention with autism. *Journal of Autism and Developmental Disorders*, **27**, 653–76.

Mundy, P., Sigman, M., Ungerer, J. A. and Sherman, T. (1986). Defining the social deficits of autism: the contribution of non-verbal communication measures. *Journal of Child Psychology and Psychiatry*, **27**, 657–69.

Mundy, P., Sigman, M. and Kasari, C. (1993). The theory of mind and joint attention in autism. In *Understanding other minds: perspectives from autism*, (eds. S. Baron-Cohen, H. Tager-Flusberg and D. Cohen), pp. 181–204. Oxford University Press, Oxford.

Mundy, P., Sigman, M. and Kasari, C. (1994). Joint attention, developmental level and symptom presentation in young children with autism. *Development and Psychopathology*, **6**, 389–401.

Ohta, M., Nagai, Y., Hara, H. and Sasaki, M. (1987). Parental perception of behavioral symptoms in Japanese autistic children. *Journal of Autism and Developmental Disorders*, **17**, 549–63.

Ornitz, E. M., Guthrie, D. and Farley, A. J. (1977). The early development of autistic symptoms. *Journal of Autism and Childhood Schizophrenia*, **7**, 207–29.

Osterling, J. and Dawson, G. (1994). Early recognition of children with autism: a study of first birthday home videotapes. *Journal of Autism and Developmental Disorders*, **24**, 247–57.

Ozonoff, S. (1997). Causal mechanisms of autism: unifying perspectives from an information-processing framework. In *Handbook of autism and pervasive developmental disorders*, (2nd edn), (ed. D. J. Cohen and F. R. Volkmar), pp 868–79. Wiley, New York.

Ozonoff, S. and McEvoy, R. E. (1994). A longitudinal study of executive and theory of mind development in autism. *Development and Psychopathology*, **6**, 415–31.

Pennington, B. F. (1991). *Diagnosing learning disorders.* Guilford, New York.

Perner, J., Leekam, S. and Wimmer, H. (1987). Three-year-olds' difficulty with false belief: the case for a conceptual deficit. *British Journal of Developmental Psychology*, **5**, 125–37.

Phillips, W., Baron-Cohen, S. and Rutter, M. (1992). The role of eye-contact in goal detection: evidence from normal toddlers and children with autism or mental handicap. *Development and Psychopathology*, **4**, 375–84.

Phillips, W., Gómez, J. C., Baron-Cohen, S., Laá, V. and Rivière, A. (1995). Treating people as objects, agents, or 'subjects': how children with autism make requests. *Journal of Child Psychology and Psychiatry*, **36**, 1383–98.

Rogers, S. J. and Pennington, B. F. (1991). A theoretical approach to the deficits in infantile autism. *Development and Psychopathology*, **3**, 137–62.

Rogers, S. J., Benetto, L., McEvoy, R. and Pennington, B. F. (1996). Imitation and pantomime in high-functioning adolescents with autism spectrum disorders. *Child Development*, **67**, 2060–73.

Seibert, J. M., Hogan, A. E. and Mundy, P. C. (1982). Assessing interactional competencies: the Early Social-Communication Scales. *Infant Mental Health Journal*, **3**, 244–58.

Siegel, B., Pliner, C., Eschler, J. and Elliot, G. R. (1988). How children with autism are diagnosed: difficulties in identification of children with multiple developmental delays. *Developmental and Behavioral Pediatrics*, **9**, 199–204.

Sigman, M., Mundy, P., Ungerer, J. and Sherman, T., (1986). Social interactions of autistic, mentally retarded and normal children and their caregivers. *Journal of Child Psychology and Psychiatry*, **27**, 647–56.

Sigman, M. D., Kasari, C., Kwon, J. H. and Yirmiya, N. (1992). Responses to the negative emotions of others by autistic, mentally retarded and normal children. *Child Development*, **63**, 796–807.

Sigman, M. and Mundy, P. (1993). Infant precursors of childhood intellectual and verbal abilities. In D. F. Hay and A. Angold (eds.) *Precursors and causes in development and psychopathology*. London: Wiley.

Smith, I. M. and Bryson, S. E. (1994). Imitation and action in autism: a critical review. *Psychological Bulletin*, **116**, 259–73.

Stone W. L. (1997). Autism in infancy and early childhood. In *Handbook of autism and pervasive developmental disorders*, (2nd edn), (ed. D. J. Cohen and F. R. Volkmar), pp. 266–82. Wiley, New York.

Stone, W. L. and Rosenbaum, J. L. (1988). A comparison of teacher and parent views of autism. *Journal of Autism and Developmental Disorders*, **18**, 403–14.

Stone, W. L., Hoffman, E. L., Lewis, S. E. and Ousley, O. Y. (1994). Early recognition of autism: parental reports vs. clinical observation. *Archives of Pediatric and Adolescent Medicine*, **148**, 174–9.

Stone, W. L., Ousley, O. Y., Yoder, P. J., Hogan, K. L. and Hepburn, S. L. (1997). Nonverbal communication in two- and three-year old children with autism. *Journal of Autism and Developmental Disorders*, **27**, 677–96.

Stone, W. L., Lee, E. B., Ashford, L., Brissie, J., Hepburn, S. L., Coonrod, E. E. and Weiss, B. H. (1999). Can autism be diagnosed accurately in children under three years? *Journal of Child Psychology and Psychiatry*, **40**, 219–26.

Swettenham, J., Charman, T., Baron-Cohen, S., Cox, A., Baird, G., Drew, A., Wheelwright, S. and Reece, L. (1998). The frequency and distribution of spontaneous attention shifts between social and non-social stimuli in autistic, typically-developing and non-autistic developmentally delayed infants. *Journal of Child Psychology and Psychiatry*, **39**, 747–53.

Ungerer, J. and Sigman, M. (1981). Symbolic play and language comprehension in autistic children. *Journal of the American Academy of Child and Adolescent Psychiatry*, **20**, 318–37.

Wetherby, A. M. and Prutting, C. A. (1984). Profiles of communicative and cognitivesocial abilities in autistic children. *Journal of Speech and Hearing Research*, **27**, 364–77.

Wimmer, H. and Perner, J. (1983). Beliefs about beliefs: representation and constraining function of wrong beliefs in young children's understanding of deception. *Cognition*, **13**, 103–28.

Wing, L. and Gould, J. (1979). Severe impairments of social interaction and associated abnormalities in children: epidemiology and classification. *Journal of Autism and Developmental Disorders*, **9**, 11–29.

World Health Organisation (1993). *Mental disorders: a glossary and guide to their classification in accordance with the 10th revision of the International Classification of Diseases (ICD-10)*. WHO, Geneva.

Yeung-Courchesne, R. and Courchesne, E. (1997). From impasse to insight in autism research:

from behavioral symptoms to biological explanation. *Development and Psychopathology*, **9**, 389–419.

Yirmiya, N., Solomonica-Levi, D., Shulman, C. and Pilowsky, T. (1996). Theory of mind in individuals with autism, Down syndrome and mental retardation of unknown etiology: the role of age and intelligence. *Journal of Child Psychology and Psychiatry*, **37**, 1003–14.

Yirmiya, N., Erel, O., Shaked, M. and Solomonica-Levi, D. (1998). Meta-analyses comparing theory of mind abilities of individuals with autism, individuals with mental retardation and normally-developing individuals. *Psychological Bulletin*, **124**, 283–307.

Zelazo, P. D., Burack, J. A., Benedetto, E. and Frye, D. (1996). Theory of mind and rule use in individuals with Down's syndrome: a test of the uniqueness and specificity claims. *Journal of Child Psychology and Psychiatry*, **37**, 479–84.

# 18

# Teaching theory of mind
# to individuals with autism

JOHN SWETTENHAM

In this chapter I will be discussing recent studies which have assessed whether it is possible to teach a 'theory of mind' to individuals with autism. One reason for conducting such training studies is that they may have important clinical implications for individuals with autism. If it is the case that a deficit in theory of mind underpins the impairments in social interaction, pragmatics and pretend play in autism, as Baron-Cohen *et al.* (1985) have argued, then a successful method for teaching theory of mind may help to alleviate the impairments in social interaction that are so debilitating in autism (Howlin *et al.* 1999).

However, as Bishop (1997) has recently emphasised, training studies are not simply the applied side of experimental research, they are also valuable experimental techniques in themselves. With respect to autism, training studies can provide direct tests of hypotheses concerning the impairments in social interaction, pragmatics, and pretend play. For example, if these impairments are caused by a lack of theory of mind, and if it can be shown that teaching theory of mind to children with autism results in a marked improvement in social interaction, pragmatics, and pretend play, this would constitute strong evidence for the theory of mind deficit hypothesis.[1]

The theory of mind training studies conducted so far have shown that some individuals with autism appear to be able learn to pass the particular theory of mind task that is taught. It is tempting to conclude that because theory of mind tasks are supposed to measure the ability to infer mental states, then a child who passes such a task must have inferred the mental states involved in that task. However, in a training study participants also have the opportunity to learn a non mental-state rule in order to pass tasks. For example, following repeated presentations of the Sally-Anne task (Baron-Cohen *et al.* 1985) a child might learn the correct answer (that Sally will look in the empty container) without really understanding why it is the correct answer, learning instead that in scenario $x$ (the Sally-Anne task) the answer is always $y$ (the empty container). This might be the case even if the child uses the word 'think' in the response.

A cautious interpretation of the child's apparent success is further underscored by the fact that children with autism seem to show limited generalisation. That is, whilst children with autism can learn to pass theory of mind tasks, this new knowledge does not generalise well to other theory of mind tasks or to everyday social interaction.

This limited generalisation may occur because the children have learned a non mental-state rule (in scenario *x* the answer is *y*) that is not appropriate to a new scenario that they have not been trained on, or because they have more general problems in generalisation. The latter could arise for several reasons, such as overselective attention to particular features of the training scenario (Lovaas *et al.* 1979); weak central coherence (Happé, Chapter 9, this volume); or poor processing of features held in common between the training situation and the transfer tests or natural social situations (Plaisted, Chapter 10, this volume). If the problem is in generalisation *per se*, it will be important to know the extent to which this is specific to autism.

There have been a wide variety of different approaches to social skills training in autism, but it is not my intention to review these studies here (see for example Matson and Swiezy 1994). The purpose of this chapter instead is to focus on training studies which have specifically targeted theory of mind ability. The following section then will be an overview of the various theory of mind training studies that have been conducted in individuals with autism of varying abilities.

## THEORY OF MIND TRAINING STUDIES

The first published study that assessed whether it would be possible to teach theory of mind to individuals with autism was carried out by Ozonoff and Miller (1995). This study included five adolescent boys with autism or pervasive developmental disorder, who were relatively high-functioning. Previous studies have shown that a minority of individuals with autism are able to pass first-order theory of mind tasks such as the Sally-Anne task (Baron-Cohen 1989), and that high-functioning individuals with autism might even pass second-order theory of mind tasks (Bowler 1992). There were grounds for optimism then that this relatively high-functioning group might have had the potential for learning to pass higher order theory of mind tasks. Four theory of mind transfer tasks were given before and after training. These were: (i) the false contents task, using Smarties (Perner *et al.* 1987); (ii) a second-order false-belief story, 'Mary thinks that John thinks *x*' (Baron-Cohen 1989); (iii) another second-order false-belief task, the overcoat task (Bowler 1992); and (iv) a third-order false-belief task, the double bluff story (Happé 1994). The children were also rated by parents and teachers on their social skills at home and at school using the Social Skills Rating Scale (SSRS).

Since the intervention took place over a relatively long period (four and a half months), it was important to know whether any improvement in performance was simply due to natural development over that time. For this reason a no-treatment control group of four adolescents with autism, matched for age, IQ, and severity of autism (as measured by the CARS), received the same pre- and post-training measures as the treatment group, but did not take part in the training programme.

The first set of seven training sessions focused on teaching interactional and conversation skills such as how to begin and maintain topics of conversation, how to choose topics of interest to others, how to interpret and express non-verbal signals, and how to listen and express interest in others. The second set of sessions focused specifically on teaching theory of mind skills. The main focus of the training was role playing exercises with the emphasis on providing underlying problem-principles that might be applied to different situations. These sessions began with a role playing exercise in which children led a blindfolded trainer around an obstacle course. This was designed to teach the children how to take another person's visual perspective. Next the children were taught that what someone sees or hears indicates what they will know (i.e. the principle that 'perception influences knowledge'). Finally the children took part in a series of role-plays which mirrored the format of second-order false-belief tasks, although the specific content was different from the transfer tasks (e.g. using different locations). For example, in one role-play children A, B, and C decide to go bowling together. After child A leaves to get changed at home, B and C revise the plan and decide to go to a film instead. B and C then go home separately. On the way home B stops at A's house to tell him of the new plan. They agree to meet at the cinema and A leaves to go there. After changing, C stops at A's house and finds he is not there. The groups members were asked to predict where C would think A had gone. After each of these scenarios the group discussed the underlying principle behind the role-plays. For example, for second-order false-belief role-plays, the principle was that 'since child C had not seen child B speak with A, he could not know that A knew of a revised plan'.

Prior to training, the group scored an average of 6 out of a possible composite score of 13, although it is not clear from the results exactly which tasks the children were failing and which they were passing. When the children who had taken part in the training were assessed on the theory of mind test battery they had improved in their performance relative to the no-training control group. However, the training appeared to have no effect on everyday social skills, rated at home or at school using the SSRS. One reason for the discrepancy between the improvement on the theory of mind tasks but lack of improvement in everyday social skills may have been because the SSRS did not provide a sensitive measure of the sort of skills one might expect to improve as a result of training. For example, the SSRS includes items such as 'is self confident in social situations' and 'is liked by other'. Alternatively, the improvement on the theory of mind tasks may have been the result of learning a specific non-mental rule which was applicable to some of theory of mind tasks in the battery, rather than learning to use mental-state terms. This is certainly possible given that the second-order role-plays involved the same scenarios as the second-order transfer tasks. This at least suggests that limited generalisation to different materials and characters can take place, even with a non mental-state rule. It is also possible that some children learned to infer mental states and to generalise this knowledge. A non mental-state rule learned for the second-order role-play scenario could not be used to pass the third-order double bluff task, and at least one child achieved this, since he achieved a maximum score after training. Unfortunately, since only composite scores were presented we cannot be sure if any of the other children improved on tasks other than the second-order false-belief tasks. However, with this small sample of relatively high-functioning adolescents with autism the results were promising.

A group of less able children with autism (CA between nine and ten years, VMA between five and six years) took part in a training study conducted by Hadwin *et al.*

(1996, 1997). In this study the intention was to assess whether it would be possible to teach children with autism in one of three domains; (i) understanding of emotion; (ii) understanding of belief; or (iii) production of pretend play.

Thirty children with autism took part in the study. Prior to the training all the children were tested on tasks from each of the three domains. In each domain there were five tasks which were ordered into 'developmental levels', so that a level 1 task was the simplest and level 5 the most difficult. In the emotion domain the tasks were: (i) photographic face recognition (Ekman *et al.* 1972); (ii) schematic face recognition (Hobson 1986*a*); (iii) situation-based emotion understanding (Harris 1989); (iv) desire-based emotion understanding (Yuill 1984); and (v) belief-based emotion understanding (Hadwin and Perner 1991). In the belief domain the tasks were; (i) simple perspective taking (Flavell 1978); (ii) complex perspective taking (Flavell *et al.* 1981); (iii) seeing leads to knowing (Pratt and Bryant 1990); (iv) true belief understanding (Wellman 1990); and (v) false belief understanding (Baron-Cohen *et al.* 1985; Perner *et al.* 1987). Finally, the five levels of play behaviour were: (i) sensorimotor play; (ii) functional play (two or fewer examples); (iii) functional play (more than two examples); (iv) pretend play (two or fewer examples); (v) pretend play (more than two examples) (see Leslie 1987 for definitions of pretend play). For the pre-training assessment each child was presented with tasks in order from level 1 onwards until two consecutive levels were failed. The pre-training assessment therefore established a 'developmental level' score for each child in each domain. (See Howlin *et al.* (1999) for the published materials).

Two additional assessments of conversation skills and use of mental-state words were also made before and after training (reported in Hadwin *et al.* 1997). Children were asked to tell a story from a picture book and the frequencies of: (i) one-word answers; (ii) two or more sentences; (iii) echolalia; and (iv) unclear statements, were recorded. Parents were instructed to ask questions and give prompts during the story telling in order to create a conversation-like interaction. The hypothesis was that improved theory of mind might help the child to understand that people know different things and that states of knowledge can be shared, so that theory of mind training would result in children expanding upon their 'conversation'. The frequency of mental-state words produced during this assessment was also recorded.

For the training itself, the children were divided into three groups, and each group was taught in a particular domain—emotion, belief, or pretence. The pre-training assessment indicated at which level teaching should begin for each child. For the emotion and belief groups each child was taught on tasks in subsequent levels by question-and-answer with corrective feedback, and in addition was given a general principle governing the understanding of the mental state involved in the task. The teaching strategy in the pretence group, by contrast, was spontaneous and unstructured. The aim here was simply to encourage children to produce and participate in pretend play acts with a series of toys related to a theme (e.g. shopping or dinner-time), and junk objects, using modelling and verbal guidance. Training took place over eight consecutive days with one half hour session per day.

The results showed that children in the emotion and belief groups improved in their performance on the tasks they were being trained on. For the children trained in pretence there was no significant improvement in performance. Of course this does not mean that pretending is therefore harder to train than emotion or belief under-standing—the children may have failed to produce more pretending because of the materials used or the type of training used, etc. All we can conclude is that the children in this study did not learn to produce more pretend play acts as a result of this particular training technique.

When children from each group were re-tested on the tasks from all three domains following training, the results revealed that children trained in one domain did not improve in their performance on tasks from another domain. That is, there was no evidence of generalisation between theory of mind domains. The children also showed no significant change in the ability to expand on conversation, and no change in the number of mental-state terms used during conversation (Hadwin *et al.* 1997). Thus, despite improvement on theory of mind tasks used during training, there was no evidence of an improvement in conversation skills. However, the children did pass tasks similar to the ones they had learned to pass during training, but which used different materials. Whilst this suggests that a limited degree of generalisation was possible, it was still not clear what was being generalised—new knowledge about inferring mental states or a non mental-state rule for passing the tasks.

What we cannot tell from either Ozonoff and Miller's (1995) or Hadwin *et al.*'s (1996, 1997) studies is whether the failure to generalise to novel tasks is a problem specific to autism. It is possible that children without autism, but with the same mental age, would show the same problems in generalising if trained on the same tasks.[2] One way to investigate this possibility is to include control groups who are trained on the same tasks as the children with autism and assessed in the same way. Swettenham (1996) attempted to do this by including eight children with autism, eight three-year-olds, and eight children with Down's Syndrome in a theory of mind training study. The aim was to teach children from each group to pass the Sally-Anne false-belief task with repeated presentations of a computer version of the task. General-isation was then assessed with five post-training false-belief tasks, all of which had been failed by all children prior to training. Two of these tasks involved the same scenario as the training tasks—a computer version without instructions and the Sally-Anne task with dolls—and were referred to as the close transfer tasks since they required minimal generalisation. The other three transfer tasks also assessed under-standing of false belief but used different scenarios to the training task. These were two versions of a deceptive-appearance false-belief task based on Perner *et al.* 1987; and the ToM (theory of mind) task, in which the child is told about a character's false belief, and asked to predict his behaviour. These tasks were referred to as distant transfer tasks as they required a greater degree of generalisation. Importantly, it was thought that the distant transfer tasks could not be passed by the use of a non mental-state rule learned during training.

In addition, the children were given four true-belief tasks before and after training. These computer presented tasks involved scenarios in which the ball is not transferred from one location to another—for example, Sally hides the ball in location A, Anne removes the ball and then replaces it in the same location (A). All the children passed these true-belief tasks prior to training.

The computer version of the Sally-Anne task was mouse driven and included music, text, and animation, with characters hiding and retrieving a ball in one of two locations as in the conventional presentation. The initial hiding place for the task varied randomly. The child was instructed to click the mouse on characters, or on a door on the screen, in order to move through the sequences of the task. Throughout each presentation prompts appeared on the screen explaining what the characters were thinking. For example, after initially hiding the ball Sally says, 'Now I think the ball is in the red/blue box', and, 'I must remember to look in the red/blue box if I want my ball.' When Anne transfers the ball she explains, and, 'Sally hasn't seen me move her ball', 'Sally will think that the ball is in the red/blue box.' At the end of each presentation of the task the child was asked to select the container where Sally thinks her ball is. If the child is correct the character approaches the container, looks inside and exclaims, 'Oh no, the ball is not there anymore.' If the child chooses incorrectly Sally replies, 'I think the ball is in the red/blue box because that's where I left it.'

Each child received a set number of 48 trials, divided into eight sessions over the course of a week. All three groups showed a steady rate of increase in the number of correct trials per session—although, surprisingly, it was the group of children with Down's Syndrome who had the lowest mean score throughout training. The children with autism and the three-year-olds consistently passed 5 out of 6 trials per session earlier than the children with Down's Syndrome. Children from all three groups were able to pass the close transfer tasks following training, suggesting that they were all capable of generalising what they had learned to tasks similar to those used for training, but which involved different materials. In contrast, none of the children with autism passed any of the distant transfer tasks, whilst five of the three-year-olds and five of the children with Down's Syndrome passed at least one of the distant transfer tasks following training. The same results were found when the children were re-tested on the transfer tasks three months later.

Since the children with Down's Syndrome and the three-year-olds were able to generalise what they had learned to pass tasks which involved different scenarios to the trained task, it seems likely that they had learned to infer mental states during training. However, the children with autism failed to generalise what they had learned to help them pass the distant transfer tasks. One possible reason for this may have been that children with autism learned the simple rule; 'Sally always thinks the ball is in the container that is empty'. This rule would always lead to success on the Sally-Anne false-belief task. However, if this rule was then generalised to a true-belief task, in which the ball is replaced in its original location, then the rule would lead to an incorrect answer. The results showed that children with autism continued to pass the true-belief tasks following training. This meant that either they had not learned that rule ('Sally always thinks the ball is in the container that is empty') during training, or that they had not applied the rule to the true-belief task. So, this study showed that children with autism could learn to pass the false-belief task, but, unlike normal three-year-olds or children with Down's Syndrome, they were unable to generalise what they learned.

There is another method that might tell us whether children with autism can learn to understand false-belief, rather than learn a non mental-state rule, without requiring evidence of generalisation. In order to learn a non mental-state rule during a training study, a child would have to be given the correct solutions to the trials. If children with autism can learn to pass false-belief tasks without being given information on or reinforcement for the correct response, then this would presumably be evidence that the children had learned to infer false belief.

Bowler and Stromm (1998) attempted to help children pass the Sally-Anne false-belief task without directly providing the correct answer on each trial. Instead, they provided action and emotional cues to the protagonists' false beliefs (based on Moses and Flavell 1990), and also gave the children the opportunity to experience their own false belief in a similar scenario. All the children in the study initially failed the Sally-Anne false-belief task. All the tasks were presented with real people playing the roles of Sally and Anne.

The study included children with autism, children with learning difficulties, normally-developing three-year-olds (nearly four years of age) and young three-year-olds (under three years, six months). Children from each group were divided into an experimental or a control condition. In the experimental condition, children received five trials. The first was the action false-belief trial in which the assistant playing the role of Sally returned to the room and stood next to the container where the ball had originally been hidden. The second was the surprise false-belief trial in which the assistant playing Sally returned to the room, looked inside the hiding place, showed a surprised expression and said 'Gosh, my (object) isn't here!'. The third was the own false-belief condition in which the child hid an object, left the room, and returned to find it had been moved. The fourth trial was a repeat of the action false-belief trial, and the final trial was a repeat of the surprise false-belief trial. The correct answer was not directly given on any of these trials. Children in the control condition were given the repeated presentations of the standard condition of the false-belief trial and the own false-belief trial.

The results showed that in the experimental condition children with autism as well as some of the normally-developing older three-year-olds, benefited to a significant extent from the enhanced action and emotional cues. Younger three-year-olds and children with learning difficulties did not benefit from the cues. In contrast, none of the children in any of the four groups, in the control condition, benefited from simple repeated presentations of the false-belief task. One explanation for the success of the children with autism and older three-year-olds in the experimental condition is that they genuinely learned about mental states as a result of the enhanced action and emotional cues. And since no direct indication of the correct result was given during training it would not be possible to learn a non mental-state rule for the correct answer. Unfortunately a simpler explanation for improved performance can be given. As Bowler and Stromm point out, the children may have been responding to the surface structure of the trials. That is, there is considerable stimulus enhancement of the correct location in the experimental condition even though it is not specifically described as the correct location for the task. Children may begin to choose the correct location simply because their attention has been drawn to it. This study therefore does not provide cast-iron evidence that children with autism have learned to employ a theory of mind as a result of being provided with action and emotion cues.

Whiten *et al.* (1993) also used real people in a theory of mind training study. In this study, adults with autism and three-year-olds matched for verbal mental age took part in a series of trials, some of which involved hiding a familiar caretaker's coat and a series which involved hiding the caretaker's cup of coffee. The participants were taking part in another experiment when the caretaker entered to see how things were going. The caretaker then announced that s/he had to leave, providing an excuse (e.g. making a phone call), and made a point of leaving his/her coat—'I'll leave my coat on this chair and come back and get it in a minute.' Once s/he had left, the experimenter suggested that they play a trick and hide the coat in a box. Having checked that the participant knew where the coat originally was, and where it was now, the experimenter asked, 'When [caretaker's name] comes back, where will s/he look for his/her coat?' If the participant was wrong, then the experimenter provided the correct answer; 'I think s/he'll look on the chair.' Participants were given up to six trials of the coat test followed by up to six trials of an equivalent test using a cup left on a table. Trials were terminated once two successive correct responses were made.

Both the adults with autism and the three-year-olds benefited from the Coat series, as fewer trials were need to achieve success on the Cup series. Both groups also showed a significant improvement on the traditional Sally-Anne task which was used as a transfer task and presented as a series of pictures. Generalisation had therefore taken place from a real life scenario to an artificial task using a very similar scenario. This means that even if they had learned a non mental-state rule, the participants must have recognised that the real life scenario was equivalent to the picture story.

It is not clear then whether any of the training studies described so far have genuinely taught theory of mind understanding to children with autism. It is certainly the case that children with autism can learn to pass theory of mind tasks, but their ability to generalise is limited. One possibility is that they can learn about mental states, but have a general deficit in generalisation. Alternatively, it is possible that children with autism have a specific deficit in understanding mental states so that they focus on non mental-state aspects of training tasks in order to acquire a rule or strategy to pass the tasks. The problem is that the rule or strategy they acquire is not useful for passing other tasks or for reasoning about mental states in everyday interactions.

## THOUGHTS ARE LIKE PICTURES IN THE HEAD

An alternative approach then might be to try to teach children with autism to employ a specific strategy, which would be useful in a variety of situations, based on an aspect of their intact abilities. Swettenham *et al.* (1996) attempted to teach children with autism the analogy that people have photos in their heads. This strategy draws on a domain of intact cognition (understanding photographic representations) in an attempt to bypass a cognitive impairment in another domain (understanding mental representations). Leslie and Thaiss (1992) and Leekam and Perner (1991) have shown that whilst children with autism were unable to understand that a person's belief can differ from reality, most could understand that a photograph can differ from reality.

That is, they were able to understand that an object's location would remain the same in a photograph, even when this had changed in reality. Of course mental states are not exactly like photos in many respects. For example, mental states are unobservable, they are only held by animate agents, and they may not be visual-image based. And whereas for adults, photos serve only as a reasonable metaphor for what beliefs are like (they are about things, they endure even when reality changes, they can be true or false, etc.), for children with autism they may be the closest approximation to what beliefs are actually like, if they cannot conceive of beliefs normally.

The aim then, was to teach the metaphor that 'people have pictures in their head' in the hope that this would be a useful prosthetic device to compensate for the lack of a 'real' theory of mind (much as Braille is used to enable a blind person to read; see Baron-Cohen and Howlin 1993). The study focused on teaching children the ability to understand false beliefs. The prediction was that if the children were able to learn the photo-in-the-head strategy, they would not only learn to solve a specific task, but would also have learned a powerful generalisable strategy that would enable them to deal with a variety of theory of mind problems. Explicit teaching of the photo strategy was given only in the context of the Sally-Anne false-belief task (Baron-Cohen *et al.* 1985). However, four different types of transfer tasks were given before and after teaching in order to assess whether children were able to generalise the strategy. These four tests were: (i) the Sally-Anne false-belief task; (ii) a deceptive contents task, the 'Smarties' task, (Perner *et al.* 1987); (iii) a 'seeing-leads-to-knowing' task (Pratt and Bryant 1990); and (iv) an appearance–reality task (Flavell *et al.* 1986).

Children with autism were gradually introduced to the photo-in-the-head analogy over the course of five separate sessions. A large manikin's head was used with a slot in the top for inserting photos. Children were taught a set of principles which govern how the photo-in-the-head analogy worked. Teaching consisted of demonstrations and questions to check that the child had learned each principle before moving onto the next. The children were taught that when the manikin (called Sally) looks at something she gets a picture of the object in her head. Next children were shown that when Sally is absent and the world changes, the picture remains in Sally's head. Children were then shown the false-belief scenario using the manikin and asked to insert the appropriate photo of an object in a location into Sally's head, and to name what the photo in Sally's head was of when she returned to look for her ball. Finally, the children were taught that by referring to the photo in Sally's head it was possible to tell what Sally was thinking (i.e. 'that the object is in the location as shown in the photo'), and that the photo would also be an indication of how Sally would act (i.e. 'that Sally would search for the object in the location shown in the photograph'). Interestingly, children had difficulty with the idea that the photo showed what Sally was thinking. This may have been lack of familiarity with the word 'thinking'.

All the children were able to learn the basic steps of the photo-in-the-head strategy. Although the strategy was not spontaneously used to predict behaviour or mental states, when an explicit link was made (that Sally will refer to the photo in her head to tell her where to look for the hidden object), seven out of eight children were able to pass the Sally-Anne task. Furthermore, there was a significant improvement in performance on the traditional dolls version of the Sally-Anne false-belief task, and an improvement on the seeing-leads-to-knowing task.

This result suggested that the children had learned the photo-in-the-head rule and that this could be generalised to a task which had not been used during training (seeing-leads-to-knowing). It would appear that the children with autism had used the rules that 'when someone sees something they get a picture in their head' and 'the picture in the head is what someone is thinking' to help them choose that the character who sees inside the box is the one who knows what is inside. However, it was also the case that there was no significant improvement on the Deceptive Appearance (Smarties) task or on the Appearance–Reality task. Lack of improvement on the Deceptive Appearance task suggests that the children's ability to generalise remains limited, whilst lack of improvement on the Appearance–Reality task suggests the limitations of the metaphor, since a sponge that looks like a rock will look the same in a photo.

McGregor *et al.* (1998) have also used a picture-in-the-head technique in a training study attempting to teach theory of mind to children with autism, and also compared this technique with another teaching method that involved highlighting the protagonists' intentions in the Sally-Anne type false-belief scenario. Two experimental groups, matched for mental age, were given training using both techniques: (i) a group of adults with autism; and (ii) a group of three-year-olds. Two non-intervention control groups were also included to control for natural change over the course of the training.

Training using this technique focused on two versions of the Sally-Anne false-belief task and involved slotting pictures of the locations of hidden objects in dolls' heads. The technique of highlighting intention also focused on the Sally-Anne scenario and involved emphasising the location that Sally hides her object and her expectation that it will remain there. Transfer tasks were given before and after training for both experimental and non-intervention control groups. These tasks were: (i) the traditional Sally-Anne tasks (without photographs); (ii) a deceptive-appearance task (Perner *et al.* 1987); (iii) the windows deception task (Russell *et al.* 1991); (iv) the coat task (a real life false-belief task in which a character's coat is moved in his/her absence—Whiten *et al.* 1993), and (v) an appearance–reality task (Flavell *et al.* 1986).

Results showed that the picture-in-the-head technique was substantially more effective for teaching theory of mind compared with the technique of highlighting intention. Both the three-year-old children and the individuals with autism who had been trained were able to pass the standard Sally-Anne false-belief task following training. The three-year-olds also showed substantial evidence of generalisation to other false-belief tasks. However, for individuals with autism generalisation was limited to being able to pass a test of their own false belief.

Another representational device that might help compensate or bypass deficits in understanding and employing mental states is 'thought-bubbles'—after all, thought-bubbles are often used to depict a person's thoughts in cartoons and magazines. In fact, typically-developing children as young as three years of age appear to have no difficulty in understanding that thoughts can be represented in 'thought-bubbles' (Wellman *et al.* 1996). Using thought bubbles to teach theory of mind has already been piloted in a single case study (Gomez *et al.* 1996) in which a child with autism successfully learned how to select thought bubbles which represented a character's thoughts in a false-belief task. Larger scale studies are currently underway to investigate the efficacy of using thought bubbles as an aid to mentalising.

## TRAINING STUDIES WITH NORMAL CHILDREN

A number of recent studies have focused on teaching theory of mind to normally-developing three-year-olds. Whilst these studies can ultimately only tell us about normal development, they may provide some clues for research with individuals with autism—what works with normal three-year-olds *might* work with children with autism. Most of the research with normal children has been conducted to test an empiricist view that theory of mind is a consciously constructed theory made up of interrelated concepts. For example, Wellman (1990) argues that a concept like 'belief' is understood in relation to other concepts like 'perception', 'action', 'desire', and 'intention'. A number of training studies have shown that emphasising the relation between 'belief' and other mental state concepts within a theory has led to improved performance on false-belief tasks (Bartsch 1991; Gopnik *et al*. 1994; Moses 1993; Slaughter and Gopnik 1996).

Gopnik *et al*. (1994) found an improvement in understanding others' false belief on a deceptive-appearance task when children were taught that their own changed visual perspective is like a change in what they thought about an object. When belief was paired with other mental states such as desires and emotions in a deceptive transfer false-belief task, Bartsch (1991) also found improved performance in three-year-olds on the false-belief task. Moses (1993) also tested three-year-olds' understanding of false belief in the context of intentions. When children were presented with a film showing an actor's surprise or sadness at having failed to complete an intended act, and then questioned about unfulfilled intentions, they performed better on false-belief tasks. Finally, Slaughter and Gopnik (1996) found that three-year-olds improved in their performance on a variety of theory of mind tasks, including false-belief understanding, when trained on the related concepts of desire and intention.

These results are interesting because they suggest that in normal development it may be possible to teach a concept such as false belief by enhancing understanding of related concepts to help children form a theory. It remains to be seen whether such methods will be successful in teaching children with autism. Hadwin *et al*. (1996) did attempt to teach children in different related concepts (pretence, emotion, and belief) but found that no benefit in belief understanding was gained by teaching about emotion or pretence.

## CONCLUSIONS

The training studies described in this chapter have all demonstrated that individuals with autism can be taught to pass theory of mind tasks. However, it is not clear what has been learned during these training studies—the ability to infer mental states and predict action from mental states, or a non mental-state rule that can be used to obtain the correct answer. Evidence of generalisation to tasks similar to the ones that had been trained does not help disambiguate these two possibilities. Children may have learned a non mental-state rule to pass the training tasks and used that rule to pass the transfer task. Individuals with autism showed limited generalisation to novel theory of mind tasks, on which they had not been trained, and no significant improvement in everyday social interaction following training. This may be because they learned a non mental-state rule during training, or because they suffer from a general deficit in generalisation.

Two studies assessed whether teaching theory of mind would lead to improvements in social interaction (Hadwin *et al.* 1997; Ozonoff and Miller, 1995), and found no difference in social interaction after training. Of course this null result does not mean that social interaction cannot be improved through training theory of mind. It is possible that more extensive training over a longer period, or the use of more sensitive assessment measures, might prove more successful, and there are some grounds for optimism. For example, although the training studies found no evidence of transfer from artificial tasks to 'real life' social interaction skills, it is worth noting that several studies showed transfer from 'real life' scenarios to artificial tasks (Bowler and Stromm 1998; Ozonoff and Miller 1995; Whiten *et al.* 1993). Furthermore, individuals who pass false-belief tasks (without training) score more highly, than those who fail, on the Vineland Adaptive Behaviour Scales (Fombonne *et al.* 1994), a correlation which suggests that theory of mind ability does relate to social communication skills. So, despite the relative lack of success in training studies so far, it would be unwise to assume that future studies will not be more successful.

Although the training studies described here do not provide a direct test of what causes the theory of mind deficit itself, they may provide clues. For example it is clear that individuals with autism have difficulty in generalising new knowledge. A general deficit in the ability to generalise, which is specific to autism, is one candidate for an underlying primary psychological deficit in autism (Plaisted, Chapter 10, this volume). However, in order to test this idea further we need to know whether individuals with autism have difficulty learning and generalising concepts or rules which don't involve mental states. If training studies that focus on teaching aspects of psychological functioning other than theory of mind lead to a genuine ability to infer mental states and predict action then this might be good evidence for a primary psychological deficit in autism. For example, if individuals with autism have a primary deficit in selective attention (Lovaas *et al.* 1979), then focusing teaching on what aspects of a social scenario to attend to and what to ignore may lead to improvement on theory of mind tasks. If there is some other psychological function or behaviour, the disruption of which early in development consequently impairs theory of mind development, then it may be preferable to conduct an early intervention to attempt to alleviate that early occurring impairment. For example, one current early intervention study is attempting to teach eighteen-month-olds with autism to attend to faces and to engage in joint attention as part of an intervention (Drew *et al.*, forthcoming), and it will be interesting to examine the effect this training has on theory of mind development. Similarly, if the perceptual and attentional impairments which seem apparent in autism (see Plaisted, Chapter 10, this volume) can be alleviated early in development, then the relationship between these apparently non-social impairments and the development of theory of mind can be examined.

One promising new approach for older individuals with autism has been to provide an analogy that 'thoughts are like pictures' (Gomez *et al*. 1996; McGregor *et al*. 1998; Swettenham *et al*. 1996). This may lead to a genuine understanding of mental states, or individuals may continue to use the analogy as a useful aid to solving theory of mind problems. Ultimately the success of the picture analogy or any other approach will be measured by how effective it is in helping individuals with autism to understand and predict the behaviour of others.

## Notes

1. Theory of mind training studies cannot however reveal much about what causes the theory of mind deficit itself, only whether a deficit in theory of mind relates to impairments in social communication.
2. It might be argued that this is less likely in the case of Ozonoff and Miller's (1995) study, because the children with autism were high-functioning. However, problems in generalisation (or any psychological process) may result from having *any* severe developmental disorder.

## REFERENCES

Baron-Cohen, S. (1989). The autistic child's theory of mind: a case of specific developmental delay. *Journal of Child Psyhcology and Psychiatry*, **30**, 285–97.

Baron-Cohen, S. and Howlin, P. (1993). The theory of mind deficit in autism: some questions for teaching and diagnosis. In *Understantding other minds: perspectives from autism*, (ed. S. Baron-Cohen, H. Tager-Flusberg and D. J. Cohen), pp. 466–80. Oxford University Press, New York.

Baron-Cohen, S., Leslie, A. and Frith, U. (1985). Does the autistic child have a 'theory of mind'? *Cognition*, **21**, 37–46.

Baron-Cohen, S., Wellman, H., Gomez, J-C., Toye, E. and Swettenham, J. Using thought bubbles helps children with autism to acquire an alternative to a theory of mind. Unpublished manuscript. University of Cambridge.

Bartsch, K. (1991). Between desires and beliefs: three year olds' theory of mind. Paper presented at the biennial meeting of the Society for Research in Child Development.

Bishop, D. (1997). Cognitive neuropsychology and developmental disorders: uncomfortable bedfellows. *Quarterly Journal of Experimental Psychology*, **50**, 899–923.

Bowler, D. (1992). Theory of mind in Asperger Syndrome. *Journal of Child Psychology and Psychiatry*, **33**, 877–93.

Bowler, D. M. and Stromm, E. (1998). Elicitation of first-order 'theory of mind' in children with autism. *Autism*, **2**, 33–44.

Courchesne, E., Townsend, J., Akshoomoff, N., Saitoh, O., Yeung-Courchesne, R., Lincoln, A., James, H., Haas, R., Schreiman, L. and Lau, L. (1994*b*). Impairment in shifting attention in autistic and cerebellar patients. *Behavioiural Neurosciences*, **108**, 848–65.

Davies, Bishop, D., Manstead and Tantam, D. (1994). Face perception in children with autism and Asperger Syndrome. *Journal of Child Psychology and Psychiatry*, **36**, 1033–57.

Drew, A., Baron-Cohen, S., Baird, G., Cox, A., Charman, T., Swettenham, J., and Wheelwright, S. (forthcoming). An early intervention study with infants with autism at 20 months of age.

Ekman, P., Friesen, W. V. and Elsworth, P. (1972). *Emotion in the Human Face.* Pergamon Press, New York and Oxford.

Flavell, J. H. (1978). The development of knowledge about visual perception. *Nebraska Symposium on Motivation 1977: Social Cognitive Development*, Vol. 25, pp. 43–76. University of Nebraska Press, Lincoln.

Flavell, J. H., Everett, B. A., Croft, K. and Flavell, E. R. (1981). Young children's knowledge about visual perception: further knowledge about the Level 1 and Level 2 distinction. *Developmental Psychology*, **17**, 99–103.

Flavell, J., Green, F. and Flavell, E. (1986). Development of knowledge about appearance reality distinction. *Monographs of the Society for Research in Child Development*, **51**, (Serial no. 212).

Folstein, S. and Rutter, M. (1988). Autism: familial aggregation and genetic implications. *Journal of Autism and Developmental Disorders*, **18**, 3–30

Frith, U. (1989). *Autism: explaining the enigma.* Blackwell, Oxford.

Gomez, J-C., Lopez, B. and Lopez, E. (1996). Applications of the theory of mind approach to assessment and intervention of children with autism. The Fifth International Congress of AutismEurope, Barcelona, 3–5 May 1996.

Gopnik, A., Slaughter, V. and Meltzoff, A. (1994). Changing your views: understanding perception as a precursor to understanding belief. In *Origins of a theory of mind*, (ed. C. Lewis and P. Mitchell). Erlbaum, Hillside, NJ.

Hadwin, J. A. and Perner, J. (1991). Pleased and surprised: children's cognitive theory of emotion. *British Journal of Developmental Psychology*, **9**, 215–34.

Hadwin, J. A., Baron-Cohen, S., Howlin. P. and Hill, K. (1996). Concepts of emotion, belief and pretence: to what extent can they be taught to children with autism? *Development and Psychopathology*, **8**, 345–65.

Hadwin, J. A., Baron-Cohen, S., Howlin. P. and Hill, K. (1997). Does teaching theory of mind have an effect on the ability to develop conversation in children with autism? *Journal of Autism and Developmental Disorders*, **27**(5), 519–37.

Happé, F. G. E. (1994). An advanced test of theory of mind: understanding of story characters' thoughts and feelings by able autistic, mentally handicapped and normal children and adults. *Journal of Autism and Developmental Disorders*, **24**, 129–54.

Harris, P. L. (1989). *Children and emotion.* Basil Blackwell, Oxford.

Howlin, P., Baron-Cohen, S. and Hadurin, J. (1999). *Teaching children with autism to mind-read.* Wiley, London.

Hobson, P. R. (1986a). The autistic child's appraisal of expressions of emotion. *Journal of Child Psychology and Psychiatry*, **27**, 321–42.

Hobson, R. P. (1986b). The autistic child's appraisal of expressions of emotion. *Journal of Child Psychology and Psychiatry*, **27**, 671–80.

Leekam, S. and Perner, J. (1991). Does the autistic child have a metarepresentational deficit? *Cognition*, **40**, 203–18.

Leslie, A. (1987). Pretence and representation in infancy: the origins of 'theory of mind'. *Psychological Review*, **94**, 84–106.

Leslie, A. and Thaiss, L. (1992). Domain specificity in conceptual development: evidence from autism. *Cognition*, **43**, 225–51.

Lovaas, O. I., Koegel, R. L. and Shreibman, L. (1979). Selective overselectivity in autism: A review of research. *Psychological Bulletin*, **86**, 1236–54.

Matson, J. L. and Swiezy, N. (1994). Social skills training with autistic children. In *Autism in children and adults: etiology, assessment and intervention*, (ed. J. L. Matson), pp. 241–160. Brooks/Cole, Pacific Grove, CA.

McGregor, E., Whiten, A. and Blackburn, P. (1998). Teaching theory of mind by highlighting intention and illustrating thoughts: a comparison of their effectiveness with 3 year olds and autistic individuals. *British Journal of Developmental Psychology*, **16**, 281–300.

Moses, L. (1993). Young children's understanding of intention and belief. *Cognitive Development*, **8**, 1–25.

Moses, L. and Flavell, J. (1990). Inferring false beliefs from actions and relations. *Child Development*, **61**, 929–45.

Ozonoff, S. and Miller, J. N. (1995). Teaching theory of mind: a new approach to social skills training for individuals with autism. *Journal of Autism and Developmental Disorders*, **25**(4), 415–33.

Perner, J., Leekam, S. and Wimmer, H. (1987). Three year olds' difficulty with false belief: the case for a conceptual deficit. *British Journal of Developmental Psychology*, **5**, 125–37.

Plaisted, K., O'Riordan, M. and Baron-Cohen, S. (1998). Enhanced discrimination of novel, highly similar stimuli by adults with autism during a perceptual learning task. *Journal of Child Psychology and Psychiatry*, **39**, 765–75.

Pratt, C. and Bryant, P. (1990). Young children understand that looking leads to knowing (so long as they are looking into a single barrel). *Child Development*, **61**, 973–82.

Rogers, S. and Pennington, B. (1991). A theoretical approach to the deficit in infantile autism. *Development and Psychopathology*, **3**, 137–62.

Russell, J. (1997). How executive disorders can bring about an inadequate 'theory of mind' In *Autism as an executive disorder*, (ed. J. Russell), pp. 256–304. Oxford University Press.

Russell, J., Mauthner, N., Sharp, S. and Tidswell, T. (1991). The 'windows task' as a measure of strategic deception in preschoolers and autistic subjects. *British Journal of Developmental Psychology*, **9**, 331–49.

Slaughter, V. and Gopnik, A. (1996). Conceptual coherence in the child's theory of mind: training children to understand belief. *Child Development*, **67**, 2967–88.

Swettenham, J. (1996). Can children with autism be taught to understand false belief using computers? *Journal of Child Psychology and Psychiatry*, **37**, 157–65.

Swettenham, J., Baron-Cohen, S., Gomez, J-C. and Walsh, S. (1996). 'What's inside someone's head?'. Conceiving of the mind as a camera helps children with autism acquire an alternative to a 'theory of mind'. *Cognitive Neuropsychiatry*, **1**, 73–88.

Wellman, H. (1990). *The child's theory of mind*. MIT Press, Cambridge, MA.

Wellman, H., Hollander, M. and Schult, C. A. (1996) Young children's understanding of thought bubbles and of thoughts. *Child Development*, **67**, 768–88.

Whiten, A., Irving, K. and Macintyre, K. (1993). Can three year olds and people with autism learn to predict the consequences of false belief? Paper presented at the British Psychological Society Developmental Section Annual Conference, Birmingham, UK.

# Part 4 Theory of mind: anthropological and evolutionary issues

# 19

# Do chimpanzees use their gestures to instruct each other?

DANIEL J. POVINELLI AND DANIELA K. O'NEILL

Several years ago, we asked ourselves the following question: when chimpanzees co-ordinate their activities to achieve what on the surface appears to be a common goal, is this co-operation mediated by an understanding of each other's mental states? In this chapter, we offer our preliminary answer to this question—a question that remains undeniably important in efforts to reconstruct the evolution of social understanding.

Co-operative behaviour among chimpanzees (and other nonhuman species) is fairly common. First, chimpanzees and other social primates form complex, shifting social coalitions which involve both related and unrelated individuals. When called into action, such coalitions typically manifest themselves as two or more individuals acting in a co-ordinated manner against another. The complexity of the behaviours that emerge from such coalitions may tempt the inference that the animals involved are reasoning about the moment-to-moment goals of their coalition partners, as well as how these tactics fit with an overall strategic objective (see de Waal 1982). Second, chimpanzees regularly hunt for food, and in many cases these hunts involve collaboration among several individuals. Here, the individuals involved may deploy different, but complementary roles in order to successfully catch the prey (see Boesch 1994).

Although the sophistication of such carefully-timed and co-ordinated behaviours among chimpanzees is impressive, recent experimental evidence has tended to suggest that these animals do not explicitly reason about the mental states of others (for recent reviews see Povinelli and Prince 1998; Tomasello and Call 1997). Despite this general trend, however, one early experimental study of co-operation among chimpanzees conducted by Meredith Crawford (1937) did provide some tantalizing (if limited) evidence that these animals might appreciate limited aspects of the attentional states of a co-operative partner. In particular, some of the results of this work suggested that the chimpanzees used their naturally-occurring gestures (albeit infrequently) to direct the behaviour of their partners. Interpreting these results has proven difficult, however. Were these gestures produced to influence the other chimpanzee's mental state, or just his or her behavioural state, or both? In reflecting on this question, we decided to investigate our chimpanzees' use of gestures in a co-operative task in which one chimpanzee would be experienced (and thus would know how to perform the task) and another chimpanzee would be naive (and thus would not know how to perform the task). We reasoned that this pedagogical context might provide greater motivation for the experienced chimpanzee to use simple instructive gestures (showing, pointing, leading) to direct his or her partner.

Before we report the results of this experimental research, we consider the emergence of human infants' use of gestures (such as pointing) to influence the mental states of others, and grapple with several theoretical problems related to comparing human and nonhuman social understanding.

## GESTURING TO MENTAL STATES?

Before children use words to direct the actions of others, they use gestures. Like words, these gestures influence various mental states of the adult to whom they are typically directed. However, because adults attribute a wide range of meanings to these gestures, it is difficult to know at what point the infants themselves are intentionally trying to influence or appeal to the mental state of the addressee. The case of pointing is particularly instructive. Elizabeth Bates and her colleagues offered a (now widely-adopted) scheme in which pointing and other gestures (such as reaching) are divided into proto-imperative versus proto-declarative acts (Bates *et al.* 1975). However, a uniform application of this distinction has proven difficult. For example, some researchers have argued that the first pointing gestures of an infant merely reflect that infant's desire to obtain a particular object, or to elicit some emotionally salient reaction from an adult, with no explicit consideration of any psychological states of the addressee (i.e. that they are proto-imperative; Moore and Corkum 1994; Vygotsky 1962). In contrast, some see even the earliest pointing gestures as motivated by the infant's understanding of the referential significance of the gesture and/or the subjective states of the addressee (i.e. that they are proto-declarative; e.g. Werner and Kaplan 1963). Other researchers have focused on the form of the gesture, and have argued for a distinction between arm extensions with and without index finger extension (i.e. points versus reaches) with only the former reflecting the infant's understanding of the psychological states of his or her communicative partner (e.g. Franco and Butterworth 1996). Still others believe that the crucial criterion for inferring the level at which an infant is considering the partner's psychological states, is whether or not the gesture is accompanied by the infant alternating his or her gaze between the object/event and the addressee (Bates 1976; Franco and Butterworth 1996; Gomez *et al.* 1993). Finally, it is even possible that proto-imperative and proto-declarative gestures imply similar levels of understanding of the psychological (i.e. attentive) states of others (Gomez *et al.* 1993).

A number of problems exist with these proposed means of determining the function/meaning of infants' early gestures. First (and perhaps foremost), it is clearly not possible to carve up reaches and points as gestures that have uniquely imperative or declarative functions, respectively. After all, the function of any given gesture would appear to depend on the context in which it is used. For example, in typical infant development, the pointing gesture is often used in a non-declarative manner (Bates *et al.* 1975). Furthermore, individuals with autism regularly use the pointing gesture in imperative contexts, but rarely, if ever, in situations in which the central goal of the social interaction is to share interest with others (Baron-Cohen 1989; Goodhardt and Baron-Cohen 1993; Mundy *et al.* 1986). In addition, reaches are deployed in situations where the child is checking the attention (and possibly even the knowledge state) of their partner (O'Neill 1996). Second, the pointing gesture itself may occur without alternating gaze, in much the same manner that reaching gestures can. There would seem to be no reason why the topographic form of the hand uniquely determines whether an infant is reasoning about the attentional state of a communicative partner. Third, monitoring the eyes or face of another (i.e. gaze alternation) may not be a reliable indicator of a capacity to understand the other's attentional state (Moore and Corkum 1994; Povinelli and Eddy 1994; Tomasello 1995). It is possible that the production of both proto-imperative and proto-declarative gestures on the one hand, and gaze-monitoring on the other, are separately functioning systems which initially become linked not because of the emergence of the infant's understanding of the mental states of others, but due to an increasing sophistication at predicting the effects of their gestures on the behaviour of others. However, several lines of research implicate eighteen to twenty four months of age as a period in which infants become explicitly aware that specific gestures such as looking and pointing are connected to internal attentional states (e.g. Akhtar and Tomasello 1996; Baldwin 1993; Moore *et al.*, in press; Tomasello and Barton 1984).

## USING GESTURES TO INSTRUCT OTHERS

In considering whether chimpanzees gesture in order to influence the mental states of those around them, we have considered the case of pedagogy. In a theoretical consideration of the topic, Premack (1984) argued that true pedagogy involves several elements: appreciating the mental state of the student, training or planned intervention into the student's behaviour, and, finally, evaluation or judgement (to determine whether further intervention is necessary). The case of pedagogy is of central interest to us because it provides a context in which communicative gestures abound, and frequently have clear external referents. For example, in the case of creating material artefacts (e.g. baskets, stone tools, clay pots), gestures by a teacher may frequently be of the type, 'I want *x*', or of the type, 'Look at *x*'), or in more complicated cases, a combination of the two ('I want you to look at *x*'). Thus, pedagogical situations may be an especially rich arena in which to examine the appearance and use of gestures that have traditionally been considered to have imperative and declarative meanings.

The remainder of this chapter is divided into three parts. First, we briefly examine the existing evidence concerning the nature of chimpanzees' understanding of their own naturally-occurring gestures. Next, we describe a study that we recently conducted to help clarify the interpretation of previous work which had examined chimpanzees' gestures during co-operative tasks. The results suggest that chimpanzees do not readily exhibit gestures which might be thought of as serving to instruct others—even in situations designed to maximize their likelihood of doing so. Third, and finally, we offer an evolutionary account of how human and chimpanzee communicative gestures can appear so similar from a structural point of view, and yet differ so dramatically in the psychologies that attend them.

## DO CHIMPANZEES UNDERSTAND THAT THEIR GESTURES INFLUENCE THE MENTAL STATES OF OTHERS?

Let us begin by asking a seemingly simple question: do chimpanzees gesture in ways that convince us that they are attending to the psychological states of others? Consider the case of pointing. If we ignore (for the moment) whether chimpanzees display the same topographic form of the pointing gesture (index finger extension), several general statements can be made. First, none of the long-term field studies of chimpanzee social behaviour have reported evidence that this species exhibits pointing as part of their natural gestural repertoire (e.g. Goodall 1986; Nishida 1970), nor have more focused investigations of chimpanzee development reported the emergence of such gestures (Plooij 1978; Tomasello *et al.* 1994).

On the one hand, chimpanzees do possess at least one gesture that structurally resembles pointing: *holding out a hand* (Bygott 1979). However, this gesture does not appear to be used as a generalized indicating or referencing device, but rather appears to be used for the purpose of food-begging, solicitations for bodily contact, or as a means of recruiting allies during conflicts (de Waal 1982; Goodall 1986). Finally, and in contrast to the previous statements, chimpanzees living in captivity do exhibit gestures that look very much like pointing, although they seem to be restricted to their interactions with humans (see Fig. 19.1; Call and Tomasello 1994; Gomez 1991; Krause and Fouts 1997; Leavens *et al.* 1996; Povinelli and Eddy 1996*a*; Povinelli *et al.* 1992; Savage-Rumbaugh 1986; Woodruff and Premack 1979).

Although there is agreement that chimpanzees exhibit the kinds of gestures depicted in Fig. 19.1, which are often accompanied by gaze-alternation between the desired object and the communicative partner, there is considerable disagreement about the nature of the psychological processes shaping and attending these behaviours. On the one hand, some researchers have leaned heavily on the *argument by analogy* and have concluded that the degree of similarity between human and chimpanzee communicative gestures is so great that the psychological processes underwriting and attending the behaviour between the two species must also be similar (for a particularly straightforward statement of this position as applied to the question of whether chimpanzees 'point', see Leavens *et al.* 1996). Simply put, the argument by analogy states that if we know that a given behaviour in humans is caused by mental state $x$, then the presence of the exact same behaviour in another species provides good evidence that this species also experiences mental state $x$ (Hume 1739–1740/1978; see also Darwin 1871; Romanes 1882, 1884; for a formal statement of the argument by analogy as a proof of the existence of other minds, see Russell 1948).

We question this conclusion from several directions. First, as a logical position, the argument by analogy (especially when applied to other species) can be shown to be inherently weak (Povinelli and Giambrone, in press). Second, there are numerous empirical reasons for doubting whether chimpanzees interpret their pointing-like

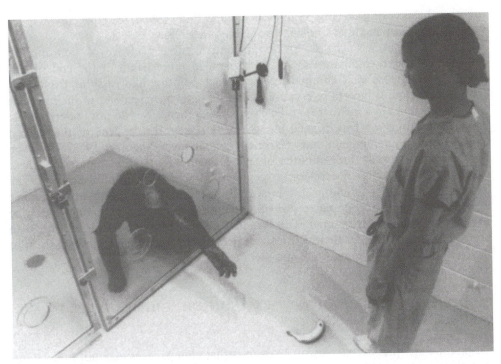

**Fig. 19.1.** In captivity, chimpanzees use gestures that resemble pointing, and these gestures are frequently accompanied by gaze-alternation between the communicative partner and the desired object. Whether they interpret these gestures in the same manner as human infants and children, however, is a separate question.

gestures in a manner similar to ours. To begin, when humans use pointing gestures to inform chimpanzees about the location of hidden food rewards, chimpanzees appear to rely not on the referential aspect of the pointing hand/finger, but upon its proximity to a particular location. Indeed, despite previous claims that chimpanzees comprehend the referential aspect of pointing (e.g. Call and Tomasello 1994; Menzel 1974; Povinelli *et al.* 1992), more recent studies which have controlled for the distance between the pointing hand and the potential hiding locations have revealed that, unlike two-year-old human children, chimpanzees use simple distance-based cues to guide their searches (see Fig. 19.2; Povinelli *et al.* 1997). Third, an extensive series of recent studies has strongly suggested that even in the context of deploying their most common pointing-like gesture (see Fig. 19.1), chimpanzees appear to be oblivious to the subjective attentional state of their communicative partner (Fig. 19.3; see Povinelli 1996; Povinelli and Eddy 1996*a*; Reaux *et al.* 1999; Theall and Povinelli in review). Finally, there is good reason to question whether the gaze-alternation that often accompanies such gestures indicates an appreciation of the communicative partner's subjective attentional state. Several lines of evidence suggest that although chimpanzees possess excellent gaze-following abilities, they do not appear to understand the attentional aspect of gaze (Fig. 19.4; Povinelli and Eddy 1996*a*, see especially, Experiment 12; Povinelli and Eddy 1996*b*; Povinelli *et al.* 1999).

How, then, can we account for the incontrovertible evidence of pointing-like gestures in captive chimpanzees? As we explain in more detail at the end of this chapter, we propose that chimpanzees construct pointing-like gestures from their existing behavioural repertoire because humans consistently respond to their actions (such as reaching) in a manner that the chimpanzees themselves do not understand or intend. Indeed, as we have argued elsewhere, this may also be true of the earliest pointing gestures in human infancy (Povinelli *et al.* in press; Vygotsky 1962). However, by eighteen to twenty four months of age human infants may 'redescribe' these gestures in light of their developing theory of mind (e.g. Karmiloff-Smith 1992). Indeed, if these later developments in social understanding are unique to humans, then the behaviours of chimpanzees which structurally resemble pointing may never be understood in a similar manner. The fact that captive chimpanzees do not seem to produce these gestures for their chimpanzee peers, but rather seem to restrict them to their interactions with humans, would seem to be consistent with this view.

## EVIDENCE OF PEDAGOGICAL GESTURING IN CHIMPANZEES IN A CO-OPERATIVE TASK?

Despite the fact that current research suggests that chimpanzees may not understand that their gestures influence the mental states of others, it is possible that this is because nearly all such studies have required chimpanzee subjects to reason about human experimenters, not fellow chimpanzees (for an elaborated discussion of this potential problem, see Povinelli 1996; Povinelli and Eddy 1996*a*, Chapter VI). Thus, one possible context in which we might search for evidence that chimpanzees are capable of reasoning about the attentional states of others is in their relatively spontaneous interactions with each other, and, in particular, during their execution of co-ordinated, co-operative tasks.

Sixty years ago, Meredith Crawford (1937, 1941) published a series of studies that examined the ability of young chimpanzees to learn how to co-operate to solve problems. Crawford defined co-operation as 'a description of behavior patterns appearing in situations requiring teamwork—the co-ordinate activity of two individuals working for a common incentive object' (Crawford 1937, p. 3). Since his two studies, there have been few experimental investigations of co-operative behaviour in chimpanzees that have been designed with the aim of determining whether they can reason about a co-operative partner's mental states (Chalmeau 1994; Chalmeau and Gallo 1996; Povinelli *et al.* 1992), despite the fact that Crawford's findings have important theoretical implications about the extent, and limitations, of chimpanzees' social understanding.

In his initial studies, Crawford (1937) reported several intriguing instances of what appeared to be one animal soliciting another animal to assist in a co-operative task. He presented five young chimpanzees with a box-pulling task which required the animals to pull in a box baited with food that was too heavy for a single animal to

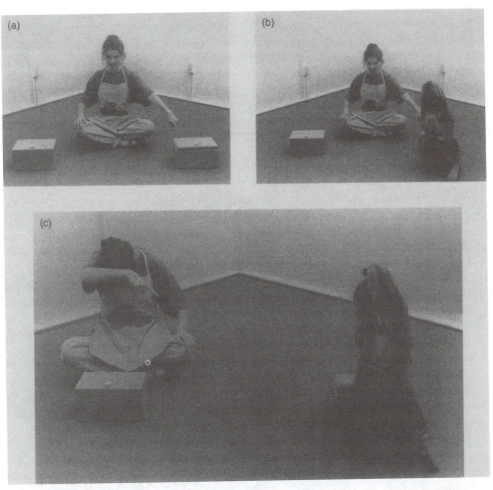

**Fig. 19.2.** Even in very unusual configurations, human toddlers will choose locations referenced by an adult pointing gesture. In contrast, chimpanzees learn and follow rules such as 'pick the box closest to the experimenter's hand/finger', ignoring the referential significance of the gesture.

move. Crawford described three stages in the development of chimpanzees' co-operative behaviour during this task. The first stage consisted of the simultaneous pulling response of the animals to an external cue (the verbal command, 'Pull!') by the experimenter. The second stage was marked by one animal watching the other animal pull in order to co-ordinate his or her pulling with that of his or her partner. The third stage was reached when 'an animal, with manual gestures, solicited from the partner help in pulling' (Crawford 1937, p. 19). These solicitation gestures included, for example, the behavioural sequence of an animal leaving the area of the box and the ropes, touching the other animal, returning to the ropes, picking up a rope, and then looking back at the animal who had just been touched. Another instance consisted of

**Fig. 19.3.** Like human infants, chimpanzees (and other nonhuman primates) follow the gaze of others. Despite this, experimental research suggests that they do not come to interpret gaze as a projection of the mental state of attention.

one animal repeatedly putting her hand around the neck of a second animal in situations where that animal was at the ropes but not pulling. This touching action appeared to have the effect of turning the animal's attention back to the task of pulling the ropes. Crawford concluded that the use of solicitation was a generalized method of problem solving that the animals readily applied with any partner, largely because when an animal began to solicit one partner, this behaviour was then shown with subsequent partners as well.

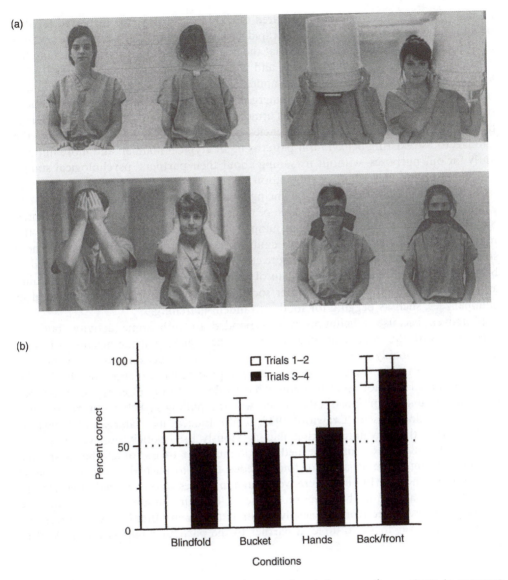

**Fig. 19.4a–b.** Chimpanzees are just as likely to deploy their requesting gestures to someone who cannot see them as to someone who can.

Although these solicitation gestures may indicate that chimpanzees are capable of manipulating each other's behaviour, there are numerous reasons to be cautious about interpreting them as evidence that chimpanzees are capable of co-ordinating their own perspective on a task with that of another conspecific. First, of Crawford's (1937) seven pairings of animals, only two used solicitation gestures, and only two other pairs reached stage 2. Second, the more precursory behaviour of simply watching the other animal was not a behaviour that appeared quickly, or one that was displayed reliably once it had emerged. Even in the most rapid case, it was only after twenty five sessions of fifteen to thirty minutes duration, that the first instance of one animal watching the other for a few seconds was observed, and it did not reliably appear again until after forty four sessions. The relatively late appearance of such behaviours in this training raises the clear possibility that they emerged from a process of conventionalization, rather than being actively deployed as a means of influencing the intentions of their partner. That is, the reward contingencies of the task itself may have caused the animals to use existing behavioural patterns in an atypical manner, and more importantly for our purposes, without reasoning about their partners' psychological states.

The behaviours described as solicitation gestures also varied quite widely in their form, with some being less than convincing as attempts to manipulate the other. For example, one animal, Bula, left the area of the box and ropes and went to her partner, Kambi, and then stood, squatted, or jumped up and down, before returning to the ropes. However, Crawford (1937) was cautious in interpreting the meaning of these solicitation gestures, noting that the more convincing solicitation gestures appeared to be largely confined to one particular pair of animals. He suggested that the behaviours appeared to be closely related to other social responses already well documented in chimpanzees, such as begging for food, or tandem-marching.

Moreover, because solicitation was responded to with some activity, but not necessarily with the same behaviours each time, he argued that the meaning of these gestures was probably most appropriately summarized as 'do something for me'. As he noted: 'Certainly there seemed to be no predicative function involved. The solicited animal did not seem to know what to do, and only after trying a number of responses under continued solicitation, was the pulling-in behaviour given, after which solicitation ceased' (Crawford 1937, p. 68). Indeed, in a later study, Crawford (1941) placed the two animals that had previously used solicitation gestures in a situation in which one animal needed to communicate to the other that a specific coloured button (from an array of four) needed to be to pushed in order to release food from a vendor. Although there were some instances of one animal appearing to push the other animal in the direction of one of the four coloured buttons, when the animals were prevented from physically manipulating each other by a wire screen, no attempts were ever made to direct a partner to the particular button that needed to be pushed.

## RE-EXAMINING CHIMPANZEES' USE OF GESTURES IN CO-OPERATIVE SITUATIONS: AN EXPERIMENTAL APPROACH

We recently conducted an experiment to clarify several ambiguities in Crawford's (1937, 1941) results, as well as those of more recent researchers (e.g. Chalmeau 1994; Chalmeau and Gallo 1996; Povinelli *et al.* 1992). We re-designed Crawford's studies to explore more directly how chimpanzees interpret the actions of a conspecific with whom they are co-operating. In particular, rather than focusing on the *acquisition* of co-operative behaviour, we sought to examine the behaviour of pairs of chimpanzees in situations in which only one member was experienced with the means to solve the problem. To this end, we modified Crawford's (1937) box-pulling task in two crucial ways. First, only two animals (of the seven participating in our study) were taught how to co-operate in order to retrieve the box. After acquiring this skill, these two 'experienced' animals were then separately paired with each of the other five 'naive' animals who had not received any experience trying to pull the box with another animal. With this method we sought to determine whether experienced animals would use their gestures to direct the behaviour and attention of naive partners to the relevant dimensions of the task, such as ushering them to the ropes, or perhaps even more specifically, (a) handing them a rope or (b) demonstrating the pulling action with a rope and then offering it to them.

A second difference between our study and Crawford's (1937) investigation, is that we elected not to overtrain the experienced animals on the task of co-operating to pull the box together. Instead, we trained them only until they were performing their co-operative acts reliably. We explicitly chose this strategy because we wanted to avoid the problem of having these two animals unknowingly train themselves to exhibit solicitation gestures in this context, and thus having these gestures become routinized. Rather, we sought to determine whether the experienced animals, when confronted with the incompetence of a naive partner, would (a) solicit the naive animal to assist them, and/or (b) attempt to direct the naive animals' attention to the relevant dimensions of the task.

## METHOD

### Subjects

The subjects were one male (Apollo) and six female (Kara, Candy, Jadine, Megan, Brandy, Mindy) chimpanzees ranging in age from six years three months (6;3) to 7;1 when the study began. Two of the subjects were selected to serve as the experienced subjects, and the remaining five served as the naive subjects. The experienced subjects were chosen by selecting the oldest subject (Kara) and then randomly selecting another subject from the group (Brandy). The subjects were born and reared at the University of Southwestern Louisiana New Iberia Research Center. The subjects had been reared together since infancy, and became part of a long-term cognitive research program when they were two to three years old. A detailed history of their rearing and experimental histories can be found elsewhere (Povinelli and Eddy 1996). Prior to the research reported here, the subjects had never participated in studies exploring co-operative abilities.

### Apparatus and test setting

A large box (52 × 40 × 57 cm) was constructed into which weights could be placed (see Fig. 19.5). A top covered the front third of the box and served as a location to place food rewards. Two 165 cm length ropes were attached to the bottom front of the

**Fig. 19.5.** General setting and apparatus for the co-operative box-pulling task. Final stages of training for the two experienced subjects (Kara and Brandy) is depicted. Box is too heavy for one subject to retrieve alone. (Figure redrawn from photograph.)

box. A graded set of weights were used to adjust the weight of the box (see below). All training and testing took place inside a plexiglas test unit, with which the animals were intimately familiar (see Fig. 19.5). The plexiglas test unit contained several holes through which the subjects could easily reach.

## Procedure

*Training to retrieve unweighted box*

This phase was conducted in two parts. In the first part, the box-and-rope apparatus was introduced to the two experienced subjects separately. The box was placed 120 cm from the front of the plexiglas partition (approximately 60 cm beyond the subjects' maximum reach), and the ropes were placed through two holes in the partition (see Fig. 19.5). A subject was then ushered into the test unit and the shuttle door was closed behind her. The trainer placed a food reward on top of the box and drew the subject's attention to it. The trainer used a variety of methods to demonstrate how to pull the box toward the partition in order to retrieve the food (e.g. using the ropes to pull the box toward the partition, pushing the box, playing with ropes, etc.). After initially experiencing the training individually, the subjects were paired together for one session in order to allow the less adept subject to witness the other subject pulling the box to within reach. Once the subjects were comfortable being closed in the test unit, pulling the box to within reach, and retrieving the food (Kara = 4 sessions, Brandy = 3 sessions), they advanced to the second part.

In the second part, formal training was conducted in sessions (typically one per day) consisting of eight trials. On each trial the box, ropes, and food were configured as before while the subject waited in the outdoor run. The trainer then opened the shuttle door, the subject entered, and the door was closed behind her. Without prompting from the trainer, the subject's task was to pull the box to within reach and retrieve the food reward. If the subject retrieved the reward within sixty seconds the trial was scored as correct; if they did not, the trial was scored as incorrect. At the end of each trial, the subjects were ushered outside so that the next trial could be configured. The subjects were required to complete two consecutive sessions with a cumulative total of 15/16 correct responses or better before advancing to the next phase.

### Training to retrieve weighted box

The purpose of this phase was to determine the maximum weight of the box that each of the two subjects could individually retrieve. Each subject was tested separately in sessions consisting of eight trials. The weight in the box was gradually increased until on two separate trials the subject tried, but failed, to retrieve the box. (Additional details of this training procedure are available from the authors.)

### Co-operative training to retrieve weighted box

Having established the maximum weight that each of the experienced subjects could retrieve on her own, we next trained these subjects to co-operate in order to pull a box that was too heavy for either of them to retrieve alone. The subjects were tested together in sessions of five to ten trials. Each trial began with the subjects waiting in the outside area, while a trainer placed food on the box and weighted it according to a predetermined schedule. The weight of the box was increased across trials and sessions in order to scaffold the animals up to their maximum combined ability. From the first session forward the subjects acted together by both pulling on a separate rope on each trial, although at the initial weight levels their actions were not well synchronized. As the weight of the boxes increased, however, the synchrony of their pulling actions improved until their efforts became fluid and well co-ordinated. The heaviest box successfully retrieved by the two subjects was 114 kg, and this was only with great difficulty. The subjects failed on four separate trials when the box was weighted to 136 kg. The subjects were trained for a total of fifteen sessions.

### Pretest orientation to box and ropes for naive subjects

To familiarize the naive subjects with the general conditions of the task, but not with the actual rope-pulling/food-retrieval process, each of the five naive subjects was paired with one of the experienced subjects and ushered into the test unit. The box was already positioned flush against the plexiglas with the ropes completely inside the test unit (thus preventing the naive subjects from pulling the box or witnessing the experienced subject pulling the box). The trainer handed both subjects food rewards *ad libitum*. Each trial lasted two minutes. The five naive subjects received two four-trial sessions of this type, one with each of the two experienced subjects. The naive subjects were thus familiarized with the procedure of being closed in the test unit with another animal, and had an opportunity to inspect and manipulate the ropes before actual testing began.

### Testing

Each of the experienced subjects was paired in an exhaustive, random order with each of the naive subjects, as well as the other experienced subject, on four separate occasions. Each pairing constituted a test session and was composed of four trials. Three of these trials were test trials in which the box was too heavy to be pulled by the experienced subject alone. On the remaining trial, the box was light enough for the experienced subject to retrieve the box by pulling it toward her, without assistance from the other subject. This trial served as a means of keeping the experienced animal motivated to at least attempt to retrieve the box during each session. This trial was randomly assigned as either Trial 2 or 3, within the constraint that across sessions it occurred equally often in both positions.

Each trial began with a pair of subjects in the outdoor waiting area. The rope-and-box apparatus was set up in front of the test unit as in Phase 2. The trainer then opened the shuttle door allowing the pair to enter the test unit. Once inside, the shuttle door was closed behind them, and remained closed for four minutes. The trainer sat in a neutral position against the back wall of the room and stared at the box. If the subjects did not successfully pull the box in after two minutes, the trainer waited for any attempt to pull the rope by either subject, and if they did attempt to pull it, he pushed the box approximately 30 cm toward the subjects, and then returned to his position along the wall. The purpose of this procedure was to maintain the experienced animal's interest in the possibility of moving the box. A visual record of each trial was acquired using a remote video system.

## Coding of videotapes

All videotapes were coded by a student who was blind to the purpose of the study. For each pair of animals, each of the four five-minute trials per session was coded. Coding began from the moment the enclosure door opened and the animals entered the test lab. Coding stopped once the animals were ushered out of the enclosure after four minutes, or once one or both of the animals first obtained the food from the box, whichever came first. During the four minute duration of the trials, the animals performed many actions that were not related to the task at hand (e.g. swinging from the top of the cage). To focus the coding process on behaviours relevant to our research questions, we defined a number of target behaviours that we believed were related to the goal of co-operatively pulling in the box:

## Solicitation

This was defined as any gestures used by one animal to indicate to the other animal to come over to the ropes or to pay attention to the ropes. These included both solicitation and proto-declarative gestures.

## Physical manipulation

This was defined as any physical contact by one animal with the other with the goal of ushering the other animal to the ropes. Physical contact in the context of fighting or playing was not included.

## Offers/takes rope

This was defined as any instance in which one animal either offered a rope to another animal, or took a rope from the other animal.

## Alone pulling at the ropes

Each instance in which either animal was alone at the ropes pulling on one or both of the ropes was noted. The pulling actions ranged from tugging at the ropes lightly (but not simply handling the ropes) to 'all-out' pulling in which the animal was upright on his or her legs and pulling forcefully with both hands in a characteristic 'tug-of-war' stance. The situation of being alone pulling at the ropes was defined in terms of the other (non-pulling) partner's distance from the ropes. If that partner was not within arm's reach of the ropes, then the pulling partner was defined as being alone pulling at the ropes.

### Looks to partner while alone at the ropes

A look was defined as a visual orientation towards the other animal of a duration of more than one second that involved a definite head turn. Each instance in which an animal at the ropes (while pulling or not) looked at their partner who was not within arm's reach of the ropes was noted.

### Looks to partner while both at the ropes

Each instance in which one animal looked at the other animal while both were within arm's reach of the ropes was noted. This variable would capture any instances of what Crawford (1937) described as one animal 'watching' the other.

### Reliability coding

Thirty per cent of the sessions were coded independently by a second student who was also blind to the purpose of the study. Percent agreement for each of the variables coded was: 100% for physical manipulation, 100% for solicitation gestures, 100% for offers/takes rope, 96% for alone pulling at the ropes, 87% for looking to partner while alone at the ropes, and 84% for looking to partner while both at the ropes. In all cases the data from the first coder were used for analysis.

## RESULTS

Our main results concern whether the experienced animals attempted to influence the attention and behaviour of the naive animals, and not so much whether the experienced–naive pairs succeeded in co-operating to retrieve the weighted boxes. Nonetheless, we begin by describing these general results to provide an overall framework for what occurred during testing.

### Successful box retrievals

First, as we expected, the experienced–experienced pair of animals (Kara–Brandy) were successful on 5/6 of the heavy box trials they received in Sessions 1 and 2 combined. Second, of the ten pairings that occurred in Session 1 (Kara with her five naive partners and Brandy with her five naive partners), eight were never successful in retrieving the heavy box. One of the pairings (Brandy–Megan) resulted in 2/3 successful heavy box retrievals, and one resulted in 3/3 successful heavy box retrievals (Kara–Megan). In both cases, an analysis of the videotape revealed that the naive animal that was involved (Megan), apparently discovered how to pull on the ropes quite independent of any actions taken by her partners. Finally, of the ten pairings that occurred in Session 2, seven were never successful. One pairing was successful on two trials (Brandy–Megan), and two of the pairings (Kara–Megan and Kara–Apollo) were successful on three trials. To summarize, in the vast majority of cases, the experienced–

naive pairs did not successfully retrieve the heavy boxes, although the experienced–experienced pair did so readily.

## Analysis of behavioural interactions

Our main results concern what the experienced animals did in response to the naive animals' lack of joint action. In order to explore this, we separately compared the behaviours of the two experienced animals (Brandy and Kara) with the behaviours of the five naive animals with whom they were each paired. (Due to extraneous factors, the results for one pairing with Brandy [Session 1, Trial 2] are not available. Thus, the results of this trial are based on her pairings with the remaining four naive animals.) Only the results for the three trials in each session on which the box was maximally weighted were used in the analyses (i.e. we excluded the one trial per session in which the box was light enough for the experienced animal to pull).

## Physical manipulation and solicitation gestures

The most critical variable coded was whether the experienced animals attempted to physically direct or solicit the naive animals' attention to the relevant features of the task. The results indicated that they did not. *Across all sessions and trials, not a single instance of physical manipulation or the use of a solicitation gesture was observed.* Thus, the most direct means by which the experienced animal could have attempted to influence the behaviour of its naive partner was simply never observed—despite the fact that these behaviours were part of their natural behavioural repertoire.

## Takes or offers rope

Another fairly direct manner in which the experienced animal might have directed the naive partner to the task would have been to hand him or her the ropes. Indeed, eight instances of taking a rope were recorded. However, five of these were of an experienced animal *taking* a rope from a naive partner, and three were of a naive partner taking a rope from an experienced partner (without a prior offer). Across all sessions and trials, there was only a single instance of a rope offer, and this was of a naive animal offering a rope to the experienced partner.

## Pulling while alone at the ropes

Figure 19.6 shows the mean frequency with which Kara and Brandy and the other animals paired with them were alone pulling at the ropes across each of the three heavy box trials of Sessions 1 and 2. Apart from Trial 1 of Session 2 for Brandy and her partners, as expected, the experienced animal was always observed to be alone pulling at the ropes more often than the naive animal. This is important because it nicely demonstrates a fact that is obvious from observing the video records; namely, that the experienced animals were motivated and interested in retrieving the box even when they were paired with the naive animals. The mean frequencies of alone pulling

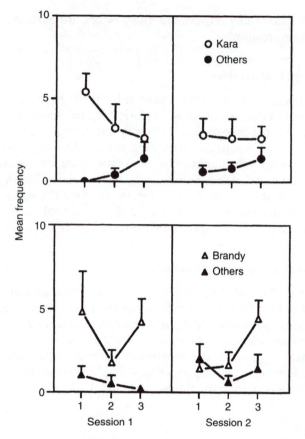

**Fig. 19.6.** Mean frequency (±SEM) of the behaviour, Alone Pulling at the Ropes, for experienced subjects (Kara, Brandy) and their respective naive partners across individual trials of Sessions 1 and 2.

at the ropes, collapsed across trials for Sessions 1 and 2 for Kara and Brandy versus their naive partners, are shown in Table 19.1.

Paired *t*-tests confirmed that Brandy was alone pulling at the ropes significantly more often than her naive partners in Session 1 ($t[13] = 2.96$, $p = .01$), but not in Session 2 ($t[14] = 1.36$, n.s.). However, Kara was alone pulling at the ropes significantly more often than her naive partners in both Session 1 ($t[14] = 3.59$, $p = .003$) and Session 2 ($t[14] = 2.63$, $p = .02$).

The effort that the experienced animals expended in generally fruitless attempts to pull in the maximally weighted box stands in stark contrast to the small number of times the naive animals attempted to do likewise. One might have expected that, over the six total trials (Sessions 1 and 2 combined), the naive animals might have attempted to mimic this behaviour. However, there was little indication that this occurred. First, on 82% of the trials, the naive animals made no attempts at all to pull at the ropes, as compared with 32% of the trials for the experienced animals.

**Table 19.1.** Mean frequency of target behaviours in Study 1 (box-pulling task)

| Target behaviour | Session | Kara | Kara's partners | Brandy | Brandy's partners |
|---|---|---|---|---|---|
| pulling (alone at ropes) | | | | | |
| | 1 | 3.73 | 0.60 | 3.58 | 0.53 |
| | 2 | 2.67 | 0.93 | 2.47 | 1.33 |
| looking to partner (alone at ropes) | | | | | |
| | 1 | 2.67 | 1.33 | 2.75 | 1.27 |
| | 2 | 3.60 | 1.73 | 2.93 | 3.20 |
| looking to partner (both at ropes) | | | | | |
| | 1 | 0.60 | 1.53 | 0.87 | 0.80 |
| | 2 | 2.60 | 3.67 | 1.40 | 2.73 |

Second, Fig. 19.6 reveals no clear pattern indicating an increase in attempts by the naive partners to pull on the ropes across trials. Finally, although 'all-out' pulling was observed with the experienced animals, this behaviour was never seen with the naive animals.

**Looking while alone at the ropes**

Figure 19.7 depicts the mean frequency with which Kara and Brandy and the other animals paired with them looked at their partner while alone at the ropes for each of the three heavy box trials of Sessions 1 and 2. Perhaps the most obvious result is that the experienced animals were more likely to look at their naive partners than their naive partners were to look at them when alone at the ropes, especially during the first trial of Sessions 1. Indeed, Kara displayed a steady decline in her looking behaviour across trials within each session. This is important, because this decline was not the result of an increase in the number of successful retrievals. In addition, for both Kara and Brandy the frequency of looks to their partner quickly declined, but this decline was not followed by an increase in solicitation or instances of physical manipulation of the partner. Thus, it seems difficult to argue that this looking behaviour was simply one of several solicitation behaviours along a spectrum from passive to active. Alternatively, this decline in looking may be because the experienced animals implicitly understood that the partner should be near the ropes, but did not explicitly represent this fact.

The mean frequencies of looking while alone at the ropes, averaged across the three trials of Sessions 1 and 2 for Kara and Brandy versus their naive partners, are summarized in Table 19.1. Kara looked more often at her naive partners than her naive partners looked at her in both Session 1 ($t[14] = 1.78$, $p = .048$, one-tailed) and Session 2 ($t[14] = 1.54$, $p = .07$, one-tailed). Similarly, Brandy looked more often at her naive partners than they looked at her in Session 1 ($t[13] = 2.139$, $p = .03$), but not in Session 2, and indeed, these results were in the opposite direction ($t[13] = 0.147$, n.s.).

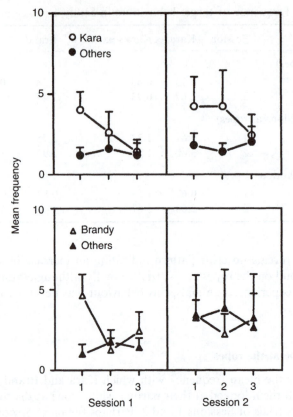

**Fig. 19.7.** Mean frequency (±SEM) of the behaviour, Looks to Partner while Alone at the Ropes, for experienced subjects (Kara, Brandy) and their respective naive partners across individual trials of Sessions 1 and 2.

This latter result was due to a large number of looks ($N = 13$) by one of the naive animals on one trial.

Overall, the behaviour of the animal at the ropes looking to his or her partner who was not at the ropes was observed on approximately the same percentage of trials for the experienced (46%) and naive (54%) animals. However, as shown in Fig. 19.7, the experienced animals were more likely to show this looking behaviour several times throughout a trial than the naive animals were (see also Table 19.1).

## Looking behaviour while both animals are at the ropes

Figure 19.8 shows the mean frequency with which the experienced versus naive animals looked at each other while both were at the ropes (pulling or not) across each of the three trials of Sessions 1 and 2. The results for this pattern of looking behaviour differ sharply from those of the previous two. Instead of the experienced animals looking more at the naive animals (see Figs 19.6 and 19.7), on nine of the

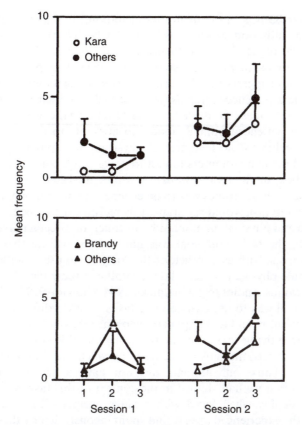

**Fig. 19.8.** Mean frequency (±SEM) of the behaviour, Looks to Partner while Both at the Ropes, for experienced subjects (Kara, Brandy) and their respective naive partners across individual trials of Sessions 1 and 2.

twelve trials shown in Fig. 19.8, the naive animals looked more often at the experienced partner than vice versa. The mean frequencies of the experienced animals and their partners (collapsed across trials within each session) of looking at a partner when both animals are at the ropes, are presented in Table 19.1. The difference in frequency between the experienced and naive animals was significant only for Session 2 for the trials involving Brandy ($t[14] = 2.142$, $p = .05$), and approached significance for the trials of Sessions 1 and 2 involving Kara ($t[14] = 1.58$, $p = .07$; $t[14] = 1.45$, $p = .08$, both one-tailed).

### Discussion

The results of our study indicated that the two experienced animals did not use their existing behaviours to either physically re-direct or manually solicit specific behaviours from their naive partners. On the other hand, they did exhibit higher rates of looking at their naive partners when they themselves were alone at the ropes (see Fig. 19.7).

This may have either been a subtle form of solicitation, or a mere recognition that something about the situation was not as it should be (i.e. there was not another animal pulling on the ropes alongside them). Indeed, the fact that the experienced animals' looks to their partners were less frequent when their partners were at the ropes (but not pulling) suggests that in terms of their understanding of the requirements for success, the experienced animals were satisfied with their partner's proximity alone. Indeed, even in the face of repeated failures to retrieve the box by simply pulling by themselves, the experienced animals made no attempts to manually solicit help from their partners, exhibited no instances of physically manipulating their partners toward the task, and made no attempts to gesture toward relevant features of the task (e.g. the ropes, the box, or the food rewards on top of the box).

The main purpose of these studies was to determine whether chimpanzees who were experienced with a given task would spontaneously recruit existing behaviours, such as solicitation gestures and physical manipulation, to solicit or direct a naive partner who was unfamiliar with the task. Our goal was not to demonstrate that chimpanzees could learn to co-operate with each other, or that they could use solicitation gestures, or even that they could physically manipulate each other—these facts have been amply demonstrated in previous studies (e.g. Chalmeau 1994; Crawford 1937; Povinelli *et al.* 1992). Rather, our goal was to use co-operative tasks to ask a different, but straightforward, question: What would a chimpanzee who was experienced on a task spontaneously do to influence the behaviour of a naive conspecific? We explicitly decided not to train the two experienced animals to the point at which they had conventionalized solicitation gestures. Thus, our animals did not have a set of highly scripted behavioural routines that we had shaped in the context of this task which they might then automatically deploy when faced with a naive partner. Thus, our aim was to determine whether the experienced apes would spontaneously deploy these behaviours, before they became conventionalized, when paired with a naive partner. Thus, our findings emerged in the context of pairing an experienced animal with a naive animal—in a sense, a 'teaching opportunity' for the experienced animal. Earlier research had involved pairings of two highly trained animals, or an animal with an adult human, in highly scripted situations.

Although in this sense our results may seem to differ from those of Crawford (1937), who did observe some limited instances of solicitation, we believe that this difference stems from our decision not to provide the experienced chimpanzees with extensive training on the task. Indeed, we have no doubt that if we had we trained our experienced animals as extensively as did Crawford, such gestures would have become conventionalized in the context of this task. However, the fact that the experienced animals did not spontaneously recruit behaviours already in their repertoire to assist them in achieving their goal, is consistent with the idea that they were not able to appreciate their partner as a separate psychological agent, whose subjective state needed to be co-ordinated with their own. Indeed, even though Crawford's (1937, 1941) animals did display some instances of solicitation and physical manipulation after extensive shaping, they never attempted to indicate what to do in particular (i.e. their communication did not appear to have a predicative function).

In any event, our results help to clarify some of these previous findings. For example, Crawford's (1937, 1941) studies found limited evidence of the use of solicitation gestures between two highly experienced animals in a co-operative problem-solving task. Köhler (1927) and Gómez (1991) both reported instances of apes leading humans to locations where the humans could act in ways that would benefit the ape. Rather than standing in contrast to such findings, our studies extend such observations by revealing important potential limitations of chimpanzees' ability to use even such solicitation gestures. In particular, these gestures may emerge through a process of conventionalization (Smith 1977), not a spontaneous reaction to a completely novel problem. Indeed, in a longitudinal project designed to track the development of the communicative gestures of chimpanzees in spontaneous social interactions, Michael Tomasello and his colleagues have concluded that conventionalization is the dominant means through which such gestures are conserved across generations (Tomasello *et al.* 1994). What does appear to emerge quite automatically, however, is the looking pattern that both we and others have observed. Either one animal learns to watch the other animal in order to co-ordinate and time its own behaviour (e.g. Chalmeau 1994; Chalmeau and Gallo 1996; Crawford 1937, 1941), or, as in our studies, the experienced animal looks repeatedly to the naive animal while alone at the apparatus. This looking pattern has also been observed between apes and humans in other problem-solving situations (e.g. Gómez 1991).

Finally, our results are consistent with the view that chimpanzees do not actively teach one another. Even among enculturated chimpanzees, no convincing attempts of teaching have ever been reported (for a range of views on this topic, see Boesch 1991; Byrne 1995; Cheney and Seyfarth 1990; Povinelli and Godfrey 1993; Premack 1984; Tomasello *et al.* 1993). In our study, the absence of attempts by the experienced animals to physically manipulate the behaviour of their naive partner strongly suggests that the chimpanzee's communicative abilities are limited, as Crawford (1937) first stated, to 'a signalizing function' and are not 'adequate for directing an animal to perform an act new to it' (p. 84). Even when these gestures are used between two animals highly trained on a specific task, they carry only the meaning 'do something for me' and thereby set off patterns of activity already well-learned and routinized.

Research with preschool human children, in contrast, suggests that by about twenty four to thirty months of age, peers are capable of co-ordinated, joint problem solving which involves one child directing the other (e.g. Brownell and Carriger 1990). This research has suggested that co-ordinated, joint problem solving is related to an ability to represent others as causing their own behaviour (Brownell and Carriger 1990), and that regulation of a peer's activity emerges only after a readiness to imitate a peer's actions (Eckerman and Didow 1996; Eckerman *et al.* 1989). The latter findings pose an especially interesting possibility with respect to potential differences between chimpanzees and children. Indeed, one recent review of the primate literature concludes that if one rules out cases in which apparent copying of motor behaviour can be explained by priming or stimulus enhancement, then few clear cases (if any) exist of one chimpanzee copying the novel acts of another conspecific (Byrne 1995; see also Tomasello and Call 1997; Tomasello *et al.* 1993). If, as Eckerman and her colleagues (Eckerman and Didow 1996; Eckerman *et al.* 1989) have found, regulation of a peer follows the emergence of a readiness to imitate a peer's actions, perhaps it is the case that the inability of chimpanzees to effectively influence a naive partner's actions is related to a more general inability (or lack of interest) in readily imitating the novel actions of another conspecific.

## UNDERSTANDING OTHER MINDS: A HUMAN COGNITIVE SPECIALIZATION?

The findings that we have reported here add to a growing body of evidence suggesting that humans may have evolved a psychological specialization in representing other minds (Povinelli and Preuss 1995; Povinelli and Prince 1998; Tomasello *et al.* 1993). Indeed, there is some reason to believe that this difference may simply be symptomatic of a much more profound difference between humans and other primates, one connected to an ability to represent *theoretical* causes of both social and physical events. For example, chimpanzees may have just as much difficulty in representing unobservable physical causes (gravity, force, space) as psychological ones (attention, desire, belief). If true, their apparent inability to use their communicative gestures in ways that would suggest that they represent the shared attention between themselves and others—the purported psychological basis for the appearance of proto-declarative gestures in human infancy—may be part of a much more fundamental psychological difference between their species and our own.

Some may object to our general conclusion, and insist that, no matter what the results of laboratory experiments, the fact that chimpanzees deploy a rich array of gestural communicative signals, the fact that they practice deception, the fact that they engage in apparently deliberate attempts to work their way up through their dominance hierarchies, and the fact that in social interactions with humans they display behaviours that are undeniably similar to our own, all provide a firm basis for suspecting that they represent each other as psychological agents. Indeed, one version of this argument indicts the entire experimental approach. This argument proceeds as follows: *Every experiment in which chimpanzees participate is contrived by humans and is thus laden with assumptions and biases which obscure the psychological operations that underwrite their more natural and spontaneous social behaviour. Furthermore, because we can use our introspective faculty to identify the psychological states that cause similar social behaviours in ourselves, it is illogical to deny the presence of similar states in chimpanzees.* As we have seen, of course, this is the argument by analogy.

Historically, one of the most persuasive aspects of the argument by analogy has been that there appeared to be no better explanation for the behavioural similarity between humans and other animals (see Povinelli and Giambrone, in press). However, there *is* an alternative point of view—one that reconciles the remarkable similarity between humans and other primates with the striking dissimilarities revealed by recent experimental research, including the research reported here (for a full treatment of this alternative, see Povinelli and Giambrone, in press; Povinelli and Prince 1998). On this view, humans and chimpanzees are seen as having inherited a wide range of social behaviours from their common ancestor—behaviours that evolved over the sixty million years of primate evolution that preceded the appearance of humans and chimpanzees. It is possible, however, that these behaviours were originally generated by low-level psychological mechanisms unrelated to an explicit representation of other minds. In short, these existing, low-level psychological mechanisms may have been recruited to support increasingly sophisticated social behaviours, which themselves became more and more tightly canalized as struggles for scarce resources became increasingly ruthless. Furthermore, these behaviours did not evolve simply to enhance the social primate's ability to emerge victorious from a particular conflict, but also to repair the damages to intra-group social relationships that inevitably follow such conflict (de Waal 1986). In any event, rather than being prima facie evidence for the kinds of social understanding present in humans, it is possible that these sophisticated social behaviours evolved and were in full operation long before the ability to explicitly represent other minds became possible.

Finally, it is possible to imagine that, for one reason or another, it may have been only a single primate lineage—the human one—that went on to evolve the ability to represent these ancient behaviours in mentalistic terms. This ability, in turn, may have put us in the unique position of being able to re-interpret behavioural acts that had been around for millions of years in new ways. One way of thinking about this 're-interpretation hypothesis' is to suppose that humans uniquely evolved a mechanism for describing behaviours in increasingly explicit ways—a hypothesized process in human cognitive development that Karmiloff-Smith (1992) has labelled 'representational redescription'. Indeed, if our reinterpretation hypothesis is correct, it may be that one of the most fundamental cognitive specializations of the human species was to evolve the neural means for redescribing behaviours that evolved tens, and in some cases, hundreds, of millions of years before humans appeared on the scene. This does not mean that these redescriptions or reinterpretations provide a less 'accurate' account of the true causes of behaviour. After all, in one sense at least, by inventing this explicitly psychological theory of behaviour (a theory of mind), humans may have come one step closer toward a fully accurate description of the causes of behaviour (Povinelli 1993). And, in terms more relevant to the evolutionary process, this kind of social understanding may have provided us with greater control over these already-existing behaviours—ultimately allowing us to reorganize those behaviours in novel, more efficient, and ultimately more productive ways (see Povinelli and Giambrone, in press ; Povinelli and Prince 1998). One illustration of this difference between humans and chimpanzees may be the inability of our chimpanzees to use their relevant, existing behavioural actions to influence the actions of their naive partners in the experiment we reported here.

This reinterpretation hypothesis places in a much clearer light our original goal of trying to identify contexts in which chimpanzees might use their natural gestures in ways that would imply that they reason about each other's mental states. It forces us to acknowledge the sterility of the debate concerning the fairness of applying different standards when evaluating the capacities of humans infants and chimpanzees. It provides a coherent theoretical foundation for not insisting on a completely uniform psychological interpretation of what appear to be the shared communicative gestures of humans and other species. The behavioural form of a given gesture and the psychological mechanism which is presumed to attend/cause it, can no longer be treated as a single, unitary phenomenon. Indeed, on close inspection, the separate evolutionary history of the low-level psychological mechanisms controlling the gestures, and our theory-laden interpretation of those gestures, may be apparent even in our species—both during the course of our development, and in our use of these gestures in our everyday adult lives.

### Acknowledgements

This research was supported in part by NIH Grant No. RR-03583-05 to the University of Southwestern Louisiana New Iberia Research Center, NSF Young Investigator Award SBR-8458111 to DJP, and a grant from the Natural Sciences and Engineering Council of Canada to DKO. Order of authorship was determined randomly. We thank James E. Reaux, Anthony Rideaux, and Donna Bierschwale for professional support, and Julie Kanter, Frank Reille, and Elicia Lacey for assistance in testing the chimpanzees. Original artwork is by Donna Bierschwale. Correspondence concerning this article should be addressed to Daniel J. Povinelli, Division of Behavioral Biology, University of Southwestern Louisiana New Iberia Research Center, 4401 W. Admiral Doyle Drive, New Iberia, Louisiana 70560, or sent by e-mail to doneill@watarts.uwaterloo.ca.

## REFERENCES

Akhtar, N. and Tomasello, M. (1996). Two-year-olds learn words for absent objects and actions. *British Journal of Developmental Psychology*, **14**, 79–93.

Baldwin, D. A. (1993). Infants' ability to consult the speaker for clues to word reference. *Journal of Child Language*, **20**, 395–418.

Baron-Cohen, S. (1989). Perceptual role-taking and protodeclarative pointing in autism. *British Journal of Developmental Psychology*, **7**, 113–27.

Bates, E. (1976). *Language in context*. Academic Press, New York.

Bates, E., Camaioni, L. and Volterra, V. (1975). The acquisition of preformatives prior to speech. *Merrill-Palmer Quarterly*, **21**, 205–26.

Boesch, C. (1991). Teaching among wild chimpanzees. *Animal Behaviour*, **41**, 530–2.

Boesch, C. (1994). Hunting strategies of Gombe and Taï chimpanzees. In *Chimpanzee cultures*, (ed. R. W. Wrangham, W. C. McGrew, F. B. M. de Waal and P. G. Heltne), pp. 77–91. Harvard University Press, Cambridge, MA.

Brownell, C. A. and Carriger, M. S. (1990). Changes in cooperation and self-other distinction during the second year. *Child Development*, **61**, 1164–74.

Byrne, R. (1995). *The thinking ape*. Oxford University Press, Oxford.

Call, J. and Tomasello, M. (1994). The production and comprehension of referential pointing by orangutans (*Pongo pygmaeus*). *Journal of Comparative Psychology*, **108**, 307–17.

Chalmeau, R. (1994). Do chimpanzees cooperate in a learning task? *Primates*, **35**, 385–92.

Chalmeau, R. and Gallo, A. (1996). What chimpanzees (*Pan troglodytes*) learn in a cooperative task. *Primates*, **37**, 39–47.

Cheney, D. L. and Seyfarth, R. M. (1990). *How monkeys see the world: Inside the mind of another species*. University of Chicago Press.

Crawford, M. P. (1937). The cooperative solving of problems by young chimpanzees. *Comparative Psychology Monographs*, **14**(68).

Crawford, M. P. (1941). The cooperative solving by chimpanzees of problems requiring serial responses to color cues. *Journal of Social Psychology*, **13**, 259–80.

Darwin, C. (1871/1982). *The descent of man*. Reprinted, 1982, Modern Library, New York.

de Waal, F. (1982). *Chimpanzee politics: power and sex among apes*. Harper and Row, New York.

de Waal, F. (1986). The integration of dominance and social bonding in primates. *Quarterly Review of Biology*, **61**, 459–79.

Eckerman, C. O. and Didow, S. M. (1996). Nonverbal imitation and toddlers' mastery of verbal means of achieving coordinated action. *Developmental Psychology*, **32**, 141–52.

Eckerman, C. O., Davis, C. C. and Didow, S. M. (1989). Toddlers' emerging ways of achieving social coordination with a peer. *Child Development*, **60**, 440–53.

Franco, F. and Butterworth, G. (1996). Pointing and social awareness: declaring and requesting in the second year. *Journal of Child Language*, **23**, 307–36.

Gómez, J. C. (1991). Visual behavior as a window for reading the minds of others in primates. In *Natural theories of mind: evolution, development and simulation of everyday mindreading*, (ed. A. Whiten), pp. 330–43. Blackwell, Oxford.

Gómez, J. C., Sarria, E. and Tamarit, J. (1993). The comparative study of early communication and theories of mind: ontogeny, phylogeny and pathology. In *Understanding other minds: perspectives from autism*, (ed. S. Baron-Cohen, H. Tager-Flusberg and D. Cohen). Oxford University Press, New York.

Goodall, J. (1986). *The chimpanzees of Gombe: patterns of behavior*. Belknap, Harvard University Press, Cambridge, MA.

Goodhart, F. and Baron-Cohen, S. (1993). How many ways can the point be made? Evidence from children with and without autism. *First Language*, **13**, 225–33.

Hume, D. (1739–1740/1978). *A treatise of human nature*, (2 Vols), (ed. L. A. Selby-Bigge), pp. 176–9. Clarendon, Oxford.

Karmiloff-Smith, A. (1992). *Beyond modularity: a developmental perspective on cognitive science*. MIT Press, Cambridge, MA.

Köhler, W. (1927). *The mentality of apes*. London: Kegan Paul.

Krause, M. A. and Fouts, R. S. (1997). Chimpanzees (*Pan troglodytes*) pointing: hand shapes, accuracy and the role of eye gaze. *Journal of Comparative Psychology*, **111**, 330–6.

Leavens, D. A., Hopkins, W. D. and Bard, K. A. (1996). Indexical and referential pointing in chimpanzees (*Pan troglodytes*). *Journal of Comparative Psychology*, **110**, 346–53.

Menzel, E. W., Jr. (1974). A group of young chimpanzees in a one-acre field. In *Behavior of nonhuman primates: modern research trends*, (ed. A. Schrier and F. Stollnitz), pp. 83–153. Academic Press, New York.

Moore, C. and Corkum, V. (1994). Social understanding at the end of the first year of life. *Developmental Review*, **14**, 349–72.

Moore, C., Angelopoulos, P. and Bennett, P. Word learning in the context of referential and salience cues. *Developmental Psychology*. (In press.)

Mundy, P., Sigman, M., Ungerer, J. and Sherman, T. (1986). Defining the social deficits of autism: the contribution of non-verbal communication measures. *Journal of Child Psychology and Psychiatry*, **27**, 657–69.

Nishida, T. (1970). Social behavior and relationships among wild chimpanzees of the Mahale Mountains. *Journal of Human Evolution*, **2**, 357–70.

O'Neill, D. K. (1996). Two-year-old children's sensitivity to a parent's knowledge state when making requests. *Child Development*, **67**, 659–77.

Plooij, F. X. (1978). Some basic traits of language in wild chimpanzees? In *Action, gesture and symbol*, (ed. A. Lock), pp. 111–31. Academic Press, London.

Povinelli, D. J. (1993). Reconstructing the evolution of mind. *American Psychologist*, **48**, 493–509.

Povinelli, D. J. (1996). Chimpanzee theory of mind? The long road to strong inference. In *Theories of theories of mind*, (ed. P. Carruthers and P. Smith), pp. 293–329. Cambridge University Press.

Povinelli, D. J. and Eddy, T. J. (1994). The eyes as a window: what young chimpanzees see on the other side. *Current Psychology of Cognition*, **13**, 695–705.

Povinelli, D. J. and Eddy, T. J. (1996a). What young chimpanzees know about seeing. *Monographs of the Society for Research in Child Development*, Vol. 61, No. 2, Serial No. 247.

Povinelli, D. J. and Eddy, T. J. (1996b). Factors influencing young chimpanzees' (*Pan troglodytes*) recognition of attention. *Journal of Comparative Psychology*, **110**, 336–45.

Povinelli, D. J. and Eddy, T. J. (1996c). Chimpanzees: joint visual attention. *Psychological Science*, **7**, 129–35.

Povinelli, D. J. and Giambrone, S. Inferring other minds: failure of the argument by analogy. *Philosophical Topics*. (In press.)

Povinelli, D. J. and Godfrey, L. R. (1993). The chimpanzee's mind: How noble in reason? How absent of ethics? In *Evolutionary Ethics*, (ed. M. Nitecki and D. Nitecki), pp. 277–324. SUNY Press, Albany.

Povinelli, D. J. and Preuss, T. M. (1995). Theory of mind: evolutionary history of a cognitive specialization. *Trends in Neuroscience*, **18**, 418–24.

Povinelli, D. J. and Prince, C. G. (1998). When self met other. In *Self-awareness: its nature and development*, (ed. M. Ferrari and R. J. Sternberg). Guilford Press, New York.

Povinelli, D. J., Nelson, K. E. and Boysen, S. T. (1992). Comprehension of role reversal by chimpanzees: evidence of empathy? *Animal Behaviour*, **43**, 633–40.

Povinelli, D. J., Reaux, J. E., Bierschwale, D. T., Allain, A. D. and Simon, B. B. (1997). Exploitation of pointing as a referential gesture in young children, but not adolescent chimpanzees. *Cognitive Development*, **12**, 423–61.

Povinelli, D. J., Bering, J. and Giambrone, S. Chimpanzee 'pointing': another error of the argument by analogy? In *Pointing: where language culture and cognition meet*, (ed. S. Kita). Cambridge University Press. (In press, *a*.)

Povinelli, D. J., Bierschwale, D. T. and Čech, C. G. (1999). Comprehension of seeing as a referential act in young children, but not juvenile chimpanzees. *British Journal of Developmental Psychology*, **17**, 37–60.

Premack, D. (1984). Pedagogy and aesthetics as sources of culture. In *Handbook of Cognitive Neuroscience*, (ed. M. S. Gazzaniga), pp. 15–35. Plenum Press, New York.

Reaux, J. E., Theall, L. A. and Povinelli, D. J. (1999). A longitudinal investigation of chimpanzees' understanding of visual perception. *Child Development*, **70**, 275–90.

Romanes, G. J. (1882). *Animal intelligence.* Keagan Paul, London.

Romanes, G. J. (1884). *Mental evolution in animals.* Appleton and Co., New York.

Russell, B. (1948). *Human knowledge: its scope and limits.* Unwin Hyman, London.

Savage-Rumbaugh, E. S. (1986). *Ape language: from conditioned response to symbol.* Columbia University Press, New York.

Smith, J. (1977). *The behavior of communicating.* Harvard University Press, Cambridge, MA.

Theall, L. A. and Povinelli, D. J. Chimpanzees deploy attention-getting behaviors independent of the attentional states of others. *Animal Cognition*. (In review.)

Tomasello, M. (1995). Joint attention as social cognition. In *Joint attention: its origins and role in development*, (ed. C. Moore and P. Dunham), pp. 103–30. Lawrence Erlbaum, Hillsdale, NJ.

Tomasello, M. and Barton, M. (1984). Learning words in nonostensive contexts. *Developmental Psychology*, **30**, 639–50.

Tomasello, M. and Call, J. (1997). *Primate Cognition*. Oxford University Press.

Tomasello, M., Kruger, A. C. and Ratner, H. H. (1993). Cultural learning. *Behavioral and Brain Sciences*, **16**, 495–552.

Tomasello, M., Call, J., Nagell, K., Olguin, R. and Carpenter, M. (1994). The learning and use of gestural signals by young chimpanzees: a trans-generational study. *Primates*, **35**, 137–54.

Vygotsky, L. (1962). *Thought and language*. MIT Press, Cambridge, MA.

Werner, H., and Kaplan, B. (1963). *Symbol formation: An organismic-developmental approach to language and the development of thought*. Wiley, New York.

Woodruff, G. and Premack, D. (1979). Intentional communication in the chimpanzee: the development of deception. *Cognition*, **7**, 333–62.

# 20

# Palaeoanthropological perspectives on the theory of mind

## STEVEN MITHEN

INTRODUCTION

During the last decade 'theory of mind' has emerged as a key concept in psychology. It has become a focus for research in many areas of this discipline including the study of non-human primates, cognitive pathologies, and child development. It has gained this status due to its apparently central role in human cognition: appreciating that other individuals have beliefs and desires, especially those which may contrast with one's own, is fundamental to possessing a 'normal' human mind. Indeed the capacity to 'mentalise', in terms of interpreting behaviour by reference to mental states, appears to be as important an element of being human as it is to use language or complex material objects. In spite of such recent attention, theory of mind remains a little understood phenomenon, as apparent from the diverse range of theories of theories of mind that currently exist (Carruthers and Smith 1996a). Research in a wide range of disciplines is required to gain an adequate definition of theory of mind, to understand its relationships to other cognitive abilities, and to explain how and why it develops in the minds of young children with such apparent cross-cultural similarities.

One discipline which will need to contribute to this further understanding is palaeoanthropology: the study of human evolution through the evidence of the archaeological and fossil record. This chapter will discuss why palaeoanthropological research on theory of mind is required, and what it may contribute to our understanding of this phenomenon. There have been very few studies which have considered how the theory of mind abilities of our human ancestors might be inferred from their archaeological remains—the work of Wynn (1993) being one example. Consequently this chapter must be exploratory and speculative. I will conclude by proposing a four-stage evolution of our theory of mind abilities during the last two million years. This will indeed be speculative and I do so largely as an attempt to provoke other palaeoanthropologists, and indeed any scholars concerned with human evolution, to begin work on the critical issues of when our theory of mind abilities evolved, why they evolved, and what impact these have had on human behaviour and culture.

## THEORY OF MIND AS PART OF OUR EVOLVED PSYCHOLOGY

Palaeoanthropology is concerned with human evolution, and is critical to those elements of our physiology, cognition, and behaviour that are believed to be universal within our species but which are either absent or less developed in our close relatives, the African apes. Theory of mind is likely to be one such feature. If it is thought that there are significant cross-cultural similarities to human theory of mind abilities and that these differ significantly to those found within the chimpanzee, it will be necessary to turn to the palaeoanthropological record to acquire a full understanding of such abilities. Scholars from diverse disciplines concerned with theory of mind recognise that there are indeed sufficient cross-cultural similarities in the nature of the theory of mind to imply an innate basis common to *H. sapiens sapiens*—although quite what is 'innate' remains unclear (Carruthers and Smith 1996*b*). While chimpanzees may have some ability at understanding other minds, this appears quite different to the human capacity. Consequently the human capacity for theory of mind must have evolved at some time during the last five to six million years, the period since the last common ancestor between modern humans and chimpanzees. Human evolution during this period is documented by the fossil and archaeological records. Attempting to draw inferences about evolving cognitive abilities from data such as stone artefacts and fossil crania is certainly not easy but is nevertheless an essential undertaking if we wish to understand the modern mind.

If the human theory of mind capacity is described as 'innate', this may be taken to imply a highly modular capacity, which is simply 'switched on' during development when particular physiological conditions are met and environmental cues are present (Segal 1996). In this regard, theory of mind abilities effectively mature within the mind, rather than having a developmental history heavily influenced by the specific environmental conditions. This modularist position contrasts with what has been termed the 'theory theory' position, in which a greater role is placed on the child's own learning abilities as he/she constructs his/her theory of mind by observation and hypothesis testing during early childhood (Carruthers 1996; Gopnik 1996). An innate basis to theory of mind is still implied, but this largely relates to the propensity to develop a theory of mind, rather than to the specific contents of that theory itself. A third position contrasts with both of the above by claiming that children do not in fact develop a theory of mind at all, but simply rely on mental simulation when attempting to predict behaviour (e.g. Gordon 1996). In this regard they imagine how they would act in any particular position, rather than deriving predictions by having a theory about the contents of someone else's mind. This position might either have an innate basis equivalent to that implied by a modularist position—abilities at simulation are simply activated at some time during development—or one equivalent to the theory theorist position in terms of a propensity to develop an ability at mental simulation.

Each of these positions, and various halfway houses between them, are currently held by different psychologists, indicating that there is no simple means of resolving which is the most accurate (Carruthers and Smith 1996*a*). Unfortunately, cross-cultural studies have not been sufficiently numerous to provide a detailed understanding of how environment influences theory of mind, and hence help to resolve whether a strong or a weak innate position is the most appropriate. Astington (1996) has noted that some non-western children, such as those from the Baku of the Cameroon, understand false-belief tasks at the same age as western children. On the other hand, the Quechura children of Peru and the Tainae children of New Guinea appear only to develop an understanding of false beliefs as they approach adolescence. This may not be surprising as, whatever theoretical position one may adopt towards theory of mind, the cultural environment must be acknowledged as being an influence over the specific timing and nature of theory of mind development.

While recognising that our data base is heavily biased to Western children, one might nevertheless argue that theory of mind abilities appear to be acquired with such regularity and so effortlessly that some innate basis appears highly probable. Indeed even the most ardent theory-theorist must acknowledge an innate propensity for children to construct a theory of mind, if that is indeed what they do. Baron-Cohen and Swettenham (1996) have suggested that this acquisition poses the same degree of a learnability problem as does the acquisition of linguistic skills, which appears to be similarly rapid, universal, and without sufficient stimulus from the environment. In this light, a modularist position appears most appropriate.

It should, of course, not be surprising that theory of mind would have a strong innate basis. The ability to predict the behaviour of other individuals by inferring their beliefs and desires is of considerable adaptive benefit. This is readily evident from the serious constraints on social interaction that arise from the loss of such abilities, as appears to be the case with autism (Baron-Cohen 1995). Being able to predict the behaviour and thoughts of other individuals transforms one's ability at co-operation and competition. Achieving such prediction by simply observing behavioural cues and learning associations between these is certainly of considerable benefit; but the possession of a theory of mind would substantially enhance the extent, detail, and accuracy of the inferences that could be made. Consequently individuals who had a theory of mind encoded within their genes—in either a strong or weak sense—would have had considerable reproductive advantage within the societies of our early ancestors.

## WHY VIEW THEORY OF MIND FROM A PALAEOANTHROPOLOGICAL POSITION?

There are two reasons why a palaeoanthropological perspective on theory of mind needs to be developed. The first derives from simply recognising that theory of mind appears to have some innate basis and as such is a fundamental part of our evolved cognitive abilities. As such, theory of mind must have an evolutionary history and we will gain a more profound understanding of those abilities by exposing that evolutionary history. A similarity can be drawn here regarding language. Our linguistic abilities also have an evolved basis and this helps us understand why language is more effective at communicating some types of information rather than others. Why, for instance, can information about complex social relationships be more easily communicated than that about spatial directions which intuitively have an equivalent, or even lower, degree of complexity? (Aitchison 1996). One possibility is that this reflects the evolutionary roots of language as a means of maintaining social cohesion (Dunbar 1996) and that its use for communicating technical information is simply an evolutionarily late by-product of this function (Mithen 1996). Similar light might be thrown on theory of mind abilities. Why is it, for instance, that understanding of desire appears to precede that of belief? (Harris 1996.) Perhaps, as I will suggest below, this reflects an evolutionary history in which the extent of theory of mind abilities were once restricted to inferences of desire, and were only extended to those concerning belief at a later stage of human evolution.

In this regard, therefore, we need a palaeoanthropological perspective on theory of mind, just as we need one on any aspect of human cognitive abilities: understanding evolutionary history may help to explain specific features of that ability.

A second reason for viewing theory of mind from a palaeoanthropological perspective is that this will facilitate our reconstruction of the behaviour and thought of human ancestors and relatives: a cognitive archaeology is an essential element of palaeoanthropology (Mithen 1996; Renfrew 1983; Renfrew and Zubrow 1993). While the exploration of our past is essential to understanding our modern condition, it is also a valid goal in its own right. Archaeologists need to explain the variability and patterning in the archaeological record. During the last decade it has become apparent that unless we make explicit reference to the mentality of past humans, species such as *H. ergaster*, *H. heidelbergensis*, and *H. neanderthalensis*, we will never gain a sufficient understanding of why tools were made and discarded in the way they were, why some hominids but not others created works of art and colonised new continents.

As theory of mind appears to be such an essential feature of the modern mind, we need to consider whether these early humans had the same, similar, or radically different theory of mind capabilities. This is by no means an easy task. As I noted above, we lack a clear understanding of quite how our modern theory of mind capacities are constituted, and there is certainly no clear methodology for drawing inferences about the nature of past theories of mind from the inert artefacts of the archaeological record. Nevertheless, if we accept that explicit reference to past mentality is an essential task when interpreting the archaeological record and reconstructing the past, we have no choice but to begin the task of adopting a palaeoanthropological perspective on the theory of mind.

## HUMAN EVOLUTION: A BRIEF RESUME

Before proceeding it is useful to provide a brief resume of human evolution to provide the chronological context for the issues I will discuss. This section will largely summarise our current understanding of human evolution as outlined in more detail in Jones *et al.* (1992), Mithen (1996), and Stringer and Mckie (1996).

Studies of molecular genetics have demonstrated that modern humans shared a common ancestor with the chimpanzee between five and six million years ago. It is unlikely that the earliest fossil hominid we have, *Ardipithecus ramidus*, dating to about four and a half million years ago, was that common ancestor, but it certainly displayed many primitive, ape-like traits. Following this species there is a diverse group of australopithecine species in the fossil record including *Australopithecus anamensis, A. afaraensis, A. africanus,* and *A. boisei* found in eastern and southern Africa. While there was considerable morphological variability between these species, and indeed within species in terms of sexual dimorphism, they shared a brain size similar to the chimpanzee today and had some degrees of bipedalism. Indeed, australopithecines can reasonably be referred to as bipedal apes.

A major split occurred in the australopithecines, with some (which are often placed into their own genus, *Paranthropus*) developing particularly robust features, and others that retained a more gracile morphology and that are likely to have given rise to the first *Homo* about two and a half million years ago. These are distinguished by an enlarged brain size, reaching *c.* 750 cc and reduced dentition. As with the australopithecines, however, they also show considerable morphological diversity and quite how many species are present in the fossil record remains unclear. At least three appear to exist, *Homo habilis, H. rudolfensis,* and *H. ergaster.* These are traditionally associated with the Oldowan industry, although strong arguments can be made that stone artefacts were also manufactured by some, or all, of the australopithecine species.

Perhaps as early as two million years ago one of these species, probably *H. ergaster,* dispersed from Africa into Asia where it appears to have given rise to *H. erectus.* In Africa *H. ergaster* (also referred to as African *H. erectus*) is likely to have been the direct ancestor of *H. heidelbergensis,* which spread into Europe by 750 000 years ago, and eventually archaic *H. sapiens.* Between *c.* two million years ago and 600 000 years ago brain size appears to have been quite stable forming a plateau with an average size of 800–1000 cc. The species during this period are associated with a range of stone artefact industries, the most important being that of the Acheulian within which handaxes were produced.

In Europe *H. heidelbergensis* gave rise to *H. neanderthalensis.* This species, in common with archaic *H. sapiens* in Africa, had a brain size within the range of modern human variation: indeed the largest brain of any known human, modern or otherwise, is that of a Neanderthal, the Amud I specimen with a brain size of 1750 cc. The average of modern humans is 1200–1500 cc. The Neanderthals are the best known of these late Pleistocene, large brained Early Humans and existed in Europe and western Asia between about 250 000 and 29 000 years ago. They are associated with the Mousterian industry, which often involved the production of stone flakes, blades, and points by the levallois method—a stone-knapping technique which demands high levels of knapping skill. The Neanderthals survived in a range of late Pleistocene environments and were generally physiologically adapted to a cold environment. Assemblages of animal bones from their occupation sites indicate that they were proficient big game hunters. Although late Neanderthals (post 80 000 years ago) appear to have intentionally buried some of their dead, there are no unambiguous traces of symbolic behaviour by this species.

In Africa one can follow a gradual evolutionary development in the fossil record from *H. ergaster* through archaic *H. sapiens* to *H. sapiens sapiens,* with the earliest of these being found at Omo Kibish, Ethiopia, at about 130 000 years ago, and at Klasies River Mouth, South Africa, at 125 000 years ago. These earliest modern humans are associated with the Middle Stone Age industry, which has similarities to the Mousterian of the Neanderthals, especially with regard to a high degree of conservatism in knapping methods and artefact design through time. At 100 000 years ago modern humans are found in the Levant, represented in the caves of Qafzeh and Skhul where they are associated with a Mousterian industries very similar to those of the Neanderthals found in the caves of Tabun at about 125 000 and Kebara at about 60 000 years ago. Only faint traces of behavioural differences between these earliest modern humans and archaic *Homo* can be found: at Klasies River Mouth there appears to be an increase in the use of red ochre, at Katanda in Zaire bone harpoons are found dating to 90 000 years ago, and in the Levant modern humans appear to have hunted in a more efficient manner than the Neanderthals, although they used a very similar technology. But in general there are very few developments in the archaeological record that can be associated with the emergence of anatomically modern humans.

After 100 000 years ago *H. sapiens sapiens* appear to have dispersed rapidly across the Old World displacing existing early human populations. By 55 000 years ago Australia had been colonised and by 30 000 years ago so had the harsh northern environments of Siberia, unexploited by archaic *Homo*. By 15 000 radiocarbon years modern humans had crossed the Beringia land bridge into Alaska and by 10 500 radiocarbon years ago they had reached Tierra del Fuego. In Asia *H. erectus* appears to have survived until about 30 000 years ago, while in Europe Neanderthals were progressively marginalised to the south west of the continent with their last dated occupations being in Spain and Gibraltar at around 29 000 years ago. As a result, the genus *Homo* is now one of very few that exist with just one species member.

The period after 50 000 years ago is also associated with considerable cultural developments. These are seen most dramatically in Europe after 30 000 years ago. There we witness the first representational art and complex bone and antler technology—with the exception of the Katanda harpoons. We also see an increased use of burial ritual which appears to have begun with the first modern humans in Qafzeh and Skhul. At the end of the last ice age, 10 000 radiocarbon years ago, several human populations in various parts of the old and new worlds appear to have independently developed farming, which provided the economic and social basis for the growth of complex societies and states.

A common assumption among those studying prehistoric populations is that the human populations after 30 000 years ago were cognitively 'modern': if one of their children was transplanted into our society they would develop just as any other child. This may also be the case for all *H. sapiens sapiens*, although some argue for a significant cognitive development occurring after 50 000 years ago.

What is clear, however, is that if we are to understand any universal patterns of cognitive development among children in the world today, this evolutionary history of our species, which I have so briefly sketched, is of vital importance. For it is during this six to five million year period that we became cognitively distinct from our closest living relative, the chimpanzee.

## A CHIMPANZEE THEORY OF MIND?

The palaeoanthropological record of the last six to five million years only becomes relevant to understanding theory of mind if it is evident that the chimpanzee theory of mind is different to that of modern humans. If there is no difference, then we must conclude that this capacity evolved prior to five to six million years ago and the palaeoanthropolgical record has no bearing on its evolutionary history.

Following what may now with hindsight be seen as an initial rush of enthusiasm for attributing chimpanzees with mind-reading skills, there has been a recent re-evaluation of the relevant observations and experimental evidence. The genuine difficulty of inferring whether chimpanzees engage in actual mind reading, or are simply very clever behaviourists in terms of perceiving many subtle cues about the states of other individuals and using these in 'clever' ways, has become apparent (*See* Povinelli and O'Neil, Chapter 19, this volume).

Perhaps the most persuasive evidence remains that of high-level tactical deception as described by Byrne and Whiten (1992), although Whiten (1996) himself now acknowledges that a very clever behaviourist may achieve the same degree of deception. Heyes's (1993) critique of the use of anecdotal evidence and of experimental designs to infer the existence of a theory of mind has had a substantial impact. Even the sophisticated experiments now undertaken by Povinelli (1996) are frustratingly inconclusive, and seem largely to raise further problems, notably the bearing of chimpanzee ontogeny on how appropriate experiments can be designed. Moreover Gomez (1996) has stressed how most experiments and observations have been designed to explore whether chimpanzees have a theory of the human mind, whereas a chimpanzee theory of mind should be about the mind of a chimpanzee. As humans do not know what the chimpanzee mind is like, we are severely constrained in trying to find out whether another chimpanzee knows what it is like. Smith (1996) has made one of the most effective summaries of the existing anecdotal and experimental data. He concludes that we cannot with certainty infer explicit mind-reading skills in chimpanzees. But we can conclude that they are at least extremely clever behaviourists.

This rather unsatisfactory and inconclusive state of affairs is nevertheless revealing. By the age of four, human children certainly engage in mind reading; indeed they appear to do it continually and compulsively. Without doubt, a profound difference between the human and chimpanzee. This must have arisen during the last five million years of human evolution.

## WHERE AND WHEN IN HUMAN EVOLUTION?

Where and when in human evolution did this change did place? Was it a gradual change or one that appeared quite suddenly? How does it relate to the evolution of other cognitive abilities, notably that of language? In the absence of any clear methodology to address such questions, a reasonable approach is to work back in time from modern humans, addressing what appear to be major developments in evolutionary history and considering whether these may have any bearing on the presence and nature of a theory of mind. The following is a brief sketch of what must be developed into a more substantive study of the palaeoanthropological evidence for the evolution of a theory of mind.


## LATE PLEISTOCENE SOCIETY

An appropriate starting point is with the later Pleistocene societies of the Old and New Worlds, of the period conventionally referred to as the Upper Palaeolithic in Europe and Late Stone Age in Africa (about 40–10 000 radiocarbon years ago). As I noted above, many of these human groups engaged in sophisticated artistic, architectural, technical, and subsistence pursuits: cave paintings in southwestern Europe, mammoth bone dwellings on the Russian plain, mega-faunal hunting in North America. These accomplishments, together with the cultural diversity and rapidity of technological change, persuade many that these late Pleistocene hunter-gatherers were 'modern' in anatomical, behavioural, and cognitive regards (Mellars 1989; Mithen 1996). There seem few grounds to doubt that such hunter-gatherers were 'like us' in their fundamental properties and as such are most likely to have had the same capacity for a theory of mind.

It is valuable, however, to have this assumption occasionally questioned, as Humphrey (1998) has recently chosen to do. He argued that archaeologists have become too complacent in their attribution of a modern human cognition on the basis of Palaeolithic cave paintings: modern individuals with severe cognitive pathologies can also produce impressive, and in some regards strikingly similar, works of art. The majority of the discussants of his views rejected them largely on the basis of contextual evidence: cave paintings were produced as one element of a complex behavioural adaptation to harsh environments. Moreover, Upper Palaeolithic art includes within it certain images that may provide compelling evidence for the presence of a theory of mind. These are the images of imaginary beings, created from the body parts of two or more different species. Classic examples are the lion/man figurine carved from mammoth ivory from Hohlenstein-Stadel, the painted bison/man figure from Chauvet cave, and the painted 'sorcerer' from Trois Frere, a composite from all sorts of animals. As Scott and Baron-Cohen (1996) argued, autistic children whose theory of mind may be inhibited appear to have immense problems in conceiving and depicting imaginary beasts, this being a reflection of their problems with engaging in pretend play. The presence of imaginary beasts in Upper Palaeolithic art, together with associated evidence for ritualistic activity—an activity that normally involves pretence—appears conclusive evidence that those cave painters were also mind readers.


### Middle Palaeolithic humans, theory of mind and the evolution of language

Prior to 40 000 years ago, unambiguous evidence of symbolic activity is absent from the archaeological record. Claimed pieces of art are no more than rather dubious incised pieces of stone and bone which seem to be dramatically over-interpreted by

Bednarik (1995) and Marshack (1997). The archaeological record also has a distinctly different appearance, lacking the high degrees of cultural and temporal variability that we associate with modern behaviour. As I noted above, this is not simply because we are dealing with pre-anatomically modern humans: *Homo sapiens sapiens* in South Africa and Western Asia are associated with a material culture that lacks a symbolic component and is essentially the same as that associated with Neanderthals and archaic *H. sapiens* (Bar-Yosef 1994). Some have argued that the dramatic change in the archaeological record 50–30 000 years ago reflects an equally dramatic cognitive change. Davidson (1991), Mellars (1989), and Bickerton (1996) have associated this with the emergence of modern language, perhaps in a catastrophic fashion, while I have argued that it relates to the replacement of a domain specific with a cognitive fluid mentality (Mithen 1996).

A third position requiring consideration is that it is only around 50 000 years ago that fully modern theory of mind abilities evolve. Could it be possible that prior to that date all species of *Homo* had a theory of mind that was more similar to that of a chimpanzee than a modern human?

An argument in favour of this position is that as the behavioural changes appear quite dramatic, no less than the appearance of symbolic behaviour, we must be dealing with a fundamental shift in human mentality. The increasingly robust anatomical evidence for a linguistic capability in the Neanderthals (Schepartz 1993), and indeed 300 000–year-old *Homo heidelbergensis* at Atapuerca (J.-L. Arsuaga, personal communication), indicate that this shift is unlikely to relate to language. As some form of linguistic ability appears likely to be a precondition for a theory of mind, either in development or evolution (Greenfield 1991; Smith 1996), the late appearance of a fully human-like theory of mind appears to be an ideal candidate as the root cause of the behavioural change around 50 000 years ago. Prior to this time technical and social skills appear already to have been highly sophisticated. What else other than the appearance of theory of mind can provide a sufficiently major development in human cognition to account for the changes in the archaeological record?

There are at least two problems with this argument, and at least one alternative answer. The first problem relates to the technical skills displayed in the levallois technology routinely employed by the Neanderthals, and indeed in other knapping techniques. These appear to be highly sophisticated; they are not easy for modern flint knappers to acquire and replicate (Schlanger 1996). Moreover, the Palaeolithic record suggests very strong social learning of such skills, as particular technical traditions have great longevity in the archaeological record (Mithen 1996). Although direct evidence is absent, it seems most probable that these technical skills and traditions were either intentionally taught from generation to generation, or acquired by passive watching and active imitation. A modern-like theory of mind appears essential to either task (Tomasello *et al.* 1993). Instructed learning requires that both the teacher and the novice take into account of what is in each other's mind—they have to see the learning from each other's point of view. Similarly, the imitation of just the actions of someone knapping stone seems unlikely to enable one to acquire skills such as the levallois technique; one must also imitate the intentions and goals of the knapper, as each specific nodule has different knapping characteristics. Indeed, the immense rarity of teaching and imitation among chimpanzees may well be attributed to the poor theory of mind that they possess.

Consequently in light of the levallois technology that appears at about 250 000 years ago, it appears likely that Neanderthals and other archaic *H. sapiens* possessed a theory of mind more similar to that which we possess today than that of the chimpanzee.

A second argument that pushes the evolution of theory of mind prior to 50 000 years ago is the presence of linguistic abilities in pre-modern humans. There is now a substantial body of anatomical evidence that before 50 000 years ago humans had vocal tracts very similar to—if not the same as—those we possess today (Schepartz 1993). This suggests that vocalisations were sophisticated and essential to the day to day lives of these hominids in a profoundly different way to vocalisation among living non-human primates. We cannot infer whether the early humans had a symbolic component to their utterances, whether they had the same massive lexicons we possess today, or whether they had grammatical complexity. Whether we should write about Neanderthal language, proto-language, speech, or vocalisations is a moot point, and one is as dependent upon one's definitions as on any evidence. But the simple fact that a modern vocal tract, and the necessary cognitive modules to make it worthwhile, had been selected suggests that we are dealing with a phenomenon far closer to modern human language than ape vocalisations.

Some would argue that this ability would act as the foundation for the evolution of a theory of mind (Smith 1996). But the relationship between language and theory of mind is likely to be more intertwined. When dealing with ontogeny, one of the continuing unresolved problems that linguists face is how children can learn the meaning of words. When a parent points to a moving stripy creature and says 'look cat', how does the child manage to associate the utterance 'cat' with the moving creature? The pointed finger might be directed at a multitude of objects, there may be several simultaneous events, and the parent may be giving a warning or command. Bloom (1997, personal communication) has suggested that to acquire words at the phenomenal rate observed during childhood, children require some type of theory of mind. They need to have an idea of what the parent is thinking and how his/her mind state differs from their own to be so very good at associating the correct utterance with the correct referent.

This is a powerful argument and one with considerable evolutionary significance. It seems unlikely that complex language abilities could have evolved within a mind that remained with a chimpanzee-like theory of mind. Conversely, and as Smith (1996) and Harris (1996) have argued, it seems quite unlikely that complex theory of mind ability would have evolved within a mind that remained with a chimpanzee level of vocal communication. In this regard, therefore, pre-50 000 humans with anatomical evidence for what is probably a modern-like linguistic capacity, should also be attributed with a modern like theory of mind capacity.

This leaves us with a dilemma. If the dramatic behavioural changes inferred from the changes in the archaeological record 50–30 000 years ago relate to neither the appearance of language nor theory of mind, then what do they relate to? As an answer I will simply invoke the argument I have made in detail elsewhere: the appearance of symbolism and cultural dynamism derive from the transition to a cognitively fluid from a domain specific mentality (Mithen 1996). In the latter there had been limited, if any, connection between discrete 'intelligences' which I conceive of as bundles of interacting mental modules. Those relating to language and theory of mind were part of a social intelligence. As I will explain below, although this transition does not appear to involve any new content to human theory of mind abilities, it transformed the contexts in which they were used.

### Middle Pleistocene encephalisation as the source of language and theory of mind

There appear to have been two 'spurts' in the growth of the human brain during the last five million years of human evolution (Aiello 1996). The first was around two million years ago which saw the brain enlarge from about 500 to 750 cc and was related to the first appearance of the Homo genus. A considerable portion of this early brain enlargement can be explained by an increase in body size (Ruff *et al.* 1997). In addition, it appears explicable by reference to a nexus of issues relating to bipedalism, tool use, diet, and group size, all of which appear to have been connected in feedback loops. The specific relationships between these and encephalisation remain unclear; but the arguments from Aiello, Wheeler, Falk and Dunbar are persuasive that relationships do exist and that the evolution of neither language nor theory of mind need to be invoked to explain the first spurt in brain growth at about two million years ago (Aiello and Dunbar 1993; Aiello and Wheeler 1995; Falk 1990; Wheeler 1991, 1994).

The second 'spurt' of brain growth occurred between 600 000 and 150 000 years ago, following a period of relative stasis in brain, anatomical, and cultural evolution (Aiello 1996; Ruff *et al.* 1997). Explaining this second period of brain growth is much more challenging. Arguments about changing group size and diet appear quite inadequate. There are no clear developments in the archaeological record that correlate with this period of brain growth; the only innovation appears to have been the presence of the levallois technique and greater use of flake (mode 3) technologies after 300 000 years ago (Mithen 1996). As noted above, hominids after this date appear to have had anatomical adaptations for speech/language. As these were not present within *Homo ergaster* at one and a half million years ago (Aiello 1996), it seems most likely that the encephalisation between 600 000 and 150 000 years ago was directly related to the co-evolution of language and theory of mind (within a relatively isolated domain of social intelligence).

### Early handaxe manufacture and the colonisation of Eurasia as pre-modern theory of mind developments

In this scenario there are at least two major developments represented in the archaeological record prior to 600 000 years ago that need to be accounted for without invoking a fully modern theory of mind. One is the earliest appearance of Acheulian technology—assemblages with high frequencies of handaxes. The first handaxes appeared at about 1.4 million years ago (Schick and Toth 1993). The biface technology required to manufacture handaxes is considerably more complex than that required to make Oldowan choppers. Moreover, handaxes are frequently described as showing considerable regularity within and between assemblages, suggesting that imitation was essential for their manufacture. Yet the examples invoked to support such claims come predominately from the later Acheulian, from sites such as Olorgesailie (Kenya) and Boxgrove (England). Both of these date to about 500 000 years ago, when some degrees of language and theory of mind may have appeared. The earliest handaxes, such as those from Upper Bed 2 at Olduvai, lack the sophistication of these later implements and would have required less advanced cognitive abilities (Wynn 1989).

The colonisation of Eurasia might also be initially taken as an event(s) likely to reflect the appearance of new cognitive abilities. The initial dispersal of hominids out of Africa where their lineage had evolved for the last about four million years is without doubt one of the major behavioural developments in human evolution. Dennell (1983) stressed the new challenges posed by moving into high latitude environments, with increased seasonality and less abundant plant foods than in African equatorial regions. Recent dating and new finds have, however, pushed the colonisation of Asia back from the one million years ago previously accepted, close to 1.8 million (Larick and Ciochan 1996). Although each piece of evidence for such an early date in Asia, such as the stone artefacts from Riwat, Pakistan, hominid tooth fragments from Longuppo cave, China, and dates on *H. erectus* from Java, is open to question, the accumulation of such evidence is impressive. As such, this development may be no more than another manifestation of the diet/tool use/sociality complex that seems to account for the first spurt of brain growth.

The date for the first colonisation of Europe is equally unclear. Fossil remains from TD6 at Atapuerca seem to indicate a hominid presence by 800 000 years ago, while stone artefacts from the Ocre basin may push the date of colonisation back by a further million years (Dennell and Roebroeks 1996). Yet these traces of early settlement appear very ephemeral when compared to those which appeared at about 500 000 years ago, marked by the occupation of northern areas, the hunting of big game, and manufacture of handaxes. This change at 500 000 years ago seems to have been the more significant development and is likely to have derived from early linguistic and theory of mind abilities.

## A SPECULATIVE FOUR-STAGE SCENARIO FOR THE EVOLUTION OF THEORY OF MIND

Modern theory of mind abilities and linguistic skills could not have evolved from an chimpanzee-like level among Plio-Pleistocene hominids in one catastrophic step. Harris (1996) has argued that a 'desire' psychology develops prior to a 'belief–desire' psychology within the child—understanding other people's desires, and that they have desires, seems easier than the equivalent for beliefs. The transition occurs, Harris argues, when children begin to engage in conversation. Perhaps we should also consider this from an evolutionary perspective. Could it be the case that there was a phase in the evolution of modern theory of mind abilities in which our ancestors and relatives had a desire but not a belief–desire psychology? I suspect that this is indeed the case, with the transition occurring around 500 000 years ago. As such the appearance of the first handaxes and occupation of Eurasia may well have had a cognitive root which distinguished the hominids responsible for these from the Plio-Pleistocene Oldowan tool makers.

In this scenario those Oldowan tool makers would have had an equivalent theory of mind ability to that found within chimpanzees today—possibly no theory of mind. As an alternative they would have been extremely clever behaviourists. This can be referred to as the first stage of an evolving theory of mind. Following this, we have a phase of early humans with a desire psychology—the second stage. This somehow allows the production of handaxes, perhaps by enabling a novice to appreciate the goals of an experienced tool maker. This in turn is followed by a belief–desire psychology, which co-evolves with language and is related to the encephalisation after 600 000 years ago leading to modern size brains by 150 000 years ago.

This third stage is not, however, the final stage of the evolution of theory of mind abilities. It is characteristic of modern humans to attribute non-human animals (especially pets), inert objects (e.g. religious icons), and natural events (e.g. thunder) with beliefs, desires, and intentions. In other words our theory of mind abilities are used in a variety of 'inappropriate' contexts—they are regularly applied to entities that a 'scientific' analysis or a moment's reflection makes clear that 'minds' are likely to be absent. This propensity for cross-modal thought appears to lie at the basis of religious beliefs (Boyer 1994). So while the third stage of the evolution of theory of mind is the appearance of our fully modern capacities in hominids before 50 000 years ago, those after this date can be attributed with a fourth stage—the application of these abilities to non-human entities. This final stage, an essential element of the emergence of cognitive fluidity, appears to have had the most dramatic consequences for behavioural and cultural evolution.

## REFERENCES

Aiello, L. (1996). Hominine pre-adaptations for language and cognition. In *Modelling the Early Human Mind*, (ed. P. Mellars and K. Gibson), pp. 89–102. McDonald Institute for Archaeological Research, Cambridge.

Aiello, L. and Dunbar, R. (1993). Neocortex size, group size and the evolution of language. *Current Anthropology*, **34**, 184–93.

Aiello, L. and Wheeler, P. (1995). The expensive tissues hypothesis. *Current Anthropology*, **36**, 199–221.

Aitchison, J. (1996). *The seeds of speech, language origin and evolution*. Cambridge University Press.

Astington, P. (1996). What is theoretical about a child's theory of mind?: a Vygotskian view of its development. In *Theories of theories of mind*, (ed. P. Carruthers and P. K. Smith), pp. 184–99. Cambridge University Press.

Bar-Yosef, O. (1994). The contributions of south west Asia to the study of modern human origins. In *Origins of anatomically modern humans*, (ed. M. H. Nitecki and D. V. Nitecki), pp. 23–66. Plenum Press, New York.

Baron-Cohen, S. (1995). *Mindblindness.* MIT Press, Cambridge, MA.

Baron-Cohen, S. and Swettenham, J. (1996). The relationship between SAM and ToMM: two hypotheses. In *Theories of theories of mind*, (ed. P. Carruthers and P. K. Smith), pp. 158–68. Cambridge University Press.

Bednarik, R. (1995). Concept mediated marking in the Lower Palaeolithic. *Current Anthropology*, **36**, 605–34.

Bickerton, D. (1996). *Human behaviour and language.* UCL Press, London.

Bloom, P. (1997). Paper presented at the 1997 Evolution of Language Conference, April, London.

Boyer, P. (1994). *The naturalness of religious ideas.* University of California Press, Berkeley.

Byrne, R. and Whiten, A. (1992). Cognitive evolution in primates: evidence from tactical deception. *Man (New Series)*, **27**, 609–27.

Carruthers, P. (1996). Simulation and self-knowledge : a defence of theory-theory. In *Theories of theories of mind*, (ed. P. Carruthers and P. K. Smith), pp. 22–38. Cambridge University Press.

Carruthers, P. and Smith, P. K. (ed.) (1996*a*). *Theories of theories of mind.* Cambridge University Press.

Carruthers, P. and Smith, P. K. (1996*b*). Introduction. In *Theories of theories of mind*, (ed. P. Carruthers and P. K. Smith), pp. 1–8. Cambridge University Press.

Davidson, I. (1991). The archaeology of language origins—a review. *Antiquity*, **65**, 39–48

Dennell, R. (1983). *European economic prehistory.* Academic Press, London.

Dennell, R. and Roebroeks, W. (1996). The earliest occupation of Europe: a short chronology revisited. *Antiquity*, **68**, 489–503.

Dunbar, R. (1996). *Gossip, grooming and the evolution of language.* Faber and Faber, London.

Falk, D. (1990). Brain evolution in *Homo*: the 'radiator' theory. *Brain and Behavioural Sciences*, **13**, 333–81.

Gomez, J-C. (1996). Non human primate theories of mind (of non human primate) minds: some issues concerning the origins of mind reading. In *Theories of theories of mind*, (ed. P. Carruthers and P. K. Smith), pp. 330–43. Cambridge University Press.

Gopnik, A. (1996). Theories and modules: creation myths, developmental realities and Neuath's boast. In *Theories of theories of mind*, (ed. P. Carruthers and P. K. Smith), pp. 169–83. Cambridge University Press.

Gordon, R. M. (1996). 'Radical' simulationism. In *Theories of theories of mind*, (ed. P. Carruthers and P. K. Smith), pp. 11–21. Cambridge University Press.

Greenfield, P. M. (1991). Language, tools and brain. *Behavioural and Brain Sciences*, **14**, 531–95.

Harris, P. (1996). Desires, beliefs and language. In *Theories of theories of mind*, (ed. P. Carruthers and P. K. Smith), pp. 200–20. Cambridge University Press.

Heyes, C. M. (1993). Anecdotes, training, trapping and triangulation: do animals attribute mental states? *Animal Behaviour*, **46**, 1023–5.

Humphrey, N. (1998). Cave art, autism and the evolution of the human mind. *Cambridge Archaeological Journal*, **81**, 165–91.

Jones, J. S., Martin, R. and Pilbeam, D. (1992). *The Cambridge encylopedia of human evolution.* Cambridge University Press.

Larick, R. and Ciochan, R. L. (1996). The African emergence and early dispersal of the genus *Homo. American Scientist*, **84**, 538–51.

Marshack, A. (1997). The Berekhat Ram figurine: a late Acheulian carving from the Middle East. *Antiquity*, **71**, 327–37.

Mellars, P. (1989). Major issues in the emergence of modern humans. *Current Anthropology*, **30**, 349–85.

Mithen, S. (1996). *The prehistory of the mind.* Thames and Hudson, London.

Povinelli, D. (1996). Chimpanzee theory of mind?: the long road to strong inference. In *Theories of theories of mind*, (ed. P. Carruthers and P. K. Smith), pp. 293–329. Cambridge University Press.

Renfrew, C. (1983). *Towards an archaeology of mind*. Cambridge University Press.

Renfrew, C. and Zubrow, E. (ed.) (1993). *The ancient mind*. Cambridge University Press.

Ruff, C. B., Trinkaus, E. and Holliday, T. W. (1997). Body mass and encephalization in Pleistocene *Homo*. *Nature*, **387**, 173–6.

Schlanger, N. (1996). Understanding levallois: lithic technology and cognitive archaeology. *Cambridge Archaeological Journal*, **6**, 231–54.

Schepartz, L. (1993). Language and modern human origins. *Yearbook of Physical Anthropology*, **36**, 91–126.

Schick, K. and Toth, N. (1993). *Making silent stones speak*. Simon and Schuster, New York.

Scott, F. C. and Baron-Cohen, S. (1996). Imagining real and unreal things: evidence of a dissociation in autism. *Journal of Cognitive Neuroscience*, **8**, 400–11.

Segal, G. (1996). The modularity of theory of mind. In *Theories of theories of mind*, (ed. P. Carruthers and P. K. Smith), pp. 141–57. Cambridge University Press.

Smith, P. K. (1996). Language and the evolution of mind-reading. In *Theories of theories of mind*, (ed. P. Carruthers and P. K. Smith), pp. 344–52. Cambridge University Press, Cambridge.

Stringer, C. and McKie, R. (1996). *African exodus*. Pimlico, London.

Tomasello, M., Kruger, A. and Ratner, H. (1993). Cultural learning. *Behavioural and Brain Sciences*, **16**, 495–552.

Wheeler, P. (1991). The influence of bipedalism on the energy and water budgets of early hominids. *Journal of Human Evolution*, **21**, 107–36.

Wheeler, P. (1994). The thermoregularity advantages of heat storage and shade seeking behaviour to hominids foraging in equatorial savannah environments. *Journal of Human Evolution*, **26**, 339–50.

Whiten, A. (1996). When does smart behaviour-reading become mind-reading. In *Theories of theories of mind*, (ed. P. Carruthers and P. K. Smith), pp. 277–92. Cambridge University Press.

Wynn, T. (1989). *The evolution of spatial competence*. University of Illinois Press, Urbana.

Wynn, T. (1993). Two developments in the mind of early *Homo*. *Journal of Anthropological Archaeology*, **12**, 299–322.

# 21

# Culture and understanding other minds

PENELOPE G. VINDEN AND JANET WILDE ASTINGTON

---

Psychology has extended its borders during the decade since the first edition of this volume was published, or at least, psychologists have been active in collaborative work at the borders. One aspect of this activity is reflected in the subtitle for this volume: 'Perspectives from cognitive neuroscience'. The addition—'cognitive neuroscience'—acknowledges a burgeoning field of research. This work focuses on the biological underpinnings of development that are universal across our species, even in cases where they may go awry. At the same time, however, there has been a flurry of activity at a very different place on the border. This is where psychology meets with anthropology, drawing attention to the different ways in which humans develop in different cultures.

It is not new to say that development occurs in a cultural context, nor that biology provides constraints on culture. Even if our concern is with the complexities of sociocultural interaction and its development, we cannot ignore their biological foundation (Astington and Olson 1995). The evolutionary and cultural–historical past are integrated in present development and together determine the individual's future. Thus the challenge is to integrate the biological and the cultural view in investigations of development (Bruner 1996). This is so difficult that one might wonder whether it is even possible. Lloyd (1996) asks how we might explain the fact that classical Greek and ancient Chinese scientists developed very different concepts and theories even though they presumably had similar brains as infants. One way, he says, is to argue that there are implicit cognitive universals, despite the differences in explicit theories and concepts developed, 'so there may be a sense in which . . . universalists and comparativists may be arguing past one another, in that the subject matter they are wrestling with is, in the one case, the postulated implicit assumptions, in the other the explicit theories the actors themselves propose' (Lloyd 1996, p. 27). That is to say, there is a danger that those who focus on biological explanations and those who focus on cultural ones cannot even talk to one another because they are grappling with essentially different issues. We hope we are not talking past other authors of chapters in this volume, but rather initiating a crossing of borders that will eventually lead to the kind of co-operation and transformation that we see as crucial to advancing our understanding.

Our aim in this chapter is to discuss theory of mind and autism from the perspective of cultural psychology. We are not sufficiently ambitious to attempt to integrate this view with the neurobiological one. Nonetheless, we believe that it is important to raise the issues we do within the context of this particular volume. It is not a question of 'Why bring culture into the picture?' Culture is always in the picture, whether or not we choose to acknowledge it. Psychology over the years, however, has tended to ignore culture, or has almost taken the attitude that it is something other people have. The ethnocentricity of psychology has manifested itself in many ways, one of which is the fact that when culture has been the focus of attention, often culture has been treated as an independent variable, something which can be controlled for or partialled out or otherwise manipulated in order to compare them to us.

The ethnocentricity of psychology is also evident in how we presently conceive of psychopathology. As several researchers have pointed out (e.g. Good 1992; Kleinman 1988), the current disease-oriented paradigm of mental illness, with its strong roots in biological psychiatry and psychopharmacology, has tended to create diagnostic categories that reify Western psychological concepts. The current DSM-IV does attempt to incorporate 'cultural variations' in the DSM classification (DSM-IV, 1994, p. xxiv). It also includes an appendix on cultural considerations, devoting a scant seven pages to the topic. While recognizing that there might be no one-to-one correspondence between diagnostic categories and 'locality-specific patterns of aberrant behavior' (DSM-IV, 1994, p. 844) the appendix attempts in its 'Glossary of Culture-Bound Syndromes' to match each folk category with the relevant DSM-IV category or categories. Likewise the specific cultural features included in the text of DSM tend to focus on alerting the clinician to how symptoms of 'our' disorders might be expressed in other cultures. A focus on categories of disorder and reliable diagnosis, however, fails to recognize cultural and social diversity and decontextualizes symptoms. To say this is not to say that the current view of autism as a biologically determined deficit in cognitive architecture will lead to less humane treatment of individuals with autism, nor is it to revisit the blame assigning that focused on social factors in explaining autism (e.g. Kanner and Eisenberg 1955). It does suggest, however, that we could benefit from directing our attention to social and cultural dimensions. In our view, explanations of behaviour that fail to take adequate account of the socio–cultural groundedness of all behaviour are missing an important point.

In this chapter we first address the question, 'What is culture?' Then we examine evidence for and against the universality of theory of mind development, through an investigation of research both from within and outside the field of theory of mind. Finally, we suggest a way that autism can be viewed from a cultural perspective.


## WHAT IS CULTURE?

A variety of definitions of culture exist, each reflecting the particular epistemological and methodological preferences of those who espouse them. One watershed among these definitions divides cross-cultural from cultural psychology. The epistemological roots of this distinction are grounded in different conceptions of what culture is, and how we come to know psychological phenomena.

Cultural psychologists, inasmuch as we can lump them into one group, tend to think of psychological phenomena as part of the shared activities and shared meaning creation that constitute the cultural process of social interaction. Human beings are cultural beings—there is no behaviour and there is no interpretation of behaviour that is not cultural. Shweder (1991, p. 74) defines cultural psychology as the idea that 'no sociocultural environment exists or has identity independently of the way human beings seize meanings and resources from it, while, on the other hand, every human being's subjectivity and mental life are altered through the process of seizing meanings and resources from some sociocultural environment and using them'. Cole (1996, p. 143) talks about culture as 'medium' and uses the metaphor of a garden to underscore the nurturing aspect of culture as an environment for linking the microworld of the child to the macroworld of the external environment. A cultural psychological point of view sees culture and psychology as mutually constitutive—Miller (1994, p. 144) describes this as the assumption that 'the individual is always a participant in a culture, with his/her subjectivity informed by cultural meanings and practices, and thus that no sharp dichotomy can be drawn between what is psychology and what is culture'.

Cross-cultural psychologists, on the other hand, tend to view culture as something that is separate and separable from human activity, something that can be viewed apart from the individual. Culture is a set of attitudes, beliefs, and scripts for action that form the basis for and context of human behaviour. Berry *et al.* (1992, p. 2) define cross-cultural psychology as 'the study of similarities and differences in individual psychological functioning in various cultural and ethnic groups; of the relationship between psychological variables and sociocultural, ecological, and biological variables; and of current changes in these variables'. Triandis (1994, p. 5) describes culture as something that influences behaviour, a set of unstated assumptions about the world and how people should act in it. It is 'an interplay of sameness and difference': all humans share certain general categories, but there are numerous differences in the way cultures apply these categories in specific situations.

These different views of culture lead to different research methodologies, which Miller (1994) and Greenfield (1997) discuss and evaluate in some detail. Cross-cultural psychologists have tended to view culture as an independent variable (or a group of independent variables), and the individual as a complex of dependent variables. Thus cross-cultural psychologists have tended primarily to use quantitative methods in their research. Cultural psychologists, on the other hand, are more interested in the process of social interaction, and tend toward more qualitative analyses of those interactions. Again, this is an oversimplification of a very complex issue. Cross-cultural psychologists today are keenly aware that culture is a global concept, and 'must be decomposed into a set of psychologically meaningful constructs, which are then used to explain the cultural differences observed' (Van de Vijver and Leung 1997, p. 260).

The difference between the two views can be seen in a description of two representative journals, *The Journal of Cross-Cultural Psychology* and *Culture and Psychology*. The cross- cultural journal describes itself as follows:

Its main emphasis is on empirical research wherein independent variables as influenced by culture may obtain different values and the subjects are from at least two different cultural groups. The concern is with individual differences and variation across cultures rather than with societal variation (e.g. sociology). Research exclusively including as subjects members of ethnic minorities within one country must be replicable among or across clearly distinguishable culture groups.

The cultural psychology journal describes itself in the following way:

. . . a genuinely interdisciplinary journal that develops a critical and socially embedded understanding of the self by drawing on diverse theoretical perspectives and empirical reflections upon psychological phenomena . . . *Culture and Psychology* rejects the static models of persons, cultures and societies that have dominated most of the discourse in the social sciences, in favour of the view that people are continuously developing dynamic systems, as are the social groups, communities and institutions in which they are enmeshed.

These two self-descriptions serve to highlight the differences between a cross-cultural and a cultural approach. The former sees culture as an outside influence on individual development which results in variation across cultures. The hope of finding underlying universals of development is implicit in the desire always to include at least two cultural groups in the analysis. This quest for universals is explicitly formulated in the self-description offered by the Society for Cross-Cultural Research, whose stated purpose is to 'support and encourage interdisciplinary, comparative research that has as its object the establishment of scientifically derived generalizations about human behaviour'. A cultural approach, however, considers psychological processes to be inextricably bound with local practices, and thus often focuses on a single culture and the multiple processes (historical, community, and so on) that constitute individual development and are themselves shaped by the developing individuals.

Culture, when viewed from a traditional cross-cultural perspective, is often a synonym for race or ethnicity. As such, it has been accorded a secondary status in mainstream psychology. Yet the cross-cultural search for universals among diverse instantiations of behaviour is really much more in accord with Western psychology's thrust than is cultural psychology's focus on diversity. The assumption has been that the basic psychological processes that we (primarily we in 'the West') have 'found' are basic to all people everywhere. The study of people in distant places, or even the study of ethnic groups within North America or Europe, while very interesting, serves only to illuminate how 'culture' can influence these basic universal processes. This concept of culture (and of psychology) serves to encourage researchers to regard culture as an independent variable. In the worst case scenario, after statistical analyses are completed, Hispanics or Koreans or Caucasians or whoever are found to perform better or worse on this or that task, and speculation begins as to why.[1] In a better case, investigators seek to identify and measure precise elements of the cultural variables that are of interest, and proceed to examine the relationships between these variables and the psychological phenomenon of interest.

A detailed discussion of the advantages and disadvantages of each of these two basic views is beyond the scope of this chapter. From our perspective, however, the cross-cultural view fails to take sufficient account of the interrelatedness and inter-dependence of culture and psychology. We should note that the way in which we describe cross-cultural psychology here corresponds most closely to early cross-cultural work and that current work by cross-cultural psychologists is moving closer toward a cultural psychological viewpoint (see Berry *et al.* 1997; the variety of approaches now represented within the cross-cultural view are thoroughly examined in their second edition of the *Handbook of cross-cultural psychology*, (Vol. 1: Theory and method)). Be that as it may, mainstream psychology still takes a primarily cross-cultural view; for example Lillard (1998) ends her masterful summary of cultural variations in the understanding of mind, by calling for more well-designed cross-cultural studies with quantifiable results to help determine whether theory of mind is universal.

Cultural psychologists, on the other hand, argue that culture cannot be reduced to a simple variable, or even a cluster of variables. Rather, culture and self, culture and mind, are inextricably tied, and all behaviour is cultural. In fact, as we will later maintain, mind is a culturally constituted entity, not a natural kind. Furthermore, viewing autism as a culturally constituted category will enable us to gain insight into understanding how individuals with autism understand social interactions within their world.

## CULTURE AND THEORY OF MIND

The majority of theory of mind research has been conducted in what we regretfully refer to as 'Western' cultures. When we use the term 'Western' we capitulate to an ethnocentricity that we do not subscribe to, which divides the world into them and us, which takes Europe or North America as the starting point and then proceeds to carve up the world as if it were flat. Many such general terms serve only to divide and marginalize, and we fear 'the West' is one of them. But we still lack a better term to describe what seem to be very real differences. 'Collectivist' and 'individualist' might start us on the way; 'Euro-American' divides along other lines; 'dominant' and 'dominated' is too politically charged, if somewhat accurate. So we shall continue to use the term 'Western,' acknowledging its limitations, fully aware that there is no single monolithic culture, and that a great variety of 'non-Western' cultures coexist in the same geographical space.

The term 'theory of mind' is also problematic (Astington 1996), because it refers to the generic field of study, but stacks the deck in favour of the child's understanding of mind being theoretical in nature. Arguing for or against the various theories of theory of mind is not our concern here, and the term will be used to indicate the understanding of mind that typically develops among middle-class Western children.

The Western research, conducted primarily in Western Europe, Canada, and the United States, has tended to produce results that point to a theory of mind developmental 'burst' occurring between the ages of three and five. Three-year-olds typically fail standard theory of mind tasks, some four-year-olds struggle, and five-year-olds generally exhibit a theory of mind, predicting the behavioural outcomes of false beliefs with relative ease. More recent research, which focuses on individual differences in development, has found that a variety of factors are associated with theory of mind development including language development (Hughes, in press; Jenkins and Astington 1996), emotion understanding (Dunn 1995; Hughes and Dunn, in press; Vinden 1999), pretend play (Astington and Jenkins 1995; Hughes and Dunn 1997), family size (Lewis *et al.* 1996; Perner *et al.* 1994), parenting style (Vinden 1997), and social class (Cutting and Dunn, in press). Yet few studies have been conducted that look at children from non-Western cultures, either living in the West or elsewhere.

Those studies that have been conducted outside the West deserve special mention here. Two were conducted in industrialized literate settings in China and Japan and support the hypothesis that a theory of mind develops universally, without regard to culture (Flavell *et al.* 1983; Gardner *et al.* 1988). Avis and Harris (1991) extended theory of mind research into a new realm, that of a non-urban group of hunters and gatherers, the Baka of Cameroon. They found that young four- to five-year-old Baka children not only passed a simple false-belief task, but also were able accurately to predict the emotional state of the person holding the false belief.

Around the time Avis and Harris were testing Baka children, one of us was conducting research in a predominantly preliterate agrarian context—among Quechua speakers in the Andes of central Peru (Vinden 1996). One challenge was that there are no separate lexical items in this Quechuan language for many mental states—notably thoughts and beliefs. For example, in this particular dialect of Quechua, the phrase 'he would say' is the closest equivalent to the English 'he thinks'. In the absence of mental-state terms, we wondered whether Quechua children would develop an understanding of minds that was similar to that developed by children in industrialized, literate, urban settings. The research plan was to administer several theory of mind tasks, including an appearance–reality task using a sponge that looks like a rock. When framing this latter task in Quechua, an abundance of words used to describe the appearances of things was discovered. Not surprisingly, the percentage of Quechua children between the ages of four and eight answering both of the appearance–reality questions correctly was above chance. Yet all the children found all questions about mental states very difficult, performing at or below chance, even on a question that simply asked where another person would look for a hidden object.

The results of this research, then, shed some doubt on the universality of a theory of mind. Not content with a single exception to the 'rule', Vinden (1999) conducted similar research in Africa and Papua New Guinea among three very different indigenous groups, as well as a group of North American, Australian, and European children living in Papua, New Guinea. This time the methodology of the Avis and Harris study was followed more closely by involving the children in creating a false belief in another person, and by including a component concerning the prediction of emotion in the other. Results showed that among two of the three non-Western groups, children eventually come to understand that people will act on the basis of what they believe, rather than merely reacting to the way the world is—although several years later than the Western children. However, one group, the Tainae of Papua New Guinea, found the direct question about the other's thoughts much more difficult than the question about where the other would look, and even children as old as fifteen did not perform above chance on the direct question about another's thoughts. On other tasks, only the oldest children performed above chance on false belief and representational change questions using their word for *think*. This raises questions whether asking about someone's overt behaviour is really the same as asking about someone's thoughts, and whether the Tainae conception of mind is really similar in all respects to our understanding of mind.

Regarding the children's ability to predict an emotion based on a false belief, the English-speaking children appeared to follow the usual path from a situation–desire understanding of emotion to a belief–desire understanding. The other three groups of children, however, did not show a clear progress toward a mentalistic understanding of emotion. These data then open the question as to whether there might be some cultures where a conception of mind shares some but not all of the features of a theory of mind.

The research in non-Western cultures presented above has a strong cross-cultural flavour to it. In each case, tasks developed in North America and Europe to study North American and European children's understanding of mind were adapted for use in the other cultures. While pains were taken in each case to ensure that the best possible translations were used, and that the objects shown to the children were culturally appropriate, the tasks themselves evolved from our prior understanding of ourselves as people who have minds, who impute mental states to others, who explain behaviour in terms of our own and others' mental states, and so on.

What would a cultural (rather than a cross-cultural) study of mind look like? There is no single established methodology for cultural psychology, but a cultural study of mind might begin by examining language acquisition, particularly the social context in which children learn language, and the particular concepts that are lexicalized within their language. Language is fundamental because it is through language that we create culture. It is a tool for interacting—language use is not an individual process, but a joint action among participants based on a common ground, which in broadest terms is a shared cultural background (Clark 1996). Children's own cognitive resources for language acquisition are crucial, but it is by virtue of growing up within Western culture that children acquire our theory of mind. We take a mentalistic stance to ourselves and other people, including the youngest of other people, that is, infants. We ascribe mental states to them in the ways we interact with them and in the lexical terms we use (Astington 1999). Thus, in acquiring our language children acquire our theory of mind, which is embedded in our speech practices. Other cultures may have quite different conceptions of mind, or the concept 'mind' may not exist in every culture. That is, there may be different ways of explaining behaviour that allow for adequate social interaction without relying on 'mind-reading'. How can we step outside ourselves to imagine such a situation?

A helpful way of conceiving of the problem of what minds might be for other cultures, or more radically, what the alternative to mind might be in other cultures, is provided by the work of Hobson (1993). Hobson turns our focus away from seeing the key issue in sociocognitive development as being the development of a theory of mind, and invites us rather view to the development of the concept of person as being more fundamental. A person, for Hobson (1993, p. 115) 'is that particular kind of 'thing' that has both a body and a mind'. Hobson claims that not all mental states are unobservable. In his discussion of the intersubjective sharing that takes places between infants and care-givers, he claims that infants do not first perceive bodies and then infer minds, but rather 'they have direct perception of and natural engagement with person-related 'meanings' that are apprehended *in* the expressions and behaviour of other persons' (Hobson 1993, p. 117).

Hobson's views provide us with a jumping-off point for thinking about how other cultures might conceive of the mind. Could the concept of person be the universal basis for all human relationships, rather than the concept of mind? If persons are conceived of as 'having' both bodies and minds in our culture, and if developing these concepts comes to govern both how we relate and how we explain, predict, and react to behaviour, could there not be other ways to divide up personhood? Not too long ago, a typical Western way to view the person was as a tripartite body, mind, and soul/ spirit, and that view is still prevalent in some circles today. Even if we were to find among other cultures concepts resembling our notions of body and mind (setting aside for now the question of souls), would they necessarily function in the same way in every culture? Could some cultures emphasize one aspect of the person much more than other cultures? Perhaps, with our focus on the understanding of mind, we reveal a cultural 'obsession' with minds that may not be universal. Perhaps children else-where develop a theory of behaviour, or a theory of body, or a theory of possession, or multiple theories that are applied in different culturally-defined contexts. There is another important question here, namely whether or not the child's understanding of mind (or behaviour or body or anything else) is really theoretical. One of us has debated this issue elsewhere (Astington 1996, 1998) and we will not enter it again now. Suffice it to say that here we use the term 'theory of mind' to refer to children's understanding of mind, however that is constituted.

Before we are accused of indulging in idle speculation that the idea of persons with minds may not be universal, let us turn to a discussion of the evidence that exists outside the theory of mind field that lends support to the notion that there might be different developmental trajectories with regard to acquiring concepts which aid us in carrying on everyday social interactions. The evidence comes largely but not exclusively from the field of psychological anthropology.

## SELF, PERSONHOOD, AND MIND: OTHER VIEWS

We begin, not with a discussion of contemporary cultures that have been studied, but with the ancient Greeks. From their language we have brought many terms into English, though, as we shall see, there is a great chasm between their concepts and ours. Whereas we place the centre of consciousness in the head, or sometimes the heart if we are talking more about the whole person, they place it in what has been colour-fully referred to by one researcher as the 'innards' (Padel 1992). We retain today perhaps a little of this Greek heritage in our expression 'to spill your guts'.

The ancient Greeks had three main terms for what we might call mental faculties—*thumos, psuche,* and *nous*. Padel translates the first term as 'spirit', noting that 'soul' or 'heart' seem to be better translations in some circumstances, and 'desire' and 'courage' in others (Padel 1992, p. 27). *Thumos* is central to anger and is described physically in a variety of ways, ranging from liquid to breath, from a container that can be filled to a site of emotion or debate. *Psuche* is also volatile and has meanings ranging from life, self, and mind, to ghost and perception. It feels, endures, can shake in agitation, fly, and wander. It is able to continue after the death of the body, but still resembles that self's body in Hades. *Nous* is most frequently translated 'mind' but it is not pure intellect—it feels emotion, depends on the fortunes that the gods send, and grows old with the body.

These are only the mind-words from the fifth century—there are many others that describe emotions, energy, and life-force. Each of the mind-words resonate at times with our concept of mind, yet each is described using bodily language. Ancient Greek words for emotions share even more of this physicalness, some being either actual words for internal organs or fluids (e.g. 'heart', for which there are three words, 'liver', and 'bile') or else described as liquids or fluids. The most interesting aspect of both the mind and emotion words, however, is how intertwined their usage is with the 'blood and guts' side of bodily existence. Reading example after example of these terms one sees that this is not mere metaphor—we might say someone is hot-tempered, or that our heart aches, but we would not examine entrails and apply what we see to ourselves. The boundary between metaphor and literal is fuzzy for the ancient Greeks, as is any boundary between mind and body.

We need not look so far back in history, however, to see a conception of person, or self, that is quite different from the one to which we are accustomed. Lutz's (1985) work among the Ifaluk, who live on an atoll in Micronesia, provides another perspective on what it might mean to have a non-Western understanding of mind. Like the ancient Greeks, the Ifaluk have a generic term for 'insides' that refers to the individual's physiological and psychological functions—thoughts, emotions, desires, illness, and physical sensations. Lutz is quick to point out that 'no sharp distinctions are made between thought and emotion, between the head and the heart, or between a conscious and unconscious mind'—to say that my insides are bad 'may mean either that one is feeling physically bad or experiencing bad thoughts and emotions, or both' (Lutz 1985, pp. 46–47). Also like the ancient Greeks, the Ifaluk have many words to describe these inner states, and these terms show an overlap and interpenetration of the psychological and the physical—for example *nunuwan*, a word for thought/emotion, which is something you can have lots of or little, many or one, it can be long or short, can be good or bad.

How do the Ifaluk explain and evaluate behaviour? To be sure, they do use terms like nunuwan in their explanations. Yet the 'causal chain' seems to proceed from situation to inner state to action. Lutz reports that 'the cause of behavior is not conceptualized as located in an inner wellspring so much as in environmental triggers. The most important facets of these situations, moreover, include the behavior of others' (Lutz 1985, p. 57). In fact, others are often seen as being responsible for one's own internal states. Other explanations include craziness (a persistent inability to act in socially prescribed ways), the spirits (though this is rare), the influence of another's thoughts or emotions, or personality traits (though this is only in exceptional cases).

Gerber (1985), in her studies of emotion among the Samoan, reports a similar lack of focus on the inner as the locus of explanations for behaviour. When an individual is asked why he or she thinks another has behaved in a certain way, the response is likely to be not about thoughts or emotions, but rather about personal gain. Gerber concludes that what prevents her informants from answering her questions is a belief about our access to the thoughts and feelings of others. Samoans frequently say 'we cannot know what is in another person's depths . . . we cannot tell what another person is thinking' (Gerber 1985, p. 133). When pressed for explanations, they give very few descriptions of internal sensations, but rather describe the actions that result from the feelings, or the kinds of situations that typically arise during which such feelings would be appropriate responses. So important is this social, external orientation of emotion for the Samoans, that they almost never talk about the internal somatic quality of emotions, even though there was plenty of evidence, according to Gerber, that bodily changes such as muscle tension and physical arousal were taking place.

The work of Fajans (1985) among the Baining of Papua New Guinea shows that this (to us) extreme external focus is not unique to the Samoans. In her words, 'evaluations of events do not invoke an internal, emotional explanation' (Fajans 1985, p. 383). It is not only people in Pacific cultures who seem to find the mind of the other in some sense unknowable—Warren (1995), for example, reports that the Kaqchikel Maya use the phrase 'each mind is a world' to explain that one cannot really know the thoughts and motivations of others. However, while not speculating on *others'* subjective attitudes is common in many non-Western societies, the Baining are reluctant to utter even their own opinions. The Baining are person-oriented, but not predominantly individualistically-oriented—'the Baining personality is social in more than the ordinary sense, and the particular Baining are unusually dependent on the surrounding sociality of their own group and the customary patterns of behavior for their self-definition' (Fajans 1985, p. 384). Idiosyncratic behaviour is tolerated, and individuality accepted, but without question or explanation. Deviant behaviour is seen as a reversion to a 'natural' state of the individual untransformed by social interaction and, though rarely discussed or even acknowledged, is often attributed to the influence of ghosts. Indeed, when asked about persons who have temporarily acted in a 'crazy' manner, other Baining give the impression of simply not remembering the incident. Interestingly, only a young man who had spent considerable time outside his culture and had greater education than most was able or willing to discuss some of the 'known' incidents.

The cultures discussed here represent only the tip of the iceberg in terms of the variety that is to be found in how different groups of people conceptualize persons and their interactions. Lillard (1998) describes a great deal more. However, even from this brief foray into non-Western views of the person, two important ideas can be gleaned. First, we see that with a collectivist or group orientation, personal, mental, and emotional states are relatively unimportant. This is not to say that either Samoan or Baining individuals are incapable of understanding these states as inner, or personal, nor is it to say that they have no concept of individuality or of persons as having some 'inner' side. Rather it is to say that these groups have 'chosen' not to go in the same direction as we have in how they make sense of social interactions. To insist that, although they do not spontaneously talk about interactions as we do, they really do conceive of these interactions in the same way as we do, would be as odd as them insisting that, although we talk about mental states all the time, we *really* see the causes of behaviour as existing in external situational and environmental influences.

The second important thing to note comes from the phrase 'customary patterns of behavior' (Gerber 1985, p. 384). In a culture where social interactions are limited, where diversity is restricted (extremely so for the Ifaluk, population 430 in 1985, who live on an atoll 500 miles from the island of Truk), patterns of behaviour will be far fewer, more confined, and highly predictable. It may be the existence of predictable behaviour that mitigates against the need to know and talk about others' mental states. More than that, to conceive of people as individuals, each with discrete thought lives and each with discrete emotional lives, could be hazardous to the well-being of the group. It is not adaptive in these cultures to think in terms of individuals each holding their own personal, private mental states. In a culture where the only Social Security is getting along with one's kin and neighbours (who are often one and the same), individuality may be a dangerous thing.

Each of the cultures discussed above makes some sort of distinction between what happens inside a person, and what happens outside. But how clear this distinction is, whether or not they draw sharp lines between mental/emotional and external causes of behaviour, whether or not they use their knowledge of the internal to predict others' actions—all this seems to vary from culture to culture. What happens when a culture does not talk about the internal states of another? It would seem natural that children would not only not talk about others' mental states, but in fact might not think about them much at all, or at least might not see their knowledge of others' inner states as particularly pertinent to their behaviour. Such a view of behaviour would help explain the results found in children's ability to predict an emotion based on a false belief (Vinden 1999). It also helps explain why Quechua children found questions about the appearance and reality of a deceptive object easier than questions about a naive viewer's belief about the object (Vinden 1996). Their language has a well-developed vocabulary for talking about the appearances of things but not for people's thoughts about them, and thus presumably the children were used to thinking about appearances of things, but did not think about beliefs. When given a forced choice of emotions, children from all three non-Western cultures did not simply refuse to answer, but the majority gave an answer which assumed the other would act is if his behaviour were not mentally motivated, but merely motivated by whatever would accomplish his goal.

The kinds of activities that we engage in most frequently serve to construct a social milieu in which certain types of behaviours, certain types of interactions, and certain ways of thinking are deemed 'appropriate'. We form, to steal a term from D'Andrade (1985), 'cultural models' of the worlds that we live in. In societies where there is constant communal living, where someone is almost always there to see what you are doing, perhaps there is less need for an extensive understanding of thought life and its relation to action because of the ever-present social control of behaviour. Under these conditions, everything that is felt or thought is in some sense prescribed by others.

Infants in our culture are, in one sense, living in a communal situation. They have little control over their private life—they are held, fed, changed, put to bed, played with, or left alone according to the desires of their caretakers. Nonetheless, from their earliest days, parents treat infants as individuals, and ascribe beliefs and intentions to their cries and gestures. As children grow older they are still in some senses under adult control—but in our culture that control extends from manipulation of behaviour to manipulation of thoughts. We want little Sarah to eat her vegetables, not simply because we want her to, but because they are good for her. So we think that if we change her thoughts about vegetables eventually she will change her own behaviour. Similarly, we want Billy to stop hitting his sister, so we often say things like 'how would you feel if you were being hit?'

Social control, then, plays an important role in the development of an understanding of mind. Because our society values individuality so highly, social control is focused on moving the child toward a particular theory of behaviour as caused by an individual's thoughts. In cultures where the community is valued over the individual, the notion of agency may develop in a radically different way. Rather than forming a 'Western' psychological theory as to the relation of thought and behaviour, children in other cultures may simply learn that an agent is someone who acts in expectable ways under expectable circumstances.

## CULTURE AND AUTISM

From a cross-cultural perspective, culture would seem to have little to do with autism. We might seek to look at the different ways different cultures view autism, for example examining how non-autistic individuals interact with individuals with autism in a variety of cultures. Or we might seek to catalogue the incidence of autism in various cultures, and study different explanations that are given to the phenomena. Note, however, that this view is entirely separate from (yet compatible with) a strictly biological maturation view of autism. Culture might have some influence to trigger the unfolding of a module, but otherwise is something quite separate from the phenomenon itself.

However, from the perspective of cultural psychology that we have developed in this chapter, human beings are first and foremost culture-makers. Culture-making is grounded in establishing connections among human beings. Making that connection seems to be hard-wired in normal individuals. The Genesis account of creation says it well, as it tells of an instant recognition between two of the species: surely this is flesh of my flesh, and bone of my bone, or, to put it in more modern terms, 'Now here is something I can relate to'. A theory of mind is not the basis for this recognition, and it is not the basis for social relationships. Rather, it is a cultural outcome of connecting. We connect, we engage in culture-making, and gradually an understanding of persons—when, how, and why they relate—emerges. Because we as infants are primarily interacting with experts in the field of relating, our 'social cognition' develops in particular directions, according to various historical, familial, and environmental forces that preceded us. The particular direction in which the social cognition of some groups of people develops has become known as a theory of mind.

If connecting through social interaction, in particular language-mediated social interaction, is crucial for the child's development, then the child with autism is in difficulty from the start. How soon this lack of ability to connect manifests itself is shown by the early age at which autistic behaviours are seen to occur. Social deficits have been noted from very early in life (see Charman, Chapter 17, this volume). It may be that whatever has gone awry in the brain predisposes the child to be incapable of participating in either the shared activities or shared meaning making from which a theory of mind arises. By not participating in the 'culture game' the autistic child has no chance to develop 'normally' but rather starts down a path which can only take him (or her) further and further from typical social interaction.

If human beings do not 'make contact' there can be no normal socialization, no co-construction of culture. Studies in autism show us how crucial intersubjective 'connectedness' is for enculturation. Teaching a child to do the right things, to act in certain ways in certain circumstances only goes so far—if there is no give-and-take, if there is not a mutuality, then the child will never truly be a part of the culture. The fact that we cannot teach children with autism to completely fit in shows us that culture is not something independent from psychological processes, that it is not just a set of scripts for behaving or a set of attitudes. If culture were some fixed thing that could be taught, we would probably be more successful in helping autistic children adjust to living normal lives.

Whatever the cause of autism, the inability to co-create culture has far-reaching effects. The care-givers of children with autism are faced with a situation in which their culture-making is not reciprocated, or at least where there is a basic mismatch in expectations. It is as if the parent is faced with a person from a radically different culture, one in which we do not speak the same language and do not make contact. Imagine yourself in this kind of situation—it is actually what very well might happen were you to be dropped into a small village in a Papua New Guinean or Brazilian rainforest. For a while, perhaps for a long while, you would experience what has been called 'culture shock'. You might react in various ways. If you were brave, you might throw yourself into the culture, imitating everything you saw, repeating words that were said to you without understanding, painfully aware that you weren't doing or saying the right thing at the right time, but unable to figure out why. If you were overwhelmed, you might retreat to your hut, and take comfort in your surroundings, trying to make them as familiar and as stable as possible, taking excessive care to keep that little space 'yours' and becoming frustrated and angry with the intrusion of the curious villagers. The villagers, on the other hand, would no doubt regard you as an oddity, and might tolerate you as a somewhat strange child, laugh at you, and, as their initial curiosity wore off, ignore you.

Children with autism may be especially out of place in our culture, which is so mentally-oriented. While their restricted capacity for language, which is a cornerstone for learning culture, would severely limit their interactions in any society, their inability to relate intersubjectively might have different outcomes depending on the culture in which they grew up. For example, their desire for sameness, for predictability, might not work against them, as it does in our highly disparate society, but in fact might help them to adjust to living in a culture where there is less diversity. An environment where everyone dresses in grass skirts and bark breech clothes, where every day the main meal consists of taro and squash and greens cooked in a bamboo tube, where daily activities are limited to hunting or gardening—in such an environment the autistic child might find less conflict and more security.

Fortunately for the normal, culture-making individual, there is hope for our culture-shock victim, for she has the ability to make contact, to come to understand the ways in which people make culture in her new surroundings. For the autistic individual, we know the story ends quite differently. People with autism are in some senses individuals without a culture (cf. Baron-Cohen 1993 in response to Tomasello *et al.* 1993), since culture by its very nature is dialogic. They are persons within a culture, persons whom we enculturate, but who are limited in their ability to reciprocate. Geertz (1973, pp. 49–50) has suggested that we complete ourselves through culture, that there is a gap between what our body tells us and what we need to know in order to function, and culture fills that gap. Individuals with autism are trying to live and function with that void still unfilled.

However, to say that the child with autism is without a culture is to return again to a view of culture as something we have and get, rather than something which pervades our interactions. Perhaps a better way to view what we interpret as isolation, distance, and aloneness is rather that the autistic child is a culture unto himself or herself. The dialogue, the meaning-making, is taking place within the self, as the self attends to detail, to pattern, to order.

If autistic individuals are a culture unto themselves, successful treatment might require learning their culture—an example would be the parent who capitalized on her child's interest in tallying numbers by giving him a counter on which he could record the number of times a day he gave appropriate greetings and so on. Many research studies involving children with autism are strongly 'cross-cultural' in the sense that tasks which have been devised for normally-developing children have been used with autistic individuals. While this research has served an important purpose in helping us to understand both populations, perhaps the time is ripe for a more cultural approach, which would endeavour to study the development of autistic children within their world—the mental processes by which they interpret behaviour, their explanations for the emotions that they see in others and that they express themselves, the culture which they create for themselves and which they may attempt to create with us.

## Note

1. One of us confesses that the reason we are able so clearly to articulate this viewpoint is that it is one which to some extent characterizes her earlier work (e.g. Vinden 1996). Though guilty as charged, a light sentence is appropriate because herein there is repentance and redress of the wrongs committed!

# REFERENCES

Astington, J. W. (1996). What is theoretical about the child's theory of mind? A Vygotskian view of its development. In *Theories of theories of mind*, (ed. P. Carruthers and P. K. Smith), pp. 184–99. Cambridge University Press.

Astington, J. W. (1998). Theory of mind, Humpty Dumpty and the icebox. (Commentary on Nelson *et al.*, Children's theory of mind: an experiential interpretation.) *Human Development*, **41**, 30–9.

Astington, J. W. (1999). The language of intention: three ways of doing it. In *Developing theories of intention: social understanding and self control*, (ed. P. D. Zelazo, J. W. Astington and D. R. Olson). Erlbaum, Mahwah, NJ.

Astington, J. W. and Jenkins, J. M. (1995). Theory of mind development and social understanding. *Cognition and Emotion*, **9**(2/3), 151–65.

Astington, J. W. and Olson, D. R. (1995). The cognitive revolution in children's understanding of mind. *Human Development*, **38**, 179–89.

Avis, J. and Harris, P. L. (1991). Belief–desire reasoning among Baka children: evidence for a universal conception of mind. *Child Development*, **62**, 460–7.

Baron-Cohen, S. (1993). Are children with autism acultural? *Behavioral and Brain Sciences*, **16**(3), 512–3.

Berry, J. W., Poortinga, Y. H., Segall, M. H. and Dasen, P. R. (1992). *Cross-cultural psychology: research and applications*. Cambridge University Press.

Berry, J. W., Poortinga, Y. H. and Pandey, J. (ed.) (1997). *Handbook of cross-cultural psychology*, Vol. 1: Theory and method. Allyn and Bacon, Needham Heights, MA.

Bruner, J. (1996). *The culture of education*. Harvard University Press, Cambridge, MA.

Clark, H. H. (1996). *Using language*. Cambridge University Press.

Cole, M. (1996). *Cultural psychology: a once and future discipline*. Harvard University Press, Cambridge, MA.

Cutting, A. and Dunn, J. Theory of mind, emotion understanding, language and family background: individual differences and inter-relations. *Child Development*. (In press.)

D'Andrade, R. D. (1985). Character terms and cultural models. In *Directions in cognitive anthropology*, (ed. J. W. D. Dougherty), 321–43. University of Illinois Press, Chicago.

Dunn, J. (1995). Children as psychologists: the later correlates of individual differences in understanding of emotions and other minds. *Cognition and Emotion*, **9**, 187–201.

Eisenberg, L. (1986). Mindless and brainlessness in psychiatry. *British Journal of Psychiatry*, **148**, 497–508.

Fajans, J. (1985). The person in social context: the social character of Baining 'psychology'. In *Person, self and experience*, (ed. G. M. White and J. Kirkpatrick), pp. 367–97. University of California Press, Berkeley, CA.

Flavell, J. J., Zhang, X-D., Zou, H., Dong, Q. and Qi, S. (1983). A comparison between the development of the appearancereality distinction in the People's Republic of China and the United States. *Cognitive Psychology*, **15**, 459–66.

Gardner, D., Harris, P. L., Ohomoto, M. and Hamazaki, T. (1988). Understanding the distinction between real and apparent emotion by Japanese children. *International Journal of Behavioural Development*, **11**(2), 203–18.

Geertz, C. (1973). *The interpretation of cultures*. Basic Books, New York.

Gerber, E. R. (1985). Rage and obligation: Samoan emotion in conflict. In *Person, self and experience*, (ed. G. M. White and J. Kirkpatrick), pp. 121–67. University of California Press, Berkeley, CA.

Good, B. (1992). Culture and psychopathology: directions for psychiatric anthropology. In *New directions in psychological anthropology*, (ed. T. Schwartz, G. M. White and C. A. Lutz), pp. 181–205. Cambridge University Press, New York.

Greenfield, P. M. (1997). Culture as process: empirical methods for cultural psychology. In *Handbook of cross-cultural psychology*, Vol. 1: Theory and method, (ed. J. W. Berry, Y. H. Poortinga and J. Pandey), pp. 301–46. Allyn and Bacon, Needham Heights, MA.

Hobson, R. P. (1993). *Autism and the development of mind*. Erlbaum, Hove, UK.

Hughes, C. (1998). Executive function in preschoolers: links with theory of mind and verbal ability. *British Journal of Developmental Psychology*, **16**, 233–54.

Hughes, C. and Dunn, J. (1997). 'Pretend you don't know': preschoolers' talks about mental states in pretend play. *Cognitive Development*, **12**, 477–99.

Hughes, C. and Dunn, J. (1998). Understanding mind and emotion: longitudinal associations with mental-state talk between young friends. *Developmental Psychology*, **34**, 1026–37.

Jenkins, J. M. and Astington, J. W. (1996). Cognitive factors and family structure associated with theory of mind development in young children. *Developmental Psychology*, **32**, 70–8.

Kanner, L. and Eisenberg, L. (1955). Notes on the follow-up studies of autistic children. In *Psychopathology of childhood*, (ed. P. Hoch and J. Zubin). Grune and Stratton, New York.

Kleinman, A. (1988). *Rethinking psychiatry: from cultural category to personal experience*. Free Press, New York.

Lewis, C., Freeman, N. H., Kyriakidou, C., Maridaki-Kassotaki, K. and Berridge, D. M. (1996). Social influences on false belief access: specific sibling influences or general apprenticeship. *Child Development*, **67**, 2930–47.

Lillard, A. (1998). Ethnopsychologies: cultural variations in theories of mind. *Psychological Bulletin*, **123**, 3–32.

Lloyd, G. (1996). Science in antiquity: the Greek and Chinese cases and their relevance to the problems of culture and cognition. In *Modes of thought: explorations in culture and cognition*, (ed. D. R. Olson and N. Torrance), pp. 15–33. Cambridge University Press, New York.

Lutz, C. (1985). Ethnopsychology compared to what? Explaining behavior and consciousness among the Ifaluk. In *Person, self and experience*, (ed. G. M. White and J. Kirkpatrick), pp. 35–79. University of California Press, Berkeley, CA.

Miller, J. (1994). Cultural psychology: bridging disciplinary boundaries in understanding the cultural grounding of self. In *Psychological Anthropology*, (ed. P. Bock), pp. 139–70. Praeger, Westport, CT.

Padel, R. (1992). *In and out of the mind: Greek images of the tragic self*. Princeton University Press, Princeton, NJ.

Perner, J. Ruffman, T. and Leekam, S. R. (1994). Theory of mind is contagious: you catch it from your sibs. *Child Development*, **65**, 1228–42.

Shweder, R. (1991). Cultural psychology: What is it? In *Thinking through cultures*, (ed. R. Shweder), pp. 73–110. Harvard University Press, Cambridge, MA.

Tomasello, M., Kruger, A. C. and Ratner, H. H. (1993). Cultural learning. *Behavioral and Brain Sciences*, **16**(3), 495–552.

Triandis, H. C. (1994). *Culture and social behavior*. McGraw-Hill, New York.

Van de Vijver F. and Leung K. (1997). Methods and data analysis of comparative research. In *Handbook of cross-cultural psychology*, Vol. 1: Theory and method, (ed. J. W. Berry, Y. H. Poortinga and J. Pandey), pp. 257–300. Needham Heights, MA: Allyn and Bacon.

Vinden, P. G. (1996). Junin Quechua children's understanding of mind. *Child Development*, **67**, 1701–16.

Vinden, P. G. (1997, April). *The effects of parenting style on theory of mind understanding*. Paper presented at the Biennial Meeting of the Society for Research in Child Development, Washington, DC.

Vinden, P. G. (1999). Children's understanding of mind and emotion: a multi-cultural study. *Cognition and Emotion*, **13**, 19–48.

Warren, K. (1995). Each mind is a world: dilemmas of feeling and intention in a Kaqchikel Maya community. In *Other intentions*, (ed. L. Rosen), pp. 47–67. School of American Research Press, Santa Fe, NM.

# Index